MUSLIM FAMILY LAW

AUSTRALIA
LBC Information Services
Sydney

CANADA and USA
Carswell
Toronto

NEW ZEALAND
Brooker's
Auckland

SINGAPORE and MALAYSIA
Thomson Information (S.E. Asia)
Singapore

MUSLIM FAMILY LAW

DAVID PEARL
AND
WERNER MENSKI

THIRD EDITION

LONDON
SWEET & MAXWELL
1998

Third Edition 1998

Third Edition published in 1998 by
Sweet & Maxwell Limited of
100 Avenue Road, Swiss Cottage, London NW3 3PF
(http://www.smlawpub.co.uk)
Typeset by Dataword Services Limited by Chilcompton
Printed and bound in Great Britain by
MPG Books Ltd, Bodmin, Cornwall

A C.I.P. catalogue
record for this book
is available from
the British Library

ISBN 0421 52980 6

Preface

It is 19 years since the publication of my introductory text on Muslim family law. The purpose of that book, and its second edition published in 1987, was to attempt to provide the English reader with a simple and short guide to the family law of the Muslim world, with a particular emphasis on the law of India, Pakistan and Bangladesh. The second edition has long been both out of date and out of print, and I was delighted when Sweet and Maxwell Ltd, who had obtained the rights to the Routledge law book titles (themselves having inherited the titles of my original publisher, Croom Helm), suggested to me the possibility of publishing a third edition.

During the very early stages of the preparation, I left the academic world on appointment to the Circuit Bench, and secondment first as Chief Adjudicator of Immigration Appeals, and now in my current position as President of the United Kingdom Immigration Appeal Tribunal. This has left me with no time to devote to writing and research, and I was both relieved and honoured when Dr Werner Menski agreed to join me as an author for this new edition. The result really is a new book, and I wish to express my gratitude to Dr Menski for all the effort he has put into this project, which he has done whilst at the same time continuing such a busy teaching load at SOAS. He has been responsible for all the new writing and updating, and whilst we accept of course joint responsibility for any mistakes contained in the book, all the praise (if there is any) must be placed on Dr Menski's head, not on mine.

Those who compare all three editions will notice that the book has grown. We have introduced much more material about *Angrezi Shariat*, the emerging Muslim law applied by the Muslim communities living in the United Kingdom. The Muslim community in the United Kingdom is increasingly a settled community with successive generations having been born, married, had children and died in this country. The first edition had little to say about all of this; the second edition had a little more; but this new book has a lot to say about it all. Much work however still needs to be done, and we hope that the book will itself provide scholars with the inspiration to seek out their own research, in order to provide concrete evidence on which to base conclusions as to whether or not our tentative views are correct.

There is much new material in the book from India, Pakistan and Bangladesh, and we hope that the book will be used by students, lawyers and others from those countries. Our coverage of other countries is not as extensive, but nonetheless we hope that there is enough here to enable the reader to find out about a particular country even if he or she may have to look elsewhere for the details.

Space is always a problem and so as to keep the book within bounds, we have resisted the temptation to write about aspects of Muslim law which are related to family law, although only in a limited way. Thus pre-emption (and land law generally), criminal law, international law, and commercial law in particular play little if no part in the passages which follow.

We have retained a large number of direct quotes in the book, and we have resisted the temptation to change the spelling, grammar and punctuation of the original. Our intention is to enable the reader to have access to original case material which may otherwise be difficult to obtain, either from a library or via the internet. We hope that the bibliography will enable the reader to delve deeper into the rich material which is now available, if the answer is not immediately apparent in this book.

Many have contributed to this book by providing information or by commenting on draft sections of the manuscript. We would like to acknowledge in particular Omar Yaqub, Abdul Hoq Mohammed, Ihsan Yilmaz, Professor Humayoun Ihsan, Professor Tahir Mahmood, Dr Lynn Welchman, Ian Edge, Judge Eugene Cotran, Martin Lau, Dr Susan Rayner, and Dr Doreen Hinchcliffe. Of these, Dr Hinchcliffe, in particular, has been a tower of strength in the teaching of, and research into, Muslim law for more than 30 years, and both of us are as grateful to her for her friendship and many kindnesses as are many generations of students. She has particularly provided material on aspects of Chapter 11.

Islamic law is taught as an undergraduate law course in the United Kingdom now only at SOAS in London University. There are few courses elsewhere in the English speaking world or indeed in Europe, although there are many in India, Pakistan, and Bangladesh where English is still used as the language of instruction. If nothing else, it would be wonderful if this book were to stimulate interest in the subject so that it can be introduced elsewhere in the United Kingdom and other countries.

DAVID PEARL
CAMBRIDGE
MARCH 1998

Table of Contents

PART II: THE SUBSTANTIVE LAW

List of Abbreviations

A.C.	Appeal Cases
A.D.	Appeal Division
A.I.R.	All India Reporter
A.J.K.	Azad Jammu & Kashmir
A.L.J.	Allahabad Law Journal
All.	Allahabad
All. E.R.	All England Law Reports
AnW.K.	Andhra Weekly Report
A.P.	Andhra Pradesh
Art.	Article
B.J.	Baghdad ul-Jadid
B.L.D.	Bangladesh Legal Decisions
Bom.	Bombay
Bom.L.R.	Bombay Law Reporter
B.S.O.A.S.	Bulletin of the School of Oriental and African Studies
C.A.	Court of Appeal
Cal.	Calcutta
Cal.W.N.	Calcutta Weekly Notes
Chap.	Chapter
C.J.	Chief Justice
C.L.C.	Civil Law Cases
Cri.L.J.	Criminal Law Journal
Cr.P.C.	Criminal Procedure Code, 1973
C.S.I.S.	Centre for the Study of Islam and Christian-Muslim Relations
def.	defendant
Del.	Delhi
D.L.C.	Dhaka Law Cases
D.L.R.	Dhaka Law Reports
D.M.M.A.	Dissolution of Muslim Marriages Act 1939
Fam.	Family
F.L.R.	Family Law Reports
F.S.C.	Federal Shariat Court
Gau.	Gauhati
Guj.L.R.	Gujarat Law Reporter
H.C.	House of Commons Rules (Immigration Rules)
Hyd.	Hyderabad
I.A.	Indian Appeals
I.A.T.	Immigration Appeal Tribunal

I.C.L.Q.	The International Comparative Law Quarterly
I.L.R.	Indian Law Reports
Imm.A.R.	Immigration Appeal Reports
I. & N.L. & P.	Immigration & Nationality Law & Practice
J.	Judge
J. & K.	Jammu & Kashmir
Kant.	Karnataka
Kar.	Karachi
K.B.	King's Bench
Ker.	Kerala
K.L.R.	Key Law Reports (Pakistan)
K.L.T.	Kerala Law Times
Lah.	Lahore
L.J.	Lord Justice
L.R.	Law Reports
Luck.	Lucknow
Mad.	Madras
M.B.	Madhya Bharat
M.F.L.O.	Muslim Family Laws Ordinance, 1961
M.I.A.	Moore's Indian Appeals
M.L.D.	Monthly Law Digest (Pakistan)
M.L.J.	Madras Law Journal
M.P.	Madhya Pradesh
Mst.	Mussammat (title for Muslim females, equivalent to Ms.)
N.L.J.	New Law Journal
N.L.R.	National Law Reports
N.O.C.	Notes of Cases
N.U.C.	Notice of Unreported Cases
n.y.	no years (of publication)
Ori.	Orissa
P.	Presate
Pat.	Patna
P.C.	Privy Council
P.Cr.L.J.	Pakistan Criminal Law Journal
Pesh.	Peshawar
pl.	plaintiff
P.L.D.	Pakistan Legal Decisions
P.L.J.	Pakistan Law Journal
p.m.	per month
P.O.	Presidential Order
Q.B.	Queen's Bench
Raj.	Rajasthan

s.	section
S.C.	Supreme Court
S.C.C.	Supreme Court Cases
S.C.J.	Supreme Court Journal (India)
S.C.M.R.	Supreme Court Monthly Review
S.C.R.	Supreme Court Reports
S.N.	Short Notes
u/s.	under section . . .
w.e.f.	with effect from
W.L.R.	Weekly Law Reports
W.P.	West Pakistan
W.R.	The Weekly Reporter (ed. by D. Sutherland)

Explanatory Note

Throughout this title there are references to works by other authors. Only the name of the author and the year of publication appear in the text. However, the full reference to each title can be found in the Bibliography. In the footnotes, the title of the work is referred to in full the first time it appears, and is thereafter to by name and year only. References to year are occasionally followed by a letter, *i.e.* (1990a). This indicates to which title by that particular author, published in that year, the text is referring.

Glossary

'adala	the quality of religious and moral probity of a witness
ad	equity (between co-wives), also means justice in the general sense
ahl al-hadith	those who base their reasoning on revelation
ahl al-kitab	'People of the Book', *i.e.* Jews and Christians
ahl al-ra'y	those who believed in the value of individual reasoning
al-walad l'il firash	legitimacy by birth (literally: the child (belongs) to the bed)
'ariyya	gift of usufruct
'asaba	agnates, usually male agnates
'asaba bi ghayriha	daughter (in inheritance)
'asaba bi nafsihi	son (in inheritance)
'awl/aul	proportionate abatement/reduction
'ayn	substance of a property
batil	void
baynuna kubra	'greater' talaq, of greater finality
biraderi	South Asian extended family/clan group
dar-al-ahd	country of treaty
dar-al-dawah	the country of mission
dar-al-harb	the land of the unbelievers, land of war
dar-al-hizmet	country of service (Turkish)
dar-al-islam	the land of Islam
darar	ill-treatment, injury
darura	necessity
dhimma	'keeping' or protection
dhimmis	protected non-Muslim minorities in a Muslim state
diwani right	local authority functions
diya	blood money
fasid	irregular
faskh	judicial dissolution of marriage
fatwa	authoritative guidance, legal opinion from a jurist/jurisconsult
fiqh	Muslim jurisprudence
firash	matrimonial bed
gharjamai	son-in-law who moves to the wife's family
ghayr sahih	'without validity' (in Iraqi law), invalid
hadd	Qur'anic punishment, plural *hudud*
hadith	saying, traditions of the Prophet, the texts of the *Sunna*
haj	pilgrimage
hakam or hakim	arbitrator
halal	ritually pure; also: legally permissible

harbi	person from the 'Land of War'
hiba	gift of substance
hiba bi'l-iwad	gift and return gift
hiba bi-sharti'l-iwad	gift with a stipulation for a return
hidona	custody (of children)
himar	donkey
hisba	religious morality
hiyal	legal fiction, device
huda	guidance
hudud	compulsory Qur'anic punishment
idda or iddat	period of waiting = three months after divorce
ijab	offer
ijma	consensus, (juristic) agreement
ijtihad	'striving', 'exerting', interpretation
ikrah	threat, coercion, duress
ila	repudiation of marriage
iman	faith
iqrar	acknowledgement
isnad	chain of transmission of a *hadith*
istihsan	equity, appropriateness of the legal decision
istislah	consideration of the public interest
iwad	return
izzat	honour and status of the family
jabr	force, coercion
jahez	dowry
jirga	local assembly, village council
jizya	poll tax for non-Muslim minorities
kabinnamah or kabhinama	marriage deed (Bangladesh)
kafa'a	equal status
kazi = qadi	judge
khalwat	seclusion, privacy
kharaj	land tax for minorities
khul or khula	release or redemption, divorce in exchange for a consideration from the wife
khiyar	option
khiyar al-bulugh	option of puberty
kitabiyya	woman 'of the book'
kubra	'greater' talaq, of greater finality, this is
lian	imprecation leading to divorce
madhab	school of law
mahr	dower
mahr al-mithl	proper dower
manfa'a	proceeds from a property
mard al-maut	death sickness
maslaha	public welfare

mazalim	court of complaints, ruler's courts, secular jurisdiction
mofussil/mufassil	hinterland of the large Indian cities
moulvi	Muslim expert adviser to British Indian courts
mubah	permissible action, indifferent in terms of religion
mubaraat	mutual discharge, divorce by mutual consent
mudda'a 'allayhi	defendant/respondent
mudda'i	plaintiff/claimant
muhsan	a married person
muhtasib	market inspector, guardian of standards?
mujtahid	person qualified to exercise *ijtihad*
mullah	religious leader
muqallid	person who is bound to practise *taqlid*, 'imitator'
musahara	prohibited degree of relations by affinity
musha'	undivided part of a property
musta'min	a foreigner, granted protection in a Muslim state
muta	temporary marriage
mutat/muta/mata	compensation payment on divorce
mutawali	administrator of an endowment
nafaqa	financial provisions, maintenance
nasab	prohibited degree of relations through consanguinity
nashiz	rebellious, disobedient wife
nushuz	disobedience
nass	textual basis, text
nikah	Muslim marriage
nikahnama	marriage deed
panchayat	South Asian village councils
pandit	Hindu law specialist advising British Indian courts
parda or purdah	seclusion
pardanashin	secluded woman
qabda	delivery of consideration
qabul	acceptance
qadi or kazi	judge
qadhf or qazf	false accusation of unchastity
qatl	murder
qiyas	analogy
rada'a	fosterage
radd/rud	return (in succession)
raji	revocable
rajm	stoning to death
ra'y	discretion, juristic speculation
riba	interest
rukhsati or rukshati	marriage ceremony leading to consummation of the marriage, also: transfer of bride to her new home
sabab	affinity, conjunction
sadaqa	gift
sahib ar-radd	criminal court or jurisdiction

sahih	valid
salih	in the general interest
samskara	sacrament of marriage
shahada	declaration of belief
shahada	also: fixed witness
shari'a	the divine law of Islam
shart	stipulation
Shi'at 'Ali	the followers of 'Ali
shubha	semblance
shurut	conditions, a branch of evidence law
siyasa shar'iyya	administrative discretion, public law doctrine of government according to shari'a, allowing certain administrative discretion to the ruler
sughra	'little method' in divorce, of smaller finality
sunna	practice of the Prophet, second source of law
tafriq	separation, divorce by judicial intervention
tafwid at-talaq	delegation of divorce
takhayyur	eclecticism, principle of selection
taqlid	imitation
talaq	unilateral divorce given by the man
talaq-al-ahsan	approved form of divorce
talaq-al-bain	final or irrevocable talaq
talaq-al-bida	disapproved form of talaq, triple talaq
talaq-al-hasan	approved form of divorce
talaq-as-sunna	meritorious form of talaq
talaq-i-tafwid	delegated talaq
talaqnama	divorce deed
talfiq	piecing together
taqadum	'an old offence'
taqlid	'imitation', following established juristic authority
ta'sib	pulling over to agnatic inheritance
ta'zir	discretionary punishments
tuhr	period between menstruations
ulema	learned men, scholars
ummah	community of all believers
usool	giving of wedding gifts (Bangladesh)
usul al-fiqh	the science of jurisprudence
vakil	legal representative, attorney
wali	guardian
waqf	endowment
waqf al-awlad	family endowment
waqf dhurri	family endowment
waqf khayri	charitable endowment
waqfnama	document establishing an endowment
waqif	dedicator of waqf, settlor
wilaya	guardianship
yamin	oath-taking, the oath

zihar	impious declaration giving rise to divorce
zina	illicit sexual relationship
zina-bil-jabr	rape

Table of Cases

Tables of Statutory Instruments

International Conventions

Tables of Statutes

Part I:

Background Material

Chapter 1

Historical introduction

The historical development of Muslim law

1–01   Joseph Schacht commenced his major work *An introduction to Islamic law* with a statement on which one can hardly improve:

> "The sacred law of Islam is an all-embracing body of religious duties, the totality of Allah's commands that regulate the life of every Muslim in all its aspects; it comprises on an equal footing ordinances regarding worship and ritual, as well as political and (in the narrow sense) legal rules." (Schacht, *An introduction to Islamic law* (1964) p. 1).

1–02   In the sacred law of Islam, the legal subject matter is but a part of the religious and ethical framework of life. This has been true from the very beginning of Islam, from the Qur'an itself. An essential feature of the Qur'an, the Holy Book of Islam revealed in the early seventh century to the Prophet (or Messenger) Mohammed, is that it is not primarily a code of law in the narrow sense of the term. Only some 80 verses refer to legal topics, and even in these verses there are both gaps as well as doubts as to whether the legal injunction is obligatory or permissive, as indeed whether it is subject to public or to private sanctions.

1–03   This should neither surprise nor shock, for the Qur'an describes itself as *huda*, or guidance, not as a code of law. The remaining nine tenths of the Qur'an are concerned with matters relating to belief or morality. On the whole, its ideas of economic and social justice, as well as its legal injunctions, are subject to its religious authority.

1–04   Thus it is appropriate to describe Islamic law as consisting of the Qur'anic foundations which were subsequently interpreted by succeeding generations and which included much of the customary law of the Arabs. Indeed, the very nature of the Qur'an is such that it could not possibly be a comprehensive code of law. Legal precepts were revealed to Mohammed to meet certain contingencies of his experience as leader, in a pragmatic and empirical fashion. For instance, the fact that increasing numbers of Muslim males fell in battle acted as a catalyst to the verses which enjoined kindness to orphans while retaining the practice of polygamy (Qur'an, Sura IV, verse 3). Another illustration is Sura XXXIII, verse 37, which abolished the pre-Islamic custom of adoption, whereby an adopted child could be assimilated in law into another family. It may well be that the revelation of this verse was designed to settle the controversy which arose from the marriage of Mohammed to the divorced wife of his own adopted son, Zayd.

1–05   A third illustration is Sura XXIV, verse 4, which lays down the penalty of 80 lashes for the offence of falsely accusing a woman of unchastity (*qadhf* or *qazf*). It is thought by some that this verse may well have been revealed after imputations of adultery against Mohammed's wife, 'A'isha.

1–06   These three examples should not in any way be seen as a challenge to the divinity of the Qur'an. Indeed, the reverse is intended; for the Qur'an is a contemporary document which reflects the life and aspirations of Mohammed and his followers in their efforts to create a new community in Mecca and Medina. The legal provisions contained in the Qur'an, therefore, are piecemeal, superseding some, but certainly nothing near a majority, of the pre-Islamic customary laws of the Arabian communities.

1-07 On the whole, the Qur'an confirmed and upheld the existing customs and institutions of Arab society and only introduced changes that were deemed necessary. Customs which do not contravene the principles of the Qur'an have been regarded as valid and authoritative on the basis that they were practised during the Prophet's time and approved by him.

1-08 In this general historical introduction we can only outline the most important of the legal reforms introduced in the Qur'anic verses. First, and certainly of paramount importance, the Qur'an provided detailed fundamental changes in the laws of inheritance. By and large, the customary law in the pre-Islamic period was patrilineal, although there were matrilineal elements. The right to inherit property belonged exclusively to the male agnatic relations of the deceased. Females were excluded from the scheme of succession, in part because they were non-combatants in the tribal disputes. The tribal unit was established so firmly that the nearest male agnate succeeded to the property to the exclusion of any other agnatic relation alive at the death of the deceased. Thus, the sons and their issue excluded the father. In the absence of lineal descendants, the father excluded the brothers and their issue. The brothers and their issue, so it is generally assumed, excluded the paternal grandfather. Finally the paternal grandfather excluded the uncles and the issue of the uncles.

1-09 The Muslim struggle against adversaries, which depleted the male members of the community leaving many scores of widows and orphans, inevitably interfered with the customary transfer of property on death. It was paramount to introduce generally a more extensive distribution system focused on the immediate family rather than the agnatic clan, and, in particular, to involve female inheritance. Thus, the most far-reaching reform in the Qur'an in the legal field is contained in those verses which provided a series of fixed fractional inheritance rights to certain close relatives of the deceased who, in the pre-Islamic customary law, may not have received any part of the estate (Qur'an, Sura IV, verses 7–14). The result was a transformation of the old tribal bond of pre-Islamic Arabia into the extended family bond of the Muslim community, politically allied by religion and legally linked by inheritance. However the new 'sharers' did not totally supersede the old agnatic system. Rather the Qur'an introduced the morality of Islam into the customary practices of the Arabs.[1]

1-10 The second major reform of the Qur'an is found in family law generally, changing the status of women in particular. Thus, much of the legal material in the Qur'anic verses concerns the very real attempt to enhance the legal position of women. In customary law, women were treated as an object of sale. A woman could be fully exploited by her father; she could virtually be sold in marriage to the highest bidder, as shown in the pre-Islamic form of the bride-price. The husband was entitled to terminate the contract of marriage on any occasion and for any whim. Various Qur'anic provisions transformed this position, for example the revelation directing the husband to pay a dower (*mahr*) to the wife (Qur'an, Sura IV, verse 19), which involved the wife as a contracting party in her own right. The absolute right of repudiation (the *talaq*) was sought to be controlled by the introduction of the 'waiting period' (*'idda*) of three menstrual cycles, during which time the husband is given the opportunity to reconsider his decision and has to pay

---

[1] For details see *e.g.* Nasir, *The Islamic law of personal status* (1990a), pp. 218–223.

maintenance. The right of polygamy is restricted to four concurrent wives, and the husband is enjoined to treat these wives equally (Qur'an, Sura IV, verse 3).

1–11 Beyond the prophetic revelations, Mohammed was concerned with the organisation of his religious community (the *umma*). To adopt one phrase of Professor Coulson (1964, p. 28), he was the judge-supreme, responsible for the interpretation of the revelations in the Qur'an to meet particular problems as and when they arose. For instance, in one case which is known to us as *Sa'ad's case*, Mohammed worked out the exact relationship between the Qur'anic 'sharers' and the pre-Islamic agnatic heirs. Sa'ad, so we are told, was one of the followers of Mohammed who fell in battle. On his death, Sa'ad's brother appropriated the whole of the estate. His widow sought assistance from Mohammed. The early commentators of the Qur'an tell us that Mohammed directed that Sa'ad's widow should take one eighth from the estate (the sum which is prescribed in the Qur'an); the two daughters should take two thirds (likewise as prescribed in the Qur'an) and the residue of five twenty-fourths should go to the brother as the closest male agnate. This case, therefore, lays down the important rule that in a competition between the Qur'anic heirs and the 'old' agnatic relations, the Qur'anic heirs have first claim on the estate. Other examples of this type of decision-making in the field of inheritance relate first to Mohammed's restriction of the power to make bequests to one third of the estate and, secondly, to his refusal to permit the making of a bequest in favour of any heir.

1–12 This type of synthesis of the Qur'anic revelations with pre-Islamic customs is almost certainly as far as one can go in the description of the early historical developments of the law without entering into controversial territory. The major question, and perhaps one which requires some sort of explanation at the outset, but to which we shall return in more detail later, is this: How much of the law now in existence which is called Muslim law or Islamic law (the *shari'a*) can be historically based on the words and deeds of Mohammed? This issue has given rise to fierce controversies in legal circles and has important practical implications, as it questions the very validity of sources which are regarded as divine and sacrosanct by Muslims. The differing views merit some discussion and we shall return to them later.

1–13 The classical formulation of the sources of Islamic law was worked out some two centuries after Mohammed's death. As we shall see, this formulation made the authentic traditions of the Prophet Mohammed (the *hadith*) the second of the classical sources of law after the Qur'an. The *hadith* is seen as evidence of what is known as *sunna*. Here it means the practice of the Prophet, the model or the normative behaviour of the Prophet. Literally, *sunna* means the 'trodden path' and the term was also used with reference to the customary law prevalent in Arabia before the advent of Islam. After the revelation, this 'trodden path' continued to be the accepted law for the Muslim community, but only in so far as it had not been abrogated by Mohammed. The Western orientalist Goldhizer in his seminal work *Muslim studies* refers to the classical concept of *sunna* as, in essence, all that could be shown to have been the practices of the Prophet and his earliest followers (Goldziher (1967–1971)). *Hadith* describe the 'report' or evidence of the Prophet's behaviour. It is self-evident that, for the classical jurist as for the religious Muslim today, *sunna* and *hadith* are consubstantial in that they refer to the same substantive source of law. The *sunna* is related by traditions known as *hadith*. In a way, the *hadith* is the vehicle for reporting the content, namely the *sunna* of the Prophet.

1–14 Some orientalists do not see the picture exactly this way. The controversy surrounding the legal innovations of Mohammed can best be described by the following question: Is it correct to refer to the *hadith* as the second source of Islamic law, remembering that the *hadith* were collected and compiled some two centuries after Mohammed's death? Or, rather, are the collections an attempt to attribute to the Prophet either the origin for the *sunna* which had developed since his death or to undermine the *sunna* which had developed in order, for political reasons, to return to what was thought to be the 'pristine purity' of the Qur'an? In other words, the issue is whether or not the *hadith* actually reflects Mohammed's words and deeds or not. Western orientalists since Goldhizer have doubted the authenticity of large tracts of the *hadith* material in their attribution to the Prophet. Particularly Joseph Schacht (1950) in his work on the origins of Muslim jurisprudence reached the conclusion that the *sunna*, by and large, is anterior to the *hadith* rather than being either the reverse or consubstantial.

1-15   Be this as it may, *hadith* material is in two parts, the text and the transmissional chain *(isnad)* which provides the names of the narrators supporting the text.[2] The classical theory is that the authenticity of the *hadith* is dependent upon the strength of the *isnad*. The text itself is not subject to critical analysis. It must be stressed, however, that even if one accepts as essentially valid the view of Schacht, and many do not, this does not in any way contradict the ideal vision of an apostolic behaviour. As a source of law, this 'behaviour' is second only to the Qur'an. Whether the mass of material reflects the seventh century of Mohammed or a later period of the jurists and administrators is, of course, at the essence of the controversy – but it is rather beside the point. No one doubts that the *hadith* collections became a vital source for all decisions in the Muslim world.

1-16   It is self-evident that it is necessary to keep firmly in one's mind the vital distinction between the 'classical' formulation of the sources of Islamic law on the one hand, and the actual or 'material' sources of the law on the other. The *hadith* collections are the second of the classical sources after the Qur'an, although the *sunna* of Mohammed – his decisions and his actions – represents the beginning of the 'material' sources. This *sunna*, in part a theoretical idealism, although it cannot be doubted that it includes actual practice, was continued by Mohammed's successors, the four Caliphs, namely Abu Bakr, 'Umar, 'Uthman and 'Ali. The Caliphs continued to solve, in an ad hoc manner, cases which came before them. The solutions were based on interpretations of the Qur'an, from where they drew their authority.

1-17   Two examples can be given and are referred to in Coulson (1964, pp. 24–25). Both examples appear in later *hadith* collections, and thus it can be postulated that they both express a decision of a later age turned into a norm by the classical exposition of that other age. It would be consistent with the development of the law, however, to accept both decisions as examples of a gradual filling in of the gaps of the Qur'anic foundations.

1-18   The first example is known as the *Himariyya* or *Donkey Case*. In this case, a woman died leaving a husband, a mother, two uterine brothers and two full brothers. In the normal Qur'anic distribution, the husband would be entitled to one half of the estate, the mother to one sixth and the uterine brothers, as Qur'anic heirs, would take one third. The full brothers, the agnatic heirs, represented the old pre-Qur'anic inheritors. The Qur'anic heirs, in this situation, exhaust the whole estate. The full brothers appealed to 'Umar against this decision on the grounds that, as they had the same mother as the deceased, indeed as they possessed the very

---

[2] For good introductions to this material, see Doi, *Introduction to the Qur'an* (1981), Doi, *Shariah: The Islamic law* (1984) and Calder, *Studies in early Muslim jurisprudence* (1993).

same quality of relationship which was the exclusive basis of the uterine brothers' right of inheritance, they should be entitled to participate in the inheritance. 'Umar accepted this argument and permitted the full brothers the right to share equally with the uterine brothers in one third of the estate. As the full brothers claimed to be entitled by virtue of their uterine relationship, this decision represented a victory for the Qur'anic sharers and a defeat for the old agnatic relationship. The case owes its name to a suggestion that the full brothers are reputed to have made to 'Umar: "Assume that our father does not count, consider him a donkey" (a *himar*).

1–19 The second example of this process of decision-making is taken from the caliphate of 'Ali and is known as the *Minbariyya* or *Pulpit case*. 'Ali was faced with the problem of the distribution of an estate between a wife, a father, a mother and two daughters. The Qur'anic distribution would have produced a situation where the estate was exhausted before all the heirs had been fully satisfied. The two daughters obtained two thirds, the father and the mother one sixth each and the wife one eighth. In solving the difficulty, 'Ali adopted the principle of proportional abatement, so that the wife's share was reduced from one eighth to one ninth and the shares of the other relations were abated in proportion.

1–20 These two decisions exemplify the piecemeal character of the Caliphs' judgments. They were content to solve problems as and when they arose. In essence, they were filling in the gaps to the Qur'anic revelations. For instance, drinking of wine is prohibited in the Qur'an, but no penalty is laid down. Abu Bakr fixed the penalty at 40 lashes but 'Umar and later 'Ali extended this punishment to 80 lashes. This result was arrived at by analogy with the offence of false accusation of unchastity (*qadhf*), where the Qur'an (Sura XXIV, verse 4) had fixed the penalty at 80 lashes. The filling-in of gaps continued at least until the founding of the Umayyad dynasty in A.D. 661.

1–21 During the second period, that is from A.D. 661 until the end of the Umayyad dynasty in A.D. 750, the essential factor contributing to the development of the law was undoubtedly the extension of Muslim rule to the non-Arab territories. Contact took place initially through war, later through the growth of trading with Byzantium and Persia. Inevitably, it appeared that Byzantine and Persian legal concepts infiltrated Muslim legal philosophy. A few well-known examples will suffice for our present purposes.

1–22 First, one can point to the development of the civil and political status of the non-Muslim communities. Certain non-Muslim citizens of the Muslim state are permitted to reside on Muslim soil in return for the payment of a poll tax (*jizya*) and the land tax (*kharaj*). Such minorities are known as the *Dhimmi* communities, comprising 'people of the book' (*ahl al-kitab*), *i.e.* primarily Jews and Christians.[3] The status of *Dhimmi* was derived or evolved from a fictional contract (the *dhimma*) and it is right to point out similar concepts both in Roman and in Jewish law. The

---

[3] Magians are referred to in the same verse (Qur'an, Sura XXII, verse 17), although it is controversial whether they should be thought of as *Dhimmis*. 'Ali is reported as saying that the Magians were once in possession of a scripture, but that they had lost this work. Most Muslim opinion would accept the Magians into the status of *Dhimmi*. The actual historical experience of the Muslims is different from the Qur'anic formulation. When the Muslims landed in India, for example, they discovered that the Hindus were so numerous that it would have been physically impossible to carry out the injunctions of Islam. In India, therefore, Hindus were quickly assimilated into the status of *Dhimmi*. One must also contrast the status of *Dhimmi* with the institution of *musta'min*. The former is a citizen of the Islamic state, whereas the *musta'min* is a foreigner who is granted protection for a period of up to one year whilst he remains in the Islamic state. If he breaks the pledge, the protection ends and he becomes a *harbi* (a person from the Land of War). For details see Lewis, *The Jews of Islam* (1984).

details of the *Dhimmi*/Muslim relationship were laid down by the Umayyad administration in a manner which highlights a major preoccupation: An organised empire with systematic tax laws, law courts and a disciplined administration. Muslim practice recognises the existence of non-Muslims, and allows them to be governed by their own laws. In this basic administrative decision, Muslim law tacitly accepts within its own territory the principle known as 'personality of laws', which we discuss in detail in Chapter 2, below. In doing this, the principles of the ancient Hebrews, the Greeks, the Romans, and the Hindus, are continued.

1-23   Similarly, the Umayyads adopted the Byzantine market inspector (the *Agoronomus*), assimilated him into Islamic practice, and granted him a new extended responsibility. He was called the *muhtasib*, and he was responsible not only for market affairs but also for safeguarding the standards of religious morality (*hisba*).[4]

1-24   The Umayyads were also responsible for the introduction of the position of the Qadi, who served as a judicial officer of the state, usually appointed by the Governor of the area in question. Quite naturally, as state appointees, the Qadis often met hostile opposition from the learned men (*ulema*) of the community. The *ulema* as a body adopted the attitude that the Qadis, especially when appointed from amongst their own ranks, tended to compromise themselves. It is indeed the case that some Qadis were open to influence, especially in the early period. However, it is far from the truth to say that all Qadis behaved in such a manner. Indeed, the reverse is true. The decisions of the Qadis on the cases which came before them contributed towards a strong local influence around certain towns. This comes down the centuries as an early vital expression of the Muslim legal process. Quite naturally, in such a diverse empire as that of the Umayyads, the development of the law by the Qadis' courts showed marked peculiarities from area to area. One can surmise that the governors did indeed interfere from time to time but, as a general rule, Qadis were free to interpret and develop the Muslim law in their own way.

1-25   At this early stage, a division can already be noticed between the practice of the Qadis in Kufa as opposed to practice in Medina. Broadly, the practice in Medina represented the stricter interpretation of Qur'anic injunctions in the light of a patrilineal society, whereas Kufa, with its more cosmopolitan outlook, provided a venue for a wider legal fusion of ideas. This resulted, for example, in a set of marriage laws which was substantially more relaxed towards the rights of women. Such differences represent the early stages of diversity in the growth of Muslim law. Indeed, these differences are the first signs of the separation of the various schools of Sunni Islamic law. All Qadis exercised discretion (*ra'y*) in the administration of the law. In strict theory, this discretion was subject to the overriding authority of the Umayyad dynasty, but it seems that such authority was rarely exercised.

1-26   It has been shown that there were three major 'material' sources of Muslim law besides the Qur'an itself and the decisions of the Prophet. First, pre-Islamic custom, secondly other legal systems, thirdly the interpretations by the Qadis through their undoubted exercise of *ra'y*. These three sources of law provided a diversity in practice which was accepted, at the time, by all as being in consonance with the requirements of Islam.

1-27   From A.D. 720, a schism is apparent in the administration of the law. The religious leaders sided increasingly with those who were to become the leaders of

---

[4] Qur'an Sura III, verses 104 and 110. For an interesting account of the Public Morality Committees in Saudi Arabia today, representing as they do a modern version of the *hisba*, see Layish, "Ulama and politics in Saudi Arabia", in *Islam and politics in the modern Middle East* (1984), p. 35.

the Abbasid regime. The Umayyad dynasty came under the combined attack of the theologians and frustrated politicians. Indeed, criticism of the Umayyads was present even amongst the ranks of the Qadis. The later Umayyad governors relied more and more heavily on the theologians as Qadis. It was natural that the theologians were less prepared to adopt their own independent judgment (ra'y) if it in any way conflicted with the injunctions of the Qur'an. Joseph Schacht (1964, p. 27) aptly states the position when he writes of the later Umayyad Qadis that, "they impregnated the sphere of law with religious and ethical ideas, subjected it to Islamic norms, and incorporated it into the body of duties incumbent on every Muslim". Schacht (1964, p. 27) goes on to suggest that the consequence of this impregnation was that "the popular and administrative practice of the late Umayyad period was transformed into the religious law of Islam". Thus for Schacht, the beginning of Islamic law proper is dated between A.D. 720 and 750 – some 100 years after the Prophetic period.

1-28 Naturally such a view is heretical for traditionally trained Muslim *ulema* who tend to regard the controversies over the authenticity of *hadiths* as suspicious, and as an attack on the Qur'an and ultimately on Islam itself. Many Muslim academics, though not going as far as Schacht, would not dispute the fact that with regard to the first century of Islam, the existing works of scholars are not free of discordance and diversity. The important jurist Shafi'i came on the scene precisely when such juristic controversies had reached a high point and it was through his work that the science of jurisprudence (*usul al-fiqh*) was articulated into an analytical and systematic framework and a coherent body of knowledge.

1-29 A systematic critique of Schacht's thesis has been undertaken by David Powers (1986) who takes issue with Schacht's approach and labels it contradictory (see in detail Powers (1986), pp. 1–8). Schacht (1964, p. 18) had accepted that many rules of Islamic law, particularly in the law of the family and the law of inheritance, not to mention worship and ritual, were based on the Qur'an from the beginning. At the same time, he had asserted that Islamic law did not develop until about 100 years after the Prophet's death. For such an argument to have force, argues Powers (1986, p. 5), in conjunction with other writers, it would have been necessary to have exhaustively examined Qur'anic provisions, *papyrii* and the Islamic science of tradition, yet Schacht devoted only eight pages in his book to the Qur'an.

1-30 Powers himself argues that Islamic law did, in fact, begin to develop during the Prophet's lifetime, "albeit not in the manner that Islamic tradition relates" (Powers (1986), p. xii). He therefore posits that:

> "Muslims living in the generations following Muhammad's death prayed on a daily basis, divorced, and divided up property, and it stands to reason on *a priori* grounds, that the Qur'anic legislation on these matters would have provided them with guidance."[5]

Certainly, the classical formulation of the sources of law was a post-A.D. 720 development. Thus the controversy, important as it is, centres around the relevance of the early material which we have described, on the Muslim law as it existed in A.D. 750.

---

[5] Powers, *Studies in Qur'an and hadith. The formation of the Islamic law of inheritance* (1986), p. 7. Endress, *An introduction to Islam* (1988), p. 2, starts his analysis by saying that already in the lifetime of the Prophet the revelation "provided . . . the elements of a legal and government system which formed the foundations of the first community".

1-31 There are some general points which do not arouse so much controversy. We know, for example, that the majority of the theologians refrained from accepting political appointments. Rather, they established schools of discussion and learning and, gradually, developed a system of *responsa* to questions which were put to them on Islamic ethics and practice. These jurist-theologians were certainly the founders of the early schools of law. In a very loose sense, 'schools' were established in a number of centres, the most important being Kufa, Medina, Basra, Mecca and Damascus.

1-32 The major area of difficulty surrounds the activity of these jurist-theologians (see in detail Makdisi (1981)). Their aim was to 'break out' of the rigid administrative machinery established by the Umayyads. Schacht argued that the theologians accepted the existence of an 'actual custom' of the local community, that they were instigators not so much for their views of the actual custom but for the creation of a normative *sunna*, or law as it ought to be. According to Schacht, it was in this way that the early theorists, through their own concept of *ra'y*, developed a normative value for the *sunna*.

1-33 It must be remarked that the discretion of the jurists differed from the empirical decision-making of the Qadi. The *ra'y* for the jurist was a composite concept based upon the consensus of opinion of a number of scholars, all of whom had worked out solutions to particular theoretical problems. This type of consensus is referred to as *ijma*, a key concept in Islamic jurisprudence to which it will be necessary to return. Another quite useful way to explain the *sunna/hadith* paradigm is that *sunna* contains within it two ideas bound together, namely continuity and normativeness. These two ideas were fused into one whole by the development of the traditions (*hadith*).

1-34 At first, the tradition was projected back to certain early specialists of the region. For instance, in Kufa, the early traditions were ascribed to Ibrahim Nakha'i. Later, in order perhaps to provide continuity with more authority, the Kufa school ascribed the doctrine to the companions of Ibn Mas'ud, a companion of the Prophet. Somewhat later, the authority is derived from Ibn Mas'ud himself. It was natural for this development to reach ultimately and inevitably the source of such inspiration, the Prophet himself. Thus, some time before the systematised reports of the Prophet's sayings and actions (*hadith*) had been accepted as a basis for the law, the Iraqis certainly had become used to the idea of *sunna* as representing the normative behaviour of the Prophet, as well as the living practice of the community.

1-35 As the schools became institutionalised, the normative *sunna* was stressed more to the exclusion of the practice of the law. The opposition of the schools to the late Umayyads, as well as the sponsorship by the early Abbasid Caliphs, stimulated this trend. It was only natural for the Abbasids, who were eager to show themselves as the true expression of Islamic piety, to encourage any philosophy which tried to cut through the Umayyad administration in order to return to the purity of the source of Islam. Thus the early Abbasid regime sponsored the views of the jurists and more of their rank were appointed as Qadis than hitherto. Abu Yusuf was an outstanding example. Such appointments naturally stimulated the movement toward the integration of practice and theory.

1-36 In order to illustrate how these early scholars developed the law, it would be useful to say a few words about the type of legal reasoning employed by them. The chief characteristic of the time was the use of analogy (*qiyas*). For instance, the characteristics of dower (*mahr*) given by the husband to the wife on marriage were not sufficiently detailed in the Qur'an, so it was necessary to develop the principles of the law on this subject, in particular to decide upon a minimum acceptable sum. In Kufa, this sum was fixed at 10 *dirhams*, because this was also the minimum value of goods which rendered a thief liable to the compulsory punishment of amputation of the hand. A parallel was here drawn between the loss of virginity and the amputation of the hand. In Medina, where three *dirhams* was the minimum value of stolen goods before the thief was subjected to the penalty of amputation, a similar analogical deduction led to the minimum dower being fixed at three *dirhams*. The Medinans probably followed the Kufan reasoning on this issue.

1–37 Around A.D. 770, the doctrinaire adherents of the normativeness of *sunna* began to make themselves more influential than the older group of scholars who, as we have seen, were prepared to accept the contemporaneity of the *sunna*. It was at this stage that the *hadith* came into their own, with those of the doctrinaire viewpoint who wished it, using the *hadith* material as a way to circumvent the practice of the Qadi and to limit the discretion (*ra'y*) of the jurists.

1–38 This conflict of legal theory was won, and won decisively, by the doctrinaire, as living traditions and independent reasoning (*ra'y*) gave way to systematic thought and more consistent doctrine. As pupil followed master, this tendency became more marked. Practical solutions, with their typical analogical reasoning, were replaced by an increasing reliance on the traditions of the Prophet and his companions. But even within this new consistency, differences of opinion were not uncommon. If there was a division of opinion in one geographical area, such as Kufa, it was natural for there to be vast conflicts of legal thought between one centre of law and another. In Medina, for instance, slaves had a right of ownership reflecting the Arab tradition, but in Kufa, possibly through Roman influences, slaves – being owned themselves – could not own. There are many other examples. For instance, in the field of inheritance, the Kufans recognised the rights of distant kindred to succeed to an estate in the absence both of Qur'anic sharers and the traditional agnatic relatives. This was not accepted in Medina.

1–39 The ancient schools of law built up around themselves a consensus (*ijma*) on a number of points which often differed in principle and certainly differed in detail from other schools. As we have indicated, the biggest controversy at this time was between the *ahl al-ra'y*, those who believed in the value of individual reasoning, and the *ahl al-hadith*, those who believed in the authority of the *hadith* to the exclusion of all independent reasoning.[6] This conflict is certainly reflected by early writers such as Malik and Ibn Abilaila, but the man who successfully integrated the two points of view was Shafi'i, who was born in A.D. 767 and died in A.D. 820. He was a student and follower of the Medina school.

1–40 It is simplest, within the context of this short historical introduction, to describe Shafi'i's concept of law by reference to a number of general statements. First, and certainly by far most importantly, Shafi'i accepted the principal contention of the traditionalists. Thus, for Shafi'i, as for the traditionalists, a *hadith* could not be overridden by a contrary practice (*sunna*) of the community. Put another way, Shafi'i's thesis, in essence, was based on the acceptance of the normative value of *sunna* and the rejection of its continuity. Secondly, it is true that Shafi'i accepted the paradox that *sunna* as he understood it could not even be superseded by the Qur'an, for the *hadith*, divinely inspired as it was, could not contradict an express revelation in the Qur'an. Once the Prophet's conduct, as embodied in the *hadith*, had been established as something like a hidden or indirect

---

[6] For an excellent detailed discussion on this topic see Coulson, *Conflicts and tensions in Islamic jurisprudence* (1969), pp. 3–19.

revelation, everything changed. Thus what may appear to be a contradiction of a *hadith* by the Qur'an was far from the case, for a further *hadith* must surely exist in conformity with revelation. Further, the authenticity of a *hadith* was to be tested by the chain of authority (*isnad*) and no other reasoning could be applied to test its veracity. Fourth, Shafi'i rejected *ijma* as the consensus of the scholars and reconstructed it as the consensus of the Muslim community. Finally, and in summary, Shafi'i rejected all forms of individual *ra'y*, only allowing independent reasoning in the form of analogical deduction (*qiyas*). Even here, however, *qiyas* was restricted in that it could only be of value in applying Qur'an, *sunna* or *ijma* to problems which had not been expressly answered. Shafi'i's work, to the extent that it was accepted by the jurists, brought to an end the uncontrolled use of *ra'y* by the early schools.

1–41 The corpus of the law introduced through *ra'y*, however, had become part of the *sunna* of the community. Shafi'i's interpretation meant the end of the dual aspect of *sunna*, but the substantive law which had been integrated into the *shari'a* was not rejected. Some people indeed believe that *hadith* were created in order to provide authority for the rules of law which had come into existence as a result of *ra'y*. Of those who believe in this development, the major exponent, of course, is Joseph Schacht. In essence, Schacht's argument is that Shafi'i was the first jurist who formulated the system of sources giving the traditions of the Prophet absolute authority, as argued earlier by the traditionalists. Before him, as for his contemporaries, traditions existed but they were interpreted in the light of the 'living tradition'. Schacht argues that the classical collections, prepared by al-Bukhari, Muslim, Abu Dawud, at-Tirmidhi, an-Nasa'i, and Ibn Maja, all in the third century of Islam, carry within their corpus many traditions which cannot be authentic. The pioneering orientalist Goldhizer had long before, originally in 1910, doubted the 'prophetic' end product of the chain of transmissions (*isnad*) and had suggested that most of the traditions belonged to the first century of Islam rather than to the period of Mohammed. Schacht went further, stating that a great deal of the *hadith* material in the classical collections was put into circulation only after Shaf''i's time. Indeed, Schacht was not prepared to date any tradition further back than the latter period of the Umayyad Caliphate. It was his view that traditionalists started to circulate *hadith* in order to overcome the administrative secularism and pragmatism of the Umayyad Qadis as well as the 'living traditions' of the early schools of law.

1–42 As indicated, the issue of the authenticity of the *hadith* has roused a great deal of controversy among Western orientalists, Muslim scholars, and between the two groups. Coulson (1964, Chap. 5), whilst accepting the broad sweep of Schacht's analysis, criticised his theory in a number of areas. Coulson argued that the immediate concerns of the Muslim community during the revelationary period involved Mohammed in the task of making *ad hoc* decisions. These decisions were necessarily publicised by word of mouth. In this way, early traditions came into existence based on authentic statements and determinations of the Prophet. This early work of Mohammed is, by and large, acknowledged by Schacht. Thus Coulson would argue that the acceptance of Schacht's thesis assumes a void in the picture of the development of law in early Muslim society. Coulson agrees with Schacht that the *isnad* is often unreliable, but that, nevertheless, the character of the classical *hadith* collections contains substantive law which is undeniably traceable to Mohammed's time. Coulson would also say that to prove the invalidity of one chain does not thereby prove the fraudulence of the entire corpus of the *hadith*. Thus, "where the rule [in the hadith] fits naturally into the circumstances of the Prophet's community at Medina, then [the hadith] should be tentatively accepted as authentic until reason for the contrary is shown". (Coulson (1964), p. 70).

1–43 Similarly, Muslim scholars, such as Kamali (1989) contend that in fact there is no dispute amongst the *ulema* over the occurrence of extensive forgery in the *hadith* literature, and that some have gone so far as to affirm that in no other branch of Islamic sciences has there been so much forgery. However, to then go and say that nearly all traditions are forged and did not, in fact, have their origins in Muhammad's time at all, sounds too conspiratorial.

1–44 Other writers have taken issue with Schacht's assertion and have, through step-by-step examination of historical documents and situations, raised grave doubts as to the reliability of Schacht's theory. Nabia Abbott undertook an exhaustive study of early documents. Her main findings were summarised by Powers (1986, p. 4) as follows: (i) *Hadith* were transmitted, both orally and in writing, from the very beginning of Islamic history; (ii) reports about Muhammad, as transmitted by his followers, were subjected to a rigorous scrutiny at each stage of transmission and (iii) the immense growth of the *hadith* literature in the second and third Islamic centuries was the result of the progressive increase of parallel and multiple chains of transmission, not of the fabrication of content.

1–45 Azami (1992) also criticised Schacht and his treatment of the sources and contended that he had failed to understand the meaning of texts, quoted statements out of context and made sweeping generalisations on the basis of scant evidence. Whatever the correct position, and of course this debate is only marginally relevant to the substantive matters discussed in this book, it could be assumed that there is an element of truth in both arguments. A safer approach would be to adopt the position taken earlier by Juynboll (1910) who contended that, with only a few exceptions, it is unlikely that scholars will ever develop a method that will make it possible to demonstrate positively the authenticity of these ascriptions. Thus, it would be better to regard *hadith* as faithfully discussing issues which were of relevance and concern to the early Muslims both during the Prophet's lifetime and after his death.

1–46 It is of course beyond doubt that Shafi'i's vision was an important contributory factor towards the further development of the schools of law. After Shafi'i, scholars devoted their time to sifting the 'reliable' *hadith* from those deemed to be 'unreliable'. It is not inconceivable that in this process previously forgotten *hadith* were brought to light. The essential point is simply this: Even if we accept the historical criticisms of Schacht, moderated or not by Coulson and other scholars, the concept of *sunna*, as Shafi'i had expounded it, was approved by the scholars and the resultant compilations of *hadith* became the primary code of Muslim jurisprudence. The study of *hadith* literature profoundly influenced the next 10 centuries of Muslim life. In essence, the previous use of independent reasoning (*ra'y*) came under control. The only permitted human reasoning in the form of analogy (*qiyas*) was so framed by Shafi'i as to be dependent entirely on the discipline of the Qur'an and the *sunna*. The law was bound to lose its accelerating pace and to become enshrined in Shafi'i's classical mould.

1–47 It is desirable, at this stage, to summarise the situation as it existed after Shafi'i's death in A.D. 820, by way of tracing, albeit in outline, the doctrine of the sources of law (*usul al-fiqh*) according to Shafi'i. There are four sources of law: Qur'an, *sunna*, *ijma* and *qiyas*. It has been argued that these sources were developed by two centuries of experience. Classical Islamic theology, however, denies this historical approach. It is important, therefore, to remember that the classical exposition of the sources of the law of Islam carries within itself the fundamental belief that the Qur'an, *sunna*, *ijma* and *qiyas* – as a theory of the *shari'a* – were laid down from the beginning of the Muslim exegesis.

1–48 The most important contribution that *ijma* made stemmed from the overarching concept of the agreement or consensus of the community (*ummah*) as represented by the scholars that the classical sources of the law – and the contents of the law at that time – were the authoritative expression of Islam. The well-known phrase that the *ummah* could not agree on an error was enshrined as a saying of the Prophet in a retrospective sense. But from that moment on, *ijma* becomes exclusionary. The Orientalist view of what happened to Islamic law is that, having agreed – or more correctly having agreed to differ – on the text (*nass*), and having worked out the interpretation, a consensus developed that all essential questions had already been discussed and settled. Thus from that time on, it was assumed that no one would have the necessary qualifications for independent reasoning in the law. The position which is taken from then on is that imitation of the doctrines of earlier jurists (*taqlid*) is to be preferred to independent reasoning. A person who is bound to practise *taqlid* is the 'imitator' (*muqallid*).

1–49 This view of the theory of the law seeks to deny the scope for *ra'y*. Of course, the actual historical experience of the Qadis, and even of the ancient schools, had been different. The use of human reasoning had played a major part in the development of Muslim law, and the jurists of the ninth century appear to have recognised this point, albeit in an indirect fashion when they acknowledge the existence of a number of subsidiary sources of law, primarily three in number: *ijtihad*, *istihsan* and *istislah*.

1–50 *Ijtihad* is defined literally as 'striving, exerting', in an effort to find the right path. Though it has been described as a most important source next to the Qur'an and *sunna*, it is not strictly a source of law at all, in the sense that *ijtihad* is a continuous process of development, whereas divine revelation and Prophetic tradition discontinued upon the demise of the Prophet. It is rather a method by which the *mujtahid*, the person who exercises *ijtihad*, recognises and makes known the legal meaning of the Qur'anic rule or the *sunna*. Put another way, *ijtihad* can be seen as a method by which the will of Allah is discovered. After the *mujtahid* exercises *ijtihad*, the consensus of opinion will either reject or accept the theory or finding. If it is accepted by *ijma*, it becomes an incorporated part of the *shari'a*. As already shown, *ijma* as a doctrine carries within it the idea of 'no contradiction'. However, there is an in-built recognition of plurality because of the well-known saying to the effect that "Difference among my community is a sign of the bounty of Allah". If one finds two or more variant opinions, they can all be accepted as equally legitimate attempts to express a particular rule.

1–51 Thus, the accepted version of history, as expounded from the late nineteenth century to almost the present day by Western orientalists (and some Muslim scholars) is that from about A.D. 950 or the end of the tenth century, the exercise of *ijtihad* exhausted itself, and that from that date the door of independent reasoning was closed. Indeed, some historians refer to the early tenth century as the date of the 'closing of the gates of *ijtihad*'.

1–52 However, writers such as Wael Hallaq [1984] deny both the closure or the narrowing of the 'gates of *ijtihad*' and, arguing on the basis of historical examples, show that in practice *ijtihad* was continuously exercised. Hallaq contends that jurists who were capable of *ijtihad* have existed at nearly all times, that the qualifications required were relatively easy to attain, and that the controversy about the closure of the gates prevented the jurists from reaching a consensus to that effect.

1–53 There are a large number of varying opinions held by commentators on this matter but it is possible to glean trends from their writings. First, early writers are in general not nearly as clear on the closure of the gates as those who wrote from 1930 onwards. Secondly, some are explicitly dismissive of the notion that *ijtihad* ever came to an end at all. It would appear that in the late nineteenth century and early twentieth century, writers were either confused, unclear or undecided about the issue and this would imply that the concept itself was not universally accepted until much later when writers such as Ostrorog (1927), seemed to have seized on the aforementioned phrase and rendered it into vogue. From then onwards, with each new utterance, the concept became more simplified, undisputed and almost cast in stone.

1-54 The other two subsidiary sources, *istihsan* and *istislah*, are essentially examples of particular forms of *ra'y*. Thus, when the early jurists, especially those of Kufa, exercised independent reasoning because of the appropriateness of the decision, a concept close to equity, then the technical term we ought to employ is *istihsan*, literally "to deem something good".[7] One example from the law relating to hire will be sufficient to illustrate the use of *istihsan*. The consideration which is required for the hire of an object or a person is considered, as a general rule in Islamic law, necessarily to involve non-fungible objects such as gold or silver. *Sunna*, however, always allowed the hire of a wet nurse in return for her food and clothing. Early jurists, faced both with the concept of hire as well as the exceptional situation relating to the hire of a wet nurse, exercised *istihsan*, the juristic preference, and thus permitted the hire of a wet nurse in return for her food and clothing.

1-55 The important concept of 'public interest', *istislah*, related to the word *salih*, 'in the general interest', is used to express the occasions when the judge or the *ulema* exercised discretion out of consideration for the public interest. One example will suffice, illustrating the Medinan attitude to the law of sale. The Islamic concept of sale is based on the belief that one contract cannot hinge upon the performance of a separate extraneous agreement. Such a contract is void (*batil*). Therefore, by strict analogy (*qiyas*) a contract between A and B, whereby A buys leather on condition that B makes the leather into a pair of shoes, is void. Well before Shafi'i's work, such a contract was seen by the jurists to be of particular benefit; thus by *istislah* the Medinans permitted the contract in question.

1-56 Shafi'i obviously disapproved of such procedures and such methods were seen by him as grave infringements upon his consistent doctrine of *usul al-fiqh*. Both *istihsan* and *istislah* permitted the use of discretion and personal reasoning, even within certain ascertainable limits. On various grounds, they were both treated as unacceptable.

1-57 It has been illustrated already that Shafi'i's theories on law were approved, although not entirely and absolutely, by those immediately after him. So it was inevitable that regardless of the adjustments and rationalisations of the previous practice which were bound to take place, the use of *istihsan* and *istislah* would be subordinated to the classical theory but not really marginalised in practice. This leads us to one of the most important aspects of the early development of Muslim law. The legal material which had been introduced by the earlier jurisprudential techniques was not abrogated. It all remained within the corpus of Muslim law, to be justified by different schools in one of two ways. First, later scholars probably 'traced back' concepts introduced by *istihsan* to a *hadith*. Secondly, by the doctrine of

---

[7] For an important article on *istihsan* and its relation to equity according to the views of various scholars, see Makdisi , "Legal logic and equity in Islamic law" [1985] 33 *The American Journal of Comparative Law* 63–92.

ijma, the *ra'y* of the scholars and Qadis in all the schools was accepted as part of the *shari'a* for all time. Further, the assumed prohibition of any further *ra'y* sought to deny the right of the *mujtahid* to change the law which had been accepted by consensus.

1–58 The subsequent history of the schools of Muslim law after Shafi'i is therefore a story of further diversification. We have already seen that centres of learning had sprung up whose purpose was to discuss law on a theoretical plane. These groups, often simply because of the impact of geographical distance, developed both their own peculiar laws and methods of reasoning. Later, due to the influence of leading scholar-jurists like Malik, Abu Hanifa, Abu Yusuf, Shaybani and others, the schools continued to grow apart.

1–59 Shafi'i's aim had been centred on his vision of the unity of Islamic jurisprudence in both theory and practice. Did he succeed? In one respect, it is possible to answer this question in the affirmative. The classical theory is impregnated by Shafi'i's doctrine, and the only major difference, although admittedly this difference is of some consequence, is that the classical system gives prominence to *ijma* and reverts to the pre-Shafi'i idea that *ijma* referred to the consensus of the scholars rather than the consensus of the community (*umma*). In another respect, Shafi'i failed, as new problems – and schools – arose as a direct result of his work. Law introduced by *ra'y*, now given the weight of acceptance through *ijma* and almost certainly having acquired *hadith* as justification, continued as orthodox doctrine within the corpus of Islam while its historical background was forgotten.

1–60 There are four Sunni schools surviving today: Hanafi, Maliki, Shafi'i, and Hanbali. A number of other schools, at one time or another, had been accepted as orthodox interpretations of the *shari'a*, but they have not survived. Dawud ibn Khalaf was the founder of a literal school, called the Zahiri, which has now become extinct. The diversity of the *shari'a* between the four schools was accepted by the classical jurisprudence under the umbrella of *ijma*.

1–61 The Hanafi school was officially adopted by the Abbasid dynasty and was subsequently brought to Afghanistan and later to the Indian subcontinent. Emigrants from India spread the school to East Africa and to Malaysia. The Ottoman Empire also recognised the Hanafi interpretation. Thus Hanafi law is today also followed in Turkey, Iraq, Syria, the Balkan countries, Cyprus, Jordan, Sudan, Israel, Palestine, Egypt and Libya. The Maliki school grew out of the school in Medina. It spread to Egypt, Sudan, Eritrea, Somalia, Libya, Tunisia, Algeria, Morocco, Central and Western Africa and Northern Nigeria. It is also followed in the Eastern coastal territories of Arabia, bordering on the Gulf. The Shafi'i school, beginning in Cairo, where Shafi'i lived for the last five years of his life, spread to South Arabia, the Indian coastline, and then via the Arab trade routes to East Africa and South-East Asia. Shafi'i Muslims predominate today in Malaysia, Singapore, Indonesia, the Philippines and Sri Lanka. The fourth surviving school, Hanbali, affirms the traditionalist approach. Before Iran became sectarian, the Hanbali school of thought had many adherents there. Often on the edge of extinction, it was revived by the puritanical movements of the eighteenth and early twentieth centuries. Hanbali law is today followed in Saudi Arabia and is also applied in Qatar.

1–62 It is true to say that whilst in the Hanafi and Maliki schools, practice came first and theory only later, in Hanbali and Shafi'i law, by contrast, the theory of law preceded the practice of the law. From this fact it might be thought that one would be correct to deduce that the content of the Hanbali and Shafi'i law would be closer to each other than Hanafi and Maliki law. Broadly, this is indeed correct. Stemming from this, the law developed by *istihsan* and *istislah* has become part of Hanafi and Maliki law. The later schools had no such wealth of historical material. The concept of consensus (*ijma*), however, acted as a unifying force which has tended to draw the substantive law of the four schools closer together.

1–63 So far, we have considered only the Sunni systems of Muslim law. Outside the Sunni law, however, there developed other sectarian schools. It is necessary in the context of this introduction to say a few words about this phenomenon. A large group within the Muslim community in the world today does not profess adherence to any of the four schools of Sunni Islam. Rather, this group belongs to one of the branches of Shi'i law; namely the Ithna 'Ashari, or the Isma'ili, or possibly also the Zaydi. This third group, the Zaydis, technically *sui generis*, are mostly to be found in the Yemen. Their legal system represents a fusion of Sunni and Shi'i beliefs. They are not numerically strong. The Ithna 'Ashari group, representing the majority of Shi'i Muslims, are to be found in Iran, Iraq and in India. The Isma'ilis, themselves divided into important sects, are present in Central Asia, Iran, the Gulf and in South Asia, from where they have spread to other parts of the world.

1–64 The Shi'i movement is rooted firmly in political schism. During the reign of the fourth Caliphate of 'Ali, a civil war resulted in victory to Mu'awiya who inaugurated the Umayyad dynasty. However, a group refused to accept the inevitable and gave their support to 'Ali and to his issue. 'Ali had married Fatima, the daughter of Mohammed. The followers of 'Ali (the *Shi'at 'Ali*) believe in the concept that the successors of Mohammed inherit the title of Imam by divine right. To this extent they deny the right of the first three Caliphs to the caliphate.

1–65 After the death of the fourth Shi'a Imam, Zayn al-Abidin, one of his sons, Zayd, was accepted as Imam by a group of followers who came to be called Zaydis. They differ from the other Shi'i groups in that they recognise that succession to the Imamate depends on election rather than on a divine right. The majority, at this period of schism, followed Muhamad al-Baqir and, after him, Ja'far al-Sadiq. When Sadiq died, another split occurred. Most adherents supported Musa al-Kazim and the six Imams after him. The twelfth leader was the last, and believers say that it is this Imam who will return to herald the Messianic age. Sadiq's elder brother, Isma'il, led the other faction. His supporters came to be called Isma'ilis or Seveners. Thus, Shi'is are divided amongst themselves. Details of their laws will be introduced, where relevant, when we turn to the discussion of the substantive law in later chapters of this book.

1–66 It is necessary, however, to return to the administration of the law as we have so far described it. The Qadis assumed jurisdiction in only a small area of the law. Jurisdiction in other courts beyond that of the Qadi emerged for a number of interconnected reasons. First, and perhaps of fundamental importance, the *shari'a* law as applied by the Qadis was, as we have seen, concerned essentially with the relationship between God and man. This relationship expresses itself with particular force in the sphere of family law and succession. It is certainly relevant in all other areas, such as public law, but comparatively less attention has been given to it. The lack of interest of the *shari'a* in public matters necessitated the development of secular courts. Different offices were created for that purpose from time to time. The *sahib ar-radd* often assumed criminal jurisdiction. The *mazalim*, those in charge of complaints, also came to control questions relating to land. In both these spheres of human enterprise, the importance of the subject-matter for the government, as well as the marked initial lack of interest by the Qadis, was responsible for the development of separate governmental courts. *Mazalim* jurisdiction, in particular, developed in Abbasid times. Indeed it has been observed by Coulson (1964, p. 122), amongst others, that the distinction between the jurisdiction of the *mazalim* and the *shari'a* came very close to the notion of a division between secular and religious courts. Thus, centuries before any reception of European law, the Muslim community was used to the separation of powers between the religious courts, which dealt with personal status matters, and the secular *mazalim* jurisdiction, which, though still within the corpus of Muslim law, was responsible for criminal law and land law (see in detail Coulson (1964), p. 129).

1–67 There is a second reason for the growth of secular jurisdiction; namely the highly formalised and complex evidential rules prevalent in the Qadis' courts. These rules are based on oath-taking (*yamin*). The Qadi, in the first instance, questions the defendant (the *mudda'a 'allayhi*). If the defendant admits the claim, then judgment is made in favour of the plaintiff (*mudda'i*). If the defendant denies the claim, then the Qadi demands from the plaintiff the production of evidence. The Muslim plaintiff is required to produce two male adult witnesses, both of whom must be Muslim, who are prepared to testify orally to their knowledge of the truth of the claim. There was bound to develop within this framework the concept of the 'fixed witness' (*shahada*), always available to give testimony, whose price depended on his alleged worth. No substitution was permitted to the oral testimony and circumstantial evidence was excluded. If the plaintiff failed to produce the necessary witnesses, the defendant was ordered to take the oath on the Qur'an. If properly sworn, judgment was given in the defendant's favour. The oath was offered to the defendant three times. On the third refusal, judgment was given to the plaintiff.

1–68 This brief description of the rules of evidence must suffice to show that the highly regulated procedure was based firmly upon the idealised assumption that a Muslim would not, indeed could not, give false testimony under oath (see Coulson (1968), pp. 67–68). The rules were so designed as to emphasise the relationship of man with God. The Qur'anic oath was the bond between the two. Balancing of evidence, as it would be understood in modern legal systems, played no part at all.

1–69 As the Muslim community extended their contacts with the Byzantine and Persian empires, it was inevitable that contracts were written and broken, and the Qadis' courts could not cater for this. Also, the stress laid on the testimony of two adult male Muslims as to their religious and moral probity (*'adala*) necessarily ensured that many hardened criminals, those who were unaffected by false oath-taking, were unjustly released. The Qadis themselves realised this difficulty. In time, but too late to prevent the flow of work from the courts, they came to accept that written documents were necessary to prove private legal transactions. A new science (*shurut*) developed as a highly sophisticated system of formularies.[8]

1–70 Further, the Islamic law of criminal justice emphasised to a considerable extent discretion in punishment (*ta'zir*). Thus the Muslim ruler was permitted, within his own policy necessities, to provide a framework for criminal law beyond the narrow confines of the compulsory Qur'anic punishments (*hudud*). This discretionary area in criminal law is perhaps only an example of the wider concept of administrative decisions (*siyasa shar'iyya*). As a basic theory of constitutional law, *siyasa shar'iyya* recognised that the sovereign, as head of the Muslim state and a man of *'adala*, fit for the office, was empowered to 'complete' or supplement the *shari'a*. However, this was to occur within limits. The ruler had no input into the content

---

[8] With reference to marriage see below, para. 6–18.

of the *shari'a*, nor did the ruler's law, at least in theory, become part of Islamic law. Both the Umayyad and Abbasid empires were thus responsible for wide-ranging legislative activities.

1–71 We conclude this brief introductory section, noting the crystallisation of the classical system of law at a period not later than the thirteenth century, emphasising the dual feature of the administration of justice between the *mazalim* courts and the *shari'a* jurisdiction. In the following section, we shall have occasion to discuss the emergence of particular Muslim legal systems from this self-imposed discipline. Our attention will be focused first on various Middle Eastern jurisdictions and then briefly on the Indian subcontinent.

Reforms of Muslim law

1–72 The first major redefinition of traditional Muslim law occurred in the Ottoman Empire in the nineteenth century. These reforms, known as the Tanzimat reforms, inspired largely by political motives, introduced into the Ottoman law a Commercial Code 1850, a Penal Code 1858, a Code of Commercial Procedure 1879, a Code of Civil Procedure 1880, and a Code of Maritime Commerce. In form, all the Ottoman Codes followed the European civil law model of attempting a comprehensive codification. There was, however, some attempt to integrate certain principles of *shari'a* criminal law. Thus Article 1 of the Ottoman Penal Code stresses that its provisions cannot in any case injure the rights of the individual consecrated by the *shari'a*.[9] In this way, the Code retained the rights of the victim's family to blood money (*diya*) in cases of homicide.

1–73 With few exceptions, the first Ottoman reforms put the *shari'a* to one side. In contrast, the Majalla, not really devised as such, but ultimately known as the Civil Code of 1876, codified the rules of contract and tort of the Hanafi branch of the Sunni law. The Majalla, although European in form, is clearly Islamic in content. After the establishment of secular courts, it became inevitable that the Islamic law of obligations required a restatement, not least so as to make the law more easily accessible to litigants and lawyers alike. The lawyers of the latter part of the nineteenth century were not trained in the intricacies of the *shari'a*. Although not seen as exclusive, the Majalla acquired a position of supreme authority from early on. Akin to a European code, the Majalla is subdivided into books, chapters and articles. It deals with contracts and with some torts, but it does not cover non-contractual obligations, family law or real property. However, it does contain some procedural rules. The Majalla is highly significant, first because it represents the earliest example of an official promulgation of large parts of the *shari'a* by the authority of a modern state. Secondly, within its specific articles, there are certain principles derived not from the consensus of Hanafi law, but rather from divergent opinions from the Hanafi traditions. It represents, therefore, an important example of creativity from within the Muslim tradition. While *ijma* had sanctioned diversity of opinion within the Sunni schools, and *siyasa shari'yya* permitted the ruler to order application of a rule from a particular school tradition, the Majalla did not consist of new rules but represented a selection (*takhayyur*) made from existing rules.

1–74 Important reforms followed when, in 1915, the Ottoman rulers started enacting legislation by Imperial edicts to improve the status of Muslim wives,

---

[9] For the relevant translation and details see Liebesny, *The law of the Near and Middle East: Readings, cases & materials* (1975).

providing them with certain, albeit limited, rights to petition for divorce. These reforms were extended and consolidated in the *Ottoman Law of Family Rights* of 1917. Such rights did not exist in the dominant Hanafi law. The authorities had based the reforms on Hanbali (and also Maliki) law and on the minority or 'weaker' Hanafi doctrine. An eclectic choice was thus made, a selection (*takhayyur*), although admittedly for a limited purpose.

1–75 These early reforms of family law in the Ottoman Empire provide the key to the legislative activity in the Muslim world in more recent times and continue to inspire the family laws of many Middle Eastern states.[10] Turkey itself went further. Only in that country has the government entirely abolished the *shari'a*, replacing it with codes of European inspiration.[11] The two major trends, both in the areas regulated by Islamic law and in those areas already subjected to secularisation, have been increased eclecticism in the selection of sources and the synthesis of Islamic and Western legal ideas. This latter development is particularly apparent in the field of contract.[12]

1–76 Perhaps the foremost advocate of these two trends has been the Egyptian scholar Dr. Abd al-Sanhuri. He approached the issues in a pragmatic way, forming the view that the Islamic system could not be reintroduced, in particular with regard to matters relating to land law and commercial law, without prior adaptation to the needs of a modern civilisation. Dr Sanhuri was primarily responsible for the drafting of the Egyptian Civil Code 1948, the Iraqi Code 1951 the Libyan Code 1953 and the Kuwaiti Code and Commercial Law 1960/1.[13] The Syrian and Libyan Codes state in Article 1(2):

> "In the absence of an applicable legal provision the judge shall decide in accordance with the principles of the Islamic Shari'a, and in the absence of these in accordance with custom. In the absence of custom, the Judge will apply the principles of natural law and the rules of equity."

Moreover, the introduction to the Syrian Code makes it clear that Article 1(2) does not limit derivation to the authoritative view of any one school. The entire corpus of relevant *shari'a* principles is available to the judge.[14] Major theoretical problems abound in the interpretation of these provisions and similar sections in other Middle Eastern codes. For instance, to which works should a judge turn? Should one be looking for principles, which will be difficult to find, or should one be looking for solutions? A judge looking for solutions will of course often find several contradictory solutions, even within one school of law.

1–77 In the field of family law, legislators faced with the need to reform an area of the law seen to be at the heart of the *shari'a* have been able to justify reforms as being wholly within the context of Islamic jurisprudence. Some expedients used have been of a procedural nature, namely the right of the ruler to confine and define the jurisdiction of his courts. This expedient was used in Egypt in 1931 to restrict

---

[10] On details see now El Alami and Hinchcliffe, *Islamic marriage and divorce laws of the Arab world* (1996); Welchman. "The development of Islamic family law in the legal system of Jordan" [1988] 37 I.C.L.Q. 868–886 on Jordan; Welchman [1994] 11 *Recht van de Islam*, on the occupied West Bank.

[11] The Civil Code and the Code of Obligation 1926 are based on Swiss models. In contrast, the Criminal Code 1926 is based upon the Italian Penal Code, the Code of Criminal Procedure 1929 is derived from the German Code, and the Code of Civil Procedure 1927 follows the Code in the Swiss canton of Neuchâtel.

[12] On this topic see in detail El Alami, *The marriage contract in Islamic law in the shari'ah and personal status laws of Egypt and Morocco* (1992).

[13] Kuwait's Civil and Commercial Code of 1961 was amended by a new Code in 1980.

[14] See in detail Anderson, "The Shari'a and civil law" (1954) 1 No. 1, *The Islamic Quarterly* 30–32 and Anderson, *Law reform in the Muslim world* (1976), pp. 86 *et seq.*

the solemnisation of child marriages by precluding the court from hearing any claim of marriage whatsoever if the husband had not reached 18 years old and the bride the age of 16 years old at the time of the litigation. Furthermore, the court could not hear any disputed claim of marriage unless that marriage contract had been registered. Earlier, in 1923, it had been made a criminal offence for a registrar to register a marriage in a case where the bride was not above 16 years old and the bridegroom above 18 years old.

1–78 Eclecticism (*takhayyur*), first seen in the Majalla, has become the most notable basis for reforms in the family law field. Some interesting examples were given by Anderson (1976, pp. 48 *et seq.*). At first, the concept of *takhayyur* was limited to the adoption of variant opinions within a particular school, or to the introduction of the dominant doctrine of another Sunni school. Later, justification for reform was based on any opinion of any jurist regardless of school. Occasionally the doctrine of one school or jurist is combined with another. This concept, known as *talfiq* or 'piecing together', permits reforms which are seen as socially desirable, yet at the same time ensures that there is no departure from the essence of Islamic law. In fact, of course, an entirely new principle has been created.

1–79 Before 1946, notwithstanding these frequent innovations, the principle of imitation (*taqlid*) was formally followed. The authority of medieval legal manuals was paramount. It was seen that these manuals contained the *fiqh*, the authoritative presentation of the corpus of Muslim law as created by consensus (*ijma*). At the same time, however, the principle of *taqlid* was beginning to be challenged, and scholars in the Muslim world propounded the view that the right to search by independent deduction (*ijtihad*) could also be invoked by modern legislators. For example, Allama Iqbal (republished in 1989, p. 134) wrote:

> "The claim of the present generation of Muslim liberals to reinterpret the foundational legal principles, in the light of their own experience and the altered conditions of modern life is, in my opinion, perfectly justified. The teaching of the Qur'an that life is a process of progressive creation necessitates that each generation, guided but unhampered by the work of its predecessors, should be permitted to solve its own problems."

This view gained considerable acceptance in the Muslim world by the end of the 1970s. Many of the reforms were based on the right to exercise *ijtihad*, although it is also true that a spirit of secular radicalism influenced the changes in countries such as Somalia and South Yemen.

1–80 It will be recalled that after Shafi'i's death in A.D. 820, there developed a process of interaction between the schools of law when concepts of one school were accepted by another school. Similarly, modern Muslim legislators went through an almost identical process of growth. Indeed, as in the ninth century, when the work of Shafi'i tended to bring the schools together, today the reformist movement has drawn the schools closer together in the search for solutions to particular problems within an Islamic framework. With an increased tendency towards codification and restatement, this trend will inevitably continue to play a dominant role in the Muslim world in the remaining months of the twentieth century and beyond.

1–81 Islamisation has been another equally fascinating development in the Muslim world today. Taking a broad view of the reforms over the last 125 years, it can be seen that there have hitherto been four distinct periods of reform: First, the nineteenth century reforms in the Ottoman Empire. Secondly, the early reforms in family law prior to the Second World War, usually, though not always, based on the doctrine of *siyasa shar'iyya*. Thirdly, the reforms based on *talfiq*, found for example in the Syrian Law of Personal Status of 1953 and the Tunisian Law of Personal Status of 1956.[15] Finally, the acceptance that some reforms can be introduced purely for social or economic reasons without recourse to juristic arguments. However, even where reforms have been based on perceived social need, at least on the surface, or even quite explicitly, juristic arguments have been adduced. For example, the abolition of polygamy in Tunisia was justified through 'neo-*ijtihad*' by a reinterpretation of Sura IV, verse 3 in the Qur'an. In that verse, the doctrine of justice is equated, in Tunisia (and now in Bangladesh), not only with financial provisions (*nafaqa*), but also with love and affection. Arguing that only the Prophet can treat two wives equally in this way, in today's conditions, an irrebuttable presumption was raised that a Muslim cannot fulfil the requirements laid down in the Qur'an. Thus polygamy was prohibited.

1–82   Fascinatingly, the same argument has now been used by the High Court of Bangladesh in *Jesmin Sultana v. Mohammad Elias* (1997) 17 B.L.D. 4, which relies on Tunisian law as well as taking a fresh look at the Qur'anic foundations to hold that polygamy is against the principles of Islamic law and that therefore section 6 of the Bangladeshi Muslim Family Laws Ordinance 1961 should be deleted and replaced by a legal provision prohibiting polygamy. Obviously, this was an eminently political decision and it can be read in various ways. It fits in, however, with other recent Bangladeshi cases which are pressing for reforms to the Muslim laws in that country.

1–83   The question which must be asked at the end of the 1990s is whether some Muslim leaders and courts have actually gone too far in the direction of reforms and whether we are not witnessing a reintroduction of *shari'a* principles long discarded. To an extent, recent developments have been based on the need to eliminate Western cultural imperialism (Mayer (1990), p. 182). This is to a large degree accompanied by the political authority managing the process of islamisation to retain supreme power and authority.

1–84   Pakistan constitutes a fascinating case study of this kind of development.[16] In 1978, the Government of Pakistan introduced Shariat Benches attached to each of the Provincial High Courts. These new courts were subsequently remodelled as a Federal Shariat Court by a new Article 203C(3) of the Constitution. The Court consists of not more than eight Muslim members. Article 203C(3) states that the Chairman shall be a person who is or has been or is qualified to be a Judge of the Supreme Court, and a member shall be a person who is or has been or is qualified to be a Judge of the High Court. The powers, jurisdiction and functions of the Court are contained in Article 203D and are worthy of citation in full:

> "203D. Powers, jurisdiction and functions of the Court.–
> (1) The Court may, either of its own motion or on the petition of a citizen of Pakistan or the Federal Government or a Provincial Government, examine and decide the question whether or not any law or provision of law is repugnant to the Injunctions of Islam as laid down in the Holy Quran and the Sunnah of the Holy Prophet, hereinafter referred to as the Injunctions of Islam.

---

[15] See Coulson (1969), pp. 46–50; Welchman [1988], pp. 870–871.
[16] For details on these reforms see Pearl, "Executive and legislative amendments to Islamic family law in India and Pakistan," in *Islamic law and jurisprudence* (1990a).

(1A) Where the Court takes up the examination of any law or provision of law under clause (1) and such law or provision of law appears to it to be repugnant to the Injunctions of Islam, the Court shall cause to be given to the Federal Government in the case of a law with respect to a matter in the Federal Legislative List or the Concurrent Legislative List, or to the Provincial Government in the case of a law with respect to a matter not enumerated in either of those Lists, a notice specifying the particular provisions that appear to it to be so repugnant, and afford to such a Government adequate opportunity to have its point of view placed before the Court.

(2) If the Court decides that any law or provision of the law is repugnant to the Injunctions of Islam, it shall set out in its decision:–

   (a) the reasons for its holding that opinion; and

   (b) the extent to which such a law or provision is so repugnant; and specify the day on which the decision shall take effect:
Provided that no such decision shall be deemed to take effect before the expiration of the period within which an appeal therefrom may be preferred to the Supreme Court or, where an appeal has been so preferred, before the disposal of such appeal.

(3) If any law or provision of law is held by the Court to be repugnant to the Injunctions of Islam,–

   (a) the President in the case of a law with respect to a matter in the Federal Legislative List or the Concurrent Legislative List, or the Governor in the case of a law with respect to a matter not enumerated in either of those Lists, shall take steps to amend the law so as to bring such law or provision into conformity with the Injunctions of Islam; and

   (b) such law or provision shall, to the extent to which it is held to be repugnant, cease to have effect on the day on which the decision of the Court takes effect."

1–85 It is important to mention that 'law' for the purposes of this Article includes any custom or usage having the force of law but does not include the Constitution, Muslim personal law, or any law relating to the procedure of any court or tribunal. Two important cases illustrated the limitations of these constitutional mechanisms. *B. Z. Kaikaus v. President of Pakistan* P.L.D. 1980 S.C. 160, was a case brought by a celebrated former Judge of the Pakistan Supreme Court. The Supreme Court had to consider the relationship between the judiciary on the one hand, and the executive and legislature on the other, in the context of the process of islamisation. The petitioners sought a number of declarations, including the following, as stated at page 164:

"(2) A declaration coupled with an appropriate injunction that the Muslims being bound only by the divine law, *i.e.* the Sharia, the Sharia is the only law in this State, the status of the remaining so called laws including the Constitution being only that of orders . . . whose validity depends on their acceptance as Allah's will by the judicial ulama or the judiciary, and that any order or any so-called law including the Constitution, which is in conflict with any part of the Holy Qur'an and Sunnah including the directions relating to justice and righteousness is null and void."

1-86 The Supreme Court refused to grant any of the reliefs sought, taking the view that the process of islamisation was the task of the government, and that the Courts had no jurisdiction to interfere, except to the limited extent laid down in the Constitution itself. The majority judgment, as expressed at page 181, emphasised that the process of islamisation of laws,

> ". . . in its very nature, is of a legislative and political character to be performed by the State by enacting the necessary laws for Islamisation of the existing laws or even to promulgate new laws on that pattern but within the hemisphere of the Holy Qur'an and the Sunnah."

1-87 The second case of interest in this context is *Federation of Pakistan v. Farishta*, P.L.D. 1981 S.C. 120. In this case, the petitioner sought a declaration that section 4 of the Muslim Family Laws Ordinance 1961 was un-Islamic and therefore void by virtue of Article 203 of the Constitution. This section introduced a system of representation into the law of inheritance to benefit the orphaned grandchild of the deceased when that person is in competition with a closer survivor, such as a son or a brother of the deceased (see in detail paragraph 11–122, below). The government relied on Article 203 itself which, in its view, excluded the court's jurisdiction from a review of the 1961 Ordinance. The Supreme Court accepted this argument, stating that the expression "Muslim personal law" was sufficiently wide to cover the special statutory laws applicable to the Muslim citizens of Pakistan. Thus the Ordinance, in this case section 4, was immune from scrutiny. These two cases illustrate the limitations of the constitutional provisions designed to reintroduce Islamic law in Pakistan. As Keith Hodkinson (1981, p. 248) has said:

> "*Farishta* reduces the potential role of the judiciary in Islamicisation by excluding from its scrutiny almost all the controversial legislation in matters of family and succession law."

1-88 Thus it has been left to the executive to realise the islamisation of the inherited laws. In this context, four important Ordinances on criminal law were introduced in Pakistan in 1979, relating to *zina, qazf*, drinking and theft. The first of these, the Offence of Zina (Enforcement of Hudood) Ordinance 1979 (VII of 1979), has had important repercussions in the family law field. *Zina* is defined as follows in section 4 of the Ordinance:

> "A man and a woman are said to commit '*Zina*' if they wilfully have sexual intercourse without being validly married to each other."

If the person convicted of *zina* is someone who at some stage was married and who had marital sexual relations (*a muhsan*), then that person is liable to the *hadd* penalty. *Hadd* is defined in section 5(2)(a) of the Ordinance as stoning to death at a public place. If the person concerned is not a *muhsan*, then the punishment is whipping by 100 lashes. Similar punishments are prescribed in the case of rape (*zina-bil-jabr*).

1-89 The standard of proof required for the draconian *hadd* penalties is very high indeed. It is laid down in section 8 of the 1979 Ordinance:

> "8. Proof of zina or zina-bil-jabr liable to hadd.–
>   Proof of zina or zina-bil-jabr, liable to hadd shall be in one of the following forms, namely:

(a) the accused makes before a Court of competent jurisdiction a confession of the commission of the offence; or

(b) at least four Muslim adult male witnesses about whom the Court is satisfied, having regard to the requirement of 'tazkiyah al-shahud' that they are truthful persons and abstain from major sins ('kabair'), give evidence as eye-witnesses of the act of penetration necessary to the offence.

Provided that, if the accused is a non-Muslim the eye-witnesses may be non-Muslims."

If proof in either of these two forms, as laid down in section 8 is not available, the accused may nonetheless be punished according to sections 9 and 10 of the Ordinance, which apply the doctrine of discretionary punishment (*ta'zir*). In these circumstances, according to the relevant parts of section 10 of the 1979 Ordinance:

"(2) Whoever commits zina liable to tazir shall be punished with rigorous imprisonment for a term which may extend to 10 years and with whipping numbering thirty stripes, and shall also be liable to fine.

(3) Whoever commits zina-bil-jabr liable to tazir shall be punished with imprisonment for a term which shall not be less than four years nor more than twenty-five years and, if the punishment be one of imprisonment, shall also be awarded the punishment of whipping numbering thirty stripes."

1-90 The Zina Ordinance has received much international publicity, especially since it had the unfortunate side-effect of criminalising women.[17] Less well-known is the Offence of Qazf (Enforcement of Hadd) Ordinance (VIII of 1979). Section 3 of this Ordinance defines *qazf* as follows:

"3. Qazf.–Whoever by words either spoken or intended to be read, or by signs or by visible representations, makes or publishes an imputation of 'zina' concerning any person intending to harm, or knowing or having reason to believe that such imputation will harm the reputation, or hurt the feelings, of such person, is said, except in cases hereinafter excepted, to commit 'qazf'."

This section allows for two exceptions. The first relates to imputation of truth "which public good requires to be made or published". Secondly, to make "in good faith an accusation of 'zina' against any person to any of those who have lawful authority over that person". These exceptions do not protect a complainant who makes an accusation of *zina* in court but who fails to produce four witnesses in support. The exceptions also do not protect a witness who gives false evidence of *zina*, or a complainant who makes false accusations of *zina*. This important provision is surely designed to keep vexatious allegations of *zina* to a minimum, for if such allegations turn out not to be proved, unjustified accusers may find themselves in considerable difficulties. The punishment for *qazf* liable to *hadd*, under section 7 of this Ordinance, is whipping by 80 lashes. In addition, after a person has been convicted for the offence of *qazf* liable to *hadd*, his evidence shall not be admissible in any court of law.

1-91 There are many cases decided under the provisions of the Zina Ordinance of 1979, in particular. The interesting case of *Noor Khan v. Haq Nawaz*, P.L.D. 1982

---

[17] See Kennedy [1988] 28 No. 3 *Asian Survey* 307–316 and [1991] 2 No. 1 *Journal of Islamic Studies* 45–55; more detail is found in Mehdi (1994).

F.S.C. 265, will be discussed in the context of divorce under section 7 of the MFLO 1961. Probably the most important cases in this area have been *Hazoor Bakhsh v. Federation of Pakistan* P.L.D. 1982 F.S.C. 145 and *Chaudry v. Islamic Republic of Pakistan* P.L.D. 1983 F.S.C. 255. The question before the court in *Hazoor Bakhsh* was whether stoning to death (*rajm*) as laid down in sections 5(2)(a) and 6(3)(a) of the 1979 Ordinance is *hadd* or obligatory under the Injunctions of Islam. In this respect, Sura XXIV, verse 2 of the Qur'an states:

> "The woman and the man guilty of adultery or fornication, flog each of them with a hundred stripes; let not compassion move you, in their case, in a matter, prescribed by Allah, if ye believe in Allah and the Last Day and let a party of the believers witness the punishment."[18]

1–92   The Qur'anic verse does not specify *rajm*, yet there are a number of *hadith* which refer to this draconian punishment when *zina* is committed by a married person. The most important of these *hadith* is cited by Doi (1984, p. 238) to the effect that,

> "For unmarried person (guilty of fornication), the punishment is one hundred lashes and an exile for one year. For married adulterers, it is one hundred lashes and stoning to death."

When the case of *Hazoor Bakhsh* first came before the Federal Shariat Court in Pakistan, two judges in particular, Salahuddin Ahmed J. and Aftab Hussain J., went in detail through the four cases from the lifetime of the Prophet in which it was allegedly reported that *rajm* had been imposed as a punishment for *zina*. Salahuddin Ahmed J. suggested that *rajm* was not imposed on the basis of injunctions in the Qur'an but rather in accordance with the then prevailing customs of the Arabs. It was therefore an imposition of a *ta'zir* penalty. This Judge stated categorically that the *hadith* cannot override a definite and clear injunction in the Qur'an. Thus it was clear that the provisions on *rajm* in the Ordinance were actually repugnant to the provisions of Islam, for the only penalty which could be imposed on a person guilty of *zina*, whether married or unmarried, is 100 lashes to be inflicted in public. The Ordinance should accordingly be brought into conformity with the injunctions of Islam.[19]

1–93   Agher Ali Hyder J., agreeing with Salahuddin Ahmed J., said that it was not possible, as he put it, to "tag on" to the punishment of *hadd* a further punishment by way of *ta'zir*. Aftab Hussain J. said that the consensus view of the relevant *hadith* was that it had been abrogated by another Qur'anic verse, Sura XXIV, verse 2. Zakrullah Lodhi J. also agreed with this view. Aftab Hussain J. disagreed with his brother judges on one issue: It was his view that stoning can be added to the provisions of *ta'zir*. Karimullah Durrani J., in a dissenting judgment, disagreed entirely with the majority view.[20] On a clear majority, however, the court held that the provisions of the Zina Ordinance were contrary to the injunctions of Islam and ordered that the necessary amendments be made.

1–94   No such amendment was introduced by the Government. In fact, the Government filed an appeal against the judgment before the Supreme Court, which

---

[18] See also Doi (1984), p. 238, with an instructive discussion of the topic at pp. 236–242.

[19] This issue has been much discussed by earlier jurists also. For details see Burton, *The sources of Islamic law: Islamic theories of abrogation* (1990).

[20] See *Hazoor Bakhsh v. Federation of Pakistan*, P.L.D. 1981 F.S.C. 145 and also *Federation of Pakistan v. Hazoor Bakhsh*, P.L.D. 1983 F.S.C. 255.

stayed the operation of the orders. A "power of review" was then added to the powers of the Federal Shariat Court by a President's Order in 1982.[21] In the review hearing, Aftab Hussain C.J. noted the point that Muslim personal law is excluded from examination by the court as a result of Article 203(B) of the Constitution of Pakistan. Thus the earlier Court had lacked jurisdiction in the matter. The other judgments add little to the fact that the original decision was *ultra vires* the Constitution. Thus the order that the necessary amendments be made to the law was withdrawn.

1–95 We have concentrated above on the trends in Pakistan. What of the rest of the Muslim world? The revolution in Iran swept away all the reforms of the Shah in the family law field. Changes in Egypt have been held by the Court there to be unconstitutional, only to be re-introduced by Law 100 in 1985.[22] Similar debates could be located in many countries, from Turkey to Malaysia. There are those who believe that the reforms in the family laws which we describe in this book have undermined the basic values of the Muslim way of life. Yet there are others who consider that the restrictions on the husband's unilateral right to repudiate his wife, and the restrictions on polygamy, and such other changes, in no way militate against the basic tenets of Islam. Nonetheless, especially reforms which outwardly improve the legal status of women in society, such as those in Somalia in relation to the rights of inheritance of the female (which are now exactly equal to the male of equal degree removed from the deceased) are often found unacceptable. From time to time, attempts may be made to repeal such supposedly Western-inspired and anti-Islamic reforms.

1–96 Writing in 1976, Sir Norman Anderson commented on the possibility of a revival of orthodoxy and fervour, although he doubted whether this would be more than a temporary phase, at least in so far as the law is concerned. Indeed, he seemed inclined to think that there may be an upsurge in secular radicalism along the lines of the reforms in Somalia and South Yemen. As in the first two editions of this book published in 1979 and 1987, it is not part of our brief to speculate on the future. But legal developments in the past few decades in Pakistan, elsewhere in South Asia and in other parts of the Muslim world, have brought about radical change in the legal framework for Muslims living in those countries. In 1987, it was predicted that further attempts should be expected to remove the Muslim Family Laws Ordinance 1961 from the statute book of Pakistan (Pearl (1987), p. 244). Indeed, this has happened in a number of important cases which we discuss in Chapter 9, below. As a social experiment, the changes brought about by provisions like section 7 in the Muslim Family Laws Ordinance 1961 of Pakistan are impressive. Indeed, they are as impressive as the reforms for instance introduced by Atatürk in Turkey in the opposite direction so many years ago. It may well be that Pakistan's islamisation will provide the inspiration for other Muslim countries over the next 20 years, rather than Tunisian *ijtihad* or Somalian secular radicalism. The debate is still ongoing and the conflicts and tensions apparent in the Muslim legal world have not been resolved. What we see at present is a co-existence of islamisation of the traditional type with reforms which are based on more liberal (which often means pro-women) interpretations of Muslim legal principles and rules.

---

[21] This is the Constitution (Second Amendment) Order (1982) (P.O. 5 of (1982), with effect from March 22, 1982).

[22] On the 1979 law in Egypt, see Ibrahim and Bakar "Recent amendments to the Egyptian family law" [1980] 7 *Journal of Malaysian and Comparative Law* 65–98. On the 1985 law, see now El Alami and Hinchcliffe (1996).

1-97 As far as the non-family law area is concerned, the trend in the Muslim world to introduce new Codes which are far more Islamic in their content than their predecessors has continued.[23] Meanwhile, new studies on Muslim jurisprudence (see Lohlker (1996)) confirm an ancient truth: It remains difficult, in fact impossible, for Muslim jurisprudence to speak with one voice on any matter of legal importance. While the religious foundations of Muslim existence are uniform, the legal systems falling under the wider label of Muslim law have, over time, grown in diversity rather than moved towards uniformity. The present edition reflects this characteristic process in the globalisation of Muslim law, focusing particularly on South Asian legal systems and the emerging Muslim law in countries like the United Kingdom.

---

[23] The example given in the previous edition was the *Law of Civil Transactions* of the UAE, enacted in 1986.

Chapter 2

Muslim law in the subcontinent

2–01 Muslim law continues to play a major role in the development of modern South Asian legal systems.[1] The Muslim law as applied today in India, Pakistan and Bangladesh is unique for a number of reasons.[2] It is based on the principles of Islamic *shari'a*, but has been subjected to considerable modification, first by the mere fact of migration to the subcontinent, then by the British colonial powers, and now by the post-colonial states, remarkably more so in Pakistan and Bangladesh than in India. Crucially, through common law influence, South Asian Muslim laws have become based, to a considerable extent, on precedent and statute rather than traditional legal sources. At the same time, local customs have played a major, often unacknowledged and resented, role in the development of modern South Asian laws and recourse to traditional *shari'a* concepts has never been entirely blocked by state-induced legal developments. After all, Islamic law has always been a matter of religion as much as law, so that formal legal changes through state law were never quite able to override the sphere of *shari'a*, even if it may appear so. The most obvious illustration of this scenario today is found in the Muslim Family Laws Ordinance, 1961 of Pakistan and Bangladesh, on which we have much to say.

2–02 The new post-colonial states in South Asia, while accepting the historically grown personal law systems, have not been immune to reform movements and social change. It would be quite wrong to assume, *a priori*, that South Asian laws are somehow 'backward' because they rely on 'traditional' laws. If one looks more closely, one finds the modern states of South Asia engaged in intense debates about modernity and development, constantly balancing many conflicting interests and concepts. In terms of wider legal policies, there has been a move towards 'purer' Islamic laws, crystallised in the concept of islamisation, particularly in Pakistan but also in Bangladesh, and not without effects in India. At the same time, secularisation has been an equally important conceptual force, with most obvious impact in India, but much relevance in Bangladesh and Pakistan, too. It is within such broad, essentially political parameters that individual cases and particular areas of Muslim law have developed distinctly South Asian characteristics over time.

2–03 As a personal law, Muslim law is the majority law in Pakistan and Bangladesh and it also governs a substantial minority in India. Like classical *shari'a*, South Asian Muslim law is internally divided into the Sunni/Shi'i branches and further into different school traditions. The majority influence in the subcontinent has been the Hanafi Sunni tradition,[3] but many legal developments in South Asia

---

[1] A brief general overview of South Asian Muslim laws is found in Menski, "South Asia Muslim law today: An overview" [1997] 9 No. 1 *Sharqiyyât* 16–36. For Pakistan see Pearl (1990a) and, "Three decades of executive, legislative and judicial amendments to Islamic family law in Pakistan", in *Islamic family law* (1990b); Lau, "Introduction to the Pakistani legal system, with special reference to the law of contract", in *Yearbook of Islamic and Middle Eastern Law* (1995a). For India, Mahmood, *Personal laws in crisis* (1986) provides a useful perspective on the Muslim personal law. For Bangladesh, usable introductions are Hoque, *The legal system of Bangladesh* (1980) and Patwari, *Legal system of Bangladesh* (1991).
[2] Hodkinson, *Muslim family law: A sourcebook* (1984), p. 13 properly emphasised that this uniqueness "makes it worthy of study in its own right and not merely as a footnote to the study of the classical law of the middle east".
[3] Another Sunni school of some importance is that of Shafi'i (mainly in South India) and there are large Shia minorities in Pakistan and India.

can only be understood by reference to other branches of jurisprudence and the potential for the combination of different doctrinal and local elements in the creative evolution of South Asian Muslim laws by various techniques. Thus, the history of Muslim law in the subcontinent is very complex. Practitioners today need not be familiar with minute details of that history, but the practical application of South Asian Muslim laws continues to be so diverse – and thus exciting and relevant for practice – that many new disputes require us to place the litigation into this complex historical framework of analysis and interpretation, which is continuing today. In other words, reading a South Asian Muslim law case or interpreting a statute on Muslim law from the region requires much more than the traditional English lawyer's skills and knowledge.

2–04   South Asian laws belong to the common law family, but they are manifestly not just common law. In the same way, South Asian Muslim law is not just classical *shari'a*, but a hybrid form of Islamic law in its own right, with many national and regional variations. The purpose of the present chapter is to provide sufficient background detail about the place of the various Muslim laws in South Asia to enable readers to get an overview and to connect such facts with legal practice today. The second edition of this book focused on explaining the influence and impact which English common law and British legislative initiatives had, in their different ways, during the period when the region was controlled by the British. Such historical material is no longer directly relevant for practice today, and has not been reprinted in the present edition (see Pearl, *A textbook on Muslim personal law* (1987a), pp. 21–33). Instead, following brief comments about the introduction of Muslim law into the subcontinent, and an equally brief account of the British period, the present section focuses on the major modern South Asian jurisdictions of India, Pakistan and Bangladesh. Outlining the place of Muslim law in these jurisdictions today, we are trying to equip practitioners, scholars and students of Muslim law with relevant background material about basic structures and key issues. These include legal developments such as 'islamisation' which have brought important new aspects to the study of Muslim laws in the post-colonial period. It continues to be a fact that some of the liveliest jurisprudential debates about Muslim law today are conducted in South Asia, where Muslim law has strong roots but is not fully indigenous, and where Muslim law is at the same time the personal law of the majority in two large countries and of a substantial minority in another. While this gives rise to potent political debates and raises difficult questions of legal policy, the Indian scenario, in particular, brings with it many instructive parallels for the development of Muslim law in the West today.

The introduction and development of Muslim law

2–05   Many South Asian Muslims are proud of the fact that Islam came to the subcontinent soon after its emergence in the seventh century. It was probably first introduced to South India (Kerala) by Muslim traders and was also brought to the Indian subcontinent on the land route in the early eighth century, when Muhammad b. Qazim conquered Sind.[4] By the thirteenth century, if not earlier, the *shari'a* had become established as the 'official law'.[5] However, it is important to

---

[4] For some details see Gadre, *The role of Islam in South Asia* (1990), pp. 35–36.
[5] The early history of this interaction is discussed *ibid.*, pp. 35–42. See also Gandhi, *V. D. Kulshreshtha's Landmarks in Indian legal and constitutional history* (1995), p. 13 and 16–17 and in detail Wink, *Al Hind – The making of the Indo-Islamic world* Vol. 1 (1990) and Vol. 2 (1997).

realise that a small Muslim minority ruling over a huge Hindu majority could not realistically hope to impose Islamic law onto the whole population. Thus, the pre-existing personal law system was continued, while the Muslim rulers developed the criminal law and tax law in particular and applied their own laws of evidence and contract. In other words, the public law sphere was restructured by the new rulers, while the areas of private law experienced minimal interference. In fact, the personal law system, in which adherents of different religions are governed by separate rules operating within one and the same official legal system, was already in existence in the subcontinent before Muslim law became the official law. Thus, the pioneers of such manifestations of pluralism have been the Hindus. The literature, however, is full of claims that the Muslim rulers,[6] and even the British, were the originators of this system.[7]

2–06 Academic opinion differs on the extent of the application of the *shari'a* during this early period, as indeed during the era of the Moghul dynasties (see Gandhi (1995), p. 14). To elucidate this is the task of historians, who face limits of evidence. There is agreement that the Hanafi Sunni school became dominant early on. As we see, in classical Sunni Muslim jurisprudence, the Qur'an as the authoritative first source of *shari'a* is followed by *sunna* (*hadith*), *ijma* and *qiyas*.[8] In practice, though, several other sources have supplemented these major foundations of Islamic law.[9] So-called minor sources such as local custom or public interest, while never entirely absent anyway, have acquired larger importance outside the heartland of Islam, almost certainly because they allowed for local peculiarities to be fitted into an Islamic framework.[10]

2–07 All major writers, whether in India, Pakistan or elsewhere, agree that reform of Islamic law is not impossible.[11] Generally speaking, it is apparent that the concept of *siyasa* or *siyasa shar'iyya* allowed for flexibility.[12] It had the effect that individual rulers could determine how strictly Islamic law was to be applied and, in particular, to what extent (as the new law of the land) it would be applied to non-Muslims. Thus Aurangzeb (1658–1707), concerned to strengthen Islamic law, applied *shari'a* to a far greater extent than Akbar (1556–1605), who pursued a more pluralist approach.[13] Another relevant concept is that of 'selection' (*takhayyur*), allowing for use of a suitable rule from another school of thought than one's own.[14]

2–08 While we are not concerned here with details of this historical process, it is important to remember that, when the British came to India from 1600 onwards,

---

[6] See now to this effect Mahmood, *Uniform Civil Code. Fictions and facts* (1995), pp. 42–45 and others before him, *e.g.* Shabbir, *Muslim personal law and judiciary* (1988), p. 1.

[7] On the British claims see generally Hooker, *Legal Pluralism* (1975) but also Mahmood, *Muslim personal law. Role of the state in the subcontinent* (1977), p. 4.

[8] See Chap. 1, above on details.

[9] On the role of these see succinctly and excellently Coulson, (1969).

[10] North African Muslim laws experienced similar processes of hybridisation. For details see in particular Rosen, *The anthropology of justice. Law as culture in Islamic society* (1989) and now Shaham [1995] 2 No. 3 *Islamic Law and Society* 258–281. On Indonesia see Geertz, *The religion of Java* (1960), Boland, *The struggle of Islam in modern Indonesia* (1982), as well as Katz and Katz "The new Indonesian marriage law: A mirror of Indonesia's political, cultural and legal systems" [1975] *The American Journal of Comparative Law* 653–681. On India see Mujeeb, *The Indian Muslims* (1985), especially pp. 58–59. On the role of custom in Muslim law generally see Rankin "Custom and the Muslim personal law in British India" [1939] *Transactions of the Grotius Society* 89–118; Mahmood, "Custom as a source of law in Islam" [1965] 7 J.I.L.I. 102–106; Mohammadi, "The custom and its significance in Islamic law" [1977] 8 No. 2 *Islam and the Modern Age* 32–38, and now Libson [1997] 4 No. 2 *Islamic Law and Society* 131–155.

[11] See *e.g.* Hidayatullah and Hidayatullah, *Mulla's Principles of Mahomedan law* (1990), p. xxvii; Mannan, *D. F. Mulla's Principles of Mahomedan law* (1990), p. xxix.

[12] On *siyasa* see Hidayatullah and Hidayatullah (1990), p. xxvi.

[13] On Akbar's policy of tolerance see Gandhi (1995), p. 27 and generally, *ibid.* p. 17, also on Aurangzeb.

[14] Hidayatullah and Hidayatullah (1990), p. xxvi.

Muslim law was the 'law of the land' and Muslim criminal law, in particular, was a key area of the 'official law'.[15] Subsequently, in the process of administration of Muslim law in South Asia by the British, the classical sources of *shari'a* have remained the basis of the religious law, but they were gradually supplemented by several other, state-sponsored sources of law. One has to understand this clearly to appreciate the hybrid nature of South Asian Muslim laws and the resultant flexibility of legal rules.

2–09 As the recent islamisation process in Pakistan has demonstrated with great clarity, the question 'Which *shari'a*?' poses a real problem for South Asian Muslims and Muslim law in view of historically grown internal diversities. Practitioners and students alike need to beware of statements that purport to project authoritative legal and uniform positions where in fact the picture is immensely complex. Contrary to popular assumptions (and frequent claims) about the uniformity of Islam, Muslims as a whole only agree among themselves about the divinity and supreme position of Allah and of the Qur'an, but differ on many other issues. As the Ahmadi *(Qadiani)* controversies in Pakistan show, sectarian disputes have arisen over the position of the Prophet Mohammed as the final prophet of Islam.[16] Quite apart from the Ahmadi controversies, Muslim law as a whole is in effect a family of laws rather than a uniform legal system. Consequently, it is hardly ever possible to state a legal rule in Muslim law without mentioning several exceptions and caveats.

2–10 The search for authoritative guidance led, in South Asia, to some form of codification by the compilation of specialist texts.[17] Two important documents must be mentioned. The *Hedaya*, a traditional Hanafi school text, was eventually translated into English from a Persian translation of an Arabic original dating from the twelfth century.[18] The *Fatawa-i-Alamgiri* is in essence a collection of *responsa* by Muslim jurists, composed from Hanafi sources in 1663 on the orders of Aurangzeb.[19]

2–11 Indian courts from the early part of the nineteenth century have tended to treat these two texts as authentic sources of Muslim law. This raised difficult problems over the relationship between the primary sources of Muslim law, namely Qur'an and *sunna*, and such compilations, since the latter were relied on to the exclusion of the earliest sources. This shows that the English judges, in particular, did not understand the nature of the texts or the law. Not surprisingly, both texts, particularly the *Fatawa-i-Alamgiri*, did not retain their authoritative status in the long run.[20] In *Imambandi v. Mutsaddi* [1917/1918] 45 L.R. I.A. 73, at page 89, Ameer Ali J. said:

---

[15] Fyzee, *Outlines of Muhammadan law* (1974), p. 49. On early British arguments in favour of replacing Muslim criminal law see Fisch, *Cheap lives and dear limbs* (1983) and Malik, *The transformation of colonial perceptions into legal norms: Legislating for crime and punishment in Bengal, 1790s to 1820s* (1994).

[16] Derrett, *Religion, law and the state in India* (1968b), p. 513 referred to the Ahmadiyas as "supposedly unorthodox". By 1974, the Ahmadis had been declared non-Muslims in Pakistan. This has created an embarrassing problem: Which personal law should one apply to the Ahmadis? Balchin (ed.), *A handbook on family law in Pakistan* (1994), p. 50 writes that "it seems the courts prefer to avoid the issue". Mannan (1990), p. 38 refers to a 1978 case as authority for the equitable proposition that Ahmadis are to be governed by Muslim law.

[17] At least it was perceived like that in the light of European concepts of law and legal development.

[18] On the Hedaya, see Mujeeb (1985), p. 58 and Mannan (1990), p. 173. The standard translation of the text is found in Hamilton, *The Hedaya, or guide: A commentary on the Mussulman laws* (1891).

[19] For some details see Mahmood, *The Muslim law of India* (1982a), p. 16 with a reference to Vol. 1 of Baillie's *Digest of Moohummadan law* (see Baillie, *A digest of Moohummudan law* (1865)).

[20] At earlier stages, these texts were held in some esteem, on which see, *e.g.* Mahmood J. in *Mazhar Ali v. Budh Singh* (1885) I.L.R. 7 All 297 at 309. However, the same learned judge in *Jafri Begam v. Amir Muhammad Khan* 1885 I.L.R. 7 All 822, at 830 treated the text with some reservation, merely as "a translation from a translation".

"Both Mr. Hamilton and Mr. Neil Baillie in their renderings have, with the object of elucidation, occasionally added phrases which do not exist in the original, but on the whole the English versions of the Hedaya and of the Fatawai Alamgiri are valuable works on Mahomedan law."

The assumption that the Muslim law is to be found in older texts, like the *Hedaya*, led to claims that new rules of law can and should therefore not be deduced by lawyers of eminence (see Fyzee (1974), p. 50). Such arguments highlight not only the specific problems relating to these two particular texts on Muslim law, but lead directly to an equally contentious issue, reflected in conflicting statements about the authority of any Muslim jurists as textbook writers, whose attempts to make authoritative statements continue to be heavily contested.[21] Clearly, the early conflicts and tensions within Islamic jurisprudence about authority (see in detail Coulson (1969)) continue today.

2–12 The peculiarities of British legal administration in the subcontinent fundamentally changed the nature and structure of South Asian Muslim law. First, the so-called 'general law' was subjected to codification and was taken outside the ambit of Islamic law and applied to all persons in more or less uniform fashion. The British policy decision to respect indigenous family laws but to administer them in a uniform civil and criminal court system, made Muslim law at first a matter for expert advisors or assessors *(moulvis)* attached to the courts until 1864, when enough judicial knowledge had supposedly accrued to allow more explicit reliance on precedent. Thus, Muslim law gradually became Anglo-Mohammedan law, a case-law system in which recourse to earlier sources was still possible but became increasingly unattractive to lawyers, since law reporting and legislative activities provided more accessible authoritative guidelines.[22] The law that emerged in this way was somewhat at variance with its original sources (Fyzee (1974), p. 51) but the post-colonial states have found it difficult to undo this long restructuring process. Attempts in that direction, such as the re-introduction of Muslim evidence law in Pakistan by the Qanun-e-Shahadat Order of 1984, are probably more significant for their political messages than in terms of legal substance.

2–13 There are few legislative enactments on Muslim law in South Asia. Some of them remain very important for legal practice and they have been incorporated into our text, where relevant. In a historical context, a few words must be said about the Muslim Personal Law (Shariat Application) Act 1937, which is still in force throughout South Asia (see in detail paragraph 2–35, below). This Act was introduced to 'islamise' South Asian Muslim laws at a time when members of the religious leadership were concerned about the reliance on local customary influence, specifically the continuation of Hindu customs among various Muslim communities. While that Act re-affirmed the supremacy of *shari'a*, it could not fully avoid the problem that *shari'a* remains what local Muslim communities say it is.[23]

2–14 The Dissolution of Muslim Marriages Act 1939, which remains in force in India, Pakistan and Bangladesh, is discussed in Chapter 9, below. It safeguarded the right of Muslim wives to demand a divorce on certain specified fault grounds, which are quite wide and have been enlarged by judicial interpretation.[24] The

---

[21] This is a phenomenon throughout the Muslim world, as Lohlker, *Scharia'a und Moderne. Diskussionen über Schwangerschaftsabbruch, Versicherung und Zinsen* (1996) confirms.

[22] A parallel process of restructuring occurred to Hindu law.

[23] This is so all over the Muslim world. For references see n.10, above, and Chap. 3, below, for British Muslims today.

[24] The leading case on this in Pakistan remains *Khurshid Bibi v. Muhammad Amin* P.L.D. 1967 S.C. 97.

Muslim Family Laws Ordinance 1961, in force in Pakistan and, with some amendments, in Bangladesh, remains extremely important and is discussed in detail in various sections of this book. Basically, it sought to improve the position of Muslim women in the two countries, but recent developments in Pakistan, in particular, show that these reforms may not have been implemented in social reality, a fact which is now increasingly recognised by the superior judiciary as well. Such recent developments in South Asian jurisprudence have many implications for legal practice in Britain which this present edition reports on and seeks to explore further.

2-15   It is important to note that Indian Muslim law has remained to a very large extent uncodified, evidently for political reasons. It is significant that law reforms in South Asia have mainly affected the respective majority personal law, while a 'hands off policy' has been applied to most minority laws. Further, lawyers should be aware that Bangladeshi law has developed quite differently from Pakistani law since 1972. In modern Indian law, but now also in Bangladesh,[25] the development of maintenance rights for divorced wives has recently become a matter of immense interest. We will examine, in Chapter 7 below, the significant implications of the Muslim Women (Protection of Rights on Divorce) Act 1986 in India, which has given rise to much political controversy and legal confusion.

2-16   In summary, Muslim law is an integral part of the modern legal systems in South Asia today. In Pakistan and also to some extent in Bangladesh, the general principles of Muslim law are deemed to inspire and influence the entire legal system. Muslim law in India, within the framework of a secular constitution which guarantees the state's equidistance from all religions, has remained a classic personal law with less state interference than in the two neighbouring Muslim countries.

The impact of English law

2-17   Apart from factors germane to Islamic law as a global but regionally flexible system of belief and laws, the unique nature of South Asian Muslim laws can be traced back to colonial influence. Three major factors have contributed to this: First, the impact of English law itself, secondly, the importance of local customary law and its use by the colonial power, thirdly, the reforms introduced into the general laws by direct legislation.

2-18   English law achieved this lasting impact because the long process of colonial administration created certain patterns which have proved impossible and perhaps unnecessary to undo. In terms of judicial administration, the British at first appointed judges directly from Britain and later used British-trained judicial personnel. This process continues today, to a large extent, when senior advocates who have studied in Britain are appointed to judicial positions. In addition, foreign-trained and locally-educated practitioners alike have been influenced by centuries of common law ideology. The Islamic rules of evidence, for example, were over time more ignored and marginalised and it appears that their recent formal revival in Pakistan has not been an unqualified success.

2-19   The second reason for this inevitably strong influence of English law was the introduction into India of the English doctrine of precedent, of the use of

---

[25] See now *Md. Hefzur Rahman v. Shamsun Nahar Begum* (1995) 15 B.L.D. 34.

English as the court language, of a hierarchical general courts structure, and subsequently of law reporting. Over time, some court decisions which were contrary to Muslim law became authoritative, leading to much criticism of Anglo-Mohammedan law in principle as well as substance.[26] This kind of historical damage has been difficult to undo.[27]

2–20 Linked to this, a third reason for the unique development of South Asian Muslim laws has been the doctrine of 'justice and right' or 'justice, equity and good conscience'.[28] Devised to fill *lacunae*, this maxim was frequently used to mask judicial ignorance of Muslim law, thus leading to further application of English law, but also Roman law and other legal rules.

2–21 For a largely legal readership, it is necessary to consider the impact of 'justice, equity and good conscience' and 'justice and right' in some detail because such flexible maxims created room for much judicial discretion in the development of South Asian laws. Importantly, this process continues today when judges justify what has come to be known as 'judicial activism' in South Asia with reference to equitable arguments.[29] The British judges in the subcontinent were generally guided in their decision-making process by what they knew and understood, rather than by the litigants' experience. This allowed some to impose English legal concepts while it did not stop some others, who were more attuned to South Asian conditions, from arguing for greater recognition of local customs and religious laws.[30] The absence of high-quality training in Islamic law for judicial personnel, then as now, impeded recourse to the principles of that law. Recourse to the classical texts, which are mostly in Arabic, was of course restricted in various ways.[31]

2–22 Already in 1668, the judges of the Court of Judicature at Bombay were directed to administer justice to all persons according to the principles of common right. The Mayor's Court Charter for Madras in 1687 enacted that all causes whatsoever, civil and criminal, between party and party, whoever they shall be, shall be adjudged according to equity and good conscience. In 1726, the Charter establishing the Mayor's courts in Bombay, Madras and Calcutta provided that judgment was to be given according to justice and right. This formula was repeated in 1753 and appears constantly in the Regulations, Acts and Charters of India from the seventeenth to the nineteenth century.

2–23 In 1886 the Privy Council held that the formulas 'justice, equity and good conscience' or 'justice and right' implied the application of English law, if found applicable to Indian society and circumstances.[32] In every situation where, by

---

[26] See in detail Mahmood (1977). A case in point is the decision in *Abul Fata Mahomed Ishak v. Russomoy Dhur Chowdhry* [1894] 22 L.R. I.A. 76, regarding *waqf dhurri*, discussed in detail in para. 11–169, below.
[27] Muslim apprehensions about misinterpretations and distortions of Muslim law are reflected not only in the writing of prominent authors like Tahir Mahmood, they have influenced also the reaction to more recent judgments. A case in point is the *Shah Bano* controversy of 1985 over the entitlement of divorced Muslim wives to post-divorce maintenance. On this see in detail para. 7–75, below.
[28] On this see in detail Derrett, "Justice, equity and good conscience", in *Changing law in developing countries* (1963), pp. 114–153, and, with further references, Derrett (1968b), pp. 311–313.
[29] This has become a matter of great importance in the recent development of South Asian laws. On details see Menski, "Introduction: The democratisation of justice in India", in *Law of consumer protection in India. Justice within reach* (1996), pp. xxv–liv, for India and Khan [1992] P.L.D. 84–95 and, *Public interest litigation: Growth of the concept and its meaning in Pakistan* (1993) for Pakistan. An overview is provided in Hossain *et al.*, *Public interest litigation in South Asia. Rights in search of remedies* (1997).
[30] A famous example is Nelson J. of Madras. For details see Derrett (1968b), p. 292.
[31] The same point must be raised for the written sources of Hindu law, which have also posed enormous problems for access to outsiders.
[32] *Waghela Rajsanji v. Shekh Masludin* [1886–1887] 14 L.R. I.A. 89.

Regulation or by an Act, the court had to apply this particular formula, if a rule of English law was relevant to Indian society or to Indian circumstances, then English law was to be applied. In fact, "so many rules of English law seemed to be merely rules of universal law" (Derrett (1968b), p. 311). In this manner substantive rules of English law found their way into the body of Indian law indirectly through the principles of 'justice, equity and good conscience' and 'justice and right'.

2-24   How did the judges deal with matters in accordance with 'justice, equity and good conscience' when the situation was completely unknown to English experience? One can conclude from a number of cases on conversion (see Pearl (1987a), pp. 29–33 and below, Chapter 5) that when the courts resort to 'justice, equity and good conscience', or 'justice and right' in a situation which is peculiar to South Asian circumstances, the judges apply the formula along lines which they, as English or English-trained judges, consider to be just. In this way, English law is introduced on what can be termed a 'third level'. The first level is obviously codification of English rules. The second level is by the application of 'justice and right' or 'justice, equity and good conscience' when English law acts as the 'reservoir law' in a case which is similar to an English situation. The third, and perhaps most interesting level, occurs in situations very different from English-type circumstances.

2-25   As British-made legislation, tailor-made for the subcontinent rather than English law itself, gained in prominence, more and more areas of law were taken outside the ambit of 'justice, equity and good conscience' and the scope for the application of that maxim, though never totally closed, was greatly curtailed. At the same time, the scope for the application of Muslim law was gradually reduced, too, so that ultimately mainly matters of family law, including succession law, came to comprise the South Asian Muslim personal law as it is known today.

Historical developments

2-26   As indicated, the present edition provides only a very brief overview (see in detail Pearl (1987a), pp. 21–33). The story of English law in India begins in 1661 with a marriage treaty between the British Crown and Portugal.[33] At that time, the politically dominant law of the subcontinent was Muslim law, while the majority of the people remained governed by the Hindu personal law.

2-27   Under the British East India Company, the British sphere of influence gradually expanded from settlements which were to become the major metropolitan cities of Bombay, Calcutta and Madras to hinterland areas, the *Mofussil* or *Mufassil*, as it came to be known. English law was originally introduced into the metropolitan areas, where British staff and their families lived and worked, so that indigenous law would not apply to Europeans. Inevitably, however, complex choice of law questions and conflicts of laws arose when disputes involved a European and a local person. To the extent that the British became more involved in legal administration and in adjudication, they had to evolve new methods of dealing with the various South Asian legal systems. In this context it is significant that the indigenous laws were recognised as laws, while at the same time Western legal systems were perceived as superior.[34]

2-28   Already in 1668, the East India Company was required in a charter to

---

[33] On the earliest period see in detail Fawcett, *The first century of British justice in India* (1934); Banerjee, *English Law in India* (1984) and Jain, *Outlines of Indian legal history* (1990).
[34] We emphasise this because, in Britain today, Muslim law is not recognised as part of the domestic law but in a number of cases Muslim law has been recognised as 'law'. For details see Chap. 3, below.

enact laws "'consonant to reason, and not repugnant or contrary to' the English laws", and "as near as may be agreeable to" such laws (Fawcett (1934), p. 6). Two important points have to be made concerning the Company's laws. First, they did not directly impose English law as the sole governing law because the British were well aware of the continuing sovereignty of the Mughal government. Secondly, a number of provisions made at that early stage showed that the jurisdiction of the court extended to non-English inhabitants. Further, there is much evidence that the direction to use 'the principles of common right' meant in practice application of local laws. Thus, "here we have the beginnings of the co-existence of English Law with Indian laws prevailing in the region concerned" (Banerjee (1984), p. 9). The example of a prostitute, whose punishment was to be shaved and paraded on a donkey (Fawcett (1934), p. 43) shows the richness of legal sources: Originally a Hindu law punishment, this had been adopted by Muslim courts and was now applied by the new legal administration.

2–29 At this early stage, too, traditional caste courts (*panchayats*) were recognised and, since 1718, appeals from them lay to the emerging colonial court structure. In fact, the 1718 Proclamation marked the beginning of the official involvement of the colonial courts in the administration of local justice. Other colonial powers have followed significantly different models, and delegated the administration of all personal law matters to the courts of the indigenous communities. But in 1718, the British had not made the complete commitment which was to develop later. Indeed, both the proclamation itself and the early reported cases prove that the British settlers in this period were fully prepared to allow the indigenous inhabitants to settle disputes, up to a point, according to their own laws. The Muslim courts at this period were better organised than the Hindu courts but, nonetheless, Hindu caste courts did exist, and were recognised by the British.

2–30 Eventually, a picture emerged that the caste courts were not often used and that the litigious Indians preferred the Mayor's courts.[35] Such observations were used to justify the extension of the colonial court structures to the *Mofussil* from 1765 onwards. In that year, the East India Company obtained *diwani* rights over some parts of Bengal, which meant that it now acted as a local authority under continued Moghul supremacy. From now on, judicial administration demanded still more attention.

2–31 In a series of proclamations between 1772 and 1793, the East India Company confirmed its policy that Hindus and Muslims were to be governed by their own laws (but not administered in their own courts) in disputes relating to inheritance, succession (since 1781), marriage, and caste and other religious usages and institutions. Interestingly, the assumption was that Hindu law was 'the laws of the Shastras' and Muslim law 'the laws of the Koran'. This focus on scriptural law was soon modified and by 1793 the Regulations referred to 'Hindu laws' and 'Mohammedan laws'. Significantly, in the actual administration of justice, from 1772 until 1864, Hindu and Muslim experts or assessors (*pandits* and *moulvis*) were enlisted to instruct the courts as to the nature of Hindu and Muslim laws.

2–32 Beyond the area of the 'listed subjects', in essence family law and caste usage, the Proclamations earmarked the 'unlisted subjects', *i.e.* the general law, for gradual codification. In these areas, there was no guarantee of continued application of Muslim or Hindu law. Instead, notice was given by the British that there would

---

[35] On the litigiousness of South Asians see Derrett (1968b), p. 286; also Galanter, *Law and society in modern India* (1989), p. xxxiv.

be legislative reforms. From 1833 onwards, various Law Commissions tackled the task of codification. Under notable Scottish influence, this led to a hybrid system of common law principles in civil law shape, with significant scope for the recognition of local customs and laws in many areas. This is why it is misleading to speak of South Asian laws in blanket fashion as 'common law systems', as English lawyers, in particular, continue to do.

2–33   The dawn of the codification era commenced with the Code of Civil Procedure 1859, followed by the Limitation Act 1859, the Indian Penal Code 1860 and the Code of Criminal Procedure 1861.[36] The report on the Law of Succession in 1863 by the third Law Commission was enacted into law by the Indian Succession Act 1865 which excluded Hindus, Muslims and Buddhists. In 1872, the Evidence Act and the Contract Act were passed. The work of the fourth, and final, Law Commission resulted in the enactment, in particular, of the Negotiable Instruments Act 1881 and the Transfer of Property Act 1882. The latter contained a special provision in section 2 that nothing in the Act relating to transfer of property should be deemed to effect any rule of Hindu, Muslim or Buddhist law. The same respect for personal laws was expressed in section 1 of the Trust Act 1882. Indeed, the British believed at this time that the personal laws were so interconnected with religious feelings that any attempt at large-scale reform, or any endeavour to codify the personal laws, would necessarily involve injury to religious susceptibilities. They were probably also worried about upsetting their colonial subjects and creating grounds for anti-colonial agitation.

2–34   Mainly for such reasons, legal reform was invoked only after considerable pressure from the communities themselves. An early example is the Hindu Widows' Remarriage Act 1856, designed to make legally possible the remarriage of Hindu widows.[37] This cautious approach was followed particularly in the case of Muslim law. Shabbir, *Muslim personal law and judiciary* (1988, p. 3) emphasises British reluctance to depart from the opinions of traditional Muslim jurists and their commentaries. It has been commented that several of the few Acts dealing with Muslim law enacted by the British actually restored traditional Muslim law. The Mussalman Wakf Validating Act 1913 is perhaps the best example of this trend.[38] It should be reiterated in addition that the orthodox Muslim community was responsible, in part, for the enactment of the Muslim Personal Law (Shariat) Application Act 1937, which sought to destroy the application of a considerable section of customary law. The only major liberalising reform of the Muslim personal law in the British period occurred in 1939 with the enactment of the Dissolution of Muslim Marriages Act.[39]

Muslim law and custom

2–35   We have already seen that the emerging colonial administration recognised Muslim law as an operative legal system and took various steps to ascertain and apply it.[40] This process was not restricted to *shari'a* law proper but

---

[36] Interestingly, this codification process took place at roughly the same time as the *Tanzimat* reforms in the Ottoman Empire, as noted at the beginning of para. 1–72, above.

[37] This Act was repealed in India by the Hindu Widows' Re-Marriage (Repeal) Act 1983 (Act 24 of 1983) but is still in force in Pakistan and Bangladesh.

[38] This Act overruled the unsatisfactory Privy Council decision of *Abul Fata Mahomed Ishak v. Russomoy Dhur Chowdhry* [1894/5] 22 L.R. I.A. 76. For details see para. 11–169, below.

[39] See below, para. 9–57.

[40] For a detailed analysis of this process see Jain (1990), pp. 617–620.

gradually extended to incorporate, to some extent, the various customs of the Muslims of South Asia.

2–36 As early as 1847, customary practice was recognised as relevant in situations where the courts were directed to apply the personal law of the parties as a governing law (see Rankin (1939)). The early leading case on this matter is a complex litigation involving Khojas and Memons, decided in Bombay in 1847.[41] In that case strong evidence of custom was soon found: It turned out that there was little or no conflicting testimony regarding the existence of a custom as stated in the plea. The principal question then arose whether such custom was valid or not (page 112). The judgment contains a brief sketch of the Khoja community, which starts as follows, in the peculiar English of the time (page 112):

> "The Khojas are a small cast in Western India, who appear to have originally come from Sindh or Cutch, and who, by their own traditions, which are probably correct, were converted from Hinduism about four hundred years ago . . . their religion is Mahomedan; their dress, appearance, and manners, for the most part, Hindu."

The plaintiff in the action, the daughter of the intestate, claimed a share in the inheritance of her father on the grounds that Muslim law governed the dispute and that under Muslim law she was entitled, as a daughter, to a share in the inheritance. The defendants countered the claim of the plaintiff on the grounds that although the Khojas are a Muslim community, and normally Muslim law would govern them, nonetheless there are Khoja customs whereby females are not entitled to any share of the father's property on his death.

2–37 Sir Erskine Perry C.J., considered, in the first instance, the enforceability of the customary rule in principle. He concluded, at page 121:

> "It appears to me that if a custom has been proved to exist from time whereof the memory of man runneth not to the contrary, if it is not injurious to the public interests, and if it does not conflict with any express law of the ruling power, such a custom is entitled to receive the sanction of a Court of law."

The obvious issue in this case was whether such a custom among Muslims would be valid despite being contrary to the Qur'anic principles of Muslim law. The learned judge found, at page 121, that "this opens up a very interesting field of enquiry". In view of the fact that the British rulers had provided Charters which expressed the legislator's will, to the effect that the laws and usages of the Muslims and Hindus should be respected, the learned Chief Justice thought it clear that this did not mean the adoption of the Qur'anic law without regard to the usages of the Muslims of India, whether they be Shi'i, Sunni or sectarian. In this sense, the Chief Justice restricted the application of the Muslim personal law, and the petition of the daughter failed. It was therefore held, at pages 124–125:

> "I am clearly, therefore, of opinion, that the effect of the clause in the charter is not to adopt the text of the Koran as law, any further than it has been adopted in the laws and usages of the Mahomedans who came under our sway; and if

---

[41] *Hirbae and others v. Sonabae* (1847) *Perry's Oriental Cases* 110, see Perry, *Cases illustrative of Oriental life and the application of English law to India* (1853), pp. 110–129; for some details see also Diwan and Diwan, *Muslim law in modern India* (1991), p. 7. This decision also involved a case on the same issue concerning Kutchi Memons, another group of Muslims with a hybrid past, on which see in detail Perry, *Cases illustrative of Oriental life and the application of English law to India* (1853), pp. 114–115.

any class of Mahomedans – Mahomedan dissenters,[42] as they may be called – are found to be in possession of any usage which is otherwise valid as a legal custom, and which does not conflict with any express law of the English Government, they are just as much entitled to the protection of this clause as the most orthodox Sunniy who can come before the Court."

2–38   This old decision, re-read today in the light of debates in Pakistan and in Western jurisdictions about the definition of 'Islamic' and 'Muslim', remains surprisingly instructive.[43] Problems of this nature were not confined to Western India. In the Panjab, custom was given statutory recognition by section 5 of the Punjab Laws Act 1872, which states:

"5. Decisions in certain cases to be according to native laws.– In questions regarding succession, special property of females, betrothal, marriage, divorce, dower, adoption, guardianship, minority, bastardy, family relations, wills, legacies, gifts, partitions, or any religious usage or institution, the rule of decision shall be –

(a) any custom applicable to the parties concerned, which is not contrary to justice, equity or good conscience, and has not been by this or any other enactment altered or abolished, and has not been declared to be void by any competent authority.

(b) the Muhammadan Law, in cases where the parties are Muhammadans, and the Hindu law, in cases where the parties are Hindus, except in so far as such law has been altered or abolished by legislative enactment, or is opposed to the provisions of this Act, or has been modified by any such custom as is above referred to."

Sections 6 and 7 of the same Act gave pride of place to 'justice, equity and good conscience' but upheld the validity of local customs and mercantile usages, unless they were contrary to that maxim or had been declared to be void by any competent authority before the passing of the 1872 Act (March 28, 1872). There is no doubt, thus, that in the Panjab, as in Bombay, provable custom took precedence over Muslim law when the court had to determine an issue before it in accordance with the personal law.

2–39   Custom was also allowed to derogate from the Muslim personal law in other areas of British India beside Bombay and the Panjab. In Madras, for example, section 16 of the Civil Courts Act 1873 contained a provision similar to the Punjab Laws Act 1872. The problem whether custom or personal law is applied as the governing law has been particularly relevant with respect to the small Mappilla Muslim community from Malabar, today's Kerala in South India.[44] The leading case concerning this group is the decision of Tyabji J. in the Madras High Court, reported as *Kunhambi v. Kalanthar* 1915 I.L.R. 38 Mad. 1052. The question before the court was whether the Mappilla community was governed by its normal personal law, the Muslim law, or by a particular variation of Hindu law, the

---

[42] The use of this particular term is interesting in view of debates about the legal recognition of non-Anglican marriage customs in Britain in the 19th century. On this, see Hamilton, *Family, law and religion* (1995) and Chap. 3, below.

[43] It is also interesting in that systematically depriving women of inheritance rights was not seen as in any way injurious to the public interest at that time.

[44] Much has been written on this community, for details see Miller, *Mappila Muslims of Kerala. A study in Islamic trends* (1992).

matrilineal Marumakkattayam law, with respect to the dispute in issue. Tyabji J. argued, at page 1062, that:

". . . the real issue to be decided is one of fact, namely, whether the particular parties have adopted the one system of law or the other and whether they have been governing their conduct in accordance with the one system or the other."

If a custom is proved, then there is no doubt that the Muslim personal law is not applicable. Finding himself unable to hold that the lower courts had approached the issue erroneously, and in the absence of positive proof to the contrary, the learned Judge dismissed the appeal and thus upheld the verdict that Mapillas are governed by Muslim law.

2–40 In contrast to the position in Madras, in Bombay and in the Panjab, custom was not granted *statutory* recognition in other areas of British India. This was particularly the case in Bengal, in the United Provinces (now Uttar Pradesh and Madhya Pradesh) and in Assam. The Allahabad High Court at first read the lack of a statutory mention of custom in the Civil Courts Acts of these areas to imply that no customary deviation should be permitted from the purity of the personal laws. These early cases were overruled in 1913 by the Privy Council in *Muhammad Ismail v. Lala Sheo-mukh Rai* [1913] 15 Bom. L.R. 76. Following this case, the general position is that custom does not have any less effect upon the Muslim law in Bengal and Assam than in other areas where it is expressly mentioned as the primary rule of decision.

2–41 We have already seen that there was a desire by the religious leadership of the Muslim community to reduce the role of local, Hindu-influenced custom. As a direct result of appeals by the Muslim community, the Muslim Personal Law (Shariat) Application Act 1937 was enacted in British India in order to reduce the instances where custom could become the rule of decision. The text of the Act lays down that in a number of specified areas of law regarding intestate succession and the laws of marriage and divorce, the rule of decision in cases where the parties are Muslims shall be the Muslim personal law (*shari'a*) save for questions relating to agricultural land. If a person satisfies the prescribed authority that he is a Muslim, he can declare, in addition, that the personal law by which he wishes to be governed is Muslim law, also in relation to testate succession and adoption.[45]

2–42 The 1937 Act was subsequently extended to all parts of independent India, but does not apply in Jammu and Kashmir (Diwan and Diwan (1991), p. 9). According to an Act of 1977, however, the courts in Jammu and Kashmir apply Muslim law in all cases specified under the terms of that Act, subject to any contrary legislation or custom.[46] As legislation relating to agriculture was not within the competence of the central legislature, agricultural land has continued to be excluded from the purport of the central Act. In so far as custom governs the law of testamentary succession, an individual has the right to opt for Muslim law, but if the option is not taken, testamentary succession is governed by the customary law.

2–43 Not surprisingly, limitations on the central state's legislative power regarding agricultural land led to the introduction of state amendments to the 1937 Act which also cover agricultural property. There have been several such amendments to the Shariat Act in India. In Madras, section 2 of Act XVIII of 1949

---

[45] Adoption is not recognised as carrying any legal consequences in Islamic law. See para. 10–25, below.
[46] The Jammu and Kashmir Sri Pratap Consolidation of Laws Act 1977. For rich detail on Kashmiri Muslim law, with special reference to the position of daughters, see Ganai [1985] 27 No. 3 J.I.L.I. 387–422.

reworded the parent Act so as to include within the scope of the Muslim personal law all *waqfs* and agricultural land.[47] A still wider extension has been introduced by section 2 of the Muslim Personal Law (Shariat) Application (Kerala Amendment) Act 1963 (Act 42 of 1963) for the state of Kerala, which provides as follows:

> "2. Application of personal law to Muslims. – Nothwithstanding any custom or usage to the contrary, in all questions regarding intestate succession, special property of females including personal property inherited or obtained under contract or gift or any other provision of personal law, marriage, dissolution of marriage, including talaq, ila, zihar, lian, khula and mubaraat, maintenance, dower, guardianship, gifts, trusts and trust properties and wakfs, (other than charities and charitable institutions and charitable and religious endowments) the rule of decision in cases where the parties are Muslim, shall be the Muslim personal law (Shariat)."

In Andhra Pradesh, a similarly titled Act (Act VIII of 1949) has made Muslim law applicable to religious institutions as well (Diwan and Diwan (1991), p. 10). Thus, it remains relevant for practitioners to check on local statutory problems. Further details on this topic are outside the scope of this book.[48]

2–44   Naturally, the 1937 Act was also adopted in Pakistan but was substantially amended and ultimately repealed by section 7 of the West Pakistan Muslim Personal Law (Shariat) Application Act 1962.[49] It appears that in Pakistan, three arguments against the continued application of local customary laws have come together. First, there was the familiar argument that Muslims should be governed by Muslim law rather than customs based on local Hindu-inspired rules. During Pakistan's recent movement towards islamisation, this reasoning has inspired further legal efforts to abolish the influence of customary laws altogether. Secondly, the Pakistani debates show concern to reduce the incidence of 'limited estates', which are linked to local customary law concepts, and to strengthen full legal ownership. Thirdly, a more recent argument, advanced by women's groups in Pakistan, is that adherence to customary law norms has disadvantaged women in their claim to absolute property rights.[50]

2–45   The application of Muslim law, rather than local custom, has been strengthened by a series of enactments. The West Punjab Muslim Personal Law (Shariat) Application Act 1948 and the Punjab Muslim Personal Law (Shariat) Application (Amendment) Act 1951 put the spotlight on the agricultural heartland of the Panjab, but other parts of Pakistan produced similar enactments.[51] Interestingly, such reforms were not introduced in the former East Pakistan, now Bangladesh.[52]

---

[47] This is the Muslim Personal Law (Shariat) Application (Madras Amendment) Act 1949.

[48] For further details see Mahmood (1982a) and Diwan and Diwan (1991).

[49] A helpful detailed compilation of material on this Act, several other Acts and related subject matters is found in Ch. M. Mahmood, *The Manual of family laws* (1991), pp. 472–508 and in Mannan (1990), pp. 4–20. The latter also reprints the full text of many of the enactments relevant to the present discussion.

[50] For this argument see now Balchin (1994), pp. 3 and 17. However, Jain (1990), p. 620, indicates that similar arguments were used by Muslim women as early as the 1930s. Whether adherence to Muslim law rather than custom guarantees, in social reality, better property rights for Muslim women remains open to question.

[51] These and other Acts were repealed and consolidated by the West Pakistan Muslim Personal Law (Shariat) Application Act 1962, as amended by the Muslim Personal Law (Shariat) Application Act 1983. For some details see Hodkinson (1984), pp. 24–25 and especially Ch. M. Mahmood (1991), pp. 474–508.

[52] In Bangladesh, the 1937 Act remains the governing statute and was not amended. Hoque (1980), p. 25 suggests generally that "a narrow margin has been left in the Codes for accommodation of customary rules".

2–46 Section 2 of the 1948 Act stated that in all questions regarding succession, including agricultural land, the rule of decision in cases where the parties are Muslims shall be the Muslim personal law. Complications were experienced in applying the 1948 Act, in particular in ascertaining the meaning of the word "succession". Did it include both intestate and testate succession, or was it restricted to intestate succession as in the parent Act? This problem was overcome by section 2 of the Punjab Muslim Personal Law (Shariat) Application (Amendment) Act 1951, which stated that notwithstanding any rule of customary usage, in all questions regarding succession, whether testate or intestate, the rule of decision shall be the Muslim personal law, in cases where the parties are Muslims.

2–47 An important focus of debate, with special relevance to women, has been the interest of a limited owner of immovable property. The 1948 Act was only prospective in operation. Moreover, it did not in any way affect the position of a limited owner as concerns powers of alienation, since only the rules governing succession to such property on the termination of a limited estate were brought under the Muslim personal law. Legal conflicts continued to occur, therefore, but even the West Pakistan Muslim Personal Law (Shariat) Application Act 1962 did not solve this conundrum. Following several further amendments (see Ch. M. Mahmood (1991), pp. 504–506), with effect from August 1, 1983, the West Pakistan Muslim Personal Law (Shariat) Act (Amendment) Ordinance 1983 (XIII of 1983) made men who had earlier inherited land as limited owners under custom, absolute owners with retrospective effect. Thus, Pakistani law has extended the provisions of the original 1937 Act to a point where a choice between the personal law as laid down by the Act and the customary law is no longer necessary. The amendments to the Shariat Act in Pakistan, more than any other reform, illustrate the attempts by the modern law to reduce the role of custom and to introduce *shari'a* law as the rule of decision in a large and important area of personal law governing Muslims. However, the current situation is still unsettled.[53] Ch. M. Mahmood (1991, p. 500) refers to continuing litigation over this matter, while the (apparently deliberate) non-attention to female owners in the 1983 Ordinance does not appear to satisfy Muslim women's claims to more secure property rights.[54]

Muslim law and the general law

2–48 The borderlines between 'personal law' and 'general law' may not always be absolutely clear. Complex conflicts arose in the development of South Asian laws because even beyond 1858, when British colonial sovereignty was more firmly established, Muslim general law was applied in important areas of the law such as criminal law and evidence which infringed on personal law topics. A most instructive example of the problems facing the British administrators and later the courts arose in respect of the rules relating to presumptions of legitimacy and of the death of a person.[55] In both cases, the critical policy question was whether these rules were to be treated as substantive rules, in which case traditional Muslim law should apply, or as rules of evidence, in which case they fell under the general law, and thus under the remit of the colonial powers for codification. The decision was taken, early on, that these rules were rules of procedure, hence they would be subject to legislative interference.

---

[53] The earlier insecurities are well-reflected in the appendices found in Mannan (1990), which contain a number of relevant statutes whose explicit purpose was to remove doubts or legal insecurities.
[54] Balchin (1994) is silent on this point.
[55] This topic is discussed in detail in para. 10–11 below.

2–49 Apart from the rules about presumptions of legitimacy of birth, another part of the Indian Evidence Act 1872 has created a similar conflict and is illustrated by an early decision from Allahabad in 1885, *Mazhar Ali v. Budh Singh* 1885 I.L.R. 7 Al. 297. Sections 107 and 108 of the Indian Evidence Act 1872 deal with the burden of proving the death of a person known to have been alive. According to traditional Muslim law, a missing person is to be regarded as alive till the lapse of 90 years (the 'natural span' of life) from the date of birth, depending on the circumstances in which s/he went missing. The Indian Evidence Act introduced a rule akin to the English law concept of proof. If it is shown that the man was alive within 30 years of the date of the presentation of the case, then the burden of proving that he is dead lies on the person who affirms this. If it is proved that he has not been heard of in the last seven years, by those who would naturally have heard of him if he had been alive, then the burden of proving that he is alive is shifted to the person who affirms that he is alive.

2–50 The dispute in *Mazhar Ali v. Budh Singh* resolved itself into whether to apply the rule of Muslim law, in accordance with section 24 of the Bengal Civil Courts Act 1871 or the rule of evidence as contained in section 108 of the Indian Evidence Act 1872. After an exhaustive analysis of the Muslim law sources, Mahmood J. concluded that the Muslim rule in question fell within the topic of evidence. Thus, although before the enactment of the Indian Evidence Act 1872 there might have been some justification for applying the Muslim law to Muslim cases, there was no doubt in the judge's mind that he was now bound by section 108 of the Indian Evidence Act 1872. If he had concluded otherwise, to the effect that the Muslim rule was a rule of substance, then he undoubtedly would have applied the Muslim law as directed by section 24 of the Bengal Civil Courts Act 1871.[56] This important case demonstrates acute judicial awareness at the time about the distinctions between personal law and general law and the fact that any decisions made should be in line with traditional Muslim law, on the one hand, while taking account of the exigencies of modern times on the other.

2–51 Sections 107 and 108 of the Indian Evidence Act 1872 have meanwhile become sections 123 and 124 of the Qanun-e-Shahadat Order 1984 in Pakistan. While the wording has not been amended, it remains to be seen how a similar case to *Mazhar Ali* would be dealt with if it came up before a Pakistani judge. The decision probably would go the other way, and there are good reasons for this. Since 1962, institutions have existed in the Pakistani constitutions for attempts to be made to bring all existing laws into conformity with the injunctions of Islam as laid down in the Holy Qur'an and Sunna. As early as 1966, the Interest Act 1839 and the Negotiable Instruments Act 1881 were being criticised by various constitutional bodies as being contrary to the principles of Islamic law. Major changes to the received laws have been introduced since 1977, especially the Qanun-e-Shahadat Order 1984. It appears that the islamisation of the laws in Pakistan, on one level at any rate, is an attempt to fuse the Muslim law with the 'general law'. In such an attempt to unify the legal system, it is perhaps only natural in the present stage of legal development in Pakistan that the Muslim law would come out the victor.

---

[56] For further details on this issue see also our discussion of the Dissolution of Muslim Marriages Act 1939 in Chap. 9, below. By s.2(i) of that Act, a woman married under Muslim law can obtain a decree for the dissolution of her marriage if the whereabouts of her husband have not been known for a period of four years. This section is confined to divorce petitions brought by the wife, and to that extent it has a limited effect on the traditional law, although it does change the Hanafi law in that respect.

Muslim law in South Asia today

India

2–52   In a secular constitutional democracy, the Muslim personal law remains of great importance and practical relevance to the substantial Muslim minority of India (about 12 per cent, now well over 120 million people). Since this personal law has remained largely uncodified, it means in practice that the laws on marriage, divorce and many other matters are decided in accordance with traditional *shari'a*, which may sometimes involve recourse to Anglo-Mohammedan law. In line with traditional legal and social expectations, however, most Muslim family law disputes in India and in the subcontinent generally are settled extra-judicially.[57] This has had the effect that Indian Muslim law has remained largely invisible. In fact, there is a strong body of opinion to the effect that this has allowed certain un-Islamic customs which damage women to thrive within the protective umbrella of the personal law system. In this respect, an important recent controversy relates to the so-called triple *talaq*, known in English legal practice as 'bare *talaq*'.[58] In India, there have been few attempts by the state to exercise greater control over the Muslim personal law for apparent political reasons. Every time such a reform is debated, the cry of 'religion in danger' is raised by vocal sections of the Muslim community.[59] In legal practice today, this means that most of Indian Muslim law remains in the extra-legal sphere. Most Muslim marriages remain unregistered, Indian *talaqs* remain 'bare *talaqs*', polygamy continues to exist without state restrictions, and recourse to documentation in many family arrangements is minimal, with obvious difficulties for lawyers, courts and some clients if documentary evidence is required at a later stage. In the context of British legal practice, many lawyers come across such problems, most frequently in immigration and family law cases. Often, this works to the disadvantage of women, so there is a strong argument for the greater use of formality and documentation in order to improve the legal position of women.[60]

2–53   While the modern Indian state, for better or worse, has not interfered in the Muslim law of marriage and divorce, one notable exception to the state's indifference to Muslim law has been the law on post-divorce maintenance. The obvious reason is a financial one, now also familiar in cash-strapped Western jurisdictions with welfare provisions which seek to protect divorced wives and children from destitution. Indian law, since the enactment of sections 125–127 of the new Criminal Procedure Code 1973, but more so through the promulgation of the Muslim Women (Protection of Rights on Divorce) Act 1986, has taken definitive steps to secure equal legal treatment for Muslim divorced wives as compared to their non-Muslim co-citizens, but without putting a financial burden on the state. Fascinatingly for Muslim jurisprudence, this has been achieved through the techniques of neo-*ijtihad*, a creative process which bypasses *taqlid* and goes back to the revealed sources.[61]

---

[57] See generally Menski [1997]. For similar observations with reference to South Asian Muslims in Britain see Pearl, *Family law and the immigrant communities* (1986a). For evidence of the re-emergence of Muslim courts or *panchayats* in India during the 1990s see Bharatiya, *Syed Khalid Rashid's Muslim law* (1996), pp. 48–49.

[58] For details on this controversy see now Furqan Ahmad, *Triple talaq. An analytical study with emphasis on socio-legal aspects* (1994). See also Pearl (1979c), p. 101; Jain (1990), p. 630.

[59] See also Pearl (1979c), p. 101; Jain (1990), p. 630.

[60] See, *e.g.* Malik [1990] 42 D.L.R. 34–40, on the scope for greater use of pre-nuptial contracts in South Asian Muslim law.

[61] On this topic see in detail para. 7–75, below.

2-54   There is little scope for the argument that the Muslim personal law of India will be superseded by a Uniform Civil Code.[62] Already in 1980, the comparative lawyer Allott (1980, p. 216) wrote:

> "This now seems no more than a distant mirage . . . there is no visible way ahead in the reduction or removal of the cleavage between Muslim and non-Muslim personal law, and the Muslim Law persists, and will persist, subject only to such minor modifications as may correspond to the reforming programmes of Muslim countries of the Near and Middle East. Now, with the re-awakening of Muslim puritanism, even on the Indian sub-continent, it is doubtful whether even this minor gain will be made."

Article 44 of the Indian Constitution stipulates that "The state shall endeavour to secure for the citizens a uniform civil code throughout the territory of India", which seems to suggest that a uniform civil code will eventually be introduced. However, the lengthy debates on this issue have been referred to as a "barren controversy" (Dhagamwar (1989), p. 71) by a leading Indian reseacher and, in the words of a Western observer, have been "rather disappointingly unedifying" (Hodkinson (1984), p. 22). The topic seems to be revived in India whenever there is a perceived crisis of the nation, but it seems as unthinkable for India to abandon the personal law system as it is for Britain to adopt it. In both cases, the respective legal system rests on a historically grown infrastructure of cultural foundations which 'modern' phenomena like national unification or mass migration cannot easily undermine. Thus, quite apart from the political and communalistic implications of restricting the scope for the application of Muslim law in India, the legal case for the continued application of *shari'a* as an integral part of modern Indian law seems unassailable. This does not mean that there is no scope for debates about reforms and modifications of Muslim law, but it does not help either side, in the often very polarised debates, to assume that there can be a future for Indian law without Muslim law input. By the late 1990s, the aftermath of the famous *Shah Bano* controversy over the rights of Muslim divorced wives to post-divorce maintenance under Indian law, which we discuss in detail in paragraph 7–75, below, shows that harmonious construction of classical *shari'a* law and modern Indian law are indeed possible. This indicates an important finding, namely that many Muslims in the world today can very well live their lives as Muslims within the parameters of a non-Muslim political structure. It would appear that the position of Indian Muslims shows significant parallels in that respect with that of Muslims in countries like the United Kingdom today.

Pakistan

2-55   Despite strong initial lip service to secularisation, which some observers misinterpreted as eventual reduction of the scope for Muslim personal law, there has never been any doubt that Muslim law in Pakistan remains an intrinsically basic ingredient of the entire legal system. Overall, the past 50 years show a clear trend towards greater explicit incorporation of Islamic values as part of the legal system as a whole. However, this was not so obvious from the start of Pakistani law

---

[62] See in detail Menski, "The reform of Islamic family law and a uniform civil code for India", in *Islamic family law* (1990b), pp. 253–293; (1990c) K.L.T. More recent official statements from the Indian government have confirmed the well-rehearsed unwillingness to supersede the personal laws and have made the point, again, that the abolition of personal laws would be an unconstitutional infringement of personal liberty.

making, when many conflicting signals were given.[63] We observe an originally implicit and now increasingly explicit rejection of the colonial legal model with its imposition of general secular law over the personal law system and, thus, over Islamic law. This re-construction of a specifically Pakistani post-colonial legal system continues today. It is a complex process, very inadequately characterised by the term 'islamisation'.[64]

2–56 This process of post-colonial rejection, as recent research shows, has been observable, as in India, since at least the mid-1970s. Pakistani courts, too, have long asserted that English law concepts and values are no longer appropriate yardsticks for adjudication of disputes. For example, in *Nizam Khan v. Additional District Judge, Lyallpur* P.L.D. 1976 Lah. 930, it was held, at pages 970–971:

> ". . . the judiciary in Pakistan, on its own part, does not at all consider the Muslim Law or its philosophy, principles and jurisprudence as opposed to 'justice, equity and good conscience'. On the basis of [the] above reasoning therefore, all aspects of law which are not covered by territorial or other enforceable law or usage, are to be governed in Pakistan by the Muslim law . . .
>
> In such a situation, it would not be permissible for Courts in Pakistan to apply and import any more the rules of English law relating to equity, justice and good conscience. In other words, all residuary law in Pakistan to be applied in fields other than those occupied by existing statutory law has to be Muslim Law and jurisprudence and philosophy underlying the same."[65]

At the same time, another focal issue in the Pakistani discourse about legal developments, though the numerous debates do not bring this out as openly as one would wish, concerns the place of minority legal systems in Pakistan and the extent to which a general legal system inspired by *shari'a* principles can safeguard minority rights. Interestingly, in Pakistan this centrally concerns the large and economically powerful Ahmadi community, who have been declared non-Muslims since 1974. Today, their precise legal position remains unclear, with strange implications especially for family law (see note 16, above). Thus, pluralism within the Muslim law sphere is as much a key issue in Pakistan as the pluralism/personal law debate is in India or in Britain today.

2–57 It appears that there has been very little open debate about such issues in Pakistan because, apart from the Ahmadi question, the non-Muslim minorities in Pakistan are numerically very small (about 2–3 per cent) and lack the political and legal representation to put their case forward. As a result, non-Muslims in Pakistan are tolerated within an Islamic framework of reference rather than accepted as an integral part of a secular state with constitutional guarantees for minority rights. In other words, Pakistan is as uncomfortable with the presence of minorities as with the personal law system itself and would appear to desire a uniform law in the personal law sphere, although at the same time it rejects the Western system of secularised legal uniformity. Seen in this light, the appeal to religion as a basis for law making is an intellectual shortcut, since Pakistani politicians have clearly remained unwilling to give up control over law making processes in favour of

---

[63] See in detail Choudhury, *Constitutional development in Pakistan* (1969); Mehdi, *The islamization of the law in Pakistan* (1994); Newberg, *Judging the state: Courts and constitutional politics in Pakistan* (1995).
[64] For a detailed analysis of the implications of this concept see especially Kennedy (1990) 63 No. 1 *Pacific Affairs* 62–77, and (1996), *Islamization of laws and economy. Case studies on Pakistan*. For various authoritative formulations of this key issue in Pakistan today see Mannan (1990), p. 35.
[65] This point is also emphasised, *ibid.* p. 3 and n.10.

religious authorities. Practitioners will need to be aware that such muddled thinking has been carried into the law courts, especially when complex questions of Muslim personal law have come up for adjudication.[66]

2-58 The sphere of the Muslim personal law was subjected to important legal reforms by the Muslim Family Laws Ordinance 1961. This seemingly modern enactment, imposed by a martial law administrator rather than passed by a Parliament, modified certain aspects of traditional Muslim family law which had come in for criticism, especially by women's groups. It was welcomed because, in essence, several provisions put restrictions on the unilateral powers of the Muslim husband to divorce (section 7) and to take more than one wife (section 6). However, the Ordinance was simultaneously criticised, right from the start, for not going far enough and for being too modern, in fact 'unislamic'.[67]

2-59 The promulgation of the MFLO has been seen as an attempt by the modern state to achieve more control over the sphere of family law. In common with the experience of many other Muslim countries, "Pakistan in the 1960s experienced a wave of governmental intervention in family law" (Pearl (1990b), p. 322). However, it must now be doubted whether such attempts, which include the promulgation of the West Pakistan Family Courts Act 1964, have been as effective as was once thought. It was assumed for some time that the provisions of the 1961 Ordinance had more or less totally superseded the provisions of traditional Muslim personal law.[68] However, during the late 1980s and early 1990s, it has become increasingly clear that this was not in fact the case and that the Muslims of Pakistan remain free to express their allegiance to *shari'a* law rather than the modern state law. Thus today, Pakistan's Muslim personal law consists of the traditional *shari'a* law *and* of the statutory provisions introduced by the modern state and it remains contested, in cases of conflict, which set of rules prevails. The side-effect of Pakistan's islamisation policies in this regard has been to make the continuing conflicts and tensions between traditional *shari'a* and modern state law more visible. In legal practice, as we shall see in Chapters 8 and 9 below in particular, this has had extremely important implications, which have influenced legal practice in Britain, too.

2-60 The current reformulations of Muslim personal law are taking place within the conceptual framework of the much-debated constitutional re-orientation in Pakistan towards islamisation. This is much more than a new round in the political chess games of different political power centres. From its inception in 1947, Pakistan has dramatically and seriously struggled to develop its own national and legal identity, seeking to reconstruct the colonial legal system into one that fits better with the socio-legal realities of a new Muslim state (see Anderson (1967)). Naturally, the place of Muslim law has been a crucial factor in this context. Starting with the formulation of the Objectives Resolution in Lahore in 1949, to its introduction as the Preamble of Pakistan's Constitutions, and its ultimate elevation from a policy declaration to a substantive part of the 1973 Constitution by Presidential Order No. 14 of 1985, the Islamic foundations of Pakistani law have been fiercely debated and contested. The current position, in light of Article 2A of the Pakistani Constitution, is best illustrated by Article 227 of the 1973 Constitution, which introduces Part IX, the Islamic provisions, and reads as follows:

---

[66] See particularly para. 9–119, below on the interpretation of s.7 of the MFLO of 1961.

[67] For details of the debates about the 1961 Ordinance see Hodkinson (1984); Mumtaz and Shaheed, *Women of Pakistan. Two steps forward, one step back?* (1987); Mehdi (1994).

[68] But see already the doubts expressed in the concluding comment to the first edition of this book, Pearl (1979c), p. 210.

"227. Provisions relating to the Holy Quran and Sunnah. –

(1) All existing laws shall be brought in conformity with the Injunctions of Islam as laid down in the Holy Quran and Sunnah, in this Part referred to as the Injunctions of Islam, and no law shall be enacted which is repugnant to such injunctions.

Explanation. – In the application of this clause to the personal law of any Muslim sect, the expression "Quran and Sunnah" shall mean the Quran and Sunnah as interpreted by that sect.

. . .

(3) Nothing in this Part shall affect the personal laws of non-Muslim citizens or their status as citizens."

The wording of Article 227 itself perceptively indicates the existing plurality of opinions in Pakistan about what precisely "Quran and Sunnah" means. In view of this ongoing struggle about the definition of Islam itself, it appears that the best a practising lawyer from a foreign jurisdiction can do is to keep an open mind about the continued relevance of traditional *shari'a* law in Pakistani jurisprudence, rather than assuming that 'modernisation' or 'globalisation' would lead to its replacement. Interestingly, some new research on Pakistani public law confirms the claims of many Pakistani jurists and key members of the higher judiciary that recourse to Islamic principles and focus on human rights are not mutually exclusive.[69]

Bangladesh

2–61 This jurisdiction presents an interesting case of a personal law system in which a large Muslim majority co-exists with substantial Hindu, Buddhist and Christian minority populations (at least 12–15 per cent of a total of more than 130 million people), thus broadly mirroring India's position.

2–62 Following its independence from Pakistan on March 26, 1971, Bangladesh inherited Pakistan's legal system through the retrospective operation of the Bangladesh (Adaptation of Existing Bangladesh Laws) Order 1972.[70] This means that Bangladesh also inherited the inherent conflicts of traditional *shari'a* and modern statutory reforms in the MFLO of 1961. However, the stronger position of non-Muslim minorities and a less vigorous politically motivated drive towards islamisation of the entire legal system in Bangladesh, coupled perhaps with greater dependence on foreign donors, has led to a less explicitly Islamic orientation of post-independence Bangladeshi laws. Further, the distance from Pakistan, both political and geographical, and the proximity to India (a classic love/hate relationship of close neighbours) has meant that, despite protests, many modern Bangladeshi legal reforms actually follow the Indian law very closely.[71] Overall, from an avowedly secular starting point, Bangladeshi constitutional law has moved towards paying lipservice to islamisation, far less so than Pakistan.[72] In the personal

---

[69] For details see Lau, "Islam and judicial activism: Public interest litigation and environmental protection in the Islamic Republic of Pakistan", in *Human rights approaches to environmental protection* (1996); Faqir Hussain, "Public interest litigation in Pakistan" (1993) P.L.D. 72–83. For South Asia generally see Hossain *et al.* (1997).

[70] For details on Bangladeshi law see Hoque (1980), Menski and Rahman, "Hindus and the law in Bangladesh" [1988] 8 No. 2 *South Asia Research* 111–131; Patwari (1991). On Bangladeshi independence see Muhith, *Bangladesh: Emergence of a nation* (1992) and Zaheer, *The separation of East Pakistan: The rise and realisation of Bengali Muslim nationalism* (1994).

[71] This is particularly so for the Bangladeshi anti-dowry law, which was copied almost verbatim from India but is not exactly the same in all respects. Bakar, *A handbook on the Dowry Prohibition Act 1980 and the Cruelty to Women (Deterrent Punishment) Ordinance 1983* (1989) is a helpful source.

[72] For details see Khosa, "Islamic provisions in the constitution of Pakistan" [1995] P.L.D. 17–22.

law sphere, where Muslim law continues to be applied, the lack of scholarship in traditional Muslim law is now felt to be a handicap and many disputes involving complex questions of Islamic law appear to be settled by recourse to provisions under the general law rather than the personal law. It has been argued that this reflects declining scholarship in the traditional personal law sphere in that jurisdiction (Menski and Rahman [1988]).

2–63 Under the MFLO of 1961, the assumption of the 1960s that the reforms introduced by this Ordinance were effective has been much stronger in Bangladesh and has been maintained much longer than in Pakistan. However, Bangladeshi jurisprudence has now also begun to acknowledge that the procedural provisions of the Ordinance and real legal life quite apparently do not match.[73] By a different route, thus, Bangladeshi law has arrived at a position similar to Pakistani law, arguing that better justice may be achieved, first, by recognition of the particular facts and circumstances of the case and secondly, by recourse to the ideal norms of the *shari'a* rather than secular modern legal provisions which purport to be morally neutral. This has led to some fascinating recent judgments which have not yet been widely noticed outside Bangladesh.[74] The present edition will incorporate such new material wherever possible. Thus, for Bangladesh, too, the future role and place of Muslim law remains undoubtedly a key issue in policy as well as legal practice, in the personal law sphere as well as regarding the general law of the country.

---

[73] In this respect, a relevant recent case is *Sirajul Islam v. Helana Begum* 48 D.L.R. (1996) 48, holding that notice of divorce is not essential for legal validity under the MLFO 1961.

[74] A case in point is the Bangladeshi position on post-divorce maintenance for abandoned Muslim wives, which mirrors the famous Indian *Shah Bano* case (see para. 7–75, below), but makes no reference to it whatsoever. See *Md. Hefzur Rahman v. Shamsun Nahar Begum* (1995) 15 B.L.D. 34 and its *neo-ijtihad* technique. The case is discussed in detail in para. 7–75, below and is currently on appeal.

Chapter 3

Muslim law in Britain

3-01 Historically, as we have seen, it is not new for Muslims to be a minority. What is new in the modern Western context is that Muslim individuals and communities and their *shari'a* are faced with state legal systems which are secular, in the sense that religion and law are seen as separate matters.[1] Western 'traditional model jurisprudence' (Chiba (1986), p. 1) appears to leave no formally recognised space for a personal law system based on different religious and cultural traditions. Viewing itself as more or less secular, and certainly as dominant, the typical Western state law thus obstructs and restricts the scope for Muslim law in a new diaspora to become part of the recognised official law. Muslim law, in such a scenario, is pushed into the realm of the unofficial, the extra-legal, the sphere of 'cultural practice' or perhaps 'ethnic minority custom' (Poulter (1986)), rather than being treated as officially recognised law.

3-02 Muslim law in the West has been still further marginalised by the fact that the typical modern Western legal system and its proponents tend to view and treat the *shari'a* value system as suspect in terms of effective human rights protection. Muslim law is, thus, often portrayed as diametrically opposed to the values of the majority community and as incompatible with modern concepts of human rights.[2] The most prominent examples, always cited when this issue arises, are the unilateral *talaq* and the male privilege of polygamy.[3]

3-03 All this leads inevitably to a basic 'clash' of values and to unprecedented conflict situations which form the conceptual backdrop to the new approach taken in the present edition. In a religious sense, it is apparent that Muslims in the West have not abandoned Islam and Muslim law, nor will they do so in future. But to what extent can Muslims in countries like the United Kingdom today be treated as secularised subjects of a uniform national legal system? We can see at once that this question resurrects age-old conflicts and tensions about the relationship between God's law and man's law (Coulson (1969)), and between the conscience of the Muslim individual and the demands of the modern state (see now King (1995)). If abandonment of *shari'a* is not an option, and Islam is seen as a way of life as well as a religion, it becomes a central issue to what extent *shari'a* can be incorporated into a secular legal system as Muslim law. It often appears that there is a sense of unbridgeable conflict between restrictive official application and full-scale social observance, between purportedly uniform English law and the continued but unofficial observance of Muslim law in Britain.

---

[1] Readers need to recall from Chap. 2, above that in South Asia and particularly in Indian law 'secularism' appears as the principle of equidistance of the state from all religions. This implies acceptance of religion as a basic factor in the legal sphere, a markedly different approach from that taken in most Western secular legal systems

[2] See, *e.g.* Poulter, "Ethnic minority customs, English law and human rights" [1987] 36 I.C.L.Q. 589–615. In more detail, see Engineer, *The rights of women in Islam* (1992); Mernissi, *Women and Islam. An historical and theological enquiry* (1993); Mayer, *Islam and human rights: Traditions and politics* (1991) and [1994] 15 *Michigan Journal of International Law* 307–404.

[3] *e.g.* Poulter, "Multiculturalism and human rights for Muslim families in English law", in *God's law versus state law. The construction of an Islamic identity in Western Europe* (1995, King (ed.)) p. 85. It is often assumed that Muslim jurisprudence has a monolithic view on such subjects but that is manifestly not so. For details, see Chaps. 8 and 9, below.

3–04 We are concerned in this chapter to understand and explain what implications this ongoing multiple conflict scenario carries for Muslim law as well as for legal practice in Britain. Before we turn to specific forms of legal regulation, it is necessary to expand a little on several interrelated issues. We tackle this task by dividing the discussion into several complex interlinking segments. In real life, they all interact. Here, we have to present them one by one, which makes it necessary for the reader to draw connections and links, which we may not always point out to avoid repetition and excessive cross-referencing.

3–05 Following a brief overview of the new scenario of Muslim presence in Britain, we first outline some relevant facts concerning Muslim settlement in Britain. We then turn to the juristic discourse on minority rights within Islamic law and find that ancient jurists probably did not think in detail about a scenario that presents itself in Britain today. The most likely explanation for this is that the modern secular model of a state legal system which purports to be separate from the religious sphere would not have made sense to those jurists.

3–06 We then examine, in more detail, the legal responses to the Muslim presence in Britain so far. This involves a survey of relevant literature and of case law and statutes which demonstrate the progression of interaction. Finally, this chapter analyses the Muslim responses to the approach taken by the official English law, explaining in detail the new concept of British Muslim law or *angrezi shariat* as a key element in this context.

The new scenario

3–07 Our starting observation must be that, from a Muslim perspective, allegiance to the supremacy of *shari'a* has continued among Muslims in Britain, while the modern state law has typically assumed – and has insisted on – the supremacy of its own rule of law models. This immediately sets up a conflict situation for which the classical tools of conflict of laws regulation among lawyers provide no meaningful remedy. For, in Britain today, recognising Muslim law is not so much a matter of giving legal validity to something 'foreign', an act that was done abroad, as in the classic conflicts scenario, which has continued to grow in importance as international migration and the emergence of transnational communities have become increasingly prominent (see Chapter 4, below). Rather, it has become necessary to think about granting – or withholding, as the case may be – official legal recognition to what Muslims do in Britain today, as neighbours, co-citizens, as purportedly equal partners in the modern business of organising a civic society, running a state and a legal system. In short, what is the place of Muslim law in modern Britain today?

3–08 It is hardly surprising that the muted debate about this issue should have led to immense tensions, much misunderstanding and, at the end of the day, palpable latent dissatisfaction and unease on all sides. By the end of the 1990s, an appropriate diagnosis would emphasise continuing lack of communication and a lingering danger of mutual intolerance. It appears that two diametrically opposed and irreconcilably entrenched positions threaten to dominate the discourse and cloud our thinking: Western legal centralism on the one hand, Islamic doctrines about the absolute supremacy of God's law and man's inability to add to it on the other. Both, as it were, are extreme positions which inevitably clash; they do not, however, represent the totality of views and possibilities.

3–09 We can locate the emergence of a British legal debate on this issue in the late 1960s and early 1970s, when Muslim migration to the United Kingdom became more prominent. The first point of relevance highlights that migration does not necessarily involve the shedding of cultural traditions and of established legal norms. The following observation remains relevant and realistic today:

> "When Pakistanis and Indians emigrate to this country, they do not discard their family customs . . . most immigrants who adopt a domicile of choice in this country still follow family customs dissimilar from those of the indigenous population" (Pearl (1972b), p. 120).

As we saw in Chapter 2, when the British migrated to the Indian subcontinent centuries earlier, they created a legal system not only for others, but first of all for themselves and their allies. While one could not suggest that Muslim migrants to Britain had the power to make official laws for themselves, let alone for others, it is unrealistic to assume that migrants setting foot on a new land will at once imbibe the laws of that new place. A Muslim, wherever s/he may be, remains subject to the main principle of Islam, total and unqualified submission to the will of Allah (Coulson (1968), p. 54). What this means in detail is a different matter; the first principle is that God's authority is perceived as superior to any form of man's law – an approach which secularising modernity purports, somehow, to have overcome.

3–10 Early comments on the legal position of Muslims in Britain, as the above quote shows, caught a glimpse of the emerging new conflict scenario. Initial scholarly reactions typically reflect an attempt to assert the supremacy of English law and its values over divergent customs and moralities, while at the same time allowing for recognition of new customs on certain conditions. Thus, continued Pearl (1972b, p. 120):

> "These customs, deeply engrained into the way of life of the immigrant population, cannot be cast aside by the English courts in an attempt to integrate the immigrants into the English community around them. This country has a multicultural history and the recognition of alien customs, so long as they do not fall below minimum standards of public policy, would appear to be a valuable contribution to the enhancement of racial harmony. Alien customs have been respected in some cases; in other cases, however, English practices appear to have been imposed."

This ambivalent approach to 'the other' persists today when English law remains willing to take account of 'cultural practices' in certain situations, but strictly imposes uniform rules in others. For example, a Muslim woman has successfully pleaded that her conviction as a drug courier should take account of the fact that many Muslim women remain subject to the strict authority of males.[4] Another Muslim woman was awarded £20,000 in damages in an action for slander against her former husband, who had falsely accused her of not being a virgin on her wedding night. The social impact of such a slur on her and her family, in view of the values of her community, must have been a factor explaining the size of the award.[5] In sharp contrast, a Muslim wife who had only undergone a *nikah* marriage

---

[4] *Regina v. Bibi* [1980] 1 W.L.R. 1193.
[5] For details see Poulter (1995) p. 83, referring to *Seemi v. Seemi* [1990], 140 N.L.J. 747. On the case see Edwards, "Vindication v. Compensation" [1990] 140 *New Law Journal* May 25, 1990, p. 747.

in Britain and never registered that marriage would still be advised today that she is not a legally wedded wife and has no standing in law.[6] One could of course say that such a wife has been negligent by not following the rules of English law, while in the first two cases the women concerned sought to defend themselves against pressures from within their particular society.

3-11   Seen in this light, the customs of immigrants and their descendants pose numerous challenges which are not fully answered by Western official legal systems today (Menski (1993a)). Nielsen (1992c, pp. 154–155) has noted an early, misguided secular assumption in Europe that Muslim immigrants would somehow be leaving their religion behind. This was soon found not to be the case. Significantly, the next assumption made was that the migrants' adherence to tradition was merely evidence of a transitory phase, perhaps a generation issue. This put the burden of assimilation on Muslims and other minorities (Nielsen (1992c), p. 164), assuming that, once Muslims and others became assimilated to an imagined 'mainstream culture', prominently through education, as Poulter (1986), p. 3) appeared to suggest, the culture of the migrants would somehow become submerged in that of the majority.

3-12   We know today that this is classic assimilationist ideology which has continuously been defeated by social realities which favour pluralism over uniformity, ethnic diversities over national stratification.[7] Such ideological posturing, or muddled thinking about law and society, comes out in leading questions about the future of ethnic minority 'customs' in Britain. Poulter (1986), p. v) posed the problem as follows:

> "Should the ethnic minorities who have come to live here conform to English ways or should they be free to continue and practise their own customs in this country? More specifically, should English law adapt its principles and rules to accommodate foreign customs or should new arrivals bear the burden of any adjustment?"

Such innocuous questions are based on the apparently sound central assumption that the state alone determines what the law is. Significantly, such an approach denies minorities the power of agency, the facility to construct their lives on their own terms. Recent anthropological research suggests that the first of Poulter's two questions misses the point (Ballard (1994), p. 8). The second question, suggesting that a modern state should adopt a policy of cultural pluralism within limits defined by the state itself,[8] sounds good but is not in fact a tolerant position, as the power to determine what is acceptable remains with the state rather than the community (Lutz [1990]). Poulter's approach, elaborated in his later writing (especially Poulter [1987] I.C.L.Q.; (1992a); (1995) and Poulter (1998)) suggests that accommodation to diversity should be made by responding positively to the requirements of ethnic minorities in Britain, but strictly within a set of shared values. Beyond this, recognition must not occur. Thus, it becomes easy to argue that there are certain

---

[6] Certain exceptions may be made, on an *ad hoc* discretionary basis, in social security contexts, especially if children are involved.

[7] See Ballard, *Desh pardesh. The South Asian presence in Britain* (1994), pp. 1–34, an excellent introduction to a study of Asians 'at home' in Britain. Parallels could be drawn to America's failed 'melting pot' ideology, on which see, *e.g.* Moore, *Al-Mughtariban. American law and the transformation of Muslim life in the United States* (1995).

[8] This was also the position taken at that time by Pearl, "Muslim marriages in English law" [1972b] 30 Part 1 *Cambridge Law Journal* 120 as quoted, above. For a similar approach see Lester and Bindman, *Race and law* (1972) p. 18, also referred to, below, n.62.

aspects of Muslim law which are capable of exceeding the bounds of tolerance, trespassing beyond the limits of multicultural recognition and of 'core values' or 'shared values' (see most clearly Poulter (1995), p. 83). In this way, the contentious international debates about universal core values (see *e.g.* Renteln (1990)) have become superimposed onto the discussions about the place of Muslim law in Britain. This has not been helpful because the fixed assumption that only ethnic minority 'customs' violate shared norms, whereas the official law is somehow exempt from such value judgments, does not match with the daily minority experience of racism and differential treatment. Thus, the official law occupies the high ground, but is perceived as dishonest in exempting itself from equal scrutiny.[9]

3–13 It is therefore manifestly too simple to assume that modern Western state law is necessarily superior to any other form of legal regulation. Yet such wishful thinking continues, based on assumptions and assertions which are not borne out by developments in reality. It is in this context that we raise important new questions – new for Britain and other Western countries today – about the recognition of Muslim law as an integral part of modern national legal systems.[10] Not surprisingly, given the social reservations about new minorities in Europe, there has been considerable reluctance on the part of English law to grant any form of official recognition to Muslim law as part of English law. However, as we began to see above, it is not true that English law has not taken notice, explicitly and implictly, of the presence of a large Muslim population.

3–14 While it is now known that South Asian migrants in the West did not throw their cultural luggage on the rubbish tip of history (Menski (1993a), p. 257), we also observe that they have been subtly, often imperceptibly to the outsider, reasserting their cultural and religious values, albeit with some modifications, in their new homeland. This process, while never without tensions, has for some time been observed among young Asians born and brought up in the West, and now occurs among the second and third generations.[11] Consequently, new research emphasises that the assimilation thesis is no longer valid today (Ballard (1994), p. 8) and that the earlier image of immigrants as lost 'between two cultures' (Watson (1977)) was inadequate and needs to be replaced by a more realistic assessment.[12] Ballard (1994, p. 30–31) suggests persuasively that many British Asians have become "skilled cultural navigators" who often effortlessly combine living in Britain with reconstructing particular Asian ways of life. Experienced researchers like Ballard emphasise the enormous difficulties which modern Western countries – and Western 'white' people – have with diversity and with multicultural approaches.[13]

---

[9] Ballard [1996] 30 No. 3 *Patterns of Prejudice* 3–33, and [1997] 20 No. 1 *Ethnic and Racial Studies* 182–194, highlights that in Britain, as exemplified by the handling of the Census of 1991, 'ethnic' still means something alien and non-white, somehow overlooking the fact that everybody is 'ethnic'. Being non-white, thus, becomes a deviation from an assumed norm, being 'the other' becomes pathogenic in itself.

[10] On Canada see now Ali and Whitehouse [1992] 13 No. 1 *Journal of Muslim and Minority Affairs* 156–172; on the USA see Moore (1995), Kelly (1998).

[11] See already Taylor, *The half-way generation. A study of Asian youths in Newcastle upon Tyne* (1976) on young people in Newcastle; Brah [1987] 7 No. 1 *South Asia Research* 39–54, for South Asian teenagers in Southall; Shaikh and Kelly [1989] 31 No. 1 *Educational Research* 10–19 for Muslim girls generally; Mirza, *The silent cry. Second generation Bradford Muslim women speak* (1989) as well as Knott and Khokher [1993] 19 No. 4 *New Community* 593–610, for Muslim women in Bradford. A new literature on citizenship and exclusion is currently emerging. See Spencer, *Strangers and citizens. A positive approach to migrants and refugees* (1994) and, *Migrants, refugees and the boundaries of citizenship* (1995); Bauböck, *From aliens to citizens. Redefining the status of immigrants in Europe* (1994).

[12] On the facile assumption of assimilation in the next generation see Kannan, *Cultural adaptation of Asian immigrants: First and second generation* (1978).

[13] Ballard (1994) p. 8. The same author (see n.9, above) shows that the British Census data collection mechanisms still assume that it is normal to be 'white'.

3–15   The critical question for lawyers, and for the law, remains to what extent the process of recognition of ethnic diversities should extend to the legal sphere. In our present study of Muslim law, we focus on the unofficial re-emergence of Muslim law in Britain.[14]

3–16   There is a powerful assumption that Muslims have found it more difficult than other minority groups to harmonise aspects of their community and family customs with the official laws of European countries.[15] Much of this, it seems, has to do with the nature of Islam.[16] However, the conceptual non-division of the 'religious' and the 'secular' is, contrary to much assertion by Muslims and non-Muslims alike, not unique to Islam. When Muslims and their spokespersons raise this issue, they do reflect concern over the basic question of God's law/man's law (which is also an issue in other religious traditions) but often this is mixed with considerable misgivings about the fact that minorities like the Jews and the Sikhs in Britain appear to have been given wider legal recognition than Muslims. The major focus of Muslim legal demands in Britain at present is therefore on remedying the exclusion of Muslims from the protective label of 'racial group' under the Race Relations Act 1976 (Modood [1993]). The focus is, then, not really on the recognition of Islam as a legal system but on the effects of exclusionary policies and politics which disadvantage Muslims, and some other minorities. Two debates and complex issues have thus been joined together, with confusing results, and often without reference to the legal sphere.[17]

3–17   It is quite apparent that English law has been facing major conceptual problems over how to handle religion as a marker of community or group identity (Bradney (1993)). Religion, not only from a Muslim perspective, is not just a matter of having places of worship or holding particular beliefs or values. Religion is also a matter of putting into practice what one believes, as well as acting in accordance with the values one holds in esteem. The fact that many Muslim authors continue to remind us of such basic issues does not mean that members of other religious groups do not face the same questions and/or come to the same conclusions.

3–18   Like British Sikhs, Muslims have attempted to raise their concerns in the public sphere (Modood [1993]; Vertovec (1996)). To some extent, this reflects disproportionate emphasis on Muslims in Britain and their concerns, creating an impression that such debates single out Islam and Muslim law as the source of the problem. That seems misguided on several counts. While all ethnic minority groups face similar theoretical and practical questions, it can be argued that the conceptual problems of legal recognition for minorities are, in the first place, caused by our dominant rule of law concepts rather than the presence of minority laws. In other words, it is the majority law, the official law, which allows insufficient space for diversity and thus drives minority communities, as it were, underground, into the

---

[14] Menski, "Legal pluralism in the Hindu marriage", in *Hinduism in Great Britain* (1987); [1988a] (1) K.L.J. 56–66; "Asians in Britain and the question of adaptation to a new legal order: Asian laws in Britain", in *Ethnicity, identity, migration: The South Asian context* (1993) discussed in detail the re-emergence of unofficial Hindu law in Britain. More detailed fieldwork about Muslim law is still to be conducted.

[15] This is also apparent from the growing French literature in this field. See Bistolfi and Zabbal, *Islams d'Europe. Integration ou insertion communautaire?* (1995); Foblets, *Les familles maghrébines et la justice en Belgique. Anthropolgie juridique et immigration* (1994b) and, *Familles – Islam – Europe. Le droit confronté au changement* (1996). For a more accessible summary see Foblets, "Community justice amongst immigrant family members in France and Belgium", in *Law and anthropology* (1994).

[16] Ballard (1994a), pp. 20–22, however, emphasises that religion as such and commitment to Islam constitute only one set of factors among others, which include economic and social forces.

[17] The most recent study in this field is Werbner and Modood, *Debating cultural hybridity. Multicultural identities and the politics of anti-racism* (1997).

realm of 'unofficial law', 'cultural practices' or custom, which modernising legal systems have been struggling to shut out.[18] However, as in South Asia, at the end of the day, people's law cannot be declared non-existent if it so manifestly exists; legal recognition in some form becomes desirable, if not inevitable. Our present study shows that the piecemeal and reluctant legal recognition of the Muslim presence in Britain has already gone much further than all players, including the official law and the Muslims themselves, seem ready to admit.

3–19 In countries like the United Kingdom, religion serves as one focal point for group cohesion and individual identity. In terms of law, one can see that the public/private distinction with respect to religion is blurred, not only in the case of Islam. As the Salman Rushdie affair demonstrated most clearly, English law only purports to be secular, it is not in fact neutral – or equidistant – to religion. Muslim authors tend to see a strong link between law and religion; it is apparent that feminist Muslim scholarship (*e.g.* Mernissi (1993); Afshar (1994)) goes along with this. Traditional authors like Abdur Rahim (1984), p. 47) emphasise the personal application of law to Muslims, wherever they may be:

> "In Muhammadan jurisprudence law is personal in its application to the Muhammadans, that is to say, it is not affected by the constitution of a particular society . . . thus, if a Muhammadan goes from one state to another, he is bound by the same law, and if he does not live within the jurisdiction of a Muslim state, the Muhammadan law still applies to his conscience."

Such statements underpin the frequently voiced view of many Muslims that they are Muslims first and citizens or residents of a particular state second. This raises profound questions of loyalty and identity, which need to be addressed. There is, on the one hand, genuine desire not to offend the laws of the country which Muslims have adopted as their own. On the other hand is strong allegiance to an entity which is regarded, because of its divine nature, as having a higher status than the state. Therefore, what should the approach of Muslims be when faced with situations of seemingly irreconcilable conflict? How should modern state legal systems react to the basic Muslim position on the superiority of God's law?

3–20 From a legal perspective, it has simply been assumed that modern Western state law would prove superior to any cultural form of legal regulation. However, such wishful thinking based on assumptions – and that is all they were and continue to be – has not been matched by developments in reality. This raises important new questions – new for Britain and other Western countries today – about the recognition of Muslim law as an integral part of their respective national legal systems. While there has been considerable reluctance on the part of English law to grant any form of official recognition to Muslim law as part of English law, it is not true that English law has not taken notice of the presence of a large Muslim population. But that is only half the story.

3–21 Open conflict has been avoided by two factors. First, modern Western legal systems, with their positivist approach to what 'law' is, and what it is not, remain purposely blind to social conventions and so-called 'cultural practices' which are perceived to operate in the 'extra-legal' sphere. This fictitious, dismissive yet reluctantly tolerant attitude has in fact allowed space for the unofficial development of new hybrid rules, but it does not make it easy to be British and

---

[18] Para. 2–35, above already discussed efforts by Muslims to restrict the scope of local South Asian customs.

Muslim at the same time (see excellently Modood (1992)). At the same time, the official legal system can afford, from a position of official superiority, to keep the legal position of British Muslims under negotiation.[19] Secondly, being faced with such intricately structured official intransigence, Muslims in Britain and their organisations have cultivated numerous avoidance strategies, so that the contact points between the official law and the unofficial Muslim law have become obscured in various ways. Thus it may appear today, from the outside, that Muslims in Britain are following English law, but in effect they are following a path which *they* consider appropriate. The classic Muslim term for this is nothing else but *shari'a*, but in the new environment of Britain, a new hybrid form of *shari'a* was needed to avoid breaking the official law of the new home.

3-22   This observation confirms for the legal realm what Ballard (1994) has recently noted with regard to the social sphere, namely that South Asian immigrants and their descendants in Britain have reconstructed *desh pardesh*, a home away from home, by rebuilding their lives "on their own terms" (Ballard (1994), p. 5). Thus, in Britain today, we find a new form of *shari'a*, English Muslim law or *angrezi shariat*,[20] which remains officially unrecognised by the state but is now increasingly in evidence as a dominant legal force within the various Muslim communities in Britain. In other words, individual and community strategies have led to the development of new hybrid, unofficial Muslim laws in Britain which have not been recognised as such but operate in social reality.[21] *Angrezi shariat* remains officially unrecognised since, from the state's perspective, its emergence is deeply offensive to established ideas about modern legal systems and their functioning. At the same time, Muslims in Britain are, to a large extent, happy to keep matters that way, arguing that traditionally the sphere of family law has not been a matter for state law (see Ahsan (1995)).

3-23   The development of *angrezi shariat* is not a new phenomenon, nor should its public emergence come as a surprise. During the late 1960s and early 1970s, English law moved further and further in the direction of recognising, through case law, that Muslims in Britain continued to act in accordance with what they took to be *shari'a*.[22] By the early 1970s, however, in line with increasing immigration restrictions and despite new anti-discrimination laws, English statute law began to demand, in effect, that the rules and procedures of the uniform domestic law were to be followed. More specifically, for example, English divorce law insisted on formal legal proceedings before an English court to bring about a legally valid divorce.[23] Soon after this, the explicit demand for the full-scale recognition of Muslim personal law, made by the Union of Muslim Organisations in 1975, apparently a reaction to the increasing assertion of English law, resulted in a straightforward negative response: There was no space for *shari'a* within the modern English legal system.[24]

3-24   This stand-off has pushed Muslim law firmly into the realm of the

---

[19] This is especially obvious in the field of education law, where persistent Muslim pressure for public funding for Muslim schools has had only limited success.

[20] This particular term for Muslim law in England is taken from Urdu, the national language of Pakistan. Its spelling reflects the South Asian majority orientation among Muslims in Britain today.

[21] The publications of the Islamic Shari'a Council (1995), for example, provide detailed evidence of this fact.

[22] The liberal high water mark in this respect appears to be the case of *Qureshi v. Qureshi* [1971] 1 All E.R. 325; [1972] Fam. 173, which was soon undone by legislation (see in detail Chap. 4, below).

[23] For details see paras. 4–14 and 9–205, below.

[24] Instructive details are found in Nielsen, *Emerging claims of Muslim populations in matters of family law in Europe* (1993a), and Surty (1991) 9 No. 1 *Muslim Education Quarterly* 59–68.

'unofficial law' and has forced Muslims and others, during the past two decades, to reorganise their legal world. Charting the emergence of *angrezi shariat* in more detail below, we show that it is possible today to trace and explain the resulting hybridisation process. It is apparent that much detailed research will need to be done in the coming years to fully understand such half-hidden processes of legal readjustment and to research their implications. The existing literature has a sociological and political focus and does not tell us much about the law. Case law and legislation, on the other hand, will need to be re-examined in the light of the emerging presence of *angrezi shariat*. Before we return to specific legal issues we turn first to a brief outline of important socio-economic factors which underpin the strength of the Muslim position in Britain.

Effects of Muslim settlement patterns in Britain

3–25   The reconstruction of Muslim law as an unofficial law within a Western context has been dependent not only on religious factors, such as the centrality of Islam to Muslims, but also on the settlement history and distribution patterns of British Muslims.[25] While this is not an issue of numbers alone, the nature, size and strength of a particular minority community are obviously relevant factors in the present context.

3–26   While the Muslim presence in Britain is of relatively recent origin, most prominently post-1945, it is known that a few Muslims have been present in Britain since the seventeenth/eighteenth century (Visram (1986)). Muslim authors tend to emphasise that Muslims have lived in Europe for a very long time and that Spain and Sicily prospered under their rule for centuries (Anwar (1994), p. 5). The Bosnia conflict brought home to a wider public that 'white Muslims' have existed in Europe for a long time and that Islam is a part of European culture, as Prince Charles and many others have pointed out.[26]

3–27   The vast majority of Muslims in Britain today are fairly recent immigrants and their descendants are mainly of South Asian origin.[27] However, especially in London there are many Arab groups, Iranians, Turks, Algerians, as well as various African communities, some American and Caribbean Black Muslims, and a growing number of converts. Most South Asian Muslims arrived as labour migrants during the 1950s and 1960s because until the passage of the Commonwealth Immigrants Act 1962 it was possible for citizens of the United Kingdom and Commonwealth to enter Britain freely.[28] Many other Muslim migrants arrived subsequently as part of various refugee movements, prominently East African Asians during the 1970s, Palestinians and Iranians, now African Muslims from various countries. In addition, the process of family reunion has been instrumental in creating a permanently settled Muslim population in Britain.[29] Today, almost 60 per cent of

---

[25] For details on the migration of Muslims see Nielsen, *Muslims in Western Europe* (1992c) pp. 1–7 and pp. 39–94.

[26] See in this respect a speech of H.R.H. The Prince of Wales "Islam and the West", (1994) 9 *Arab Law Quarterly*, pp. 135–143.

[27] For an analysis of the South Asian presence in Britain see Ballard (1994), pp. 1–34. For the 1991 Census data see Peach, *Ethnicity in the 1991 Census. Vol. 2: The ethnic minority populations of Great Britain* (1996).

[28] This necessarily brief account does not refer to migrants other than workers and refugees. Many Muslims came (and come) to Britain for studies, business and other purposes.

[29] For a detailed analysis and breakdown of statistics see Wahab, *Muslims in Britain: Profile of a community* (1989), pp. 7–11.

Muslims in Britain are below 25 years old, part of a "burgeoning British-born second generation" (Ballard (1994), p. 6).

3-28 Determining the size of the Muslim community in Britain is an impossible task because the statistical collection mechanisms are, typically, not geared towards ascertaining religious allegiances but remain based on place of birth as a primary statistical criterion. The 1991 Census, which included for the first time an 'ethnic question', still only yielded approximate figures.[30] It has been discussed whether the next Census should contain a question on religion, which is favoured by Muslim organisations but widely resisted. It is estimated that there are about 1 million to 1.5 million Muslims resident in Britain, about 2–3 per cent of the population, with an upward trend,[31] making Muslims the largest minority group in Britain and Islam the second religion after Christianity. There is widespread agreement that in the absence of precise statistics it remains difficult for public agencies and the communities themselves to assess the extent of their needs (Anwar (1994), p. 18). Some local initiatives have attempted to rectify this, but much remains to be done (see Ellis [1991]).

3-29 Early labour migration by Muslims involved mostly male individuals who ultimately aimed to buy property and improve the lives of their families in their home country. This is why so many early migrants were involved in rotating labour, staying in Britain only for some time before a kinsman took their place. This observation is relevant for questions of domicile, establishing an early pattern of no intention to stay permanently in Britain and, in sociological terms, the famous 'myth of return' (Anwar (1979)). However, the gradual restrictions on free movement for Commonwealth citizens after 1962 resulted in more or less permanently settled Muslim communities, when individuals present in Britain found they could not return home, as before, to be replaced by an overseas successor. Thus, the immigration restrictions forced many Muslims to stay in Britain for much longer than anticipated, often more or less permanently.[32] The inevitable corollary has been the emergence of family reunion, especially during the 1970s and 1980s. Sikhs and Hindus took to this strategy much faster than Muslims, in particular Bengali Muslims, some of whom never called their wives to Britain (Gardner and Shukur (1994), pp. 153–154).

3-30 The re-establishment of Muslim families and whole communities in Britain involved also the reconstruction of Muslim ways of life, influenced by traditional local, caste and family customs as well as the new British environment. Among South Asian Muslims, certain communities are strongly represented in Britain, while others are virtually absent. In essence, the majority of South Asian Muslims in Britain are Panjabis and Mirpuris, with significant Gujarati and Bengali groups.[33]

3-31 It appears to be a common element that many Muslims view the lifestyle of the majority with some distaste (Ballard (1994). pp. 2–5). While this reflects an

---

[30] Ballard and Kalra, *The ethnic dimensions of the 1991 Census. A preliminary report* (1994); Peach (1996); Peach and Glebe, "Muslim minorities in Western Europe" [1995] 18 No. 1 *Ethnic and Racial Studies* 28, give a figure of 1 million Muslims for the U.K.

[31] Poulter, *English law and ethnic minority customs* (1986) p. 2 does not attempt to give any figures for Muslims as such. The statistics provided are generally too conservative, while some community leaders have a tendency to inflate the numbers of 'their' people, *e.g.* Ahsan, "The Muslim family in Britain", in *God's law versus state law. The construction of an Islamic identity in Western Europe.* (1995), p. 21 with an estimate of 2–3 million Muslims in Britain today. On the picture in Europe see Peach and Glebe [1995].

[32] There is now a significant return migration of 'retired' migrants and, often, their families, further illustrating the continuing strong links within what are now called 'transnational communities'.

[33] For details on these groups see helpful bibliographical details in Ballard (1994).

assertion of religious and cultural values, often more explicitly than was the case 'back home', where so much was simply taken for granted, it also implies a feeling of superiority of one's own system. As Ballard (1994, p. 2) emphasised, "all the new minorities are strongly committed to cultural and religious reconstruction". We have already seen that this is not the kind of assimilation that was expected to occur over time.

3–32   Such psycho-social factors must be seen as related to the current picture of Muslim residential segregation in Britain. Overall, Muslims may be about 2–3 per cent of the population, but they are not thinly spread over the whole country. British Muslims today are heavily concentrated in London, in several large industrial cities like Birmingham, Glasgow, Manchester, Leeds/Bradford and in the old textile towns on either side of the Pennines. Within those cities, one finds many local Muslim centres of settlement and concentration, now not only in the classic 'inner city' areas.

3–33   Two complex processes need to be highlighted in this regard. First, even if they were not initially settling in close proximity, many Muslims have during the past two decades chosen to live in more or less Muslim-dominated areas because of all kinds of structural advantages, like easy access to mosques, after-school education facilities, shops and the homes of relatives and friends. At the same time, other Muslims have moved out of the 'inner city' areas to suburban residences, where they may again recreate community structures or where they may live more or less remote from other Muslims.[34]

3–34   Muslim residential segregation often reflects purposive distancing from the majority community, based on active initiative rather than victimised submission, a complex mixture of self-protection and a desire to be among one's own people. This trend is extremely relevant for legal analysis. Locally, if not nationally, the recreation of large Muslim communities in Britain has had important legal implications, given that community mores, *shari'a* and specifically South Asian concepts of honour (*izzat*) are perceived as superior to those of other communities.[35] At the same time, not all British Muslims are closely linked with such community structures and there is no unity among Muslims in Britain, reflected in many divergent opinions about how *shari'a* and legal life in Britain should be reconciled. Far from being socially homogenous, divided by ancient sectarian groupings and regional affiliations (see also Nielsen (1992c), pp. 164–165), Muslims are at the same time part of the universal Muslim community of all believers (*ummah*) as well as members of distinct families and clan groups (*biraderi*). Leading sociologists like Roger Ballard have commented that kinship loyalties amongst Muslims dominate over loyalty to one's co-religionists (see also Shaw (1994), p. 50). Young Muslims, in particular, constitute an increasingly vocal British-born second generation with a self-perception as hyphenated Britons or British Muslims and Muslim women have developed their own voice in this respect.[36] While much has been written about the outward and inward islamisation of British Muslims, it has remained unclear how this is, or can be, translated into the legal sphere.

---

[34] See, *e.g.* Werbner [1979] 7 No. 3 *New Community* 376–389, on Pakistanis in Manchester.
[35] Nielsen (1992c), p. 51, rightly emphasises that many of the practical problems faced by Muslims have had to be sorted out at the local level. An example of some prominence are burial practices, on which see Anwar, *Muslim burials — A policy paper* (1975).
[36] See groups like Women Against Fundamentalism; Sahgal and Yuval-Davis, *Refusing holy orders. Women and fundamentalism in Britain* (1992).

Islamic law and minorities: The juristic discourse

3-35   Before we turn to the approach of Western legal systems, it is useful to consider in a little more detail what Islamic jurisprudence has had to say about the minority status of Muslims. While questions about recognition of the Muslim 'other' arise today prominently in European states, it is also relevant to consider the traditional Islamic views on this difficult issue. After all, the history of Islam and of its legal systems starts from a position where Muslims were in various types of minority situation. Indeed, the status of Muslim minorities in non-Islamic territories has been an important subject of debate from the very beginning of Islamic history.[37] Lewis (1992, p. 6) has argued that it received only minor attention from Islamic jurists, relating mainly to migration necessitated by persecution or by the forced occupation of Muslim territory. The main reason for this particular slant may well be that in the historical context of gradual Muslim expansion it became necessary and inevitable for many Muslims to live under non-Muslim rule. It would appear that this scenario continues today.

3-36   Early Muslims, including the Prophet of Islam himself, became refugees having to migrate to avoid persecution for their religious beliefs. Later, sometimes the territory in which Muslims lived was conquered by a non-Muslim power or, increasingly during the period of Muslim expansion, Muslims migrated to territories which were not yet under Muslim rule. To these more historical categories we must now add the phenomenon of settled Muslim communities as 'ethnic minorities', resulting from voluntary migration to non-Muslim, secular states, most of which have a Christian ethos.[38] Lewis argues that there was no precise precedent in Islamic history for this particular phenomenon. The jurists, notes Lewis (1992, p. 13):

> ". . . discussed the predicament of the Muslim under a non-Muslim government under several headings: the new convert . . . the temporary visitor, taken as a captive or travelling . . . the unhappy inhabitant of a Muslim country conquered by unbelievers."

Not surprisingly, the possibility never seems to have entered their minds that a Muslim would voluntarily leave a Muslim land in order to place himself in this predicament.[39] This may not be the whole list of agenda. At any rate, as both Fadl and Lewis acknowledge, the juristic discussions relate to "the ethical and legal duties that these Muslims owe to the Shari'a and to their host polity" (Fadl (1994), p. 143). Some jurists argue, with considerable force, that Muslims and non-Muslims can live together only on the basis of peaceful co-existence which involves being able to profess and preach their respective religions. If circumstances should arise where Muslims are unable to defend and maintain their faith, they are obliged to emigrate, following the example of the Prophet himself, preferably to a Muslim country.[40] If this was the settled, authoritative position, it would carry with it enormous implications for Muslim communities in the West today.

---

[37] It is significant that the topic has received fresh attention recently. See Kettani [1990] 1 No. 2 *Journal of Muslim Minority Affairs* 226–233, and Lewis [1992] 13 No. 1 *Journal of Muslim Minority Affairs* 1–16, and in considerable detail Fadl [1994] 1 No. 2 *Islamic Law and Society* 141–187.

[38] The case of early Muslim traders in Kerala (see, above, para. 2–05) would appear to be different.

[39] Lewis (1992) p. 6 also notes that the jurists probably did not devote much attention to the minority scenario because in the age of Muslim expansion this was a largely hypothetical matter.

[40] See in detail Kettani, *Muslim mimnorities in the world today* (1986), pp. 3–4.

3–37   After thorough examination of the Qur'an, Sunna and juristic works, Fadl (above) concludes that early juristic opinions on the position of Muslims in non-Muslim lands are characterised by ambivalence and great diversity of thought. No one conclusive view has been offered by the various jurists of different schools. They generally appear to discourage such residence but never forbid it outright. Indeed, many jurists considered the issue mainly with reference to converts to Islam in non-Muslim countries.

3–38   Apart from early historical precedent,[41] two Qur'anic verses offer guidance. The most relevant source, verses 4.97–100, calls upon Muslims to escape persecution by migrating in the cause of God. Verse 5.44 instructed not only Muslims but also Jews and Christians to govern themselves by what God had decreed for each of them.

3–39   Fadl (1994, p. 144) rightly asks whether it is fair to conclude from such verses that oppression is synonymous with living in non-Muslim lands. What, for example, if a Muslim encounters oppression in an Islamic land?[42] Fadl (1994, p. 145) takes issue with the finding of Lewis (1992, p. 6) that Sunnis insisted on migration whereas Shi'is (because of their particular historical experiences) allowed a Muslim to remain in a hostile environment. In fact, even the Sunnis disagreed among themselves and, writes Fadl (1994, p. 150): "It seems that different jurists were addressing different scenarios in their expositions without specifically indicating the issue they had in mind".

3–40   Thus, while earlier juristic opinion discouraged but never outrightly forbade residence in a non-Muslim country, subsequent historical events, in particular the *reconquista* in Spain during the fifteenth century, may have meant that more definite stances were taken. Notably the Malikis, who were most affected by such conquests, adopted a hard-line position, saying that Muslim populations who find themselves under the rule of non-Muslims, whether it be good or bad, must follow the Prophet's footsteps and migrate to a Muslim state.[43] For Malikis then, as Fadl (1994, p. 163) has written, "choosing to reside in a non-Muslim land was a religious and ethical decision as much as a political one".

3–41   Hanbali and Shi'i jurists appear to have taken a less extreme view and generally held that such residence was permitted, as long as Muslims were secure from harm, would suffer physically or financially if migration took place, and were able to manifest or practise their religion (Fadl [1994], p. 157). However in their view, too, it was always better to reside in a Muslim territory, however poor or despotically governed it may be. Fadl notes the problem that words such as 'manifest' and 'practise' are nowhere defined. Thus, at what point is a Muslim being prevented from following Islam? Is the critical issue ability to perform acts of worship, such as prayer or fasting, or permission to apply the laws of Islam in their totality? Fadl ([1994], p. 158) rightly notes that "while it might be feasible to pray or fast in non-Muslim lands, it is far more difficult to apply Islamic criminal, commercial and personal status laws". Such comments have an obvious bearing on the development of modern state laws in South Asia as well as the kinds of demands which can be legitimately made by Muslims in Britain today.

3–42   Fadl has also shown that the opinions formulated by the Hanafi and Shafi'i jurists went further than any of the other schools. Their more flexible stance

---

[41] The emigration of the Prophet from Mecca to Medina and a group of Muslims who escaped persecution in Mecca by seeking sanctuary in Abyssinia, then a Christian state.

[42] On this question see also Kettani [1990] p. 226, who makes the point that Muslims in a non-Muslim society often discover that they can live their Islam better than in many 'Muslim countries'.

[43] For details see Fadl [1994], pp. 153–157.

is reflected in a less rigid view of what constitutes *dar al-islam*, the territory or abode of Islam. It is likely that this flexibility was influenced by the experience of Hanafi and Shafi'i Muslim expansion into South Asia and South East Asia. Some jurists contended that even where sovereignty vested in non-Muslim hands, the territory in question may still be a part of *dar al-islam* and where the conditions were right, it might in fact be good for a Muslim to reside in such a state. Hanafi jurists saw the free exercise of prayer and respect for the precepts of Islamic law as key conditions, whereas the Shafi'is remained more ambiguous.[44]

3–43 One of the leading experts on Muslims in Europe, Professor P. S. van Koningsveld, in the well-received Annual Lecture of the South Asian Studies Centre at the School of Oriental and African Studies in London on November 6, 1996, showed in detail that different answers about the position of Muslim minorities had been given by Muslim jurists in different historical situations.[45] Distinguishing a range of approaches, from pragmatic to utopian, he demonstrated that the classic distinction between *dar-al-islam* and *dar-al-harb* was not in fact a simple binary model, since there was another way of looking at the issue: He gave prominence to the intermediary concept of *dar-al-dawah* ('the country of mission') or *dar-al-ahd* ('the country of treaty'), where Muslims could live as a minority in a non-Muslim state, yet could organise their lives in accordance with *shari'a*.[46] This concept probably comes closest to the current Muslim experience in most Western countries. It is significant that this model was not prominently discussed in the Islamic literature before, indicating that scholarly concern was really more focused on those members of the *ummah* who faced real persecution.

3–44 Muslims as members of minority communities in the West today, then, have no clear, authoritative, uniform juristic guidance available to them. Muslim jurists, in both classical and modern times, were not and are not in a position to pronounce on this issue with certainty, and they do not explain unambiguously what Muslims are to do in case of a conflict, whether perceived or real, between the laws of a non-Muslim state and Muslim law. The only consistent advice appears to be that Muslims remain bound in conscience to God's law and must retain their separate identity, thus safeguarding *shari'a*. Modern jurists have referred in this context to the expedients of compromise (*ikrah*), necessity (*darura*) and public welfare (*maslaha*). These are concepts developed within Islamic jurisprudence to facilitate and allow for actions which ordinarily would be forbidden. The use of such jurisprudential tools is justified on the basis that refusal to compromise would lead to a weakening of Muslims and thus of Islam. It appears, at the same time, that the main justification put forward for Muslim migration to the West is of an economic nature, assuming that such migration is conducive to the welfare of the community. Such an intricate mixture of socio-economic and religious reasoning should not escape notice. The equally ambivalent approach of Western legal systems, which legally de-recognise Muslim law while tolerating its social presence, has clearly been conducive to the hidden growth of unofficial Muslim law in Western countries.

3–45 The demand for the full-scale recognition of Muslim personal law in

---

[44] For details see, *ibid.* p. 162.
[45] The title of this lecture, "Islamic policies of the Western colonial powers: Their relevance in the European Union in the post-colonial era", does not immediately point to the detailed analysis of traditional Muslim jurisprudence given by the speaker. This paper will be published in a journal on Muslim law.
[46] In Turkey, the concept of *dar-al-hizmet* ('the country of service', meaning service of Islam) was used to maintain an Islamic identity despite outward westernisation of the legal system.

Britain during the mid-1970s (see Poulter (1990b)) showed most clearly that Muslims in the West have been increasingly reasserting their religious and legal values and have been willing to challenge the official legal system rather than neglecting what they perceive as their religious duties. While it was a tactical mistake to demand full-scale legal recognition for *shari'a* in Britain, from a Muslim perspective one can see the ongoing bargaining process between Muslims and the British state as an exploration of the limits of *darura* among Muslims. The official negative response to this struggle, manifested most obviously in rejecting the claim for recognition of the Muslim personal law in Britain, leads directly to the private strategy of individual Muslims, now more manifestly of the various Muslim communities, to restructure their lives in accordance with *shari'a* as well as the requirements of English law.[47]

3-46 Studies of Muslim law in Britain today must therefore take notice of the fact that British Muslims have begun to deal with such conflicts internally, but not entirely without reference to English law, in an attempt to work out a feasible solution for themselves as a Muslim minority in a non-Muslim state. The result, it appears, has been the creation of *angrezi shariat*. But quite how does this operate in practice? In the following section we concentrate our attention on the reactions of English law to this new hybrid legal phenomenon.

English law and Muslim minorities

3-47 Western legal systems have long been facing major conceptual problems over how to handle 'religion' in relation to law, but the dominant models of Western jurisprudence have shut out religion and have pursued secular agenda. Today, modern secular legal systems are again uncomfortable with religion, and the relationship of law and religion appears to demand a fresh analysis.[48] With the so-called 'resurgence' of ethnicity, legal systems are again seen to be under intense pressure to define the role of religion in the marking of community or group identities. This has gradually become a much bigger issue than many lawyers realise.

3-48 The debate is not, as many people believe, a direct result of recent mass migration of non-Western people to Western countries; it has a much longer history.[49] While, as we saw earlier, from a Muslim perspective religion may not just be seen as a matter of having places of worship or holding particular beliefs or values, the dominant Western theories of law have shut out references to religious systems of law and to higher forces like divine authority, treating any religious authority as devoid of legal relevance. Conversely, if one views religion also as a way of life, as most Muslims clearly do, putting into practice what one believes and acting in accordance with particular ethical value systems become perceived as legal matters. In view of such universal predicaments, at the end of the day, some legal recognition for people's perceptions of right or wrong appears to become inevitable, whether we think of the reluctant concessions for unmarried cohabitants in English

---

[47] An obvious recent example is the attempt to guide British Muslims on how to make wills which harmonise the rules of Muslim and English law, as documented in Haqq, Aisha and Thomson, *The Islamic will: A practical guide to being prepared for your death and writing your will according to the Shari'a of Islam and English law* (1995).

[48] Significantly, A. Bradney stated in 1993 that to write a book on religion and law would have been unthinkable a few years before.

[49] On this see excellently and in detail Kelly, *A short history of Western legal theory* (1992).

law, or the still more cautious recognition of the fact that cultural factors do play a role in the assessment of crime or in sentencing policies.[50]

3-49 The present study shows that the process of reluctant legal recognition of actions which Muslims and other ethnic minorities in Britain perform, has already gone much further than all players, including the Muslims themselves, seem ready to admit. In countries like the United Kingdom, despite lipservice to secularism, religion continues to serve as a focal point for group cohesiveness, forming an important factor of identity formation for individuals as well as groups. It might be healthy to recognise this more fully rather than to perpetuate convenient myths about the segregation of law and religion.

3-51 Turning to the question whether the English legal system is really as uniform as it purports to be, we find that this is not a prominent area of research as yet, although the underlying theoretical issues have been much debated.[51] A brief examination of three key concepts would appear relevant – first, the notion of 'law' and of 'common law' as a national uniform legal system and its role in obstructing the inclusion of 'extra-legal' factors; secondly, the concept of legal centralism, closely linked to the above; thirdly, the notion of legal pluralism or multiculturalism in a legal sense, which searches for a more inclusionary approach towards 'new minorities' like the Muslims of Britain.

3-51 Our starting point is that the English legal system is manifestly not as uniform as it claims and is widely perceived to be. As a complex system of rules it is in fact composed of many sub-systems which only apply in certain situations, to certain facts, and often to particular groups of people. It is manifestly not the case that all rules of the law relate to all subjects of the law in equal measure. Thus 'legal system' and especially the notion of 'common law' itself are convenient labels rather than reflections of reality.

3-52 The assumption that uniform laws are desirable and are the pinnacle of legal development, fit for universal application, is clearly Eurocentric, a point which we need not discuss here in detail.[52] Authors who have thought about the subject, especially if they have had exposure to non-Western concepts of law, speak of "normative legal theory" (Cotterell (1992), p. 3) or of Western "model jurisprudence" (Chiba (1986), pp. 1–2), contradicting universalistic claims. The history of South Asian laws demonstrates that basic assumptions about legal uniformity, and about the separation of law and religion, are not shared in that part of the world, as elsewhere in 'the South'. It is significant that the European colonial powers respected this, at least to a large extent, when they became involved in law making overseas.

3-53 The current debates about Muslim laws in Europe are still influenced by colonial experiences and the persistent view that overseas concepts and values are inferior (Kelly (1992), pp. 303–304). Thus, while it was acceptable and appropriate to respect Islamic law for colonial subjects 'out there', restrictions on the application of Islamic law in Britain today are justified by relying, *inter alia,* on convenient notions of the uniformity and commonality of Western state law.[53] This has led to many uneasy compromises in Britain (Shah [1994]).

3-54 Kelly (1992, p. 306) rightly emphasises that the claim of the modern state

---

[50] See with useful examples Poulter [1989] 16 No. 1 *New Community* 121–128.
[51] A recent pathbreaking study, Hamilton, (1995), shows the way for further work.
[52] For the history of such concepts see in detail Kelly, (1992).
[53] The same, with slight variations, would go for France and other continental countries. See Rutten, *Moslims in de Nederlandse rechtspraak* (1988) for the Netherlands; Foblets (1994a); (1994b) for France and Belgium.

to a larger and interventionist role went hand in hand with an increasing interest in regulating family relationships and their consequences.[54] It has been assumed for a long time that the post-colonial states of Asia and Africa would follow such modern strategies. Indeed, as indicated in Chapter 2, above, the post-colonial South Asian states appeared to do just that. During the 1950s and 1960s, South Asian family laws became, to some extent, a typical lawyers' creation, stipulating the supremacy of legal regulation, shutting out virtually everything else, attempting to override customs and traditions, whether religious or social.[55] By the 1990s, as we shall see in detail in the following chapters, South Asian family laws have returned to a position of greater respect for the religious and social sphere, not only as a result of islamisation, as is often assumed, but because the Western model of uniform legal regulation is increasingly seen and experienced as inadequate for vastly diverse populations. Being Asian countries, and treating religion as an integral part of the law-making process, South Asian jurisdictions today are in many respects no longer even attempting to follow Western models of legal development.

3–55 In the United Kingdom, the impact of legal positivism and its conceptual underpinnings has been that English law, as the official legal system, largely ignores what Chiba (1986, pp. 6–7) has called the "unofficial law" and "legal postulates", particular value systems of certain groups of people. Within its own realm, English law simply grants no space for any other legal system. This approach still allows for the creative development of conflict of law rules (see Chapter 4, below) but that is quite different from recognising the presence of foreign laws within the physical space of one's own jurisdiction. As we began to see, many Muslims – but not only Muslims – find this unacceptable.

3–56 In view of the experience of other increasingly multicultural countries, notably Australia and Canada, some authors have argued that this fictional uniformity is unreal in social terms (see already Griffiths (1986, p. 4) and that a new conceptualisation of equity is required in the world of today to handle ethnic diversity (Castles (1994), pp. 15–16).[56]

3–57 Legal pluralism is the antithesis of legal centralism and has been defined authoritatively as "that state of affairs, for any social field, in which behaviour pursuant to more than one legal order occurs".[57] For a pluralistic analysis of English law today, this means that apart from the official law there are many other normative orders, such as local customs, but now also Muslim law and others, which cannot be merely disregarded.[58]

3–58 At first sight, multiculturalism may appear to be a utopian and vague sociological concept which has little relevance to our discussion of the law. Poulter has emphasised that the three key elements of multiculturalism are equal opportunity, cultural diversity and mutual tolerance, and that the law's role in terms of the maintenance of cultural diversity is "to allow and, where appropriate,

---

[54] In Britain, this is first reflected in the Marriage Act 1836 and its provision for secular marriages as well as the liberalisation of divorce procedures by the Matrimonial Proceedings Act 1857.

[55] On this see excellently Derrett, (1968b) with particular reference to India. On various jurisdictions see Anderson, *Islamic law in the modern world* (1959); Anderson, *Family law in Asia and Africa* (1968a); Mahmood, *Family law reform in the Muslim world* (1972a).

[56] The Australian Law Reform Commission (1991) reflects a fascinating debate in that country about the limits of law and the movement towards legal pluralism.

[57] So Griffiths, "What is legal Pluralism?" [1986] 24 *Journal of Legal Pluralism and Unofficial Law* p. 2. The author manifestly disregards the distinction of 'legal' and 'non-legal' orders and thus shows himself to be a 'strong' legal pluralist. He does not, however, analyse what practical effects that approach will have in any given society or legal system.

[58] The present scenario must be distinguished from colonial pluralism, on which see in detail Hooker, (1975), expounding the concept of 'weak' legal pluralism.

facilitate the continued practice of ethnic minority customs and traditions" (Poulter (1992a), p. 175). Crucially, Poulter then went on to emphasise the limits to the acceptance of cultural diversity where the belief or practice in question falls below certain perceived standards and thereby clashes with the "overriding public interest in promoting social cohesion" (Poulter (1992a), p. 176). These limits, still referred to in his later writings (Poulter, (1995)), go to the heart of our understanding of plurality. For, who determines the criteria for what is acceptable and what is not? If this particular approach is taken, Muslims would appear to have to renounce or modify certain beliefs and practices which are perceived to be contrary to the limits of acceptability as defined by the modern state. Very similar questions constantly arise in Indian law, where the acceptability of Muslim norms is also a prominent issue.

3–59 Recognising the presence of other normative orders does not mean that the dominant legal system abdicates its claim to overriding authority. This, however, appears to have been a major fear, reflecting concern about losing control. But what is preferable? Should the official law restrict itself to controlling the limited space that it recognises, knowingly ignoring the rest of the social field, or should it attempt to control the entire field while being prepared to make concessions to diversity? The section below explores this issue in some more depth and shows the consequences for the legal position of Muslim law in Britain today.

The legal approach to Muslims and Muslim law in Britain

3–60 The critical question for lawyers, and for the law, is whether and to what extent the legal sphere should take notice of the fact that today millions of people resident in Britain, and subject to English law, are Muslims. From a pluralistic legal perspective, there can be no doubt that this should lead to some creative development. From a traditional positivist viewpoint, this is not a legal matter and there is not much to debate.

3–61 The key problem remains, therefore, that any analysis of this complex issue depends on the basic definition of 'law' which one uses. We have already emphasised that the prevailing approach so far has been to study Muslims and others as objects of the official law, not as active players and agents in real conflict of laws situation. This has been widely resented. In a book on South Asian Muslim laws in the late 1990s, this imbalance would appear to demand some critical attention.

3–62 While it appears to be the case that English law excludes rather than incorporates Muslim law and Muslims in Britain, it would be quite wrong to accept this as a blanket statement. We have already said that, in certain respects, English law has made significant allowances for Muslims in Britain. However, these have neither been coherent, nor have they been systematically researched in depth.[59] Recent research in the context of debates about citizenship (see Spencer, (1995)) portrays a scenario of muddled criteria for inclusion and exclusion of minorities, as well as deliberate drawing of distinctions between individuals and groups of people for the sake of demonstrating and asserting political and legal power. Poulter ((1992a), p. 183) has commented on the piecemeal approach of English law to diversity and the fact that the law appears to be responding to needs depending on

---

[59] For some brief but helpful early attempts see Nielsen, *Islam in English law and administration. A symposium* (1981); Poulter [1989] and in detail Poulter (1986). Some of Nielsen's work during the 1990's has focused on this topic, too.

the strength of demands and the urgency of the needs. However, this does not mean that those who shout loudest will achieve the best results. Muslims in Britain experienced the opposite when the demand for full-scale recognition of *shari'a* in the mid-1970s was simply thrown out,[60] while British Sikhs appear to have won legal concessions through persistent low-key, less dramatic lobbying.[61]

3–63   Looking at the official status of Muslim law in Britain, we therefore find a complex, somewhat dual picture. As a foreign legal system, under the rules of private international law, various forms of Islamic law are fully recognised as law, but only as overseas law (see Chapter 4, below). When it comes to Muslims in Britain itself, the continued basic non-recognition of *shari'a* remains a fact because of the official law's technique of treating all ethnic minority laws as customs or cultural practices. This approach, more or less completely, tries to ignore the presence of Muslim and other ethnic minority legal perspectives.

3–64   The key argument in the official legal position, represented with deceptively liberal persuasiveness in Poulter's pioneering 1986 study, has been that all ethnic minority practices, in order to qualify for legal recognition, must not offend the 'core values' (Poulter (1986), p. vi) or 'shared values' (Poulter (1995), p. 83) of British or even English culture. This approach has been more and more prominently justified by human rights arguments.[62] As Poulter (1992a, p. 176) put it:

> "There are, therefore, limits to the acceptance of cultural diversity which need to be imposed in support of the overriding public interest in promoting social cohesion. Cultural tolerance cannot become a 'cloak for oppression and injustice within the immigrant communities themselves',[63] nor must it endanger the integrity of the 'social and cultural core' of English values as a whole ... English judges have emphasized that tolerance is bounded by notions of reasonableness and public policy and that foreign customs and laws will not be recognized or applied here if they are considered repugnant or otherwise offend the conscience of the court."

It has been argued that this purportedly liberal, not entirely culture-blind but still culture-biased approach preserves the status quo of English law as the dominant law. This assessment relies on the assumption that non-Western laws, including Islamic law, cannot be trusted to uphold universally accepted human rights values. In a sense, this approach seeks to protect members of ethnic minorities from their own rule systems. Indeed, it is an issue, not the least among Muslim scholars themselves, how injustice to any one segment of Muslims can be avoided.[64]

---

[60] A similarly brash Muslim demand in India, to the effect that Muslim ex-husbands should not (like all other Indian men) have to pay maintenance to their ex-wives till their death or remarriage, ended in the implementation of the Muslim Women (Protection of Rights on Divorce) Act 1986, which does not accept the traditional Muslim position, but imposes, as it turned out, the general law rules in personal law form. For details see para. 7–75, below. More recently, Indian debates about the triple *talaq* (see F. Ahmad (1994)) show that Indian Muslims now prefer a restrained level of debate rather than provoking further legal reforms.

[61] See in particular the Motor-Cycle Crash Helmets (Religious Exemption) Act (1976) and the effects of the House of Lords decision in *Mandla v. Dowell Lee* [1983] 1 All E.R. 1062.

[62] See already Poulter, (1986) pp. v–vi and in detail Poulter [1987].

[63] N.16 at this point in Poulter's text refers to Lester and Bindman (1972, p. 18) as the original source of this phrase.

[64] This issue is particularly relevant for the debates generated by Muslim feminists, *e.g.* Helie-Lucas, "Strategies of Women and women's movements in the Muslim world *vis-à-vis* fundamentalisms", in *The rights of subordinated peoples* (1994); Afshar, "Islam empowering or repressive to women?", in *God's law versus state law. The construction of an Islamic identity in Western Europe* (1995); Kabbani, "Family matters", in *God's law versus state law. The construction of an Islamic identity in Western Europe* (1995).

Significantly, the assumption that foreign systems like Muslim law allow the violation of basic human rights lingers in this context as an immediate response to anyone advocating legal pluralism or the recognition of Muslim law in whatever form.

3–65 In essence, then, recognition of diversity is seen as acceptable in the social sphere, but not in the realm of the law. However, as Hamilton (1995) shows for various Christian groupings of 'dissenters' and Jews, the English legal system has for a long time been making numerous exceptions to the general law theory by allowing adherents of certain religious or ethnic minorities to do what their belief system requires of them (see also Poulter (1989), pp. 123–124). Seen in this light, Muslims in Britain are simply one of the most recent claimants to specific forms of separate legal recognition. This time factor seems quite relevant: New minorities do not win concessions overnight; they have to be carefully negotiated, and this takes time. As the Muslim example in Britain has already shown with great clarity, a less than diplomatic approach which simply demands huge, rapid changes leads to defensive reactions and swift refusal.

3–66 The policy of the English legal system towards recognition of ethnic minority laws has been inconsistent, haphazard and unco-ordinated. The response has very much depended on the nature of the particular rule or conflict in question and is undoubtedly linked to cultural factors. Thus, English law criminalises bigamy, but has found itself making more and more allowances for unmarried cohabitation, which would in many cases be considered a crime under Muslim law, given the powerful prohibitions on sex outside marriage (*zina*). The English legal system has extended the provisions of section 1(2) of the Slaughter of Poultry Act 1967 and section 36(2) of the Slaughterhouses Act 1974 from Jews alone to include Muslims. The current law allows Muslim butchers to procure and sell *halal* meat, provided it is for the consumption of Muslims only (Poulter (1989), p. 124). Such assumptions of the law clearly do not match with social and commercial realities. It is a well-known fact that *halal* butchers are popular with all kinds of customers. Hindus and Sikhs, in particular, as in their original homelands, are in fact largely relying on Muslim butchers to carry the *karmic* burden of killing animals and handling their meat. In this particular case, then, English law has unwittingly gone much beyond recognising a 'religious' need for Muslims.

3–67 On the other hand, the state seems unwilling to recognise the existence of Muslims as a 'racial group' under the Race Relations Act 1976, a matter of great concern to Muslims who point to preferential treatment for other groups (Modood (1993)). Well-used earlier examples are the exemptions for Jews and Quakers in the Marriage Act 1949 and its predecessors when it comes to solemnising marriages. Such explicit legal permission to practise particular usages points to established precedents for the recognition of non-secular and non-Anglican beliefs and practices by statute under the general umbrella of English law. This appears to support the assertion that "English law is a reasonably flexible system" (Poulter (1995), p. 82). The critical question remains, however, to what extent the law and its spokespersons may be willing to accommodate Muslim concepts and Muslims themselves. An analysis of Poulter's writing points to remarkable strictness. He identified as key flashpoints polygamy, divorce by repudiation (*talaq*) and prohibitions on interreligious marriages, which "would seem to me to be points of absolutely irreducible conflict" (Poulter (1995), p. 85).[65]

---

[65] In this respect, it must not be overlooked that so-called 'modern' forms of divorce, *i.e.* the breakdown principle, have exactly the same effect of unilateral repudiation and it has been forgotten that many Muslim women can also claim the right to unilateral divorce.

3–68 Where it is felt that certain acts are not contrary to public policy, they will be allowed to go on unhindered and without legal regulation. Many actions remain permitted in English law simply because there is no law against them. Thus, it is not prohibited by English law to enter into an Islamic contract of marriage in Britain, showing that even in relation to key areas of family law, English law has remained almost exclusively concerned with its own formal expectations. As we shall see in subsequent sections of this book, for Muslims (and especially for Muslim women) the matter is generally not that simple.

3–69 The law's piecemeal and limited adaptation to what is nowadays often called the multicultural reality of modern Europe is now increasingly perceived to be unsatisfactory. An obvious example may be the legal reaction to Muslim demands that pupils should be allowed to wear certain types of dress, including the headscarf. In the absence of clearly stated and coherent official policies for dealing with such issues, the results are often subjected to accusations of discrimination.[66] Many Muslims, noting the differential treatment of Jews, Quakers and Sikhs, see this as repudiating and undermining the state's claim of equal treatment. This has the unfortunate side effect that the Muslim community has begun to feel excluded and even victimised by the English legal system.[67]

3–70 Poulter (1992a, p. 187) has argued that there should be a continuation of the current approach. Is this just a status quo argument, does it signify fear of recognising 'the other', or is this indeed the only way forward? The argument that recognition of ethnic and religious diversities should be withheld because the dominant policy goals are legal uniformity and equality before the law may be flawed in view of incontrovertible evidence that English law continues to discriminate between different minorities.[68]

3–71 It is obvious that allowing Muslim claims for the full-scale recognition of Muslim personal law would necessitate a fundamental restructuring of English law, introducing a system of concurrent family laws for different religious communities, along lines familiar to the British colonial experience of governing other people. This is an unrealistic expectation, as it would be a major change (Nielsen (1992a), p. 98), affecting the entire structure of the English legal system, which helps to explain further why this particular debate was terminated in its embryonic state.

3–72 However, this view seems too simple. If, in the shape of *angrezi shariat*, we now find evidence of the existence of an unofficial British Muslim law, how should the official law deal with this? Not surprisingly, the judiciary have been at the forefront of attempts to harmonise the official law and 'ethnic customs'. Experienced authors suggest that, of all establishment institutions, the judiciary "has shown the greatest degree of practical flexibility" (Nielsen (1992a), p. 93).

3–73 To resolve the conflict, it may help to turn to history. The development of Islamic law as a legal system shows that family law issues, in particular, were never treated as a matter for the state. This is a common pattern, also found in Hindu law, classical Chinese law and many other legal systems.[69] All of these know

---

[66] Shah [1994] Nos. 66/67 *Retfoerd* 18–33 , highlights this perception of uneasy compromises.

[67] Zingel and Zingel Ave Lallement, *Pakistan in the 80s. Ideology, regionalism, economy, foreign policy* (1985), pp. 532–533 highlight the encapsulation of Pakistanis in Britain.

[68] The most obvious example continues to be *Dawkins v. Department of the Environment* [1993] I.R.L.R. 284. This case concerned a Rastafarian driver who was told that unless he cut his long hair he would not be given a job. Dawkins lost his appeals on the ground that Rastafarianism was not a cultural tradition of sufficient age to be legally recognised. Earlier, in the almost identical scenario in *Mandla v. Dowell Lee* [1983] 1 All E.R. 1062, Sikh claims to recognition were granted by the House of Lords. As indicated, Muslims are still not fully recognised under the 1976 Act as a 'racial group'.

[69] On other non-Western legal systems see Derrett, *An introduction to legal systems* (1968a).

long-established systems of what is misleadingly called 'extra-legal' regulation of family affairs and many other local matters, avoiding outsider interference and officialdom by setting up internal regulatory mechanisms to settle disputes within the community.[70] One could cite a plethora of opinions to the effect that this may be very satisfactory.[71]

3–74   Naturally, this informal strategy has resulted in considerable ignorance on the part of state legal systems as to how order is maintained at various local levels. The corollorary of this scenario, therefore, has been a certain powerlessness of the central state in virtually all matters of family law, including succession and property laws. It appears that historically, because of their economic importance, succession laws attracted more state interest. Modern legal systems, anywhere in the world, claim a right to regulate ultimately all forms of behaviour, which must inevitably clash with traditional concepts of informal dispute settlement and legal regulation from within society. If a state legal system is unwilling to recognise this purportedly 'extra-legal' sphere, it is bound to face opposition and obstruction.

3–75   Most pertinent to our present discussion, the modern Pakistani state has tried to achieve greater state control over societal processes by using statute law, prominently the MFLO 1961 (see Chapter 2 above). Such obvious attempts to gain control over the sphere of family law have only been possible for modern Asian (and African) states because they have been willing to recognise the continuity of the Muslim personal law as an integral part of the official legal system, albeit in reformed shape. In Pakistan, and to some extent in Bangladesh, as this book shows, it is now obvious that this has led to intense clashes between two types of Muslim personal law, the traditional *shari'a* rules and the state-sponsored codified Muslim personal law. In Britain, the non-recognition of Muslim personal law as an integral part of the official legal structure has avoided the emergence of such a conflict, but it has not resolved the same, difficult practical problems, often centred on 'limping marriages'. For example, as we explore in detail in Chapters 7 and 9 below, when is a Muslim woman married, and when is she divorced? Is it only when she (or her husband, as the case may be) has complied with the modern state law, or is recourse to the principles and rules of Muslim law sufficient?

3–76   Seen from this perspective, it is obvious that Britain's *a priori* refusal to accord validity to Muslim law does not solve the family law problems arising among Muslims in Britain. Direct intervention and reforming activity are, however, to a large extent closed to modern Western legal systems unless they are willing to take explicit legal notice of the presence of large Muslim communities, and of Muslim law, within their jurisdiction. How this can be done without giving official recognition to Muslim law remains a conundrum.

3–77   So far, the effect of the dominant assimilationist approach of the English legal system towards Muslims in Britain has been to cloud our views of what Muslims in Britain actually do and what *their* concerns are.[72] Since Muslims in Britain have been unwilling to abandon *shari'a* and Muslim law as a way of life, many individuals appear to have ended up ignoring state law, which cannot be a healthy approach. The phenomenon of British Muslim law has made a public

---

[70] Today, such mechanisms are being studied under the fashionable label of A.D.R. (alternative dispute resolution), which now involves legal supervision of such processes, while in traditional circumstances the state law and its agents played no role at all in this context.

[71] See to this effect Pearl, (1986a), p. 32, emphasising that "conciliation within the family and community circle is well understood amongst South-Asian families".

[72] See further Menski (1993a); Poulter, *Ethnicity, law and human rights* (1998); Pearl, "A note on Islamic law and the child", in *Children's rights and traditional values* (1998).

appearance only recently and the official law's disregard of so-called 'cultural practices' or 'customs' in Britain has perhaps been a useful cloak under which the sphere of Muslim family law could remain outside formal legal regulation. Thus, it has been surprisingly convenient for both parties in this ongoing struggle over the extent of official legal recognition to perpetuate a breakdown of communication scenario. It is our argument here that mutual non-recognition is not a viable option from either perspective.

Muslim responses

3-78 The various reactions of Muslims in Britain to the non-recognition of Muslim law as an integral part of the English legal system and to assimilation pressures appear to have one element in common. Such developments have taken place on terms set by Muslim individuals and representatives of the Muslim communities themselves, rather than by official agents (see Badawi (1995)). This is confirmed in recent anthropological literature when Ballard (1994, p. 8) writes:

> "Short of comprehensive ethnic cleansing – which one hopes is not an option – nothing can alter the fact that the new minorities have become an integral part of the British social order, and that they have done so *on their own terms*. Hence the underlying challenge is simple: how – and how soon – can Britain's white natives learn to live with difference, and to respect the right of their fellow-citizens to organise their lives on their own preferred terms, whatever their historical and geographical origins?"

Emphasising the agency of British South Asians in the process of reconstructing their communities in Britain, Ballard implicitly raises the question of conflict between Muslim socio-legal systems and the state. For him as an experienced observer, the answer has already been given: Muslims and other South Asian minorities have organised their own response to this dilemma, seeing that the state was not willing to compromise. This reconstruction process appears therefore, at least to some extent, as a counter-reaction to the failed demand for full-scale recognition of Muslim family laws in Britain.

3-79 We have already explained why this demand was roundly refused. Several authors have discussed these proposals, dismissing them as unsuitable for Britain.[73] Nielsen (1993a, pp. 2–3) emphasised that old struggles over the definition of *shari'a* and its practical application would be revived in Britain, creating immense practical problems. It is difficult to evaluate the extent of popular support for such proposals. Nielsen (1993a, p. 4) has argued that they appear to be of an opportunistic political nature, while Tariq Modood (1993) observed that the demand for a separate Muslim personal law in Britain has slipped off the immediate agenda. This indicates that public strategies of working towards the official integration of *shari'a* into English legal structures have been abandoned, if only for the moment. It is also possible to argue that the official discourse has been overtaken by informal, more individualised adjustment processes within the Muslim communities. The

---

[73] For details see Nielsen [1992a] 10 *Recht Van de Islam* 92–99; Nielsen (1992c); Nielsen (1993a); Pearl (1987a); Poulter, "The claim to a separate Islamic system of personal law for British Muslims", in *Islamic family law* (1990b).

argument would then be that the demand for official legal recognition of Muslim personal law is not fully supported by many British Muslims today because they have found their own private ways, through *angrezi shariat*, of reconciling *shari'a* and English law.

3–80 Two types of non-public actions to ensure harmonisation of potentially or actually conflicting rule systems have therefore gained prominence, the more individualised creation of *angrezi shariat* and the slightly more official development of informal Muslim dispute settlement systems in Britain. Both constitute forms of recreating *shari'a* in Britain.

Assimilation on their own terms: *Angrezi shariat*

3–81 We saw already that unilateral assimilation to the rules of English law cannot be a realistic strategy for Muslims in Britain. If following English law is supposed to mean abandoning *shari'a*, it cannot be a viable option for them to 'do as the Romans do'. Modood (1992) has analysed in depth why and how many Muslims feel, as a result, more or less excluded and marginalised. Official insistence on legal uniformity and efforts to "confine all residents of England to English law even where this conflicts with people's personal and religious law",[74] have created intense resentment, increasing the sense of alienation and isolation. Consequently one finds various avoidance reactions, a form of inner migration, coming out publicly as heightened emphasis on religion and, in turn, on ethnicity.[75] It misses the point of this complex debate to simply label this as 'fundamentalism' and to blame Muslims for this.

3–82 The necessity to make adjustments on all sides in the process of creating space for the new identities of European Muslim communities has been identified by some scholars (see Nielsen (1992b), p. 150). While most legal researchers stubbornly cling to old paradigms and resist the challenges of the post-modern focus on respect for diversity, many immigrants have now become "skilled cultural navigators" (Ballard (1994), p. 31) who often effortlessly combine living in Britain with reconstructing their specific ways of life. Nielsen (1992b, p. 156) has emphasised that many young European Muslims "are developing new forms of expressing their Islam, which they consider more appropriate to the European context". The resulting processes of constructing hybrid rule systems have allowed many Muslim individuals to feel more or less at ease in two worlds. As part of this complex process, redefined Muslim laws in Britain have become hybrid obligation systems peculiar to British Muslims as a matter of social practice rather than legal fact.

3–83 An analysis of the position of Muslim law in relation to the English legal system today has to take account of the emergence of *angrezi shariat* and other forms of hybrid legal cultures among ethnic minorities in Europe and North America.[76] The terminology chosen signifies that the reconstruction of British Muslim law was not merely a matter of continuing an ancient form of *shari'a* familiar to all Muslims. Rather, we find a variety of locally influenced sub-forms, in this case prominently

---

[74] Berkovits [1988] 104 L.Q.R. 92, see in more detail Berkovits, "Get a talaq in English law: Reflections on law and policy", in *Islamic family law* (1990).

[75] Several writers have noted that Islam is defined much more as an ethnic phenomenon in diaspora situations.

[76] For the USA see Haddad and Lummis, *Islamic values in the United States* (1987); Moore, (1995).

South Asian British Muslim law. Hence the term *angrezi shariat*,[77] signifying the re-emergence of various forms of South Asian law, different from their prototypes, because they take explicit account of the presence of English law in the same field (Menski (1993a), p. 244). In the realm of family law, in particular, we now have significant evidence, discussed in the relevant chapters of this book, that virtually all ethnic minorities in Britain marry twice, divorce twice, and do many other things several times in order to satisfy the demands of concurrent legal systems. There is currently much research work in progress showing that such diversities exist in all minority communities, not just among Muslims.

3–84 As a matter of fact, then, Muslims in Britain operate today a form of unofficial legal pluralism. Muslim individuals and whole communities, irrespective of state law or in explicit reaction to it, have developed their own hybrid legal system in Britain, which *they* perceive as a form of Muslim law. Significantly, English law today is under pressure to find remedies in new legal conflict situations that have arisen because of such hidden unofficial developments.[78]

3–85 What is *angrezi shariat?* The leading Japanese jurist Masaji Chiba (1986) offers a useful model for explaining this phenomenon in jurisprudential terms. While English law is clearly the 'official law', Muslim law in Britain today has become part of the sphere of 'unofficial law'. This analytical paradigm indicates that Muslims continue to feel bound by the framework of the *shari'a* and value it more highly than Western concepts.[79] They operationalise what Chiba (1986, pp. 6–7) has called "legal postulates", ethical-philosophical concepts which are culture-specific and include religious notions. Thus, rather than adjusting to English law by abandoning certain facets of their *shari'a*, South Asian Muslims in Britain appear to have built the requirements of English law into their traditional legal structures. As evidence of the continued vitality of South Asian legal traditions in a new environment, the reconstruction of *angrezi shariat* is a consequence of Muslim migration to Britain which started immediately on arrival.

3–86 This evolutionary process appears to have developed in three stages.[80] First, when immigrants arrive in a new place, they do not normally know about the official laws of their new home while, unknown to them, the demands of English law affected the immigrants the moment they set foot on the British Isles (Menski (1988a), p. 14). In their own little world, especially in segregated settlements, many new migrants would appear not to notice that they have become subject to a different legal system. This process can still be observed in Britain today where such cases come up in practice, but rarely reach an official forum.[81] Muslims would

---

[77] On *shariat* as an appropriate term for South Asian forms of Muslim law see Mahmood, (1982a), p. 7. The concept of *angrezi shariat* was tested by Menski in a number of conferences and presentations. Acknowledgements for constructive criticism are due, in particular, to Chief Justice Siddiqi of the Sindh High Court in Karachi, Pakistan (as he then was), to Professor Humayoun Ihsan in Lahore, and to Roger Ballard.

[78] A pertinent example here is the claim for legal recognition of the Muslim *mahr* payment as an obligation on the husband which can be enforced by an English court. There are indications that the courts would react positively: see *Shahnaz v. Rizwan* [1965] Q.B. 190. On the same scenario for Belgium, with reference to *talaq*, in particular, see in detail Foblets, (1994a). It remains to be seen what is the effect of recent legislative changes in English marriage law which appear to reflect a more liberal approach to ethnic minority needs, in particular the Marriage (Registered Buildings) Act 1990 and the Marriage Act 1994.

[79] On this see Ballard (1994), pp. 13–14 and Wahab (1989), pp. 4–5.

[80] See earlier Menski (1988a); (1993a).

[81] Many such cases appear to involve Muslim women who have recently come to Britain and painfully learn about such legal conflicts. On the vulnerability of such women see Barton, *The scarlet thread. An Indian woman speaks* (1987) and evidence produced by Southall Black Sisters in London. There are many indications, however, that South Asian men can be similarly victimised. For India, see Kusum, *Harassed husbands* (1993).

get married, at this early stage, by simply contracting a *nikah*, a contract of marriage before God.[82] Similarly, a Muslim man would divorce his wife by *talaq*, irrespective of whether she was in Britain or Pakistan, and she would then be treated as free to remarry. In this first stage, neither does English law take cognisance of such actions, nor are Muslims aware of the conflicts which this is bound to cause.

3–87 Inevitably and sometimes very quickly, the first stage leads to the second when individuals realise that non-compliance with English law may lead to problems and when confusions arise over legal statuses. Within the rule system of Muslim law, individuals would know who is married to whom and whether a person is divorced or single. According to English law, however, there would be a number of serious questions: Is the *nikah* the equivalent of a legal marriage under English law? Does a *talaq* uttered in Britain dissolve a marriage? There is much evidence that Muslims are just as nervous about the phenomenon of limping marriages as English law. After all, such legal insecurity gives rise to cases of illicit sexual intercourse (*zina*), one of the seriously prohibited acts under Muslim law (Miftahi (1993)).

3–88 The next stage in the development of *angrezi shariat*, however, has not simply been recourse to English law and abandonment of *shari'a*, as assimilationist assumptions suggested. Rather, it involved a combination of the rules of English law and of Muslim law. If the state law clearly lays down that a legally valid marriage must be registered in a prescribed form, the intended message would appear to be that a simple *nikah* contracted in England does not constitute a valid marriage. But this does not mean that Muslims would not have a *nikah*, just as much as the official registration requirement does not rule out a Christian 'white wedding'.

3–89 Registration of marriage is of course not entirely unknown to Muslims. There are no prohibitions against it and it was easy for Muslims in Britain to learn the English law on registering marriages. However, the prevailing picture today is that most Muslim couples register their marriage first in accordance with English law and then, either soon afterwards, or after some time, enter into the *nikah*, which is socially marked as the wedding, is treated as the operative date of the marriage, and before which there is, most significantly, normally no cohabitation between the couple. Fieldwork confirms that the current trend is to bring the secular registered ceremony and the religious marriage as close together as possible, avoiding the legal and social insecurities of another form of limping marriage.

3–90 This second stage in the development of *angrezi shariat*, however, brings out a potential conflict of loyalties: are individuals and whole communities bound by Muslim law, or now by English law? Should a Muslim in Britain just follow English law, or is the *shari'a* still the dominant yardstick for legal recognition? Basically Muslims had three alternatives – first, one could avoid English law altogether. Indeed, there is evidence that some Muslims are following this strategy, probably relying on the universality of Muslim legal concepts. The second approach would simply be to follow English law, to the extent that a couple would solemnise their marriage in a secular and administrative form and do nothing else. It appears that extremely few British Muslims would choose this path.

3–91 The third alternative is the one chosen by most Muslims (and other ethnic

---

[82] Of course, many Muslims returned earlier to the subcontinent to get married there. The effect, in our context, would be to delay the development of *angrezi shariat*. At the same time, this increased the plurality of legal actions and led to interesting new legal developments abroad, which do not concern us at this point. One particular legal problem which still arises is whether a couple who have been party to a marriage abroad would then also register their marriage in Britain.

minorities) in Britain today. The development of *angrezi shariat* is here marked by awareness of the need to combine the requirements of both legal systems. At first sight, this looks quite simple, as most British Muslims today marry twice and divorce twice to satisfy both legal systems.[83]

3–92 In the view of some English legal professionals and a number of scholars, the third stage, following classic assimilation concepts, should be the eventual abandonment of Muslim 'cultural practices' in favour of compliance with the rules of English law. Thus, there would be no third stage. However, the construction of *angrezi shariat* as hybrid British Muslim law, no longer a haphazard and uneasy effort, points to a process of consciously building the English legal requirements into the framework of localised *shari'a* rules. This third stage in the development of *angrezi shariat* is evidence that Muslims view the *nikah*, the *talaq*, and in general the rule system of Muslim law, as dominant to that of English law and treat it as such.[84]

3–93 Because the presence of *angrezi shariat* has not been officially recognised, disputes which reach the courts often appear in a twisted form. Solicitors and barristers involved may not be aware of the Muslim dimension in a particular case, or may be inadvertently or purposely misled about the full extent of the problem. Frequently, thus, it becomes difficult for judges to ascertain the full facts and to reach an adequate verdict. In this respect also, current attempts by the Judicial Studies Board in particular to increase the awareness of the judiciary to ethnic minority cultural practices are a welcome advance. An equally prominent scenario, however, is the Muslim strategy to avoid direct recourse to the structures of English law in cases where conflicts between the rules of English law and those of Muslim law are seen to arise.

Informal Muslim dispute settlement processes

3–94 This second strategy to reconstruct Muslim law in Britain on the terms of the community also arises as a consequence of the refusal by English law to accept *shari'a* as a personal law component. It is very practice-focused, designed to solve difficult social and legal problems which may and do arise as a result of the application of English law to British Muslims, while the principles of Muslim law remain in the unofficial sphere.

3–95 Answering such real needs has by now led to the emergence of a complex informal network and hierarchy of Muslim dispute settlement fora in Britain.[85] This process has been facilitated by the residential concentration of British Muslims (see paragraph 3–25, above), providing informal social security networks which include mechanisms for settling disputes (see already Pearl (1986a), p. 32).[86]

---

[83] On how this operates in detail see paras. 6–90 and 9–205, below.

[84] Hindus in Britain have clearly taken that approach, in that the official registration of the marriage is becoming ritually incorporated into the drawn-out process of the religious marriage rituals (see in detail Menski (1993a)). Some field research among Muslims has been conducted since the mid-1980s, but it is still too early to draw definite conclusions.

[85] Historically, this is not a new experience. For example, Kettani (1990) p. 229, refers to the fact that the Muslims of Bulgaria had at some time 22 *shari'a* courts. New writing from India refers explicitly to the re-establishment of Islamic courts during the 1990s. For details on this see Bharatiya (1996), pp. 48–49 who seems to say that this is a strategically planned development, which incidentally fits in well with the customary Indian model of the local dispute settlement forum, the *panchayat*.

[86] On similar evidence from Belgium and France see Foblets (1994a). On Britain see Ahsan (1995) and now, Carroll "Muslim women and 'Islamic divorce' in England" [1997] 17 No. 1 *Journal of Muslim Minority Affairs* 97–115.

3–96   Inaction on the part of the state, while religious leaders recognised the gravity of the problem, has led to concerted efforts from within the Muslim communities to address certain practical issues. In this context, the phenomenon of 'limping marriages' appears to have had a catalytic function, propelling self-help mechanisms. Badawi (1995, p. 77) illustrates clearly why Muslims had to act:

> "A common problem was that you get a woman seeking a divorce in the courts and obtaining it. She becomes therefore eligible for marriage in accordance with the civil law, but her husband has not given her a *talaq* which is the prerogative of the husband within an ordinary contract of marriage, so the woman becomes unmarried according to the civil law but still married according to the Sharia law."

Limping marriages occur, and their frequency is likely to increase, when an unscrupulous husband realises the damaging effects this can have on the woman.[87] Thus:

> "He leaves the woman hanging there, unable to remarry, because in conscience she does not want to challenge the law of Islam because she is a committed Muslim or because she is frightened as a Muslim from doing so. Also socially she does not want to lose face and honour in her community by marrying someone else when she is still married in the eyes of God." (Badawi (1995), pp. 77–78).

Making efforts to deal with this problem "in a manner that would resolve the dispute without breaking either the Sharia or the law" (Badawi (1995), p. 78), Muslim leaders found that they themselves had to get involved in such disputes in order to find an acceptable solution. The result has been the establishment of a variety of informal Muslim dispute settlement fora and the setting up of formal bodies like the United Kingdom Islamic Shari'a Council. Founded in 1980 and consolidated at a Muslim jurists' meeting in Birmingham in 1982,[88] it provides professional conciliation services to couples and gives authoritative guidance on aspects of Islamic family law.[89] In essence, it is modelled on the Beth Din, a quasi-judicial body, which regulates the affairs of a large number of British Jews. The Islamic Shari'a Council has started to make its presence felt by resolving difficult marital disputes, for example those relating to enforcement of dower. It also provides expert advice to lawyers and courts on aspects of Islamic law from its panel of 25 jurists, who represent all the major Islamic schools of thought.

3–97   The need to act was keenly felt, as "sitting back and waiting for the civic local authorities to solve the problems of the Muslim community does not present a positive response to the challenges facing Muslims".[90] In terms of family law, the objectives of the Council are to advise and assist in the operation of Muslim family matters, to establish a bench to operate as a court of Islamic *shari'a* and to make

---

[87] It appears that in the USA the occurrence of limping marriages has reached such alarming proportions that in a number of states the legislature has taken action to remedy the situation. For a discussion of this issue and further references relating to the Jewish community see Hamilton (1995), pp. 82–139. Much of this can be applied to the Muslim community.

[88] For details on this see Surty (1991) 9 No. 1 *Muslim Educational Quarterly* 59–68.

[89] A description and analysis of the Council's work is found in Badawi, "Muslim justice in a secular state", in *God's law versus state law. The construction of an Islamic identity in Western Europe* (1995), pp. 73–80.

[90] See Islamic Shari'a Council 1995 p. 9.

relevant decisions, to safeguard the identity of Islamic family laws and to encourage their recognition for the Muslim community by the English legal system.[91]

3–98 This is clearly a complex response, focused on Muslim self-organisation, designed to solve practical problems, but with much wider implications for the future of Muslim laws in Britain. While it would be alarmist to speak of a parallel Muslim court structure in Britain, there is much evidence that many disputes among Muslims in Britain are today settled in the context of such informal family or community conciliation, involving senior family members or community leaders, depending on the length and seriousness of the dispute. This appears to be a preferred method, the focus being on healing wounds and bringing the parties together, whereas adversarial proceedings in English courts risk exacerbation of such difficulties (see already Pearl (1986), p. 32).

3–99 More complicated matters, or protracted disputes, may be referred to bodies like the Islamic Shari'a Council. The practical impact of this strategy appears to be quite considerable. By March 1995, the Council had dealt with 1500 cases presented to it (Islamic Shari'a Council 1995, p. 5), the majority concerning divorces where the wife had obtained a civil decree but the husband refused to release her from the Muslim marriage.

3–100 It appears that the Council tries to deal with this problem of limping marriages through mediation, but where the husband persists in his refusal to grant the wife a *talaq*, it may grant a *khula* to the wife.[92] This technique of dissolving a Muslim marriage is immediately effective and a divorce certificate is provided which is recognised as authoritative in several countries, notably Pakistan (Islamic Shari'a Council 1995, p. 19). Significantly, this method reflects recent judicial practice in Pakistan of granting *khula* to wives who claim that they cannot live with the husband 'within the bounds of Allah'.[93]

3–101 This strategy to end a broken Muslim marriage raises significant points for any discussion about the position of Muslim women in Britain. It could be argued that it virtually involves the wife in purchasing her freedom, since she has to return to the husband any dower *(mahr)* given to her on marriage. Thus, there is a critical financial penalty against the wife, while the husband is absolved from financial liabilities. It is not surprising, therefore, that this strategy should find favour with some Muslim husbands. It seems that this particular issue has barely been noticed in Britain.[94]

3–102 The other solution to the problem of limping marriages, imposing a financial penalty on the husband, is reflected in one well-known case decided in 1969, involving a Jewish couple.[95] The Court of Appeal, whilst making an assessment of the quantum of maintenance due to the wife, thought it right to make provision in the award for the possibility of the husband persisting in his refusal to grant the *get* (the religious divorce), which was to be increased quite substantially if, within three months, the husband still had not granted the *get*. It is thought that the same technique could be applied to Muslim husbands, but if the informal Muslim dispute settlement fora offer Muslim husbands a cheaper alternative, it is

---

[91] For details see, *ibid.*, pp. 3–5.
[92] For situations in which this remedy is chosen see, *ibid.* pp. 17–18.
[93] For details on this see paras 9–82—9–119, below.
[94] It has, however, become a matter of growing concern in South Asia (see below, Chap. 9). In the British Parliament, assurances were given by the Solicitor-General that such problems would be looked at in more detail (*Hansard* June 13, 1984, cols. 926–932). It appears that no further action has been taken. For details see Hamilton (1995), pp. 119–120.
[95] *Brett v. Brett* [1969] 1 All E.R. 1007. Note also *Berkovits v. Grinberg (Attorney-General Intervening)* [1995] 1 F.L.R. 477, [1995] 2 All E.R. 683.

likely that this strategy will be followed. Thus, as Poulter (1995) and others have observed,[96] there may be inadequacies in the informal Muslim methods of conciliation. They are patriarchal in nature and tend to put undue pressure on women, either to pay for their freedom or to go back to their husbands, so as to avoid dishonour through the violation of *izzat*. While Poulter (1995, pp. 85–86) has also argued that the state should encourage settlement of family disputes between Muslims by mediation, conciliation and arbitration through some kind of tribunal such as the Islamic Shari'a Council, he seeks (at pp. 84 and 86) to make such agreement conditional on safeguards to protect the rights of women and to monitor the maintenance of human rights standards. In his view the Council "merely operates as a facility for those who feel that the English courts are not responsive enough to their religious needs or cultural needs" (Poulter (1995), p. 86) and could, if the party or parties wished, be completely bypassed, since recourse to the English court remains fully available.

3–103   The critical issue remains, however, that Muslim wives whose husbands do not wish to release them from the Muslim marriage will not find that recourse to English law alone will solve their problem, unless of course they are prepared to ignore *shari'a* concepts. Few will wish to go this route.

3–104   In the view of the Council itself, the fact that it is gaining prominence within the Muslim community, and the satisfaction of those who dealt with it, confirm that Muslim law is capable of developing viable mechanisms for settling matrimonial disputes (Islamic Shari'a Council 1995, p. 8). This increased recognition is not limited to the Muslim community, as members of the 'bench' at the Council often provide expert advice on matters of Islamic law.[97] Badawi (1995, pp. 78–79) illustrates the wide range of cases that are brought to another conciliatory and advisory body, the Muslim Law Council, while at the same time referring to the dangers of official state sponsorship for certain Muslim bodies.[98]

3–105   It must be noted again that this approach clearly reflects the strategy of inner emigration. Like the communities themselves, these semi-official Muslim bodies are pursuing a strategy of operating *angrezi shariat*, aspiring for its eventual official recognition without claiming this as a definite right at the present time and lobbying vigorously for it. In other words, by the creation of social facts, a quiet process of legal restructuring is being achieved from within the community, very much along the lines of *dar-al-dawah*, as identified in paragraphs 3–43, above.

The future

3–106   Our discussion has identified a latent conflict which is not easy to resolve. We saw Poulter (1995, p. 82) emphasising that English law is a reasonably

---

[96] Pearl (1987a), p. 168, reported official reservations against separate Muslim courts.

[97] Islamic Shari'a Council 1995, p. 3 and Badawi (1995), p. 79.

[98] *ibid.*; p. 80. Readers should note that the French government has been making concerted efforts to liaise with an authoritative body of French Muslim representatives, only to find that this has increased the level of political tensions among different Muslim groups. On French Muslims and their organisations see also Kettani (1990) p. 231 as well as Bistolfi and Zabbal, *Islams d'Europe. Integration ou insertion communautaire?* (1995). Chirane, "Conflict and division within Muslim families in France, in *God's law versus state law. The construction of an Islamic identity in Western Europe* (1995) and Boumidienne, "African Muslim women in France: The emergence of a new identity", in *God's law versus state law. The construction of an Islamic identity in Western Europe* (1995) throw important further light on the situation of Muslims in France.

flexible system, providing examples which suggest that the English judiciary is becoming more sensitive with regard to ethnic minority values and traditions, not the least through the efforts of the Judicial Studies Board. At the same time, as we saw, he also identified definite flashpoints (Poulter (1995), p. 85). In addition, the growing presence of *angrezi shariat* puts limits on what can be done by the English judiciary, in two ways. First, if more and more complex cases are in fact settled by Muslim fora rather than state legal institutions, the English judiciary will rarely get sight of important Muslim cases. Indeed, there appears to be now a disproportionately low profile of matrimonial case law involving Muslim parties, in marked contrast to the 1970s and early 1980s. Secondly, since the official policy appears to be to do as little as possible, even if the judiciary wanted to see changes, charges of judicial legislation and excessive activism could easily be raised. This dilemma is illustrated in a recent case concerning recognition of the Jewish *get*. Wall J., while refusing such recognition, commented:

> "The question as to whether or not in an increasingly multi-racial and multi-ethnic society the refusal to recognise the . . . divorce can or should continue is a matter for Parliament, and should not influence my interpretation of the statute."[99]

This and similar judicial pronouncements show that the state is, finally, worried about the issue as such, but lacks sufficient insight and political will to fully address the difficult questions which arise. The official law, thus, still closes its eyes to the somewhat unpalatable reality of different Asian laws in full, though unofficial, operation on British soil. The reaction so far has been to retain the present policy of adapting a uniform legal system on an ad hoc basis, perhaps with some liberal rhetoric about the somewhat charming nature of 'ethnic customs' in a multicultural, multi-faith state. It appears that a more courageous approach from both Muslims and the state is required.

3–107   One could go further and adopt Nielsen's suggestion (1985, p. 17) that the courts should, as a matter of course and by law, be made aware of the parties' religious identity and that this should be a material factor in deciding a case. Nobody is denying the possibility of discrimination in religion-based laws but explicit recognition of the presence of other normative orders, as well as a search for solutions which attempt to harmonise *shari'a* and English law rules may help to develop practical and mutually acceptable solutions. We need to examine in subsequent chapters to what extent this is perhaps already being done.

3–108   Suggestions for the future, thus, relate both to steps taken by the state and by Muslims themselves. For example, the use of Muslim marriage contracts which contain clauses protecting the rights of women could probably easily be encouraged within the communities.[1] Courts in England may then consider the terms of such a contract in deciding what orders to make (Badawi (1995), p. 79; Poulter (1995), p. 86). Such examples also show that Muslims in Britain need to become more directly involved in the process of law reform by positive contributions to policy discussions. So far very little in this direction has been done (Poulter (1995), p. 87). The Law Commission operates long periods of consultation and invites contributions. It appears that more detailed input

---

[99] *Berkovits v. Grinberg (Attorney-General Intervening)* [1995] 1 All E.R. 681, at 696.
[1] See already Carroll (1982) 20 No. 1 *Journal of Commonwealth and Comparative Politics* 57–95, and Pearl (1986a), pp. 35–37. On the importance of such strategies in the Bangladeshi context see Malik (1990).

from Muslims is required. Nielsen's earlier suggestion (1985, p. 17) that there should be a Muslim member of the Law Commission seems too ambitious and certainly clashes with traditional reservations about recognising special interest groups in English legal processes. Major reforms in the divorce law have recently been made. Despite the Law Commission's reference to Islamic law, it appears that Muslim organisations have rarely come forward to offer comments, unlike their Jewish and Christian counterparts (Poulter (1992), p. 269). To some extent it is this lack of a co-ordinated response and the absence of a single authoritative body, representative of all Muslims, which hinders the official interaction of Muslims and English law, so that Muslim views often go unheard and the state remains unaware of Muslim needs. What is required is a two-way dialogue. At the same time, academics have noted a growing perception of the need for change. King (1995, p. 12) writes:

> "Just as Islam has successfully adapted itself to different countries and different cultures, so the institutions of the West *are* changed by the environments in which they operate. The very fact that the legal, political, economic and educational systems in many European countries are now obliged to confront the demands of Muslim communities for recognition of their differences *is* a significant development of recent years, even if those demands are not always fully met."

There is growing realisation, however, that this process has not gone far enough. Nielsen (1995a, p. 154) refers to the "unreality of cultural encounter" in today's European context, where the burden of assimilation is still on the new ethnic minorities (Nielsen (1995a), pp. 155–156). Ballard (1994), as we saw, used strong language to analyse the new skilled cultural navigation processes among the transnational communities of Britain. The official legal system, however, hiding behind public policy arguments, does not show sufficient willingness to incorporate 'the other' and clearly lags behind knowledge in the social field. It appears, therefore, that the English legal system would benefit from taking more explicit notice of Muslim needs. While it remains doubtful whether this can be done through a total restructuring of English law into a personal law system with separate rules for British Muslims, Bernard Lewis (1992) has argued for a kind of 'communal autonomy' similar to that given to non-Muslims or *dhimmis* in Muslim countries. This would probably apply at least to Muslim family law, though Fadl (1994, p. 158) argues that the language used by jurists does not admit of any definitive conclusion. While a process described by Anwar (1994, p. 16) as "pluralistic integration" is apparently well under way, the key issue remains to what extent the official legal system is willing to take account of new phenomena like *angrezi shariat* and the informal Muslim dispute settlement processes which we have analysed here.

3–109 Only more informed consideration of the effective presence of *angrezi shariat* would appear to enable English law to fulfil its own public policy demands of overall control. In particular, if the official law wishes to protect Muslim women in Britain against discriminatory treatment on the basis of gender, it is not a viable option to ignore the operation of unofficial Muslim laws. Thus, it appears inevitable, in the long run, to think in more detail about how to harmonise *angrezi* *shariat* with official English law. This kind of adaptation policy on the part of English law may not instantly appeal, but mutual non-recognition, as we emphasised before, is not a viable strategy for a harmonious future.

Chapter 4

Conflicts of laws

4–01 The second edition devoted a large chapter (Pearl (1987a), pp. 207–233) to this important topic. In the present edition, the material relating to conflict of laws is placed among the introductory sections to facilitate treatment of the more general conceptual questions concerning conflicts of laws before we come to specifically practice-related questions which arise with regard to Muslim family law in South Asia and in Western jurisdictions today.

4–02 We need to distinguish basically three types of conflict here. Sometimes, problems arise when a court has to decide whether to apply Muslim law or possibly some other legal system which may be appropriate to a case involving a Muslim element. This is the classic international conflict of laws scenario, also covered by the term 'private international law'.

4–03 Private international law or international conflict of laws has a long history. Over time, rules were developed to control the application by the judiciary within the municipal system of alien systems of law.[1] Readers should turn to standard textbooks on this specialist subject for historical background material and general principles.[2] It is pertinent to emphasise here that there is no such thing as one universal private international law (McClean (1993), p. 2; North and Fawcett (1992), p. 9).

4–04 We therefore need to examine this particular subject from several angles. First, it is relevant to consider briefly what the general rules of English law concerning conflict of laws are, and to what extent these rules have taken account of the presence of other rule systems, whether abroad or in the same social field. With particular reference to Muslim laws, we must ask to what extent modern English law has reacted to the legal rules of particular Muslim jurisdictions and/or jurisdictions which include Muslim law. We see today that far from facilitating blanket recognition of legal effects arising in foreign jurisdictions, English conflict of laws principles and techniques have, in practice, at least to some extent, sought to control and restrict the effects of Muslim law. This has become especially obvious in relation to polygamous marriages and immigration. Private international law can therefore be used as a means to circumscribe non-Western concepts of law and to fit them into the dominant Western model of international standards. To some extent, as we shall see, this restrictive approach has been based on various public policy arguments.

4–05 On the other hand, an examination of private international principles from the perspective of Muslim law and non-Western jurisdictions brings out the fact, already identified above, that Muslims, wherever they may be in the world, tend to claim that they remain governed by *shari'a* principles. Where these have become part of a particular national legal system, we encounter new tensions and modified forms of the traditional conflict of laws scenario. In Britain, during the

---

[1] For details on legal history and current theories see North and Fawcett, *Cheshire and North's Private international law* (1992), pp. 14–40; Diwan and Diwan, *Private international law. Indian and English* (1993), pp. 53–72.

[2] See in particular North and Fawcett (1992); McClean, *The Conflict of laws* (1993). The leading Indian textbook on this subject is Diwan and Diwan (1993).

past few decades, particular attention has focused on new legal conflict issues concerning Muslims, sometimes related to polygamy and, more prominently, to the recognition of various forms of Muslim divorces. Because of new phenomena like *angrezi shariat*, it has become virtually impossible to draw neat dividing lines between the principles of private international law and other conceptualisations of legal conflicts.

4–06   The second type of conflict of laws comprises what a specialist study has called 'interpersonal conflicts of laws'.[3] Courts in the Indian subcontinent (and in many other parts of the world) are quite familiar with such conflicts, for instance between Muslim and Hindu law. They typically arise when, in one and the same national jurisdiction, different legal systems co-exist as officially recognised personal law systems and conflicts occur between them, or between one particular personal law and the general law of that state. The South Asian jurisdictions offer plenty of examples of such scenarios and the place of Muslim law has often been an issue in this context.

4–07   Sometimes, the conflict is between a particular personal law, such as Muslim law, and the law of some other country, possibly the law applied in England. Those problems fall again under 'international conflict of laws' because the personal law is here treated as a part of the official law of that particular state. While judges in the Indian subcontinent have fairly frequently come across such issues, members of the higher judiciary in England have also increasingly had to examine such issues because of the prolonged presence of Muslims from India, Pakistan, Bangladesh and elsewhere in the United Kingdom. Their marriages and divorces, in particular, have been the subject of judicial hearings. Again, we shall examine the general principles here but turn to a more detailed discussion of relevant cases in the substantive chapters in Part II of this book.

4–08   A third type of conflict, not as yet adequately covered in the literature, evidently because it is not perceived and treated as falling under 'conflict of laws', relates to conflicts between the official law of a country and officially unrecognised personal laws. In Indian, Pakistani or Bangladeshi law, of course, this type would fall under the 'interpersonal' or internal conflict of laws category because the respective personal law is recognised as 'law'. Since English law is structured differently, we find here precisely the scenario of *angrezi shariat* in Britain today, paralleled by new developments in other Western countries. As we saw in Chapter 3, above, English law as the law of the land has been officially juxtaposed to 'ethnic minority customs' (Poulter (1986)), so that English law and conflict lawyers would not treat this as a legal conflict scenario.

4–09   Evidently, however, this approach does not solve the complex conflict of laws which arise among Muslims living in Western countries today. By refusing to recognise the laws of ethnic minorities as laws, and declaring them as customs or 'cultural practices', English law appears to avoid a meaningful discussion about the place of Muslim law and other ethnic minority laws. The dominant view so far appears to be that English law does not accept its own transformation into a personal law system, and that consequently Muslims in Britain (and other ethnic minorities) will have to adjust accordingly and will be officially bound by English law alone.

4–10   We saw already in Chapter 3 that this is certainly not how the matter looks from a Muslim perspective and in social reality. If *shari'a* is actually being followed by British Muslims, *as well as* English law, we need to examine here in

---

[3] See in particular Pearl (1981a); also Pearl (1978a) and Pearl (1987a), pp. 208–214.

more detail how the English legal system should react to this new challenge. In addition, it is possible today to think about the consequences of the official non-discourse about this kind of conflicts issue. In Chapter 4.5, below, we will do so briefly in theoretical terms, while details of the practical effects of the different types of conflict in cases of marriage, divorce and other areas of the law are to be examined in the respective sub-chapters in Part II of this book.

The English conflicts perspective: Public policy and polygamy

4–11   Leading textbooks (*e.g.* North and Fawcett (1992), p. 5) reiterate the basic rule that conflict of laws arises when a foreign element is present in a case. This foreign connection can be of many types. Theoretically, it is possible for legal systems to shut out consideration of such facts and circumstances, to ignore foreign laws and to disregard foreign judgments (McClean (1993), pp. 3–4). However, quite apart from questions of 'comity of nations' or the need to cultivate harmonious relationships, there seems to be agreement that to simply ignore foreign law would mean inflicting grave injustice "not only on foreigners but also on Englishmen" (McClean (1993), p. 3). This shows familiar tensions between preserving one's own sphere of jurisdiction and allowing elements of a foreign jurisdiction to be considered. Narrow nationalism has no place here, since application of foreign laws or concepts does not involve loss or abdication of sovereignty (North and Fawcett (1992), p. 38). An older study stated clearly that "the dominant motivating principle is the desire to do justice in cases involving a foreign element" (Graveson (1974), p. 7). While that principle itself appears sound and important,[4] the precise meaning of 'justice' can indeed be problematised (see Diwan and Diwan (1993), p. 46).

4–12   An important consideration in defining the limits of recognition of foreign laws has been public policy.[5] It is here that special consideration of Muslim law can and has become an issue. If the public policy argument is emphasised, a domestic court in a secular jurisdiction may seek to exclude the application of foreign religious laws or legal principles on public policy grounds related to secularism. More prominent recent considerations have been the protection of human rights and of women's rights. Within the wider context of recognition of overseas marriages,[6] an issue of particular relevance in this context has been polygamy, *i.e.* the recognition of polygamous marriages, not only among Muslims, as well as the treatment of potentially polygamous unions. Here English law attempts to follow modern, supposedly liberal principles of private international law by recognising (albeit reluctantly) as legally valid polygamous marriages which were entered into under a foreign law and are recognised by that law as valid. However, public policy arguments have more recently been used to restrict recognition of the consequences of such marriages, so that, for example, British immigration law today no longer allows all spouses and offspring of a polygamous marriage to enter the United Kingdom.[7]

---

[4] It is discussed in detail in Graveson, *Conflict of laws. Private international law.* (1974), pp. 7–10.
[5] See in detail McClean (1993), pp. 41–46; North and Fawcett (1992) pp. 128 *et seq.* include a consideration of repugnance. See also Pilkington [1988] 37 I.C.L.Q. 137–141.
[6] On this see in detail relevant textbooks, *e.g.* McClean (1993), Chap. 11; North and Fawcett (1992), Chap. 21; Bromley and Lowe, *Family Law* (1992), pp. 59–67.
[7] This restriction was introduced by the Immigration Act 1988. The relevant rules are now found in *Hansard* H.C. 395, paras 278–280, the current Immigration Rules, laid before Parliament on May 23, 1994, under s.3(2) of the Immigration Act 1971 which came into effect on October 1, 1994.

4–13 At an earlier stage of development of such public policy principles, the treatment of potentially polygamous marriages in English conflicts law led to real difficulties, discussed in paragraph 8–9, below. Most recently, the Private International Law (Miscellaneous Provisions) Act 1995 has been promulgated to settle a long-standing controversy over the legal validity of overseas polygamous marriages. Sections 5 and 6 of that Act are of particular relevance to questions of polygamous marriages. This area of the law will remain of considerable interest to policy makers and practitioners alike.[8]

English conflicts law and recognition of Muslim divorces

4–14 In this prominent area of the law, researchers have noted a shift of emphasis from case law to statute and even international conventions,[9] though the latter seem to be limited because of concerns about loss of national sovereignty.

4–15 It is significant that much attention in this area has been directed towards the *talaq* forms of Muslim divorce, reflecting social and legal concern about the Muslim husband's unfettered discretion to divorce and about the informal and extra-judicial nature of the procedures involved (see in detail Poulter (1986), pp. 98–102). The development of English statutes and cases in this field can therefore be studied through the example of the recognition of *talaq* divorces. This immediately mixes the principles of private international law with public policy considerations about how to control the effects of unofficial use of personal laws, such as Muslim law, in England itself.[10] To some extent, therefore, the English legal debates about recognition of foreign divorces have had to account for the continued presence of foreign elements in the United Kingdom itself.[11] To complicate matters further, the discussions about *talaq* divorces in English law reflect on similar confusions and tensions about divorce in Muslim jurisdictions, particularly in Pakistan.[12]

4–16 English statutes and cases are of course important for the Muslim communities living in the United Kingdom, but they also have considerable influence on legal developments in the subcontinent. For instance, the enactment of the Domicile and Matrimonial Proceedings Act 1973 resulted in the Pakistan government withdrawing facilities for Pakistani citizens resident in England to give notice of their pronouncement of *talaq* to the Head of Chancery of the Pakistan Mission in London.

Statutory regulation: The old regime

4–17 The relevant domestic legislation is common to the entire United Kingdom. Two older Acts require consideration here, the Recognition of Divorces and Legal Separations Act 1971 and the Domicile and Matrimonial Proceedings Act 1973. The 1971 Act and certain provisions of the 1973 Act were subsequently

---

[8] At the time of writing, a Bangladeshi widow's pension case, decided negatively by the Court of Appeal on June 26, 1997 represents the latest evidence of continuing legal insecurities. See *Bibi v. Chief Adjudication Officer and another*, The Times, July 10, 1997, which decided that neither of the two widows of a deceased was entitled to the widow's state benefit. There are indications that this case may be taken to the European Court of Human Rights; the reaction to the case has been very negative.
[9] See in this respect particularly McClean (1993), p. v.
[10] Pilkington [1988] pp. 137 *et seq.* elaborates on public policy grounds and rightly highlights the importance of financial provisions and considerations.
[11] This is well-reflected in the treatment of the subject by Poulter (1986), Chap. 5.
[12] On this, see in detail para. 9–205, below.

repealed by Part II of the Family Law Act 1986, discussed in paragraph 4-44, below.

4-18 Sections 2 and 3 of the 1971 Act introduced what has been termed a 'jurisdictional code', stating in essence that a divorce shall be recognised in the United Kingdom if it has been "obtained by means of judicial or other proceedings" (section 2) in any country outside the British Isles where either spouse is a national, where either spouse is habitually resident, or where either spouse is domiciled within the meaning of that term in the foreign law. The divorce must also be effective under the law of the country in which it was obtained (section 2). This legislative provision, designed to implement the Hague Convention on Recognition of Divorces and Legal Separations 1970, was evidence of a desire to respect the rules of foreign jurisdictions, allowing foreign nationals living in England to avail themselves of their respective overseas jurisdiction, while restricting, at the same time, the access by British citizen habitual residents of the United Kingdom to such overseas laws. At first sight, this seems innocuous and straightforward. However, the effect of the 1971 Act has been to create 'limping marriages' in contravention of the Hague Convention (Pilkington (1988), p. 131).

4-19 In addition to this 'jurisdictional code', the old common law rules of recognition were retained. Section 6 of the 1971 Act (as amended) saved those old common law rules, so that a divorce obtained 'abroad' would be recognised if it was obtained in the country of common domicile, or in the country of domicile of one party if recognised in the country of domicile of the other, or in a third country when recognised in the country of common domicile, or if the parties had separate domiciles, recognised in both domiciles.

4-20 Section 8(2)(b) of the 1971 Act enabled a court to withhold recognition to a foreign divorce when it considered that recognition would manifestly be contrary to public policy. An early indication of reservations about Muslim divorce procedures (or the lack of them) is found in section 8(2)(a) of the 1971 Act, to the effect that recognition of the validity of a divorce may be refused if the divorce was obtained by one spouse without notice to the other spouse or without reasonable involvement of the other spouse in the proceedings. Muslim divorces were probably not explicitly mentioned because such procedural concerns arise also in other non-Western forms of divorce.

4-21 The Domicile and Matrimonial Proceedings Act 1973 contained provisions in section 16 dealing with the recognition of non-judicial divorces. These were therefore particularly relevant to the law on *talaq*:

"16.—(1) No proceeding in the United Kingdom, the Channel Islands or the Isle of Man shall be regarded as validly dissolving a marriage unless instituted in the courts of law of one of those countries.

(2) Notwithstanding anything in section 6 of the Recognition of Divorces and Legal Separations Act 1971 (as substituted by section 2 of this Act), a divorce which –

(a) has been obtained elsewhere than in the United Kingdom, the Channel Islands and the Isle of Man; and

(b) has been so obtained by means of a proceeding other than a proceeding instituted in a court of law; and

(c) is not required by any of the provisions of sections 2 to 5 of that Act to be recognised as valid, shall not be regarded as validly dissolving a marriage if both parties to the marriage have throughout the period of one year immediately preceding the institution of the proceeding been habitually resident in the United Kingdom.

(3) This section does not affect the validity of any divorce obtained before its coming into force and recognised as valid under rules of law formerly applicable."

Thus, notwithstanding the survival of the common law grounds for recognition in section 6 of the 1971 Act, a non-judicial divorce obtained 'abroad' (other than such a divorce where recognition would be required by the 'jurisdictional code'), was not to be regarded as validly dissolving the marriage if *both* parties had been habitually resident in the United Kingdom. It follows that if only one of the parties had been so habitually resident, or indeed neither of them, then the validity of such a non-judicial divorce depended on the law of the domicile of both parties. One sees here how English law struggled, at that point, with the distinction between normal conflict of laws rules and the emerging scenario of resident immigrant or ethnic minority populations who continued to rely on a foreign domicile but had become long-term residents of the United Kingdom. The attempted modification of criteria or connecting factors, in favour of residence rather than domicile, reflects some unease about the fact that Muslim ethnic minority populations may continue to use some form of Muslim law in England, although they should be bound by English law. Such early legislative attempts to control the situation indicate real practical problems which are yet to be solved today. It could be argued that such problems are structurally inherent in Western legal systems with their exclusive focus on state law and their consequent insistence on a uniform, secular-type family law.

4–22　To sum up, the statutory regime of the early 1970s in Britain clearly aimed to curb the emergent trend for Muslims in Britain, in particular, to rely on *talaq* divorces rather than the judicial process of English divorce law to bring about a divorce.[13] In addition to de-recognising the legal effects of any form of extra-judicial divorce executed in Britain, the statute law also sought to prevent abuse of recourse to foreign jurisdictions which would tend to favour the husband and might damage the public purse. It appears, as Pilkington (1988) has explained, that gender-focused arguments as well as financial considerations played a key role in this regard.

4–23　Muslims themselves, as victims of this restrictive approach, have probably tended to avoid litigation in the official fora of English law, favouring settlements within the unofficial sphere. However, that has not always been possible. While there has been very important case law in the 1970s and 1980s, it is noteworthy that during the 1990s very few reported cases on conflicts of law have involved Muslims. In light of our discussion in paragraph 3–94, above, this may be taken as further evidence of 'inner migration' rather than assuming that important legal conflicts questions have now been settled or resolved.

The case law

4–24　Based on the statutory regime of the early 1970s and various policy considerations, the English courts appear to have taken a tough line since the mid-1970s. Many commentators (*e.g.* Pilkington (1988), p. 131; North and Fawcett (1992), p. 666) have been critical of this, indicating that the law has probably gone too far in its declared aim to prevent abuse and to enforce compliance with domestic law by persons who could, through various connecting factors, and therefore probably quite legitimately, avail themselves of foreign laws. In other words, there is some apprehension about the fact that English conflict of laws

---

[13] It is apparent that the statute law was passed to reverse the implications of the judgment in *Qureshi v. Qureshi* [1972] Fam. 173. See in detail para. 4–30, below.

regulation has become too concerned about not losing control, particularly in transnational conflict situations, overlooking in the process the fact that the principles of private international law are not uniformly agreed everywhere in the world and that different forms of family law regulation continue to co-exist in today's world.

4–25 A brief consideration of the English case law concerning recognition of overseas divorces shows first of all that important cases, many of them involving Muslim law, arose under the 1971 and 1973 Acts, while there is not yet any prominent case law under the new regime of the 1986 Act.[14] Earlier, issues arose in many different contexts. Cases have come before English courts, for example, when a respondent filed a defence to a divorce petition on the ground that the marriage had already been effectively terminated under Muslim law. In other cases, Superintendent Registrars of Marriages may have refused to grant permission for a marriage because the Registrar General took the view that an earlier marriage was still in existence. Immigration officers and social security personnel increasingly have had to consider these issues, too.

4–26 Apart from an important later immigration case,[15] the leading case in this field is considered to be *Quazi v. Quazi*, a decision of the House of Lords.[16] The *ratio* of this case is that a *talaq* pronounced in Pakistan and fulfilling the procedural requirements of the Muslim Family Laws Ordinance 1961 comes within the requirements of the 1971 Act and is therefore capable of recognition in the United Kingdom. Lord Diplock said in the House of Lords [1979] 3 All E.R. 897, at 903:

> "It is rightly conceded on behalf of the wife that the divorce by talaq which was obtained in Pakistan followed on acts which though not judicial do fall within the description 'other proceedings officially recognised' in that country."

The English courts have drawn a distinction between the Pakistani *talaq* on the one hand, and the so-called 'bare *talaq*' on the other. It appears that this distinction was first made by Wood J. at first instance in *Quazi v. Quazi*.[17] In the case of the 'bare *talaq*', where there is no official intervention at all to the traditional form of unilateral and extra-judicial pronouncement, Wood J. felt that the 'jurisdictional code' does not apply because this code only applies to 'judicial or other proceedings', and that a 'bare *talaq*' cannot constitute such proceedings. Such divorces therefore were to be recognised only under the common law provisions in section 6 of the 1971 Act, based on the validity of the divorce in the domiciliary law of both parties. However, if either party was domiciled in England, no such *talaq* would be recognised as valid.

4–27 This view was later followed by the Court of Appeal in *Chaudhary v. Chaudhary*.[18] In this case, the husband was a national of Pakistan originating from the territory of Kashmir. The parties were married in Kashmir and lived there until 1963, when the husband went to the United Kingdom leaving behind him his wife

---

[14] To some extent, this may be taken as further evidence of what we called 'avoidance reactions' by Muslims in Britain today, a strategy to prevent contentious issues from reaching the higher echelons of the official court system (see para. 3–94, above).

[15] *R. v. Secretary of State for the Home Department, ex p. Fatima* [1984] 2 All E.R. 458, and *Fatima v. Secretary of State for the Home Department* [1986] 2 All E.R. 32, see Pilkington [1988], p. 131 and para. 4–30, below.

[16] [1980] A.C. 744; [1979] 3 All E.R. 897; [1979] 3 W.L.R. 833; 10 Fam. Law 148.

[17] [1979] 3 All E.R. 424; [1979] 3 W.L.R. 402; 9 Fam. Law 219.

[18] [1984] 3 All E.R. 1017, [1985] 2 W.L.R. 350.

and children. Having settled in England, the husband then established a relationship with another woman and went through a register office marriage with her in 1967. In 1969, they solemnised a religious marriage in Beirut, Lebanon. The husband purported to divorce his first wife on two occasions. First, he made an oral pronouncement of *talaq* at a mosque in London. Secondly, he pronounced a *talaq* divorce in Kashmir when he went there in 1978. The marriage at the register office was declared void by a High Court judge in proceedings in 1980.

4–28   In 1979, the first wife, who had arrived in the United Kingdom in 1976, had filed a petition for divorce based on the fact of the husband's adultery with the other woman. The husband had then presented a petition for a declaration that the marriage had been lawfully dissolved prior to the petition filed by the wife, either by the *talaq* pronounced in England or by the second *talaq* pronounced in Kashmir. The issues surrounding the *talaq* pronounced in England, which Wood J. at first instance did not recognise, are discussed in paragraph 4–30 immediately below. So far as the second *talaq* was concerned, Wood J. held that this was a 'bare *talaq*' because the 1961 Ordinance does not apply to the territory of Kashmir, and that it could not be regarded as 'judicial or other proceedings' within the meaning of the 1971 Act. As the 'jurisdictional code' does not apply to the 'bare *talaq*', Wood J. went on to consider whether the *talaq* could be recognised under the provisions of section 6 of the 1971 Act. This section was wider in scope than the 'jurisdictional code' because there are none of the requirements of 'judicial or other proceedings' or effectiveness in the country where the divorce was obtained. However, the *talaq* can only be validated by section 6 if it is valid by the law of the parties' domiciles. Wood J. decided that, at the relevant date, the husband had acquired a domicile of choice in England. He was also satisfied that the wife had acquired a domicile of choice in England. As no English domiciliary can pronounce or be a recipient to a non-judicial divorce under the common law, the provisions of section 6 had no application. Wood J. therefore refused the declaration sought by the husband and granted the wife a decree nisi of divorce on her petition based on the husband's adultery with the other woman.

4–29   The husband appealed on the ground that the *talaq* pronounced in Kashmir in 1978 should be recognised as valid under the provisions of the 'jurisdictional code' of the 1971 Act.[19] His appeal was dismissed and Cumming Bruce L.J. said, at page 483:

> "But neither respect for the divine origin of the procedure nor respect for the long enduring tradition which over the centuries had rendered the bare talaq effective as terminating marriage by the law of Muslim countries necessarily or sensibly should convert the procedure into a proceeding within the intent of section 2 of the 1971 Act. So I conclude that . . . a divorce obtained by a bare talaq would not be construed as not 'obtained by means of judicial or other proceedings' within the intendment of section 2 of that Act."

This case takes the same position as subsequently adopted by the Family Law Act 1986, refusing to recognise the legal validity of informal and extra-judicial divorces despite the fact that they are considered legally valid by a number of foreign jurisdictions. It has been argued that this particular point will need to be reconsidered under the Family Law Act 1986 and in the light of more recent policy discussions (see to this effect Pilkington (1988)).

---

[19] *Chaudhary v. Chaudhary* [1985] F.L.R. 476; [1985] 2 W.L.R. 350.

Talaq pronounced in England

4–30 Prior to the 1971 legislation, in *Qureshi v. Qureshi*,[20] Simon P. had held that a *talaq* obtained by a husband who was domiciled in Pakistan should be recognised by the English courts even though this *talaq* was pronounced in England. Finding himself in agreement with leading textbook writers on conflict of laws at the time, the learned judge held:

> "In my view, therefore, the fact that there has been no judicial intervention or even presence is irrelevant if the purported divorce is effective by the law of the domicile to terminate the marriage in question, and it should be recognised as such, unless the result would be offensive to the conscience of the English court."[21]

This was a matter decided under the common law, prior to statutory intervention. The learned judge explicitly recognised the fact that "the rule of foreign law under which the husband has proceeded has the authority of the holy scriptures of the common faith of himself and the wife" (p. 540).

4–31 The Recognition of Divorces and Legal Separations Act 1971 did not deal with this particular issue, concerned as it was with overseas divorces. The Domicile and Matrimonial Proceedings Act 1973, however, was partially enacted to reverse the implications of *Qureshi v. Qureshi*.[22] The courts have stated that section 16(1) of that Act excludes both 'bare *talaqs*' and 'procedural *talaqs*'. This is why the first *talaq* pronounced in *Chaudhary v. Chaudhary* [1985] 2 W.L.R. 350, which we discussed in paragraph 4–24, above, could not be recognised. Oliver L.J. said in that case, at page 369:

> "The obvious intention of section 16 was to deny by statute the recognition accorded by the decision in *Qureshi v. Qureshi* [1972] Fam 173 to informal divorces effected in this country. The *Qureshi* case was, it is true, not a case of a 'bare' talaq, but it cannot reasonably be supposed that the legislature intended to exclude from the operation of the section and thus to permit the continued recognition of even less formal divorces obtained here, such as, for instance the consensual agreement recognised by the law of Thailand."

Recent textbooks see *Qureshi v. Qureshi* as the high water mark of liberalism as far as English legal recognition for ethnic minority divorces executed in the United Kingdom is concerned. It seems to have been widely assumed that the effects of subsequent restrictive legislation and the legal refusal to recognise such divorces would somehow filter down to Britain's ethnic minority populations, thus ensuring compliance with the domestic law in the long run. We have already seen in Chapter 3 above that this has been an unrealistic assimilationist assumption. There appears to be a need for some new thinking and new case law on this matter.

4–32 In this context, the issue of transnational *talaq* divorces has assumed particular relevance (see Pilkington (1988)). In an increasingly mobile world, and given the nature of divorce, what of a *talaq* pronouncement in England, which is subsequently communicated to the chairman of a Union Council in Pakistan, or which is 'perfected' (Pilkington (1988)) by some kind of proceedings overseas?

4–33 This problem came before the English courts for the first time in a case in 1977 which contains facts that must actually have been quite common among

---

[20] [1972] Fam. 173; [1971] 2 W.L.R. 518.
[21] *ibid.*, at p. 538.
[22] See *Chaudhary v. Chaudhary* [1985] F.L.R. 476, at 483, para. c.

Muslims in Britain during the 1970s.[23] Mr Minhas, a Pakistani national living on his own in Lancashire and now an English domiciliary, was anxious to divorce the wife he had left behind in Pakistan and to marry a Pakistani woman living in Britain. He decided to divorce his wife 'back home' by *talaq*. He pronounced a triple *talaq* in England and then sent a notice of it both to the chairman of the Union Council where his wife lived in Pakistan and to his wife. Interestingly, he then travelled to Pakistan and actually attended a meeting of the Arbitration Council which had been summoned by the chairman. Predictably, attempts at reconciliation proved unsuccessful. He returned to England and sought a licence to marry from the Superintendent Registrar of Marriages in his home district. This official was not satisfied that Mr Minhas was free to marry, and therefore sent the papers to the Registrar General. The Registrar General determined that Mr Minhas was still married. Mr Minhas therefore sought an order of mandamus against the Registrar directing him to perform his duty under the law. The Divisional Court refused to grant the application, for it held that the divorce was obtained in England and therefore fell outside the ambit of the 1971 Act. The mandatory provisions of the Pakistani law, the pronouncement of the *talaq*, and the sending of notices of the *talaq* to the chairman and to the wife, had all taken place in England. The subsequent activities in Pakistan, in particular the reconciliation attempts by the Arbitration Council, were not mandatory. Mr Minhas had even gone to the trouble of travelling to Pakistan. If he had divorced his wife by *talaq* in Pakistan, the position would have been entirely different.

4–34   While this may be a technically correct decision, it is not surprising that such judgments by the English courts will be found acceptable to the Muslim communities, for a number of reasons. The main argument, of course, is that such divorces are treated as perfectly valid in Pakistan. The fact that Mr Minhas even travelled to Pakistan could have been taken to signify that he was taking part in Pakistani judicial or other proceedings which validly terminated this particular marriage. Intransigence of the English law in the context of such transcontinental proceedings is not likely to inspire confidence in the law as an adequate and fair means to sort out interpersonal relationships.

4–35   Not surprisingly, the same issue arose again in the immigration context of three cases, one of which ended up in the House of Lords.[24] In this case, and the others, the applicants were Pakistani women who sought leave to enter the United Kingdom as fiancées of their sponsors, who were United Kingdom residents of Pakistani nationality. Again, this is a fairly common situation among the Pakistani community in Britain. In each case, there had been previous marriages to Pakistani women which the male sponsors had purported to dissolve by pronouncing a *talaq* in England, making statutory declarations before solicitors in England that they had done so, and then sending copies of these documents to Pakistan, both to their wives and to the appropriate local officials. The response of the immigration officers was to find that they could not be satisfied that these marriages had been effectively dissolved according to English law. The immigration officials therefore found that they could not be satisfied that the intended marriages between the applicants and the sponsors could take place within a reasonable time, and accordingly refused entry. The applicants sought review of these decisions. One lady, Ghulam Fatima,

[23] *R. v. Registrar General, ex p. Minhas* [1977] Q.B. 1.
[24] See *R. v. Immigration Appeal Tribunal, ex p. Secretary of State for the Home Department* [1984] 1 All E.R. 488; [1984] 2 W.L.R. 36, QBD; *R. v. Secretary of State for the Home Department, ex p. Ghulam Fatima* [1984] 2 All E.R. 458; [1984] 3 W.L.R. 659, CA; [1985] Q.B. 190; See *R. v. Secretary of State for the Home Department, ex p. Ghulam Fatima* [1986] A.C. 527; [1986] 2 W.L.R. 693.

fought her case unsuccessfully right up to the House of Lords. The House of Lords had no hesitation in upholding the negative decision of the Court of Appeal. Lord Ackner referred to section 16(1) of the 1973 Act and said[25]:

> "It is thus clearly the policy of the legislature to deny recognition to divorces obtained by persons within the jurisdiction, and therefore subject to the laws of the United Kingdom, by any proceedings other than in a United Kingdom court. It would seem contrary to that policy to encourage the obtaining of divorces essentially by post by Pakistani nationals resident in this country by means of the talaq procedure."

It is apparent that this decision produced two anomalies. First, the more wealthy (or simply more circumspect) Pakistani national can travel to that country and pronounce a *talaq* there. The decision in *R. v. Registrar General, ex p. Minhas* [1977] Q.B. 1 appears to indicate that this should be done without taking any action whatsoever in Britain itself. Given the relaxed nature of the Pakistani rules relating to notice to the appropriate chairman, Muslim husbands could easily comply with the relevant Pakistani law. There was a discretion to refuse recognition inherent in section 8 of the 1971 Act, but subject to this provision, such a *talaq* would have to be recognised in England. This is what Mr. Minhas should have done in his situation, rather than pronouncing the *talaq* in England and then travelling to Pakistan.

4–36   One may ask if there is any way for a person to divorce his wife by the traditional Muslim form without the expense of going back to the country of his nationality. Three possibilities suggest themselves. First, to pronounce the *talaq* over the telephone to the wife in Pakistan. Secondly, to delegate the right to someone in Pakistan. Thirdly, to pronounce the *talaq* in another more convenient Muslim country. As to the first suggestion, the divorce is still of course a *talaq* divorce pronounced in England. In classical law, a *talaq* need not be communicated to the wife; thus the fact that the wife hears or does not hear of the pronouncement in Pakistan is of little consequence.

4–37   Instead, then, the husband might be able to avoid the expense of going to the subcontinent by delegating his right of *talaq* to someone else, either absolutely or conditional on the occurrence of a particular event. Courts in the subcontinent are reluctant to infer delegation, but so long as this essentially evidential hurdle was overcome, it could be argued that the divorce subsequently pronounced was validly obtained in Pakistan and is therefore an overseas divorce capable of recognition under the 'jurisdictional code' of the 1971 Act. Against this view, it could be argued that the delegation was created in the United Kingdom, and that this in effect is an essential step to the pronouncement of this divorce. Also the discretionary provisions which enable an overseas divorce not to be recognised may be particularly relevant in this context.

4–38   In the third situation, the divorce is pronounced in a country other than the United Kingdom, the country of nationality, habitual residence or domicile within the meaning of that term in the foreign law of one of those parties. The 'jurisdictional code' of the 1971 Act did not apply. The common law rules as saved by section 6 of the 1971 Act, however, did apply, as well as another important provision, namely section 16(2) of the 1973 Act. For example, if a Pakistani national divorces his wife in Kuwait by the *talaq* form of divorce, informs the chairman of an appropriate Union Council in Pakistan that he has done this, and sends a copy of

---

[25] *ibid.*, at p. 698.

this notice to his wife, the legal position under the old law would appear to be as follows: If both husband and wife have been habitually resident in the United Kingdom for more than one year prior to the pronouncement of the *talaq*, then that *talaq* will not be recognised. The situation will be different, however, if both arrived in the United Kingdom within one year of the pronouncement, or one of them arrived in the United Kingdom within the year. In this case, the *talaq* could be recognised if it is valid in the country of domicile of both parties. If they are both domiciled in Pakistan and, assuming that the husband complied with Pakistani law, then such a transnational Kuwaiti/Pakistani *talaq* is capable of recognition in the English courts. If, in contrast, either party is domiciled in England, then the *talaq* cannot be recognised. These complexities illustrate how concerned English law has become to protect its domiciliaries from the potentially negative effects of applying a foreign legal system. In addition, as Pilkington (1988) convincingly shows, concerns over implications on public funds have become an increasingly prominent public policy issue, helping us to explain why English law has become so restrictive when it comes to recognition of foreign divorces.

The 'bare *talaq*', public policy and financial provisions

4-39 While cases in the English courts concerning Pakistani or Bangladeshi Muslim divorces under the relevant procedures of the Muslim Family Laws Ordinance 1961 have given rise to much controversy, the vexed question of the 'bare *talaq*' continues to pose a much more serious and, in practice, much greater difficulty. Under the old legal regime of the 1971 and 1973 Acts, an Indian national or a Pakistani Kashmiri Muslim husband would not be able to secure recognition of his 'bare *talaq*', even when pronounced in India or Kashmir, unless both parties were still domiciled in that country, or at least domiciled in countries whose law recognises the effectiveness of termination by such means.[26] Regarding exemptions from recognition, section 8(2) of the 1971 Act stated that the validity of a divorce or legal separation obtained outside the British Isles may be refused if, and only if:

"(a) it was obtained by one spouse –
    (i) without such steps having been taken for giving notice of the proceedings to the other spouse as, having regard to the nature of the proceedings and all the circumstances, should reasonably have been taken; or
    (ii) without the other spouse having been given (for any reason other than lack of notice) such opportunity to take part in the proceedings as, having regard to the matters aforesaid, he should reasonably have been given; or
(b) its recognition would manifestly be contrary to public policy."

Case law suggested that paragraphs (a)(i) and (a)(ii) were of little importance in the context of the 'bare *talaq*' and of only limited significance in the case of the Pakistan procedural *talaq*. As Bush J. said in the case of a 'bare *talaq*' in *Zaal v. Zaal* [1983] 4 F.L.R. 284, at p. 288:

"So far as para. (a)(i) is concerned . . . there does not seem much point in giving notice that the husband is about to undertake a unilateral act in which the wife can play no part and have no standing for objection. So far as para.

---

[26] For further discussion, also with reference to Indian law, see Carroll [1981a] 23 No. 4 J.I.L.I. 588–595.

(a)(ii) is concerned what part in the proceedings could the wife be expected to play when the law applicable to this talaq permits a unilateral decision?"

More important was the common law provision, contained in section 8(2)(b) of the 1971 Act. The earlier case law suggested that the courts would exercise their discretion in this area sparingly.[27] However, the courts had discretion to be tougher and recognition might well be refused, on what would appear to be several interrelated public policy grounds. There is indeed little evidence of 'bare *talaq*' cases in which this was an issue. Prominently, Oliver L.J. stated the following in *Chaudhary v. Chaudhary* [1985] 2 W.L.R. 350, at 371:

> "In my judgment it must plainly be contrary to the policy of the law in a case where both parties to a marriage are domiciled in this country to permit one of them, whilst continuing his English domicile, to avoid the incidents of his domiciliary law and to deprive the other party to the marriage of her rights under that law by the simple process of taking advantage of his financial ability to travel to a country whose laws appear temporarily to be more favourable to him. This, as it seems to me, is precisely the sort of situation which the legislature must have had in mind in enacting the provisions of section 8(2)(b)."

The learned judge here pinpoints what, from an official legal perspective, must appear like a growing form of abuse, namely making a convenient choice of jurisdiction on the part of (mainly male) members of ethnic minorities in Britain who belong to transnational communities. We find here confirmed, in the legal field, what Roger Ballard (1994) so instructively highlighted, writing about British Asians re-creating a home abroad on their own terms. Part of this re-creation process appears to be the self-empowerment to utilise facilities of the relevant overseas legal system in the process of sorting out difficult family situations. Regarding divorce, this might involve recourse to an individual's respective overseas legal system despite the fact of permanent residence in Britain, apparent assumption of an English domicile, and even acceptance of British nationality.

4–40 Obviously, such strategies flatly contradict official legal assumptions about how members of ethnic minority communities assimilate to and interact with the official laws of their new home. Following the virtual ban on extra-judicial divorces in Britain through the operation of the 1971 and 1973 Acts, overriding the liberal approach in *Qureshi v. Qureshi* [1972] Fam. 173 and rendering informal Muslim forms of divorce in the United Kingdom legally invisible, the official focus shifted, thus, towards banning – or at least curbing – the next best alternative for members of ethnic minorities resident in Britain, namely direct access to their respective 'native' overseas legal systems. It became, thus, a growing policy concern in Britain during the 1980s to prevent access to overseas jurisdictions for members of ethnic minority communities.

4–41 This is well-documented in the academic debates about divorce law reforms in Britain during the 1980s.[28] Gordon (1988, p. 94) states very clearly that the general policy of the Family Law Act 1986 became "to restrict the recognition of extra-judicial divorces". Gordon documents notable judicial intolerance in the run-up to the new legislation, mainly reserved for the 'bare *talaq*'.[29] Hamilton (1995,

---

[27] *Qureshi v. Qureshi* [1972] Fam. 173; *Quazi v. Quazi* [1980] A.C. 744.
[28] See also Gordon [1986a] 37 No. 2 *Northern Ireland Legal Quarterly* 151–169; [1986b] 16 *Family Law* 169–172.
[29] See the particularly unsympathetic comments of Cumming-Bruce L.J. in *Chaudhary v. Chaudhary* [1985] 2 W.L.R. 350, at 365–366, referred to by Gordon, *Foreign divorces: English law and practice* (1988, p. 107) and Hamilton (1995, p. 109).

p. 103) notes that while Jewish divorces were treated as acceptable, "public policy objections were raised, particularly in England, to Muslim talaq divorces". Such evidence reflects growing judicial strictness and official reservations towards the legal recognition of overseas divorce proceedings generally, whether these were following certain proceedings or the 'bare *talaq*' model.

4-42 Two important areas of concern to the law have, thus, become intersected in this complex way. Having introduced a virtual ban on extra-judicial divorces in the United Kingdom itself, English law now moved against recognition of overseas divorces. The result has been the fairly restrictive regime under the Family Law Act 1986 which has virtually driven ethnic minority practice in Britain 'underground' and now focuses on controlling access to what are perceived as minimal divorce procedures in overseas jurisdictions.

4-43 The academic response to this development has not been generally favourable. Pilkington (1988), argued against the growing strictness and has helpfully pointed to underlying public policy arguments and financial considerations, in particular, while pleading for a more refined approach to the recognition of transnational divorces by English law. Gordon (1988, pp. 114–115) points to the practical difficulties created by the new strict regime. Arguing in favour of greater tolerance (especially page 145), he highlights the fact that a very strict approach is neither good for race relations nor bilateral relations with a number of countries (Gordon (1988), p. 141). Hamilton (1995, p. 90) recognises that these are matters of immense concern to ethnic minorities and joins those who criticise the new provisions as too strict (Hamilton (1995), pp. 112–113). In the light of such arguments, which we shall discuss further in the section immediately below, it would appear that the official treatment of 'bare *talaq*' divorces requires reconsideration.

The new regime: The Family Law Act 1986

4-44 This Act could not be incorporated into the previous edition of this book. Its aims and ambit were briefly outlined in the preface to that edition and in a subsequent article (Pearl (1987c)). More recent editions of textbooks on conflict of laws contain useful sections for readers who wish to have more detail than the present chapter can provide.[30]

4-45 The Family Law Act 1986 served a number of purposes. Part II of that Act, which alone is relevant here, repealed the Recognition of Divorces and Legal Separations Act 1971 and various provisions of the Domicile and Matrimonial Proceedings Act 1973. The Act sought to consolidate the English law on recognition of overseas divorces. The Preamble to the Act indicates that its purpose is "to amend the law relating to the recognition of divorces, annulments and legal separations". While this was a consolidating exercise, it was only another piecemeal effort, not a comprehensive code, rather an attempt to tidy up a very difficult area of the law. It remains a fact that the 1986 Act tackles only certain problems and leaves others unsolved (Pearl (1987c), p. 38).

4-46 The Act clearly continues the earlier ban on extra-judicial divorces obtained in the United Kingdom itself. In this respect, section 44(1) of the Family Law Act 1986 provides:

---

[30] See in particular McClean (1993), pp. 190–202 and North and Fawcett (1992), pp. 655–690, with references to further writing. Gordon (1988) is a very useful specialist study of the subject. Hamilton (1995), pp. 89–139 contains a detailed discussion of various aspects of religious divorces.

"No divorce or annulment obtained in any part of the British Isles shall be regarded as effective in any part of the United Kingdom unless granted by a court of civil jurisdiction."

As indicated already, the main focus of the other relevant provisions concerns restrictions on the recognition of overseas divorces. The English and Scottish Law Commissions had made detailed recommendations in this regard, but their advice was not followed in all respects. Thus, the distinction between procedural and 'bare' *talaq*, established by case law, was retained, with a much tougher approach to informal divorces, justified by public policy grounds (Pilkington (1988), pp. 137 *et seq.*; Gordon (1988), pp. 120–148). Parliament rejected clear proposals of the Law Commissions that the 'bare *talaq*' should be treated in the same way as other types of divorce. Commentators have been critical about this and about the lack of definition of the phrase 'judicial or other proceedings' and have noted that the 1986 Act implicitly rejects the more liberal approach taken by several leading judges earlier (see McClean (1993), p. 195; Hamilton (1995), p. 112). This remains unsatisfactory and has important implications in legal practice.[31]

4–47 McClean (1993, p. 191) finds the 1986 Act "in almost all respects a distinct improvement on the legislation it replaced" but refers critically to "the troublesome distinction" between divorces 'obtained by means of judicial or other proceedings' and other divorces (*id.*). This distinction is clearly in response to Muslim *talaq* divorces and the Jewish *get* and their various forms.[32]

4–48 One major difficulty in operating this distinction has been that it is based on a certain understanding of what the Pakistani and Bangladeshi law on *talaq* divorces actually is, or more correctly, was. It has been overlooked in Britain (but see the warning by Pearl (1987c, p. 38) that Pakistani law itself (and also Bangladeshi law, unnoticed in Britain so far) has changed quite considerably during the late 1980s and early 1990s. These changes have not been reflected in the English legislation of 1986, which operates on the basis of certain mental images of Pakistani law and in particular an understanding of Pakistani case law which is now out of date.[33]

4–49 Under sections 46(1)(a)(b) and 46(5) of the 1986 Act, a divorce obtained abroad 'by proceedings', through what was then assumed to be the Pakistani or Bangladeshi process of getting divorced under the provisions of section 7 of the MFLO 1961, will be recognised in the United Kingdom if it is effective in the respective country and if, at the relevant date, either party was habitually resident in, domiciled in, or a national of that country. This respects the need for Pakistani nationals, for example, to avail themselves of Pakistani law in a moment of crisis, but for how long after they have left Pakistan? The continued use of domicile and nationality as connecting factors in this context may still be abused by long-term residents of Britain who have the financial means to move to the subcontinent for some time to 'arrange' their family affairs without supervision by any state legal system but claiming subsequent legal recognition of such arrangements.

4–50 The official approach to the 'bare *talaq*' was clearly less favourable for exactly that underlying policy reason. Such a *talaq*, most frequently from India or Pakistani Kashmir, will be recognised by English law only,

---

[31] On further details in this regard see para. 9–206, below.

[32] Hamilton (1995) repeatedly highlights the fact that this is not only a question of Muslim divorces and refers to some evidence of African case law.

[33] See in detail Chap. 9, below, particularly on the question whether notice of *talaq* is actually essential to bring about a legally valid Muslim divorce under Pakistani law. The answer to that, today, must be in the negative, so that the assumptions on which English legal regulation has been built during the 1970s and 1980s need to be re-examined.

"if it is effective by the law of the country where it was obtained (this is a new provision) and if at the relevant date each party was domiciled in that country (or if only one was domiciled in that country, then the other is domiciled in another country where the talaq is recognised . . ." (Pearl (1987c), p. 36).

The relevant provisions in section 46(2) read as follows:

"(2) The validity of an overseas divorce, annulment or legal separation obtained otherwise than by means of proceedings shall be recognised if –
  (a) the divorce, annulment or legal separation is effective under the law of the country in which it was obtained;
  (b) at the relevant date –
    (i) each party to the marriage was domiciled in that country; or
    (ii) either party to the marriage was domiciled in that country and the other party was domiciled in a country under whose law the divorce, annulment or legal separation is recognised as valid; and
  (c) neither party to the marriage was habitually resident in the United Kingdom throughout the period of one year immediately preceding that date."

The crucial proviso in section 46(2)(c) of the 1986 Act above represents a tightening of the jurisdictional screw, since prior to the 1986 Act recognition would only be denied if both parties had been so resident. McClean (1993, p. 196) concluded:

"This last provision is designed to prevent easy circumvention of the rule that no extra-judicial divorce can be obtained in England; an English resident obtaining such a divorce on a short trip abroad will find that it will not be recognised."

This would appear to confirm our observations in paragraph 4–39, above, to the effect that the 1986 legislation is very much focused on controlling the use by Britain's ethnic minorities of their respective 'personal laws', which are of course not recognised as law by the English legal system. Put the other way round, this legislation seeks to encourage (perhaps one should rather say, force) members of ethnic minority communities to make use of the domestic English legal provisions rather than taking recourse to overseas laws and then seeking recognition of such actions through private international law.

4–51   Procedural aspects were used to reinforce such messages. A further hurdle was put in the path of divorcing couples by requiring documentary evidence of the overseas divorce. It has of course long been known to lawyers and legal advisers that the absence of official documentation of a change of legal status in another jurisdiction may cause problems.[34] If there is no official documentation certifying that the divorce is valid and effective under the respective foreign law, recognition of legal validity may be refused. It has been argued that given the difficulty in obtaining documentation from countries such as India, this provision may form a considerable stumbling block (Pearl (1987c), p. 36).

4–52   The practical problems surrounding transnational unilateral divorces have not been solved by the 1986 Act, either. Commentators have not been unanimous

---

[34] See Pearl (1986a), p. 70 with reference to divorce and Mole, *Immigration: Family entity and settlement* (1987), pp. 39 and 41 with reference to marriage and divorce documentation, especially from the subcontinent and Africa.

on this issue. Pearl (1987c, p. 36) assumed that the 1986 Act has not disturbed the position established earlier by the case law. It is certain that section 44(1) of the 1986 Act retained the virtual ban on extra-judicial divorces in Britain itself and that the 1986 Act seeks to stop persons resident in Britain from going on a short trip abroad with the purpose of bringing about a divorce. Following this reasoning, a *talaq* pronounced in the United Kingdom which is then, for example, communicated to a local official in Pakistan, would be hit by section 44 of the 1986 Act (Pearl (1987c), pp. 36–37). In light of the fact that for Muslims, in accordance with *shari'a*, a *talaq* may be instantly valid and effective, irrespective of what modern Pakistani or Bangladeshi state law might say, this particular reasoning used several implied British public policy grounds to argue against the recognition of transnational divorces.[35]

4–53   In contrast, Pilkington (1988, p. 133) suggested that the recognition of transnational divorces may have been affected because the 1986 Act focuses much more on the place where the divorce was actually obtained than on the proceedings. She argued, in essence, that transnational divorces (provided the relevant criteria are fulfilled) should not be denied recognition under the 1986 Act because they fall under the category of 'divorce by proceedings' and were obtained abroad.[36] Observing that section 46 of the 1986 Act does not place any restrictions on the place where the proceedings may occur, her argument was that section 46(1) did not require "that the proceedings should be commenced in the same country as that in which the divorce is finally acquired" (Pilkington (1988), p. 134). Critical of what she called "linguistic gymnastics" in the new legislation (page 135), she found therefore that reform may well have been intended, but this was not made obvious in the wording of the statute.

4–54   In this context, Pilkington brings out a very important discussion about when (and therefore *where*) a transnational divorce is actually obtained.[37] Relying on the assumptions underlying English case law,[38] she deduces that a *talaq* is of no legal effect until and unless the officially required notices have been given and the formal proceedings have been completed.[39] Assuming that a *talaq* initiated in England but perfected elsewhere would actually be 'obtained' in that other jurisdiction, Pilkington (1988, p. 136) reaches the conclusion that such a *talaq* "can no longer be denied recognition merely because part of the proceedings occurred in the United Kingdom".

4–55   While this seems logical and would appear to have been the correct interpretation at some point in the past with reference to Pakistani and Bangladeshi law, it can very well be argued that in *shari'a* law, and thus in Indian Muslim law, for Pakistani Kashmiri Muslims, as well as now for Pakistanis and Bangladeshis as Muslims rather than citizens of Pakistan or Bangladesh, a final or triple *talaq* pronouncement becomes instantly valid. If one takes that view, any such *talaq* uttered in England would of course immediately fall foul of the ban on extra-judicial divorces in section 44(1) of the 1986 Act, as argued by Pearl (1987c) and could not become a truly transnational divorce. But it remains valid as a Muslim divorce.

---

[35] Gordon (1988, p. 118, n.52) questioned this interpretation.

[36] For a similar argument see Berkovits (1988).

[37] On this issue see also, in terms of 'effectiveness', McClean (1993), p. 191; North and Fawcett (1992), pp. 670–671.

[38] The reference here is to *Quazi v. Quazi* [1979] 3 All E.R. 897 and the views expressed by Lord Ackner in a later case.

[39] McClean (1993, p. 196) assumes that a 'bare *talaq*' "would seem to be located where the husband speaks the required formula", while he makes a distinction with the Jewish divorce, which "is probably located where the document is delivered to and accepted by the wife".

4–56 In the recent case of *Berkovits v. Grinberg and another (Attorney General Intervening)* [1995] 2 All E.R. 681, the recognition of an overseas divorce by the English courts under section 46 of the Family Law Act 1986 was again an issue before the Family Division of the High Court in London. The case concerned a Jewish *get* divorce involving two Israeli nationals who had married in Israel in 1975. The husband was habitually resident and domiciled in England. In 1988, a *get* was written in London in accordance with Jewish law and was delivered to the wife in Israel, where she was domiciled and resident. This divorce was treated as effective under Israeli law. However, when the husband applied to remarry in Britain, the Registrar General took the view that the Jewish *get* was not recognised as a valid divorce under English law because the divorce proceedings had taken place partly in England and partly in Israel.

4–57 The Registrar's intervention was challenged by Dayan Berkovits in his capacity as an ecclesiastical judge for the Federation of Synagogues. In this test case of considerable importance, Wall J. held that an overseas divorce would be treated as valid under section 46 of the Family Law Act 1986 if it had been obtained by means of one set of proceedings instituted in the same country as that in which the divorce was ultimately obtained. Given the facts of the case, the *get* was not entitled to recognition as a valid overseas divorce under section 46 of the Act, although it was effective as a divorce decree under Israeli law.

4–58 This decision followed *Fatima v. Secretary of State for the Home Department* [1986] 2 All E.R. 32. The learned judge found that the 1986 Act has not altered the law. In what appears to be a technically correct decision in terms of statutory interpretation, it was therefore held that a transnational divorce is not entitled to recognition by English law. The case contains an excellent discussion of the procedures for effecting a *get* divorce and clearly distinguishes these from *talaq* divorces, though it does not go into detail on the latter.

4–59 In his closing comments, Wall J. pointed to the fact that the decision in *Berkovits* has not resolved this difficult and complex matter and that there is a need for Parliament to act again.[40] It remains unsatisfactory that limping marriages are being created by the law itself. This, said the learned judge finally, can of course be remedied simply by recourse on the part of the spouses to the provisions of the domestic English divorce law. The message to members of ethnic minority communities in Britain has once again clearly been given: Learn to use the relevant provisions of English law; worry about the aspects of your respective overseas law later. Undoubtedly, it will take time for such legal messages to filter through.

4–60 In general, under section 51(3)(c) of the 1986 Act, judges have at their disposal discretionary grounds to refuse recognition on public policy grounds.[41] As Pilkington (1988, pp. 137–138) has clearly shown, the objections to the use of transnational divorces appeared to relate to some extent to their unilateral nature. In other words, the 'bare *talaq*' was and is considered unacceptable because it does not allow the other party, in most cases the wife,[42] any real say in the matter. However, it is argued that this is hypocritical, since the effect of modern English divorce law has actually been to facilitate unilateral repudiation of the marital tie, so that "since the Divorce Reform Act 1969, it has been possible to achieve precisely

---

[40] *Berkovits v. Grinberg and another (Attorney-General Intervening)* [1995] 2 All E.R. 681, at p. 696.
[41] See in detail Gordon (1988), pp. 120–148. For an example of this negative approach see *Zaal v. Zaal* [1983] 4 F.L.R. 284.
[42] However, in Pakistani law, following the important case of *Khurshid Bibi* P.L.D. 1967 S.C. 97, Muslim wives can divorce the husband unilaterally, either under the Dissolution of Muslim Marriages Act 1939 or by using s.8 of the MFLO 1961, under which there is now a huge case law. For details see para. 9–82, below.

this result by judicial process in England" (Pilkington (1988), p. 138). There is now little to distinguish the old 'bare *talaq*' and the supposedly modern breakdown principle, and some English judges appear to be aware of this.

4-61 With added force, an English court might invoke the residual rule of public policy to refuse recognition to a *talaq*, whether pronounced in Pakistan or in England, by a Pakistani national domiciled in England, where his wife is a non-Muslim and where the marriage was solemnised under the provisions of the English marriage legislation. Analysis of the case law shows, however, that the overriding concern has been focused much more on financial considerations, reflecting the desire to protect the British welfare state from unwarranted expense. Pilkington (1988, p. 139) argued very perceptively that this has in fact been the most powerful argument against easy recognition of *talaq* divorces in any form:

> "The concern is therefore that a husband may be able to evade an obligation placed upon him by English matrimonial law and leave his wife destitute to be supported by the British taxpayer. Financial provision for the wife is at the heart of the matter . . ."

4-62 Today, following important recent pro-women developments in the laws of post-divorce maintenance in the subcontinent,[43] and under Part III of the Matrimonial and Family Proceedings Act 1984 in England, Muslim women are, at least officially, much better protected by modern state laws than in the recent past.[44] Many of the cases considered above arose because of the husband's attempt to prevent the wife from seeking financial relief in England. The enactment of Part III of the Matrimonial and Family Proceedings Act 1984 has removed some of the juridical advantages for a husband in that situation because an ex-wife can now, with leave, seek ancillary relief from an English court despite the fact that her marriage has come to an end and recognition of the overseas divorce has been granted.[45] This has certainly been a welcome development.

4-63 The provisions of the 1986 Act show, then, that English law at that time was not ready to take a broad view of the conflicts scenario and remained instead fixed on the desire to regulate this complex area of the law restrictively, despite clear evidence that full control over foreign and transnational divorces would be impossible to achieve. It was soon observed that this law would have limits, too, as explained by Pearl (1987c, p. 37), to the effect that "the new Act has limited the situations where nonjudicial divorces can be recognised by the law in this country. But there is no doubt that there will still be problems."

4-64 The situations referred to in this context are when the relevant overseas law states that a 'bare *talaq*' is sufficient to bring about a legally valid divorce in the overseas jurisdiction, but the party concerned uses certain procedures which are available locally. Pearl (*id.*) has highlighted this problem concerning Kashmiri Muslims, but also refers to cases from Bangladesh and to Jewish cases. In all such situations of transnational divorces, legal validity may be refused because the divorce process is deemed to fall under the restrictive provisions of section 44 of the

---

[43] See in detail Chap. 7, below. It is important to highlight here that these reforms, in India and now also in Bangladesh, seek to protect the public purse rather than women. The consequence is the same: the new laws put a definite obligation on the divorcing male spouse of whatever religion (at least in the Indian case) to provide for the divorced woman till death or remarriage.

[44] On this see North and Fawcett (1992) p. 666; MacClean (1993), pp. 208 *et seq.*; Pilkington (1988), pp. 140–141.

[45] *id.*; for further details see North and Fawcett (1992), pp. 708–718.

1986 Act.[46] Apart from entry clearance and other immigration problems (Pearl (1987b), pp. 37–38), which are inevitably going to arise, English law should perhaps be more concerned about the position of those Muslim wives who face the common scenario of being validly divorced in an overseas jurisdiction but not according to English law.

4–65 Despite lipservice to the need to avoid 'limping marriages', the 1986 Act continues a fairly restrictive regime, offending, according to some, the first principle of private international law, namely that one state should recognise the effectiveness of the laws of another state.[47] The English approach also appears to contain a deliberate message to South Asian jurisdictions to reform their law on divorces and to follow the English model of requiring a state-controlled registration system for all divorces. This could be seen as evidence of using conflict of laws provisions to put other jurisdictions under pressure to conform to certain patterns or techniques of handling conflicts. However, Pakistan's experience of the practical operation of the MFLO 1961 and the almost corresponding Bangladeshi experience do not warrant a finding that such suggestions are realistic. It is even more apparent that a country like India will not be in a position to introduce fully bureaucratised registration systems for marriages and divorces. Indeed, registration of marriages and divorces remains optional for most Indians today.[48] This is not going to change, since the modern states of South Asia have neither the means nor the political will to enforce a comprehensive registration system along Western lines.[49]

4–66 Also North and Fawcett (1992, pp. 664–670) show in their detailed examination of the position of extra-judicial divorces that, while the Law Commissions had taken a more liberal approach to the recognition of various forms of extra-judicial divorces, the 1986 Act retained a quite restrictive approach towards informal divorces which do not involve specific judicial proceedings. Significantly, these learned authors, too, find these arguments not wholly convincing (North and Fawcett (1992), p. 666). It appears that the refusal to grant recognition to 'bare *talaq*' divorces will remain problematic, given that Indian law, and now also Pakistani and Bangladeshi law in most circumstances, accept the full legal validity of such divorces. The problem of 'limping marriages' will simply not go away.

4–67 In the light of Pilkington's analysis, however flawed by the incomplete understanding of the implications of *talaq* divorces, but also following the decision in *Berkovits v. Grinberg* [1995] 2 All E.R. 681, new arguments can be developed for why transnational divorces in any form should in fact be granted judicial recognition by the English courts. Following our discussions in Chapter 3, above, an important point to emphasise here is perhaps that this should happen not in explicit reaction to Muslim demands for separate legal regulation but as a matter of uniform English legal policy, *i.e.* under the umbrella of a uniform family law which is phrased in such a way that it allows members of different communities to be protected by one and the same law rather than different legal regimes. To achieve that result, draftsmen of parliamentary legislation will probably need to be more sensitive to the legal needs arising in Britain's new multicultural environment. Significantly, Wall J. in *Berkovits* [1995] 2 All E.R. 681, at 696, said just that:

---

[46] The decision in *Berkovits v. Grinberg*, discussed above, has of course confirmed this view.

[47] On 'comity' see Hamilton (1995), pp. 101–102.

[48] While Indian Muslim law remains *shari'a* law, thus formally extra-judicial, the secular Special Marriage Act 1954 insists on compulsory registration of marriages and divorces. However, that Act is, for most Indians, an optional uniform civil code, used by very few people indeed.

[49] Before readers assume an element of backwardness or lack of development here, a reminder that English law has not been successful in its endeavour to enforce full registration may be in order. The law clearly faces limits here, as discussed by Allott, *The limits of law* (1980), pp. 259–286.

"Accordingly, the question as to whether or not in an increasingly multi-racial and multi-ethnic society the refusal to recognise the transnational divorce can or should continue is a matter for Parliament and should not influence my interpretation of the statute."

In the present debate, we have not yet raised another important practical aspect of conflicts of laws, namely the discussion about limping marriages as it relates to religious divorces. The issue here is whether a modern Western state law should also concern itself with dissolution of the religious element of Muslim (and Jewish) marriages, rather than just concentrating on the secular, legal processes of divorce. A brief affirmative answer to this question is given in the section immediately below, which considers the potentially beneficial impact of Britain's most recent family law legislation in this respect.[50]

The potential of the Family Law Act 1996

4–68   The latest English legislation on the process of divorcing may have begun to move a little further towards a better understanding of the socio-legal needs of certain ethnic minority communities (see Hoggett *et al.* (1996), pp. 248 *et seq.*). The 1996 Act is not yet in force and is being tested first in a pilot project in certain areas of the country (Hoggett *et al.* (1996), p. 259). The relevant provisions of this Act are as follows:

> "9.–(1) The requirements as to the parties' arrangements for the future are as follows.
>
> (2) One of the following must be produced to the court –
> - (a) a court order (made by consent or otherwise) dealing with their financial arrangements;
> - (b) a negotiated agreement as to their financial arrangements;
> - (c) a declaration by both parties that they have made their financial arrangements;
> - (d) a declaration by one of the parties (to which no objection has been notified to the court by the other party) that –
>   - (i) he has no significant assets and does not intend to make an application for financial provision;
>   - (ii) he believes that the other party has no significant assets and does not intend to make an application for financial provision; and
>   - (iii) there are therefore no financial arrangements to be made.
>
> (3) If the parties –
> - (a) were married to each other in accordance with usages of a kind mentioned in section 26(1) of the Marriage Act 1949 (marriages which may be solemnized on authority of superintendent registrar's certificate), and
> - (b) are required to co-operate if the marriage is to be dissolved in accordance with those usages, the court may, on the application of either party, direct that there must also be produced to the court a declaration by both parties that they have taken such steps as are required to dissolve the marriage in accordance with those usages.

---

[50] This subject has also been vigorously debated in North America. For some details see Hamilton (1995). A number of recent publications from the Law Society of Upper Canada focus on this topic; lack of space prohibits further detail at this point.

(4) A direction under subsection (3) –

    (a) may be given only if the court is satisfied that in all the circumstances of the case it is just and reasonable to give it; and

    (b) may be revoked by the court at any time.

(5) The requirements of section 11 must have been satisfied.

(6) Schedule I supplements the provisions of this section.

(7) If the court is satisfied, on an application made by one of the parties after the end of the period for reflection and consideration, that the circumstances of the case are –

    (a) those set out in paragraph 1 of Schedule 1,

    (b) those set out in paragraph 2 of that Schedule, or

    (c) those set out in paragraph 3 of that Schedule, or

    (d) those set out in paragraph 4 of that Schedule,

it may make a divorce order or a separation order even though the requirements of subsection (2) have not been satisfied."

This must be read in the context of legislative attempts to ensure that divorce proceedings are not unduly prolonged and complicated and that situations akin to limping marriages are avoided. Significantly, section 9(3) makes a more or less explicit reference to Jewish divorces, suggesting that Jewish parties to a marriage should co-operate in the parallel termination of the religious divorce. This refers to the problem of the 'recalcitrant spouse' which arose in *Brett v. Brett*,[51] and in a more recent case.[52] Hamilton (1995, pp. 113–139) has discussed this particular issue in considerable detail and confirms that English law has been willing to recognise the legal needs of Jewish people living in the United Kingdom. Thus, the two English cases referred to here have been showing the way towards official legal acceptance of ethnic minority cultural practice. Section 9 of the Family Law Act 1996 puts this official recognition into statutory form.

4–69 Hoggett *et al.* (1996, p. 261) cite an extract from a recent article which is relevant to the present discussion. In it, Helen Conway (1995) neatly pinpoints the key issues:

"The failure of the legal system to allow a religious law influence in the dissolution of marriages has the potential to cause injustice to members of religious minorities.

A prime example of this is where a civil divorce is obtained but the Jewish Get is not forthcoming. In Jewish law a divorce can be obtained by consent without the commission of a matrimonial offence. A wife is divorced when a husband executes and delivers a Get to her, Get being the Aramaic word for a formal deed of severance.

It is only the husband who may formally initiate the divorce. There are set grounds on which parties may compel the other to either execute or accept a Get . . .

Problems occur when a civil divorce exists but one party refuses a Get. If the wife refuses to accept a Get, the husband has certain religious solutions . . . However, a wife is left in a position where she would be forbidden by religious law to contract a second Jewish marriage. Such women are known within their community as the *agunot* or 'the chained'.

. . . there is an argument to say that the English civil law ought to address this issue and offer some assistance to potential *agunot*."

---

[51] [1969] 1 All E.R. 1007. For details see Gordon (1988), pp. 46–51 and Berkovits (1990).

[52] *Berkovits v. Grinberg (Attorney-General Intervening)* [1995] 2 All E.R. 681; [1995] Fam. 142.

Precisely the same problem exists for a Muslim wife in Britain who may have obtained a divorce from an English court but whose husband refuses to release her from the Muslim marriage. As we showed in paragraph 3–94, above, the evidence that is beginning to transpire concerning Muslim wives in that situation is that they need to seek the assistance of informal, officially extra-judicial Muslim organisations which can help them out of this predicament, either by putting some pressure on the husband or by making the wife give up any financial entitlements she may have under Muslim law. Too little is known about these kinds of processes at the moment, and this particular issue is not of central concern to the present chapter, but we need to point out here that the wording of section 9 of the Family Law Act 1996 might eventually be taken to cover Muslim divorces as well. It is at least a model for the incorporation of ethnic minority practices into the statutory framework of modern English law.

South Asian perspectives on conflicts of laws

4–70 From the perspective of South Asian laws, we find first of all a reflection of the view that there is no universal system of conflict of laws rules and that "every country has its own private international law" (Diwan and Diwan (1993), p. 37). In the case of India, one of the repercussions of British rule has been a tendency to emphasise heavy reliance on English law in this respect (Diwan and Diwan (1993), p. ix). However, this has been vigorously criticised in the leading Indian textbook on the subject (Diwan and Diwan (1993), p. xvii). One senses some emphasis on national pride in an important post-colonial jurisdiction. The following passage reflects the powerful recent Indian re-assertion of judicial independence and creativeness, ultimately focused on the search for 'justice, equity and good conscience' which was so apparent in Chapter 2 above:

> "Indian courts have almost blindly, apishly, followed and adhered to English precedents. Probably in a dependent India nothing else was possible. But now after independence it is not at all necessary or logical to ape any country and follow its rules. Now we are in a position to develop the rules of private international law in accordance with the social needs and circumstances of our contemporary society and in accordance with the ideas and notions of world justice" (Diwan and Diwan (1993), p. 61).

In Indian law, too, arguments about public policy or 'public order' have been given some prominence.[53] Diwan and Diwan (1993, p. 127) provide a useful discussion of this concept:

> "It is submitted that the states have used the concept as a device under which otherwise applicable foreign law is precluded. Already there are many devices under which courts tend to apply the law of forum. The public policy is used as something like a residual head for the exclusion of application of foreign law. The stock justification for the doctrine is that no country will give effect to laws which are 'repugnant to its ideas of social justice'. Looked at in this perspective, the doctrine becomes a question of values."

---

[53] See in detail Diwan and Diwan (1993), pp. 126 *et seq.*; interestingly, Perry C.J. in the 1847 case of *Hirbae v. Sonabae* (see Perry 1853), p. 110, at 120), referred to public policy as "an unruly horse", adding the advice that "wherever public policy is a matter of controversy, a lawyer should be the last to express any opinion on it".

Going on to discuss the development of English law in this respect, the authors refer to several examples, state at page 129 that "justice and morality are subjective and relative notions" and refer to early cases in which the English courts have refused to recognise the status arising out of polygamous marriages.[54]

4–71 Similarly, Pakistani jurisprudence has been exploring its creative potential, with a definite focus on Islamic justice. However there is, as yet, no single Pakistani textbook on conflict of laws, and the subject is regrettably very much neglected in Pakistani legal education.

4–72 In the sections below, which illustrate South Asian approaches to conflicts of laws, we focus on Pakistani law, since the relevant Indian cases concern Hindu and Christian law and their details would not be relevant to the present study.

Extra-territoriality of Pakistani Muslim law: Succession

4–73 We have already seen that Muslim authors often emphasise the applicability of *shari'a* law to Muslims wherever they may be. Problems of international conflicts of laws are often posed in courts faced with questions of the recognition of a divorce or a marriage or in the case of inheritance disputes. These questions are, to a large extent, outside the scope of this book but one or two observations may be useful. An interesting case which illustrates the problem is *Yusuf Abbas v. Ismat Mustafa* P.L.D. 1968 Karachi 480. In graphic form this complex case scenario looks as follows:

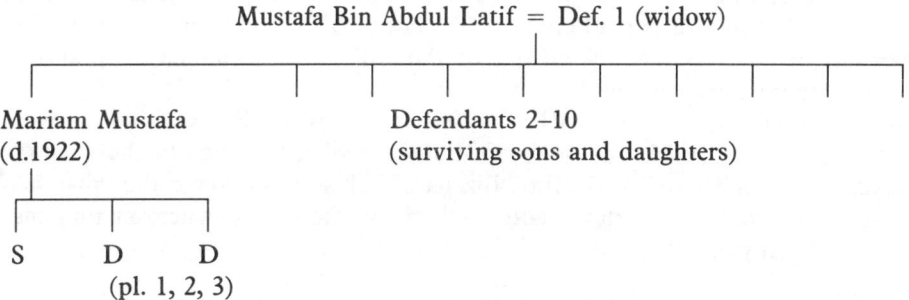

Mustafa Bin Abdul Latif = Def. 1 (widow)

Mariam Mustafa
(d.1922)

Defendants 2–10
(surviving sons and daughters)

S   D   D
(pl. 1, 2, 3)

The case arose out of a claim by the plaintiffs for shares in the assets of Mustafa Bin Abdul Latif under the provisions of section 4 of Pakistan's MFLO 1961. This section substantially amended the traditional Muslim law of Pakistan, providing the orphaned grandchild with a share of the grandfather's estate equivalent to the share the parent would have received if alive. The section reads as follows:

> "4. Succession. – In the event of the death of any son or daughter of the propositus before the opening of succession, the children of such son or daughter if any, living at the time the succession opens, shall *per stirpes* receive a share equivalent to the share which such son or daughter, as the case may be, would have received, if alive."

The defendants contested the plaintiffs' action because they denied that the plaintiffs were legitimate heirs and contended, in the alternative, that even if the plaintiffs were heirs of the deceased, then the MFLO was not applicable to the property which was the subject of this dispute.

---

[54] See Diwan and Diwan (1993): p. 130. *Ibid.*; pp. 130–131 discusses in detail how English law has changed its approach to polygamous marriages and their consequences. For further details see para. 8–91, below.

4–74   The deceased had died in 1964, holding both movable and immovable property situated in Pakistan and in the Gulf. At the time of his death, he was a national of Pakistan and was domiciled there. On the preliminary point of jurisdiction, Noorul Arfin J. held that the Court had jurisdiction under section 20 of the Civil Procedure Code 1908 to entertain an action with respect to properties situated outside Pakistan. The Judge then went on to consider the principles which should apply to the succession of the deceased's estate situated within the foreign territory. He held that Muslim law, the personal law of the deceased, does not recognise any principle of scission between movables and immovables for the purposes of succession. He then went on to make the following proposition, at page 502:

> "Thus, if a Moslim dies domiciled in England, the Courts in this Country, will apply, not *lex domicilii* but his personal law, that is Islamic law as administered in this country to succession to his movables in Pakistan. Even the will with regard to these movables, though valid in English law, will be recognised by the Courts of this country only so far as it is consistent with Islamic Law."

This suggestion represents the concept of the universal applicability of Muslim law to Muslims, wherever they may be.[55] We have already seen that this raises important issues for English lawyers today in relation to Muslims. There seems no doubt that, in Pakistan, both the movable and the immovable property of a Muslim deceased devolves on the heirs in accordance with the Muslim personal law of the deceased and no regard is paid either to the law of his domicile or to the *lex situs*. Questions of construction arising out of the will or the intestacy may also be governed by the personal law.

4–75   Section 1(2) of the MFLO 1961 provides explicitly for the extra-territoriality of the provisions of the Ordinance, which "extends to the whole of Pakistan, and applies to all Muslim citizens of Pakistan, wherever they may be." Not surprisingly, Noorul Arfin J. laid emphasis on the phrase 'wherever they may be' and held, at page 503:

> "If a Muslim citizen of Pakistan dies domiciled in a foreign country, the law of his domicile cannot, by the force of the words used in section 1(2) and 4 of the Ordinance, be applied to his estate in Pakistan. On the same principle, if a Muslim citizen dies domiciled in Pakistan and leaves property, both immovables and movables, in foreign jurisdiction, the succession to his estate will be according to the rule of Islamic law as modified by section 4 of the Ordinance. The Courts in Pakistan, in matters of succession to the estate of [a] Muslim citizen, can apply only his personal law, irrespective of the rules of the *lex domicilii* or *situs*."

In the event, the judge held that the plaintiffs had a cause of action in the suit and that the defendants were liable to render account to the plaintiffs for their share in the estate. As the deceased was held to be domiciled in Pakistan at the time of his death, the judge's comments are obiter. Nevertheless, the only limitation which the judge was prepared to accept in a case where the deceased was not domiciled in Pakistan was the effectiveness of the judgment of the Pakistani court.

---

[55] On this, the learned judge, at p. 502, cites an authoritative statement from Amir Ali: "Mussulman Law generally is a personal law; that is, its incidents remain attached to the individual Mussalman whatever the domicile, so long as [he] continues even outwardly faithful to the Islamic faith. 'Mussalman' says the Kifaya, is absolutely subject to the laws of Islam, whatever the domicile".

Extra-territoriality of the *talaq*

4–76 *Yusuf Abbas* has echoes in the position in Pakistan regarding capacity of a Pakistani Muslim to invoke the procedures of the MFLO 1961 with respect to *talaq*. The leading case in this context is *Marina Jatoi v. Nuruddin K. Jatoi*, P.L.D. 1967 S.C. 580. In May 1959, a marriage had been solemnised in a register office in London between Marina, a Christian woman domiciled in Spain, and Nuruddin K. Jatoi, then a Muslim Bar student domiciled in Pakistan. The marriage was not a happy one and within a year the husband had returned to Pakistan, while the wife and their newly born son remained in London. In March 1961 Jatoi married a second wife, a Swedish woman, who had converted to Islam. That marriage was solemnised in a mosque in Karachi in Muslim form. Meanwhile, Marina applied to the Magistrates' Court in London for maintenance under the Matrimonial Proceedings (Magistrates' Courts) Act 1960.[56] Marina obtained a maintenance order, which was then registered in Pakistan and confirmed by the Karachi District Magistrates Court.[57] The husband failed to remit any maintenance to the wife. In 1965, she travelled to Karachi with the intention of seeking enforcement. Whilst she was in the city, Jatoi repudiated his wife by *talaq*, and sent a copy of the *talaqnama* to the chairman of his local Union Council as required by section 7(1) of the MFLO. After the requisite 90 days, Mr Jatoi applied to the District Court for rescission of the English maintenance order on the ground that he was no longer married to Marina. In doing so, he relied on juristic interpretations of Muslim law, according to which a Muslim husband is not obliged to maintain an ex-wife beyond a three month period, known as the *iddat* period, after the *talaq* has become irrevocable.[58] The District Court refused to rescind the registration of the order, but on appeal to the High Court of West Pakistan the ruling of the lower court was reversed. Marina then appealed to the Supreme Court of Pakistan. Her appeal was rejected by the majority, Yaqub Ali J. dissenting. The majority took the view that the *talaq* was effective to dissolve the marriage between Marina and Jatoi. Pakistani law was applied as the *lex domicilii*. Mr Justice S. A. Rahman held in this regard, at page 599:

> "Under the rules of Private International law, the *lex loci celebrationis*, as such has nothing to do with the question of divorce which is a matter solely for the law that happens to be the *lex domicilii* of the parties, at the time of the suit. This may very well be different from the law that governed the solemnisation of the marriage."[59]

4–77 Faced with the possibility of an internal conflict between the Muslim law, the personal law of the husband in this case, and the provisions of the Indian Divorce Act 1869 (since the marriage was celebrated under the English Marriage Act 1949 and the wife was at all times a Christian), the majority clearly chose to apply the Muslim law of Pakistan. There is no provision in the Divorce Act 1869 or the Christian Marriage Act 1872, said the majority, which, in express terms, prevents a Muslim husband of a Christian woman from having resort to his own personal law for the purpose of the dissolution of marriage. S. A. Rahman J. said in this regard, at page 602:

---

[56] This Act was subsequently replaced by the Domestic Proceedings (Magistrates Courts) Act 1978.
[57] This was done under the Maintenance Orders (Facilities for Enforcement) Act 1920. The Maintenance Orders Enforcement Act 1921 is in force in Pakistan.
[58] Today, this position is increasingly under scrutiny. For details see below, Chap. 7.
[59] See in this respect the English cases of *Har-Shefi v. Har-Shefi* [1953] 2 All E.R. 373 and *Qureshi v. Qureshi* [1972] Fam. 173.

"If a Muslim husband is married to a Christian woman in a form recognised by
Muslim law, or to a non-citizen Muslim woman, there is no reason why the
provisions of section 7 of this Ordinance, should not apply, if he wants to
divorce his wife by *talaq*."

The majority took the view that the Jatoi marriage, which had been solemnised in a
London register office, would be recognised in Muslim law because the declaration
and the acceptance by the couple at one and the same meeting in the presence of
witnesses complied with the minimum formalities under Hanafi Muslim law.
Yaqub Ali J., dissenting, interpreted the relevant statutes in a different way. He
rejected the argument accepted by the majority that section 2 of the Divorce Act
1869 is an enabling Act.[60] The dissenting judge stated, at p. 592:

"The language . . . has, therefore, to be construed in the sense that if one of the
parties to the marriage professes the Christian faith the marriage can be
dissolved only by a decree of the Court under the Act and not otherwise. A
contrary view would lead to anomalous results, such as, if a Muslim husband
petitions to Court under the Divorce Act for dissolution of his marriage with a
Christian wife he shall have to prove to the satisfaction of the Court that she
has been guilty of adultery and shall also be obliged to pay to her alimony
pendente lite and costs of the suit as well as permanent alimony on obtaining a
decree for dissolution. On the contrary if the Muslim law applies he can avoid
all these obligations by pronouncing *talaq* and bringing to an end the marriage
by his unilateral act. No husband would, therefore, ever make resort to a Court
for dissolution of marriage."

The dissenting judge also rejected the argument, advanced by the majority, that
there are no specific ceremonies or rites for solemnising a marriage under Muslim
law and therefore the register office marriage in England can necessarily be equated
with a Muslim ceremony. In the judge's opinion, the Christian and the Muslim
marriage are essentially different types of status, one a voluntary union for life
dissoluble only by a judicial decree, and the other a potentially polygamous
marriage dissoluble on the unilateral declaration of the husband.

4–78 One could argue that the distinction suggested by Yaqub Ali J. confuses
the concept of a status of marriage with the incidents of that status. The judge
might have been on stronger ground if he had simply recognised that an English
civil ceremony of marriage possesses attributes within it of a Muslim marriage valid
by Muslim law, but that so long as the wife retained her personal law, and so long
as she had not married in an outwardly Muslim ceremony, her vested rights must
be protected by the Divorce Act 1869.

4–79 Another question can be posed. Supposing Marina had petitioned for a
divorce in Pakistan. Presumably, the courts would have assumed jurisdiction under
section 2 of the Divorce Act 1869 rather than the Dissolution of Muslim Marriages
Act 1939. Marina was not 'a woman married *under* Muslim law'.[61] It is slightly

---

[60] s.2 of the 1869 Act reads: "Nothing hereinafter contained shall authorise any court to grant any relief
under this Act except where the petitioner or respondent professes the Christian religion." This is the
amended version of the Act. As originally enacted, the Indian Divorce Act 1869 gave the court
jurisdiction only where the petitioner professed the Christian religion. The words "or respondent" were
added by s.2 of Act XXX of 1927. For Bangladesh, Ordinance XVIII of 1969 has altered and clarified the
position so far as that state is concerned. A proviso added to s.2 of the Divorce Act in that country states:
"Provided that nothing in this paragraph shall be deemed to authorise any Court to grant relief under
this Act where the petitioner or the respondent is a Muslim".
[61] The majority state that a register office marriage is *recognised* by Muslim law as a Muslim marriage.
Even so, there would appear to be a difference, even by the majority argument, between a marriage *under*
Muslim law and a marriage *recognised* by Muslim law as a Muslim marriage. See S. A. Rahman J. at
p. 602.

inequitable to permit the husband the choice between Muslim law and the Divorce Act, when the wife is denied this choice. The majority decision can only be explained in terms of the public policy of an Islamic state, thus as early evidence of a tendency in Pakistan to islamise the legal system and to give predominant consideration to Muslim law in cases where there is a potential conflict.

4–80 Earlier cases, all cited in *Jatoi v. Jatoi*, actually support the dissenting judgment.[62] In the first of those cases, an Indian Christian (Dukhiram) had married a Christian girl (Sudakshina) under the Indian Christian Marriage Act 1872. Subsequently, the husband converted to Islam and contracted a second marriage in a mosque with a Muslim woman. The Court had to decide whether the second marriage was valid, but in the course of the judgment, Henderson J. said: "It might be difficult to say whether Dukhiram could have divorced Sudakshina by *talaq*."[63]

4–81 In *Farooq Leivers v. Adelaide Bridget Mary*, P.L.D. 1958 (W.P.) Lahore 431, the husband and wife were Christians who had married according to Christian rites. Many years later the husband embraced Islam, asked his wife to join him in his new faith and, on her refusal, purported to divorce her by *talaq*. The suit arose out of an application by the husband seeking a declaration that he was no longer married to his Christian wife. Changez J., in the Lahore High Court, refused to grant the husband such a declaration and said, at p. 447:

> ". . . the position that emerges is that on the one hand under the Muslim law, a Christian husband, on his conversion to Islam, is authorised to give *talak* to his Christian wife by pronouncing the formula of *talak*, but on the other hand, the Courts in Pakistan cannot recognise such a *talak* in view of the provisions of the Divorce Act of 1869 and other existing laws. In such a conflict of the personal law of the parties to the suit, there does not appear to be any justification to prefer the personal law of the plaintiff than to the personal law of the respondent. The essential function of adjudication is to decide only according to law between the conflicting claims."

In view of this conflict, the judge applied section 6 of the Punjab Laws Act 1872 which enabled him to solve the conflict according to the principles of justice, equity and good conscience. According to the application of this principle, the *talaq* could not be recognised in the Pakistani courts. Almost a decade later, Yaqub Ali J. in *Jatoi*, of course, held that he was bound by the substantive law itself which created a statutory choice of law rule, as it were, in section 2 of the Divorce Act 1869.

4–82 In the important Pakistani Supreme Court decision of *Ali Nawaz Gardezi v. Muhammad Yusuf*, P.L.D. 1963 S.C. 51, Rahman J. stated that the Christian wife had been fully aware of the position that the marriage celebrated in an English register office could not be dissolved by the Muslim husband's pronouncement of *talaq* unless she herself converted to Islam. Reference may also be made to the Ceylonese case of *Attorney General for Ceylon v. Reid*, where counsel for the appellant-husband admitted that "a person who has embraced Islam [cannot] unilaterally succeed in divorcing the former wife by going through the procedures which are recognised in Muslim marriages."[64]

---

[62] For details see *(John Jiban) Chandra Datta v. Abinash Chandra Sen* I.L.R. [1939] 2 Cal. 12; *Farooq Leivers v. Adelaide Bridget Mary*, P.L.D. 1958 (W.P.) Lah. 431; *Ali Nawaz Gardezi v. Muhammad Yusuf* P.L.D. 1963 S.C. 51. See also *Keolapati v. Harnam Singh* I.L.R. [1937] 12 Luck. 568; *Budansa Rowther v. Fatma Bi* (1914) [26] M.L.J. 260; *Sainapatti v. Sainapatti* A.I.R. (1932) Lah. 116.

[63] *(John Jiban) Chandra Datta v. Abinash Chandra Sen*, I.L.R. [1939] 2 Cal. 12 at 16.

[64] [1965] A.C. 720 at 728. See also *Abdoolie Drammeh v. Joyce Drammeh*, [1970] *Journal of African Law*, 150.

4–83 If both parties to a Christian marriage convert to Islam, there is no objection to applying the Muslim law of divorce. Indeed, section 2 of the Divorce Act 1869 is couched in such terms that this Act would no longer be available to either of the parties. The non-application of the Divorce Act is aknowledged by *Khambatta v. Khambatta* 1935 I.L.R. 59 Bom. 278. Section 7 of that Act, however, as amended by section 2 of the amending Act of 1912, provides the court with jurisdiction if the facts upon which the claim to relief is founded occurred at a time when both parties were Christians.

4–84 The legal position in India is affected by the Foreign Marriage Act of 1969 (Act No. 33 of 1969). A decision from Bombay, *Abdur Rahim Undre v. Padma Abdur Rahim Undre*, A.I.R. 1982 Bom. 341, illustrates the problems associated with that Act, which applies potentially to all marriages solemnised outside India when one of the parties to the marriage is an Indian citizen. If a marriage is registered or solemnised under that Act, then it can only be dissolved under its terms, *i.e.* on judicial application in accordance with section 18(1) of the 1969 Act. If a marriage is not solemnised or registered under the terms of the Act, then the provisions on dissolution do not apply. However, section 18(4) of the 1969 Act is a particularly cryptic provision:

> "Nothing contained in sub-section (1), shall authorise any Court to grant any relief under this Act in relation to any marriage in a foreign country not solemnized under it, if the grant of relief in respect of such marriage whether on any of the grounds specified in the Special Marriage Act 1954 (43 of 1954), or otherwise is provided for under any other law for the time being in force."

It was this provision which arose for interpretation in *Abdur Rahim Undre v. Padma Abdur Rahim Undre* A.I.R. 1982 Bom. 341, where the parties, both Indian citizens, had married in the United Kingdom in a register office in 1966. The plaintiff-husband was a Muslim, whereas his wife was a Hindu. The court found as a fact that at the time of the marriage both parties were domiciled in India. The parties returned to India in 1969. The husband, in his evidence, stated that the wife had converted to Islam on December 29, 1969 and that a subsequent *nikah* ceremony had been performed. Relations between the two then deteriorated, and the husband's allegation was that on April 20, 1978 he divorced his wife by *talaq*, after which the husband attempted to restrain the wife from entering the matrimonial apartment. He brought proceedings for a permanent injunction, together with an application for a declaration that the lady was no longer his wife. He argued also that even on the assumption that she had not embraced Islam and had remained a Hindu, nonetheless the Muslim personal law was applicable to their relationship, and thus he was entitled to divorce his wife by *talaq*.

4–85 The defendant-wife denied that any conversion had taken place and also denied the facts relating to the *nikah* ceremony. Indeed, she even put in issue the *talaq* pronouncement itself. At first instance, the trial judge decided that the law which governed the parties to this marriage was the Special Marriage Act 1954 read with the Foreign Marriage Act 1969. On the contested facts relating to the conversion, the *nikah*, and the *talaq*, the trial judge decided in favour of the defendant-wife. Both suits were dismissed and the husband appealed. This appeal was dismissed and a further appeal was taken by way of Letters Patent to a bench of two judges.

4–86 This appellate court decided, first, that the marriage solemnised in 1966 in England was a valid marriage recognised as such by Indian law, notwithstanding that the wife was a Hindu and the husband was a Muslim at that time. Secondly, the judges went on to consider the question whether the effect of section 18(4) of the Foreign Marriage Act 1969 was to exclude from the operation of that Act marriages where the husband was of the Muslim faith. The court rejected this view at page 352:

> "The Shariat Act or the Shariat Act read with Muslim personal law cannot be said to be the law in force contemplated by Section 18(4) of the Foreign Marriage Act."

The court decided therefore that the courts below had been correct in concluding that the marriage in this case was governed by the Foreign Marriage Act 1969 and could be dissolved only under its terms. As to the questions of fact, the court upheld the findings of the courts below. There was no evidence to sustain the contention that the defendant had converted to Islam or that a *nikah* had been performed. But even if the facts had been otherwise and the court had decided that the wife had actually converted to Islam and that a religious ceremony of marriage had been performed, the court would still have held that the Special Marriage Act 1954 would have been the applicable legislation governing the dissolution of this marriage. One doubts whether the court in those circumstances would have followed *Khambatta v. Khambatta* [1935] I.L.R. 59 Bom. 278. Although the court did not consider that case, it is implicit in the judgment that *Khambatta* is not relevant in the context of a foreign marriage in civil form.

4–87 The decision has been subjected to some criticism. For instance, Neeru Sehgal (1982, p. 309) concluded in her study of civil and religious marriages:

> "Parties who are Indians may be in some western country for a short or temporary period. Their *lex domicilii*, we submit, must be their personal law and when they come back to India and go through a religious ceremony it should be taken as a manifestation of their intention to be governed by their personal law. In such a case the first civil ceremony should not be allowed to govern the nature of the marriage for ever, as they had no choice but to undergo that form of marriage. It would be patently unfair to impose upon them a form of marriage in respect of which they had no choice and to prevent them from changing its nature by undergoing a subsequent religious ceremony."

This comment raises the question of unfair discrimination against spouses who had no option but to undergo a secular marriage ceremony after they had moved outside India. However, Sehgal overlooks the fact that there may also have been a religious marriage, albeit not in *Undre v. Undre*, raising the issue of the official non-recognition of what in Britain today would be called 'ethnic minority customs'. In South Asia, obviously, such diversity would be treated differently because of the different basic structure of South Asian legal systems, which has given rise to particular forms of conflict of laws, which we discuss below.

Interpersonal conflict of laws

4–88 Interpersonal conflict of laws has an even older pedigree than private international law. It was known to the ancient Greeks and to the Romans. It is of course also an ancient and well-known system in South Asia, where various personal law systems have co-existed for many centuries (see p. 31, above).

4–89 As a separate branch of legal science, it survived the fundamental changes in European society of the early Middle Ages. A eurocentric focus today may lead textbook writers to the wrong assumption that personal law systems are now more or less a thing of the past.[65] While it remains correct to say that "the system of personal laws gradually disappeared from the European scene to be replaced by the territorial concepts of law" (Pearl (1981a), pp. 16–17), this observation would not be true for many non-European legal systems. Pearl (1981a, p. 23) emphasises that the Muslim experience involves study of the personal law. In addition, we see today that international migration and the pluralising side-effects of globalisation put pressures on European legal systems to recognise Muslim law under the guise of different conflict of law concepts. As we shall see in the following sub-section, this process today has to take more explicit account of personal law systems.

4–90   As to the question what is a personal law, for South Asian legal systems as well as Muslim law, the dominant criterion in this respect appears to be religion. The laws of sovereign nation states may also, however, employ racial, religious or tribal criteria,[66] or they may rely on a different category of connecting factors, such as nationality, domicile and residence.

4–91   In this context, Pearl (1978a; 1981a) made various distinctions. First of all, conflicts within the laws of the first three groups, which can be classified as interpersonal conflict of laws within one class, in other words, conflicts between different personal laws in one and the same state. In contrast, conflicts between the law of the first class (race, religion or tribe) and laws of the second class (that is nationality, domicile or residence) can be classified as interpersonal conflict of laws between two classes. In other words, they are conflicts between a personal law and the general law within one and the same state. It needs to be emphasised that the second category contains problems of interpersonal conflict of laws. Thus, despite the apparent territorial connection, we are not concerned with international conflict of laws proper, but with interpersonal conflict of laws. To use another expression, the interpersonal conflict of laws between two classes are nonetheless 'internally mixed' questions as opposed to 'internationally mixed' questions.[67]

4–92   Problems of interpersonal conflict of laws between two classes have already been considered in Chapter 2. Problems of interpersonal conflict of laws within one class have arisen in connection with the discussion of the rules of apostacy and conversion and the effects of these rules on a pre-existing marriage. Interpersonal conflicts within one class arise on the subcontinent because the operation of a personal system of law creates a situation where advantage can sometimes be taken of a more sympathetic legal solution by one rather than another personal law. In particular, there may be a temptation for an unhappily married spouse to change his or her religious persuasion and thus invoke certain procedures for bringing the union to an end, which may not have been available if the status quo had been maintained. Although our discussion is largely confined to cases involving Muslims, it is as well to remember that interpersonal conflict situations of a similar kind arise whenever two persons to a marriage allege that they are governed by different personal laws. Such problems were supposed to be avoided in India if there was a marriage solemnised under the terms of the Special Marriage Act 1954 or if there had been a marriage in religious form which was subsequently registered under that Act. However, registration of a marriage under a secular law does not make the religious element non-existent; it creates a variant form of legal pluralism. The issue is not new to Western authors. Graveson (1974, p. 4) wrote:

---

[65] See, *e.g.* North and Fawcett (1992), p. 16.
[66] Today, it would appear that ethnicity is becoming a more prominent, if complex, distinguishing criterion. We have already explored this in Chap. 3, above.
[67] For further details see Pearl (1981a), pp. 1–26.

"The personal religious law of oriental countries transcends national or territorial legal frontiers, for it is based on the identity of law and religion in certain fields, most notably in family law and succession."

Stating that such personal religious laws rarely raise questions of conflict of laws for any English court except the Privy Council, Graveson (1974, p. 4, note 3) interestingly pointed to the existence of some early cases in England, especially *Mehta v. Mehta* [1945] 2 All E.R. 690, a nullity case, and several cases on polygamy. Several decades later, we know that there has been a considerable number of such cases, many of which have raised complex questions about various forms of conflict of laws. Generally speaking, Western legal systems have continued to struggle with the official recognition of non-state law and have sometimes had specific problems with Muslim law.

4-93   We return, finally, to one particular scenario of conflict which has arisen as a result of the fairly recent migration of Muslims and other 'ethnic minorities' to Western countries. This scenario involves conflicts between the official laws of the receiving states and the personal laws of the country of origin, which the receiving state may not officially recognise as 'law'. Focusing on the example of the United Kingdom and South Asian Muslims, we recognise that many other jurisdictions experience similar conflicts which remain incompletely understood and deserve further scholarly and legal attention.

Official law v. unofficial law

4-94   In legal disputes involving Muslims with a South Asian domicile or residence, or in cases where particular actions have taken place in a South Asian country, but are now litigated before the British courts, English law purports to apply standard conflict of laws rules, using complex concepts like residence, domicile and nationality. However, the use of such criteria sometimes fails to produce acceptable and just solutions in relation to the growing number of British Muslims resident and domiciled in the United Kingdom who are British citizens and yet, for one reason or another, have not followed the rules of English law. The reason for this is, in essence, that the law tends to be 'culture-blind', thus denying that a dispute involving British Muslims in Britain has a foreign or 'ethnic' element.

4-95   It appears, then, that the prevailing assimilationist approach has been used to deny legal recognition to what British Muslims do in Britain, rather than to accept their cultural patterns of life as evidence of operative legal norms. The official message to Muslims and other ethnic minorities has been outlined earlier: If you live in England, you must follow English law; being Muslim is a matter of religion, of belief, rather than of legally relevant practice. We have already seen that, from a Muslim perspective, this division of the legal and non-legal spheres does not make sense.

4-96   Apart from conflicts about different conceptualisations of law and religion, Western legal systems today refuse to recognise 'ethnic minority' legal issues and the resulting conflicts, while they remain more open to arguments that new conflicts arising in the majority communities should be addressed. To take one prominent example, modern English law increasingly makes allowances for cohabiting couples who have not formally married, while refusing to accord meaningful legal recognition as spouses to Muslim individuals who have undergone only a *nikah* in Britain. This raises the question whether English law should not at least consider recognising some form of 'multicultural cohabitation' to take account of Muslim law and practice in Britain in this regard. Similarly, it is significant that in 1991 the English judiciary refused to consider extension of the offence of blasphemy to protect the faith of Muslims (*R. v. Chief Metropolitan Stipendiary Magistrate, ex p. Choudhury* [1991] 1 All E.R. 306), *inter alia* on the ground that this would mean judicial creation of a new offence.[68]

4–97 Such examples show clearly that modern English law is willing, albeit reluctantly, to take account of new socio-legal patterns and conflict situations arising within the majority community. However, when it comes to the legal recognition of ethnic minority customs, the law displays symptoms of reluctance, even hostility, and it may take a long time to overcome these.[69] Newcomers to the territory of a legal system, new ethnic minorities as a result of migration movements, appear to experience particularly apparent conflicts in cases of religious difference and cultural distance. The strategy of non-recognition of ethnic minority concerns as an initial reaction on the part of the official legal system to newcomers may eventually give rise to specific forms of legal organisation of 'the other', as the phenomenon of *angrezi shariat* shows.

4–98 In the present context, there is pressure on the English legal system to take legal cognisance of the fact that a Muslim *nikah* is treated by Muslims anywhere in the world as a structural and functional equivalent of a state-endorsed, legally valid marriage. The same could be said about *talaq* divorces. However, accepting the *nikah* or the *talaq* as a valid legal concept in English law could imply that English law has switched into the mode of concurrent personal laws, rather like non-European legal systems. It remains difficult to envisage this, and more complicated to accept this for only one particular community rather than all 'ethnic minority' communities.

4–99 In social reality, as shown in paragraph 3–78, above, British Muslims have *suo moto* begun to harmonise conflicting elements of English law and Muslim law. In the perception of Muslims themselves, the new hybrids appear as a form of Muslim law, in this case *angrezi shariat*. If modern English law wants to be constructively involved in this process of harmonising potentially conflicting systems of legal regulation among minority communities in diaspora, one needs to retain an open mind about the nature of legal conflicts and, ultimately, about the nature and purposes of law itself.

4–100 While there appears to be much scope for harmonious reconstruction and co-existence, the potential for conflict is often overstated by both sides. The norms and values of Islam are often simplistically portrayed as conflicting head-on with the standards and perceptions of Western civilisation. Islamic rules relating to marriage, divorce and polygamy, in particular, are often in sweeping fashion regarded as completely contrary to the principles of Western law and undeserving of legal recognition. Some Muslims use similarly antagonistic strategies, pitting the concept of the God-given legal system against the man-made constructs of Western laws (see King (1995)). Another strategy, increasingly prominent at present, is to declare Muslim law and other non-Western systems of law as inherently violative of international principles, a charge which is now almost ritually answered by assertions that Islam stands for justice and protection of human rights.

---

[68] However, in the very same year the House of Lords forcefully overrode reservations of the Law Commission and created the new offence of marital rape (*R. v. R. (Rape: Marital Exemption)* [1991] 4 All E.R. 481. See Hayes and Williams, *Family law. Principles, policy and practice* (1995), pp. 306–307. This not only shows that judicial law-making is possible in English law but that the social need for change has to be present first.

[69] See on this the excellent study of Carolyn Hamilton (1995), with numerous examples from English and U.S. law and specific focus on the legal position of Jews.

4-101 The policy of the English legal system towards official recognition of Muslim law has evidently been inconsistent and somewhat uncoordinated. Responses have very much depended on the nature of the particular rule or conflict in question. It is apparent that much more work needs to be done in this field. Some unresolved conflicts are not healthy and may lead to unnecessary tensions. If English law wishes to retain overall control of the broad social field within which multicultural Britain and its legal system are evolving, lawyers and policy makers need to take more account of the perceived socio-legal needs and concepts of minority communities such as the Muslims.

Part II

The substantive law

Chapter 5

Application of Muslim law

5–01 In this chapter, a new element in the present edition, we focus on the question of Muslim identity and the application of Muslim law. In legal practice, this issue is unlikely to cause many difficulties but there are certain issues which warrant some scrutiny because there sometimes may be room for arguing whether a particular person is a Muslim or not and, more so, whether Muslim law should be applied to a dispute or not.

5–02 We consider first how a Muslim is defined, starting from the classical position, then moving to the more complex South Asian legal scenario. It is evident that in South Asian laws there have been important debates about Muslim identity and the application of Muslim law. These are briefly retraced in the second subsection. Finally, we take a brief look at the question of application of Muslim law to Muslims in Britain today.

Definition of a Muslim

5–03 The definition of a Muslim is more a matter of religion than of law. Lawyers will find that many textbooks on Muslim law do not pay close and direct attention to this issue.[1] This does not mean, however, that the matter is clear and requires no comment. Rather it is perhaps a question of different agenda and of authors' preferences for certain topics. Legal textbooks tend to focus immediately on the various sources of law, the history of Islam, and the development of Islamic law.[2] Especially outside the Middle Eastern heartland of Muslim law, there has been much focus on exploring and clarifying the position of Muslim law, as well as emphasis on ascertaining the status of individuals as Muslims.[3] There are few studies which place our present topic in a prominent place. A good example of this approach is a leading Indian textbook written by a non-Muslim (Diwan (1977); Diwan and Diwan (1991)).

5–04 It appears that Middle Eastern authors are less concerned about this question than writers on South Asian laws. One major reason for this could be that there are so many different sects and groups of converted Muslims in the subcontinent who fall under the label of 'Muslim' but follow particular local or regional traditions, raising critical questions about Muslim identity. Some of these questions have already arisen in Part I of this book – are Ismaili Khojas in India governed by Hindu succession law? Are South Indian Mapillas to be treated in law as Muslims, or are their legal transactions covered by Hindu customs? More difficult, and politically explosive, as we saw, remains the question whether Ahmadis or Quadianis are Muslims or not.

---

[1] Nasir (1990a) discusses personal status in the Arab states in Chap. 2 (pp. 29–40) but does not find it necessary to define 'Muslim'. Nasir (1990b) also makes no attempt at definition and focuses only on the substantive law with reference to women.

[2] For an example see Tayyibji, *Muslim law. The personal law of Muslims in India and Pakistan* (1968); Fyzee (1974) focuses much on Muslim history.

[3] The various editions of *Mulla's Principles of Mahomedan law* (Hidayatullah and Hidayatullah (1977)) for India, Mannan (1990) for Pakistan devote much space to the applicability of Muslim law.

5–05   Questions of religion, politics and law become, thus, intermingled in this field of enquiry. It is useful to turn to some non-legal writing to obtain a broader perspective. The chapter on Islam in the *Penguin Handbook of Living Religions* represents a good starting point. The introduction lays out the complexity of the question:

> "For Muslims Islam has been from the beginning much more than what is usually meant by the Western concept 'religion'. Islam, meaning in Arabic 'submission (to God)', is at the same time a religious tradition, a civilization and, as Muslims are fond of saying, a 'total way of life'. Islam proclaims a religious faith and sets forth certain rituals, but it also prescribes patterns of order for society in such matters as family life, civil and criminal law, business, etiquette, food, dress and even personal hygiene. The Western distinction between the sacred and the secular is thus foreign to traditional Islam. In the Muslim view there are few if any aspects of individual and social life that are not considered to be expressions of Islam, which is seen as a complete, complex civilization in which individuals, societies and governments should all reflect the will of God." (Welch (1984), p. 123.)

The same author rightly emphasises that "the task of understanding Islam is immense" (Welch (1984), p. 125) and pinpoints later the critical issue of the existence of many different groups within the Muslim community.[4] A recent edition of a Muslim law textbook from India indicates that "there is a lot of difference between the viewpoint of law courts and theologians" (Bharatiya (1996), p. 41).

5–06   Regarding definition, a combination of belief and of practice indicates whether a particular person is a Muslim or not, with much obvious potential for conflict.[5] With regard to belief, the key element has been expressed in various ways. Many studies emphasise that the essence of an individual's commitment to Islam is found in the *shahada*, the express declaration of belief in the unity and authority of Allah and the eminent position of the prophet Mohammed (see *e.g.* Mannan (1990), p. 21). Some studies list three basic theological positions:[6] (i) belief in the prophethood of Muhammad[7]; (ii) belief in God *and* the Prophet Muhammad as his messenger; and (iii) the above in (ii) *and* conformity to certain other standards, which do not appear to be capable of clear, unambiguous definition.

5–07   Rahim (1994, p. 47) says that the first postulate of Islamic law is *iman* or faith, belief in God and acknowledgment of His authority over human actions. One of the leading writers on Muslim law in this century, in his typical clear style, focused on the essential element of total and unqualified submission to the will of God as the fundamental tenet of Islam and immediately linked this to the understanding of law as a comprehensive code of behaviour covering all aspects of life. In this way, *shari'a* becomes "a divinely ordained path of conduct which guides the Muslim towards fulfillment of his religious conviction in this life and reward from his Creator in the world to come" (Coulson (1968), p. 54). This kind of

---

[4] For details see Welch, "Islam", in *A handbook of living religions* (1984), pp. 149 *et seq.* under the heading of 'unity and diversity'. With particular reference to custom in Muslim law, see now Libson (1997).
[5] A crisp summary of the main points about the definition of a Muslim is found in Edge, "A comparative approach to the treatment of non-Muslim minorities in the Middle East, with special reference to Egypt", in *Islamic family law* (1990), pp. 35–36. See also Diwan, "Who is a Muslim" [1978] 4 No. 1 *Indian Socio-Legal Journal* 75–85.
[6] So Bharatiya (1996) p. 42; see also Fyzee (1974) p. 60.
[7] This clearly implies unquestionable belief in God.

understanding illustrates that ideally there would be close links between essential belief (orthodoxy) and correct practice (orthopraxis).

5–08 In real life, though, virtually everywhere in the Muslim world, but especially outside the Middle East, there are many communities which are "not wholly Muslim in character".[8] In other words, there are many Muslims who fulfill some but not all aspects of a strict cultural Middle East-focused definition of 'Muslim'. It does not appear that Muslim theologians or lawyers have ever resolved this issue. The complexities of life, and the internal diversity of Muslims as a global faith community with very many different socio-cultural characteristics work against simple uniformity and standardisation. The assertion that the universal Muslim community (*ummah*) is simply 'equal' is not helpful for socio-legal analysis, since this assertion refers first of all to the equality of all Muslims before God, not *inter se*.

5–09 To some extent, therefore, the absence of discussion about the problems of defining 'Muslim' in Middle Eastern textbooks indicates implied recognition of global diversity, as well as an awareness that there is often no scope for questioning whether a person is Muslim – the issue simply being that a particular individual might be a 'bad' Muslim, but still unquestionably a Muslim. Islam as a belief system does not necessarily see a role here for state law, as retribution for deviating from the right path remains first of all a matter for God rather than human agencies. This line of argument opens up a huge debate about the nature of the Muslim state, a topic which we cannot pursue here.[9]

5–10 Muslims at the periphery of Islamic territory, and perhaps still more so Muslims in Western diaspora today, have to struggle with such questions in much more explicit terms since the scope for divergence between belief and practice is so much larger. In a situation of insecurity, especially when a siege mentality develops, the critical issue becomes not just whether a particular person is a 'bad' Muslim, but whether that individual has actually abandoned the basic tenets of Muslim law and of the Muslim way of life, however perceived.

5–11 Much material on the question of Muslim identity appears, in various scenarios, in chapters on the relationships between Muslims and non-Muslims. Here one finds important pointers in terms of Muslim ethnicity, relating to self-definition and being defined by others. These are also issues which we cannot explore here further.[10]

5–12 In practice, therefore, traditional Islamic thinking on the question of who is a Muslim has focused on a combination of belief and practice. The five pillars of Islam are often mentioned as a key element,[11] but lack of adherence to them does not automatically disqualify an individual from being a Muslim.[12] To allow for greater flexibility, it has apparently been convenient for the law (and re-assuring for Muslim communities) to apply a number of important presumptions, particularly

---

[8] This is the phrase used by Bharatiya (1996), p. 45. Fyzee (1974), p. 65 speaks in this context of "amphibious communities which cannot be said to be either wholly Hindu or wholly Muslim".

[9] For details see the introduction to Mallat and Connors, *Islamic family law* (1990); Mallat, *Islamic and public law* (1993a); Ullah, *The administration of justice in Islam. A introduction to the Muslim conception of the State* (1986); Ahmed, *The concept of an Islamic state: An analysis of the ideological controversy in Pakistan* (1987); Esposito, *Islam in Asia, Religion, politics and society* (1987) for various Asian jurisdictions; with particular reference to Pakistan see Newberg (1995).

[10] For useful details on different sects among Muslims in Egypt and the Middle East see Edge (1990); Bharatiya (1996), pp. 41–49 produces a good discussion on Indian sub-groups; see also Diwan and Diwan (1991), pp. 1–10.

[11] For details see Welch (1984), pp. 136–149; Esposito, *Islam, The straight path* (1988), pp. 90–95.

[12] This must be true, since the requirement to go on pilgrimage, in particular, cannot be realistically followed by many millions of Muslims.

for persons and communities who converted to Islam (Bharatiya (1996), pp. 44–45).
It is again apparent that, historically, this has been a much bigger issue in South
Asia than in the Middle East.

South Asian laws and the definition of 'Muslim'

Muslims in the South Asian legal context

5–13   Naturally, studies on South Asian Muslim law build largely on the
conceptual framework of older writing and there is a similar prominence of
historical investigations, with detailed outlines of the Qur'anic foundations, the role
and place of *hadith*, and of subsequent jurisprudential developments. Important
differences need to be brought out, however. As indicated, there appears to be much
concern in South Asian legal textbooks with the question of Muslim identity. This
reflects not only the contentious reality of conversions to and from Islam in the
region, but also a much greater involvement of the courts in a situation where
personal law systems inevitably throw up interesting conflicts of laws. Some of these
have been discussed in Chapter 4, above.

5–14   In addition, the presence of the general law system means, of course, that
Muslims in South Asia are not governed by Muslim law in all respects.[13]
Significantly, the recent trend towards islamisation in South Asia has sought to
change this, particularly in Pakistan, working towards a situation where the self-
respect of Muslims was increased through being governed by laws that are within
the ambit of Islam. In Pakistan, a historical re-appraisal is currently underway, as
Mannan (1990) and many other authors indicate in various ways. The history of the
administration of Muslim law during British rule has been revisited.[14] The
important concept of 'justice, equity and good conscience' has long been given an
Islamic slant,[15] and the more recent developments in Pakistani public interest
litigation must also be seen in this light (see paragraph 2–55, above). Professor
Mannan, the Pakistani editor of *Mulla's Principles of Mahomedan law*, has explained
this new trend:

> "Pakistan in a way is passing through a developing state of transformation
> from English to Islamic judicial norms and the process must . . . follow its own
> rules of natural justice as contained in Islamic "accepted judicial norms" and
> fundamental principles and basic concepts of Islam, and seek inspiration from
> its own Constitution, ideology, history and environment." (Mannan (1990),
> p. 35.)

The movement towards indigenisation of the legal system has been an important
phenomenon in all of the three South Asian countries that we are concerned with
here; these three jurisdictions have however taken quite different approaches. In
India, despite periodic agitation by Indian Muslims against their 'subjugation' by
the general law system, the modern secular state has found various ways to assert its
supremacy. A case in point has been how the Muslim protests in India against
sections 125–127 of the Criminal Procedure Code 1973 in relation to the rights of
divorced Muslim wives to maintenance beyond the *iddat* period have developed

---

[13] On the interaction between general law and Muslim personal law see Mahmood (1982a): pp. 29–32;
Bhattacharjee, *Muslim law and the constitution* (1985) and (1994) are very useful, too.
[14] See in detail *B. Z. Kaikaus v. President of Pakistan* P.L.D. 1980 S.C. 160.
[15] An important case in this regard is *Nizam Khan v. Addl. District Judge, Lyallpur* P.L.D. 1976 Lah. 930;
see also Mannan (1990), pp. 3 and 35.

over time. Of course, this controversy rather concerned the duties of Muslim ex-husbands to provide for such wives till they die or remarry (see in detail paragraph 7–75, below). The highly publicised and controversial *Shah Bano* case gave rise to arguments that Indian Muslims should be governed by their own law, not by the general legal system. The reaction of the modern secular state has been to grant Muslims that wish in terms of formality, but the newly formulated Muslim personal law on the subject, the Muslim Women (Protection of Rights on Divorce) Act 1986 has not given in, as we shall show in detail in paragraph 7–75, below, to pressures from Muslim men. There is hardly any room for doubt now that Muslim men are required by Indian law to provide for their former wives beyond the *iddat* period.

5–15   In Bangladesh, starting from socialist secular foundations, the legal system has shifted some way towards islamisation, but the price to pay for total islamisation was clearly considered too high. It has been all too apparent that in Pakistan, where islamisation was taken to its logical conclusion with signal changes to the Constitution itself, the non-Muslim minorities have become more like second-class citizens, despite well-sounding constitutional guarantees. It was easier for Pakistan to go down that route because the non-Muslim minorities are demographically small. Crucially, however, islamisation has also turned against Muslim minorities in Pakistan. The focus on the Islamic nature of the legal system as a whole brought out the definitional problems of what 'Islamic' means. In the process, not only were the Ahmadis subjected to renewed violence as traitors of Islam, but sectarian and communal violence has been targeted at non-Hanafi groups, in particular the Shi'a minority. Rather than uniting the Muslims as a community, islamisation as an exercise in focusing on the Islamic nature of the entire legal system in Pakistan has therefore brought out the latent conflicts over diversity within various Muslim communities. Whether it was devised with this aim in mind or not, islamisation appears to have failed in uniting the nation and its people. It has also put tremendous pressure on the legal system to become more involved in questions of religion.

5–16   In the light of such evidence, it is apparent that in South Asia the historical experience of mass conversion to Islam is still fresh and that legal and socio-religious questions cannot be treated in strict isolation. In many cases the process of conversion to Islam appears to have extended to the sphere of belief rather than practice. This is of course typically South Asian, in that diversifying local cultural elements continuously assert themselves against globalising, uniformising concepts like the unity of the divine. During the 1920s and 1930s, vigorous debates about the Muslim Personal Law (Shariat) Application Act 1937 and subsequent legislation, which we have already traced in various parts of Chapter 2, reflected tensions over precisely what laws Muslims were to be governed by.[16] Today, such conflicts and tensions continue at various levels and allowances continue to be made for persons and communities who converted to Islam. Over time, South Asian Muslims have developed their own hybrid cultural characteristics, coexisting in some degree of tension with the strict monotheistic ideals of Islam. In terms of practice, in particular, South Asian Muslims follow many paths which orthodoxy may consider unacceptable, but which local practice and normative value systems underwrite.

---

[16] A case in point is the Caste Disabilities Removal (West Pakistan Amendment) Act 1963 (Act of 1963), which amends the Caste Disabilities Removal Act 1850 to the effect that "nothing contained in this Act shall apply to the rights of inheritance to the property of a Muslim".

Legal strategies of definition

5-17 The critical question for our present study is whether a simple declaration of faith, *i.e.* an express commitment to the basic tenets of Islam, such as the *shahada*, is sufficient to attract the application of Muslim law. Bharatiya ((1996), p. 42) suggests that the South Asian law courts have never ventured to decide the complex disputes among theologians about who is a Muslim. Instead, the courts took an easy-going, middle-of-the-road approach. It was held in *Jiwan Khan v. Habibi*, A.I.R. 1933 Lah. 759, a case in which it was argued that Shias were not really Muslims:

> "Every person who believes in the unity of God and the mission of Muhammad as a Prophet is a Mussalman to whatever sect he may belong."

Thus, it was found that Shias are undoubtedly Muslims, and this particular test has been applied in other cases to similar inclusive effect. Most Muslims would probably not protest against decisions that included an individual or a group of persons in their fold. Problems have, however, arisen more recently in Pakistan with reference to the exclusion from Islam of the Ahmadis or Qadianis, who have been held to be Muslims by Indian and Bangladeshi courts,[17] but who have been declared non-Muslims by the Pakistani state through the Constitution (Second Amendment) Act 1974 and in much subsequent legal activity.[18] This shows that the issue of the definition of a Muslim has come more alive recently, with unpleasant consequences.[19]

5-18 In Pakistan, the entire legal system has been influenced by the agitation against the Ahmadis, leading to important constitutional amendments which bring law and religion closer together. Today, the Pakistani Constitution of 1973 provides, in Article 260(3), a definition of 'Muslim' which clearly excludes any form of Quadiani or Ahmadi doctrine:

> "260(3) In the Constitution and all enactments and other legal instruments, unless there is anything repugnant in the subject or context, —
>
> (a) "Muslim" means a person who believes in the unity and oneness of Almighty Allah, in the absolute and unqualified finality of the Prophethood of Muhammad (peace be upon him), the last of the prophets, and does not believe in, or recognize as a prophet or religious reformer, any persons who claimed or claims to be a prophet, in any sense of the word or of any description whatsoever, after Muhammad (peace be upon him); and

---

[17] On India see *Shihabuddin Imbichi Koya Thangal v. K. P. Ahammed Koya*, A.I.R. (1971) Ker. 206, holding that Ahmadis are Muslims. On the position of Ahmadis in Nigeria see in detail Balogun, *Islam versus Ahmadiyyah in Nigeria* (1977).

[18] On islamisation and legal reforms in Pakistan generally see Kennedy (1990). *Abdur Rehman Mobashir v. Amir Ali Shah Bokhari* P.L.D. (1978) Lah. 113 is an early leading case distinguishing Ahmadis from Muslims. The Anti-Islamic Activities of Quadiani Group, Lahori Group and Ahmadis (Prohibition and Punishment) Ordinance 1984 is relevant in this context. In *Mujibur Rehman v. Federal Government of Pakistan* P.L.D. (1985) F.S.C. 8, it was held that this Ordinance is not un-Islamic. On this case, see the somewhat triumphant study entitled *Quadianis are not Muslims* (1987). An important recent case is *Khurshid Ahmad v. Government of Punjab*, P.L.D. 1992 Lah. 1. It was confirmed, in essence, that Ahmadis and Muslims are two separate and distinct entities. On July 3, 1993, the Supreme Court of Pakistan decided by a majority that the 1984 Ordinance was not *ultra vires* the Constitution of Pakistan. On this occasion, a large number of criminal and civil appeals were brought together in *Zaheeruddin v. The State* (1993) S.C.M.R. 1718. See Lau (1995b) for details.

[19] It is now well-known known that many Ahmadis have been seeking asylum in various countries of the world, often successfully. Details on this issue are beyond the ambit of the present study. For a case in the U.K. see *Kaleem Ahmed v. SSHD* (12774).

(b) "non-Muslim" means a person who is not a Muslim and includes a person belonging to the Christian, Hindu, Sikh, Buddhist or Parsi community, a person of the Quadiani Group or the Lahori Group (who call themselves 'Ahmadis' or by any other name), or a Bahai, and a person belonging to any of the Scheduled Castes."[20]

The import of religious definitions into the country's constitution marks a significant shift away from secularism in Pakistan and the growing concern with defining religious boundaries. Earlier, as the useful discussion in Fyzee (1974, pp. 60–64) shows, the courts in South Asia attempted to keep such issues as uncomplicated as possible and preferred to stay out of religious doctrinal controversies and religious politics. This is, of course, entirely in line with general secular legal policy, whether under the colonial regime or in accordance with the modern Indian Constitution.

5–19   In this regard, Mahmood (1982a, p. 31) emphasises that 'Muslim' has in fact never been defined by Indian statute law and that the judiciary carries the burden of having to define relevant categories:

"In India there is no statutory definition either of the word 'Muslim' or of the term 'Islam'. No legislative enactment has ever defined the word 'Muslim' or enumerated the essentials of Islam. In the absence of any statutory guidance in this behalf, the judicial decisions on the subject constitute the law."

Several authors discuss elements of judicial decisions. A coherent analysis is found in Fyzee (1974, p. 60–64), suggesting that the following propositions have emerged as authoritative in Anglo-Indian and modern Indian law:

- It is for the courts to decide whether a person is or is not a Muslim, and this depends upon the facts of each case. (page 61)
- A court of law is not concerned with peculiarities in belief, orthodoxy or heterodoxy, so long as the minimum of belief exists. (page 61)
- The essential doctrine of Islam is (i) that there is but one God and (ii) that Muhammad is His Prophet.[21] This is the indispensable minimum; a belief short of this is not Islam; a belief in excess of this is, for the law courts at least, a redundancy. (page 61)
- It is not necessary that a Muslim should be born a Muslim; it is sufficient if he is a Muslim by profession or conversion. According to the theory of Islam, religion depends upon belief. (page 61)
- Islam depends upon belief, but it is well-known that no hard and fast rules can be laid down so far as external tests are concerned. (page 63)
- Therefore it may be said that a formal profession of Islam is sufficient, unless (i) the conversion is a pretended or colourable one, for the purpose of perpetrating a fraud upon the law, or (ii) the whole of the man's conduct and the evidence of surrounding facts is such as to run counter to the presumption of conversion to Islam. (page 64)

---

[20] This particular wording was introduced by the Constitution (Third Amendment) Order 1983 with effect from March 19, 1985 and replaced an earlier wording to similar effect which was introduced by the Constitution (Second Amendment) Act 1974 with effect from September 17, 1974.
[21] Fyzee (1974, p. 61) refers at this point in a footnote to an old Indian case and several textbook writers, as well as the Pakistani case of *Atia Waris v. Sultan Ahmad*, P.L.D. 1959 (W.P.) Lah. 205, which also follows this basic approach.

By trying to keep the issue as simple as possible, the Indian courts have clearly avoided entanglement in theological discussions (Mahmood (1982), p. 32). Thus, an individual's assertion, to the effect that s/he is a Muslim, would be accepted by a court in the absence of evidence to the contrary.[22] Significantly, as Fyzee's discussion shows, the earliest contentious questions immediately focused on Ahmadis.[23]

5-20   Indian textbooks cover familiar ground on the present topic. Like many other authors, Mahmood (1982a, pp. 33–44) focuses on different schools and classes of Muslims in India, providing a detailed socio-legal analysis. As indicated, Diwan (1977, pp. 1–9) starts with a chapter on the application of Muslim law, thus marking the importance of definitional questions in the Indian context.[24] Distinguishing Muslims by origin and Muslims by conversion, Diwan (1977, pp. 1–2) reiterates the basic principles of the definition of a Muslim. He then argues that Muslims by origin are governed only by *shariat* law, while Muslims by conversion may, in certain circumstances, be governed by custom.[25] Focusing therefore on the questions relating to conversion (see further below), he comes to those Muslim communities of India which have been professing the Muslim faith but have continued to regulate some of their day-to-day matters by reference to Hindu customs. The key issue regularly is which law to apply, rather than whether the individuals concerned possess Muslim identity.

The consequences of conversion

5-21   The question whether a person is a Muslim assumes potentially critical importance in cases of conversion, significantly not only for the individual in question but also for members of his or her family. As a result of an individual's conversion questions may arise about the validity of a marriage or divorce, or in the context of property disputes, often after a person's death, so that succession cases often arise in this context. The topic has also become relevant, particularly in India, with reference to polygamy, since there appears to be evidence that by converting to Islam, men may take advantage of the right to have more than one wife.[26] There may be other reasons why individuals find it convenient to change their religion and to fall under the ambit of a different personal law.

5-22   Not surprisingly, one finds a section on such problems in many textbooks.[27] Since we have already outlined some of the basic principles, we can fairly swiftly turn to the case law to illustrate several important points. Generally

---

[22] This would appear to be the same in Pakistan. See Mannan (1990), p. 21 on who is a Muslim and on the simplicity of conversion to Islam.

[23] The case cited is *Narantakath v. Parakkal* (1922) I.L.R. 45 Mad. 986, a Mapilla (here spelt Moplah) polygamy case, in which it was held that Ahmadis are Muslims. It was held that a Mapilla woman whose husband of the same community had become an Ahmadi was not automatically divorced from him on account of his alleged apostasy. Evidently, this case was as much about sexual morality and the security of marriage as about religion.

[24] This is virtually the same as Diwan (1978).

[25] Readers should note the ambivalent approach to customs in this respect. Diwan clearly overstates the contrast with Hindu law, in which custom was held to override the written letter of the law. His position on the place of custom in Muslim law is therefore too rigid and is contradicted by more recent writing, as already cited.

[26] Diwan and Diwan (1991), p. 4. This became an issue in the much-publicised Indian case of *Sarla Mudgal v. Union of India* A.I.R. 1995 S.C. 1531. For details see below, para. 8–312. For earlier indications of the latent potential for abuse see, *e.g.* Diwan and Diwan (1991), p. 5.

[27] On the simple procedures for conversion to Islam see succinctly Diwan and Diwan (1991), pp. 3–4. A good discussion on conversion and custom is found in Fyzee (1974), pp. 64–68; Hidayatullah and Hidayatullah (1977), pp. 19–26 consider particularly the consequences of conversion in the context of marriage and divorce law.

speaking, there are few reported cases regarding conversion. The basic position remains that a non-Muslim may become a Muslim by professing Islam, and such a person will then be governed, with immediate effect, by the relevant provisions of Muslim law. Conversion is mainly a question of fact (Fyzee (1974), p. 64). These basic principles were applied in an instructive case from South India which is typical of the legal problems and questions which can arise in this context. In *Syed Amanullah Hussain v. Rajamma*, A.I.R. 1977 A.P. 152, the brother of a deceased Shia Muslim man challenged the validity of his brother's marriage and the legitimacy of the only son of the deceased on the ground that the lady in question was a Hindu and had therefore not been party to a valid marriage which now entitled her son to succession to the property of the deceased. In the High Court of Andhra Pradesh, the case turned first of all on evidence of the alleged conversion of the wife to Islam. It was held, at page 157:

> "In this connection, it must be remembered that under Mohamadan Law or religion, there is no particular ceremony or ritual for conversion. Any person who professes Mohamedan religion and acknowledges that there is but one God and Mohammad is his prophet, is a Mohammedan. It is not necessary that he should observe any particular rites or ceremonies or be an orthodox believer in the religion."

Applying, in addition, a presumption of marriage between the deceased husband and the converted wife, who had also died in the meantime, the judge found in favour of the son's right to inheritance. This case illustrates how tempting it may be for Muslim parties in a dispute to allege that the other party is not in fact a Muslim. Obviously, these are tactical considerations in property-related disputes, often of a petty nature, rather than questions of religious identity and personal salvation. It remains a fact that South Asian judges have to be very alert about the potential for abuse in such arguments.[28]

5–23 From a European perspective, it does not seem to help the formal legal process that neither conversion to Islam nor marriage need to be fully documented. However, as the above case illustrates and confirms, South Asian laws have their own mechanisms to handle informal legal processes, tend to give full recognition to oral evidence, and the judges apply a well-established set of presumptions in many different contexts.

5–24 In the earlier case law, one important line of decisions deals with the effects of a religious conversion by one of the parties to a marriage. By Sunni Islamic law as applied in India, a Muslim male has capacity to marry either a Muslim woman or a Jewish or Christian woman. Jews and Christians, as 'people of the book' (*kitabiyya*) are deemed to possess revealed scriptures and are thus seen as more acceptable than adherents to other religions. In South Asia, it became a well-known rule, very important in practice, that a Muslim male cannot marry a polytheist, *i.e.* first of all a Hindu.[29] It has always been considered an important provision that a Muslim woman can marry only a Muslim male.[30]

---

[28] We shall argue in para. 5–44, below that this has also become a matter of importance in the English context.

[29] This is mainly a reference to Hindus and explains why the case of *Syed Amanullah Hussain v. Rajamma*, A.I.R. (1977) A.P. 152, discussed above, arose in the first place. It was alleged, *inter alia*, that this lady had been buried as a Hindu, so she could not have been a Muslim. This contention was accepted by the judge in light of a sensible explanation why this should be so, but it did not mean that at an earlier stage the lady had not converted to Islam. Again, the point needs to be made here that judges who lack cultural sensitivity and knowledge would not be able to sift through such arguments and counter-claims.

[30] For details see, *e.g.* Doi (1984), p. 138.

5–25   The general principles in this field have been discussed by several authors. An important preliminary consideration is clearly that conversion to Islam is generally welcome.[31] While a conversion cannot be fully tested since, as several authors emphasise, the thought of man is not triable,[32] as a general rule "it is necessary that the conversion should be bona fide, honest, and should not be colourable, pretended or dishonest".[33]

5–26   If a married person converts, it appears to make some difference whether the spouses concerned live in a jurisdiction in which Muslim law is the law of the land or not. In this regard, the textbooks make a distinction between a country subject to Muslim law and a country where Muslim law is not the law of the land.[34] In the first case, when one of the parties to a marriage converts to Islam, s/he should offer Islam to the spouse. If this offer is refused three times, the marriage can (and probably should) be dissolved. In the second case, the rule is that the marriage is dissolved automatically after a period of three months, unless the other spouse also converts to Islam (Hidayatullah and Hidayatullah (1977), p. 20; Mannan (1990), p. 23).

5–27   This is not the rule in Indian law, however. Diwan and Diwan ((1991), p. 5) comment that for the purposes of application of Muslim law, "India is considered neither a Muslim country nor a non-Muslim country".[35] Interestingly, there are now important differences between Indian and Pakistani law in this respect. The Indian position, established in a number of cases (see further below) is that the spouse who has converted to Islam cannot seek a judicial dissolution of the marriage or a judicial declaration that the marriage is dissolved on the ground that the other spouse refused to convert to Islam. The textbooks do not tell us why this should be so. In many cases it is the husband who will have become Muslim. If he remains married to his wife, whatever her religion, subsequent children in particular, but probably also existing children will be governed by the provisions of Muslim law.[36] Conversion here takes a larger effect with regard to the next generation and Muslim law seems prepared to tolerate the temporary violation of the rule against marriage with a non-*kitabiyya* woman. This legal position also reflects, of course, the general position that an inter-religious marriage is not, *per se*, perceived as legally problematic and socially questionable.

5–28   This is apparently viewed quite differently in Pakistan. An important case in this context is *Farooq Leivers v. Adelaide Bridget Mary*, P.L.D. 1958 (W.P.) Lah. 431. This case must be read in the light of *Jatoi v. Jatoi*, P.L.D. 1967 S.C. 580, already discussed above. In *Jatoi v. Jatoi* the husband was a Muslim at all times. He contracted a civil ceremony with a Christian woman in England. His subsequent divorce by *talaq* was recognised by the Pakistani Supreme Court. *Farooq Leivers v. Adelaide Bridget Mary* was referred to in the judgement of the majority, but the case was not expressly overruled. The husband and the wife in this case were Christians

---

[31] We are not concerned here with conversion from Islam, which falls under the heading of apostasy and is a subject in its own right. For a new Indian study on that topic see S. A. Rahman, *Punishment of apostacy in Islam* (1996).

[32] On this see an interesting discussion in Tayyibji (1968), p. 7, with references to old English cases.

[33] Diwan and Diwan (1991), p. 4, with reference to an old Indian Christian case, in which conversion was an obvious device to facilitate a pleasurable liaison without violating the legal rules against polygamy.

[34] See Hidayatullah and Hidayatullah (1977), p. 20; Mannan (1990), p. 23; Diwan and Diwan (1991), p. 5.

[35] This relates well to the argument highlighted by Professor van Koningsveld that Muslim law knows and applies finer distinctions than just *dar-al-islam* and *dar-al-harb*.

[36] There are various positions on this. For details see Diwan, *Muslim law in modern India* (1977), p. 2 and para. 10–32, below.

married in British India according to Christian rites. The husband later converted to Islam, asked his wife to embrace the Muslim faith and, on her refusal, purported to divorce her by *talaq*. The husband then sought a declaration that he was no longer married to his former wife.

5–29 In the Lahore High Court, Changez J. found (at page 435) that the point raised in this case had not so far been decided by any High Court in South Asia. The learned judge proceeded to consider the general effects of conversion, examining the legal consequences for the convert as well as the persons closest to such a convert. He touched briefly on religious bars against inheritance and then turned to the effects upon a convert's existing marriage. Relying on the *Hedaya* and juristic writing, the judge drew a distinction between the conversion of a man and that of a woman. While the conversion to Islam of the husband of a *kitabiyya* woman does not bring about separation, according to such sources a Muslim woman can only be married to a Muslim. Thus, after her conversion, if the husband does not wish to convert as well, "the Judge must pronounce the dissolution of the marriage" (page 438). Focusing on the question of polygamy (page 438), the judge then proceeded to a discussion of the case law, showing that Indian courts had held that conversion to Islam of one of the parties did not bring about an automatic dissolution of the marriage.[37] It is noteworthy how the judge then abandons this enquiry and turns to Islamic authorities instead, reproducing an analysis of the classical position, according to which a Muslim male may remain married to a *kitabiyya* woman, but "this choice is . . . not given to the Muslim woman" (page 441).

5–30 That point having been settled, the really important question in *Farooq Leivers* was whether he could legally divorce his wife by *talaq*, now that he was a Muslim. In view of the injunctions of the Qur'an, the learned judge found (at page 442) that a Muslim husband has such a right in Muslim law. However, under the legal system of Pakistan, given that the wife was a Christian and was party to a Christian marriage, Muslim law itself, *i.e.* the *shari'at* law, did not apply. The learned judge examined the relevant provisions of Pakistani Muslim law and found, indeed, that they applied only to marriages where both parties were Muslims.

5–31 Turning therefore to sections 5 and 6 of the Punjab Laws Act 1872, Changcz J. found that he was required to decide this novel point according to 'justice, equity and good conscience' (page 444). The case makes reference to the full application of the Divorce Act 1869 in Pakistan and the non-recognition of a *talaq* divorce by the English High Court in an important early case,[38] all of which leads to the conclusion, at page 448, that "it will be against the dictates of justice, equity and good conscience to grant a decree to the plaintiff in terms of the relief sought for".

5–32 This case is as significant for what it says as for what it does not make explicit. On the one hand, the learned judge uses strong language to oppose the very idea of interreligious marriages (pages 439–441) and regrets the fact that Pakistan has not islamised its legal system (pages 444–445). On the other hand, and the two views are clearly not mutually exclusive, the judge finds firmly in favour of the non-Muslim wife, protecting her position and status. It seems quite certain that he looked through the husband's plan and therefore did not view his conversion to Islam as entirely bona fide. It seems all too apparent from the facts of the case that the husband, married under Indian Christian law, and thus virtually tied to his wife for life, devised the route of conversion to Islam to get rid of her through a *talaq*

---

[37] On this see *Robaba Khanum v. Khodadad Boman Irani* I.L.R. (1948) Bom. 223, discussed further below.
[38] *R. v. Hammersmith Superintendent Registrar of Marriages, ex p. Mir Anwaruddin* [1917] 1 K.B. 634.

divorce and, more crucially perhaps, to free himself from the financial liability of having to maintain a woman with whom he did not want any further relationship. Changez J. very diplomatically leaves such points unmentioned and uses instead the creative avenue of recourse to 'justice, equity and good conscience'. This leads to what looks like a socially desirable result but also creates a 'limping marriage', so the result is not altogether satisfactory.

5–33   In Pakistani law, then, the conversion to Islam of a man married to a Jewish or a Christian woman will not affect the validity of the existing union.[39] In contrast to this position, the conversion to Islam of a man married to a polytheistic woman, or the conversion to Islam of a woman married to a non-Muslim, regardless of his faith, will bring into play the Muslim law rules which demand either the conversion to Islam of the non-Muslim partner or the termination of the union. When the wife is the one who converted to Islam, not surprisingly, Pakistani law has very clearly taken the position that the marriage of such a woman should be dissolved on the completion of three monthly courses, without any decree or order of a court.[40] More recently, this position has been confirmed in several reported cases.[41]

5–34   In Indian law, two older important decisions discuss in considerable detail the question of conversion to Islam and its consequences.[42] In both cases, however, this was clearly not the only matter of concern influencing the decision of the judges. In *Robaba Khanum v. Khodadad Boman Irani*, I.L.R. 1948 Bom. 223, decided in 1946, the parties were Parsis who had married in Iran in 1927 and had subsequently settled permanently in India. In 1944 the wife converted to Islam and requested that her husband should adopt her new faith. The husband refused the wife's request, whereupon she instituted proceedings in the High Court for divorce or, in the alternative, for a declaration that her marriage was at an end. The wife argued that by the classical Islamic law as applied in India, a marriage celebrated in non-Muslim form between non-Muslims is brought to an end usually three months after the wife's conversion to Islam, without any intervention from the court. The wife argued that this legal result applied to her situation. She submitted that after her conversion she had become a Muslim and was now governed by Muslim law. Blagden J. rejected this plea and said, at page 232:

> "The law of India is not Mahomedan law any more than it is Hindu law or Christian ecclesiastical law, but the Mahomedan law is by virtue of the general law of India (in so far as it is not inconsistent therewith) the personal law of a minority of Indians, regulating their relations with one another. It differs in degree but not in kind, from (say) the by-laws of the Willingdon Club."[43]

The learned judge went on to say, at page 233:

> "It is true that a convert is generally subject to the personal law appropriate to his new religion as against that appropriate to his old one . . . But why should this apply to the wife or husband of the convert any more than to his or her aunt?"

---

[39] However, see the case of *Viswalingham v. Viswalingham* [1980] 1 F.L.R. 15, where the Court of Appeal in England considered a different view of this area of the law in the context of Shafi'i law as applied in Malaysia.

[40] Mannan (1990), p. 23 refers to the case of *Faiz Ali Shah v. Ghulam Abbas Shah* P.L.D. 1952 A.J.K. 32.

[41] *Sardar Masih v. Haider Masih* P.L.D. 1988 F.S.C. 78; *Zarina v. The State* P.L.D. 1988 F.S.C. 105. It is also apparent from newspaper reports in Pakistan that conversion of the non-Muslim minorities is an ongoing process and receives constant, favourable publicity.

[42] These are *Robaba Khanum v. Khodadad Boman Irani*, I.L.R. (1948) Bom. 223 and *Rakeya Bibi v. Anil Kumar Mukherji*, I.L.R. [1948] 2 Cal. 119.

[43] This argument, in rephrased form, is also given at p. 235 of the judgment.

5–35   In the context of a personal law system such as the British Indian law, therefore, the judge recognised the duty to take account of the position of both parties to this marriage. In other words, he recognised that there was a conflict of laws. Having held Muslim law, *i.e.* the classical *shari'a* law, to be inapplicable to the case, he found that the case had to be decided according to 'justice, equity and good conscience'. There are subtle indications in this case that the judge was actually quite suspicious of the motives of the wife for her conversion. Apparently, a handsome Muslim man played a role in this context (see page 230). The learned judge, however, did not attempt to question the sincerity of the wife's conversion to Islam and instead phrased his decision in terms of 'justice and right'. According to this criterion, the wife's contention that she should now be entitled to a declaration of divorce, so the learned judge at page 235, was not a logical conclusion from her factual situation,

> ". . . for there is nothing in "justice and right" or in "justice, equity and good conscience"which requires that a marriage, once validly celebrated, should be judicially dissoluble or otherwise capable of being terminated, except by death."

The language of the judgment points to strong feelings about the repugnance of divorce, as then conceived. The judge was quite scathing in his refusal to accept the wife's arguments and said, at pages 235–236:

> "Do then the authorities compel me to hold that one spouse can by changing his or her religious opinions (or purporting to do so) force his or her newly acquired personal law on a party to whom it is entirely alien and who does not want it? In the name of justice, equity and good conscience, or, in more simple language, of common sense, why should this be possible? If there were no authority on the point I (personally) should have thought that so monstrous an absurdity carried its own refutation with it, so extravagant are the results that follow from it."

The learned judge here used what we have referred to above as 'public policy arguments', pinpointing precisely that to allow the legal effect which the wife claimed would immediately bring alive other issues, such as the Muslim male convert's claim to polygamy (page 236).

5–36   The wife appealed and, on appeal, the decision of Blagden J. was upheld.[44] Chagla J. also found that Muslim *shari'a* law as such was not the law of India and said, at pages 253–254:

> "It is not possible to take the view that India is a country subject to the laws of Islam. It is true that the Courts in British India administer the Muslim law as altered and amended by statute law to Muslim parties. But the Courts of law do so pursuant to the directions contained in the laws of India. Complete religious neutrality obtains in our country and our Courts administer laws irrespective of the creed of the parties who appear before them. The Courts do not administer the laws of any particular community, but they administer such laws as are valid in British India, Muslim law is administered only in those cases where it happens to be the law of British India in cases where the parties are Muslims."

---

[44] This decision is printed as part of the same judgment, starting from p. 252, with the decision of Chagla J.

According to traditional Muslim law, the plaintiff would have been entitled to a court declaration, but in the present situation there was a conflict of laws under Indian law because the husband was a Parsi. Going through a number of earlier decisions, the learned judge confirmed that this case would have to be decided in accordance with 'justice and right'. Interestingly, the judge also comments on the viability of inter-religious marriages (see pages 257–258) and expresses quite different views from those referred to by judges in Pakistani cases at page 258 of the report:

> ". . . the Indian legislature has departed from the rigour of the ancient Muslim law and has taken the more modern view that there is nothing to prevent a happy marriage notwithstanding the fact that the two parties to it professed different religions."

It was therefore confirmed (*id.*) that "it is not in accordance with justice and right that on the conversion of one of the parties to the marriage to Islam it should be held that the marriage stands dissolved".

5–37   A similar result was reached in *Rakeya Bibi v. Anil Kumar Mukherji* I.L.R. [1948] 2 Cal. 119. Here the parties, both of them originally professing the Hindu faith, had married in 1944 in accordance with Hindu rites. The marriage was never consummated because of the husband's impotence. In 1945 the wife converted to Islam, evidently as a tactical device to allow herself to be freed from this marriage which, under traditional Hindu law, would be treated as an indissoluble union for life. She offered Islam to her husband, who refused the invitation. The wife then sought a declaration from the court that her marriage be dissolved because of her conversion to Islam or, in the alternative, that the marriage be annulled because of the husband's impotence. The case was heard by a Special Bench of the Calcutta High Court, which examined the relevant rules of Muslim law relied upon by the plaintiff, but rejected the wife's plea that her conversion should be a basis for divorce.[45] Chakravartti J., giving the decision of the Special Bench, asked himself the critical question at page 130:

> ". . . if one of the parties to a marriage brings about a conflict of personal law by forsaking their common religion and adopting another, can the new personal law of the converted spouse prevail over the old personal law retained by the unconverted partner, under which the marriage was celebrated?"

He ultimately answered this question in the negative, deciding that the personal law of the converted spouse could not govern the case because there were two persons and two different personal laws involved in the matter, not one. The plaintiff was unable to prove to the satisfaction of the Bench that there was any law in force in India which brought the rule of Muslim law into prominence as the law governing the dissolution of this marriage. It was not just nor right to apply the rule of traditional Muslim law to this case (page 136). The Bench decided, therefore, that the extra-judicial Muslim law could not govern the dispute and that, instead, it fell under 'justice, equity and good conscience'.

5–38   Apart from the consequences of conversion for the marriage, the learned judges were rightly concerned, at page 124, about the question "whether her conversion was a bona fide one or a mere device adopted for the purpose of avoiding

---

[45] The wife still managed to extricate herself from this hopeless marriage by arguing successfully that, under modern Hindu law, a marriage to an impotent husband should be annulled because there was no meaningful remedy, as had existed earlier.

the marriage". There are some relevant comments in this case about how to test the genuineness of a person's conversion to Islam. Chakravartti J. found, at page 126, that the conversion in the present case "appears to have been a very casual affair" and that the lady concerned did not really follow her alleged new way of life. Thus, it was held at page 127, "the plaintiff must grievously fail on the issue of *bona fides* of her conversion".

5–39 In this case, too, the decision of an Indian High Court on the consequences of a conversion to Islam has been reached by an analysis of the facts and circumstances of that particular case as much as by wider policy issues. The question of religion and of conversion is only one of several factors which the courts will take into account.

5–40 The two cases discussed above provide detailed reference to earlier cases decided by the British Indian courts on the implications of conversion to Islam. These cases also serve as examples of the use of the formulas 'justice, equity and good conscience' or 'justice and right' and they came to the same conclusion as the cases reported in 1948. In *Sayeda Khatoon v. M. Obadiah* [1944/45] 49 Cal. W.N. 745, both parties were members of the Jewish community domiciled in India. They married in Calcutta in 1943 according to Jewish rites. In December 1943, the husband deserted the wife, and in 1945 the wife embraced Islam. She petitioned the court for an order that her marriage be declared at an end by reason of the conversion. Lodge J. asked, however, why Islamic law should be preferred to Jewish law in a matrimonial dispute between a Muslim and a Jew, particularly when the relationship was created under Jewish law. He decided, first, that Muslim law should not govern the dispute, and second, that by the principle of 'justice and right' the marriage still subsisted.

5–41 There are a few isolated cases where the courts in this situation have applied the Muslim law as the governing law. The most important case, so far as India is concerned, is *Ayesha Bibi v. Subodh Chandra Chakrabarty*.[46] This case was decided by Ormond J. in the Calcutta High Court. The husband and wife in this case both came from backgrounds referred to in the judgment as 'respectable' Brahmin families. They were married according to Hindu rites in 1941. They then went to live in the wife's parents house and the husband became, as the judgment puts it, 'a domesticated son-in-law'. Nevertheless, the husband mistreated his wife. In 1943, perhaps in desperation, the wife converted to Islam and invited her husband to accept her new faith. On his refusal, she petitioned for a declaration that the marriage had been dissolved. Ormond J. granted her the declaration. Clause 19 of the 1865 Letters Patent establishing the High Court directed him to give judgment according to 'justice and right'. The Government of India Act 1915 directed him that in certain matters he must decide according to the laws of the defendant, but he held that the Government of India Act did not apply to the case before him because it did not cover suits relating to marriage. Thus the case must be governed according to 'justice and right', and in his view it was just and right to apply the Muslim law, primarily because, in his opinion, under the Hindu law the wife-apostate would be reduced to the position of an untouchable menial servant. It was also just and right in the circumstances of the case to separate the parties because no rights of the husband would be transgressed and the husband, too, would be liberated from an intolerable position. Under the umbrella of 'justice, equity and good conscience', therefore, in certain cases the Indian courts have been willing to accept that conversion to Islam can lead to a severing of the marital tie.

---

[46] I.L.R. [1945] 2 Cal. 405. See also the older case of *Budansa Rowther v. Fatma Bi* [1914] 26 M.L.J. 260. Some other, unreported cases are referred to by Basu [1948] 2 Nos. 3–4 *The Indian Law Review* 249.

This is by no means, however, as appears to be the case in Pakistan, a general rule; in fact it is rather an exception.

5–42   Since it is a well-known fact in South Asia that conversions to Islam occur on a considerable scale, the legal issues which conversion gives rise to will continue to engage lawyers. It will be interesting to watch new developments in this field. The general position seems well-settled, though: if it is the husband who converts to Islam, depending on the status of the wife as a *kitabiyya* or non-*kitabiyya*, the matter will probably not go to court and the marriage will be allowed to subsist. If, however, the wife is the one who converts to Islam, and the husband is unwilling to follow her in this, then there is a greater likelihood of litigation.

5–43   In the context of this discussion, it has been notable that there is now a considerable divergence between the laws of Pakistan and of India in respect of the consequences of conversion to Islam. In the latter case, although Muslim law as such is not the law of the land, it is still an integral part of the official legal system as the personal law of an important minority. We shall now briefly take a look at the British legal scenario to see how English law would handle such questions if they arose.

Application of Muslim law in Britain

5–44   The general rule would appear to be that under English law today, Muslims in Britain are governed by English law, as anybody else, unless we are dealing with a conflicts of laws situation, in which case Muslim law will be applied as a matter of foreign law. In the domestic British arena, Muslim law is reduced to 'custom' or 'cultural practice', is treated as extra-legal and thus not immediately recognised. In this regard, the author of the leading British study in this field to date has written:

> "Broadly speaking, if an event occurs in this country its direct legal consequences will, in the vast majority of cases, be governed exclusively by English domestic law" (Poulter (1986), p. 4).

This confirms that there is, first of all, no conceptual space for the application of Muslim law. Even in the field of conflicts of laws, as Chapter 4, above showed in detail, Muslim law and its effects have been more and more curtailed by English legal rules, which appear to have the purpose of exercising some kind of control or supervision.

5–45   As far as English domestic law is concerned, following from our discussion in Chapter 3, above, we can summarise the current position as follows:

(1) English law does not operate a personal law system, as all South Asian countries, for example, clearly do.

(2) Because English law offers no conceptual space for any form of Muslim law as an integral part of the English legal system, questions of Muslim identity will probably not be brought before English courts, in the first place.

(3) When it comes to defining a Muslim, the same criteria will presumably apply as are used in other jurisdictions. This is because they are theological and religious criteria, rather than legal ones.

(4) If such questions were brought, English lawyers would probably be in need of taking expert advice.[47] The role of expert opinions would inevitably become a critical element in such cases but there would be reservations about the interference of religious authority.[48]

(5) Cases that come before English courts and tribunals could in fact involve key questions of Muslim identity. This is because, not only in the modern world, legal issues concerning the position of religious minorities have sometimes been carried to foreign domestic courts. It is likely, for example, that disputes about the position of Ahmadis will arise before English courts.[49] If the past colonial policies offers any useful pointers, it may be predicted that English law today would prefer to stay out of such disputes, especially if they are of a religious nature.[50]

Other cases have arisen, however, in which disputes among Muslims in Britain were carried before English courts, such as several recent controversies about mosque leadership, some of which have been treated as criminal law matters under English law rather than cases involving religious controversies (see Badawi (1995), p. 79). In such circumstances, English judges will probably restrict themselves to the technical legal aspects of the case before them, rather than getting involved in questions of theology. Again, it needs to be emphasised that conflicts of such a nature will probably not be raised before an English court in the first place.

5-46   Arguments of the 'cultural defence' type have already been alluded to in Chapter 3, above, where reference was made to the case of *R. v. Bibi* [1980] 1 W.L.R. 1193. In that case, a Muslim wife argued successfully for a reduction in penalty for trafficking drugs, on the grounds that she had been subject to the authority of male members of her family when she committed acts which turned out to be against the law of the land. It is doubtful whether such cultural defence arguments will be widely acceptable.

5-47   However, the potential is always there for Muslims in Britain to argue that they are not really bound by English law. In other words, the argument is that as a member of the *ummah* they are bound by God's law (King (1995)). Of course, this is a matter of conscience, always present, but would and should this override adherence to English law? We know what the theological answer must be. The official legal answer, no doubt, would be in the negative. It seems apparent that modern, so-called secular legal systems have found a way round this conundrum by dividing the legal sphere into the private and the public, and by assuming that individuals can be bound by religion in private, as a matter of conscience, while at the same time the law insists on being the superior authority. This is clearly an unresolved issue which continues to give rise to conflicting claims. The example of a recent case, resolved by consent before reaching a judicial forum, may be instructive. It highlights the limited potential for relying on Muslim identity in the context of English legal proceedings today.

---

[47] On the crucial role of expert evidence see Poulter (1986), pp. 6–7.

[48] We note, for example, the reservations expressed about the use of religious expert opinions in Mannan (1990), p. 2. Read in context, these probably indicate judicial concern about the latent potential for conflicts between law and religion in British India as well as in Pakistan today. Similar concerns would arise in Britain.

[49] This has already happened in asylum cases in Britain and elsewhere. For examples see *Mohammad Suleman Malik v. Secretary of State for the Home Department* (Appeal Number TH/40604/93, heard on May 26, 1995) and *Kaleen Ahmed* (12774). There is a comparatively much larger amount of material on Ahmadi cases in German asylum law.

[50] On the reservations of English law about religion generally see Bradney, *Religions, rights and laws* (1993).

5–48 Mr and Mrs X were a Pakistani Muslim couple living in England. Over several years, the wife gave birth to a number of children and the family acquired a larger house with the help of a mortgage from a building society. After some years, the husband decided to leave the family, the wife fell into arrears with the mortgage payments and the building society started proceedings for the recovery of those arrears and for repossession of the property. The wife opposed this action on the ground that, as a Muslim wife, she had not really been a party to the mortgage deed and she should not be bound by it. Her argument, somewhat similar to that used in *R. v. Bibi*, was that as a dutiful Muslim wife, she simply signed anything her husband put before her without questioning him.

5–49 This kind of argument, apparently untested in the English courts so far, is not likely to succeed. It will be general legal policy to treat a contract entered in Britain as a binding agreement, whose presence overrides any consideration of the religious arguments used by any particular individual.

5–50 The wife in the above case was obviously relying on extremely idealistic interpretations of the role of Muslim family members. However, the husband's desertion of the family, for whatever reason, showed that this particular family had not exactly exhibited characteristics of strict adherence to 'pure' Islamic norms. The case was bound to fail but the temptation to juggle with the competing authorities of the state's law and Muslim religion will probably continue to motivate claims for the recognition of particular Muslim cultural practices. Particularly in employment law and in education law, among others, such disputes will continue to arise. It appears that at present no comprehensive analysis of the place of Muslim law in such contexts is available.[51] It remains, as we pointed out before, not easy being British for Muslims living under the jurisdiction of English law.[52]

5–51 As concerns the specific topic of conversion to Islam, and its legal implications in Britain, the absence of a personal law system within English law precludes the emergence of officially recognised interpersonal conflicts of laws, such as we studied for India or Pakistan. In the eyes of the official law, converts to Islam in Britain would remain governed by the same legal system that applied to them before their conversion. However, this is probably not the end of this story in Britain today. In the absence of official documentation of such important questions, it is apparent that issues such as this one remain to be covered in more depth and detail through further studies.

---

[51] For a conceptual discussion see King, *God's law versus state law. The construction of an Islamic identity in Western Europe* (1995). On the question of Muslim headscarves in schools in England and France see now Poulter [1997] 17 *Oxford Journal of Legal Studies* 43–74.
[52] See on this, with instructive examples, Modood, *Not easy being British. Colour, culture and citizenship* (1992).

Chapter 6

Muslim marriage: Form and capacity

6–01 This chapter considers the legal framework of the marriage contract in Muslim law. The material is divided into sections that outline and discuss first the classical principles and then focus on South Asia. In the third sub-section, we consider these issues with reference to the legal position of Muslims in Britain today. The material in this chapter concentrates on the formal requirements for entering into a valid Muslim marriage, focusing on registration, capacity, and guardianship in marriage before we discuss the prohibitory rules which prevent certain relationships from being given the imprint of a fully valid and lawful union.

Marriage according to the classical system

The *nikah*

6–02 In this section, we turn first to the basic elements of this concept and then consider how one documents such a contract.[1] The Muslim marriage ceremony is normally referred to as the *nikah*. In view of the informality of pre-Islamic marriage customs,[2] the Islamic system of Muslim marriage sought to regularise relations between the sexes. Muslim definitions of marriage therefore emphasise "the lawful entitlement of each of the parties thereto to enjoy the other in a lawful manner" (Nasir (1990a), p. 41). Other authoritative sources give a slightly wider interpretation, considering also the implications on the children from such a union. Fyzee (1974, p. 90) says in this regard that it is "a contract for the legalisation of intercourse and the procreation of children". Nasir (1990a, p. 41; 1990b, p. 3) provides a number of comprehensive definitions of marriage taken from various North African and Middle Eastern jurisdictions.[3]

6–03 A Muslim marriage is in essence a solemn civil contract between a man and a woman.[4] Middle Eastern writers like Nasir (1990a, p. 41) distinguish it from the sacramental concept of Christian marriage, while South Asian authors almost always contrast the Muslim contract of *nikah* with the Hindu concept of marriage as an indissoluble sacrament or *samskara*. Referring to a leading case, Fyzee (1974, p. 90) stresses that "marriage among Muhammadans is not a sacrament, but purely a civil contract".[5] It is apparent, however, that a Muslim marriage also has religious elements and is not purely a matter of contractual arrangement between two

---

[1] We are not discussing here the topic of betrothal, on which see in considerable detail Nasir (1990a), pp. 42–45.
[2] On this see Engineer (1992), pp. 20–40; Miftahi, *Modesty and chastity in Islam* (1993), pp 8–17; Bharatiya (1996), pp. 50–51.
[3] For a comparative study of Moroccan and Iranian laws of marriage see Mir-Hosseini, *Marriage on trial. A study of Islamic family law: Iran and Morocco compared* (1993).
[4] On Muslim marriage see in detail El Alami (1992). An overview of many jurisdictions is provided in El Alami and Hinchcliffe (1996).
[5] This has given rise to misunderstandings, criticised by Mahmood (1986), pp. 63–66 (see below para. 6–41). Such a simple contrast underplays the contractual elements of Hindu marriage, while the element of indissolubility of Hindu (and Christian) marriages has been overstated.

individuals.[6] Indeed, as a contract before God, it has a character of sanctity (Nasir (1990a), p. 42; (1990b), p. 4).

6–04 In terms of formal requirements, the *nikah* is effected quite simply by the two essential elements of offer and acceptance.[7] The declarations, which must be made conceptually 'at the same meeting' (for details see Nasir (1990a), p. 46) are pronounced by the parties themselves, or by an attorney (*vakil*) acting on their behalf, or by their guardians when they lack the capacity to contract themselves in marriage. The first speech, from whichever side it emanates, is the offer, and the second speech constitutes the acceptance. Nasir (1990a, p. 46) emphasises that "mutual hearing and understanding of the offer and acceptance are essential to establish a marriage contract". Muslim law has therefore made provisions for contracting marriages in different languages, even sign language (Nasir (1990a), p. 46), and a proxy marriage, for example over the telephone, is possible in Muslim law.

6–05 Another essential element of a valid Muslim marriage contract, except for Shi'as,[8] is the presence of witnesses. It has been said that this element of publicity makes the difference between lawful wedlock and fornication (Nasir (1990a), p. 54). The particulars of this requirement depend on school tradition, but the general rule is that there must be either two males or one male and two females.[9]

6–06 The simple contractual form of marriage is almost always accompanied by religious and customary ceremonials.[10] However, as emphasised by Anderson and Coulson (1967, p. 62):

> "Those formalities which are usually attendant upon a Muslim marriage, such as the performance of the ceremony in the presence of a religious official like the Imam of the mosque, are matters of customary practice and in no sense legal essentials."

However, proof of such forms of celebration of a Muslim marriage may become part of the evidence required to demonstrate the existence of a particular marriage in law. This is important since there may be no written evidence of the simple contractual arrangements, which may have been entirely oral.

6–07 The understanding of the traditional concepts of Muslim marriage and the simplicity and informality of the contract do not take account of the need, especially in complex and highly mobile societies today, to have definitive formal proof of the existence of a legally valid marriage. While official registration is considered of paramount importance today, in traditional societies, instead of formal registration, the publicity of the marriage contract serves as an important safeguard. Further, the public celebration of the marriage through feasting and other social rituals leads to public recognition of the married status of the individuals concerned. In this context, certain presumptions of marriage have developed in practice.

---

[6] See Doi (1984), p. 117. On the fact that Muslim marriage is much more than just a formal contract, a good discussion is found in Bharatiya (1996), p. 55.

[7] *ibid.* p. 56 neatly summarises all the basic requirements. There are different terms in Arabic and other relevant languages for these essential elements. For details on Middle Eastern laws see Nasir (1990a), p. 45; for South Asian laws see, *e.g.* Fyzee (1974), p. 91.

[8] Tayyibji (1968), p. 54 states that Maliki law strongly recommends the presence of witnesses but does not make it necessary for the validity of the marriage.

[9] For particulars see Nasir (1990a), pp. 54–55; *ibid.*; 55 and Fyzee (1974), p. 91 emphasise that witnesses are not required in Shi'i law, they are merely desirable.

[10] We do not have the space here to refer in detail to Middle Eastern and other Muslim marriage customs. For details see nn.3 and 4, above. On traditions in the Middle East an important study is Smith (1907).

6–08 Attempts to introduce registration procedures have met with considerable opposition. The present position in most Muslim countries is that facilities exist for registration of marriages, but non-compliance with these merely involves criminal sanctions and does not invalidate the marriage. A device which has been employed in Egyptian law, for example, has been to remove the ability of the courts to adjudicate over matrimonial disputes, inheritance problems and the like, in cases where a marriage has not been registered.[11]

Capacity

6–09 Considering questions relating to the capacity of persons to contract a valid Muslim marriage, we find that three issues, apart from sanity, are of particular relevance here.[12] First, the age of the spouses. Secondly, the question of consent, *i.e.* whether a minor spouse can contract himself or herself into marriage or whether a guardian of some kind is required. Thirdly, the so-called 'option of puberty' is an important issue in this context. These questions continue to be of considerable relevance in legal practice and have also given rise to important recent cases in South Asian law (see paragraph 6–50, below).

6–10 The general rule is that both parties to the marriage must possess legal capacity (Nasir (1990a), p. 47). Emphasising that under modern state laws legal capacity for marriage need not be the same as full legal capacity or the age of majority, Nasir (1990a, pp. 47–49) provides relevant details about minimum marriage ages from many Middle Eastern and North African countries.[13]

6–11 The reason for the discrepancy between legal capacity for marriage and full legal capacity is that classical Islamic law provides that every Muslim of sound mind who has reached puberty has thereby attained majority. Muslim law, therefore, is not in principle opposed to what modern jurisdictions call 'child marriage'. It is apparent that the criteria for defining a person as a 'child' differ in important respects.

6–12 In Hanafi law, the general rule is that a person can contract a marriage as soon as he or she has attained the age of puberty. Emphasising that celibacy is not considered a virtue in Islam, Doi (1984, p. 115) relates that "the Prophet orders Muslims to get married as soon as they can" and links this to the statement that "extra-marital relations are categorically condemned and prohibited" (*id.*). A key argument for early marriages is therefore, clearly, the avoidance of any form of extra-marital relations, which would fall under the prohibitions of *zina*. In Muslim law, the presumption is that puberty is reached at 15 years old, but evidence can certainly be produced to the effect that it has been reached at an age earlier than this. Minimum ages would appear to be 12 years old in the case of males and nine years old in the case of females (Fyzee (1974), pp. 93–94).

6–13 Of course there are legitimate concerns about the marriages of children at such a young age. In addition, Nasir (1990b, p. 12) makes reference to what he calls an "emotionally charged issue" in parts of the Muslim world, namely the custom of pre-arranging marriages while the parties concerned are still very young. He emphasises that such practices are not in accordance with the *shari'a* and often conflict with the laws of modern states, so that this may even become a crime. In South Asian laws, too, this is an important issue and even in Britain cases of child betrothal and of 'child marriage' among Muslims have given rise to legal intervention (see paragraphs 6–50 and 6–106, below).

---

[11] For details of many jurisdictions see Nasir (1990a), pp. 70–76. With particular reference to Egypt see Ibrahim and Bakar (1980) and now Shaham (1995).

[12] Sanity is a basic precondition for a Muslim marriage. On this see briefly Nasir (1990a), p. 49.

[13] See now in detail El Alami and Hinchcliffe (1996).

6–14 Nasir (1990b, p. 12) argues that "the freedom of both parties reigns supreme in the choice of the partner" but does not back this statement up with further references. He does make the important point, however, that:

"Guardianship, even with the right of compulsion, is not intended to coerce any party into acceptance of another in wedlock, but to guard the ward's best interests. Even that authority is not absolute. . . . it is subject to appeal before the judge, who holds the welfare of the ward as of paramount importance" (*id.*).

This topic, predictably and inevitably, has led to complex, fierce debates about the question of guardianship in marriage, which relate to children as well as women generally and are often discussed under the separate heading of 'guardianship in marriage'.[14] Nasir (1990a, pp. 50–51) summarises the general *shari'a* rules on marriage guardianship and highlights the important distinction between 'guardianship with the right of compulsion' and 'guardianship without the right of compulsion' (*ibid.*, p. 50). The latter, as stated *id.*, is exercised when the woman is an adult and possesses full legal capacity,

". . . but in deference to social customs and traditions, delegates the conclusion of her marriage to a guardian. In fact this is more of an authorization of agent than guardianship. Some Islamic jurists call it joint guardianship when the woman has been previously married."

It is obviously difficult to draw precise distinctions between the two types of guardianship and it is not surprising that social customs and traditions should have coloured juristic interpretations. Indeed, the four major Sunni schools also differ in important respects in their interpretation. The Shafi'i and Maliki schools consider approval of the guardian as an essential element in a marriage, while the Hanafi and Hanbali schools do not insist on this.[15]

"Nevertheless, the general consensus of jurists is that the woman shall not conduct her own marriage contract, whether she is a virgin or previously married, even when she possesses full legal capacity. Only the Hanafis do not require a guardian to conclude the contract on behalf of the woman unless she is of no or limited legal capacity."[16]

6–15 In contrast to the more liberal Hanafi law, in both Shafi'i and Maliki law, even an adult virgin has been taken to have no capacity to contract herself in marriage.[17] She needs the consent of her guardian, and indeed it is possible for a guardian to contract into marriage his daughter who has reached puberty without any necessity of obtaining her prior consent. The woman only becomes capable of contracting herself in marriage when she ceases to be a virgin by reason of a consummated marriage or an illicit sexual relationship.[18] Nasir's outline of various

---

[14] See, *e.g.* Bharatiya (1996), pp. 67–68.

[15] This is a very early distinguishing feature of different school traditions, as Coulson, "Islamic law", in *An introduction to legal systems* (1968), p. 60, confirms. For details see Doi (1984), pp. 140–142; Nasir (1990a), pp. 50–53; similarly Nasir, *The status of women under Islamic law and under modern Islamic legislation* (1990a), pp. 9–12;

[16] Nasir (1990a), p. 50; virtually identical Nasir (1990b), p. 10.

[17] Moroccan law, for example, was built on that doctrine, as in the Moroccan Code of Personal Status and Succession of 1957–1958. However, a new law, passed on September 10, 1993, amended the traditional provisions and now allows a woman in certain circumstances to contract her own marriage. The general rule now appears to be that a woman has the right to authorise a guardian of her choice.

[18] See for the Shafi'i law the decision of the Singapore Appeal Board in *Syed Abdullah Shatiri v. Sharifa Salman* (1959) Malaysian L.J. 137.

modern Middle Eastern and North African laws on the subject shows that this is an important issue in Muslim countries on which there continues to be much debate.[19]

6–16 Classical Islamic law would appear to have provided a remedy to a spouse who had been forced into a marriage in the form of the so-called 'option of puberty' (*khiyar-al-bulugh*). Of course, this right may not be very meaningful in social reality. It is not found in the Qur'an nor in the Prophet's *sunna*, but is based on juristic opinions in the various schools. Although Hanafi law does permit a guardian the right to contract his minor ward in marriage, the child on attaining puberty has a right himself or herself, under certain conditions, to avoid the union by exercising this option. In classical Hanafi law, the option exists only in cases where the child is married by a guardian other than the father or grandfather. The exercise of the option of puberty is the only situation in Hanafi law where a marriage can be avoided unilaterally and extra-judicially at the option of one of the parties. A marriage made by way of jest, or under duress, or without any intent to contract a marriage is, in Hanafi law, nevertheless lawful.

6–17 The other Sunni schools recognise the right of *khiyar* in the area of jest and duress. The person who was induced into performing the marriage, for instance through threat, can in effect rescind the contract by the exercise of the *khiyar*. This topic seems to have a very low profile in classical Islamic law and is debated in detail mainly with reference to South Asian Muslim law.[20]

Classification of marriages

6–18 We now turn briefly to the classification of different kinds of marriage found in Sunni law.[21] Most modern jurists in India and Pakistan (see paragraph 6–69, below) adopt a threefold classification between the valid union (*sahih*), the void union (*batil*) and a middle classification, the irregular union (*fasid*). This type of classification is not necessarily acceptable to non-Hanafi Muslims and even some Hanafi jurists, not least the two disciples, Abu Yusuf and Shaybani, who were not prepared to adopt a rigid demarcation. Nevertheless, the classification technique has gained acceptance. At the very least, it does provide a framework within which one can discuss the effects of irregularities in the form of a marriage or the capacity of the parties to contract a marriage.

6–19 The *sahih* marriage is a valid and fully effective union. It has a total effect in law in that sexual intercourse is lawful. In addition, the wife is entitled both to a dower (*mahr*) and to maintenance by the husband during the marriage. The husband acquires certain specific rights relating to the organisational aspects of the relationship, based primarily upon his patriarchal power to control the activities of his wife, although she retains rights with respect both to ownership and control over her own property (see also paragraph 7–31, below).

6–20 At the other end of the spectrum is the *batil* or void marriage, which does not create any rights or obligations between the parties other than that there is no *zina*, the technical term for any illicit sexual relations outside marriage, if the parties were unaware that the marriage was void. If there is consummation in a *batil*

---

[19] For details see Nasir (1990a), pp. 51–53; Nasir (1990b), pp. 10–12. Further material is found in El Alami (1992).

[20] For details see also Carroll (1981b) and para. 6–50, below.

[21] For details see Nasir (1990a), pp. 53–70; Nasir (1990b), pp. 12–28. Siddiqui, *Studies in Muslim law. Vol. I. Batil and fasid marriages* (1955) is an early specialist study of this subject. The discussion in Doi (1984), pp. 155–157 is quite limited. The topic of the temporary (*muta*) marriage has fascinated many writers but is only an element of Shi'a law. For details see Nasir (1990b), pp. 16–18; Nasir (1990a), pp. 57–59; Doi (1984), pp. 155–156.

marriage, it could be argued that there should be a right of dower, similar to a consummated *fasid* marriage. However, this is a doubtful proposition. The factor which makes the union *batil* is that there is a permanent irregularity preventing the relationship from being regularised.

6–21 An irregular (*fasid*) marriage, like a *batil* marriage, is also no marriage at all, but it can be regularised in certain circumstances. A *fasid* marriage, however, is not capable of ratification by simple approbation, there must be a separation of the parties first. While there is a clear irregularity in a *fasid* relationship, in contrast to the *batil* relationship, the irregularity in this situation is of a temporary nature. Thus, if the parties were to separate and the temporary bar removed there would be no reason why the marriage between the parties should not be reconstituted as a *sahih* union. If the *fasid* marriage is consummated, certain legal effects arise, primarily that children of the union are legitimate, a dower is due to the wife, and on separation, the wife is obliged to observe an *'idda* period from the date of separation. The parties are also not liable to any penalties for committing *zina*. The distinction between *batil* and *fasid* was well described by Professor Anderson (1950, p. 359) who, in commenting upon Abu Hanifa's view, stated:

> ". . . there was a clear and logical distinction between *batil* and *fasid* contracts of marriage. In the former the contract was vitiated in essence and there was no legal effect; in the latter the contract was good in itself, and would have been valid in different circumstances, but was illegal in this particular instance by reason of some divine prohibition."

A *fasid* marriage therefore is good in itself, but the particular circumstances render it irregular. Thus it is the responsibility of the parties, or in the absence of any move by the parties themselves, the responsibility of the Qadi, to separate the couple.

6–22 The two disciples, as well as the Shi'i schools and the other Sunni schools, recognise no real distinction between *batil* and *fasid* unions. Rather they recognise the doctrine of 'semblance' (*shubha*) of the marriage which confirms that although a systematic distinction between *batil* and *fasid* appears from some of the texts, nonetheless this distinction is blurred at the edges. Some jurists state that neither an irregular nor a void marriage has *any* validity whatever in law unless it is consummated. If the union is consummated in a situation where the parties were acting in good faith, then any children of such a union are legitimate and there is no *zina*. The 'wife' is entitled to the appropriate dower and the *'idda* period has to be observed by her on separation. The jurists often classify types of marriages under five different conditions (*shurut*). These conditions are:

   (a) *shurut al-in'iqad,*
   (b) *shurut al-sihha,*
   (c) *shurut al-madaidh,*
   (d) *shurut al-luzum,*
   (e) *shurut al-sijill.*

The first *shurut* deals with the necessity to comply with the formal conditions, namely that offer and acceptance must be pronounced at the same meeting, and must issue from persons competent to make the contract. The second *shurut* deals with the conditions which decide whether the contract, valid as to form, actually creates a marriage valid as to essence. For instance, are the parties outside the prohibited degree of relationship? Thirdly, the *shurut al-madaidh*, which deals with the matter of effectiveness, relates primarily to questions of capacity of slaves and, as such, is no longer of significance. Fourthly, the *shurut al-luzum* concerns itself with the question whether the contract is binding, for example, the option of puberty and the ability of the husband to consummate the marriage. The fifth *shurut* refers to the modern innovation of registration. Here, a new category has been created, the illegal marriage, whereby criminal penalties and sanctions are imposed in the absence of registration, although the marriage may well be valid, if it can be proved by other means.[22]

Void (batil) marriages

6–23 Under this heading, we need to consider prohibited degrees of blood relatives (*nasab*), prohibited relationships by affinity (*musahara*), relationship by fosterage (*rada'a*), illicit sexual impropriety, remarriage to a triply divorced wife and differences of religion.[23]

6–24 The first heading of *batil* marriages relates to the prohibitions which stem from consanguinity. In outline, the rules prohibit a man from marrying his own ascendants or descendants; or his father's or mother's descendants, *i.e.* his sister and her descendants. A complete list of the prohibitory degrees indicates that there is a permanent impediment of marriage between a man and:

    (i)   his mother and all female ascendants;
   (ii)   his daughter and all female descendants;
  (iii)   his sister, whether germane, consanguine, or uterine;
  (iv)   his paternal aunt and the paternal aunt of any ascendant;
   (v)   his maternal aunt and any maternal aunt of any ascendant;
  (vi)   his brother's daughter (of whatever degree of descent);
 (vii)   his sister's daughter (of whatever degree of descent).

The only immediate relatives with whom the man is free to marry are his mother's brother's/sister's daughter and his father's brother's/sister's daughter, *i.e.* his cousins. Such marriages are of frequent occurrence in the Indian subcontinent, especially in Pakistan.

6–25 Relationships by affinity are, in certain circumstances, likewise not allowed. A man is prohibited from marrying, first, any ascendant or descendant of his wife and second, any former wife of any ascendant or descendant. The only exception which is permitted in Hanafi law is that a man, if he so desires, can marry a descendant of his wife by another marriage so long as he had not consummated that marriage with her.[24] If the first marriage is itself *fasid* or *batil*, then there is no prohibition on marrying a descendant of that woman from the first *batil* or *fasid* marriage unless the union had been consummated. If this has in fact occurred, then the prohibition is operative.

6–26 Historically, a third major prohibition arises in Muslim law in situations where there is a relationship of 'fosterage'.[25] This prohibition, introduced by jurists, stemmed from the not uncommon situation of the woman providing breast milk not only for her own child but for someone else's child as well. The two children are then prohibited from intermarrying, as is the male child with the foster mother.

[22] A relevant case from Pakistan is *Nasim Akhtar v. The State* P.L.D. 1968 Lah. 841.
[23] For further details see Nasir (1990a), pp. 60–63; Nasir (1990b), pp. 19–22.
[24] *Hedaya* Vol. 1 Book II, Chap. 1.
[25] Nasir (1990a), pp. 62–63 and Nasir (1990b), pp. 21–22 also provide examples of modern statutory regulation.

The link arising out of the mother's milk is therefore given a force similar to that of the blood tie.[26]

6–27 Illicit sexual impropriety between a man and a woman also creates a bar to marriage, about which there appears to be more debate in South Asian law than elsewhere. Although the man, at least in the Sunni schools, can marry the girl in question, the improper association is seen by the Hanafi and the Hanbali jurists, in particular, as an association which creates a permanent bar to a marriage between the man and those relatives of the girl with whom he is prohibited by the bar on affinity (*musahara*). The man can, however, marry the girl's sister, for there is no such bar in that situation based on *musahara*, as indicated in the Pakistani case of *Sakina v. The State*, P.L.D. 1981 F.S.C. 320.

6–28 Moreover, the impropriety is caused not only when there is actual proof of sexual intercourse. It arises also when there is privacy (*khalwat*) between the parties. The Hanafi and the Hanbali jurists, therefore, treat the sexual act, or an actual period of privacy, as equivalent to a *nikah* to create a *musahara* impediment. This view of illicit sexual contact being equated to a *nikah* was rejected by the Shafi'i and Maliki jurists. The Shi'i jurists accept the Hanafi view with regard to actual illicit intercourse, but if there is privacy only, the Shi'i jurists do not have any consensus view, some favouring the Hanafi viewpoint and others preferring the Maliki law.

6–29 If a Muslim husband divorces his wife by *talaq* and repudiates her for a third time, whether in a single, final pronouncement or in the 'triple *talaq*', a prohibition on marriage between the two arises. Thus any marriage between the couple *inter se* is void unless and until, first, the woman has observed her *idda* or waiting period. Secondly, there has to be a supervening marriage between the woman and another man. Thirdly, the rule is that this supervening marriage must itself have been consummated and effectively terminated. There is some dispute as to whether a remarriage between the man and his first wife without the intervening union is *batil* or *fasid*.

6–30 Although polygamy within certain limits is permissible, polyandry, where the woman takes a second husband whilst still married to her first husband, is treated by Muslim law as utterly reprehensible and such a second union is definitely *batil*.[27]

6–31 As for differences of religion, the general rule in Hanafi law is that a Muslim male may marry a 'woman of the book' (*kitabiyya*), while a Muslim female can marry no one other than a Muslim male.[28] Most Shi'i sects, traditionally, do not permit any flexibility. The status of *kitabiyya* is granted to Jewish and Christian girls, and also to Magians or Zoroastrians.[29] The important question is whether a marriage solemnised between a Muslim husband and a non-*kitabiyya* or between a Muslim girl and a non-Muslim is *batil* or *fasid*. In the Qur'an, Sura II, verse 221, it is said: "Do not marry unbelieving women until they believe". This is generally taken to show that a union of the type referred to is a *batil* union. However, the distinctions between this view and the acceptance of such marriages as irregular are

---

[26] Doi (1984), p. 157 laments in this context what he calls the curse of the modern milk bank, which leads to confusion.

[27] See *In the Matter of Ram Kumari*, I.L.R. [1891] 18 Cal. 264; *Budansa Rowther v. Fatma Bi* [1914] 26 M.L.J. 260. Carroll [1981b], 23 No. 2 J.I.L.I., p. 163 shows that judges in British India took an extremely negative view of polyandry.

[28] See Nasir (1990a), p. 69 and Nasir (1990b), p. 27 with the relevant verses from the Qur'an.

[29] However, in *Viswalingham v. Viswalingham* [1979] 1 F.L.R. 15, the English Court of Appeal decided that the unilateral termination of a marriage, under the law of Malaysia, by the husband's change of religion from Hindu to Muslim did not constitute a divorce within the meaning of the English legislation. In the context of this case, the court heard evidence of a restrictive approach taken by Shafi'i law to the definition of a *kitabiyya*.

not very clear, and they have been further blurred in South Asian Muslim law (see paragraph 6–69, below).

Irregular (fasid) marriages

6–32 As we saw, Muslim law developed the position that there can be several situations in which a marriage is not treated as entirely void but as irregular.[30] In most of these scenarios, the marriage can fairly easily be regularised in certain ways. The main situations we are dealing with here are the absence of witnesses, the fact that a woman married during her *idda*, situations concerning unlawful conjunction with close relatives of the wife, where a man oversteps the limits of polygamy, and the lack of equality of status between the spouses *(kafa'a)*.

6–33 Absence of witnesses to a Muslim marriage may make that marriage irregular, depending on school tradition and circumstances.[31] It will be recalled that one of the few essential formalities to be observed in a *nikah* is that witnesses, two males, or one male and two females, must be present at the moment the marital tie is created. Thus the Sunni jurists agree unanimously that the presence of witnesses is essential to ensure publicity. The witnesses must be adult, sane and Muslim. A man and a woman who contract a marriage without witnesses are under a duty, as in all *fasid* marriages, to separate. This bar is not permanent, however, and the matter can be resolved by the husband and wife contracting a fresh marriage in the presence of the appropriate witnesses.

6–34 Muslim law permits the proof of marriage on the basis of a prolonged and continuous cohabitation by the parties and thus applies a presumption of marriage. There must be evidence that the man acknowledged the woman as his lawful wife, and equally acknowledged any children by the relationship as being his legitimate children. The presumption does not arise in a case where no lawful marriage could have been solemnised in any event. Nasir (1990b, p. 22) helpfully summarises several other situations in which a marriage will be treated as irregular (see also Nasir (1990a, p. 64):

> "An existing married status is an impediment to a valid marriage in three situations: (a) a woman married or in her iddat; (b) unlawful conjunction; (c) polygamy."

A *fasid* relationship arises therefore when a man marries a woman who is still in her *iddat* period. The *iddat* must be observed by the woman after her divorce or on the death of the first husband. The *iddat* provides a period of time for the parties to 'ascertain the state of the womb' at the moment of divorce or death. This is important in order to establish parentage and thus to protect the rights both of the first as well as of a potential second husband, and of course of any child born to such a woman. In addition, the *iddat* period enables the wife to observe mourning in the case of her husband's death. If the wife is pregnant, it is seen to be correct for tenderness to be shown to the foetus.

6–35 Therefore, during the *iddat* period the wife cannot remarry.[32] If she does so, the marriage is *fasid*, there must be a separation, and the parties must contract a

---

[30] Siddiqui (1955), p. 68 shows that early jurists made no distinction between *batil* and *fasid* marriages. Nasir discusses relevant situations under the heading of 'temporary impediments'. For details see Nasir (1990a), pp. 63–70; Nasir (1990b), pp. 22–28. His treatment shows that there is no universal agreement about the severity of several of these impediments and their precise classification.
[31] *ibid.*, pp. 12–14 treats this topic in a different context altogether; see also Nasir (1990a), pp. 54–55.
[32] On this topic, see in detail Siddiqui (1955), pp. 289–339.

fresh ceremony of marriage after the expiry of the *iddat*. The need to observe an *iddat* period is linked closely with the Islamic notion of consummation, and it is interesting to note that no *iddat* period is required when a marriage, dissolved by a *talaq*, has not been consummated. However, as we have seen, Islamic law does not demand definitive evidence of the sexual act, *i.e.* of consummation of the marriage. If it is shown that the husband and the wife were together in a room on their own, and that the circumstances of their meeting were such that there was no possible impediment to the performance of the sexual act, then this situation, often referred to as 'undue familiarity', 'privacy' or 'valid retirement' (*khalwat*), is for certain purposes, including the present matter, deemed to have the same consequences as consummation. If the marriage has not been 'consummated' in this extended sense, no *iddat* period is necessary on divorce; thus the wife on divorce can immediately remarry. Otherwise, she has to observe an *iddat* period of three menstrual cycles (or three months in the case of a woman who does not menstruate or whose menstruations are irregular) before she can remarry. Furthermore, the prohibition extends to cases of separation from a *fasid* union itself. If the woman is pregnant at the time of repudiation, or death of the husband, the *iddat* period is prolonged until the delivery. If the husband dies, an *iddat* period of death (four months and 10 days) has to be observed in any event regardless of whether the marriage has or has not been consummated. Thus any marriage solemnised by a man with a woman who is observing an *iddat* period is *fasid*.

6–36   The prohibition on unlawful conjunction is simply stated. A man may not validly contract in marriage his existing wife's sister or any woman so related to his wife that if one of those two ladies were male they could not lawfully marry. The source for this rule is Sura IV, verse 23 in the Qur'an: "And two sisters in wedlock at one and the same time, except for what is past; for Allah is oft-forgiving". This verse includes the prohibition based on consanguinity; some interpret the verse collectively as creating permanent prohibitions based on *nasab* (consanguinity) and *sabab* (other cause, namely affinity and conjunction).

6–37   The third prohibition which results in a *fasid* marriage concerns polygamy. It arises when a man, whilst already married to the maximum permitted four wives, marries a fifth wife. This fifth contract of marriage is *fasid*.[33]

6–38   The doctrine of equality (*kafa'a*) is different from the other *fasid* situations so far discussed.[34] The inequality of the parties provides the guardian in certain circumstances with the right to exercise the option (*khiyar*) to set the marriage aside. Thus, *kafa'a* is closely analogous to the option of puberty (*khiyar al-bulugh*). Nonetheless, the effect of the successful exercise of the *khiyar* and its application by the court produces a separation of the parties. Thus *kafa'a* is best discussed today within the context of *fasid* marriages.

6–39   The principle of *kafa'a* was peculiar to the ancient school of law of Kufa, where, because of the freedom of an adult girl to contract herself in marriage, it was seen to be necessary to protect the interests of the guardian (*wali*). After Shafi'i's thesis had been accepted by the scholars, the principle of *kafa'a* found its way into Maliki law, although in a rather restricted sense. In Maliki law, women require the consent of their guardian for marriage. Thus, there was no real danger that the girl would be influenced to marry a man not her equal, unless there was fraud. Thus, fraud came to be regarded as an essential ground in Maliki law on an application by

---

[33] *ibid.*, pp. 227–236. See in more detail para. 8–04, below.
[34] Indeed, it is discussed separately by Nasir (1990a), pp. 59–60 and Nasir (1990b), pp. 18–19.

the *wali* for a separation of the parties based upon inequality. This is not the case in Hanafi law.

6-40 Six matters, all to some extent interrelated, would appear to provide grounds in Hanafi law for inequality. These are: family, Islamic adherence, occupation, freedom, character and financial resources.[35] As to family and freedom, these are of no real significance today. Slavery is abolished and the view that only a man of the tribe of Qur'aysh (Mohammed's tribe) is suitable for a woman of that tribe cannot really be extended to a system which, in theory, although not in practice, is caste-free. As to Islamic adherence, a Muslim husband whose father is a non-Muslim would seem not to be *kafa'a* with a woman whose parents were both Muslim. This form of *kafa'a* must be of only limited application today and is not observed in countries such as Egypt.[36] With regard to the other three factors, namely occupation, character and financial resources, certain guidelines were developed by the jurists. First, the husband should have the probability of matching the financial means of the wife's father. Secondly, the husband should have a similar occupation as the wife's father, and thirdly, if the wife's father is pious, the husband must not be irreligious. A misalliance is not of itself *fasid*, and acquiescence by the guardian will enable the marriage to continue. It is of considerable relevance at this point to emphasise that social concerns like the above have played a large role in legal disputes over Muslim law in South Asia. We now turn our attention specifically to that part of the world.

Muslim marriages in South Asian law

The *nikah* and registration of marriages

6-41 Building on the classical definitions of Muslim marriage as a simple solemn contract,[37] South Asian legal textbook writers add a number of comments, showing how the basic Islamic concepts of marriage have been amalgamated with local customary traditions to create distinctly South Asian Muslim marriage customs.[38]

6-42 Textbooks and cases reiterate that "there are no special rites, no proper officiants, no irksome formalities" (Fyzee (1974), p. 91). The South Asian local elements added to the contractual format of a Muslim marriage are of two kinds. First, they consist of recitations from the Qur'an, underpinning the solemnity and sanctity of the marriage contract. However, they have no legal significance, as Mahmood (1986, p. 65) explains:

> "These are superfluous as far as the legal theory is concerned, but have great social significance and add an aroma of solemnity to the occasion and to the newly created relationship between the two individuals and their families."

Secondly, they consist of locally coloured rituals, feasting and the ritualised involvement of representatives or agents of the spouses (*vakil*) and the religious

---

[35] For the different criteria according to various schools see *id.*

[36] For details see Khadduri and Liebesny, *Law in the Middle East. Vol. I. Original development of Islamic law* (1955), Chap. VI by Abu Zahra.

[37] A good restatement of the basic principles is found in Fyzee (1974), pp. 91–92. The contractual nature of Muslim marriage is discussed in detail by Shabbir (1988), pp. 9–30. Mahmood (1986), pp. 63–66 complains vigorously of the misunderstandings about Muslim marriage as a pure contract.

[38] Much good writing exists on this topic. See, *e.g.* Husain, *Marriage customs among Muslims in India* (1976); Hastings, *Marriage among Muslims: Preference and choice in Northern Pakistan* (1988).

functionaries such as *mullah*. Such individuals are supposed to be conversant with the requirements of the law and will probably recite Qur'anic verses and give benedictions to the parties. The *kazi* is merely a keeper of the marriage register and his function is evidentiary (Fyzee (1974), p. 92). Mahmood (1982a, p. 54) refers to these additional features of Muslim marriage as "extra-legal practices" and says that they, too, are "superfluous as far as the theory of Islamic law is concerned". However, as the learned author adds (*id.*), "being fully established as the marriage-procedure of Muslims in this country, it has come to acquire an evidentiary value and is so recognized by the courts".[39]

6–43   There are many local variations of such practices and it would be wrong to assume that all South Asian Muslims follow the same customary patterns.[40] A description of the usual marriage ceremony in Northern Pakistan appears in the case of *Ghulam Kubra Bibi v. Mohammad Shafi Mohammad Din*, A.I.R. 1940 Pesh. 2. It is customary for a relation of the bride to be sent to the bride accompanied by two witnesses. The relation asks the bride within the hearing of the witnesses whether she authorises him to agree to the marriage offered by the prospective husband. When the bride signifies her consent, the relation and the two witnesses go to the prospective husband, who is in another house, another part of the building, or in the mosque. A religious leader (*mullah*) then asks the prospective husband whether he is offering to marry the bride. After an affirmative reply, the *mullah* will then ask the relation if he is the agent of the bride and to communicate to him the views of the bride. As soon as both the prospective husband and the relation have replied in the affirmative, the marriage is complete. Normally, certain scriptures are then read before the conclusion of the ceremony, although this is not essential.[41]

6–44   Muslim authors, in particular, are often concerned to emphasise that all these customary ritualisations do not have the force of law, thus clearly distinguishing Muslim marriage from its Hindu counterpart.[42] Mahmood (1982a, p. 55) wrote in this regard:

> "It must be noted that none of the above steps in the customary procedure of marriage among Indian Muslims, or any other additional or alternative steps that may be followed by any group of Muslims in any part of the country, constitutes a legal requirement. Holding so would strike at the very root of the Islamic legal concept of marriage."

While the essentials of a Muslim marriage remain very simple,[43] it is a well-recognised fact that these so-called extra-legal actions constitute important elements of proof in cases where the existence of a Muslim marriage is doubted. Mahmood

---

[39] In contrast, as already noted, given the nature of the marriage as a civil contract, it is possible for the contract to be concluded entirely by proxy, for instance over the telephone. This has become an issue in English law (see para. 6–106, below).
[40] See Mahmood (1982a), p. 54 with further references. Rashida Patel describes in her study of 1979 how in Pakistan many families resort to wild spending, feasting and singing, dancing and music. Pakistani law has sought to control such excesses by legislation, found in the Dowry and Bridal Gifts (Restriction) Act 1976 and the Dowry and Bridal Gifts (Restriction) Rules 1976 and the Dowry and Bridal Gifts (Restriction) (Amendment) Ordinance 1980. Ch. M. Mahmood (1991), p. 269 suggests that there is no explicitly Islamic sanction behind this legislation.
[41] See *Shahzada Begum v. Abdul Hamid*, P.L.D. 1950 Lah. 504.
[42] Even the modern statutory Hindu law, in s.7 of the Hindu Marriage Act 1955, retains the dominant position of customary rites and ceremonies as the key determinator of legal validity.
[43] On this see *Syed Amanullah Hussain v. Rajamma*, A.I.R. 1977 A.P. 152, a property dispute in which the validity of a Muslim marriage was an issue.

(1982a, p. 56) provides a helpful list of factors which may constitute proof of a Muslim marriage. These are registration of the marriage, a written record of the marriage,[44] evidence of a *kazi* that he was present at the marriage, and evidence of witnesses who can testify to the *nikah*. Nowadays, evidence in the form of photographs and video recordings is often available. Mahmood (1982a, p. 56) also refers to the important element of presumption of a valid Muslim marriage in cases where the parties have lived as husband and wife and have been treated as a married couple, where either party has acknowledged the marriage and the other party has acquiesced in this and, thirdly, where the man acknowledges paternity of the woman's child or children.

6–45   Registration of a Muslim marriage under any statutory law in India is treated as conclusive proof of its existence, but not necessarily of its validity (Mahmood (1982a), p. 56). Registration of the marriage will be good evidence and in the absence of registration it may be difficult to prove a valid marriage. It is a fact, however, that most Muslim marriages in South Asia remain unregistered and a marriage which is not registered can often be proved by the production of other evidence.[45]

6–46   Indian Muslim law does not require compulsory registration of marriages,[46] but Indian state law provides some facilities for the voluntary registration of Muslim marriages. In some states, old statutes exist to facilitate this. The earliest statute of this nature is the Registration of Muhammedan Marriages and Divorces Act 1876 (Act 1 of 1876) which is still in force in the states of West Bengal and Bihar, while some neighbouring states have modelled their own Acts on this earlier statute.[47]

6–47   In Pakistan,[48] registration of Muslim marriages was introduced by section 5 of the Muslim Family Laws Ordinance 1961, which provides as follows:

"5.   Registration of marriages.–
   (1) Every marriage solemnized under Muslim Law shall be registered in accordance with the provisions of this Ordinance.
   (2) For the purpose of registration of marriage under this Ordinance, the Union Council shall grant licence to one or more persons, to be called Nikah Registrars, but in no case shall more than one Nikah Registrar be licensed for any one ward.
   (3) Every marriage not solemnized by the Nikah Registrar shall, for the purpose of registration under this Ordinance, be reported to him by the person who has solemnized such marriage.
   (4) Whoever contravenes the provisions of sub-section (3) shall be punishable with simple imprisonment for a term which may extend to three months or with fine which may extend to one thousand rupees, or with both.

---

[44] In South Asia, different names are used for such documents. The most common term in India and Pakistan is *nikahnama*, in Bangladesh *kabhinama*.
[45] For Pakistani cases, see *Nasim Akhtar v. The State*, P.L.D. 1968 Lah. 841; *Habib v. The State*, P.L.D. 1980 Lah. 791 and *Sher Afzal v. Shamim Firdaus*, P.L.D. 1980 S.C. 228.
[46] Nor does Indian law generally. Professor Tahir Mahmood has argued vigorously in favour of a national law for compulsory registration of all marriages. On a strange case involving an Indian Muslim male, punished for registering a polygamous marriage, see Menski (1993b (2) K.T.L. 19–22).
[47] The Assam Moslem Marriages and Divorces Registration Act 1935 (Assam Act IX of 1935) and the Orissa Muhammedan Marriages and Divorces Registration Act 1947. For Bangladesh see further below.
[48] For a good discussion see Mehdi (1994), pp. 158–160. The author concludes, at p. 160, that 'compulsory' registration of marriages in Pakistan has not been successful.

(5) The form of *nikahnama*, the registers to be maintained by Nikah Registrars, the records to be preserved by Union Councils, the manner in which marriage shall be registered and copies of *nikahnama* shall be supplied to the parties, and the fees to be charged therefor, shall be such as may be prescribed.

(6) Any person may, on payment of the prescribed fee, if any, inspect at the office of the Union Council the record preserved under sub-section (5), or obtain a copy of any entry therein."

On a close reading of this statutory provision, one does not find a definite legal requirement of registration to bring about legal validity of a Muslim marriage. In other words, a Muslim marriage in Pakistan and Bangladesh still becomes legally valid when the contract of marriage has been properly completed in accordance with the personal law, not when the marriage is registered. All that the state law can do, therefore, is to encourage Muslims to register their marriages. Non-compliance with the legal requirement to register may be penalised. Indeed, section 5(4) of the 1961 Ordinance, cited above, stipulates punishments. However, these are quite lenient fines (see also Mehdi (1994), p. 160) and there is no evidence that either Pakistani or Bangladeshi law are treating non-registration as a serious offence warranting heavy penalties.

6–48 Bangladesh introduced a new Act regarding registration of Muslim marriages and divorces in 1974, which has given rise to the misguided argument that Bangladeshi Muslim marriages must now be registered to achieve legal validity. The Muslim Marriages and Divorces (Registration) Act 1974 repealed the Registration of Muhammedan Marriages and Divorces Act 1876, deleted section 5 of the Muslim Family Laws Ordinance 1961 in Bangladesh and made some other smaller amendments. The 1974 Act provides in section 3 for the registration of marriages:

"3. Registration of marriages. –
     Notwithstanding anything contained in any law, custom or usage, every marriage solemnized under Muslim law shall be registered in accordance with the provisions of this Act."

In section 4, the Act lays down a mechanism for the granting of licences to Nikah Registrars who will be licensed for a particular area. Significantly, section 5 of the Act allows explicitly for the fact that Muslims in Bangladesh will not routinely register their marriages with such registrars and provides for an alternative mechanism:

"5. Marriages not solemnized by Nikah Registrars to be reported to them. –
(1) Every marriage not solemnized by the Nikah Registrar shall, for the purpose of registration under this Act, be reported to him by the person who has solemnized such marriage.
(2) Whoever contravenes the provision of sub-section (1) shall be punishable with simple imprisonment for a term which may extend to three months, or with fine which may extend to five hundred taka, or with both."

6–49 It must be noted that these punishments are as lenient as under the MFLO 1961.[49] Nowhere is it provided, however, that an unregistered Muslim marriage is not legally valid. For Pakistan, while it has been said that the non-registration of a marriage casts a doubt on the solemnisation of the marriage itself, and the law provides for punishment of non-registration, all textbooks are quite clear on this point (see Pearl (1990a), p. 206). The position is confirmed by Ch. M. Mahmood (1991, p. 33):

> "Under Islamic Law *nikah* can be performed orally and such a *nikah* is not invalidated merely because it is not registered according to the provisions of the Muslim Family Laws Ordinance 1961."

The use of the phrase "shall be registered" in section 3 of the Bangladesh Act 1974, as cited above, clearly also does not allow a conclusion that unregistered marriages are invalid. It remains a fact in all South Asian jurisdictions that any unregistered Muslim marriage is valid in Muslim law and may be proved by other means than registration. There is actually growing evidence of registration of marriages, not necessarily in compliance with the provisions of section 5 of the 1961 Ordinance, or of section 3 in the Bangladesh Act, but this occurs probably in recognition of the Islamic guideline that important contracts should be made in writing (Mehdi (1994), p. 158). Recent local fieldwork evidence in Pakistan, which remains unpublished, has suggested that the higher rate of marriage registrations in some parts of the country may be due to the activities of local functionaries who have learnt to make a small business out of producing marriage registration documents.[50] Clearly, there is nothing contrary to Islam about registering one's marriage with the state, or in any other form, but it is evident that the traditional informal elements of Muslim marriage law continue to prevail over the stipulated legal requirements of modern state laws.

Guardianship in marriage

6–50 South Asian Muslim law follows the classical law in its basic rules about puberty and capacity to marry. The Anglo-Indian courts accepted such rules and even the Privy Council held that majority in the case of a Shia girl was reached at the age of nine years.[51] However, the complicated Muslim law rules about majority in the sense of capacity to marry and capacity to act as an independent individual have been further coloured by local practice, which denies many individuals, not only women and children,[52] the status of legal majors. In South Asian Muslim law, therefore, the general rule is that the marriages of minors can be contracted only by their guardians, but such marriages, although valid, can also be repudiated through the 'option of puberty'.[53] It has remained contested, socially rather than legally, whether the right of the guardian is a matter of 'guardianship with the right of

---

[49] The Act was amended by the Muslim Marriages and Divorces Registration (Amendment) Ordinance 1982. However, this is merely an administrative amendment, adding a second proviso to s.4 of the 1974 Act, to the effect that the government may alter the limits of any area for which a Nikah Registrar has been licensed. For relevant case law see Monsoor, *From patriarchy to gender equality: Family law and its impact on women in Bangladesh* (1994), pp. 237–242.

[50] This is further evidence of the privatisation of services which in many countries are provided by the state.

[51] See Fyzee (1974), p. 94 with further references.

[52] In the context of South Asian joint family laws, many fully adult males never achieve the status of full majority all their life, since their legal affairs are handled by a 'manager' of the family affairs.

[53] Fyzee (1974), pp. 94 and 208–209. On this subject, Carroll (1981b) is useful.

compulsion' or 'guardianship without the right of compulsion', *i.e.* more in the nature of agency.[54] If an under-age boy or girl contracts himself or herself in marriage without the consent of the guardian, provided he or she has attained 'discretion' (intellectual maturity) at the time of the marriage, the union can still be validated by acts of ratification after the minor has attained sexual maturity. The general rule appears to be, however, that "under the Muhammadan law of all schools, the father has the power to give his children of both sexes in marriage without their consent, until they reach the age of puberty" (Fyzee (1974), p. 208–209). Details of who precisely can act as a guardian in marriage are provided by many authors.[55]

6–51 Dealing particularly with the Shafi'i community, it appears that the strictness of the classical Shafi'i law in respect of marriage guardianship has not been followed in modern Indian law. A different view of the Shafi'i law appears to have been taken by the High Court of Kerala, which emphasised the consent of the wife, rather than the guardian. In the case of *Kammu v. Ethiyumma* 1967 K.L.T. 913, the judge made comments to the effect that it was advisable that the consent of the girl be given through a *wali*, while accepting that the consent of the girl herself was the critical element. In *K. Abubukker v. V. Marakkar*, A.I.R. 1970 Ker. 277, at 279, the judge said as follows:

> "Marriage among Muslims being a contract and the contracting parties being the husband and the wife the consent contemplated in the Shafei sect is that of the wife and not of the father or grandfather or any other person who acts as the wali at the time of the marriage. The person who acts as the wali only communicates the consent of the wife to the Kazi who conducts the marriage and the husband."

Under Hanafi law, the guardian's power of giving the child of both sexes in marriage comes to an end when the child attains the age of puberty, and this was reiterated by South Asian Muslim law (see Diwan and Diwan (1991), p. 53). Socially, however, this rule retains much potential for conflict, as is illustrated by the case of Saima Waheed in Pakistan.[56]

6–52 In this case, a Hanafi Muslim woman aged 22 years, Saima Shah, had married a man of her own choice in February 1996. He was a college lecturer and Saima's father, a rich and powerful businessman, did not consider him an appropriate choice.[57] It appears that, using his considerable influence, he filed a suit to secure his daughter's custody and a petition under Pakistan's notorious Zina Ordinance 1979 to harass his unwanted son-in-law. This case was not only seen as a legal test case but as a rallying point in the ongoing tussle between Muslim conservatives and women's rights activists in Pakistan. It should have been clear throughout that under traditional Hanafi law, the father had no right to make his claims because his daughter was not a minor. Indeed, a three-member bench of the High Court of Lahore ultimately held, in a majority judgment delivered on March 10, 1997, that marriage without the consent of a guardian is not invalid and that the father's case was not maintainable. The case, and the controversy it raised,

---

[54] On this see already para. 6–09, above. Tahir Mahmood (1982a), p. 50, always concerned to clarify the various misunderstandings about Muslim law, distinguishes guardianship in Muslim marriage from the Hindu concept of giving a girl in marriage.

[55] See Fyzee (1974), pp. 209–210; Carroll (1981b); Mahmood (1982a), pp. 49–50; Diwan and Diwan (1991), pp. 53–55.

[56] *Hafiz Abdul Waheed v. Asma Jahangir*, K.L.R. 1997 *Shariat* Cases 121.

[57] In a sense, therefore, here is also an element of lack of 'equality' between the spouses.

illustrates to what extent public opinion in South Asia has become agitated about such important social, rather than legal matters. The judgment in this case, as well as protecting individual rights and women's rights, would also appear to uphold the sound basic principle that every Muslim is entitled to marry.[58]

6–53 The way in which this case has been handled should be compared with a very recent decision from India on the same subject which clearly protects the rights of Muslim women to decide for themselves whom they should marry. In *Abdul Ahad v. Shah Begum*, A.I.R. 1997 J.L.K. 22, a Muslim husband had sought restitution of conjugal rights but the wife refused to live with him and claimed to have repudiated the marriage. Bilal Nazki J. said, at page 24:

> "Even the father of the girl cannot contract a marriage of his daughter against her will if she is a major. This is the settled principle of law in Islamic law that once the girl becomes major, she has absolute right to contract the marriage and this right cannot be exercised by any one else including the father of the girl."

In this case, it was found that the *wali* had been the girl's uncle who happened to be the father of the groom, and the court had no hesitation to declare this marriage null and void, noting, at page 24, that "there was not even a repudiation needed . . . to annul the marriage because the marriage in itself had been invalid".

6–54 Technically, the issue of guardianship in marriage should no longer be a matter of much concern to the law in view of legislation in the Indian subcontinent in the form of the Child Marriage Restraint Act 1929 which was specifically designed to restrain (not, however, to abolish) the solemnisation of child marriages. It has been argued that this legislation has taken away the practical importance of the present discussion (Tayyibji (1968), p. 89). That is not quite correct, however, since child marriages, in all South Asian countries, continue to be solemnised and are everywhere, with few exceptions,[59] treated as valid marriages. The short explanation for this, as far as Muslims are concerned, is probably that it has been recognised that a valid Muslim marriage contract, once entered into, cannot be refused legal recognition by any form of state law.[60]

6–55 Already in British India, the Child Marriage Restraint Act 1929 laid down minimum ages for the marriage of boys and girls.[61] Originally, these were 14 years old for females and 18 years old for males. The Act applies to persons of any religion. While very early marriages are widely perceived as socially undesirable, and the average marriage ages in South Asia are in fact slowly going up, most child marriages never come to the notice of the authorities, hardly anybody gets penalised, and such marriages have consistently been recognised as legally valid.[62]

---

[58] See Tayyibji (1968), p. 45 n.18 with a reference to the important case of *Muhammad Yamin v. Razia Begam* [1919] 17 A.L.J. 1138.

[59] Thus, under the secular Special Marriage Act 1954 in India, a child marriage would be void, in fact it could not be registered under that Act.

[60] A very similar argument would appear to apply for Hindu marriages of minors, reinforcing and, as it were (at least in India), protecting the Muslim argument from legislative intervention.

[61] This Act is still in operation in all three countries, with a variety of different amendments. In India, the Child Marriage Restraint (Amendment) Act 1949 raised the female minimum age to 15 years old. The Child Marriage Restraint (Amendment) Act 1978 then raised the minimum ages further to 18 and 21 years respectively and also increased the penalties for violation of the provisions in the Act. In Pakistan, the 1929 Act was amended by s.12(1)(a) of the Muslim Family Laws Ordinance 1961 and the minimum ages are now 16 years old for the woman and 18 years old for the man. In Bangladesh, the minimum ages stipulated have been 18 years old for the woman and 21 years old for the man since the Child Marriage Restraint (Amendment) Ordinance 1984.

[62] The earliest leading case on the subject is *Munshiram v. Emperor*, A.I.R. (1936) All 11. For Pakistan see *Bakhshi v. Bashir Ahmed*, P.L.D. 1970 S.C. 323 and *Sughran Mai v. The State* P.L.D. 1980 Lah. 386. For Bangladesh, see also *Bakshi v. Bashir Ahmed*, reported as 22 D.L.R. (1970) S.C. 289.

6–56   Concern continues to be expressed about the fact that many children in South Asia are still getting married too early, often with little say in the matter.[63] One early case in Pakistan, decided under Muslim law, actually held that the marriage of a Muslim girl before puberty was void. In *Allah Diwaya v. Kammon Mai*, P.L.D. 1957 (W.P.) Lah. 651, a young woman alleged that she had been abducted, subjected to sexual intercourse, and fraudulently married before she reached puberty. The court found, at page 653, that this case raised questions of law "of considerable importance from the point of view of Muslim women". It was held, at page 658, that a marriage entered into while the girl had not even attained puberty "was no marriage at all in the eye of the law and was, therefore, void". This case also made very pertinent comments on the law regarding 'option of puberty' when it was held, at page 660, that "if the girl has not attained the age of fifteen years her consent to the consummation of marriage will not amount to consent in the eye of the law".

6–57   It is noteworthy that Pakistani law has, in one particular case, taken a negative stance against very early child marriages. In *Ghulam Qadir v. Judge, Family Court, Murree* 1988 C.L.C. 113, it was held that a marriage entered into by a female who has not even yet attained puberty is no marriage at all in the eyes of the law and is void. While early marriages continue to be a matter of some relevance, the recent *Saima* case in Pakistan points to much social concern about the freedom of young people who are no longer children to select their own marriage partners. The fact that traditional Muslim jurisprudence did not speak on this subject with one voice assists young Muslims today in trying to ascertain what they consider, in today's world, the right path.

6–58   For our present discussion, this means in particular that the issue of guardianship in marriage is not fully settled by the intervention of modern laws. In many problematic cases, nobody goes to court, while in other cases, wide publicity is part of at least one of the litigants' strategy, as recently witnessed in the drama surrounding the *Saima* case in Pakistan. In Indian law, too, some recent cases have involved the question of consent in Muslim marriages. In the noted case of *Adam v. Mammad* 1990(1) K.L.T. 705, the Kerala High Court referred to *Abubukker v. Marakkar*, A.I.R. 1970 Ker. 277 and expounded further on the basic concepts of Muslim marriage in terms of consent.[64] Here the father of an adult girl was arguing that only he was entitled to consent to the marriage, relying not only on his interpretation of Muslim law but also on local custom. Pareed Pillay J. soundly rebuked these arguments and held, at page 707:

> "The principle is that when a girl is adult and discreet, no one has a right to be her guardian to give consent for the marriage. Nevertheless it is always open to her to authorise her father or guardian to settle the terms of the contract for her. That does not mean that the father or guardian without her consent can give her in marriage. Whenever it is found that the consent of the parties has not been obtained it has to be held that there is no valid contract of marriage."

---

[63] There is little, if any, research, on child marriages in South Asia. See Korson [1965] 5 *The Pakistan Development Review* 586–600, and Alam [1968] 8 *The Pakistan Development Review* 489–498, for Pakistan. Mehdi (1994), pp. 193–196 is more concerned with forced marriages than with child marriages. Sagade [1981] 1 S.C.J. 27–35 remains the best analysis on Indian law.

[64] For detailed comments on this case see Latifi, "Muslim law", in *Annual survey of Indian law* (1990), pp. 156–158.

This, of course, is precisely the concept of agency, rather than guardianship in marriage.[65] Under Indian law, therefore, the question of guardianship in marriage has appeared settled for some time. Latifi (1990, p. 158) in his comment on the decision in *Adam*, states the position very clearly:

"The principle is that where the girl is an adult and discreet no one has the right to be her guardian to give consent to the marriage. Nevertheless it is always open to her to authorise her father or guardian to settle the term of the contract for her."

In *Noor Mohammad v. Mohammad Jiajddin*, A.I.R. 1992 M.P. 244, we find a convoluted case involving two men in a public battle over status and money. In this case, a minor girl had been given in marriage by her father. The families fell out almost immediately over the nature of the arrangements made for the marriage celebrations, which involved a dancing girl and other entertainment.[66] The father of the girl sought reimbursement of the marriage expenses. Muslim law is only a minor issue in this case. The marriage was without question treated as valid but the girl repudiated it, no doubt at the behest of her father, under the provisions for option of puberty.

6–59   Where a young Muslim has been given in marriage by a guardian and objects to this marriage, the 'option of puberty' offers a remedy. In India, Pakistan and Bangladesh this doctrine has been affirmed in its classical mould.[67] In traditional Hanafi law, when fraud or negligence by the father or grandfather can be proved, there is a way out of an unwanted marriage.[68] The option is lost by the affirmative act of consummation of the marriage, at least if consummation has taken place without duress and after the girl has reached puberty. This principle was applied in the Bombay case of *Abdul Rahiman v. Aminabai*, I.L.R. [1935] 59 Bom. 426. There is also one Pakistani case which suggests that when a woman above the age of puberty has not consented to the marriage, then there is no valid subsisting marriage, for the simple reason that there has been no effective acceptance.[69]

6–60   There is an additional right available only to a young Muslim girl to avoid the marriage within the terms laid down by section 2(vii) of the Dissolution of Muslim Marriages Act 1939, which stated originally that a woman married under Muslim law shall be entitled to obtain a decree for the dissolution of her marriage on the ground that she, having been given in marriage by her father or other guardian before she attained the age of 15 years, repudiates the marriage before attaining the age of 18 years. In Pakistan, the relevant age was increased to 16 years old by section 13(b) of the Muslim Family Laws Ordinance 1961. Again, the option is not lost when consummation occurs without the woman's consent.[70]

6–61   Interestingly, in Bangladeshi law, which also had a minimum age of 16 under section 2(vii) of the DMMA 1939 as amended in 1961, the interaction

---

[65] On the concept of agency for marriage, see a good detailed discussion in Verma, *Muslim marriage, dissolution and maintenance* (1988), pp. 32–38.

[66] The comments of the judge, Dr T. N. Singh, are instructive in terms of law as well as social criticism. At p. 248 he said that: "Indeed, it is no part of a marriage-contract under Mahomedan Law that the bride or the bride's father is to bear any expenses incurred by the bridegroom or his father in connection with the marriage solemnized at [the] bride's house . . . no religious ceremony or the intervention of any priest is necessary for a valid Muslim marriage".

[67] See in detail Carroll (1981b).

[68] This was confirmed in *Noor Muhammad v. The State*, P.L.D. 1976 Lah. 516, which is discussed below. See also *Muhammad Sharif v. Khuda Bakhsh*, A.I.R. (1936) Lah. 683.

[69] *Sughran Mai v. The State*, P.L.D. 1980 Lah. 386.

[70] *Behram Khan v. Akhtar Begum*, P.L.D. 1952 Lah. 548; *Muhammad Bibi v. Raja*, P.L.D. 1962 A.J.K. 7. For details see Carroll (1981b).

between higher minimum ages for marriage and the 'option of puberty' is reflected in a further amendment to section 2(vii) in 1986. The sole purpose of the Dissolution of Muslim Marriages (Amendment) Ordinance 1986 was to provide that a Muslim girl, having been given in marriage by her father or other guardian before the age of 18 years, can repudiate the marriage before the age of 19 years. No such amendment exists in India.

6–62   In addition to the ground now available under the Dissolution of Muslim Marriages Act 1939 in its various forms, it is interesting to note that the classical law and the statutory law appear to exist side by side, as held in an interesting pre-1961 case.[71] The promulgation of the 1961 Ordinance in Pakistan and other legislation have highlighted this conflict of laws within the sphere of the Muslim personal law. It poses interesting questions about the 'limits of law' for legal scholars but makes the practising lawyer's task very complicated indeed.

6–63   South Asian Muslim laws continuously confirm their position as a laboratory of social and legal interaction. This can be shown with reference to many examples. In the present context of 'option of puberty', one problem brought about by the 1939 Act is whether the option operates by itself to bring the marriage to an end, or whether it is mandatory to obtain a decree from the court. A reading of the 1939 Act would make it appear that the latter position prevails. However, there has been a line of Pakistani authority which decides that a court decree is not necessary. In *Muni v. Habib Khan*, P.L.D. 1956 (W.P.) Lah. 403, the judge said at page 409:

> "Such repudiation puts an end to the marriage without the aid of any Court and when the matter comes to Court, the Court does not dissolve the marriage by its own act but recognises the termination of marriage. This proposition is well established."[72]

A similar point was made in *Noor Muhammad v. The State*, P.L.D. 1976 Lah. 516. In this case, a husband had brought a private complaint alleging that Noor Muhammad, the woman's father, had committed a criminal breach of trust under section 406 of the Pakistan Penal Code 1860 by arranging a second and bigamous marriage between the wife and another man. The husband alleged that he had married the woman, Amiran, in 1958 and that there had been an agreement that they would commence living together in 1974. Ten days before Amiran was due to move to the husband's house, Noor Muhammad told the 'husband' that he was giving her in marriage to Bashir Ahmad, and that marriage was duly performed. The court decided that there was no bigamy, thus no criminal breach of trust, since the woman had exercised her option of puberty. The mere fact of her entering into a subsequent marriage on attaining puberty amounted, in the view of the court, to repudiation of her earlier marriage. There was no need to communicate the decision to exercise the option to a court, and any court decree is therefore only confirmation of an established fact.[73]

6–64   The same matter came up again in a Pakistani case in the context of a criminal prosecution for *zina*. In *Said Mahmood v. The State*, P.L.D. 1995 F.S.C. 1, the facts were that a girl, soon after puberty, had been married to a young man on

---

[71] *Daulan v. Dosa*, P.L.D. 1956 (W.P.) Lah. 712.
[72] See also *Muhammad Bakhsh v. Crown*, P.L.D. (1950) Lah. 203 to the same effect, as well as several older cases referred to at p. 409 of the judgment. For further details see Carroll (1981b).
[73] See in similar terms and to the same effect *Abdul Ahad v. Shah Begum*, A.I.R. (1997) J.L.K. 22, discussed at para. 6–53 above.

July 13, 1987.[74] Since the *nikah* had been performed, but not the *rukhsati*,[75] the girl had not yet started cohabiting with her husband when he was jailed for a criminal offence on May 13, 1987. In April 1993, she was arrested by the police together with another young man who claimed to be her husband. A prosecution for illicit sexual intercourse (*zina*) was filed and the two young people were convicted and sent to jail.

6–65 On appeal, before the Federal Shariat Court, the legal question was whether the young woman had exercised the option of puberty and could therefore claim that she was validly married to her alleged lover rather than her former husband. The court first stated the classical position, at page 4:

"There is no express verse of the Holy Qur'an and Hadith of the Holy Prophet (p.b.u.h.) wherein exercise of option of puberty may have been mentioned. However, Muslim scholars have recognised this right."

Nazir Ahmad Bhatti C.J. further restated some of the classical juristic positions and found that "the jurists concur that this is a weak right" (page 5), heavily circumscribed by the rule that the option has to be exercised on reaching puberty. He then turned to section 2(vii) of the Dissolution of Muslim Marriages Act 1939 which provides that a woman, having been given in marriage before she attained the age of 16 years, may repudiate the marriage before attaining the age of 18 years, provided the marriage has not been consummated.

6–66 Based on the facts of the case, it was swiftly decided that the accused woman was only 15 or 16 years old when she married her co-accused, so her marriage to him amounted to repudiation of the first marriage and she had validly exercised her right of option of puberty. Thus, no offence had been committed by the accused and they were both set free.

6–67 The learned judge also went into the important question whether the woman concerned could just exercise her option, or was there a need for a declaration from a quazi to say whether the repudiation was appropriate or not? Two arguments were used to come to the finding that no such declaration was needed. First, there was no provision in the traditional Muslim law to that effect. Secondly, the courts of Pakistan had held in several cases that mere exercise of this right by the wife was a perfect repudiation. Thus, what the accused in the present case had done did not offend against the injunctions of Islam and was perfectly justified. Reference was made to a number of earlier cases on this matter, including *Noor Muhammad v. The State*, P.L.D. 1976 Lah. 516. The position was authoritatively summed up, at page 6:

"The unanimous opinion of the Courts was that no judicial approval was necessary for having exercised the right of option of puberty by a wife and the first marriage subsequently stood dissolved when the wife contracted the second marriage after attaining puberty."

---

[74] Significantly, the girl's mother and the young woman herself tried to claim, without success, that she was only engaged, not married. Obviously, viewing the *nikah* of a young girl merely as an engagement is not in line with traditional Muslim law but it appears to reflect local practice. On the flexibility of perceptions about when someone is married see the reference to *rukshati* immediately below. We return to this concept in para. 6–106 while discussing British Muslim perceptions of a full marriage.

[75] This is the actual transfer of the bride to the husband's home and is normally followed by consummation of the marriage. While the Muslim marriage is valid after the *nikah*, it could be argued that it is not a complete marriage.

This particular case is remarkable for the way in which it handles the allegation of *zina* and frees the young couple from such accusations by law enforcement officers.[76] Three comments should be made. First, the judicial position in this case (and the other cases discussed here) is in marked contrast to other cases on the 'option of puberty' which involve female inheritance rights (see Mannan (1990), pp. 385–386). In such cases, a stricter approach would appear to protect the position of women, so it seems to depend on the constellation of the facts and circumstances whether judges will hold that some form of official documentation is essential to accept an option of puberty as valid. It appears that a fuller analysis of this particular subject is now required and, at least for India and Bangladesh, the position is not clear.[77] The strict general position as stated in older texts is no longer correct,[78] certainly not for Pakistan, on which see now in detail Mannan (1990, pp. 382–386).

6–68   Secondly, cases on the 'option of puberty' confirm that Pakistani courts, including (and in fact often particularly) the Federal Shariat Court, are not as unconcerned about Muslim women's rights as some studies have made out.[79] Thirdly, the cases cited here reinforce the general picture that much of South Asian Muslim law today remains in the so-called extra-legal sphere and that court involvement remains optional. This remains a significant difference between Western laws and modern South Asian laws, confirming that it is not an inevitable step of legal development that the latter will follow Western models of formalised legal processes. Official acceptance of informal laws, as *Said Mahmood v. The State*, P.L.D. 1995 F.S.C. 1, confirms, can clearly work in favour of Muslim women.

Classification of marriages

6–69   Although the distinction between *batil* and *fasid* marriages is somewhat blurred in many cases, and has been rejected even by some opinions in the Hanafi school, it is generally recognised in South Asia as the basis of jurisprudential discussion (see in detail Siddiqui (1955)). It is confusing and inconvenient for anyone wishing to ascertain the law that different writers use a variety of classifications for the various disabilities. Fyzee (1974, p. 96) lists seven main limitations to the unfettered capacity of a Muslim to marry any person of the opposite sex but does not attempt to make a clear distinction between permanent and temporary disabilities. Verma (1988, pp. 38–76) contains an extremely detailed and helpful discussion of all major elements in this context. Tayyibji (1968, pp. 71–87) presents a well-focused analysis of the relevant topics. Mahmood (1982a, pp. 56–68), discusses this topic under the heading 'basic conditions for marriage'. Diwan and Diwan (1991, pp. 47–49) and Hidayatullah and Hidayatullah (1977, pp. 284–291) present brief discussions, the latter with much emphasis on the distinction between void and irregular marriages. Mannan (1990, pp. 366–376) provides an updated discussion of the law on this topic in Pakistan. The most recent, but very brief, treatment of the subject by a Pakistani author is found in Balchin (1994, pp. 36–39).

6–70   As to the distinction between void and irregular marriages, Balchin (1990,

---

[76] An earlier, important case with an erudite exposition on Muslim marriage law in Pakistan is *Muhammad Azam v. Muhammad Iqbal*, P.L.D. 1984 S.C. 95.
[77] On the unsettled position in Indian law see already Hidayatullah and Hidayatullah (1977), pp. 299–300. A good discussion is found in Mahmood (1982a), pp. 65–67.
[78] *E.g.* Fyzee (1974), p. 95; Tayyibji (1968), p. 93.
[79] But see, *e.g.* Mehdi (1994), p. 195 arguing that the option of puberty is only a theoretical right. For a recent activist judicial decision on the need to protect women's rights in Pakistan see the forthright comments and lucid reasoning by Dr Ghous Muhammed J. in *Rani v. The State*, P.L.D. 1996 Kar. 316.

p. 37) clearly reiterates that "the obstacle in void marriages is permanent and perpetual and cannot be remedied". She lists under this category the three forms of prohibited degrees by consanguinity, affinity and fosterage, as well as marriage with a woman who is still married to another man, *i.e.* polyandry, as well as the marriage of an adult and sane person brought about without his or her consent. While there are no doubts about the first four scenarios, the final one appears to reflect modern pro-women concerns, such as arose in the recent *Saima* case in Pakistan.[80]

6–71 Mannan (1990, p. 366) prefers the term 'irregular' to 'invalid' to avoid confusion with the term 'void'. This is helpful because most irregular marriages can in fact be regularised, albeit after separation of the couple, although this point is debatable, especially for the irregular situation where there were no witnesses, which would not appear to require separation of the couple, just a fresh contract of marriage before witnesses. As for irregular marriages, Balchin (1994, p. 38) lists six different situations and says that:

> "An irregular (*fasid*) marriage is one that suffers from a temporary bar or informality. An irregular marriage has no legal effect before consummation and can be terminated by either party . . . In certain instances, once the temporary bar or informality has been removed or corrected, the marriage becomes valid with all the incumbent rights and obligations on both the parties."

Below, we now concentrate on those aspects of the law in this field which have given rise to debate and/or case law in South Asia. It appears that most emphasis has been given to questions concerning irregular marriages rather than void marriages, which we briefly discuss first.

Void marriages

6–72 There is not much scope for disagreement over the *batil* marriages which involve prohibited degrees, they are simply void and offspring from them illegitimate; all schools of law agree on this. Diwan and Diwan (1991, p. 48) highlight that under Muslim law the matrimonial cause of nullity of marriage is simply not available.

6–73 Regarding prohibitions arising from fosterage, the *Hedaya* lays down the following general rules[81]:

> "It is not lawful for a man to marry his foster-mother, or his foster-sister, the Almighty having commanded, saying, Marry not your mothers who have suckled you, or your sisters by fosterage; and the Prophet has also declared, Every thing is prohibited by reason of fosterage which is so by reason of kindred."

In Hanafi law, at least, even one drop of milk will create this bar. The detailed discussion in Verma (1988, pp. 44–48) indicates the vast potential for legal arguments on this particular topic, which is probably today more of academic concern than a field of current interest for family lawyers. Indeed, Fyzee (1974, p. 106) confirms that the rules as to fosterage are now to a large extent obsolete.

6–74 Some other situations may give rise to a void marriage. There is some juristic opinion to the effect that a marriage with a woman undergoing *iddat* is void

---

[80] See *Hafiz Abdul Waheed v. Asma Jahangir*, K.L.R. (1997) *Shariat* cases 121, discussed in para. 6–52, above.

[81] *The Hedaya*, Vol. I, Book II, Chap. 1, Hamilton (1891), p. 28.

(Fyzee (1974), p. 109), but that is clearly a minority view, the majority view would be that it is irregular and that such a couple may validly marry in due course. With regard to difference of religion, the rule that a Muslim woman must not marry a non-Muslim man is upheld in South Asian Muslim law but we have already seen (in paragraph 5–21, above) that in cases of conversion there is ample scope for debate over how strictly this rule should be applied.

Irregular marriages

6–75 The discussions in various legal textbooks from South Asia show that on some topics under this heading, in particular *iddat* and marriages with non-Muslims, an extended discussion could be produced. Other subjects receive only minimal attention and do not appear to have posed serious practical problems which have required judicial clarification. This would suggest, again, that South Asian Muslim laws remain capable of resolving many insecurities of status through the informal sphere rather than formal legal processes.

6–76 Verma (1988, pp. 81–84) discusses different types of irregular marriages in terms of how they can be converted into valid marriages and distinguishes basically two types. In the first, an irregular marriage becomes a valid marriage after certain defects are removed. Several such situations are listed, the most obvious ones being the absence of witnesses and the absence of consent. Other defects cannot be so easily remedied and it becomes essential for the parties to be separated and to undergo a fresh marriage once the defect has been remedied.

6–77 Regarding the absence of witnesses, Siddiqui (1955, p. 237) starts his discussion by showing that the Qur'an "is absolutely silent on the point of witnesses", which has given rise to much juristic activity. In legal practice, there are many cases where the essential formalities of marriage are beyond positive proof. Such cases, having been considered by judges who are familiar with the cultural patterns of Muslim communities and the informal and extra-legal nature of most aspects of Muslim family law, are very instructive. The judicial decisions in South Asia tend to lean in favour of a valid *sahih* marriage. Not many cases on this topic will reach higher courts and be reported because it is so very well-settled that a Muslim marriage may be proved by a variety of evidentiary material. In addition, the use of presumptions of marriage is a frequent feature (see Fyzee (1974), pp. 114–115). Thus in one case, the court said:

> "There is ample evidence to show that both Mst. Qadul and Haji Qadir Bakhsh had for years lived as husband and wife in the eyes of the public and nobody seems to have raised his little finger on the nature of their relationship which by no means appears promiscuous."[82]

As far as Indian law is concerned, there is not much evidence of debate about this issue,[83] which can, however, be of considerable practical importance and regularly comes up in legal practice in the United Kingdom. Some helpful details on Pakistani case law are provided by Mannan (1990, p. 367).

6–78 We have already seen that when a woman is still married to another man, any fresh marriage would be void under Muslim law (see also Verma (1988), pp. 79–80). However, if a woman enters a new marriage while she is still in her *iddat* period, the marriage would most probably be irregular, not void.[84] Since one of the

---

[82] *Mst. Qadul v. Allah Bachaya*, P.L.D. 1973 B.J. 48.
[83] For some cases see Verma (1988), p. 78.
[84] For details of the debates about this see *ibid.*, p. 81; Fyzee (1974), pp. 107–109.

major purposes of the *iddat* is to avoid confusion about paternity, this is a potentially very serious matter. Fyzee (1974, p. 108) confirms that the question whether a particular union, valid or invalid, has been consummated is "of prime importance in the law relating to *'idda*". Textbook writers leave it open precisely how such a marriage is regularised. The defect in this type of irregular marriage is obviously easily cured through the efflux of time, but this may not take care of all difficult situations. It appears that intense concern in Muslim law about legitimacy, focused on subjects such as the normal length of pregnancy, intersects with the present topic, and there is some evidence of scholarly debate on this topic.[85]

6–79 Where a Muslim man already has four wives and contracts a marriage with a fifth woman, this is an irregular marriage.[86] Here again, if one of the four wives were to die or to be divorced, the irregular union would be capable of simple regularisation. This appears to be a fairly settled issue.[87]

6–80 The issue of unlawful conjunction has arisen only infrequently. This prohibition is based on a Qur'anic provision (Sura IV, verse 23), which formed the basis for early Indian decisions holding such marriages void.[88] Logically, the prohibition of 'unlawful conjunction' should be characterised as a temporary prohibition. For, on the separation of the parties to the second union and a subsequent divorce from the first wife, or the death of the first wife, there would be no reason why the man could not remarry his second partner. This indeed is the more appropriate solution in modern jurisprudence, which has been accepted by Indian cases since the early part of the twentieth century.[89] Interestingly, Fyzee (1974, p. 107) objected to this, in view of the Qur'anic provisions, on the ground that "legislation and not 'elastic interpretation' is the proper remedy".

6–81 On the topic of intervening marriage, which concerns the question of re-marriage between the husband and wife after a final *talaq*, there has been some development in South Asian Muslim law, basically to allow spouses in that situation to circumvent the strict *shari'a* rules about the need for an intervening marriage.[90] The Hedaya goes into great detail on the possibility of an intervening marriage with a person who marries her solely to free her from the impediment of a remarriage with her former husband. In particular, attention is given to marriage with a boy below the age of puberty. In these cases, the intervening marriage is valid and a second marriage with the first husband (after a valid dissolution of the intervening marriage) is *sahih*. Another opinion on this issue is based on the point that as the impediment is actually temporary – the marriage would be correct so long as the procedures with regard to the intervening marriage have been gone through – the remarriage after a triple *talaq* and without any intervening marriage should be *fasid* rather than *batil*. Indian case law, however, treats such marriages as *batil*.[91]

6–82 Not surprisingly, there is much South Asian law material on the question of marrying a non-Muslim partner.[92] We have already seen the basic rules about

---

[85] For further references see Verma (1988), pp. 79–80 and the discussion in Siddiqui (1955), pp. 237–250.
[86] See *ibid.*, 227–236.
[87] Hidayatullah and Hidayatullah (1977), p. 290; Verma (1988), p. 80 with references to some old cases.
[88] See briefly Siddiqui (1955), pp. 197–199. The discussion in Fyzee (1974), p. 107 refers to cases, including *Aizunnissa Khatoon v. Karimunnissa Khatoon*, I.L.R. [1896] 23 Cal. 130.
[89] See for instance *Tajbi v. Mowla Khan*, I.L.R. [1917] 41 Bom. 485.
[90] For considerable detail see Tayyibji (1968), pp. 81–84; the topic is not covered by several other authors.
[91] See *Rashid Ahmad v. Anisa Khatun* [1931] 59 L.R. I.A. 21.
[92] Fyzee (1974, p.96) confirms that marriages between Muslims of different schools do not fall under this prohibition and are fully valid. *ibid.*, pp. 97–100 contains a detailed discussion of this subject. See also Verma (1988), pp. 50–52;

kitabiyya women (see paragraph 6–23). The strict position would be that a Muslim man can only marry a *kitabiyya* woman, *i.e.* a Christian or Jewish woman, but not a Hindu woman, for example. Significantly, the Indian jurist Ameer Ali did not accept the strict interpretation of the Qur'anic verse (Sura II, verse 221) on marrying non-Muslim women. This can be explained by the realities of South Asian life, at a time when many Hindu individuals, in particular, would convert to Islam during their lifetime. Ali suggested that these marriages should be considered *fasid*. He placed emphasis on the temporary nature of the irregularity, presumably because the non-Muslim partner could easily convert and thus regularise the marriage.

6–83 Several writers discuss this issue, which created much interest, as is documented in Fyzee (1974, p. 98), where a most interesting reference is made to the older argument that many Hindus could in fact be taken to believe in one God and that marriages with Hindu women would therefore be lawful. On accepting such marriages as irregular unions, Verma (1988, p. 51) takes the view that a liberal position is not likely to be accepted, while Hidayatullah and Hidayatullah (1977, p. 287) rely on an old case to say that marriages with non-*kitabiyyas* are irregular, not void. Mannan (1990, p. 371) falls back on Fyzee's stricter opinion, but says clearly that the question will have to be judicially decided. Bharatiya (1996, p. 65) argues that only legislative intervention could get around the strict position of the Qur'anic foundations. However, given that religion is such a politically sensitive issue in South Asia today, it is unlikely that a test case will be brought or legislation passed on this matter. At the same time, it is not a surprise that a vigorous parallel debate about this issue has been conducted under the heading of 'conversion' (see paragraph 5–21, above).

6–84 The question about difference of religion was left open in the interesting if slightly puzzling decision of the Privy Council in *Abdool Razack v. Aga Mahomed Jaffer Bindaneem* [1893/1894] 21 L.R. I.A. 56. The case concerned the inheritance claim brought by a Muslim, Abdool Razack, to the property of his uncle. On the death of the uncle, no immediate Muslim heirs could be discovered. Abdool Razack was the son of a relationship between the half-brother of the deceased and a Burmese Buddhist lady, Mah Thai. The case is somewhat coloured by the peculiar circumstances in which it was brought before the court. When the uncle died, certain Calcutta gentlemen 'discovered' Abdool Razack, who was living rough in the jungle, and adopted his claim as a speculative enterprise. The success of the action, of course, depended on whether there had been a valid marriage between the half-brother and the Burmese lady. Out of this curious case, two principles appear to be established. First, a marriage between a Muslim male and a polytheistic or atheist female is *batil*. Thus the classical view of the Qur'anic texts is accepted, and the views of Ameer Ali, the nineteenth-century Indian jurist, rejected. Secondly, the issue of such a *batil* relationship is illegitimate and, as such, no such child is capable of being acknowledged as a legitimate child.

6–85 Unfortunately, both these principles were really obiter in this particular case, since the court decided on the facts that the half-brother and Mah Thai had simply cohabited and had not even married. In fact, the court refused to apply a presumption of marriage and the question of difference of religion became irrelevant. It could be argued, therefore, that it is still an open question whether by Muslim law as applied in India, Pakistan and Bangladesh the marriage of a Muslim man to a Hindu or Buddhist woman is a *fasid* rather than a *batil* union.

6–86 The point is perhaps academic now, at any rate in India, for the Special Marriage Act 1954, as amended in 1976, permits a marriage to be solemnised under its provisions between any two persons regardless of religious affiliation, provided the marriage is monogamous and both parties have full capacity to enter into a monogamous relationship. Under the secular 1954 Act, either a Muslim male and a non-*kitabiyya* female, or a Muslim woman and a non-Muslim male may enter into a valid marriage and the spouses may choose to ignore the fact that Muslim law either does not recognise this union as legally valid at all or has reservations about its full legal validity.

6–87 The position in Pakistan and Bangladesh, however, is quite different. If a Muslim male in either country wishes to marry a Hindu woman, for example, the couple can do one of three things, all possibly unattractive. First, the woman can adopt Islam; secondly, the couple can marry in a secular form outside the country[93]; thirdly, the couple can take advantage of the provisions of the Special Marriage Act 1872 which is still in force both in Pakistan and Bangladesh. The 1872 Act, however, is very limited in its scope. It is available, first, for persons both of whom profess one or other of the Hindu, Buddhist, Sikh or Jaina religions. Secondly, it provides a form of marriage for persons neither of whom professes the Christian, Jewish, Parsi, Muslim, Sikh, Buddhist or Jaina religions. In effect, therefore, two people, unless they are both members of the Hindu or associated faiths, who wish to marry under the Act, are forced to renounce their religion. It is a matter of controversy whether such a renunciation, made solely for the purposes of enabling a solemnisation of an inter-community marriage, is valid. Old Indian cases decided before partition suggest that it is not necessary to enquire into the bona fides of a renunciation; the test therefore is purely subjective. For example, in the case of *Mohan v. Mohan*, A.I.R. 1943 Sind 311, it was decided that whether the parties to a marriage solemnised under the terms of the 1872 Act were, or were not, at heart adherents to a particular faith was irrelevant for the purpose of the Act and the only relevant criterion was the declaration made at the time of the celebration of the marriage. The Dacca bench of the old Pakistan High Court was not as tolerant and the authority which would presumably prevail today both in Bangladesh and Pakistan is the case of *Muhammad Mustafizur Rahman Khan v. Rina Khan*, P.L.D. 1967 Dacca 652. In this case, both parties at the time of the marriage, which was celebrated under the 1872 Act, declared that they did not belong to a specified religion. Subsequently, however, they denied having renounced respectively the Muslim and the Christian religions. It was held, therefore, that the marriage which was purported to have been solemnised under the 1872 Act was null and void.

6–88 While the ancient issue of religious differences is not likely to go away, the question of social and economic distinctions also remains a topic of perennial interest among Muslims in South Asia and may sometimes be raised as an argument against the validity of a Muslim marriage. In fact, this is what happened in the *Saima* case in Lahore, where a rich businessman and other members of his family objected to what they saw as the young woman's improper marital selection of a mere college lecturer. Even where arranged marriages are the norm, this may become an issue, but it is more likely to arise in today's context of 'love marriages', where the parties may face a lot of social pressure after marriage (Mehdi (1994), p. 194).

6–89 The basic underlying principle of the doctrine of *kafa'a*, supposedly a Hanafi concept, is that ideally the husband should be the equal of the woman in

---

[93] The capacity of such parties to marry abroad in this way has not yet been tested in the Pakistani or Bangladeshi courts, though such marriages appear to occur.

social status.[94] Several authors ignore the topic altogether, presumably because it is not a strictly legal issue.[95] Fyzee (1974, pp. 109–111) produces a good discussion but indicates that it is among the topics which are "perhaps not quite so important, . . . rules of prudence rather than mandatory provisions of law" (page 109). The South Asian courts have not given any clear indications of the status of this rule. They have a wide discretion and will only terminate a marriage when it would be inequitable to permit continuation having regard to the best interests of the two parties and their respective families. Fyzee (1974, p. 111) likens this remedy to a voidable contract. Only the guardian can apply for separation, although in at least one Pakistani case the court appears to have given the wife *locus standi* to apply on her own behalf for separation based on *kafa'a*. That application was unsuccessful.[96] This topic also appears under the rubric of *faskh* or judicial dissolution of a marriage (see Chapter 9, below).

Muslim marriages and English law

6–90   Given the theological and social nature of many of the questions raised in this chapter, it is not surprising that disputes over the legal status of a particular marriage, or a party to a marriage, will rarely reach an official English legal forum. Matters of religious doctrine are likely to be kept out of the reach of an official legal system which purports to be secular but for historical reasons favours one particular Christian denomination. Matters of social control, in a scenario where Muslims are *de facto* an ethnic minority, are likely to be settled within the various communities and rarely will evidence of such conflicts spill over into the arena of the official law. Moreover, if that happens, the issues are likely to be distorted and will be made to fit the parameters of the dominant legal system. In that way, a Muslim marital dispute may appear officially as a criminal law case; a struggle over guardianship in marriage could end up as a criminal case, too. Disputes over prohibited relationships in marriage, especially in view of powerful concepts like *izzat*, the honour and status of the family, sadly could easily turn into murder cases.

6–91   Conversely, the English legal system is more interested to exercise control in the legal field than to understand and define details of Muslim law. While the official law would, in this way, claim jurisdiction over many matters, the self-conscious distancing of British Muslims from the official legal system inhibits full interaction. It would appear that lack of knowledge and trust do not constitute a healthy basis for a harmonious relationship between the state and its institutions and the Muslim communities in Britain. The mutual avoidance reactions which we identified in the discussions of Chapter 3, above, lead to practical consequences in all the substantive chapters of this book. Much of the literature concerned with such questions emphasises how little we know but stresses at the same time how very important key questions of family law actually are for the daily life of Muslim individuals and communities living in the West.[97]

---

[94] The converse is not required, showing that hypergamy, 'marrying up', is an asset for the woman.

[95] Given that Islam is said to stand for equality, the doctrine of *kafa'a* is of course politically embarrassing.

[96] *Shazada Begum v. Abdul Hamid*, P.L.D. 1950 Lah. 504. In *Sughran Mai v. The State*, P.L.D. 1980 Lah. 386 at 397, the judge said that *kafa'a* might provide a ground for annulment for the wife herself "if she was misrepresented by the husband regarding any element of his social status". This comes close to the concept of 'option of puberty'.

[97] For details see, *e.g.* Pearl (1986a), Nielsen (1992c), pp. 95–115, various essays in King (1995) and *Pakistanis in Europe* (1982).

Muslim marriages in the United Kingdom

6–92 Early writing on Muslim marriages in Britain immediately identified the problem of mutual lack of knowledge and understanding (Pearl (1972b)) and pinpointed some problems arising from the observation, at that time, that "many immigrants ignore the provisions of English law" (Pearl (1972–1973), p. 69). More than 20 years later, there is still not much writing on the subjects we address here.[98] The social science literature emphasises, generally, that marriage and in particular the selection of marriage partners, is a major topic of concern (Ahsan (1995), pp. 22–23). At the same time, it remains significant that despite the size of the Muslim communities in Britain today there is hardly any reflection of Muslim presence in the case law. This observation would appear to confirm the impact of officially invisible dispute resolution mechanisms within the Muslim communities, as highlighted in paragraphs 3–94—3–105, above.

6–93 A major reason for the low profile of this issue is that the official law is actually quite clear. Under English domestic law, the performance of a Muslim marriage contract, the *nikah*, is simply not recognised as leading to a legally valid marriage (Ahsan (1995), p. 22). It has been stated authoritatively that all marriages performed in England, other than those which are performed in foreign missions and which are technically extraterritorial, must comply with the statutory provisions of the English Marriage Acts 1949–1994.[99] Therefore, a Muslim couple who merely went through a *nikah* in the United Kingdom would not, in English law, be seen and treated as validly married, while they are certainly married according to Muslim law. If such a couple also consummated the marriage and there were no impediments or disputes of any kind, this would be a perfectly valid Muslim marriage, but it would still be denied legal recognition in English law.

6–94 The consequences can be dramatic. Take the case of Ms. S, a Muslim woman who married P, a Muslim male, in a mosque in London. The couple then cohabited, but after a short time P left S and she does not know his whereabouts. Let us assume that S has in her possession a copy of a marriage certificate, headed Nikah (Marriage) Certificate, issued by the Muslim Law (Shariah) Council (United Kingdom) in London. This certificate confirms that the *nikah* was solemnised between P and S according to Muslim law, with due particulars given, their respective signatures and the signature of two witnesses. The form further specifies the amount of *mahr* in British pounds and also contains the name and signature of the person who conducted the *nikah*, the date, and the signature of the Chairman or Secretary of the Muslim Law (Shariah) Council (U.K.). An official seal has been affixed.

6–95 Notwithstanding this impressive certificate, S will have to be advised that she is not party to a valid marriage under English law.[1] The Certificate of Marriage, however formal and authentic, is simply not recognised by English law. Ms S may well have known this, in which case she would probably not approach any English lawyer for legal advice and her case would be one of those many legal problems which remain entirely within the sphere of the unofficial law.[2] In practice, however, one does come across Muslim women who believed themselves to be fully married

---

[98] A useful summary of the key issues is found in Ahsan (1995).

[99] See to this effect Pearl (1972b), p. 131; Ahsan (1995), pp. 22–23; Poulter (1986), pp. 33–35.

[1] On the authoritative position in English law see also Poulter (1986), pp. 46–47 with a reference to the relevant case that governs this matter, *R. v. Bham* [1966] 1 Q.B. 159; [1965] 3 All E.R. 124.

[2] Such a woman would then seek to obtain a Muslim divorce (see para. 9–235, below) and would be free to marry again in a *nikah*. Her status, as far as English law is concerned, is not 'divorced' but 'unmarried'.

and who trusted this official documentation, only to find at some stage that they have lost their virginity and reputation, the Muslim husband, and all forms of security which they thought they had acquired through marriage.[3] There are cases of women who have been 'married' as Muslim wives for many years and suddenly face enormous social, economic and legal difficulties.[4] Such cases do not appear in law reports because the official law takes the view that they are clear-cut matters which require no legal debate. The English law on this subject, as officially stated, is indeed simple and clear: A woman like Ms S has no married status and no meaningful remedy. She can expect only minimal help from social service departments, depending on her status.[5]

6–96 Whether S would wish to view herself as a cohabitant must be doubted in view of South Asian concerns about *izzat* and Muslim concerns about the prohibitions on illicit sex (*zina*). To be sure, S has not committed *zina*, because she believed herself to be married, and was validly married to P according to Muslim law. The discovery that her marriage was in fact not legal in the eyes of English law may have come as a shock to S and she will feel distressed and vulnerable. Experience suggests that such women have been unwilling to offer themselves as the subject of a test case in English law.

6–97 While such problems have remained in the realm of unofficial regulation, it is a fact, not yet well-researched, especially where children are involved, that English social welfare legislation can be used to assist such women, and certainly their children.[6]

6–98 It may be relevant whether S has members of her natal family in Britain, but this can be a mixed blessing, given that the negative repercussions in terms of *izzat* will also affect the family. In either case, the burden of shame and distress for the individual is enormous.[7] Today, such cases have become rare but they do still occur, sometimes when a woman without close family contacts in Britain is brought over from the subcontinent or elsewhere. If she then marries a Muslim man in England in a Muslim ceremony, which she accepts as sufficient, she has fallen into the same trap as Ms S. Pearl (1972b, p. 130) highlighted this problem about Muslim marriages in Britain:

> "A fundamental question is whether a marriage celebrated in England according to Muslim rites between two Muslims domiciled in Pakistan is to be recognised as creating a valid status of marriage for the purposes of English law. Some mosques are now registered under section 41 of the Marriage Act 1949 as registered buildings for the purposes of the solemnisation of marriages, but the problems concern ceremonies which take place in unregistered buildings and which are not preceded or followed by any civil ceremony."

Nearly 30 years later, it is apparent that Muslim families and communities in Britain have, over time, learnt that the *nikah* by itself is not sufficient to bring about a legally valid marriage under English law. In consequence, we find today an intricate combination of Muslim *nikah* and English registered marriage. This, as we shall see, satisfies both legal systems; most importantly, it protects the social and

---

[3] The Law Commission became aware of this problem (see Poulter (1986), p. 62 with some details) but no legislative action has been taken to implement the proposals which were made, designed to protect women in such situations.

[4] Naturally, many of those cases involve matters of social security.

[5] Some such women may in fact become subject to deportation procedures.

[6] See para. 10–97, below, and details in Pearl (1986a), pp. 48–52.

[7] For a typical case study of an Indian woman with hardly anyone to turn to see Barton (1987). There are also cases of men, including Muslim men, in a similar situation of isolation and legal insecurity.

legal status of the woman. British Muslims have, in this way, developed their own ways of combining the religious and moral requirements of *shari'a* with the legal requirements of English law. The result, a key element of *angrezi shariat*, as discussed in paragraph 3–81, above, has been that Muslims in Britain effectively marry twice. There will be a variety of modifications, depending also on whether a particular mosque is a 'registered building' for the purposes of marriage solemnisation,[8] but the overall picture of the need to marry twice to satisfy English law and Muslim law is today absolutely clear.[9] Since the status of being married, in a modern society, is important for all kinds of legal and administrative processes, there is increasing pressure on individuals to follow *angrezi shariat* rather than simply *shari'a*. At present, it is not yet known how the most recent changes to English marriage law will impact on Muslim patterns of marriage in Britain.[10]

6–99   It is instructive to analyse this process of double marriage because it is not a haphazard duplicity. It is clearly a systematic attempt to fulfil the requirements of two different legal systems. Fieldwork and observation over many years have shown that there have been significant developments during the past few decades which have created today's very complex picture. First, let us note that some Muslims in Britain will still only undergo the *nikah* and will altogether refuse to register their marriage in accordance with English law. They would appear to be a definite minority today, because the benefits of following the process of marrying twice have become so patently obvious.

6–100   If most Muslim couples now marry under both legal systems, the question arises which marriage to enter into first. Ahsan ((1995), p. 22) appears to suggest that the Muslim marriage comes before the registered marriage, but emphasises correctly that "the couple start their life as husband and wife only when the proper Islamic ceremony of marriage takes place". Significantly, today most Muslims in Britain will not have the *nikah* first. They will first register their marriage in accordance with English law. However, this will not normally allow the couple to consummate the marriage, since there is no Islamic marriage. Thus, the couple are seen – and normally view themselves – as husband and wife only according to English law, but not under Muslim law. In fact, most Muslims in Britain probably still treat the registration procedure as an equivalent of engagement.[11] The 'real' marriage which confers full legal validity on the union of husband and wife is the contract before God, the *nikah* and all that goes with it (see also Ahsan (1995), p. 22). This is a clear indication that in the minds of many Muslims *shari'a* remains superior to the secular *lex loci*.

6–101   There is of course a further reason why *angrezi shariat* has a rule that one should register the marriage first and then undergo the *nikah*. Concerns about *izzat*, about the position of the woman and the avoidance of *zina* are clearly dominant in this respect. It has proved inconvenient, in fact quite impracticable and dangerous,

---

[8] On this see already Nielsen (1981) and numerous references in Nielsen's work. On religious buildings see in detail Pearl [1972–1973], 2 No. 1 *New Community* 68–69; Poulter (1986), pp. 214 *et seq.*
[9] See also Ahsan (1995), p. 22. Whether one lists English law first, or Muslim law, is a matter of some interest. It would be useful to conduct systematic research on this point among young Muslims. Preliminary indications are that Muslim law is valued above English law, thus confirming the findings of Ballard (1994) and others about British Asian reconstructions of a new identity 'on their own terms'. (see already para. 3–81, above).
[10] s.1 of the Marriage Act 1994 introduced a procedure whereby local authorities may be permitted to approve premises other than their own register offices for the purpose of solemnisation of marriages. It is not known at present to what extent this offer has been taken up by Muslims in Britain.
[11] This was observed in fieldwork during the (1980)s (see Menski (1987), p. 194). Some couples registered their marriage virtually in a lunchbreak, both spouses returning to their work and their respective homes, without marking the occasion in any form. This appears to be changing today and the registration ceremony is gaining more popular acceptance.

to keep spouses who are legally married according to English law apart for very long periods. To avoid this kind of limping marriage, the originally separate elements of formal registration of the marriage and solemn *nikah* have now in most cases been brought as closely together as possible to avoid the dangerous limbo period, which not only gave rise to social and moral concerns, but also to legal problems which surfaced in the English case law on nullity, especially during the 1970s.[12]

6-102   Therefore, unless the couple marry in a 'registered building',[13] the most common pattern today is for the register marriage to occur first, followed very soon by the *nikah* and those customary ceremonies which the couple and their families may choose to follow. The registration of the marriage is arranged first to ensure that the female partner is not subject to the risk of sudden abandonment and consequent disgrace. This may not be expressed in so many words but is clearly the underlying motive for insisting on the registration under English law, which has therefore become a formal legal device to protect the social standing and status of the female party, in particular. For it was the painful experience of individuals and families during the 1960s that, following a *nikah*, Muslim husbands could just abandon the woman after a few days of cohabitation.[14] The woman and her family, where close relatives existed, were often deeply shocked, hurt and shamed. The idealistic framework of Muslim law was seen to be open to abuse by unscrupulous individuals and the resulting legal learning process has been swift, it appears. However, this assimilation to English law did not lead to the abandonment of the *nikah*.

6-103   Today's majority pattern of arranging for the registration first and the *nikah* as closely thereafter as possible also has the effect that those Muslim figures of authority who supervise the *nikah* can be sure that the Muslim marriage they witness is actually valid in English law.[15] In this way, new links are drawn between the secular ceremony and the Muslim contract but the two are kept conceptually apart. This is probably in contrast to the experience of other ethnic minority communities in Britain.[16] It appears, then, that Muslims in Britain continue to fall back on the old principles of Muslim law to the effect that the basic solemn contract of the *nikah* is all that two Muslims need to comply with to be validly married before God. The same arguments as in South Asia are being used by Muslims in Britain today to brush aside local South Asian customs as folk rituals of no legal significance and, equally forcefully, to refuse any legal relevance in terms of Muslim law for the secular registration ceremony. For many Muslims, the basic position remains that a Muslim marriage in Britain today is still, in essence, nothing more and nothing less than the solemn offer and acceptance of the two parties in front of witnesses at the same meeting. There are, of course, positive advantages for a Muslim couple to solemnise a marriage also in accordance with English law and writers have since long advised on the benefits of following that strategy.[17]

---

[12] Remarkably, the relevant English case law is comprised for the most part of Sikh and Hindu cases. For a clear indication that the English courts understand the need for the religious ceremony to achieve full legal validity see the early precedent of *Singh v. Singh* [1971] P 226; [1971] 2 All E.R. 828; [1971] 2 W.L.R. 963.

[13] In that case, the Muslim *nikah* normally precedes the formal registration of the marriage.

[14] In fieldwork, it was found that few people are willing to speak about such problems.

[15] There appears to be evidence that in some mosques the parties have to provide documentary evidence of their marriage registration before they will be allowed to undergo the *nikah*.

[16] There is now much evidence that Hindus, Jainas and Sikhs in Britain have begun to incorporate, often through specific rituals, the secular registration procedure into the rituals of their religious marriage. See in detail Menski (1987); (1988a); (1993a).

[17] For details see Pearl (1972–1973), p. 69. Poulter (1990a), p. 7 merely stipulates the need to follow the rules of English law as well.

6–104 One particular issue has come up in the context of immigration and social security cases, namely the so-called 'marriage by proxy'. A number of English cases have expressly recognised this form of marriage and there has been an instructive debate about this question.[18] It has been concluded that:

"So far as the Muslim communities are concerned . . . it is possible for a proxy marriage to take place, although all the evidence suggests that they are fairly infrequent . . . all that is necessary to establish a marriage in Muslim law is an offer and an acceptance before witnesses. The offer or the acceptance can be delegated to a proxy who can then pronounce the necessary words before witnesses." (Pearl (1986a), p. 56.).

Concerns about the legal position of a 'transnational marriage' are likely to arise in this context under English law. As far as Muslim law is concerned, as long as the other contractual elements are fulfilled, a marriage by proxy should be treated as perfectly valid. The other concern that is likely to arise relates to the position of the proxy as someone who gives a person in marriage, in other words, the proxy may be acting as a marriage guardian as well. This issue is addressed in the section below.

6–105 In quite a few cases, absence of witnesses or more generally lack of documentation of a Muslim marriage entered into in South Asia has been an issue for determination before the British courts and tribunals. While the South Asian courts, as we saw in paragraph 6–02, above, lean in favour of recognising such marriages as valid, European judges appear to need constant reminders of the existence of a strong presumption in favour of marriage in Muslim law.

Consent and guardianship

6–106 Under this heading, the extremely contentious issue of 'arranged marriages' and the problem of child marriages arise for discussion. Both have led to some debate because they are a key issue of family life (Ahsan (1995), p. 22; Nielsen (1992c), p. 98) and are also of considerable relevance to legal practice in Britain.[19] While this is also, as indicated earlier, "an emotionally charged problem" in Middle Eastern countries (Nasir (1990a), p. 49, note 13), and of course in South Asia (see paragraph 6–50, above), in Britain the combination of persuasion, if not force, used to bind young people in marriages and the question of minimum age has led to a debate about human rights violations through forced marriages.[20]

6–107 The Muslim law rules are reflected in some of the English writing on the subject. Ahsan (1995, pp. 22–24) discusses the problem of arranged marriages among Muslims in some detail. Poulter (1986, p. 16) focuses on the fact that marriages of girls under 16 years old are not uncommon in many parts of the world.[21] In fact old English common law also used puberty as the main criterion and there was no statutory minimum age for marriage until the Age of Marriage Act 1929 laid down that a marriage with a person under the age of 16 years is void. It is not a coincidence that at the very same time the Child Marriage Restraint Act 1929 was promulgated in India, at the insistence of some sections of the Indian elite, but

---

[18] See the unreported (1981) case of *Nasreen Akhtar v. Secretary of State for the Home Department*, referred to in Pearl (1986a), pp. 55–56; Bradford [1975] 4 No. 2 *New Community* 254–255, discusses this topic, too.

[19] For details see Pearl (1971a); Ballard (1978), Bradley (1983); Poulter (1990a), pp. 10–11.

[20] See especially Poulter (1986), (1987), (1992a), (1995) and (1998).

[21] Interestingly, Poulter fails to include Europe in this context. He should also have written about early marriages for boys. Examples of rather early marriage ages in countries like Austria (14 years old), Turkey and France (15 years old) are given elsewhere (Poulter (1986), p. 17).

also against much local opposition. The Indian law, as we saw, did not provide that under-age marriages are void.

6–108   Poulter's discussion of the subject highlights the element of "free and informed consent" (Poulter (1986), p. 17) and leads to a human rights debate which has a definite Western bias. This is especially obvious in the section on forced marriages and arranged marriages (Poulter (1986), pp. 22–33), which appears to concentrate particularly on forced marriages in the Muslim world and among South Asians. While some Muslims have found this approach offensive, recent press reports have confirmed the existence of a real problem when young British Muslim women are pressurised into marriages, in Britain or abroad, with men they never saw or did not like.

6–109   With regard to the question of consent, the English case law on nullity of marriage on the grounds of duress is very instructive, although it does not involve many Muslims and is heavily focused on Sikh and Hindu cases. The only early Muslim evidence is the unreported 1968 case of *Khusai ja Bi*.[22] Here, a Muslim woman aged 20 had been given in marriage by her brothers, following an advertisement in a newspaper. The marriage was solemnised in a register office in Britain. The judge found, as a matter of fact, that the woman had never consented to the union and the marriage was therefore annulled. This decision was out of line with the earlier case law and was in fact not even considered in a number of later Sikh cases when similar issues came up.

6–110   Commenting on this case, Pearl (1986a, p. 17) speaks of the fact that "the reality of consent had been destroyed". This phrase is used in explicit reference to the leading case of *Hirani v. Hirani* [1982] 4 F.L.R. 232, CA, in which the Court of Appeal applied a relaxed, more socially perceptive test of duress than in the earlier leading case law, according to which there had been a need to prove real danger to life or limb. It was held, at page 234:

> "The crucial question in these cases, particularly where a marriage is involved, is whether the threats, pressure, or whatever it is, is such as to destroy the reality of consent and overbears the will of the individual."

While the low-key message to Muslims from the *Khusai ja Bi* case had clearly been that a marriage in English law could be avoided in the absence of consent, the leading case of *Hirani v. Hirani* has reinforced that message in a much more public way.[23] The reaction of English law was clearly to the effect that an Asian individual who sought the protection of the English law against overbearing parents or guardians would be sympathetically treated.

6–111   This approach was more vigorously followed in a series of nullity cases in Scotland which involved young Muslims, significantly not only women. The case of Nasreen Akmal, in particular, received wide press coverage between 1990 and 1993. She claimed that at the age of 14 years, she had been virtually abducted to Pakistan by her parents and had been forced into an arranged marriage there in 1983. Applying for nullity of her marriage to the Court of Session in Scotland in 1990, she relied on the argument that she had remained domiciled in Scotland throughout and that, therefore, her marriage should be treated as void since it violated the provisions as to minimum age under her domiciliary law. At the same time, it was apparent that she had been party to a full-fledged marriage according to Pakistani law, out of which three children had been born.

---

[22] This case was decided by Park J. For some details see Pearl (1972–1973), p. 72; Pearl (1986a), p. 17.
[23] The case has been intensely debated. See, *e.g.* Bradley (1983), Poulter (1986), pp. 29–32.

6–112   The case, therefore, involved a complicated question of choice of law. Under Pakistani Muslim law, as we saw in paragraph 6–50, above, this marriage would be legally valid. Under Scots law, it could be treated as void *ab initio*. It was ultimately held by Lord Coulsfield in October 1992 that the Scottish courts could interfere with such an arranged marriage. Nasreen Akmal was therefore granted an annulment on the ground that she was only 14 years old at the time of her Pakistani marriage. This decision is in obvious contradiction to the Muslim law and must be interpreted in the context of wider policy concerns about abuses of the arranged marriage system by Asian parents in Britain today. Press reports at the time correctly identified that this judicial decision was seen as a deliberate interference in British Asian culture. On the other hand, it was obvious that Asians of the younger generation welcomed this kind of decision. Two other cases brought by young Scottish Asians concerned the same issue but have shown that the age factor has been taken as less important than the element of compulsion. When in June 1993 the forced marriage of a young Scottish Muslim man, Shahid Mahmood, was annulled by Lord Prosser, the case did not turn on the question of his age at the time. Rather, the principle was reiterated that physical or psychological force had to be in evidence, vitiating the consent of the parties to the marriage.

6–113   These unreported cases show, as did the much-publicised case of *Hirani v. Hirani* in 1983, that British judicial authorities are willing to disregard and override the principles of a particular Asian legal tradition, even where a marriage was lawfully entered into under an overseas jurisdiction. It is obvious that these decisions have created interesting new legal conflict situations which remain unresolved but intervene in the social sphere of marriage arrangements among Muslims in Britain today.

6–114   The much earlier case of *Alhaji Mohammad v. Knott*[24] involved a potentially polygamous Muslim marriage contracted in Northern Nigeria in which the wife was only 13 years old at the time of the marriage.[25] That marriage was legally valid under Nigerian law as the *lex loci celebrationis* and was therefore recognised by English law when the couple went to live in Britain, where the husband was a student. The case came to light when a medical practitioner became concerned about the wife's welfare and legal proceedings were brought under child protection provisions at the time.[26] The lower court had found this arrangement, as well as the facts of the case themselves, deeply repugnant. Expert evidence had been provided by Noel Coulson, outlining relevant elements of Muslim law, as stated at pages 6–7 of the report:

> "In brief, the marriage is effected by a simple contract between the parents or guardians of the bride and bridegroom . . . Sometimes, but not always, the signing of the contract is succeeded by a religious ceremony and a marriage feast; thereafter there is a formal handing-over of the bride to the bridegroom by the bride's parents. There is no minimum age for the marriage of a girl, but . . . it is unlawful for the bridegroom to live under the same roof or consummate the marriage until there are decisive indications of pubertal maturity in the bride. It is conclusively presumed that a girl cannot attain puberty below the age of nine and has attained it at the age of 15."

---

[24] [1969] 1 Q.B. 1; [1968] 2 W.L.R. 1446; [1968] 2 All E.R. 563.
[25] Poulter (1986), p. 33, n.1, suggests that this was probably a 'forced marriage'.
[26] These were s.62 of the Children and Young Persons Act 1933 combined with s.2 of the Children and Young Persons Act 1963. For details see Poulter (1986), pp. 19–21; Hamilton (1995), pp. 60–62.

However, the justices in this case were of the view, whether or not the marriage was recognised as valid by English law, that the girl was exposed to moral danger and made what was then called a 'fit-person order', which enabled them to admit the girl into the care of a local authority. It was held, as reported at page 9:

> "In our opinion a continuance of such an association, notwithstanding the marriage, would be repugnant to any decent-minded English man or woman. Our decision reflects that repugnance."

6–115   On appeal, the unchallenged evidence on Muslim marriage law, as cited above, was taken as a basis for deciding, first of all, that the marriage was recognised as valid by English law. The court then went on to reverse the decision of the magistrates. Lord Parker C.J., at page 15, expressed the view that the magistrates had misdirected themselves and said:

> "I cannot myself think that decent-minded English men or women, realising the way of life in which this girl was brought up, and this man for that matter, would inevitably say that this is repugnant. It is certainly natural for a girl to marry at that age. They develop sooner, and there is nothing abhorrent in their way of life for a girl of 13 to marry a man of 25. Incidentally, it was not until 1929 that, in this country, an age limit was put on marriage."

It was therefore concluded, at page 17 that this was indeed "a case of husband and wife validly married, recognised as validly married according to the laws of this country".

6–116   This case gave rise to some interesting debates.[27] The negative attitudes to early marriages among Muslims, in particular, found further expression in changes to the Immigration Rules since 1986, which have banned the entry into the United Kingdom of spouses below the age of 16 years.[28] Poulter (1990a, p. 10) succinctly states the legal position in English law today that "no-one can marry under the age of 16, even if their religion allows it". It would appear that this rule is well-known also among the ethnic minority communities in Britain. Cases involving under-age Muslim spouses have become virtually invisible to the law for several reasons. First, as marriage ages have generally gone up and ethnic minority communities in Britain have 'learnt' the law, such cases have become quite exceptional, while one does come across reports of very early engagements. Secondly, some British Muslim parents who are desperate to marry off their daughters as early as possible appear to be sending them abroad while they are still of school-going age. It seems that this particular legal problem has been virtually exported from Britain by members of a transnational community who can use several legal systems for their family arrangements.

Classification of Muslim marriages in Britain

6–117   Pearl (1972b, p. 129) indicated that courts in England would find it difficult to draw neat distinctions between valid, void and irregular marriages according to Muslim law. This particular problem has certainly not been resolved and courts in the United Kingdom would need to rely on expert evidence to draw such distinctions. The absence of reported case law in this field is a clear indication

---

[27] For details see Poulter (1986), pp. 20–21 and Pearl (1995).
[28] This was first done in H.C. 306 of May 22, 1986. See now para. 277 of H.C. 395, the Immigration Rules of October 1, 1994.

that, similar to South Asian societies, British Muslim communities may be finding social rather than official legal solutions to problems of prohibited or irregular relationships that may arise.

6–118 It is extremely unlikely, in the first place, that an English court would be asked to adjudicate on a complex matter of Islamic jurisprudence involving prohibited degrees, for example. This would be seen as a matter under the jurisdiction of expert religious bodies, such as the Muslim Law (Shariah) Council (U.K.) and decisions would probably appear in the form of authoritative guidance (*fatwa*) which Muslims may obtain from a suitably qualified expert in *shari'a*.

6–119 One matter of considerable social and medical rather than legal concern has been the issue of cross-cousin marriages among some South Asian Muslim communities in Britain. Such marriages clearly do not fall under the prohibited degrees according to English or Muslim law; their prevalence depends on local customary practices and family traditions. In some cases, such arrangements have been made over several generations, which has led to genetic problems. In Britain, such cases appear to be sufficiently frequent to have sparked off debates and research in the medical field, since there is strong, worrying evidence of a higher incidence of deformity and neo-natal mortality in new-born children from such unions. It appears that no explicitly legal issues arise in Britain in this respect.

Chapter 7

Marriage: Legal effects

7–01 This chapter concentrates on the legal effects which arise on the solemnisation of a valid (*sahih*) Muslim marriage. A *sahih* marriage is based on a binding and fully valid contract. It is also a status and carries with it a number of rights, duties and responsibilities. Many of these fall into the domain of the religious and the spiritual. However, strictly legal consequences play a significant part in the description of the totality of a marriage in Muslim law. A leading Pakistani writer and judge, Tanzil-ur-Rahman ((1978–1980), Vol. I: 18) put it this way:

> "The rights arising out of an Islamic marriage contract are not the gifts of any legislative body of a country; they emanate from the proposal and acceptance of the parties made at marriage time. The rights and obligations arising thus are a cohesive whole based on the biddings of God and traditions of the Prophet. Hence Muslim jurists regard Nikah to be both temporal and religious at the same time."

The concepts underlying a Muslim marriage follow a patriarchal pattern firmly based on particular historical and geographical roots.[1] Although the status of marriage should be seen as a composite unit, for the purposes of our present discussion it is possible to identify a number of specific issues. Five matters require some discussion in this chapter, again with particular reference first to general Muslim principles, then South Asian Muslim law and finally the legal position of Muslims in Britain today:

(1) sexual relations;
(2) the extent of the husband's control over the wife;
(3) the dower (*mahr*), as distinct from dowry;
(4) the entitlement of the wife to maintenance;
(5) the question of ownership of property.

Effects of valid marriage in classical Muslim law

Sexual relations

7–02 While Nasir (1990a), p. 76) indicates generally that "the effects of marriage depend on the quality of the marriage contract", *i.e.* this depends on whether a marriage is valid, irregular or void, there is agreement in terms of *shari'a* about the centrality of sexual relations and marital fidelity.[2]

---

[1] For details on the effects of a Muslim marriage and Middle Eastern and North African legislation in this regard see especially Nasir (1990a), pp. 76–81; Nasir (1990b), pp. 33–38; El Alami (1992); Mir-Hosseini (1993); Doi (1984), pp. 129–143, dedicates a whole chapter to the marriage relationship in Islam.

[2] On this see in impressive detail Miftahi (1993); see also Engineer (1992); Chaudhry, *Women's rights in Islam* (1991); Schleifer, *Motherhood in Islam* (1986).

"The first duty of the spouses is faithfulness and chastity in that the man and the wife should not enter into any extra-marital relationship. Failure to observe this duty constitutes adultery which can constitute a ground for divorce. This is based on the Quranic verses: "And who guard their modesty – save from their wives or the (slaves) that their right hands possess, for then they are not blameworthy. But whoso craveth beyond that, such are transgressors.""[3]

The Qur'an contains many verses proscribing the severe offence of *zina*, the sexual connection between a man and a woman outside a valid or an irregular union. Typical of such verses are Sura XVII, verse 32 and Sura XXIV, verses 2–3:

"32. Nor come nigh to adultery:
For it is a shameful (deed)
And an evil, opening the road
(To other evils)

2–3. The woman and the man
Guilty of adultery or fornication
Flog each of them with a hundred stripes."

Sexual intimacy is only permitted, therefore, in the context of the marital union. Outside this union, sexual connection is referred to as *zina*, and exposes the perpetrators to the *hudud* (compulsory) punishments.[4]

The extent of the husband's control over the wife

7–03   Closely linked to the sexual bond between husband and wife is the element of joint residence. Nasir (1990a, p. 81) speaks in this context of the common matrimonial home and emphasises the duty of the husband to provide a suitable and agreeable residence according to his means.[5] This duty is matched by the Muslim wife's right to such a home and is the foundation for the general principle that a Muslim wife is bound to reside with her husband unless there is a valid reason for her refusal to do so.

7–04   Nasir (1990a, p. 81; 1990b, p. 39) lists the various criteria for assessing whether a matrimonial home is of the appropriate standard. This is important in litigation, because a dissatisfied wife may have a case for refusing to live with her husband. A wife who leaves the matrimonial home without permission or legal reason is seen by traditional Muslim law as a rebellious wife (*nashiza*) who loses important rights as a result of her disobedience. What exactly constitutes disobedience is subject to interpretation and depends to a large extent on the socio-economic circumstances of the parties.

7–05   Muslim law, being based on patriarchal principles, assumes that the husband has some control over the movements and actions of his wife. Traditional authors like Doi (1984, pp. 129–130) seek to justify this by reference to male physical power and the need to have a figure of authority. Engineer (1992, p. 51) emphasises that the Qur'an itself does not give men an edge over women and then

---

[3] Nasir (1990a), p. 81, with a reference to Qur'an, Sura XXIII, verses 5–7. Nasir (1990b), p. 38 repeats this almost verbatim but confusingly provides a wrong Qur'anic reference.
[4] For details on this topic, which has become very prominent in Pakistan as a result of islamisation and the introduction of the Offence of Zina (Enforcement of Hudood) Ordinance 1979 see Jahangir and Jilani, *The Hudood Ordinances. A divine sanction?* (1990); Mehdi (1994).
[5] He cites in this regard Qur'an, Sura LXV, verse 6.

refers to South Asian interpretations that the element of female obedience relates to breaches of sexual conduct rather than any form of movement.

7–06   The concept of obedience is closely related to the wife's physical presence in the matrimonial home and her duty not to leave it without the husband's permission or for a legitimate reason. Concerns about the wife's right to go out to work and participate in any form of wage-earning labour have an ancient history. While the classical position is that the husband has the right to prohibit this, women may stipulate certain conditions in the marriage contract.[6] The power of the husband certainly does not extend to refusing the wife the right to visit her parents or other close relatives. Equally, unreasonable requests by the husband that the wife should accompany him on long journeys can be refused by the wife. More recently, Engineer ((1994), p. 52) has argued that the particular social conditions at the time of the Qur'anic revelations were later "eternalised" by the Muslim jurists, who subsequently "declared the status of women to be inferior to men under all conditions". In addition, the basic Muslim principles were overlaid by local perceptions and customs, often with the effect of restricting the movements of women further.

7–07   Similarly, the very contentious question of the Muslim husband's right to chastise his wife is not a matter purely of Muslim law. Verma (1988, pp. 107–108) refers to the Qur'an, Sura IV, verses 30–33, some jurists, an unspecified *hadith* and two old Indian cases,[7] supporting the proposition that Muslim law confers a right to moderate chastisement of the wife on the husband. Doi (1984, p. 130) indicates in this respect that wife-beating is generally discouraged by Muslim jurists but suggests, like several other writers, that if a Muslim husband finds that his wife's behaviour goes against the basic principles of Islam, "beating her in a light manner may become necessary". The literature indicates that this is an ancient controversial matter of great complexity.[8]

7–08   This necessarily short summary shows that Muslim law sees the system of rights and duties within the marriage as a carefully balanced appraisal of the needs of both men and women. If a Muslim wife were to refuse her company to the husband, but did not want to be divorced, this would not be acceptable to traditional Muslim law. There will be several reasons for this. First of all, such an arrangement defeats the purposes of marriage. Secondly, it may give rise to *zina*, because if a wife is not willing to stay with her husband, the presumption may arise that she prefers to stay with someone else. This reflects again that Muslim law does not accept the possibility of self-imposed chastity and abstinence.

7–09   If a wife abandons her husband without seeking divorce, he would have the right to demand her return to him. The classical law discusses this, but not so much in terms of conjugal relations as in relation to the wife's duty to return to, or remain in, the matrimonial home.

The dower (mahr)

7–10   If the Muslim wife is conceptually required to be obedient, the corresponding duty of the husband is to provide a dower (*mahr*) and adequate

---

[6] In her research on *shari'a* court records in the occupied West Bank, Welchman, *The Islamic law of marriage and divorce in the Occupied West Bank* (1992, p. 145) found that between 1965 and 1975, the subject on which women made the most stipulations in the marriage contract was the geographical location of the wife's residence. By the 1980s and early 1990s, it is notable that a growing number of stipulations relate to the wife's right to continue her studies.

[7] *Abdul Kadir v. Salima* I.L.R. [1886] 8 All 149; *Asha Bibi v. Kadir Ibrahim Rowther* I.L.R. [1910] 33 Mad. 22.

[8] Verma (1988), p. 108 refers to a *hadith* which indicates that some Muslim women complained to the Prophet about domestic violence.

maintenance for the wife. Dower is mentioned in the Qur'an and is in essence "a sum of money or other property which becomes payable by the husband to the wife as an effect of marriage" (Nasir (1990a), p. 86). Dower is therefore "neither an essential nor a condition for the validity, binding or effectiveness of the marriage contract".[9] A fairly accurate description which expresses clearly the basis of the dower in Muslim law is the definition adopted by Abu Zahra found in Chapter VI of Khadduri and Liebesny (1955, p. 141):

> "The bride-price (mahr) is a due which the husband must pay to the wife in accordance with the marriage contract, but it is not a condition which affects the validity of the contract nor is it an essential requisite. Therefore, if the bride-price is not mentioned in the contract, the contract is still valid."

In view of the use of the term 'bride-price' above, it needs to be emphasised at once that *mahr* is not a *consideration* for the contracting of the marriage.[10] The dower must be clearly seen as an *effect* of the contract of marriage rather than the *price* paid by the husband for acquiring the various rights which accrue to him on marriage. *Mahr* is often discussed also in terms of a sum paid to the wife as a mark of respect to her. Doi ((1984), p. 159) emphasises its character as a "free gift by the husband to the wife, at the time of contracting the marriage". Nasir ((1990b, p. 43) suggests in the words of a Hanafi jurist that "dower has been ordered to underline the prestige of the marriage contract and to stress its importance".

7–11 One should not confuse dowry and dower. Dowry payments are not a part of Muslim legal tradition, while the *mahr* is an integral element of Muslim matrimonial law. Dowry payments have been outlawed and criminalised in South Asia, where they still are a huge legal problem (see paragraph 7–50, below). Dowry not being an element of traditional Muslim law, where it occurs, it is part of customary traditions.

7–12 Unlike dowry, which passes from the woman's side to the man's side, the Muslim law element of dower is designed to protect the woman and is therefore paid by the husband (or on his behalf) to the wife.[11] It is for this reason that some confusion has arisen with the concept of bride-price or bridewealth.[12]

7–13 Having underlined the point that the obligation to pay a *mahr* is an effect of the marriage, rather than an incident to it, we must now turn our attention to the question of classification. The *mahr* is usually classified either as a specified or an unspecified ('proper') *mahr*. The specified *mahr* is further sub-classified, first customarily and now legally, into 'prompt' and 'deferred' dower.

7–14 In principle, there is no fixed amount of *mahr*, there are no maximum limits to its size, and anything lawful may be given or stipulated as *mahr*. According to all schools, Sunni and Shia, "the dower may consist of anything that can be valued in money, is useful, and ritually clean".[13] The early Hanafi and Maliki jurists developed a minimum limit to the specified dower, by the use of analogy with the minimum value of stolen goods which rendered a thief liable to one of the *hudud* penalties, namely amputation of the hand. The sum was 10 *dirhams* in Hanafi law

---

[9] Nasir (1990a), pp. 86–87; Doi (1984), p. 158 suggests that it is "an essential part of a Muslim marriage" and asserts on p. 159 that according to the Qur'an and Hadith it would appear that it is necessary for a valid marriage.

[10] This has been a much-debated issue in South Asian laws, on which see para. 7–50, below.

[11] On the historical antecedents of *mahr* in Muslim law see Fyzee (1974), pp. 132–133.

[12] On these concepts see also Poulter (1986), pp. 40–43 with further references, and Doi (1984), p. 158.

[13] Nasir (1990a), p. 88; Nasir (1990b), p. 45. For details on different school traditions and modern legislation see *ibid.*, pp. 44–45 and Nasir (1990a), pp. 88–89.

and three *dirhams* in Maliki law, while the Shafis and Shias specified no fixed minimum.[14] The use of this analogy raises the suspicion that the dower is a consideration for the marriage. However, as we have already stated, it should rather be seen as an effect of the creation of the relationship and the analogy probably arose because ancient jurists compared the loss of virginity to the loss of a limb.

7–15 The distinction of 'prompt' and 'deferred' specified dower is very important in theory and practice.[15] The prompt dower is payable immediately on marriage, which confirms that the dower is an inalienable right of the wife (Nasir (1990a), p. 87; Nasir (1990b), p. 44). More commonly some of the dower, if not the entire amount, will be deferred. It is then payable on the dissolution of the marriage by divorce or death, or on the happening of a specified event. Many marriage contracts do not specify whether the dower is to be prompt or deferred. In these circumstances, the presumption, in the absence of any usage of the particular community, is that the dower is prompt. Nasir (1990a, p. 89–90; 1990b, p. 46) confirms that this is largely a matter of custom.

7–16 As concerns the unspecified dower, it is discussed and treated as the 'proper' dower and its size is to be determined in view of the socio-economic conditions of the parties involved. If no *mahr* has been agreed or expressly stipulated by the parties, the contract of marriage is still valid. This also means that if no *mahr* sum is specified in the marriage contract, the husband is not thereby released from his liability to pay a dower. Even a statement that no dower shall be paid does not change the position. In these circumstances, what is known as the 'proper dower' *(mahr al-mithl)* becomes due. It is worked out on the basis of the *mahr* agreed for women of a similar social status to the wife. Particularly relevant will be the *mahr* paid to other female members of the wife's family, for instance sisters, paternal aunts and female cousins.[16]

7–17 Several related issues concern the extent of the wife's entitlement to dower. The general principle is that the whole dower shall become due to the wife either on the actual consummation of the marriage or the death of either spouse before consummation.[17] To claim it, the wife need not prove actual consummation, seclusion *(khalwat)* will suffice.[18] In the event of the husband's death prior to consummation, all the jurists agree that the wife will be entitled to the dower payment (Nasir (1990a), p. 93; Nasir (1990b), p. 49). In certain situations, the wife will be entitled to only half the dower or to a present.[19]

7–18 The wife may lose the whole dower in two situations: First, if the marriage is dissolved by the husband before consummation, in various situations akin to annulment (see Nasir (1990b), p. 54).[20] Secondly, if the marriage is dissolved by an action of the wife before consummation, the most common example being probably her exercise of the 'option of puberty', she is not entitled to any dower (see Nasir (1990b), pp. 54–55).

7–19 There is much evidence of debate about legal disputes in this respect

---

[14] See Fyzee (1974), p. 134. In *Asma Bibi v. Abdul Samad Khan* I.L.R. [1910] 32 Al. 167, 10 *dirhams* was treated as equivalent to three or four Indian rupees.

[15] For details see Nasir (1990a), pp. 89–90; Nasir (1990b), pp. 45–46; Fyzee (1974), pp. 136–140 is useful. See also Hinchcliffe (1973), p. 5.

[16] For relevant details see Nasir (1990a), pp. 90–92 and Nasir (1990b), pp. 46–48 with numerous details of modern legislative provisions and Hinchcliffe (1973), p. 5.

[17] Doi (1984), p. 160 correctly emphasises that the Hanafi school treats dower more or less as a debt. For details see para. 7–50, below and Hinchcliffe (1973).

[18] On details see Nasir (1990a), pp. 93–96; Nasir (1990b), pp. 50–51.

[19] For details see Nasir (1990a), pp. 96–98; Nasir (1990b), pp. 52–54.

[20] However, if an unconsummated marriage is dissolved by the husband's *talaq*, the wife is entitled to half the dower.

(Nasir (1990a), pp. 99–101; Nasir (1990b), pp. 55–58). Hinchcliffe (1973, p. 5) emphasised that most wives would not seek the help of a court while the marriage is still subsisting, so most cases arise after the termination of the marriage through divorce or the husband's death. If it was the wife who died, her heirs could sue for recovery of the dower-debt.

7–20 Certain contentious situations may be briefly highlighted here. One must distinguish the pre-nuptial agreement releasing the husband from his obligation to provide the wife with a dower – which is a void contract in Muslim law – from the remission of the dower which can be made after the marriage by the wife. She can enter into an agreement remitting the obligation to pay the dower either in whole or in part. Such a remission in this context is equivalent to a gift. This rule confirms that the wife is the absolute owner of the dower, and she can do with it what she likes (Nasir (1990a), p. 91; Nasir (1990b), pp. 47–48).

7.21 Reduction of dower is a complicated sub-topic, an area of the law in which much depends on local customs.[21] Relevant details are also found in some older cases.[22] There are particular rules which apply to a *fasid* marriage. If a *fasid* marriage is consummated, the husband is also under an obligation to pay a dower, although the obligation is restricted to the payment of either the specified dower or the proper dower, whichever is the lesser sum (Nasir (1990b), pp. 48–49). Even the Shias, who treat a *fasid* marriage as a void marriage, maintain that after consummation a woman becomes entitled, on separation, to the 'dower of the equal', even if a specified dower has been agreed (Nasir (1990a), p. 92; Nasir (1990b), p. 49). Such rules would appear to enable a man to pay a more realistic amount in these admittedly few cases.

7–22 On enforcement of dower, a useful, detailed discussion is found in Hinchcliffe (1973). Problems arise in relation to the payment of the prompt dower, not least when wives refuse to have sexual relations until the prompt dower has been paid. The matter will often come to court on the basis of a suit initiated by the husband for a decree for restitution of conjugal rights (see paragraph 7–50, below). The defence raised by the wife will invariably be that she has denied sexual intercourse to the husband because the dower has not been paid. Such a defence will be accepted by the court in cases where the marriage has not been consummated. The wife in these circumstances will not be forced to live with her husband until such time as the prompt dower has been paid. Thus refusal to have sexual intercourse under these circumstances does not constitute disobedience (*nashuz*), and the husband remains under a duty to continue to provide his wife with maintenance. Difficulties arise, however, in cases where the marriage has actually been consummated and, subsequent to the consummation, the wife refuses any further sexual contact until the prompt dower is paid. Abu Hanifa argued that the wife can always refuse consortium until such time as the dower is paid. The two disciples, Abu Yusuf and Shaybani, as so often, disagreed with the view of their teacher and gave priority to the actual consummation of the union. According to them, the wife's right to demand the payment of the prompt dower by refusing consortium comes to an end as soon as the marriage has been consummated. The right to refuse consortium, therefore, is in the view of the two disciples a very limited right indeed. This links in with the subject matters discussed in paragraph 7–03, above.

---

[21] For details see especially Nasir (1990a), pp. 96–97; Nasir (1990b), pp. 52–54.
[22] *Tajbi v. Nattar Sheriff* A.I.R. (1940) Mad. 888. In this case the court applied the provision stated in the *Hedaya*, Vol. I Book II, Chapter 3, at p. 124.

Maintenance (nafaqa)

7–23   This has probably always been a topic of great interest to the public and to lawyers, because it concerns key financial provisions. In earlier times these financial matters were mainly the subject of informal family arrangements and rarely generated case law. More recently, however, there have been significant developments in various legal systems and especially in South Asian laws concerning women's rights to maintenance after divorce. These are analysed in detail in paragraphs 7–75—7–125, below. Here, we discuss first maintenance during marriage, then the rules about post-divorce maintenance. On maintenance during marriage, the Qur'an, Sura IV, verse 34 states:

> "Men are the protectors
> And maintainers of women
> Because God has given
> The one more (strength)
> Than the other, and because
> They support them
> From their means."

This verse has been treated as the basis of Muslim law in this area. Doi (1984, pp. 207–208) emphasises the necessity of providing maintenance by reference to words of the Prophet and to some *hadith*. The general rule is that a wife is entitled to maintenance, *e.g.* food, clothing and lodging, during the subsistence of a valid *(sahih)* marriage and during the period of *iddat*. Nasir (1990a, p. 102; 1990b, p. 59) says that maintenance is "the lawful right of the wife under a valid marriage contract on certain conditions". These conditions relate in particular, as we saw already, to the contract of marriage itself and the wife's obedience, and they involve spouses above the age of puberty.[23] Maintenance is the wife's right irrespective of her means or her religion, but in certain situations the wife may be expected to fall back on her own resources.[24] Nasir (1990a, p. 103) also shows that "maintenance of the wife is deemed a debt on the husband from the date of withholding it once it is due".

7–24   The right to maintenance may be lost in certain situations.[25] The general rule is that a wife loses her right to maintenance if she is 'disobedient' *(nashiza)*. This certainly occurs when she leaves the home without the husband's consent or without a lawful excuse. The non-Hanafi schools are of the opinion that even if she stays at home she will not be entitled to maintenance if she refuses sexual intercourse. Conflict has arisen, more so in today's conditions, where the wife goes out to work against the wishes of the husband, obviously an issue of great controversy in the Middle East and North Africa as well as in South Asia. Where a wife is otherwise uncooperative or, as most textbooks call it, disobedient or rebellious *(nashiza)*, especially in terms of staying with the husband and subjecting herself to his authority, much depends on the specific conditions in which the dispute arises.[26] There is a strict approach to wives who abandon Islam (Nasir (1990a), p. 108; Nasir (1990b), p. 65).

---

[23] Doi (1984), p. 204 and again at p. 208. Nasir (1990a), p. 104, n.3 and Nasir (1990b), p. 61, n.1, raise in this context the position of child brides too young for consummation of the marriage, arguing that since modern Islamic laws of marriage now prohibit such marriages, the problem has become irrelevant. On the position of the wife under irregular contracts of marriage, see Nasir (1990a), pp. 104–105.

[24] See, *e.g. ibid.*, 103, where some exceptions to this general rule are given.

[25] These are listed by Doi (1984), p. 205 and discussed in detail by Nasir (1990a), pp. 104–109 and Nasir (1990b), pp. 61–66.

[26] In the case of a co-wife, she must have a separate apartment from the other wife. We discuss questions relating to co-wives in Chap. 8, below.

7–25 Past maintenance is not easy to claim in classical Hanafi law. In this school past maintenance only becomes a true debt if the court has authorised the wife to borrow money on the strength of the debt. In essence, maintenance can only be payable during the continuance of the marriage, and only from the date of the decree.[27] The Shafi, Hanbali, Maliki and Shi'i schools are more flexible in this area, and arrears are seen as a debt on the husband which can be claimed however much time has elapsed. Doi (1984, p. 208) writes that the Shafi and the Shi'a schools assume that the wife is not entitled to past maintenance.

7–26 Concerning the quantum of maintenance, socio-economic conditions, customs and traditions and the individual circumstances of the spouses have obviously a key bearing on the issue. The various schools have developed different criteria to assess the extent of a wife's entitlement.[28] All schools agree that if both the husband and wife come from wealthy backgrounds, then the level of maintenance should be in accordance with their standard of living. Likewise, if both are from poor backgrounds, the level of maintenance will reflect this position. If, however, one party is from a poor background and the other one from a wealthy background, the schools have arrived at slightly differing interpretations of the level of the appropriate maintenance. The Maliki and Hanbali schools adopt the view that the average and medium level should be maintained in all cases. The Hanafi school adopts the same position when the husband is wealthy and the wife poor. When the wife is wealthy and the husband poor, however, the Hanafi school believes that it is unreal to look to an average position. This school adopts the view that the husband's condition alone should be the guiding factor.

7–27 As we shall see in our analysis on South Asian Muslim law, there is considerable controversy as to whether the Muslim husband's obligation to maintain the wife extends beyond the *iddat* period.[29] Doi (1984, p. 206) states generally:

> "The responsibility of maintenance of the husband is not only when she lives as a legal wife and towards his children by that wife, but it is important to maintain her even in the event of divorce."

There is no dispute that the husband remains under a duty to support his wife during the period of *iddat* following a revocable pronouncement of *talaq* by him. This is because the wife is then not yet finally divorced and the purpose of the *iddat* period, namely to avoid confusion over paternity in the event that the wife is pregnant, would be defeated. Doi (1984, p. 206) vigorously criticises the selfishness of some people in this regard.

7–28 So far as the irrevocable *talaq* is concerned, the extent of the wife's entitlement depends to some extent on whether she is pregnant or not. The schools have differed much in this respect.[30] In Hanafi law, which appears to have been widely accepted also in modern legal systems (Nasir (1990a), p. 153), a woman divorced by her husband in a form which is held to be irrevocable is entitled to full maintenance during the *iddat* period for as long as she does not leave the home. In contrast to this view, the Maliki law states that such a woman is entitled to full maintenance only when she is actually pregnant. Maintenance is extended to

---

[27] See *Abdool Futteh Moulvie v. Zabunnessa Khatun* I.L.R. [1881] 6 Cal. 631.
[28] For relevant details on the traditional rules and modern legislation see Nasir (1990a), pp. 109–111; Nasir (1990b), pp. 66–68; Doi (1984), p. 208.
[29] The discussion on this topic is found in chapters on *iddat*. For details see Nasir (1990a), pp. 152–154; Nasir (1990b), pp. 104–105.
[30] For details see Nasir (1990a), p. 153; Nasir (1990b), pp. 104–105.

pregnant women even when they leave the former matrimonial home. According to the Maliki view, a non-pregnant woman is only entitled to lodging during the *iddat* following a pronouncement of an irrevocable divorce.

7–29   There has been remarkably little comment on the position of the divorced Muslim wife after the *iddat* period in classical Muslim law, probably because the traditional expectation is that a woman in that situation would return to her natal family, or would remarry. It also appears that the topic has traditionally been discussed in relation to divorce rather than maintenance. Nasir (1990a, pp. 143–144; also Nasir (1990b), p. 96) states the general position that, under the strictest *shari'a* provisions, the divorcee has no entitlement other than the whole dower, if the marriage was consummated, and the *iddat* maintenance. But the matter does not rest there. Can a Muslim husband rely on what nowadays would be called a 'clean break' in this way?

7–30   It appears that a key element in this context is the compensation payment of *mutat*. Relying on Qur'an, Sura II, verse 236, Nasir (1990a, p. 144; 1990b, pp. 96–98) shows that the amount of *mutat* is a matter of goodwill and of custom. Applicable, first of all, in situations where a woman was not entitled to a *mahr* payment and thus received a compensation 'present', it had the potential to be applied to a divorce situation where *mahr* and *iddat* maintenance had been paid. Indeed:

> "The Hanafi jurists hold that the mutat is desirable for every divorcee after consummation, but that there is no mandatory or desirable mutat, prior to consummation, for a divorcee who is entitled to half the dower, nor for a widow."[31]

Nasir then shows how, in various modern Muslim states, the wife's entitlement to the *mutat* compensation has been incorporated into modern statutes. Many of these laws set minimum or maximum levels.[32] It is important to note, however, that this remedy is treated as compensation for an arbitrary *talaq* and is not an automatic, general entitlement. For example, the new Article 52*bis* in Law No. 1.93.347 of September 10, 1993 in Morocco now provides:

> ". . . If it is proven to the *qadi* that the husband exercised *talaq* without an acceptable justification then he shall, when assessing the level of compensation (*mut'a*), take into consideration the injury that the wife may thereby sustain."

It is apparent that such immensely useful and constructive provisions have not been taken notice of in the recent South Asian legal debates about maintenance for divorced Muslim wives.

Property

7–31   The fifth of the legal effects of a Muslim marriage relates to ownership of property. The wife is, as a basic principle, entitled to full ownership of her property. This is often held up by Muslim authors as proof of the modern and advanced nature of Muslim legal regulation, for the simple reason that many so-called modern legal systems did not allow women independent property rights until fairly recently. However, it has already become obvious that this ideal principle, in

---

[31] Nasir (1990a), p. 144; identical Nasir (1990b), p. 96. This is said to be based on the Qur'an and on *shari'a* rulings, but is not further specified.
[32] For details on this important topic see Welchman (1988), pp. 881–883 and (1992); El Alami and Hinchcliffe (1996).

practice but not in law, creates tensions with the ideal principle that a married woman should be 'obedient' to the husband.

7-32 There is no concept either of a doctrine of unity between husband and wife as known in common law, or the concept of community in matrimonial property. The Qur'an, Sura VI states that "to men is allotted what they earn. And to women what they earn".

7-33 We saw already that a wife can give away her *mahr* as she pleases, which confirms her absolute right over this kind of property. Restrictions on the right of alienation of the widow's dower debt in South Asian laws are discussed in paragraph 7–50, below. If one looks at the Muslim system of marriage, the rules about puberty and majority, and the concept of a solemn contract between the two parties suggest full legal capacity on the part of the wife. We have seen, however, that especially younger women may be expected to let a guardian or agent act on their behalf, which opens up various possibilities for arguing that women are not, in fact, treated as full legal personalities. Local customs and traditions, which had already influenced the major early school traditions, have continued to play an important role in this regard, too. We shall see in paragraph 7–126, below what South Asian traditions have to say on this matter.

7-34 Mutual rights of inheritance accrue on the solemnisation of a valid *sahih* marriage.[33] Here again, the idealistic principles of the Qur'anic foundations and social reality for many Muslim women show a wide divergence.

Effects of Muslim marriage in South Asian laws

Sexual relations

7-35 In South Asian Muslim law, too, the first major effect of a valid marriage is seen to be the lawful nature of sexual intercourse and the legitimacy of any children from that union (Fyzee (1974), p. 116; reiterated in Bharatiya (1996, p. 57). While some authors have written about Muslim marriage as though it denotes a union of two souls which are essentially one (Shabbir (1988), p. 23), Tahir Mahmood (1982a, p. 88) opposes this idea as being influenced by Hindu concepts and proposes that Muslim spouses are to be seen as "associates" of each other, with neither party losing their respective individual identity. Several writers emphasise the potential for stipulating certain conditions in the marriage contract, indeed Muslim jurisprudence distinguishes between valid and illegal conditions in this respect.[34] Few of these conditions relate directly to sexual relations, they are more focused on questions of living arrangements, maintenance, property rights, entitlements to divorce, and perhaps the husband's discretion to enter a polygamous marriage.[35]

7-36 Concerning sexual relations, the concept of *zina* is very powerful in South Asia, too. Linked with various local notions of social standing and status, as exemplified in the key concept of *izzat*, concern about sexual impropriety is very prominent. Much has been written about the impact on women in this regard. Verma (1988, p. 88) emphasises that "conjugal fidelity is of course a moral duty of both parties". However, he also highlights the fact that the husband's conjugal infidelity would not lead to any direct legal consequences while a much higher burden is on the wife:

---

[33] For details see Nasir (1990a), p. 83; Nasir (1990b), p. 40 and further, below, Chap. 11 on succession.
[34] See in detail Bharatiya (1996), pp. 58–59; Mahmood (1982a), pp. 84–85.
[35] Excellent comparative material is found in Welchman (1992).

"A wife is bound to observe strict conjugal fidelity from the time of the marriage contract even though the dower has not been paid. She must refrain from improper familiarity with strangers and from any unnecessary appearances in the public. Infidelity of the wife may affect her rights of maintenance." (Verma (1988), p. 88.)

Not surprisingly, the islamisation of laws in Pakistan strongly reflects such concerns. It is notable that in sections 5 and 6 of the Offence of Zina (Enforcement of Hudood) Ordinance 1979, the punishments for married persons (*muhsan*) are in every case much more severe than for unmarried persons.[36]

7-37   Social science research has shown that this kind of legal intervention has had disparately negative and discriminatory repercussions on Muslim women.[37] However, the picture is by no means uniform and clear. Kennedy (1990, p. 71) has argued that the Islamic reforms in Pakistan "have had only a minor impact on the corpus of Pakistan's legal system". He further argued that courts in Pakistan have been protecting women against allegations of *zina*, finding gender bias in favour of women (Kennedy (1991), p. 49). Such apparently disparate and contradictory conclusions can actually be harmonised. At one level, that of local society and the lower courts, there is no doubt that women suffer greater surveillance and are easily blamed and falsely accused of sexual improprieties. In particular poor, unprotected women may end up in jails on trumped-up charges. However, when cases come to the superior courts, there is indeed much evidence of balanced thinking and a definite concern to protect women against negative social forces.[38]

The husband's right to control the wife

7-38   Few South Asian legal textbooks devote any space to this topic, which is a matter of growing concern today in the context of debates about domestic violence and more equitable treatment of women.[39] Such discussions, however, are not as new and 'modern' as many observers assume. Verma (1988, pp. 88–91) produces a good extended discussion of this issue and cites (at page 89) two old Indian cases to the effect that the husband has been given powers to control the movements of the wife to a degree.[40] He also states that the Muslim wife is under a duty to reside with the husband and specifies a long list of arguments which are not open to a Muslim wife wishing to live separately, such as that she wishes to live closer to her natal family,[41] or that she cannot get on with her mother-in-law.[42] Verma (1988, p. 90) also asserts that the husband has a right to reasonable control over the personal behaviour of the wife and can exercise some degree of disciplinary control over her. As to the critical question of chastisement, he refers again to some old cases which support this right of the husband under Muslim law.

7-39   However, already in British India the question arose whether wife beating

---

[36] This is in line with classical Islamic law. The stipulated *hadd* punishment in those cases is stoning to death (*rajm*), the precise method being specified in s.17 of the 1979 Ordinance.
[37] See, *e.g.* Mehdi (1994), p. 226; Singh, *Women in Muslim personal law* (1992), pp. 31–32 provides case studies of young Pakistani rape victims accused of *zina*.
[38] See in this regard the recent cases of *Said Mahmood v. The State*, P.L.D. 1995 F.S.C. 1 and *Rani v. The State*, P.L.D. (1996) Kar. 316.
[39] On the concept of gender equity rather than absolute equality see in detail Monsoor (1994) and (1998).
[40] *Asha Bibi v. Kadir Ibrahim Rowther*, I.L.R. [1910] 33 Mad. 22 at 25, and *Abdul Kadir v. Salima*, I.L.R. [1886] 8 Al. 149 at 156.
[41] *Ghulam Fatima v. Nur Mohammed*, A.I.R. (1933) Lah. 721.
[42] *Mohammed Ali Akbar v. Fatima*, A.I.R. (1929) Lah. 660.

was really acceptable for Muslims in view of the new secular criminal laws.[43] In a brief article (Datta (1940)), which essentially asks for clarification from Muslim law experts, following an unreported case in which the High Court of Dacca had held that a Muslim husband had no right to chastise his wife, the author finds that it appears to be lawful for Muslim husbands to chastise their wives. In support of this view he cites a number of traditional Muslim sources and also relies on the argument that the then recently promulgated Muslim Personal Law (Shariat) Application Act 1937 had reinstated the matrimonial rights of Muslim men in British India.[44] According to one juristic opinion, only a toothbrush may be used to beat the wife, on which Datta (1940, p. 26) comments that "this symbolic beating may be with a view to insult her".

7–40   Verma (1988, p. 108) also cites an Indian case report from 1955 which opposes the right of the husband to chastise his wife.[45] In that case, it was held that at page 202 that "neither the Koran nor the prophet Mohammad approved of the beating of the wife" and (id.) that "thus there is no sanction in law to beat the wife and the practice must be held to be cruel and a relic of barbarism". It was even suggested that escalation of such beating could ultimately deliver the husband to the hangman's noose. The husband's application for restitution of conjugal rights was refused.

7–41   Numerous recent studies from South Asia focus on the question of gender equality and some of them deal specifically with domestic violence.[46] We cannot go into such studies in any detail. Shams (1991, p. 16) contrasts the religious equality of Muslim men and women with social reality:

"Alas the role which has been assigned to woman in the laws of the religion of Islam is being minimised in practice. The practical subjection of the wife to her husband is almost complete and absolute. Her personality is being crushed and now she is in a quandary. The sooner the fallacy of this attitude is realised the better."

In a seminar on the problems and prospects of Muslim women, held at Aligarh Muslim University in 1990, M. Fathima Beevi, then India's first female Muslim Supreme Court judge, sought to find a harmonious balance for the greater good:

"Great importance is given in Islam to husband-wife relationship. The supremacy of the husband in family affairs is conceded. He is charged to support, feed and clothe his wife and speak to her words of kindness and justice and treat her gently. The wife on her part has to appreciate that the husband is a degree higher than her because he has to spend a part of his wealth on her and take care of the financial burden of their children. She has to give to her husband not only love and care but also obedience because that alone can ensure harmony in the family. Harmony in the family is essential to keep the institution of family intact. On this institution of family rest the pillars of civilization. If the husband and wife live as ordained with mutual love and harmony, no matrimonial problem arises." (Beevi (1993), pp. 8–9.)

---

[43] Verma (1988), p. 108 points to evidence of discussions during the 1940s; see Datta [1940] A.I.R. 25–27, below.

[44] The general classical interpretation appears to have been that chastisement is a matter of final recourse, that blows must be non-violent and must leave no mark.

[45] *Shakuran Abdul Majeed v. Abdul Majeed Ghafurkhan*, A.I.R. (1955) N.U.C. 202 (M.B.).

[46] With reference to Muslim women in India see Gani, *Reform of Muslim personal law. The Shah Bano controversy and the Muslim Women . . . Act 1986* (1988); Shams, *Women, law and social change* (1991); Singh (1992); Sarkar and Sivaramayya, *Women and law. Contemporary problems* (1994). On Pakistan see Mumtaz and Shaheed (1987); Mehdi (1994). On Bangladesh see Chaudhury and Ahmed, *Female status in Bangladesh* (1981); Ahmad, *Situation of women in Bangladesh* (1985); Matin, *The women's law* (1993b).

Questions about the extent of the Muslim husband's control over his wife have prominently arisen in South Asian laws under the heading of 'restitution of conjugal rights'. This has been a much-debated topic and it would go too far here to provide full details.[47] There is widespread agreement that the concept of restitution of conjugal rights itself owes its origin to those ancient days when the concept of marriage was based on proprietary rights of the husband. On the other hand, it is also arguable that the fundamental right of the spouses to 'consortium' leads to a basic principle that one spouse is entitled to the society and comfort of the other (see *e.g.* Fyzee (1974), p. 121).

7–42   As regards Muslims in South Asia, the rights and duties of the spouses in this regard were determined early on through case law. Mahmood (1986, p. 121) criticises the early leading case of *Moonshee Buzloor Raheem v. Shumsoonnissa Begum* [1867] 11 M.I.A. 551, decided by the Privy Council in 1867, "under the influence of the English juristic obsession with the so-called contractual element in Muslim marriages". Muslim marriage being treated as a civil contract, it was held that a civil court had the power to enforce all rights and obligations arising from it. A suit for restitution of conjugal rights was classified as a suit for specific performance of contract, based on the principles of justice, equity, and good conscience. Shabbir (1988, p. 90) also criticised the fact that this case still dominates the legal scene notwithstanding the fact that it finds no place in Islamic matrimonial jurisprudence. Significantly, this Muslim author also opposes restitution decrees on the ground that the primary sources of Muslim jurisprudence do not recognise the intervention of the state in matrimonial matters through the judiciary or another remote party (Shabbir (1988), p. 100). It has further been argued that the remedy has its genesis in a mercantile theory of transactions and is grossly repugnant to the matrimonial sphere, so that "its retention on the statute book militates against the positive dictate of an educated and civil conscience" (Shabbir (1991), p. 97). Such comments must be read in the wider context of recent Indian debates about the abolition of the remedy and in the light of a number of recent high-profile cases which did not involve Muslims.[48] The resulting academic discussion about this topic in South Asia also did not concern Muslim law.

7–43   It remains a fact that restitution of conjugal rights is a remedy aimed at preserving the marriage, rather than terminating it. The remedy must therefore be seen in a wider context and it is particularly noteworthy that most petitions for restitution of conjugal rights only arise after the wife files a suit for separate maintenance or, as shown in paragraph 7–50, below, when questions of dower payments arise. Verma (1988, p. 109) correctly states that there is no absolute right to restitution vested in the Muslim husband, so it could not be argued that modern state law in South Asia creates a situation where Muslim women can be simply ordered back to their husbands because the latter demanded this.[49]

7–44   Courts have had to find a balance between the rights and duties of both spouses. In the leading case of *Itwari v. Asghari*, A.I.R. 1960 Al. 684, a Muslim husband filed a suit for restitution of conjugal rights against the first wife after he had taken a second wife. The court refused to grant the husband's petition, finding it inequitable to demand that the first wife should continue to live with the

---

[47] For a detailed discussion see, *e.g.* Verma (1988), pp. 109–116.

[48] For details of the ensuing debates on constitutional principles see Bhattacharjee (1994), pp. 79–81. For a critique of the continued reliance on old British concepts and rules see Bhattacharjee, *Matrimonial laws and the Constitution* (1996), pp. 16–19, and 123–125.

[49] Although it probably remains correct to say that the concept of the 'house of obedience' as a result of the marriage contract should not be overlooked.

husband in those circumstances.[50] The court used strong language to criticise the husband and held (at page 687) that his actions amounted to cruelty against the wife, which entitled her to separate residence.[51] Fyzee (1974, p. 124) has commented that since the Dissolution of Muslim Marriages Act 1939, "the courts have leaned heavily in favour of the wife in all such cases, and restitution cannot be had by the husband unless the wife is clearly in the wrong".

7–45 In *Raj Mohammad v. Saeeda Amina Begum*, A.I.R. 1976 Kant. 200, the learned judge confirmed the principle that there is no absolute right in a husband to claim restitution of conjugal rights, relying on *Itwari v. Asghari*, A.I.R. 1960 All 684, an old Privy Council case of 1867, and other cases. The principle was thus confirmed that, especially since the appellant had taken another wife and had not maintained his first wife and their children, the wife had reasonable cause to stay away from her husband.

7–46 In *Shahina Praveen v. Mohd. Shakeel*, A.I.R. 1987 Del. 210, the facts were that the husband had filed a suit for restitution of conjugal rights against the wife in 1981 and had been successful in 1983. Apparently, the wife's family had put pressure on the husband to stay at their residence and, when he refused, the wife preferred to remain at her parents' house rather than return to the husband. There were allegations of dowry demands and related violence, and the wife claimed that she feared for her physical safety if she were forced to return to her husband. She therefore filed an appeal in the Delhi High Court under the DMMA of 1939, alleging cruelty as a ground for divorce under that Act. The petition was granted and it was clearly held that in such circumstances a Muslim wife cannot be ordered back to the matrimonial home. Notably, this case has given rise to a critical comment in the *Annual Survey of Indian Law* of 1987 (Latifi (1987), pp. 314–315) to the effect that Indian courts should follow the more liberal approach of Pakistani courts to the dissolution of marriage at the behest of a Muslim wife, with a reference to the leading case of *Khurshid Bibi v. Md. Amin*, P.L.D. 1967 S.C. 97.

7–47 In Pakistan itself, *Sahi Bi v. Khalid Hussain* 1973 S.C.M.R. 577 serves by way of example to illustrate the balance between the competing claims of spouses. The Supreme Court of Pakistan here considered a case which, one suspects, occurs all too frequently. Irshad Begum was married to Khalid. They lived together for a month after their marriage. It was then suggested by the wife's mother that the husband was cruel to her daughter, and she therefore left the marital home and returned, indeed 'took refuge', in the maternal home. It is alleged that some time later, the girl was forcibly removed by the husband and his family. The mother brought a habeas corpus petition under section 491 of the Pakistan Penal Code. In effect, this criminal action complained that the husband was not allowing the woman to move freely, that she was confined within the four walls of the house, that she was maltreated and tortured. The court took the view that a wife cannot be forced to live with her husband against her wishes. The judge said, at page 579:

> "We are satisfied that under the Mohammadan law, a *sui juris* woman cannot be forced to live with her husband against her wishes. Quranic injunction is against it. According to the Mohammadan Law, if there is disagreement between the husband and the wife, the wife is entitled to live separately from her husband."

---

[50] Other case citations are found in Desai, *Indian law of marriage and divorce* (1993), pp. 136–138.
[51] Indeed, under classical law, the husband is obliged to accommodate the co-wives separately. As clearly shown by Welchman (1992 and 1994), this issue is of major concern to many women in the Middle East.

However, notwithstanding this statement of general principle, the judge went on to state that it was open to the husband to file a suit for restitution of conjugal rights. In that context, unless the wife is able to show that the husband has treated her with cruelty, a decree will be ordered. Although the decree cannot be enforced, and to that extent the remedy may not be viewed as effective, refusal by the wife in these circumstances to return to the husband releases him from any obligation to provide maintenance. In addition, any property owned by the wife can be attached.

7–48 Balchin (1994, p. 63) confirms the current legal position in Pakistan, which has primarily arisen in divorce cases under the DMMA 1939 and under section 8 of the MFLO 1961 (see Chapter 9, paragraph 9–57, below) that forcing a Muslim woman into a hateful union is perceived to be against Islamic principles. Thus, a wife would be entitled to a *khula* divorce if there was any attempt to force her to return to such a marriage through a decree for restitution of conjugal rights.

7–49 In Bangladesh, too, Muslim women are well-protected by judicial alertness to the rights of women in marriage and the desire to balance the rights and duties of the spouses within the context of a modern constitutional and rights-based framework. In the leading case of *Nelly Zaman v. Giasuddin Khan*, 34 D.L.R. (1982) 221, it was held by S. M. Hussain J. at page 225:

"A reference to Article 28(ii) of the constitution of Bangladesh guaranteeing equal rights of women and men in all spheres of the state and public life would clearly indicate that any unilateral plea of a husband for forcible restitution of conjugal rights as against a wife unwilling to live with her husband is violative of the accepted state and public principle and policy."

The more recent case of *Hosne Ara Begum v. Rezaul Karim*, 43 D.L.R. (1991) 543 at 545, further reiterated the principle that a wife has, under Muslim law, a right to refuse conjugal relations to the husband if she is treated by him with cruelty or if there is failure to pay the prompt dower. This confirms, for all three South Asian jurisdictions examined here, that Muslim wives have a strong voice in proceedings for restitution of conjugal rights and are not treated as though they were merely the property of the husband.

Dower in South Asian laws

7–50 South Asian law books generally start the discussion of *mahr* with a standard definition of dower which has given rise to considerable debate concerning the precise nature of the concept. This standard definition is, for example, found in the various editions of Mulla's textbook and runs as follows:

"*Mahr* or dower is a sum of money or other property which the wife is entitled to receive from the husband in consideration of the marriage."[52]

It is the term 'consideration' which has led to vigorous discussion about the nature of the Muslim marriage contract and the position of the wife in this respect. As we saw in Chapter 6, there has long been widespread agreement that a Muslim marriage is much more than a purely commercial contract. Mahmood (1982a, p. 69) distinguished *mahr* from 'consideration' and also from 'dowry', emphasising that the Muslim dower has a unique position of its own. Mahmood (1982a, p. 70) identified

---

[52] Mannan (1990), p. 397 and Hidayatullah and Hidayatullah (1977), p. 308. Mahmood (1982), p. 69, writes that *mahr* is the most important aspect of the Muslim law of marriage. On the debate see Diwan and Diwan (1991), pp. 62 *et seq.*

the elements of 'effect of the marriage', 'essential incident' and a legal responsibility of the husband towards the wife as key components for an appropriate understanding of the term.

7–51 Such definitional problems have arisen as a result of early judicial decisions, some of which have been criticised as being out of line with *shari'a* principles. Mahmood J.'s dictum in *Abdool Kadir v. Salima*, I.L.R. [1886] 8 Al. 149 has been criticised as misleading. He said, at page 157:

> "Dower, under the Muhammadan Law, is a sum of money or other property promised by the husband to be paid or delivered to the wife in consideration of the marriage, and even where no dower is expressly fixed or mentioned at the marriage ceremony, the law confers the right of dower upon the wife as a necessary effect of marriage."

Although he also used the offensive word 'consideration', Lord Parker produced a description of dower in *Hamira Bibi v. Zubaida Bibi* which has been useful and important[53]:

> "Dower is an essential incident under the Mussulman law to the status of marriage; to such an extent this is so that when it is unspecified at the time the marriage is contracted the law declares that it must be adjudged on definite principles. Regarded as a consideration for the marriage, it is, in theory, payable before consummation; but the law allows its division into two parts, one of which is called "prompt", payable before the wife can be called upon to enter the conjugal domicil; the other "deferred", payable on the dissolution of the contract by the death of either of the parties or by divorce . . . But the dower ranks as a debt, and the wife is entitled, along with other creditors, to have it satisfied on the death of the husband out of his estate. Her right, however, is no greater than that of any other unsecured creditor, except that if she lawfully, with the express or implied consent of the husband, or his other heirs, obtains possession of the whole or part of his estate, to satisfy her claim with the rents and issues accruing therefrom, she is entitled to retain such possession until it is satisfied. This is called the widow's lien for dower, and this is the only creditor's lien of the Mussulman law which has received recognition in the British Indian Courts and at this Board."

More recent decisions from Pakistan have appropriately captured the essence of the concept, while it appears that some Indian judges are still too fixed on the contractual element.[54] In a 1980 case in Karachi, it was held:

> "The dower, therefore, is a right which comes into existence with the marriage contract itself except that in case the dower is deferred its enforcement is held in abeyance till a certain event, *i.e.* dissolution of marriage by death or divorce, occurs."[55]

Emphasising that *mahr* is the exclusive property of the woman,[56] Fyzee ((1974), p. 133) outlined the financial and social benefits it brings for the wife under Muslim law:

---

[53] [1915–1916] 43 L.R. I.A. 294, at 300–301, cited in full at Fyzee (1974), p. 134.
[54] See an unclear reference to this effect in Diwan and Diwan (1991b), p. 63.
[55] *Anwarul Hassan Siddiqui v. Family Judge, Court No. III Karachi*, P.L.D. 1980 Kar. 477, at 483. In *Zarin Qaisha v. Arbab Wali Mohd*, P.L.D. 1976 Pesh. 128 at 130, *mahr* was referred to as "a mark of respect" to the wife.
[56] Several authors stress this, see Mahmood (1982a), p. 71; see also Fyzee (1974), p. 132.

"Thus Islam sought to make *mahr* into a real settlement in favour of the wife, a provision for a rainy day and, socially, it became a check on the capricious exercise by the husband of his almost unlimited power of divorce. A husband thinks twice before divorcing a wife when he knows that upon divorce the whole of the dower would be payable immediately."

No maximum limits on dower were laid down by the early jurists. In South Asia, as in some Middle Eastern countries and now in Britain, the recent trend has been for very large *mahr* sums to be announced.[57] There are probably three reasons for this trend. First, the fathers of brides will often demand high *mahr* sums for status purposes. Secondly, in many cases the bridegrooms themselves encourage the insertion of large *mahr* sums in the marriage contract *(nikahnama)* for their own aggrandisement. Finally, a large dower sum can be viewed as an insurance for the wife against the possibility of an unjustified divorce by the husband or a provision in case of his early death.

7–52   The *mahr* system imposes substantial financial strains on young men who often find that it is simply impossible for them to raise the money required, and who in consequence delay their marriage for considerable periods of time.

7–53   An unfortunate result of the lack of a maximum sum of dower is that the publicly acclaimed *mahr*, in many cases, is never intended to be paid, for there is a private arrangement for a lesser sum agreed between the parties. In any dispute over the payment of dower, there is ample scope for the husband to allege such an agreement. If the court believes him, it is the private agreement which will be enforced. If the dower is *intended* to be paid, then the dower is enforceable against the husband. Indeed, it is only in Oudh (now part of Uttar Pradesh in India), under section 5 of the Oudh Laws Act 1876 and in both Jammu and Kashmir (India) and Azad Kashmir (Pakistan) under the Muslim Dower Act 1920, that a dower is only enforceable if it is a reasonable figure in the circumstances of the particular parties.[58]

7–54   A comment on the institution of private dower agreements was made by the Pakistani Commission on Marriage and Family Laws in its report in 1955. The Commission stated, at page 1218:

"A vicious custom has grown up in our society of fixing an inordinately high sum as *Mehr* without any intention of paying it. It is often stated that a large sum had been fixed as *Mehr* merely as a matter of prestige of the husband or to do honour to the status of the wife. The result is that even in cases where a larger amount of dower has been genuinely fixed, a defence is taken, if litigation ensues, that the *Mehr* was not meant to be paid and that the intention of the parties was that it shall never be claimed. This necessitates the framing of a number of unnecessary issues by the court, and the civil suit relating to dower lasts sometimes for 10 years . . . If such a defence is ruled out by law, cases of dower instituted by women would be decided promptly and the vicious process alluded to above will gradually disappear. It should, therefore, be enacted that a husband will have to pay the *Mehr* fixed in the marriage contract however high it may be."

The Commission clearly believed that the possibility for husbands to argue that the agreement in the *nikahnama* was really a sham had created a social evil. The

---

[57] For some examples see *ibid.*, pp. 135–136.
[58] On Oudh see *ibid.*, p. 137; Hodkinson (1984), p. 137.

recommendation that the law should require the husband to pay the fixed *mahr*, no matter how high it was set in the document, was criticised and never became law. The principle was discussed in detail by Daud Khan J. in the Peshawar case of *Nasir Ahmad Khan v. Asmat Jehan Begum*, P.L.D. 1967 Pesh. 328, at 334–335:

> "Broadly speaking, this principle recognized that when a real dower has been fixed between the parties privately and in some cases publicly the second dower is fixed in inflated amount just for the enhancement of the prestige of the family of the bridegroom, and for its glorification, but in such a case the intention was never to enforce the dower announced in public and the real intention was to enforce the dower agreed upon privately between the parties . . . it is abundantly clear that the principle of As-Sum'at recognizes the fixation of two agreements with respect to the dower. One agreement is in private for a real amount and the other agreement for inflated amount is in public for the glorification of the bridegroom and his family, and if this is proved, then the real dower, which has been fixed in private should alone be allowed."

The presence of the dower must be seen in the context of the absence of alimony after divorce, and within the background that although the dower can be either prompt or deferred, the greater part of it is usually deferred. In Pakistan, it is important to distinguish dower from 'dowry and bridal gifts'. The latter are sums of money and presents given either by the bride's family (*jahez* or dowry) or by the groom's family (bridal gifts). In Pakistan, section 3 of the Dowry and Bridal Gifts (Restriction) Act 1976, places restrictions on the amounts that can be given as dowry, presents and bridal gifts. In section 7 of the Act, there used to be a requirement of display of dowry (see Hodkinson (1984), pp. 138–143). This was removed by section 3 of the Dowry and Bridal Gifts (Restriction) (Amendment) Ordinance, 1980 (Ordinance 36 of 1980).[59] Section 5 of the 1976 Act provides that all such property vests absolutely in the bride. Under section 2(a), dower (*mahr*) is expressly excluded from the operation of this Act.[60] Criminal penalties are laid down for breach of the Act but it continues to be a feature of Pakistani society that husbands, after divorce, refuse to let women have access to items of dowry and bridal gifts that are rightfully theirs.

7–55   Balchin (1994, pp. 132–133) provides a long list of reported cases under the Act and argues that the Act "has had absolutely no impact on social norms" (page 92). Balchin's case analysis shows that Pakistani Muslim husbands regularly rely on the argument that their former wives obtained dowries and bridal gifts in violation of the law and should, therefore, not be entitled to their enjoyment. Fortunately, it appears that the courts have been alert and have, in every case, upheld the wife's appeal for return of dowry and bridal gifts.[61] The Act itself, and the few available comments on it, suggest the presence of a huge unresolved social problem at the periphery of the dower complex, for there is no doubt that the various financial transactions involved in a Muslim marriage are closely interlinked and go much beyond the dower.

---

[59] This Ordinance sought to tighten up some of the earlier rules. Ch. M. Mahmood (1991), p. 269 makes the point that there is no Islamic sanction behind this Act.
[60] See *ibid.*, pp. 269–280 and Abid, *Manual of family laws in Pakistan* (1993), pp. 317–332, with further details on the Dowry and Bridal Gifts Restriction Rules 1976 at pp. 322–324. The most recent enactment in Pakistan on this subject has been the Marriages (Prohibition of Wasteful Expenses) Act 1997.
[61] For details see Hodkinson (1984), pp. 138–143; Balchin (1994), pp. 92–93. A full analysis of this area of the law does not yet exist.

7–56   For Pakistan today, Balchin (1994, p. 42) confirms that a Muslim marriage is valid even if no dower is mentioned, but "the exact legal implications and legal effects flowing from it remain controversial". Since dower concerns money and property, it has inevitably been an area of much interest for legal practice. As for classification of dower, the standard principles apply, as discussed in paragraph 7–10, above. The dower is usually specified at the time of the marriage and the *kazi* or *mullah* performing the ceremony enters details of the *mahr* on the *nikahnama* or other documentation of the marriage.[62] Absence of such details on documents does not render the marriage invalid in any form but requires that the dower be specified at a later stage.[63] In this regard, the minimum value of a dower has been a controversial issue.[64]

7–57   When the 'proper' dower of a woman is to be fixed, the main criteria are the social position of her father's family and her own personal qualifications.[65] One may detect an element of the doctrine of equality (*kafa'a*) in this context.

7–58   As for the distinction of prompt and deferred dower, this is a matter of contractual arrangement and there is no hard and fast rule (Diwan and Diwan (1991), p. 66)). In Pakistan and Bangladesh, at any rate, the presumption is that dower is prompt, for section 10 of the MFLO 1961 lays down that when no details of the mode of payment for the dower are specified, the entire amount shall be presumed to be payable on demand.

7–59   Not surprisingly, case law has arisen in South Asia on the important question whether a Muslim wife whose prompt dower has not been paid is entitled to refuse consummation of the marriage. The problem came up before Mahmood J. in *Abdul Kadir v. Salima*, I.L.R. [1886] 8 Al. 149, and it was held that a Muslim wife whose prompt dower had not been paid had no right to refuse herself to her husband if the marriage had earlier been consummated with her consent. This reasoning was based on the views of the Disciples of Abu Hanifa, thus on later juristic opinion, rather than on the view of Abu Hanifa (see paragraph 7–10, above). The same matter was discussed at length in *Anis Begam v. Muhammad Istafa Wali Khan*,[66] a case which followed the normal pattern of a petition by the husband for restitution of conjugal rights, defended by the wife on two grounds, first that the husband had been guilty of cruelty and further, that the husband had not paid the prompt dower to the wife. On appeal, Sulaiman J. followed *Abdul Kadir v. Salima*, and also adopted the views of the Disciples that a wife, once the marriage had been consummated, had lost the right to deny her company to the husband. To that extent, the learned judge dismissed the wife's appeal and said, at page 763:

> "To allow to the wife the right of refusing to live with her husband, even after consummation, so long as any part of the prompt dower remains unpaid would, in many cases, where the husband and wife quarrel, amount to an absolute option to the wife to refuse to live with her husband and yet demand a maintenance allowance. This would dislocate domestic life."

More recently in India, in *Rabia Khatoon v. Mohd Mukhtar Ahmad*, A.I.R. 1966 All 548, it was argued that the opinion of Mahmood J. in *Abdul Kadir v. Salima*, I.L.R.

---

[62] Diwan and Diwan (1991), p. 63 emphasise that no deed is necessary, although it is normally put in writing.

[63] Fyzee (1974), p. 137 succinctly puts this into the formula "if marriage, then dower", an old principle developed by the Privy Council.

[64] See Mahmood (1982a), p. 71; Fyzee (1974), p. 138.

[65] Fyzee (1974), pp. 137–138; Diwan and Diwan (1991), p. 68. Notably, the husband's social position is not a criterion.

[66] I.L.R. [1933] 55 Al. 743; also reported at A.I.R. (1933) Al. 634.

[1886] 8 Al. 149, was only an obiter dictum, in other words, that the law was not clear and this question needed to be looked at afresh.[67] The facts of this case are unremarkable and typical, the wife relying on a combination of domestic violence and non-payment of the prompt dower despite repeated demands on her part. While the lower courts did not accept the wife's claims of cruelty, they did find in her favour regarding the prompt nature and the size of the dower and had granted the husband a decree for restitution of conjugal rights, on condition that he paid the outstanding high sum of dower. In the wife's appeal case before the High Court of Allahabad, we find a very detailed judgment, which makes interesting comments about the nature of juristic law making in Muslim law, traces the development of the relevant law and also refuses to open up this question afresh. The reasons are obviously of a social nature, rather than grounds based on Muslim jurisprudence. It was held by Uniyal J., at page 551, that if the old legal position were to be modified,

> "it would not only create uncertainty in the law but also disturb the domestic peace of Muhammedan families throughout India. According to one school of Mahomedan Law a Muhammedan wife governed by Hanafi law has the right to refuse to go to her husband even after the consummation of marriage with her consent if her dower remains unpaid, but it would be dangerous to adopt this view at the present time having regard to the prevalent practice and the modern conditions of life."

Apparently, in this case, it also helped the learned judges that they were not persuaded by the wife's evidence to the effect that she had demanded the payment of her prompt dower. Thus the decision of the lower court was confirmed, asking the husband to pay Rs. 5000/- to the wife if he wanted to claim the restitution of conjugal rights which the court had granted him. It is not known what happened to this couple thereafter.

7–60   In Pakistan, the same question was argued before the High Court of Lahore in the important case of *Rahim Jan v. Muhammad*, P.L.D. 1955 Lah. 122. The parties had stayed together only for a month and a half. The wife had subsequently petitioned for divorce on the ground that the husband had failed to maintain her without reasonable cause for more than two years. This ground is available to the wife under section 2(ii) of the DMMA 1939 (see below, paragraph 9–57). The husband defended the petition arguing that the wife had not given him the benefit of her conjugal society; thus he was under no obligation to maintain her. In reply, the wife said that the prompt dower, fixed at Rs. 500/-, had not been paid to her. The lower courts had sided with the husband throughout.

7–61   On appeal, the High Court had to decide whether, in Hanafi law, the wife is entitled, even after consummation, to refuse to live with her husband when the prompt dower has not been paid to her. The court reviewed the case law and produced a detailed discussion of *Abdul Kadir v. Salima*, I.L.R. [1886] 8 Al. 149, finding that the comments in that case about the wife's right to refuse conjugal relations after an unfulfilled dower demand are *obiter*. Kaikaus J. therefore dissented from *Anis Begam v. Muhammad* and adopted the view of Abu Hanifa rather than that of the Disciples. The learned judge held, at pages 134–135:

> "I do not find any principle of justice or reason by which the right of the wife to refuse the performance of marital obligations on account of non-payment of prompt dower may come to an end by her once surrendering herself."

---

[67] This was also noted in *Anis Begam*, but the learned judge considered it too dangerous to unsettle the law.

It was therefore firmly held, at page 136, that "even after consummation the wife retains the right to refuse the performance of marital obligations till the prompt dower is paid". Thus, as stated at page 137:

"It is true that unless she makes a demand for her prompt dower the husband is entitled to conjugal rights, but if a demand for prompt dower has been made and the dower is not paid, the refusal of the wife to live with the husband would be justified even though this is not assigned as the reason of her refusal. The husband being in default is not entitled to the exercise of conjugal rights and the failure of the wife to live with the husband cannot be a wrong."

However, in the present case the judge held that the wife had never demanded the payment of the dower and, most fatally for her case, there was a decree for restitution of conjugal rights against her. Her appeal, thus, had to fail.

7–62 In *Nur-Ud-Din Ahmad v. Masuda Khanam*, P.L.D. 1957 Dacca 242, we find a wife's suit for dissolution of marriage and recovery of her prompt and deferred dower. The couple had married according to Muslim law in 1947, the marriage had been registered and the *kabinnamah* specified a dower of Rs. 5.000/-, half of which was prompt. There was also a condition in the marriage contract that if the husband should fail to pay the wife the monthly maintenance allowance, she should obtain the whole *mahr* from the husband and would have the power to divorce him. The wife alleged that despite these protective conditions the husband had maltreated her, so that she had to stay in her parental home. The husband's petition for restitution of conjugal rights was resisted, *inter alia*, on the ground of non-payment of *mahr*. The husband had twice been asked by the lower courts to deposit the prompt *mahr* in court, but he had not done so; his suit was thereafter dismissed but he continued to appeal. The wife claimed that she was entitled to a decree of divorce and the entire amount of dower. In the course of these protracted proceedings, it was found by Rahman J., at page 248:

". . . the right to prompt dower given to a wife is a right which cannot be defeated by the husband even on the ground of his being denied the society of his wife. The wife is under the Muhammadan Law entitled to refuse herself to her husband until and unless the prompt dower is paid to her. This right she can exercise even when residing in the house of her husband. Indeed all authorities on Muhammadan Law are unanimous on the point that the right to maintenance cannot be defeated if the wife has demanded her prompt dower and the husband has not paid it to her."

Considering various authorities on the point, including the *Hedaya*, Baillie's *Digest* and the similar case of *Najiman Nissa Begum v. Serajuddin Ahmad Khan*, A.I.R. 1946 Patna 467, the court found a continuing liability of the husband to maintain the wife and to pay her the dower. In view of his persistent refusal to do so, the case was clear-cut and the husband's appeal failed.

7–63 In *Muhammadi v. Jamil-Ud-Din*, P.L.D. 1960 (W.P.) Kar. 663, the key issue was whether a wife whose dower had not been paid and who therefore refused to cohabit with the husband still had a right to maintenance. In other words, did such a wife have a reasonable excuse to withhold her company and to live separately? In this case, too, it was held that the husband's failure to pay the prompt dower entitled the wife to stay away from him without penalty. At page 666, it was found, relying also on *Nur-Ud-Din Ahmad v. Masuda Khanam*, P.L.D. 1957 Dacca 242:

"It is [a] well settled rule of Muhammadan Law that a wife is entitled to stay away from her husband if there is reasonable cause for her to do so. Amongst others, maltreatment by the husband is a ground on which the wife can refuse to go to her husband's house. Another ground on which she can refuse to go to her husband's house is the non-payment of the prompt dower. All the Muslim Jurists are unanimous on the point that the right of maintenance of a wife cannot be defeated if she has demanded her prompt dower and her husband has not paid her."

More recently, Professor Mannan (1990, p. 404), the Pakistani editor of Mulla's *Principles of Mahomedan law*, has mentioned the old authority of *Rahim Jan v. Muhammad*, P.L.D. 1955 Lah. 122, but does not give it much importance. Instead, he has tried to argue that if a suit is brought in Pakistan after sexual intercourse has taken place with the consent of the wife, "the proper decree to pass is not a decree of dismissal, but a decree for restitution conditional on payment of prompt dower". This view was supported by reference to the old Anglo-Indian case law and even the 1966 Indian case of *Rabia Khatoon*, discussed above.

7–64   However, there is also further Pakistani evidence of the other view. Balchin (1994, pp. 53–54) shows that there are at least three reported cases from the 1980s which support the proposition that even after consummation has taken place, the wife may refuse to live with her husband unless he pays her the prompt dower.[68] In *Muhammad Ishaque v. Rukhsana Begum*, P.L.D. 1988 Kar. 625, the couple were married on March 23, 1986 with a prompt dower of Rs. 25.000/- which the husband did not pay. The wife stayed with him for five days and claimed "complete retirement for several days" (page 626). The court circumscribed 'complete retirement' and held, dismissing the husband's case, at page 627:

"According to Hanafi law where there is a complete retirement the husband is liable to pay the full amount of dower . . . In the present case the admitted position is that the petitioner and respondent No. 1 were in complete retirement for five days and nights."

In *Chanani Begum v. Muhammad Shafiq*, 1985 M.L.D. 310, there was a marriage between cousins with a prompt dower agreed at Rs. 5.000/- which was not paid by the husband. The couple lived together for two and a half years but then fell out and the wife moved to her parental home, filing suits for the recovery of dower, maintenance allowance and dissolution of the marriage on various grounds. The husband claimed that the wife had relinquished her dower. The learned judge in this case found, at page 313:

"It is true that [a] wife cannot claim maintenance if she lives separate from her husband without any justification but it is equally well-recognized that a wife can refuse herself to the husband and also live separate from him until the prompt dower is paid by the husband and that during such separation the husband is duty bound to maintain her."

The case was therefore remitted to the lower court, which came in for some critical appraisal, for reconsideration and fresh decision. This case, too, confirms that a woman in Pakistan today, finding that her dower has not been paid years after the

---

[68] The cases cited are *Muhammad Ishaque v. Rukhsana Begum*, P.L.D. (1988) Kar. 625, *Chanani Begum v. Muhammad Shafiq*, (1985) M.L.D. 310, and a case reported at P.L.J. (1985) Lah. 232. Balchin (1994), pp. 101–102, lists a total of 25 reported dower cases from Pakistan during the 1980s.

marriage, may use this fact as a reasonable ground to withdraw from the husband's society, while she remains entitled to maintenance. It is of course debatable whether a woman in that situation would be wise to use this argument to put pressure on her husband for paying the prompt dower. It seems preferable to insist on instant payment of the prompt dower, but economic restraints may not permit that strategy. As always, spouses have to find a delicate balance between insisting on legal rights and considering their social and economic circumstances.

7–65 In the previous edition (Pearl (1987a), p. 68) it was argued that Pakistan and Bangladesh are almost certain to follow *Rahim Jan,* but that in India *Anis Begam* seemed to be the better authority. It is evident that Pakistani law today gives a larger right to women in this respect than Indian law appears to do.

7–66 In Bangladeshi law, it is not quite clear what the precise position is on this point. The leading case of *Hosne Ara Begum v. Rezaul Karim,* 43 D.L.R. (1991) 543, an extremely instructive rich person's case,[69] would appear to suggest, at p. 545, that a Muslim wife has a right to withdraw herself from the husband's company at any time if the dower has not been paid. In this case, the lower court came in for severe criticism for having been "guided by the archaic concept of absolute dominion of the husband over the wife and children" (page 545), as in Roman law, while:

> "under the Muslim law several rights have been recognised to the wife and she can refuse to subject to the conjugal domain of the husband if the husband treats her with cruelty when it is of such a character as to render it unsafe for the wife to return to her husband and her prompt dower is not paid on demand" (*id.*).

In this case, there was evidence that the lady had received gold ornaments worth many thousands of Takas, which the husband unsuccessfully tried to declare as equivalent to dower. The non-payment of prompt dower appears to be more or less customary in Bangladesh. Monsoor (1994, p. 5) reports on a recent study in the metropolitan district of Dhaka which showed that 88 per cent of Muslim wives did not actually receive any dower at all and rightly wonders what the situation would be like in rural districts. Monsoor (1994, pp. 286–289) also shows in detail how the customary concept of *usool,* counting all kinds of wedding gifts as elements of dower, does not actually allow women to raise the argument that their dower has not been paid. In contrast, Balchin (1994, p. 52) cites a 1990 case from Pakistan in which it was held that various amounts paid by the husband to the wife during the marriage should not be presumed to be in lieu of dower.

7–67 Relating to remission of the dower by the wife, there is some older case law which confirms not only the position of the wife as absolute owner of the dower but also that all gifts are subject to the general rules relating to threats or coercion (*ikrah*). Mannan (1990, p. 402) confirms for Pakistan that remission must have been made with free consent. If coercion is proved, the remission will be treated as involuntary and will be set aside by the court. In *Shah Bano Begum v. Iftikhar Muhammad Khan,* P.L.D. 1956 (W.P.) Karachi 363, the wife had remitted the dower so as to prevent the husband from taking a lover. It was held by the court that in the circumstances of the case the remission or waiver was void and was therefore of no effect.[70]

---

[69] This is obvious from the large sums of dower agreed upon and the amounts of jewellery involved, as well as the wife's argument that compelling her to do housework was evidence of cruelty.

[70] See also Balchin (1994), pp. 55–56. A good discussion of the case law is found in Mannan (1990), p. 402. There appears to have been no recent development on this point. See also Hidayatullah and Hidayatullah (1977) to the same effect. Diwan and Diwan (1991), pp. 69–70 confirm the absence of new Indian case law.

7–68 The widow's dower-debt has been discussed in great detail and has been rightly distinguished from the kind of 'limited estate' that Anglo-Indian law was so fond of. Nevertheless, it appears that the Muslim law on this subject has been influenced by the South Asian legal environment, especially the parallel development of protective legal provisions for Hindu widows. The general position in Muslim law is that an unpaid dower represents an unsecured debt and a widow may sue to enforce payment (Hinchcliffe (1973), p. 5). In all South Asian jurisdictions covered here, the period of limitation for the recovery of dower-debt is three years.[71] Where, however, a widow enjoys possession of property in lieu of dower, the limitation of three years from the date of the death of the husband does not operate.[72] On the death of the widow, either her heirs or her legal representatives are entitled to sue for the debt.[73]

7–69 Hinchcliffe's study highlighted the creation of an additional right for a widow under Anglo-Muhammadan law.[74] The widow herself has a right to retain possession of the deceased husband's property until the dower debt is paid to her. She may hold the property of her husband, of which she has lawfully and without force or fraud obtained possession, until her debt is satisfied. This right, which must be distinguished from the right to the dower itself,[75] was discussed in the leading case of *Maina Bibi v. Chaudhri Vakil Ahmad*.[76] In this case, a Muslim husband, Muin-ud-din, had died in 1870 survived by a widow, Maina Bibi. The widow remained in possession of certain immovable property. In 1902, the other heirs sued the widow, claiming immediate possession of their share of the estate. The widow defended the application on two grounds. First, she said that the property had been gifted to her. Secondly, and in the alternative, she argued that she was entitled to remain in possession of the property until the dower had been paid. The judge made a decree for possession on condition that the heirs paid to the widow Rs. 25387/- within six months. The decree provided that in default of payment the suit should be dismissed. The heirs did not pay the money and the widow remained in possession.

7–70 In 1907, well before the case had been finally decided, the widow executed gifts of the property in favour of a third party and gave possession of the property to this third party. In 1915, the heirs filed a further suit against the widow and the alienees. The Judicial Committee of the Privy Council, before which the case eventually arrived, advised that although the widow had a right to remain in possession of her former husband's property until the dower debt had been paid, she had no *absolute right* in the property. Thus the alienation in this case was treated as *ultra vires*. Further, the failure of the heirs to comply with the original order did not convert her into the absolute owner of the immovable property of her deceased husband.

---

[71] For details see Mannan (1990), p. 403; Hidayatullah and Hidayatullah (1977), p. 313.

[72] This was held, it is submitted correctly, in *Syed Yousuf Akbar Hussaini v. Syed Murtuza Akbar Hussaini* A.I.R. (1983) A.P. 225.

[73] See *Janudul Haque v. Zubair Haider* A.I.R. (1981) Patna 345.

[74] Hinchcliffe [1973] 4 No. 3 *Islam and the Modern Age* 6. This must probably be seen in the context of comparative jurisprudence, since Hindu widows in India have enjoyed a similar right, which has been enlarged over time. The relevant statutory basis for this right today is s.14 of the Hindu Succession Act 1956, which has generated a considerable case law and strengthens the position of the widow *vis-à-vis* the joint family.

[75] Hence very correctly Hinchcliffe's reservations, at p. 6, about the use of the term 'widow's lien', which would indicate that this right is in the nature of a limited estate.

[76] [1924/1925] 52 L.R. I.A. 145. Hinchcliffe (1973), p. 6 refers to the Privy Council case of *Mussumat Bebee Bachun v. Sheikh Hamid Hossein* [1871] 14 M.I.A. 377 as the leading authority. Bharatiya (1996), pp. 88–89, discusses another leading case, *Hamira Bibi v. Zubaida Bibi* [1916] 43 I.A. 294.

7–71   The Judicial Committee here followed the decision of Sir Montagu Smith in *Mussumat Bebee Bachun v. Sheikh Hamid Hossein* [1871] 14 M.I.A. 377. The judge in that case had defined the right to retain possession in the following manner:

> "It is not necessary to say, whether this right of the widow in possession is a lien in the strict sense of the term . . . Whatever the right may be called, it appears to be founded on the power of the widow, as a creditor for her dower, to hold the property of her husband, of which she has lawfully, and without force or fraud, obtained possession, until her debt is satisfied, with the liability to account to those entitled to the property, subject to the claim for the profits received."[77]

Although a widow's right is only a personal right, and she is therefore not able to convey a good title to third parties, the right is probably heritable and a wife's heirs can themselves remain in possession.[78] There is a Mysore case which has held that the right to retain possession was not only heritable but also transferable, provided it was done by a deed of conveyance, and the transferee is put in possession.[79] Bharatiya (1996, pp. 90–91) discusses the older judicial decisions and also points to the most recent reported case on the matter, *Ghouse Yar Khan v. Fatima Begum*, A.I.R. 1988 A.P. 354. It was held in that case, dissenting from the position of the Patna High Court in *Zobair Ahmad v. Jainandan Prasad Singh*, A.I.R. 1960 Patna 147, that the widow's right to retain possession of property in lieu of dower debt was heritable and alienable. This decision also relies on an important earlier judgment of a Full Bench of the Madras High Court. It appears that the trend of the Indian case law on this matter is in favour of an enlarged right for the widow, which is well in line with the general development of Indian law.

7–72   The right to remain in possession is conditional on being in possession of property at the moment of the husband's death.[80] In all other respects, the widow is in the same situation as other creditors of the estate.[81] Indeed, if there are any profits arising from the property in her possession, she has to account for the profits to the other heirs.[82] The Indian Supreme Court has held that a widow is not entitled to priority as against her husband's other unsecured creditors.[83]

7–73   Scholarly opinion on this position in Indian law has been favourable. Diwan and Diwan (1991, p. 71) comment that "the widow's interest should be the paramount consideration" before a court. Making protective provisions for widows fits in well with general legal policy in South Asian jurisdictions, where of course a social welfare system financed by the state does not exist. The burden of providing for widows falls on families, not on the state.

7–74   For Pakistan, an extended discussion and the best summary of the law is found in Mannan (1990, pp. 407–417). The learned author emphasises that in Islamic law the widow has no special claim to retain her husband's property in lieu of dower and stands on the same footing with other creditors (Mannan (1990, p. 407). In *Sardar Begum v. Iqbal Ahmad*, 1986 C.L.C. 1151, the widow's right was

---

[77] At p. 384. See also Hinchcliffe (1973), p. 6. In *Zobair Ahmad v. Jainandan Prasad Singh*, A.I.R. (1960) Patna 147, the widow's right was treated, at p. 148, as "an interest restricted in its enjoyment to her personally within the meaning of s.6(d) of the Transfer of Property Act, and . . . not capable of alienation".

[78] *Kapore Chand v. Kidar Nissa Begum*, A.I.R. (1953) S.C. 413.

[79] *Hussain v. Rahim Khan*, A.I.R. (1954) Mys. 24.

[80] Again, this is exactly parallel to the corresponding rule in Hindu law.

[81] A more recent case is *Ghouse Yar Khan v. Fatima Begum*, A.I.R. (1988) A.P. 354, just mentioned above.

[82] A useful article on this area of the law is Ganai [1985] 27 No. 3 J.I.L.I. 387–422. See also the case of *Syed Yusuf Akbar Hussaini v. Syed Murturza Akbar Hussaini* (1983) 1 An. W.R. 273.

[83] *Kapore Chand v. Kader Unnissa Begum* (1950) S.C.R. 747.

fully recognised, but it was also held that on payment of her dower debt, her right was extinguished. Several recent cases have acknowledged that husbands may give their wives property in lieu of dower.[84] The discussion by Professor Mannan indicates that the old uncertainties about many questions of detail still persist in Pakistani law and have not been vigorously tested in recent litigation. For Pakistan, it is in line with developments in other areas of the law that this particular question about the extent of property rights of women is left open and remains largely within the unofficial sphere.

Maintenance in South Asian Muslim law

7-75   Older South Asian legal textbooks spend little time on the topic of maintenance. For example, the various editions of Mulla's, *Principles of Mahomedan law* and Fyzee (1974, pp. 211–216) do not give it much importance.[85] This particular topic has become 'alive', as it were, only quite recently. As we shall see, the law is today very different in Pakistan, on the one hand, and India and Bangladesh, on the other. This is so largely because of the impact of legislative provisions in criminal law which protect the rights of women to maintenance during the marriage, and now increasingly after divorce, too. This legal development must be understood in the context of South Asian conditions today, where many millions of people live in abject poverty and where desertion of wives, in any community, has become a growing social problem against which religious injunctions offer little help. In such a situation, neither may a Muslim wife be properly divorced, nor will she be able to rely on supposedly positive effects of her marriage, such as entitlement to *mahr* or maintenance during the marriage, not to speak of post-divorce maintenance.

7-76   Indian law, in particular, has experienced rapid growth in this field in the past decade and has produced pioneering judgments and statutory provisions which deserve wide notice in the Muslim world and beyond. Very recently, Bangladeshi law, too, prima facie based on principles of Muslim jurisprudence, has given some fresh interpretations to this central area of family law, which concerns protective mechanisms for women and children who, without any fault of their own, have been abandoned by men. The pressing socio-economic problems of South Asia, it appears, have given rise to a fresh look at the Qur'anic foundations of Muslim maintenance law, with very positive results for women. It can certainly be argued that this is another form of islamisation, counterbalancing the otherwise prominent fundamentalist movement.

7-77   The basic principle that during a valid marriage a wife remains entitled to maintenance has also been operative in South Asian Muslim law. This extends to past maintenance where there are arrears.[86] Mahmood (1982a, p. 78) emphasises that "under no circumstances is a wife legally liable to maintain her husband howsoever indigent".[87] Fyzee (1974, p. 212) suggests that the husband's duty to

---

[84] *Fazal-ur-Rehman v. Sosan Jan*, 1989 S.C.M.R. 651; *Roshan Ara v. Badri Kamala*, 1989 S.C.M.R. 1981.
[85] Hidayatullah and Hidayatullah (1977), pp. 300–304, discuss this topic in a few paragraphs. Verma (1988), pp. 328–331, provides a succinct summary of the traditional law. See also Malik, *Muslim law of marriage, divorce and maintenance* (1988), pp. 20–21. For Pakistan see, also with reference to some recent cases, Mannan (1990), pp. 386–392.
[86] On a case involving Shafi'i law, see *M. Abdul Karim v. P. K. Nabeesa*, A.I.R. 1988 Ker. 288, where it was held that the wife is entitled to past maintenance even in the absence of any agreement to that effect.
[87] Several writers note that this is different from Hindu law and some Western laws. However, Welchman (1988), p. 876 shows that South Yemen's code of family law makes the expenses of shared marital life the responsibility of both spouses. She sees this, at p. 877, as "a huge departure from classical Islamic law, and one that modern-day jurists would find very hard to justify in Islamic terms".

maintain commences only when the wife attains puberty and not before, a reference to the existence of child marriages in South Asia also among Muslims. Diwan and Diwan (1991, p. 135) state that in India, in all the schools of Muslim law, a wife who has not attained puberty is not entitled to maintenance. Verma (1988, p. 328) explicitly links the question of age with fitness for conjugal intercourse.

7–78   When the husband has no means at all, this is a misfortune which has to be shared by the wife. This point was made in an Indian Hindu law case; in the light of social circumstances, this principle could also be applied to Muslim cases.[88] In a recent case involving a Muslim Keralite who had earlier worked in the Gulf, it was held that under Muslim law a man's obligation to maintain his wife and children cannot be denied on the ground of his pecuniary incapacity or indigence so long as he has the ability to earn.[89] The general rule being that "a husband is bound to maintain his wife and children even if he is necessitous" (page 563), this case illustrates the stresses of the migratory labour movement and the resulting emphasis on cash economy.

7–79   The wife may lose her otherwise absolute right to maintenance in certain situations. South Asian writers seem less fixed on the terminology of disobedience and emphasise the combination of sexual contact and submission to the husband's authority, with a stress on reasonableness. Diwan and Diwan (1991, p. 135) write that "the husband's obligation to maintain his wife exists only so long as the wife remains faithful to him and obeys all his reasonable orders".[90] We have already seen that, in turn, non-payment of prompt dower is a reasonable ground for a wife to refuse cohabitation to the husband.

7–80   An instructive Pakistani case on the subject of maintenance is *Resham Bibi v. Muhammad Shafi*, P.L.D. 1967 A.J.K. 32. Following a childless first marriage, which ended in divorce, Muhammad Shafi had married Resham Bibi, but no children were born to her either. The husband then married another woman, who also remained childless. Resham Bibi at first stayed with her husband and the new wife, but after some time she left him and asked for dissolution of the marriage and maintenance. The lower courts had held that she was to blame for her separation from the husband, and was not entitled to maintenance. On appeal, it was held, at page 37, dismissing the wife's claim for divorce on the ground of failure to maintain her:

> "Under Mohammedan Law there is no obligatory duty cast upon the husband to maintain the wife when she refuses to live with him. The right of the wife to obtain maintenance from the husband is subject to her living with him and if she refuses to live with him without reasonable cause, then she is not entitled to maintenance and the failure of the husband to provide her with maintenance in these circumstances would not entitle the wife to dissolution of the marriage tie."

On the quantum of maintenance, the old differences of opinion persist as to whether the husband's means alone are to be taken into account. While the *Hedaya* provided that the quantum of maintenance should be determined by taking into account the position of both spouses, thus reflecting the Hanafi position, under Shafi'i law the husband's means are taken to be the main criterion. In Shi'a law, the emphasis is on the need of the wife and her requirements in accordance with her

---

[88] See *Sivankutty v. S. Komalakumari*, A.I.R. (1989) Ker. 124.
[89] *Kadeeja v. Aboobacker*, (1995)(1) K.L.T. 563. This is very much in line with other cases in Indian law on the same subject.
[90] For discussion of this concept see *Ahmed Ali v. Sabha Khatun Bibi*, P.L.D. 1952 Dacca 385.

status. In changed social conditions, the criteria have remained flexible and therefore constantly contested in society; the Hanafi principle appears still useful.

7–81   After the dissolution of the marriage by death, the wife's right to maintenance ceases. If the marriage is dissolved by divorce, depending on circumstances, the widely understood general rule is that the wife is entitled to maintenance during the *iddat*,[91] unless she is pregnant, in which case the husband's liability continues. In Pakistan, it has been held recently that the expenses of the delivery of a child fall within the definition of "other necessary expenses for mental and physical well-being" of the wife and must be borne by the husband.[92] In normal circumstances, the *iddat* period starts from the date of pronouncement of *talaq*, and the wife's right to maintenance for three months is not lost or diminished if she files a suit at some time during the *iddat* period.[93] However, if the wife does not have knowledge of the *talaq*, her entitlement starts when she comes to know of the divorce (Verma (1988), p. 330). As we shall see, post-divorce maintenance has become a bone of contention in modern South Asian Muslim laws.

7–82   Apart from the basic principles of Muslim law, South Asian laws on maintenance are governed by statutes of a general nature, with a criminal law emphasis. The first relevant enactment to consider here is section 488 of the Code of Criminal Procedure 1898. This enables a wife of any religion to apply for maintenance if she can prove that her husband, having sufficient means, neglects or refuses to maintain her. Concerning Muslim wives, it has been held that their rights under such provisions are independent and irrespective of their rights under Muslim law.[94] Section 488 is no longer in operation in India,[95] and in most of Pakistan.[96] The original section read as follows:

"488.   Order for maintenance of wives and children. –

(1)   If any person having sufficient means neglects or refuses to maintain his wife or his legitimate or illegitimate child unable to maintain itself, a Magistrate of the first class may, upon proof of such neglect or refusal, order such person to make a monthly allowance for the maintenance of his wife or such child, at such monthly rate, not exceeding five hundred rupees in the whole,[97] as such Magistrate thinks fit, and to pay the same to such person as the Magistrate from time to time directs.

(2)   Such allowance shall be payable from the date of the order, or if so ordered from the date of the application for maintenance."

The original purpose of this section was to provide a remedy to all Indian wives neglected by their husbands. The various provisos of this section enabled a wife, including a wife whose husband had taken another wife or wives, to refuse cohabitation to the husband and yet to claim maintenance under this section. Not surprisingly, this provision was challenged by Muslim husbands as conflicting with

---

[91] *Mohd. Shamsuddin v. Noor Johan Begum*, AIR (1955) Hyd. 144; *Chandbi Badesha Mujawar v. Badesha Balwad Mujawar* [1960] 62 Bom. L.R. 866.

[92] Balchin (1994), p. 88, and *Maqsood Ahmad Sohail v. Abida Hanif*, 1992 M.L.D. 219, at 220. This is in line with traditional Muslim law, where the expenses of childbirth could always be claimed back from the husband. In the Jordanian Law of Family Rights of 1951, the claim for medical expenses was an innovation, since carried into Egyptian law.

[93] *Maria Munnisa Begum v. Noore Mohammad Saheb*, A.I.R. 1965 A.P. 231.

[94] *K. Raza Khan v. Mumtaz Khatoon* [1976] 1 An.W.R. 1.

[95] The relevant provisions were replaced by ss.125–127 of the Criminal Procedure Code 1973 (see below).

[96] It was repealed by the Criminal Law (Amendment) Ordinance (No. XXVII of 1981), but is still in operation in Azad Jammu and Kashmir.

[97] In Pakistan, this was reduced to Rs. 400/- by Act 2 of 1958.

the *shariat*, but almost all of these petitions were turned down.[98] It soon became obvious that the simplest remedy for a Muslim husband faced with such claims to maintenance from a 'disobedient' wife was to divorce her, and thus to free himself from the burden of maintenance.[99] The section thus lost, for Muslim wives at any rate, much of its protective force through the easy device of the instant *talaq*. Early judicial criticism of the fact that a Muslim husband could defeat a wife's claim for maintenance under section 488 of the Criminal Procedure Code 1898 by exercising his unfettered right to *talaq* is found in the interesting case of *Ahmad Kasim Molla v. Khatun Bibi*, I.L.R. [1932] 59 Cal. 833, at 848, where it was held by Costello J.:

> "I am bound to say that, in my opinion, it does seem harsh that, at any time, a Mahomedan husband can, of his own power, put an end to any proceedings his wife may take under section 488 of the Code of Criminal Procedure, and it may be that some day this matter will have to be seriously considered by the members of the Mahomedan community and the legislature with a view to determining whether such arbitrary power in the hands of the husband is not now an anachronism inconsistent with present day ideas and incompatible with modern conditions."

Starting in the 1930s, various enactments sought to strengthen the position of wives in terms of maintenance during the marriage. Section 2(ii) of the DMMA of 1939, which applies in India, Pakistan and Bangladesh, gives a Muslim woman the right to claim divorce if her husband fails to maintain her for a period of two years. In Pakistan and since 1971 in Bangladesh, section 9 of the MFLO 1961 has become the main statutory provision placing an obligation on the Muslim husband to maintain his wife or wives during marriage. The Ordinance entitles the wife to seek a certificate specifying the due amount. In both Pakistan and Bangladesh, such amounts are recoverable as arrears of land revenue. There are significant procedural differences between Pakistani and Bangladeshi law in this respect today.

7–83   Under sections 5 and 20 of the West Pakistan Family Courts Act 1964 in Pakistan, the Family Court now has exclusive jurisdiction to entertain, hear or adjudicate upon matters relating to maintenance.[1] Pakistani cases appear to have adopted the flexible attitude of the non-Hanafi schools. For instance, in *Rashid Ahmad Khan v. Nasim Ara*, P.L.D. 1968 Lah. 93, it was decided that maintenance which is awarded to the wife after the reconciliation and arbitral procedures implicit in section 9(3) of the MFLO 1961 can include payment for past maintenance as well as future obligations. In *Hajiran Bibi v. Abdul Khaliq*, P.L.D. 1981 Lah. 761, it was held that this court could award past maintenance. Although this case produced a result contrary to the generally held view of the law under section 488, its effect was certainly welcome. It provides consistency between the more arbitral, localised procedures under the MFLO 1961 and the formal judicial proceedings in the Family Court.

7–84   Early fieldwork in Pakistan (Pearl (1971b), pp. 566–567) showed that these provisions were the only effective protective mechanism at the time. Later research (see Mehdi (1994), pp. 185–186) has pinpointed a number of practical difficulties. Monsoor (1994, pp. 296–311) reports from Bangladesh that Muslim wives remain in essence inadequately protected because the husband can of course, at any time, just divorce the wife, in which case he would probably assume that his liability to

---

[98] For details see a good discussion in Mahmood (1986), pp. 82–83.
[99] For some case references see *ibid.*, p. 83.
[1] See *Adnan Afzal v. Sher Afzal*, P.L.D. 1969 S.C. 187.

maintain her ceases after the expiry of the *iddat*.[2] Recent, unpublished fieldwork from Pakistan shows a pattern of abuse of the *iddat* maintenance entitlement in that women are sent back to their parental home, to be maintained there, while the husband may or may not inform the wife of the fact that he has divorced her. Few such cases end up in courts and almost all writers indicate the practical obstacles faced by Muslim women seeking to enforce their legal rights to maintenance.

7–85   In view of such difficulties, and the resulting socio-economic problems, both India and now Bangladesh have activated further legal mechanisms to protect the maintenance rights of wives generally, and of Muslim wives in particular. This has raised very interesting jurisprudential questions in Indian law about the role and position of the Muslim dower and its relationship with other financial consequences of a marriage. In short, the question has been whether the *mahr* is linked to divorce, and thus whether it is a form of maintenance payment, or whether it is a more general entitlement. These particular questions have not been fully settled, but there have been many attempts to answer them.

7–86   Given that a Muslim husband could easily defeat a wife's claim for maintenance under section 488 of the 1898 Code by simply divorcing her,[3] Indian law extended the statutory definition of wife for the purposes of maintenance law in 1973 to include a divorced wife. This, of course, at once raised a fresh conflict with traditional Muslim law principles. Would a Muslim husband in India now have to pay maintenance to his divorced wife till she died or remarried? The new statute law tried to find a compromise between social welfare concerns and respect for the Muslim personal law. Twenty years later, it is obvious that the compromise that was found favoured the social welfare of women but led, in turn, to a re-assessment of the basic principles of Muslim law in this respect. It has been established in Indian law that there is actually no real conflict between the Qur'anic foundations on the husband's obligations towards a divorced wife and the modern welfare-based statutes which place an obligation on divorcing husbands to look after the future welfare of their ex-wives. The recent decision of the Dacca High Court in *Md. Hefzur Rahman v. Shamsun Nahar Begum* (1995) 15 B.L.D. 34, confirms this social reasoning, which is, after all, as in India, a self-protection mechanism for a welfare state which does not have the money to support the indigent victims of broken marriages. However, by placing an Islamic interpretation on this modern social welfare rationale, the Bangladeshi legal decision vindicates the basic reasoning of the Indian courts to the effect that a Muslim husband has, ever since the Qur'anic foundations were created, been under an obligation towards the woman he divorces. We saw already, in paragraph 7–23, above, that this basic message has not been totally lost in the Muslim heartland either, but has been overlaid with much juristic reasoning to the effect that the liability of Muslim husbands ceases at the end of the *iddat* period. As we shall see in more detail below, modern Indian and Bangladeshi Muslim law today have made creative use of the Qur'anic foundations about a husband's obligations to his former wife to establish a tightly framed and time-bound system for identifying and implementing the divorcing husband's liabilities.

7–87   The story of modern South Asian Muslim law on maintenance rights for divorced wives began to unfold when section 488 of the Code of Criminal Procedure 1898 was replaced in India by section 125 of the new Code of Criminal Procedure 1973. The relevant parts of this section read as follows:

---

[2] More recent case law, as we shall see further below, places a continuing obligation on the Bangladeshi ex-husband.
[3] For a good commentary see, *e.g.* Diwan and Diwan (1991), p. 137.

"125. Order for maintenance of wives, children and parents. –
    (1) If any person having sufficient means neglects or refuses to
    maintain –
        (a) his wife, unable to maintain herself, or
        (b) his legitimate or illegitimate minor child, whether married or
        not, unable to maintain itself, or
        (c) his legitimate or illegitimate child (not being a married
        daughter) who has attained majority, where such child is, by
        reason of any physical or mental abnormality or injury unable
        to maintain itself, or
        (d) his father or mother, unable to maintain himself or herself,
a Magistrate of the first class may, upon proof of such neglect or refusal,
order such person to make a monthly allowance for the maintenance of
his wife or such child, father or mother, at such monthly rate not
exceeding five hundred rupees in the whole, as such Magistrate thinks fit,
and to pay the same to such person as the Magistrate may from time to
time direct.
    Provided that the Magistrate may order the father of a minor female
child referred to in clause (b) to make allowance, until she attains her
majority, if the Magistrate is satisfied that the husband of such minor
female child, if married, is not possessed of sufficient means.
    Explanations. – For the purposes of this chapter, –
    . . .

        (b) "wife" includes a woman who has been divorced by, or has
        obtained a divorce from, her husband and has not remarried."

By including a divorced wife in the definition of 'wife', this section opens the way
for maintenance payments to be awarded to a divorced woman until her death or
remarriage.[4] As we have seen, according to the classical juristic interpretations of
Muslim law, maintenance to a divorced wife is assumed to cease after the *iddat*
period. The Muslim husband is unquestionably responsible for his wife's
maintenance during the *iddat* period. As a result of political pressure from Muslims
(see, *e.g.* Parashar (1992), pp. 9–10), an additional provision, section 127(3)(b), was
therefore inserted into the Code, taking account of customary Muslim institutions
like *mahr* and *iddat* money. This section states:

"127. Alteration in allowances.–
    (1) On proof of a change in the circumstances of any person, receiving,
    under section 125 a monthly allowance, or ordered under the same
    section to pay a monthly allowance to his wife, child, father or
    mother, as the case may be, the Magistrate may make such alteration
    in the allowance as he thinks fit: Provided that if he increases the
    allowance, the monthly rate of five hundred rupees in the whole
    shall not be exceeded.
        . . .

    (3) Where any order has been made under section 125 in favour of a
    woman who has been divorced by, or has obtained a divorce from,
    her husband, the Magistrate shall, if he is satisfied that

---

[4] Parashar, *Women and family law reform in India* (1992), p.164, confirms that it had been brought to the
notice of the government that in some cases, when Muslim women asked for maintenance, men had
avoided the application of s.488 of the 1898 Code by divorcing their wives extra-judicially.

    (a) the woman has, after the date of such divorce, remarried, cancel such order as from the date of her remarriage;

    (b) the woman has been divorced by her husband and that she has received, whether before or after the date of the said order, the whole of the sum which, under any customary or personal law applicable to the parties, was payable on such divorce, cancel such order. –

    . . .

    (c) the woman has obtained a divorce from her husband and that she had voluntarily surrendered her rights to maintenance after her divorce, cancel the order from the date thereof."

The precise meaning of section 127(3)(b) read with section 125 was the subject of much litigation in Indian law between the mid-1970s and until 1985. It raised afresh the key question whether dower was an amount payable by the Muslim husband to the wife on divorce.[5]

7-88 In the Bombay High Court, it was originally held that the payment of the dower on divorce will satisfy section 127(3)(b), and that therefore a magistrate would have no jurisdiction to make an order under section 125.[6] However, it was soon held in Kerala that the dower payment is outside the purview of section 127(3)(b). The obvious basis for this reasoning was that such dower payments were found insufficient to take care of the needs of divorced women. In *Muhammed v. Sainabi*, 1976 K.L.T. 711, Khalid J. first restated the traditional understanding of Muslim law and then turned to the impact of the 1973 Code when he said, at page 712:

> "Under the Muslim Personal Law, as applied by Courts in India, a divorced wife is entitled to claim maintenance after divorce only for the period of iddath. Even here, there is difference between Shaffi and Hanafi Law. S. 125 Cr.P.C. imports a legal fiction, which is that a divorced wife continues to be a wife notwithstanding the divorce, in her claim for maintenance until she remarries. The husband, under the new clause, can successfully resist the claim of the wife for maintenance only if he establishes a custom, that certain customary dues, if paid, at the time of the divorce, would disentitle the wife from claiming maintenance. What exactly is meant by customary dues I do not propose to examine here."

However, concerning the role of *mahr* in this context, the learned judge said, at page 713:

> "Mahar is an amount payable by the husband to the wife either prompt or deferred. Payment of Mahar will not effect a discharge of a claim for maintenance, because the claim for mahar is a valuable right available to the wife and this claim is a charge over the properties of the husband. Therefore, mention of payment of mahar . . . will not also operate as payment of customary dues in discharge of the claim for maintenance."

In the earlier case of *Kunhi Moyin v. Pathumma*, 1976 K.L.T. 87, the constitutional validity of section 125 of the 1973 Code had been challenged. Khalid J. characterised the new legislation as "a milestone in the social legislation conferring

---

[5] A useful discussion on this is found in Bharatiya (1996), pp. 92–96.
[6] *Rukhsana Parvin v. Shaikh Mohomed Hussein Mohomed Akbar* (1977) 79 Bom. L.R. 123.

benefits to a particular group of women who is in need of help . . . the object being to prevent vagrancy and to protect such women from poverty and starvation" (page 91). As to the charge that the new law violated Muslim law and was "an invasion of the personal law of Muslims" (*id.*) because it effectively changed, with retrospective effect, the conditions under which Muslim spouses had entered their marriages, the judge responded with a discussion of the social conditions of divorced women in India and the abuse of liberal divorce laws. Finally, it was held, at page 96, concerning the import of section 127(3)(b):

> "We would like to make it clear that section 127(3)(b) refers not to maintenance during the period of iddat or payment of dower . . . It is therefore not a sum of money which under the personal law is payable on divorce."

These decisions were much debated at the time and it was widely felt that some form of judicial legislation and social engineering was being attempted (see, *e.g.* Derrett (1977)). A number of further High Court cases followed.[7] Among them, one case deserves special mention because here the wife refused to accept the meagre sum offered by the husband and had thus, according to section 127(3)(b) of the 1973 Code, not 'received' the customary dues.[8] The husband had paid the wife Rs. 27.50 as prompt *mahr* at the time of the marriage, had offered to pay her Rs. 100/- as deferred dower and had actually deposited that money in court, claiming that he was now no longer liable to maintenance payments under the 1973 Code. The judge held that in view of the social welfare objectives of the new law, any liberal interpretation was uncalled for.

7–89   Three Supreme Court cases then took up the debate, which went in favour of the socially activist Kerala decisions.[9] In *Bai Tahira*, the wife had earlier received a divorce settlement through a consent decree. A flat had been transferred into her name, as well as shares of a housing society and there was reference to a *mahr* of Rs. 5000/- and Rs. 180/- as *iddat* money. Following the change in the law, and suffering from the effects of inflation, the woman then made an application under section 125 of the 1973 Code for a decree of maintenance in favour of herself and her son. Krishna Iyer J. said, at pages 365–366:

> "Payment of mehar money, as a customary discharge, is within the cognisance of that provision. But what was the amount of mehar? Rs. 5000/-, interest from which could not keep the woman's body and soul together for a day, . . . unless she was ready to sell her body and give up her soul! . . . Where the husband, by customary payment at the time of divorce, has adequately provided for the divorcee, a subsequent series of recurrent doles is contra-indicated and the husband liberated. This is the teleological interpretation, the sociological decoding of the text of s.127. The key-note thought is adequacy of payment which will take reasonable care of her maintenance. The payment of illusory amounts by way of customary or personal law requirement will be considered in the reduction of maintenance rate but cannot annihilate that rate unless it is a reasonable substitute. The legal sanctity of the payment is certified by the fulfilment of the social obligation, not by a ritual exercise rooted in custom. . . . The proposition, therefore, is that no husband can claim under s.127(3)

---

[7] *e.g. Hajuben Suleman v. Ibrahim Gandabhai*, 18 [1977] Guj. L.R. 133; *Khurshid Khan Amin Khan v. Husnabanu*, 1976 (78) Bom. L.R. 240.

[8] *Hajuben Suleman v. Ibrahim Gandabhai*, 18 [1977] Guj. L.R. 133.

[9] *Bai Tahira v. Ali Hussain*, A.I.R. 1979 S.C. 362, *Fuzlunbi v. K. Khader Vali*, A.I.R. 1980 S.C. 1730 and finally *Mohd. Ahmed Khan v. Shah Bano Begum*, A.I.R. 1985 S.C. 945, the famous *Shah Bano* case, which gave rise to legislation, as discussed further below.

absolution from his obligation under s.125 towards a divorced wife except on proof of payment of a sum stipulated by customary or personal law whose quantum is more or less sufficient to do duty for maintenance allowance."

7–90   Kusum (1980, p. 412) called this an "enlightened judicial approach" and opposed the action of an Indian MP to bring a Private Member's Bill, which would have had the effect of restricting the maintenance rights of divorced Muslim wives.[10] Krishna Iyer J., giving the judgment of the court in another case, *Fuzlunbi v. K. Khader Vali*, A.I.R. 1980 S.C. 1730, where the husband had paid his wife Rs. 500/- by way of dower and now claimed exemption from the effect of section 125 of the 1973 Code, said at page 1731:

> "No one in his senses can contend that the mahar of Rs. 500/- will yield income sufficient to maintain a woman even if she were to live on city pavements! What is the intendment of s.127(3)(b)? What is the scheme of relief for driftwood and destitute wives and divorcees discarded by heartless husbands? . . .
> What, in short is the text and texture of the provision, if read in the light of the mischief to be avoided, the justice to be advanced?"[11]

The learned judge answered his questions, as he had done a year before in *Bai Tahira*, by stating categorically that the payment of illusory amounts by way of customary or personal law requirements would be considered in the reduction of maintenance awarded, but that it could not 'annihilate' the liability unless it was a reasonable provision for the former wife.

7–91   Another case in the Supreme Court of India, *Zohara Khatoon v. Mhd. Ibrahim*, A.I.R. 1981 S.C. 1243, permitted a Muslim wife who had earlier obtained a divorce under the Dissolution of Muslim Marriages Act 1939 to secure maintenance under section 125 of the 1973 Code. An important point of contention in this case was whether a wife who had herself divorced the husband, rather than being divorced by him, would still be a 'wife' for the purposes of the 1973 Code and thus entitled to maintenance. The court referred to section 127(3)(c), as cited at page 207, above. Unfortunately, various obiter remarks in this judgment appeared to contradict the views of Krishna Iyer J. in the earlier cases. It was therefore assumed that there was still some doubt as to the exact meaning and extent of section 127(3)(b).

7–92   It was hoped that this chapter of uncertainty would be brought to an end by the Supreme Court decision in the *Shah Bano* case of 1985, about which some comment is required, particularly since this case caused immense political tensions and its aftermath has been wrongly interpreted by many writers.

7–93   The basic facts of the Shah Bano case, reported as *Mohd. Ahmed Khan v. Shah Bano Begum*, A.I.R. 1985 S.C. 945, were that the husband, a senior advocate by profession, was married to the respondent wife in 1932. Three sons and two daughters were born to the marriage, which was never a happy one. The husband took a second wife and, in 1975, drove Shah Bano, the first wife and now an old

---

[10] That Bill was never passed. The M.P. in question wrote a book on the subject, see Banatwalla, *Religion and politics in India* (1992). For details see Kusum [1980] 22 No. 3 J.I.L.I. 412–413 and Jain (1988), pp. 291–292.

[11] See to the same effect *Thilothama v. Kunjappan*, (1983) K.L.T. 90, which concerns customary dues under a specific Hindu enactment. This confirms that the legal development discussed here was not simply directed against Muslim men, but was promoted to protect indigent women of all communities.

lady, out of the house. She filed a petition for maintenance in April 1978 under the provisions of the 1973 Code, claiming Rs. 500/- per month. It speaks volumes for the legal position even of privileged Muslim women that the magistrate awarded her Rs. 25/- per month. However, in November 1978 the husband divorced the respondent by irrevocable *talaq* and his defence to the lady's claim for maintenance was now that she had ceased to be his wife, that he had paid her Rs. 3000/- by way of *mahr*, and that he was under no further obligations to her. The High Court of Madhya Pradesh eventually awarded the ex-wife maintenance at the rate of Rs. 179.20 per month and the husband appealed against that. A Supreme Court bench of two judges took the view that *Bai Tahira* and *Fuzlunbi* were incorrectly decided and that the law was not clear. Therefore, they referred the matter to a bench of five judges, headed by Chandrachud C.J., which dismissed the husband's appeal and confirmed the decision of the High Court. The fact that these five judges were Hindus became a political issue, since the case involved an analysis of Muslim law.[12]

7–94   The learned Chief Justice first reiterated the well-established position that section 125, as an element of general law, overrides the personal law if there is any conflict between the two (page 949). While that was hardly new, on the extended definition of 'wife' under the 1973 Code there was also little to discuss, since the law on that point had already been clarified. Chandrachud C.J. then went on to examine the question whether there was in fact any conflict between the Muslim personal law and the general law. This is a new element in the case law, which led to intense confrontation thereafter, partly because here were five Hindu judges interpreting the principles of Muslim law, in a case that would hit the pockets of many Muslim men.

7–95   The learned judges went through the statements of several specialist authors and found that "these statements in the text books are inadequate to establish the proposition that the Muslim husband is not under an obligation to provide for the maintenance of his divorced wife, *who is unable to maintain herself*" (underlined in the original at page 950). Chandrachud C.J., speaking for the court, then stated, at pages 950–951:

> "Since the Muslim Personal Law, which limits the husband's liability to provide for the maintenance of the divorced wife to the period of iddat, does not contemplate or countenance the situation envisaged by section 125, it would be wrong to hold that the Muslim husband, according to his personal law, is not under an obligation to provide maintenance, beyond the period of iddat, to his divorced wife who is unable to maintain herself . . . The true position is that, if the divorced wife is able to maintain herself, the husband's liability to provide maintenance for her ceases with the expiration of the period of iddat. If she is unable to maintain herself, she is entitled to take recourse to section 125 of the Code. The outcome of this discussion is that there is no conflict between the provisions of section 125 and those of the Muslim Personal Law on the question of the Muslim husband's obligation to provide maintenance for a divorced wife who is unable to maintain herself."

These statements were immediately backed by reference to relevant Qur'anic verses (Sura 2, verses 241 and 242), to the effect that for divorced women, maintenance should be provided on a reasonable scale and that this was a duty on the righteous

---

[12] However, one of the two judges who referred the case to the larger bench was a Muslim.

Muslim.[13] Having gone through various English translations of these verses,[14] the Chief Justice concluded, at page 952:

> "These Aiyats leave no doubt that the Quran imposes an obligation on the Muslim husband to make provision for or to provide maintenance to the divorced wife. The contrary argument does less than justice to the teachings of the Quran."

7–96 The learned Chief Justice then turned to the issue of *mahr* and refused to accept the argument that *mahr* is the amount payable by the husband to the wife on divorce (page 952). Having discussed the issue, he held at pages 952–953:

> "If Mahr is an amount which the wife is entitled to receive from the husband in consideration of the marriage, that is the very opposite of the amount being payable in consideration of divorce. Divorce dissolves the marriage. Therefore, no amount which is payable in consideration of the marriage can possibly be described as an amount payable in consideration of divorce. The alternative premise that Mahr is an obligation imposed upon the husband as a mark of respect for the wife is wholly detrimental to the stance that it is an amount payable to the wife on divorce. A man may marry a woman for love, looks, learning or nothing at all. And, he may settle a sum upon her as a mark of respect for her. But he does not divorce her as a mark of respect. Therefore, a sum payable to the wife out of respect cannot be a sum payable 'on divorce'."

After a brief reference to two old Privy Council cases, the court finally turned to political issues, which appears to be the main reason why the *Shah Bano* case became so notorious, including unnecessary, unfortunate obiter dicta about the desirability of a uniform civil code, thus raising an implied threat to the future of Muslim law in India. These parts of the judgment do not otherwise concern matters of Muslim law.

7–97 The reactions to the *Shah Bano* decision have been mixed, to say the least.[15] It was argued in the second edition (Pearl (1987), p. 74) that there is little justification for describing the Muslim law obligation as was done in the *Shah Bano* case. It was an unorthodox approach, and the Qur'anic authorities cited by the judge were given by him a novel interpretation. At roughly the same time, Tahir Mahmood (1986, pp. 82–93) wrote an elaborate discussion of this subject, which he introduced by saying that a "*Shari'at* vs. Cr. P. C. war is being fought in the judicial corridors of this country" (page 82). Mahmood vigorously opposed the social welfare-oriented interpretations of the various judgments discussed above on the ground that Muslim law had, as usual in Indian law, been misunderstood. He made much of the conceptual difference between Hindu and Christian concepts of marriage on the one side and Muslim law on the other.[16] According to him, a

---

[13] At p. 951 of the judgment. It is illuminating to study the reactions of official bodies like the All India Muslim Personal Law Board, suggesting that this was a rule only for the more pious Muslims. For details see, *e.g.* Diwan and Diwan (1991), pp. 138–139; Latifi (1985); Mahmood (1990), pp. 305–306.

[14] Compare the discussion in Nasir (1990a), pp. 143–145; Nasir (1990b), pp. 96–98, on the concept of the wife's compensation for divorce (*mutat*). The Indian Supreme Court evidently did not have the benefit of access to current Middle Eastern writing and legislation as outlined by Nasir.

[15] For an extended discussion see Latifi (1985); Mahmood (1986), pp. 88–94; Gani (1988); Mahmood (1990).

[16] Unfortunately, in the process Mahmood (1986, p. 85) overstated the Hindu law principle that on marriage "every girl would be *finally and perpetually* transferred to her husband's family" to achieve the familiar contrast effect between Hindu and Muslim law. There is no such binding and universal principle in Hindu law, nor does this accord with general practice.

Muslim husband has no obligation towards his divorced wife once the *iddat* period is over. Mahmood (1986, pp. 86–87) wrote:

> "The fact is that in the Islamic matrimonial culture neither there is an interfamilial transplantation of the girl on her marriage, nor are her parents or guardians perpetually absolved, after that, of their liabilities towards her. In Islam, since marriage is always a dissoluble union, the parents' liability to maintain the unmarried daughter remains only *suspended* during her married life. On the dissolution of her marriage, whether by her husband's death or by divorce and, in the latter case, whether at her own instance or otherwise, the liability is *revived* and must continue to be discharged until she remarries.
>
> . . . As a natural corollary to its concept of marriage and policy on divorce, after the dissolution of a marriage Islam does not keep the parties tagged to each other for the rest of their lives. It encourages both of them [depending on their age] to get remarried – against the remarriage of a divorcee, either male or female, there being no taboo in Islamic law or culture. The law keeps both parties to a dissolved marriage wholly free to look after their new responsibilities."

These arguments must be interpreted in the context of concerns that the modern Indian judiciary had gone too far, as Mahmood (1986, p. 127) put it, in "gradually turning divorce into a sort of an insurance deal offering far more lucrative benefits than available in marriage". In the view of the author, this was so because the modern Indian laws of divorce, as judicially interpreted, absolved divorced wives from all kinds of traditional obligations "without depriving them of the benefits that were available to them in married life" (Mahmood (1986), p. 127). Thus, Mahmood argued that women were being treated too favourably by the law and that the basic principles of Muslim law were being violated in the process.

7–98 In contrast, the elaborate discussion of the *Shah Bano* case in the 1985 issue of the Annual Survey of Indian Law (Latifi (1985), pp. 385–400) supports not only the decision but also the argument that Indian judges may, in certain cases, have to interpret Muslim law to do justice to the parties before them. For:

> "To deny the Indian courts the jurisdiction to look, in appropriate cases, at the Holy Quran, would be to deny the Indian Muslims the right to be governed by Islamic laws." (Latifi (1985), p. 399).

This discussion emphasises and documents in detail the differences between the classical concept of maintenance (*nafaqa*) and the provision to be made by a divorcing Muslim husband to compensate the former wife (*mata*). Latifi concludes this discussion at page 398, saying that,

> ". . . there appears ample and respectable Islamic authority for the proposition that under the Muslim law the divorcing husband, in appropriate cases, is bound to provide maintenance for his divorced wife until death or remarriage. He may also be liable to pay compensation particularly in cases of *talaq ul bidaat*."

We shall see below that this distinction has been further clarified more recently in the case law under the Muslim Women (Protection of Rights on Divorce) Act 1986 which was promulgated very soon after the *Shah Bano* decision and in explicit reaction to it. For, the decision in the *Shah Bano* case led to riots, generated much concern among certain sections of the Muslim community in different parts of

India and deeply divided the community.[17] Traditionalists urged amendments to this law in two directions. First, it was suggested that in a situation where a Muslim divorced woman has no blood relatives who would normally support her, the magistrate should ask a Waqf Board to make a monthly allowance for her maintenance. Secondly, Waqf Boards should be authorised to raise money for this purpose from *waqfs* within their jurisdiction. The problem with this argument is that the Waqf Boards may be unable to help women with living relatives who perhaps simply do not wish to maintain the divorced kinswoman. Numerous demonstrations and riots led to political considerations which in turn contributed to the rapid passing of an Act in May 1986, which was widely understood at the time to prohibit a Muslim woman from going to court to seek a maintenance payment from the man who divorced her (Pearl (1987a), p. 74).

7–99   As we now know, the Muslim Women (Protection of Rights on Divorce) Act 1986 has done precisely what its name suggests and has proved rather beneficial to divorced Muslim wives who were unable to maintain themselves appropriately after the *iddat* period. The 1986 Act has not taken away the divorced Muslim woman's right to claim maintenance from the former husband but has in fact strengthened it. At the same time, it is correct that this Act, being a legislative provision under Muslim personal law rather than under the general law, violates the Directive Principle of legal uniformity as found in Article 44 of the Indian Constitution of 1950. However, that is more a point of communal politics. It is more important for the present discussion, and for the development of Muslim law on this point, to understand clearly that section 3 of the Muslim Women (Protection of Rights on Divorce) Act 1986 offers a more or less instant remedy today to any divorced Muslim wife in India who, at the end of the *iddat* period, finds that her ex-husband has not made reasonable provisions for her future maintenance.

7–100   This statement requires some explanation, since it is a fact that almost all the literature on the 1986 Act proceeds on quite misguided assumptions about the effects of that Act. Political commentators, it seems, do not normally read Indian High Court judgments, and even many legal writers followed the *Shah Bano* bandwagon and could not at first see the beneficial effects of the 1986 Act.[18]

7–101   The Muslim Women (Protection of Rights on Divorce) Act 1986 is the first codification of Muslim law in India after the Dissolution of Muslim Marriages Act 1939 and the only Indian Act on Muslim law after independence. It is a very short piece of legislation with only seven sections, out of which only three contain substantive rules. It seems that in the heated debates about the Act, attention was deliberately focused on sections 4 and 5 of the Act. Section 4(1) concerns the obligations of a divorced woman's relatives to maintain her in the event that she is not able to maintain herself after the *iddat* period. Section 4(2) provides that, in the absence of such financial support from the family, the State Wakf Board may be directed by a magistrate to support such a woman. Thus, in the outcry over the new obligations on the Wakf Boards as found in section 4(2), in particular, it was

---

[17] For details on the reactions see Agarwala, *Plight of a Muslim woman. The Shah Bano case* (1986) and Naseem, *The Shah Bano case x-rayed* (1988). On opinion surveys at the time see Rao [1985] 27 No. 4 J.I.L.I. 575–577. Singh (1992), pp. 142–143 confirms that many Muslims were in favour of the *Shah Bano* decision and provides details at pp. 160–161.

[18] The list is too long to cite here. An early example of rushed reaction is Agarwala (1986). Latifi (1986), used strong language to criticise the key provisions of the 1986 Act, which "could mean almost anything" (Latifi (1986), p. 617). Iyer (1987), p. 13 complained about "long clauses and crude drafting", asserting at p.12 that alimony cannot be claimed under s.3 of the (1986) Act for the period beyond the brief *iddat*. Diwan and Diwan (1991), pp. 155–165 provide a curious, interesting mixture of old and new views, but at least this is explained by the authors in a note at p. 155.

forgotten by most campaigners that the Act also has a section 3, in which it is made crystal-clear that the first source of support for a divorced Muslim wife remains her former husband. Section 3 of the 1986 Act provides:

"3. Mahr or other properties of Muslim woman to be given to her at the time of divorce.–

(1) Notwithstanding anything contained in any other law for the time being in force, a divorced woman shall be entitled to -

(a) a reasonable and fair provision and maintenance to be made and paid to her within the iddat period by her former husband;

(b) where she herself maintains the children born to her before or after the divorce, a reasonable and fair provision and maintenance to be made and paid by her former husband for a period of two years from the respective dates of birth of such children;

(c) an amount equal to the sum of mahr or dower agreed to be paid to her at the time of her marriage or at any time thereafter according to Muslim law; and

(d) all the properties given to her before or at the time of marriage or after her marriage by her relatives or friends or the husband or any relatives of the husband or his friends.

(2) Where a reasonable and fair provision and maintenance or the amount of mahr or dower due has not been made or paid or the properties referred to in clause (d) of sub-section (1) have not been delivered to a divorced woman on her divorce, she or anyone duly authorised by her may, on her behalf, make an application to a Magistrate for an order for payment of such provision and maintenance, mahr or dower, or the delivery of properties, as the case may be.

(3) Where an application has been made under sub-section (2) by a divorced woman, the Magistrate may, if he is satisfied that -

(a) her husband having sufficient means, has failed or neglected to make or pay her within the iddat period a reasonable and fair provision and maintenance for her and the children; or

(b) the amount equal to the sum of mahr or dower has not been paid or that the properties referred to in clause (d) of sub-section (1) have not been delivered to her, make an order, within one month of the date of the filing of the application, directing her former husband to pay such reasonable and fair provision and maintenance to the divorced woman as he may determine as fit and proper having regard to the needs of the divorced woman, the standard of life enjoyed by her during her marriage and the means of her former husband or, as the case may be, for the payment of such mahr or dower or the delivery of such properties referred to in clause (d) of sub-section (1) to the divorced woman:

"Provided that if the Magistrate finds it impracticable to dispose of the application within the said period, he may, for reasons to be recorded by him, dispose of the application after the said period.

(4) If any person against whom an order has been made under sub-section (3) fails without sufficient cause to comply with the order,

the Magistrate may issue a warrant for levying the amount of maintenance or mahr or dower due in the manner provided for levying fines under the Code of Criminal Procedure, 1973, and may sentence such person, for the whole or part of any amount remaining unpaid after the execution of the warrant, to imprisonment for a term which may extend to one year or until payment if sooner made, subject to such person being heard in defence and the said sentence being imposed according to the provisions of the said Code."

These intricately worded provisions in India's newly codified Muslim law on the subject soon gave rise to a large number of petitions. The numerous challenges to the constitutionality of the 1986 Act, filed immediately in 1986, have been kept pending before the Supreme Court and an ominous silence is all that can be reported.[19] The previous edition speculated on whether this Act would be struck down as unconstitutional (Pearl (1987a), p. 74). It seems now that these petitions have been treated as lacking bona fide status and have been lost in the long queue of appeals pending in the Indian Supreme Court. As we shall see below, the case law which has grown up under the substantive provisions of the 1986 Act actually renders these constitutional challenges otiose.[20]

7–102   It could be argued that there was perhaps an attempt to protect the Act from allegations of unconstitutionality through inserting section 5, which enables the husband and the wife (or ex-wife, as she would be) to opt jointly to be governed by sections 125–128 of the 1973 Code of Criminal Procedure rather than the 1986 Act. However, litigation activity under that section has been minimal. Since the financial limit of Rs. 500/- under the 1973 Code is more stringent than under the 1986 Act, it may actually be to the advantage of Muslim husbands to opt for the 1973 Code.[21]

7–103   A first substantive issue arose in numerous petitions where a case had been pending under section 125 or section 127 of the 1973 Code when the 1986 Act was promulgated on May 19, 1986. Section 7 of the 1986 Act provided in this regard:

"7. Transitional provisions. –
Every application by a divorced woman under Section 125 or under Section 127 of the Code of Criminal Procedure, 1973 pending before a Magistrate on the commencement of this Act, shall, notwithstanding anything contained in that Code and subject to the provisions of Section 5 of this Act, be disposed of by such Magistrate in accordance with the provisions of this Act."

In *Abdul Gafoor Kunju v. Pathumma Beevi*, 1989(1) K.L.T. 337, it was held that a divorced Muslim wife is no longer entitled to invoke the provisions of section 127

---

[19] Jain (1988), pp. 289–290. See also Mahmood (1990), p. 310, with details on the pending petitions *ibid.*, p. 305. Mahmood (1989), p. 227 also refers to the lack of progress on the project of a draft code for Indian Muslim law.

[20] Challenges of the kind which question the *vires* of the Indian state to legislate on matters of Muslim law are, of course, lacking standing as well as bona fides.

[21] See on this the discussion in Mahmood (1990), p. 304.

of the 1973 Code after the 1986 Act came into force.[22] It has also become clear that cases concerning the maintenance of children and of parents are still governed by sections 125–128 of the 1973 Code.[23]

7-104   The judicial interpretation of section 3 of the 1986 Act is still not backed up by a Supreme Court judgment, but there is now a plethora of High Court cases which support the view that the divorcing husband remains liable for his former wife's welfare.[24] Only very few cases go the other way.[25] The Kerala High Court's detailed verdict in *Ali v. Sufaira*, 1988(2) K.L.T. 94 was not the first such case to be decided under the 1986 Act,[26] but it has had probably the most impact, being cited later several times as the leading case on the matter. *Ali v. Sufaira* is actually a cluster of several cases. In the main petition, the divorced woman had claimed Rs. 30,000/- as reasonable and fair provision for her life, Rs. 22,500/- as *iddat* money, Rs. 11,500/- as *mahr* and the return of properties to the value of 1.5 million rupees. This shows at once that the litigants here are, again, not some impoverished desperately poor Indian Muslims, but middle-class people who can afford to argue over principles of jurisprudence. The magistrate had accepted the wife's case but had granted her substantially lower sums, so both the husband and the wife appealed. Sreedharan J. clearly identified, at page 95, that the most important issue before him was the extent of the liability cast on a Muslim husband at the time of divorce.

7-105   Referring back to the *Shah Bano* case, the learned judge first considered section 3 of the 1986 Act, as cited above, highlighting that in section 3(1)(a) the Muslim woman is entitled to "a reasonable and fair provision and maintenance to be made and paid to her within the *iddat* period". In *Ali v. Sufaira*, the former husbands were pleading that their liabilities had ended after the *iddat* period, thus implying that 'provision' and 'maintenance' were one and the same thing. The learned judge therefore identified for himself a task of statutory interpretation: What was the precise import of the chain of words chosen in section 3(1)(a) of the 1986 Act? Considering the Preamble of the 1986 Act, as well as the Statement of Objects and Reasons as published in the *Official Gazette* of February 25, 1986, Sreedharan J. found, first of all, that the unmistakable object of the 1986 Act was to

---

[22] Various procedural points have arisen but lack of space prevents expansion. For material on the very early cases under the Act, including excerpts from unreported cases, see Jain (1988). For details and references to other cases see Mahmood (1989), pp. 230–232. In *Anwaruddin Ahmad v. State*, (1989) Cri.L.J. (N.O.C.) 20 (Cal.) it was held that in a case filed by the husband s.7 of the (1986) Act did not apply. In *Shamsudeen v. Sabhiya*, 1988(2) K.L.T. 392, it was held that an earlier final order for maintenance under the (1973) Code would not be disturbed by the promulgation of the 1986 Act. See also *Idris Ali v. Ramesha Khatun*, A.I.R. 1989 Gau. 24. *Mytheen v. Saphiya*, 1993(2) K.L.T. 322 suggests that if a wife has signed away her right to maintenance, she cannot reclaim it later.

[23] For the position of children see para. 10–83, below.

[24] See in detail Mahmood (1990) and Menski (1994) with further case references. Other important cases on the same lines are *Aliyar v. Pathu*, 1988(2) K.L.T. 446; *Arab Ahemadhia Abdalla v. Arab Bail Mohmuna Saiyadbhai*, A.I.R. 1988 Guj. 141; *Ahammed v. Aysha*, 1990(1) K.L.T. 172; *Alavi v. Safia*, 1992(1) K.L.T. 649, defends the rights of a divorced woman who allegedly lives 'in adultery', a frequent, convenient allegation used by Indian men to defeat maintenance suits; *Hyderkhan v. Meharunnissa*, 1992(2) K.L.T. 330, held that the 1986 Act has retrospective operation and, at p. 333, that "there is no logic in holding that the Act for the first time introduced a burden on the Muslim husband to provide for reasonable and fair provision and maintenance to the divorced wife". This was established by reference to Qur'anic sources as well. *Syed Fazal Pookoya Thangal v. Union of India*, 1993(1) K.L.T. 860 holds that s.4(2) of the 1986 Act is not unconstitutional; *Hassainar v. Raziya*, 1993(2) K.L.T. 805 is a case on limitation. *Amjum Hassan Siddiqui v. Salma B.*, A.I.R. 1992 All. 322 concerns the lack of jurisdiction of Family Courts in such proceedings but does not question the positive interpretation of the 1986 Act.

[25] The main decision holding that a husband is not liable to maintain his ex-wife beyond the *iddat* period appears to be the High Court case of *Usman Khan Bahamani v. Fathimunnisa Begum*, A.I.R. 1990 A.P. 225. Even the more patriarchal North Indian High Courts have very recently begun to fall in line, as reported in the press.

[26] For the very first decisions under the 1986 Act see Jain (1988) and Mahmood (1990), pp. 306–307.

protect the interests of divorced Muslim women. Then, looking afresh at the wording of the section, he held, at pages 97–98:

> "In interpreting a provision in a statute it is important to remember that the Parliament does not waste its breath unnecessarily . . . The courts are duty bound to examine and give meaning to every word of the statute in its context . . . We cannot assume a mistake in an Act of Parliament . . . The presumption is always against superfluity in a statute . . . The Parliament must be taken to have decided to provide the divorced woman with maintenance for the period of iddat and also a reasonable and fair provision for her. Both of these should be made and paid to her during the iddat."

Interestingly, it was also held, at page 98, that section 4 of the Act "does not absolve the former husband from making a 'reasonable and fair provision' for the lady's life". More relevant for our present discussion is the fact that this learned judge, too, having distinguished 'provision' and 'maintenance', turned to the Qur'anic foundations, citing Sura II, verses 236–237 and 241–242.[27] He concluded, at pages 99–100:

> "From this it is clear that the Muslim who believes in God must give a reasonable amount by way of gift or maintenance to the divorced lady. That gift or maintenance is not limited to the period of iddat. It is for her future livelihood because – God wishes to see all well. The gift is to depend on the capacity of the husband. The gift, to be paid by the husband at the time of divorce, as commanded by the Quran, is recognised in sub-clause (a) of Clause (1) of s.3 of the Act. This liability is cast upon the husband on account of the past advantage received by him by reason of the relationship with the divorced woman or on account of the past dis-advantage suffered by her by reason of matrimonial consortium, it is in the nature of a compensatory gift or a solatium to sustain the woman for her life after the divorce. In accordance with the principles of Islamic equity the said provision or compensation or support from the former husband is [the] wife's right. This right has been given legislative recognition in the above provision. So, I find it difficult to accept the argument that the only liability of the former husband is to pay maintenance to the divorced Muslim woman during the period of iddat only."

It was therefore held, at pages 100–101, that under section 3(1)(a) of the 1986 Act "a divorced Muslim woman is not only entitled to maintenance for the period of iddat from the former husband but also to a reasonable and fair provision for her future". The approach in *Ali v. Sufaira* could not be clearer. The same position was subsequently further developed in a number of cases from different Indian High Courts, as cited in note 24, page 216, above. The basic principle today is that a divorced Muslim woman in India, when she finds at the end of the *iddat* period that her former husband has not made reasonable and fair provisions for her, has an instant case against him, which is to be decided within a tight time-frame (see section 3(3) of the 1986 Act as cited above).

7-106 Several cases illustrate that when it comes to the quantum of maintenance awarded, much depends on the financial standing of the spouses. But which spouse? In *Ahammed v. Aysha*, 1990(1) K.L.T. 712, it was claimed that the wife was better off than the husband, so her claim to maintenance should fail. Jagannadha Raju J. held, at page 174:

---

[27] Bhat J. in *Aliyar v. Pathu*, 1988 (2) K.L.T. 446, at pp. 457–458, also made reference to these sources.

"If we compare and contrast the provisions of s.3 of the Act with similar provisions in the other enactments, we find that even a millionaire wife who lives in luxury and affluence is certainly entitled to claim maintenance and other reliefs from her former husband under s.3. There is no requirement of the wife being unable to maintain herself for granting maintenance or for payment of fair and reasonable provision as contemplated under s.3."

As indicated, only very few reported cases oppose the pro-women interpretation of the 1986 Act.[28] In *Usman Khan Bahamani v. Fathimunnisa Begum*, A.I.R. 1990 A.P. 225, a long majority decision from a bench of three judges, two major questions arose. First, what was the position of maintenance applications under sections 125–128 of the 1973 Code which were pending when the 1986 Act came into force? Secondly, what was the extent of the divorced woman's right under section 3 of the 1986 Act? The answer on the first point was contained in section 7 of the 1986 Act itself, which provided for this situation and this matter was therefore uncontroversial. As to the extent of the husband's liability, the learned judges, taking a wide historical sweep, examined the precise wording of section 3(1)(a) of the 1986 Act, in particular the phrase "within the iddat period" and concluded at p. 231 that "there is nothing in the section which can be read to mean that the husband is liable to make reasonable and fair provision and maintenance beyond the period of Iddat". Thus, the majority verdict continued, at page 231:

"The word "within" indicates two things that the liability of the husband to make a reasonable and fair provision and maintenance is limited to the period of Iddat only and it is already seen in the statement of the objects and reasons that the principle of Muslim law limits the husband's liability to provide maintenance to the divorced wife for the period of Iddat only."

7–107 This lengthy judgment contains a detailed analysis of Muslim law principles, textbooks and various judicial decisions. It looks like an impressive piece of judicial work, but it is submitted that the majority decision in this case is based on faulty, circuitous reasoning which neither reflects the intended social purposes of the 1986 legislation nor the idealistic spirit of the Qur'anic provisions, which certainly suggest that divorcing men should be kind to the women they divorce. It would only be correct to argue for a basic rule of Muslim law that a divorced woman has no entitlement beyond the *iddat* period if one could assume that all divorcing Muslim men provided well enough for their former wives. This, in the light of the various Qur'anic verses, which are also looked at in this case, is clearly not the underlying assumption of the earliest sources of Muslim law, while later juristic statements are concerned to limit the extent of the husband's liability to the *iddat* period. Despite the length of this judgment, this part of the analysis of Muslim law is open to criticism and was rightly challenged by Latifi (1991b, p. 29) who comments that the learned judge who delivered the majority verdict in *Usman Khan* virtually refused to give due meaning to the expression 'fair and reasonable provision' and behaved as though these words had been deleted from section 3 of the 1986 Act. The minority view of Bhaskar Rao J. in *Usman Khan* is clearly based on extended consideration, as documented by various commentators. The contested wording 'within the iddat period' was interpreted very differently by this judge on page 245:

---

[28] One of these is a Short Note from a case decided by the Madras High Court, see *Raja Mohammed v. Moimoon*, 1992 (2) K.L.T. S.N. 1. This strange case appears to rely on the wording employed in *Usman Khan*, but does not say so. For early case references see Mahmood (1990), pp. 306–307.

"The words in s.3(1)(a) "within the Iddat period" lay stress on the urgency in making or paying and they cannot be read as confining the liability to the limited period of iddat, save in so far as maintenance is concerned since the Muslim Law is settled on that aspect. Interpreting the distinct liability of making a reasonable and fair provision as having been confined to the period of Iddat would not only render the very Section 5 on the statute otiose but also defeats the specific purpose of casting that liability on the former husband . . ."

Since there was a clear distinction between 'maintenance' on the one hand and 'provision' on the other, the dissenting judge concluded on page 246:

"Accordingly, I am of the firm view that the maintenance contemplated by Sec. 3(1)(a) of the Act is limited to the Iddat period while the fair and reasonable provision to be made in terms of the same section runs for the future much beyond the iddat period."

Tahir Mahmood's extended comment on this case in the 1989 *Annual Survey of Indian Law* contains an instructive analysis. At first, Mahmood (1989, pp. 228–229) refers to an earlier ruling of Bhaskar Rao J. to the effect that a Muslim husband's obligation to provide maintenance and to make provision extended beyond the *iddat* period. Then Mahmood shows, as we saw above, that the same judge modified his view in *Usman Khan* and held that maintenance was restricted to the *iddat* period only, while the 'reasonable and fair provision' under the 1986 Act was different from maintenance and was clearly not restricted to the *iddat* period. Mahmood (1989, p. 230) then introduces his own view, which is very relevant to the present discussion:

"The author is convinced that the 'fair and reasonable provision' spoken about in the Muslim Women Act is different from maintenance of *'iddat* period – it rather represents what the Qur'an calls *mata'* [compensation for an arbitrary divorce or for a woman divorced for none of her fault]. However, since under the Qur'anic law *mata'* is payable in deserving cases *only* and not unconditionally to every female divorcee – guidelines for ordering and fixing 'fair and reasonable provision' under the Act should be provided either by legislation or by the process of judicial law-making. It will be wrong on the part of courts to take it as a mandatory provision of general application; but in a suitable case *mata'* must be awarded in addition to maintenance of *'iddat.*"

7-108 In this subtle argument we see further confirmation that in Indian Muslim law, too, the concept of some kind of compensation for the divorced Muslim wife is not unknown.[29] There continues to be social concern, however, about the fact that this general provision could be abused by women. Professor Mahmood has reiterated in various publications, as in the quote above, that since under the Qur'anic law *mata* is payable in deserving cases only, and not unconditionally to every female divorcee, guidelines for ordering and fixing a fair and reasonable provision should be provided either by legislation or by the process of judicial law-making.[30] The protective cloak of the 1986 Act should, thus, not give

---

[29] Nasir (1990a), pp. 143–145, as discussed in para. 7–23, above, spoke in this context of *mutat*. For the legal position in Syrian and Jordanian law today, which make provision for up to a year's maintenance for the divorced wife in cases of arbitrary *talaq*, see Welchman (1988), p. 881.

[30] See in particular Mahmood, "Muslim law", in *Annual Survey of Indian Law 1989* (1989), p. 230 and Mahmood, "Islamic family law. Latest developments in India", in *Islamic family law* (1990), p. 300.

an absolute right to all divorced women irrespective of circumstances.[31] After all, according to Mahmood (1990, p. 304), a man who wants to provide maintenance to his divorced wife periodically for the rest of her life is not prevented from doing so by any provision of Muslim law.[32]

7–109 It can be hardly doubted that the underlying reason for the recent litigation and legislative activity in this area of law in India has been that many Muslim men did not act with such magnanimity as Mahmood assumes and proved to be unwilling to share their resources fairly with former wives. In this context, it is certainly not a reasonable argument to advance in South Asia today that the modern state should be held responsible for divorced women and their children. However, it has been argued, in the context of section 4(2) of the 1986 Act:

> "According to the principles of Islamic law a member of the society who is unable to maintain himself or herself is the liability of the State. Where the Muslims are not the rulers and therefore the State cannot be compelled to fulfil this legal obligation, this liability passes on to the Muslim community in general." (Mahmood (1990), p. 304.)

It is submitted that in modern Indian law the combined effect of creative judicial interpretation of cases under sections 125 and 127 of the Criminal Procedure Code 1973 and the skilful legislative drafting in section 3(1)(a) of the Muslim Women (Protection of Rights on Divorce) Act 1986 has been to ensure, first of all, that no financial liability falls on the state. At the same time, the new scheme for the protection of divorced Muslim wives appears to have developed the very framework of reference that Professor Mahmood has called for. It is manifestly not the case that every divorced Muslim woman in India would automatically have a claim under the 1986 Act today. At least two safeguards have been provided. First, if the provisions which a divorcing Muslim man makes are in fact fair and reasonable, in the particular circumstances of the couple, the divorced woman can raise no further claim. An ex-wife of a poor husband, as we saw, will have to suffer, like her former husband, and section 3(3)(a) of the 1986 Act clearly says that the husband must have sufficient means, in the first place. Secondly, as is clearly specified by the wording of section 3(1)(a) in the 1986 Act, a divorced Muslim woman only has a claim for further provisions when her former husband has not made available to her such provisions at the point when the *iddat* period expires. If he has made fair arrangements at this point, or he has no means, the woman has no case.

7–110 While even recent writing on the 1986 Act maintains a politicised critical stance, often uninformed by the undoubted progress in the case law,[33] the Kerala High Court has confirmed in an authoritative judgment in 1995 that the leading 1988 cases of *Ali* and *Aliyar* are still good law and that the legislature has deliberately used the terms 'provision' and 'maintenance' to stress that these are two

---

[31] In this context, *M. Alavi v. T. V. Safia* A.I.R. 1993 Ker. 21, may raise a few eyebrows. It was held that s.3 of the 1986 Act does not say that a woman who had been living in adultery is not entitled to maintenance from the former husband.

[32] It must be noted, though, that this comment is made in the context of s.5 of the 1986 Act, allowing the spouses to opt for the 1973 Code instead. Mahmood apparently realised, by then, that the 1973 Code could be better for men than the 1986 Act, obviously because the latter stipulates no financial upper limit.

[33] See, *e.g.* Parihar, "Right to maintenance of Muslim divorcees", in *Women and law. Contemporary problems* (1994), p. 227, who still complains that the language of the 1986 Act is "clumsy and ambiguous" and simply asserts *ibid.*, p. 234 that "the Act of 1986 is in fact against the protection of Muslim women's rights".

different entitlements of divorced Muslim wives.[34] As noted, the Indian Supreme Court has kept a strangely low profile on this issue and questions about the constitutionality of the 1986 Act have now probably been overtaken by events.[35]

7-111 Two Supreme Court decisions after the *Shah Bano* case deserve brief mention here. In *Subanu v. A. M. Abdul Gafoor*, A.I.R. 1987 S.C. 1103, the question was whether a Muslim wife whose husband has married again is worse off in terms of maintenance than a former wife whose husband merely took a mistress. The husband's case was that since Muslim law allowed him to marry again, the first wife should not be allowed to live separately and claim maintenance from him. This was not really a new issue and, predictably, this argument failed.[36]

7-112 A most interesting, very recent case decided by the Supreme Court concerns section 4 of the 1986 Act.[37] Notably, this very first case on the matter from the apex court,[38] carefully omitting any reference to the existence of section 3 of the same Act, holds that sub-sections (1) and (2) of section 4 of the 1986 Act are not mutually exclusive but that the State Wakf Board comes "last in line to bear the burden" (page 413) of the woman's maintenance. In this case, a divorced Muslim wife had claimed Rs. 750/- per month as maintenance from the Wakf Board because none of her relatives was in a position to maintain her. The social welfare dimension of the 1986 Act is underlined by Punchhi J. at page 414:

> "It is futile for a divorced woman seeking succour to run after relatives, be it her children, parents or other relatives, who are not possessed of means to offer her maintenance and in fighting litigations in succession against them, dragging them to courts of law in order to obtain negative orders justificatory to the last resort of moving against the State Wakf Board. In our considered view, she would instead be entitled to plead and prove such relevant facts in one proceeding . . . It is . . . open for the State Wakf Board to controvert that the relations mentioned in the provision, or some of them, have the means to pay maintenance to her."

For obvious reasons, this decision from the highest court of the land does not make any reference to the liability of the welfare state. For reasons which are not quite clear from the report, however, this case also does not say a word about the role of the ex-husband!

7-113 In terms of Muslim law, our conclusion about the current legal position in India must be that a Muslim ex-husband is undoubtedly expected to maintain his wife during the *iddat* period and is in addition required to make reasonable provisions for his former wife for the period beyond the *iddat* period to the best of his abilities. We have seen that if such provisions have not been put into place by the end of the *iddat* period, the wife may have a claim under section 3 of the 1986

---

[34] See *Kunhammed Haji v. Amina* 1995(1) K.L.T. 765.

[35] On these petitions see Jain (1988). Interestingly, the High Court of Orissa, in *Bishnu Charan Mohanty v. Union of India*, A.I.R. 1993 Or. 176, upheld the constitutional validity of s. 5 of the 1986 Act. It was held that it does not discriminate on the basis of religion and as such does not violate Art. 15 of the Constitution.

[36] This case is further discussed in para. 8–31, below.

[37] See *Tamil Nadu Wakf Board v. Syed Fatima Nachi*, 1996(2) K.L.T. 410 [SC]. See earlier *The Secretary, Tamil Nadu Wakf Board v. Syed Fatima Nochi*, A.I.R. 1995 Mad. 88.

[38] There have been a number of High Court cases in which various Wakf Boards claimed that it would be against their constitution to have to provide for indigent Muslim wives. In *Syed Fazal Pookoya Thangal v. Union of India*, A.I.R. 1993 Ker. 308 it was argued without success that s.4(2) of the 1986 Act is unconstitutional. On this see Latifi (1993), p. 170. Parihar (1994), p. 229, wrote that the 1986 Act "is a sin against the constitution of Wakfs", since they are religious and charitable trusts created to perform specified holy acts.

Act. Since the actual extent of the husband's financial liability continues to depend on the facts and circumstances of each case, and Muslim husbands may choose to ignore the basically idealistic principle of their continued liability, one can still only say, in conclusion, that the former husband has a liability *in principle*. It remains a fact, and will remain a problem of growing dimensions in South Asia, that many women can expect precious little support from a former husband. It is, however, no longer possible to claim that divorcing Muslim husbands have no such responsibility.

7–114 In fact, the long, intensive debates in Indian law have clearly shown that the Muslim husband's responsibility beyond the *iddat* period was well-established already in the Qur'anic foundations. Modern Indian Muslim law has creatively used these foundations to make it easier for divorced women to come to the courts claiming a fair provision if they feel that they are being treated unfairly. Whether one calls this 'compensation', 'provision' or some form of 'maintenance' does not really matter. What seems to count most is whether a particular arrangement is fair and reasonable. Traditional Muslim law, as well as modern Indian law, at the end of the day, seem to concur in agreeing that what is fair and reasonable depends on the circumstances of the spouses.

7–115 In Pakistani law, there has also been a continuing, albeit low-key debate about the maintenance rights of divorced Muslim wives but the result is very different. The underlying socio-religious problems are clearly the same, but in Pakistani law a divorced wife is no longer a 'wife' and thus the catalytic element of criminal law support to remind Muslim husbands of an ancient duty was never activated. The issue itself was clearly identified by the Commission on Marriage and Family Laws in the 1950s when Pakistan began to contemplate reforms in Muslim family law. In the context of divorce reforms, the issue was phrased as follows[39]:

> "5. *Should it be open to a Matrimonial and Family Laws Court, when approached, to lay down that a husband shall pay maintenance to the divorced wife for life or till her remarriage?*
>
> The Commission was of the opinion that such a discretion should be vested in the Matrimonial Court, and that a large number of middle-aged women who are being divorced without rhyme or reason should not be thrown on the street without a roof over their heads and without any means of sustaining themselves and their children. Of course it would be open to a Matrimonial Court to refuse to sanction any maintenance if the woman is at fault."

This was the majority response, while the views of the lone dissenting member of the Commission, Maulana Ehtisham-Ul-Haq Thanvi, were published separately. On the question of post-divorce maintenance, the Maulana focused entirely on the interests and needs of the new wife of a divorcing husband, rather than the woman he had divorced:

> "The moment *talaq* severs all lawful ties between man and wife, the parties become complete strangers to each other. In the matter of *ihsan* this strangeness comes to assume even more dangerous significance. In the first place the present wife, whose expenses have been declared wholly a liability of the husband by *Shariat*, is as much a woman as the one divorced. So the attempt to help a woman who has been divorced and paid her dower and

---

[39] Report of the Commission, *Gazette of Pakistan*, "Extraordinary", June 20, 1956, p. 1215.

deprive the present wife of her due share is like trying to rob Peter to pay Paul. This is no virtue in this world . . . curiously enough, they still want to help a woman who has been justly and properly divorced and deprive the present wife of her due share. This certainly means an injustice to other women. The grant of maintenance, etc., to the divorced wife would not only mean monetary injustice to the present wife but also lead to the moral degeneration of the beneficiary. The aid especially from a man who has lived as a husband for a long time would mean a standing threat to the chastity of the divorced woman. The members of the Commission look only to the monetary aid while Islam aims above all at safeguarding the chastity of women. Moreover, the continued payment of maintenance to the divorced woman would keep the mind of the present wife constantly vexed with suspicion. The proposal is, therefore, ill-advised and harmful to women. The right that *Shariat* has not seen wise to confer on women cannot be granted to them by any Commission or Court."[40]

This submission combines exclusive concern for the welfare of the new wife of a divorcing husband with a strangely worded interest in the chastity of divorced wives. It does not address the socio-legal key issue, the need to protect divorced, mainly middle-aged ex-wives from destitution. It also merely asserts a *shariat* position which is clearly not underwritten by the Qur'an itself. In a brief reference to the Commission's report, Latifi (1985, pp. 398–399) noted, at page 399, that the Muslim Family Laws Ordinance 1961:

". . . is silent on this point perhaps because the responsible persons concerned were confident that Pakistani courts would give the same interpretation to *Alquran* II. 241 as has been done by the Supreme Court of India in *Shah Bano* and that, consequently, legislative interference was unnecessary. Speculation will only be set at rest when the Pakistan courts consider the matter."

7–116 This, in 1985, was speculation indeed! Neither the Pakistani law makers (a functioning legislature being the exception rather than the rule) nor the Pakistani courts had considered this matter in any depth, nor have they done so since. It seems, however, that Pakistani law has purposely avoided discussion of this important issue and it is remarkable that Pakistani law on this subject seems to be entirely unaffected by the recent developments in Indian Muslim law in the same field.[41] Apart from reluctance to copy trans-border laws, there are several other reasons for this. It seems certain that the approach to the continued parental liability for married daughters, as outlined by Mahmood (1986, pp. 86–87, cited above, p. 211) appears to dominate in Pakistani society. This would imply an understanding of a particular division of labour in society which is different from that in India and Bangladesh. The Report of the Commission in 1956, as well as recent unpublished fieldwork, suggest that this has for a long time been a standard pattern, so that the burden of maintaining divorced women is normally borne by the natal family, rather than the divorcing husband and/or his family. In 1956, the Commission stated, in the context of claims for past maintenance:

"At present if a wife is expelled by the husband and she goes to live with her parents, the husband generally stops paying maintenance to her. Even if she

---

[40] *Gazette of Pakistan*, "Extraordinary", August 30, 1956, p. 1589.
[41] In other areas of law, there is a similar reluctance in Pakistan to learn or copy from 'the other country'. This barrier is probably higher when it comes to accepting Indian interpretations of Muslim law.

and her children are compelled to live with her parents or she maintains herself and her children by earning a little money in some profession she cannot claim any past maintenance. The husband therefore resorts to various subterfuges so that the wife may not sue him. He feels that the longer the suit for maintenance is delayed the less will be the amount of maintenance that he will be compelled to pay."[42]

Recent fieldwork in Pakistan has confirmed that this pattern continues today and that almost all divorced women have to rely on their natal families for survival. While there has been an ongoing debate in Pakistan about reforms to Muslim family laws,[43] it is a fact that divorced women face an uphill struggle even to obtain their *mahr* and any provisions for the *iddat* period. Various governments have done nothing beyond appointing formal bodies to consider the position of women. The Women's Rights Committee of 1976 and the 1983 Pakistan Commission on the Status of Women (which published a report in 1986) have both recommended the introduction of a right to maintenance for divorced Muslim women in Pakistan, but nothing has been done about this. The 1983 Commission was well aware of the relevant Qur'anic verses and their import, as well as developments in Indian law, but the status quo in the Pakistani Muslim law on maintenance has been retained, continuing to disadvantage divorced women and to expose many of them to the kinds of moral dangers that Islam seeks to control.

7–117 In Bangladesh, where there is evidence of a fairly large body of reported cases on maintenance issues,[44] there have been recent developments which deserve more than a brief notice. While earlier it seemed that Bangladesh, too, was unwilling to follow the liberal trend of the Indian case law and statutory protection mechanisms, the recent case of *Md. Hefzur Rahman v. Shamsun Nahar Begum* (1995) 15 B.L.D. 34, reflects and displays a new-found judicial activism in that country, following Indian models but not admitting this in so many words.[45]

7–118 In *Md. Hefzur Rahman*, the parties had married in March 1985, a dower of Takas 50,001/- had been fixed, and a son was born in December 1987. In August 1988, the husband divorced the wife. Three months later, the wife filed a suit for recovery of her dower and for maintenance for herself and the child at Takas 2,000/- per month. The Family Court directed the husband to pay Takas 48,000/- as the balance of the *mahr*, Takas 1,000/- per month for maintenance of the child, and a sum of Takas 3,000/- for the *iddat* period of three months. The husband appealed against this to the District Judge and managed to have the maintenance payments reduced to Takas 600/- per month each for the wife and the son. The husband then filed a further appeal to have the maintenance payments reduced still further.

7–119 Mohammad Gholam Rabbani J., delivering the judgment, stated that nobody appeared to support a further reduction. He found that the lower courts had not explained how the sums were arrived at, nor had any reasons been cited for the reduction. Finding that the husband was a government servant in stable employment, he decreed, at page 35, that the award of Takas 1,000/- each per month should be restored, criticising the District Judge for his illegal action.

---

[42] Report of the Commission, *Gazette of Pakistan*, "Extraordinary", June 20, 1956, p. 1220.

[43] For details see, *e.g.* Weiss [1985] 25 No. 8 *Asian Survey* 863–880, and Weiss [1990] 30 No. 5 *Asian Survey*, esp. pp. 441–443.

[44] See in particular *Nur-Ud-Din Ahmad v. Masuda Khanam*, P.L.D. 1957 Dacca 242; *Amena Khatun v. Sherajuddin Sardar*, 17 D.L.R. (1965) 687; *Md. Ebrahim Hossain Sarkar v. Solemanessa*, 19 D.L.R. (1967) 751; *Begum Hamida v. Abdul Hamid*, 26 D.L.R. (1974) S.C. 26.

[45] See also the still more recent case of *Jamila Khatun v. Rustom Ali*, 48 D.L.R. (1996) A.D. 110, which is a limitation case focused on maintenance entitlements under Muslim law.

7-120   The judge then immediately took up, *suo moto*, the question whether the divorced wife could have claimed maintenance beyond the *iddat* period. Citing the relevant Qur'anic passages, the *Hedaya* and other sources, he commented that the Qur'an itself says that it is easy to understand, thus it prescribes a rule of literal construction of its verses (page 35). This leads to a discussion of the role and scope of *ijtihad* (page 36), with a reference to an old Privy Council case,[46] in which the judges had refused to interpret the Qur'an. Rabbani J., a Muslim judge in a Muslim majority country, felt entitled to take a fresh look at the Qur'anic injunctions, in fact he argued that under Article 8(1A) of the Constitution of Bangladesh he had a positive obligation to do so (page 36). Further, he cited a case from the Lahore High Court to support the propositions that reading and understanding the Qur'an is "a privilege granted to every Muslim which cannot be taken away from him by anybody, however highly placed or learned he may be to read and interpret Qur-an" and that interpretation must be "in the light of the existing circumstance and the changing needs of the world".[47] Thus it was concluded, at page 37, not in very clear terms but very much in line with current Bangladeshi trends of islamisation:

> "We, thus, come to the conclusion that a civil court has the jurisdiction to follow the law as in the Qur-an disregarding any other law on the subject, if contrary thereto even though laid down by the earlier jurists or commentators may be of great antiquity and high authority and though followed for a considerable period. Under the Hindu Law clear proof of usage can outweigh the written text of law. But it is not in the case of Islamic Law. For it is an article of faith of a Muslim that he should follow without questioning what has been revealed in Qur-an and disobedience thereof is a sin."

Having taken another close look at Qur'an, Sura II, verse 241, Rabbani J. then changed, with a stroke of his pen (at page 37), the law of Bangladesh on maintenance for divorced wives:

> "Considering all the aspects we finally hold that a person after divorcing his wife is bound to maintain her on a reasonable scale beyond the period of iddat for an indefinite period that is to say till she loses the status of divorcee by remarrying another person."

7-121   Notably, this decision makes no reference whatsoever to Indian legal developments.[48] The end result, however, even goes beyond it: A divorced Muslim wife in Bangladesh today, depending on the facts and circumstances of the case, can rely on the Qur'anic foundations to claim permanent alimony from the former husband, more so if she has a child to look after. This case will be criticised by some observers for its obvious legal activism, judicial legislation and the comments about the use of the Qur'an as law of the land. However, at the same time, this case gives a clear indication of social stress in the current Muslim society of Bangladesh, where desertion of wives and children unhappily is not uncommon and where husbands, as this case illustrates, do not fulfil even their basic obligations without being compelled to do so by courts. Regrettably, Rabbani J. did not enlighten us on the social rationale for this pioneering decision, but this judgment and the way in

---

[46] *Aga Mahomed Jaffer Bindanim v. Koolsom Beebee*, I.L.R. [1898] 25 Cal. 9.
[47] At p. 36. The case cited is *Rashida Begum v. Shahan Din*, P.L.D. 1960 Lah. 1142.
[48] Other recent cases from Bangladesh show similar activism and are similarly concerned to keep a distance from Indian legal developments, emphasising the unique nature of the Bangladeshi legal system.

which it was reached represent much more than simply islamisation of current Bangladeshi law.

7-121   A very recent case, decided by the same judge of the Dacca High Court, is *Jesmin Sultana v. Mohammad Elias* (1997) 17 B.L.D. 4. This is a wife's suit for payment of prompt dower and maintenance but the case is also important with regard to polygamy. The marriage was very short, lasting from May 27, 1992 to August 2, 1992. Dower had been fixed at Takas 150,000/- altogether, with a prompt dower of Takas 60,000/-. The trial court had held the husband liable for payment of the full prompt dower, and for Takas 500/- as monthly maintenance, while on appeal he succeeded in having the dower sum reduced to Takas 40,000/-. The wife appealed to the High Court against this reduction of the prompt dower.

7-123   Apparently, the lower appellate court had reduced the amount of *mahr* based on the argument that the Qur'an does not support fixation of a dower which the husband cannot pay. Examining relevant sources, Rabbani J. held that there was no evidence of remission of dower, so the lower court had been wrong to reduce the amount of the prompt dower.

7-124   Turning to the question of maintenance, Rabbani J. referred to *Mosammat Nur Akhtar v. Abdul Mabud Chowdhury* (1996) 16 B.L.D. 396, where it had been held that a wife who voluntarily leaves her husband and is unwilling to return to him is not entitled to maintenance. The husband in the case before him was pleading just this, while the wife produced documentation to show that the husband had in fact sought permission from the local Union Council to marry another woman, alleging that his wife was "sickly and incapable to perform conjugal relation" (page 5). In view of these facts, the maintenance decree of Takas 500/- per month was affirmed. It is not absolutely clear whether this is a permanent decree or whether it is restricted to three months, but the former appears to be the case.

7-125   The learned judge then, again, took up the related issue in the case before him, this time polygamy, and embarked on comments of great relevance to current Bangladeshi law on this subject. This aspect of the case is examined in paragraph 8-77, below. It must suffice here to say that Rabbani J. hit out at section 6 of the MFLO 1961, saying that it is against the principles of Islamic law and should be deleted from the Ordinance, to be replaced by a section which prohibits polygamy.

Property rights

7-126   Some South Asian authors refer back to the Qur'anic foundations to make the point that husband and wife are two independent yet mutually interdependent entities.[49] Therefore, "in Islam the husband and wife are equal partners in a sacred relationship of trust and confidence" (Mahmood (1986), p. 68). Mahmood (1982a, p. 88) emphasised that, in Muslim law, spouses retain their independent legal status and that, apart from retention of their respective school of law and retention of the wife's maiden name, the wife's authority to own property in her own right was unquestioned:

> "The husband has no right to interfere with the property of the wife, and the wife does not become the owner of the husband's property during his life-time. Contrary to the rules of the western law, a Muslim spouse dishonestly removing the property of the other spouse from the latter's possession will be

---

[49] See, *e.g.* Mahmood (1986), p. 68, with a reference to Qur'an, Sura II, verse 187.

guilty of the offence of theft and, in India, will be punishable under section 379 of the Penal Code, 1860. This rule of Muslim law has been applied by the courts in some old cases." (Mahmood (1982a), p. 89.)

Given the realities of South Asian Muslim societies, however, the combined effects of patriarchy-dominated juristic interpretations, of mostly patriarchal local customs and of socio-economic stress are often felt. This leads to practical difficulties in all areas of law, since women may not be treated as *sui juris* for many purposes. This will often become a contested issue, not only when female minors are given in marriage, but also when adult women have difficulties securing their independent property rights and asserting themselves *vis-à-vis* men, or other women, as the case may be.[50] The recent *Saima* case in Pakistan was a case in point, showing that even today middle-class, educated, city-based women have to struggle against attempts, in the name of Islam and Muslim tradition, to control their most intimate feelings and their authority to make independent decisions. One could cite numerous references to confirm that situations like this constitute complex socio-legal problems for which no easy solutions can be found.[51]

7–127   In the extreme, linked to South Asian local traditions rather than any Muslim concepts, women may be treated as the property of men, which has of course the effect that any property they may be entitled to in law would then also be perceived and counted as the property of the person who claims ownership of the woman. Although this is not supposed to happen in Muslim societies, not the least because this approach was a hallmark of pre-Islamic societies, the extended litigation over women's rights to dower and maintenance, and the male claims over females, as illustrated in restitution of conjugal rights cases and questions over when a woman may refuse cohabitation, demonstrate very clearly that Islamic theory and socio-legal Muslim practice exhibit wide divergencies. Mahmood (1986, p. 68) emphasises correctly the ideal rules:

"The Muslim wife legally retains her maiden name, her property, her independent legal status and even her school of law (*madhab*) if different from the husband's. The latter, by marrying her, does not acquire any right to tamper with any of these."

Many South Asian legal provisions stress that women should be the absolute owners of property. For example, in Pakistan section 5 of the Dowry and Bridal Gifts (Restriction) Act 1976 provides clearly that:

"All property given as dowry or bridal gifts and all property given to the bride as a present shall vest absolutely in the bride and her interest in property however derived shall hereafter not be restrictive, conditional or limited."

---

[50] It should perhaps be emphasised again here that South Asian concepts of joint family life, and the resulting property relations and interdependencies, do not allow many individuals the absolute and permanent status of independent legal personality. However, the obligation to subject oneself to 'managers' of various descriptions is matched by the rights and claims one has towards such fuller legal personalities and towards the family as a unit. Another topic of relevance here is of course the continued presence of various forms of slavery or bonded labour, with no boundaries of religion. On South Asian women as virtual chattels in a historical context, see excellently Dhagamwar, *Law, power and justice. The protection of personal rights in the Indian Penal Code* (1992). Numerous cases could be cited on the complications created for South Asian Muslims by the pervasive influence of the joint family system. See, *e.g. Md. Zafir v. Amiruddin*, A.I.R. (1963) Pat. 108.

[51] Lateef, *Muslim women in India. Political and private realities* (1990), p. 205 highlights that in India women leaders were particularly concerned at the difficulties Muslim women faced in getting their share of property rights, *mahr*, maintenance, and custody of children and makes the valid point that there is a need for such laws as already exist to be implemented to give women a fair chance.

A similar rule exists in section 6 of the Indian Dowry Prohibition Act 1961. Also in sections 3(1)(c) and (d) of the Muslim Women (Protection of Rights on Divorce) Act 1986 (as cited above, p. 214) it has been explicitly provided that any amount of dower, and any properties given to the wife in connection with the marriage, shall be the absolute property of the wife. Such provisions are obviously required because many South Asians do not follow the ideal principles of their respective personal laws. Such forms of property are often the subject of fiercely contested cases, even involving murder.[52] In the context of litigation over maintenance, it has been confirmed in Pakistan that the wife is entitled to own property independent of the husband and that she has the power to exercise her rights over such property.[53]

7–128 Local sentiments of course fully support a patriarchal and dependent structure for the simple reason that most women have few opportunities to obtain financial rewards other than through inheritance, and even here the entitlement is often much smaller than that of the male members of the inner family circle. By custom, the management of her property will often fall into the hands of the husband, or the wife will readily give up her rights to own property in return for other privileges, for example the right to visit relatives, which is particularly common in Bangladesh.

7–129 With regard to Islamic theory and local Muslim practice, therefore, one can find huge divergencies. The legal effects of marriage among South Asian Muslims, in social reality, continue to exert much pressure on the wife to submit not only herself but also her property to the overriding authority of the husband.

Legal effects of Muslim marriages in Britain

7–130 English law itself says very little about the legal consequences of a Muslim marriage solemnised in Britain other than holding that it is not a legally valid marriage in its own right. As we saw in paragraph 6–92, above, however, Muslims in Britain now normally marry under English law as well as Muslim law, which has led to some evidence of interaction between the two legal systems. The literature emphasises, as we saw, the central nature of the family in the Muslim way of life. Nielsen (1992c, p. 98) stresses that the increasing involvement of Muslims in Europe in various aspects of the public sphere has created new difficulties for Muslim families and individuals, especially women and writes, at page 99:

> "This put Muslim families into situations which were usually difficult, often embarrassing and occasionally traumatic. Women had to go through ante-natal care and give birth in the impersonal surroundings of city hospitals without the accustomed support and presence of female relatives. Occasionally, a young son may be the only available interpreter. The bureaucracy involved in entry and residence formalities, in dealing with the welfare services and housing authorities and in arranging schooling for the children, were all daunting and often frightening."

---

[52] For evidence of Pakistani cases see Mahmood (1991), p. 274; Balchin (1994), p. 93. In Indian law, none of the leading cases involved Muslim parties. In Bangladesh, the right of the woman to own the otherwise illegal dowry was originally introduced by the Dowry Prohibition Act 1980, which was virtually copied from India. However, for some reason which is not obvious, and has not been explained, s.6 of the 1980 Act was deleted by the Dowry Prohibition (Amendment) Act 1984 in Bangladesh.
[53] See already *Said Ahmad v. Sultan Bibi*, A.I.R. 1943 Pesh. 73. For more recent evidence see Balchin (1994), p. 88 and *Muhammad Younus v. The Collector, District Sialkot*, 1988 S.C.M.R. 1346.

In contrast, there is little direct evidence of such tensions in the sphere of family life itself, since such difficulties arise and are dealt with in the context of the private, informal, unofficial sphere. It appears that little published research of direct legal relevance exists on such matters at present.[54] Nielsen (1992c, p. 102) emphasises correctly that "Muslims bring with them to Europe a complex of perceptions about the norms of family life" which are in essence rooted in the broad concept of shari'a, based on Qur'anic injunctions, customs, as well as later more formal, legal sources. A handbook on family law and the immigrant communities (Pearl (1986a)) advised generally that the importance of the informal sphere should never be underestimated. Many of the legal conflicts discussed here are therefore not officially visible, as solutions are negotiated, informally and from case to case, within the conceptual framework of shari'a, which does not require, and does not include, recourse to the dispute settlement fora of the respective state. In other words, the central area of Muslim family law remains firmly anchored within the private so-called extra-legal sphere.

The position of the Muslim wife

7–131 In the wider context of feminist debates, human rights discussions and related topics, the rights of Muslim women vis-à-vis men have recently become more of a public issue, a much-discussed subject of growing relevance to legal and ethnic minority studies. We do not propose to enter that debate here in any detail.[55] It is noticeable, however, that male authors tend not to discuss such issues.[56] At the same time, it is apparent that having moved to Western societies and being exposed to their different value systems, Muslims in Europe and North America find themselves confronted with conflicts which also arose in more traditional circumstances but are now highlighted more prominently by the fact that 'the others' appear to be allowed to do things that Muslim women are not expected, and are often not permitted, to do. Ahsan (1995, p. 21) suggests in this regard that Muslim migrants "were not fully equipped to meet the multipronged challenges of Western society to many aspects of their life, in particular to the institution of the family". This may explain, to some extent, the partly exaggerated concern over the control of Muslim women's movements. It is by now a well-known observation that South Asian British Muslim women often find that their sisters 'back home' appear to be given more freedom than is granted to them in the diaspora situation.

7–132 Given the delicate nature of sexual relations, it is not surprising that the existing literature does not say much on the subject under the present heading and that this issue remains invisible to the law. Only rather vague references will be found here and there, barely indicating the potential for, and the reality of, huge stresses and tensions. Thus, in an interesting book on Pakistanis in Europe one finds a brief article on the problems of women and young people. Malik (1982a, p. 79) states:

"Contrary to the permissive society of the West, religion and cultural values prohibit Pakistani women from observing total freedom in dress, diet and behaviour. Their problems and difficulties in Western society are wide and of various natures."

---

[54] For a very brief overview see Ahsan (1995), pp. 21–28.
[55] For details see Sahgal and Yuval-Davis (1992); Knott and Khokher (1993); Afshar (1995). An insightful study based on fieldwork is Mirza (1989).
[56] For example Ahsan (1995) does not mention the issue of wifely obedience.

Similarly, at page 81, Mrs Malik states that "the much freer relations between the sexes in this country" are a matter of surprise and shock to Pakistani parents. It appears that this is as far as we can go in the present discussion. No specific writing appears to exist on the sexual relationship of Muslim spouses and the husband's right to control the wife in this respect. Problems in this regard would be hidden issues in petitions for divorce, for example, and are unlikely to be raised explicitly. However, sometimes it is part of the strategy of one of the litigants to destroy the other party's reputation (*izzat*), in which case wild allegations about sexual deviations may be brought. An instructive and relevant case in this respect is *Seemi v. Seemi* [1990] 140 N.L.J. 747, referred to by Poulter (1995, p. 83) as an example of the flexibility of English law in taking account of the religious and cultural background of litigants. In this case, a young Muslim woman argued successfully that she had been falsely accused by her former husband of not having been a virgin on the wedding night. She was awarded £20,000 in damages for slander and Poulter (1995, p. 83) rightly comments that the size of this award reflects the seriousness of the slur on the family in view of the values of the community (see also Edwards (1990)). In such situations, some men resort to murder. The potential for some very instructive research on such 'honour killings' in Britain must be stressed.[57] Such work would also be relevant for the topic immediately below.

Female obedience and male authority

7–133   Beyond the intimate sphere of sexuality, old and new tensions are bound to arise over the element of female obedience. In today's parlance, the issue of domestic violence is clearly relevant in this context but we cannot explore this in the present study. An English court will perhaps rarely come to hear of such problems. The issue will probably be hidden away under the catch-all rubric of 'unreasonable behaviour' in divorce proceedings. There is the potential, however, for full expert evidence to be brought before the court, in which case an English court might agree to consider the Muslim law principles. This does not appear to have happened so far with specific reference to the husband's right to control his wife's movements.

7–134   Pearl (1986a, p. 35) provided examples of stipulations in a Muslim marriage contract and indicated that "terms in the contract dealing with the right of the wife to visit parents and friends will be very relevant when considering the question of whether the husband is guilty of unreasonable behaviour".[58] An English court in this situation would do well to take account of the religious and cultural practices of Muslim litigants, but the obvious risk is that traditional male-dominated concepts might predominate over more liberal concepts. There are certainly dangers in using Muslim legal concepts, for precisely what is the position of Muslim law on the husband's right to control over his wife's movements? We saw in paragraphs 7–03 and 7–38, above that the position is not simply that the wife has to be unconditionally obedient and that the husband has some kind of absolute right. As always, much depends on the facts and circumstances of the case, and the scope for arguments is huge. It is doubtful whether many Muslim spouses would want to spend valuable resources to clarify what are essentially points of social arrangement in an English court of law.

---

[57] Such cases, from Jordan and Pakistan, have been reported in the press recently.
[58] Welchman (1992) and (1994) shows in detail how stipulations in modern Muslim marriage contracts reflect social change and the changing needs of women. Of particular relevance here is growing evidence of stipulations designed to allow the wife to continue her studies.

7-135 The social problems in this regard are well-known and have been documented in the literature, some of which has been cited above. Malik (1982, p. 79) drew a distinction between women born in Pakistan who came to the West, experienced "cultural shock" and often continue to suffer immense isolation, and Muslim women born and raised in the West who run the risk of being confused and of acquiring "shattered personalities".[59] As for the younger Muslim women, Malik (1982, pp. 79–80) writes:

> "They live in two different worlds; in schools everything under the sun is allowed to be discussed freely, whereas at home, orders are given and expected to be obeyed without objection. They are supposed to behave like an ideal good Pakistani girl at home, without really knowing how an ideal Pakistani girl should behave.
>
> But owing to their Western school education they are not submissive; they reason and argue. The result is tension at home . . .
>
> One of the common complaints of these girls, brought up in Great Britain, is that they are denied the right to receive higher education or good professional training. They argue that according to the Qur'an and the Sunnah, it is incumbent on every Muslim man and woman to seek knowledge. No one has yet convinced them that Muslim men and women have different duties to perform and that they should be trained to fulfil their obligations separately and independently."

Discussing the restrictions faced by Muslim girls growing up in Britain, Malik (1982, p. 80) raised a further point of relevance. She clearly identified that parents are much more permissive about the behaviour of young men and observed:

> "The girls are also irritated at the fact that their parents have double standards, one for boys and one for girls. It appears that this would not be accepted by the second generation of Pakistani girls being brought up in the U.K.
>
> . . . Even before marriage, boys are allowed much freedom and their behaviour is less subject to scrutiny, but girls do not receive the same treatment."

As a result, observes Malik ((1982), p. 80), "some Pakistani women have also started to argue that they should have the same rights and privileges as men have, in all walks of life". If such well-known arguments were to be brought before an English court, they would probably be supported on the basis that the litigants are governed by English law and that Muslim law has, in the United Kingdom, become a matter of cultural practice rather than legal principle in this respect.

7-136 Some Muslim women have tried to use the argument of female subordination in English courts to their advantage, relying on their supposedly dependent and restricted status to explain why a particular act was done. We have already seen, in Chapter 3, above, that such arguments are unlikely to succeed in most situations, but they may represent mitigating circumstances in criminal proceedings. Thus, in *R. v. Bibi* [1980] 1 W.L.R. 1193, the Court of Appeal reduced a Muslim widow's sentence for her involvement in smuggling drugs on the ground

---

[59] This phrase is used at p. 79. While this kind of assumption, that young people are lost somewhere 'between two cultures' is now widely treated as outdated (see in particular Ballard (1994), discussed in Chap. 3, above), it remains a fact that not every young Muslim is, or would want to be, a 'skilled cultural navigator'.

that, as a Muslim woman who led a completely secluded life and was under the control of her male relatives, she was entitled to recognition of her special circumstances. However, this does not amount to an explicit recognition by English law of Muslim conceptualisations of female obedience.

The Muslim dower and English law

7–137 Several writers indicate that this is a matter of considerable legal relevance in Britain, too.[60] While English lawyers and judges still appear to know very little about the various manifestations of South Asian dowry problems and their potentially grave consequences for women,[61] the concept of the Muslim dower has actually been the subject of litigation, and a higher level of judicial knowledge and official cognisance may be presumed on this subject. Pearl (1986a, p. 32) reiterates the importance of *mahr* as an element of Muslim marriage law and discusses its features, including reference to some prominent Bangladeshi customs in this respect.

7–138 Pearl (1972a, p. 133) referred to English cases which had considered the Muslim law relating to dower.[62] The most prominent case is *Shahnaz v. Rizwan*.[63] The parties in this case had been married under Muslim law in India on January 21, 1955, and a deferred *mahr* had been agreed, evidenced by a marriage contract. The wife in this case, following her divorce given by the husband and documented on November 16, 1959, had brought an action in contract for the recovery of £1,400, the sterling equivalent of her *mahr*. Since this was a Muslim marriage, and therefore a potentially polygamous union, Winn J. had to consider in some detail whether the wife's action could be heard at all.[64] He preferred to treat the wife's case as a contractual rather than a matrimonial matter and said, at page 400:

> ". . . what is being sought to be enforced here is a contract entered into in contemplation of, by reason of, and – as has been said in at least one decided case, though I doubt if it be very accurate – in consideration of a marriage which was indeed polygamous."[65]

Since it was obvious from the evidence that the right to dower is a right in action, enforceable by a civil action and well-recognised in Indian law, the judge found himself satisfied that he could deal with the wife's case on that basis, holding at page 401:

> "This right is far more closely to be compared with a right of property than a matrimonial right or obligation, and I think that, upon the true analysis of it, it is a right *ex contractu*, which, while it can in the nature of things only arise in connection with a marriage by Mohammedan law (which is *ex hypothesi*

---

[60] Relevant details are found in Poulter (1986), pp. 40–42; 127 and 129; Pearl (1986a), pp. 32–37; Gordon (1988), pp. 23–24 and 207; Hason (1998); Poulter (1998).

[61] For some, not very clear, indications see Poulter (1986), pp. 40–41. Gordon (1988), p. 24, mentions *jahez* as presents which should belong to the wife but effectively says nothing about the dowry problem. The topic is not even mentioned by Ahsan (1995), obviously because it is not a matter of Muslim law, although Muslims also engage in dowry abuses, as a recent, unreported case from North England confirms.

[62] Whether one calls this *mahr, mehr* or *mehar* is really immaterial, but see the struggles of Winn J. in *Shahnaz v. Rizwan* [1965] 1 Q.B.D. 390, at 395. See also Hason (1998).

[63] [1965] 1 Q.B.D. 390; [1964] 2 All E.R. 993; [1964] 3 W.L.R. 1506.

[64] This part of the judgment is not relevant for our present discussion. For details see, however, para. 8–91, below.

[65] Readers will note how the confusions over the word 'consideration' are also reflected in the English case law.

polygamous), it is not a matrimonial right. It is not a right from the marriage but is a right in personam, enforceable by the wife or widow against the husband or his heirs."

7–139 A further comment by the learned judge on why he should decide this matter arose from the fact that in an earlier case on dowry, involving Greek law, it had been held that an English court should leave complicated matters of foreign law to the overseas jurisdiction. Winn J. emphasised the need for English courts to take up the challenge of dealing with Muslim law cases and thus threw out the husband's case completely, saying at page 401–402:

"As a matter of policy, I would incline to the view that, there being now so many Mohammedans resident in this country, it is better that the court should recognise in favour of women who have come here as a result of a Mohammedan marriage the right to obtain from their husband what was promised to them by enforcing the contract and payment of what was so promised, than that they should be bereft of those rights and receive no assistance from the English courts."

Following this important case, in *Qureshi v. Qureshi* [1971] 2 W.L.R. 518, a Muslim wife was awarded what was then a quite substantial sum of money by the President of the Family Division, on the ground that she was better off with this sum of money than a meaningless status of wife in a limping marriage. It was held, at page 540:

". . . it is only if the marriage is recognised as dissolved that the wife is entitled to dower. Whatever the judgment of this court, the husband will not return to the wife. I trust that it will not be thought cynical if I feel that she is really better off with a judgment for a considerable sum of money, which is likely to be more easily enforceable while the husband is in this country, than with a largely meaningless right to be recognised locally as his wife. Lastly, the rule of foreign law under which the husband has proceeded has the authority of the holy scriptures of the common faith of himself and the wife."

In this case, the institution of dower was virtually taken as judicially known and the absence of subsequent case reports may be taken as an indication that *Shahnaz v. Rizwan* is applied as the law on the subject. It is not known how many such actions are being brought by Muslim women in Britain today, although Hason (1998) refers to a particularly interesting case.

7–140 The two cases which have been reported confirm that some Muslim husbands in Britain will seek to avoid honouring their obligations in terms of *mahr*. The husbands in the two reported cases used intricate arguments to defend themselves against the actions of their former wives but were not successful. The case law shows that English courts will give judgment in favour of the wife, who can now claim any *mahr* dues through English court proceedings. In view of such evidence, it should at least be asked whether the absence of any further case law is not to some extent due to pressure being placed on Muslim wives, or ex-wives as the case may be, not to approach English courts for relief of this kind. It appears that research is needed on this matter, since there is growing evidence that the operation of Muslim divorce procedures in Britain is being used to divest Muslim women of dower claims (see now Carroll (1997a)). The manner in which this is done is to encourage the wife to ask for divorce – with the effect that she loses her entitlement to dower. We discuss this further in paragraph 9–235, below.

7–141　In the two reported cases, the contractual status of the wife's dower entitlement was not really in question. Pearl (1972a, p. 134) distinguished this scenario from the situation where a dower had not been specified at the time of the marriage ceremony. As we saw, in that situation Muslim law implies the agreement of a 'proper' dower, determined on the basis of the social status of the wife and her relatives (see also Pearl (1986a), pp. 33–34). In 1972, the argument was that "there would appear to be no reason why the courts should deny jurisdiction to declare on the rights relating to the dower solely because the sum is unspecified" (Pearl (1972a), p. 134). In view of some doubts whether the court would asssume jurisdiction to assess the amount of the 'proper' dower (Pearl (1972a), p. 135), the advice was, similarly, that the English courts should assume jurisdiction. In line with the comments of Winn J. in *Shahnaz v. Rizwan*, the positive approach at that time was, therefore, even more open, to the extent that "English courts should become slightly more adventurous in the determination of issues involving concepts unknown to English law" (Pearl (1972a), p. 142).

7–142　We have seen in Chapter 4, above, how since the mid-1970s this earlier phase of multicultural legal exploration in English law has been fundamentally changed by restrictive legislation. It is likely that the official invisibility of legal actions among Muslims over dower payments today is at least partly a consequence of this more negative approach. It may be possible to argue that dower arrangements simply fall within section 25 of the Matrimonial Causes Act 1973. The question whether in a marriage contract, where no *mahr* is mentioned, an English court will enforce the wife's claim, will almost certainly elicit a negative answer (Pearl (1986a), p. 34). On the other hand, it has been asked what an English court would decide if a Muslim couple marrying in England had a marriage contract which stipulates that no *mahr* should be paid (Pearl (1986a), p. 34–35). In this case, it is probable that the English court would accept this contract for what it says, and would not apply the Muslim law rule that a 'proper' dower was due to the wife.

7–143　Today, especially in view of the evidence that Muslims in Britain have been developing *angrezi shariat*, which also involves dower arrangements,[66] including purposely inflated dowers to protect the woman from quick divorce, there would appear to be even stronger arguments for English courts to get involved in matters of Muslim law, if they are brought before the judicial forum.

7–144　Actually, this is not a new issue. Pearl (1986a, p. 33) indicated with reference to disputes about dowry and other presents that occasionally there may be difficulties over such litigation in the English courts. The advice given was that if *jahez* is in dispute on the termination of a marriage, it is likely that the district judge will pay only scant regard to the legal entitlement and that it would be far better to resolve the matter outside the court. With regard to stipulations of unrealistically high sums of *mahr* the advice was that "the presumption must be that the amount inserted in the contract was the amount to be paid unless there is evidence to the contrary" (Pearl (1986a), p. 34). Such comments reinforce the widespread view among British Muslims today that the English courts probably lack sufficient cultural insight and detailed knowledge of Muslim law to be able to adjudicate on matters that involve difficult issues of Muslim law and cultural practice.

---

[66] It has also been reported that payment of dower among North African Muslims in France continues to be a part of the marriage proceedings, while other elements are weakening. For details see No. 1097 [November 15, 1986] *Hommes et Migrations*, referred to in No. 38 [June 30, 1987] of *News of Muslims in Europe*.

Maintenance

7-145   On this important topic, there is virtual silence as far as British Muslims are concerned. Schleifer (1986, p. 67) merely reiterates the traditional Muslim position when she writes:

> "It is an accepted principle in Islam that within the context of marriage the father is fully responsible for the *nafaqah* (support) of his wife, whether she is the mother of his child or not, and whether she is rich or poor."

Given the debates in South Asia about the maintenance rights for divorced Muslim wives, however, there are bound to be important, more or less hidden repercussions for English legal practice. In *Shahnaz v. Rizwan*, at page 401, Winn J. clearly, and of course very rightly, distinguished dower from maintenance, so there is some judicial knowledge of these topics and it is somewhat surprising that such matters have not attained a higher profile. There are several possible reasons for this.

7-146   First, the presence of a developed social security system has contributed to this silence. The impression one gets is that there was no perceived conflict between Muslim assumptions that a divorcing husband has an obligation to maintain his former wife only until the end of the *iddat* period and the English welfare state's readiness to foot the bill after that time, if not in fact before. There appears to be no research at all on how *iddat* arrangements are being made in Britain. Ahsan (1995, pp. 24–25) discusses *iddat* as an important problem area for British Muslims, but seems only concerned about female chastity and the undoubtedly important issue of ascertaining paternity in case the divorced wife or the widow is pregnant. Interestingly, Ahsan (1995, p. 25) confirms that "during the waiting period, the wife is entitled to have full maintenance from the husband or members of his family". We saw in paragraph 7–75, above, how differently Indian/Bangladeshi and Pakistani Muslim law have developed in this respect and have analysed the underlying social concepts. In Britain, where the majority of Muslims are Pakistanis of various descriptions, the view that the wife's natal family has a role to play in maintaining the divorced wife or the widow (see page 212, above) has probably been modified by the impact of the welfare state.

7-147   In the context of divorce, Ahsan (1995, p. 24) writes that Islam "exhorts the husband to be especially generous towards the wife" and that he "should not take back from her whatsoever he has given her 'even if it be a heap of gold' (Qur'an, 4:20)". This statement, apart from being rather idealistic, also avoids the critical issue of post-*iddat* maintenance for divorced wives. It appears, therefore, that we have no clear response on this subject from official spokespersons of Muslims in Britain and no evidence from decided cases about how Muslim spouses in Britain handle this particular consequence of a marriage.

Property

7-148   We have already seen that the idealistic statements about the equality of men and women in Islam relate to equality before God rather than socio-economic equality. Similarly, the independent property rights of women in Muslim law are a conceptual fact but are not always transposed into social reality. Again, there is extremely little academic comment on this subject in relation to Britain, although some research appears to be in progress.

7-149   In practice, it is often difficult for Muslim women, especially South Asian women, to assert that they are *sui juris* and are not the property of men. Writing on the problems of Pakistani women in Britain, Malik (1982, p. 80) found it "a matter of great regret that, even today, women in our society are considered as second-class citizens and as the property of men". She further argued that "Islam gives the right to women to earn money and possess property but in practice it is usually denied" (*id.*). She clearly saw this as the root cause of many problems between young Muslim women and their families.

7–150   Pearl (1986a, pp. 29–30) discussed this problem, emphasising that the family plays a key role in any disputes over property, for a number of interconnected reasons:

> "Indeed, the very presence of the extended family will often impose on the legal adviser an obligation to attempt to resolve the dispute over the chattels if at all possible outside the court. Advisers should realize that a settlement imposed by a court may well produce unfortunate results extending beyond the problems of the immediate dispute. It may become difficult for other marriages to be arranged; long-term financial arrangements including future marriages may be jeopardized; and so on. In order at least to attempt a settlement without the need to go to court, advisers need to have some familiarity with the various principles relating to dowers, dowries and bridal gifts and the like. The parties should then be able to negotiate an amicable settlement through the good offices of community leaders. Only if this fails will legal proceedings be necessary. If proceedings do take place, the customary rules can be placed before the . . . judge, and proved if possible by an affidavit sworn by a religious or community leader or someone else with knowledge of the practices of the community in question. The . . . judge may take these matters into account, but he is not bound to and, as we have stated, experience is that these matters are usually disregarded."

Here again, then, it is the largely unresearched extra-legal sphere which contains the evidence of how Muslims in Britain negotiate the consequences of a Muslim marriage.

Chapter 8

Polygamy

8–01 It is well-known that polygamy is a controversial issue in Islam (Mehdi (1994), p. 161). This is not only so because of principled objections to polygamy as an institution, but because the classical Muslim position on polygamy itself is not as simple and uncomplicated as is often assumed. It could be said that Muslim law does not simply allow any man polygamous marriages with up to four women unconditionally. The law as classically interpreted did allow men such freedom, although subject to conditions which were not judicially enforceable but related to the individual's conscience. However, it is correct to say that "in Islam, monogamy is a general rule while polygamy is only an exception".[1] Because the conditions in which polygamy is seen as permitted are not strictly circumscribed, the effect has been that the nature and extent of these conditions have become the subject of fiercely contested debates in modern Muslim jurisprudence and in the socio-legal literature.

8–02 Coming out in favour of limited polygamy, rather than purporting to prohibit it altogether, Muslim law, like other non-Western legal systems, has of course put itself in contrast to Christian law and to modern Western legal systems which insist on monogamy as the basic principle, demanding legal separation from an existing wife before any new legal union can be entered into. There has always been ample room for debating whether strict legal monogamy is preferable – and better for women – than a legal scheme which allows for polygamous arrangements in certain situations and on specific conditions. This chapter as a whole shows that most Muslims accept the argument that monogamy should be the norm but remain unwilling to underwrite a total prohibition of polygamous arrangements, perhaps because this would require the toleration of extramarital relations for men in a number of situations. The so-called Western solution to male promiscuity, freely allowing unmarried cohabitation, is seen as a dishonest legal fiction that merely maintains the facade of monogamy.

8–03 By continuing to prohibit and criminalise extra-marital relations while allowing for polygamous arrangements within the concept of *nikah*, official and unofficial Muslim laws in the world today claim to place the requirements of social harmony and order above individualistic human rights arguments. This approach and argumentation, not surprisingly, continues to be contested. At the same time, even in Britain today, Muslims claim the right to arrange polygamous marriages and thus expose themselves to fresh criticism.

Polygamy in classical Muslim law

The foundations

8–04 Before the advent of Islam, unlimited polygamy was a general practice among the Arabian tribes.[2] Thus, it is definitely correct to say that Islam has not

---

[1] Bharatiya (1996), p. 74. The author also asserts (*id.*), somewhat apologetically but probably with much justification, that "neither Islam favours polygamy nor the Muslims prefer polygamous unions".
[2] For some details see Doi (1984), p. 144.

developed polygamy (Bharatiya (1996), p. 76). In fact, relevant Qur'anic verses as interpreted by the first jurists restricted the man's right of polygamy to four concurrent wives, which has been widely seen as "an achievement of a high order, a definite step towards the amelioration of the harsh lot of woman and a definite advancement in the then prevailing juristic thought" (Diwan and Diwan (1991), p. 43). It has been said of Mohammed that:

> "The Prophet was not an impractical visionary who simply made high-sounding moral pronouncements. It was a central function of the Prophet and his mission, after having made these moral pronouncements, to be effective in society and to move it in a certain direction. In other words, the Prophet was a seer-cum-reformer. But at any given time a reformer, however zealous, cannot change society beyond a certain point." (Rahman (1966), p. 418.)

Whether this limited recognition of polygamy is perceived as appropriate today is a different matter. In its own time, this was an important reform, which did take some time to implement.[3] The most relevant Qur'anic text relating to this subject is Sura IV, verse 3:

> "If ye fear that ye shall not
> Be able to deal justly
> With the orphans,
> Marry women of your choice,
> Two, or three, or four;
> But if ye fear that ye shall not
> Be able to deal justly (with them),
> Then only one, or (a captive)
> That your right hands possess.
> That will be more suitable,
> To prevent you
> From doing injustice."

8-05   As a result of this fairly ambiguous Qur'anic foundation,[4] evidence from the Sunna and massive support from *ijma* in the form of juristic consensus, all schools, Sunni and Shia, are agreed that a Muslim man can have up to four wives at the same time, subject to certain conditions.[5] It is the nature of those conditions which has been heavily contested. Hinchcliffe (1970, p. 13) emphasised that the restriction in terms of equitable treatment "was construed as a matter for a man's own conscience, not as establishing a condition precedent for a polygamous marriage". Thus, the general and unanimous position of all schools is that a Muslim man does not require permission from anyone to enable him to contract a second or subsequent marriage up to a maximum of four. Polygamy in classical Muslim law, therefore, is a matter of conscience and, as many critics of this system would say, convenience and male discretion. It needs hardly be emphasised that no corresponding right was given to Muslim women.[6]

---

[3] Several authors relate *hadith* accounts of early Muslims who had large numbers of wives and were told to restrict themselves to four.

[4] For example, it was interpreted by the Tunisians in the 1950s to amount to a prohibition on polygamy.

[5] Nasir (1990a), p. 66; Nasir (1990b), p. 24; Doi (1984), pp. 144–145; Malik (1988), pp. 57–58. The Shias make an allowance for any number of temporary wives under the concept of *muta* marriage. Various restrictions on who can be a partner in marriage apply, as discussed in various parts of para. 6–02, above. See also Hinchcliffe [1970] 1 No. 3 *Islam and the Modern Age* 14.

[6] On this see Diwan and Diwan (1991), p. 44, and n.13.

8–06 The requirement in Sura IV, verse 3, as cited above, to treat the two or more wives equally is construed, again by all schools, as a requirement to be decided upon by the husband himself. It is his responsibility to treat the wives equally and he has no need to submit himself to examination by any person or institution in advance of the final decision to contract a second or subsequent marriage. Whether this moral injunction – for so it was interpreted – to treat up to four wives equally relates only to *nafaqa* (material support and maintenance) or also to equal affection has remained heavily contested.[7] The Qur'an itself appears to suggest that the latter is an impossible task. Sura IV, verse 129 says that "ye shall not be able to deal in fairness and justice between two women however much ye wish". It has therefore been possible to argue, as we shall see, that polygamy was never really allowed in Islam and should consequently be prohibited by modern Muslim law.[8]

8–07 The prevalent view, however, has been all along that polygamy is allowed for Muslim men, albeit within limits, and that equality of financial support is the deciding criterion. Of course, this indicates in several ways that "the traditional law gives only a limited effect to the principle of equal treatment" (Hinchcliffe (1970), p. 14). It also means that the focus of legal attention has shifted to the relative material conditions for wives who are party to a polygamous marriage. In this context Doi (1984, p. 147) writes:

> "Once a Muslim marries more than one wife, it is essential for him to treat them equally in the matter of food, residence, clothing and even in sexual relationship as far as is possible. If one is a little doubtful in showing equal treatment in fulfilling their rights, he must not take more wives. If he feels able to fulfil his responsibilities to only one, he should not marry two."

Hinchcliffe (1970, pp. 14–15) stresses that the legal right of polygamous wives to equal and impartial treatment arises as a consequence of the marriage. The first requirement she highlights is the right to a separate dwelling for each wife.[9] If this is not provided, the wife has a valid ground for refusing to begin cohabitation, and this will not be considered disobedience.[10] There seems to be less agreement among the schools about whether the polygamous husband is obliged to provide all wives with maintenance (*nafaqa*) on exactly the same basis.[11] Doi (1984, p. 149) emphasises the impact of different living standards. Another aspect of equal treatment is the amount of time a polygamous man spends with his wives. This appears to have been a topic of great interest to traditional jurists.[12]

8–08 The legal remedies for women whose husband decides to take a further wife, or for the woman who joins an existing marriage, are limited.[13] Thus, under the traditional rules, still operated in some Muslim countries, as highlighted by Welchman (1988, p. 883),

---

[7] For details see Nasir (1990a), p. 66–67; Nasir (1990b), pp. 24–25; Doi (1984), pp. 147–148. The argument that polygamy is really not permitted by the Qur'an arose well before the 20th century. See Mahmudunnasir [1968] P.L.D. 64 with reference to the third century of Islam.

[8] On some details see Hinchcliffe (1970), p. 14. Traditional writers like Doi (1984), p. 149, vigorously oppose this view.

[9] Welchman (1994) confirms that this remains a matter of major concern for Muslim women today.

[10] Hinchcliffe (1970), p. 15. This leaves open the question whether a wife can, after consummation of the marriage, still withdraw from the society of the husband on this ground. This is a point which relates to the discussion about non-payment of the prompt dower in para. 7–50, above.

[11] For details see Hinchcliffe (1970), p. 15.

[12] See *ibid.*, pp. 15–16; Malik (1988), p. 58.

[13] Notably, Nasir (1990a), p. 66–67, and Nasir (1990b), pp. 24–25, do not contain much detail on polygamy, nor does the author discuss the topic in any depth.

"the only protection a wife may afford herself in Jordanian law is to insert a stipulation in her marriage contract ensuring that she may seek divorce should her husband take another wife."

Hinchcliffe (1970, p. 16) had commented earlier that "for the vast majority of Muslim women who find themselves in this unfortunate situation the law, unhappily, provides no solution whatever". She also provided detailed evidence of how the Sunni schools treat a husband's violation of the promise that he will not marry another wife and concluded, at page 17:

"Thus a non-Maliki wife who reluctantly finds herself a co-wife will have no recourse at all unless her husband has agreed to delegate to her (or to someone acting on her behalf) the right to repudiate herself if he takes a second wife, or if he has himself pronounced a repudiation conditional upon taking a subsequent wife."

If a husband marries a fifth wife, this is an irregular (*fasid*) marriage, invalid but not a complete nullity (Hinchcliffe (1970), p. 17). The various effects flowing from such a marriage show that Muslim law has been concerned to keep this borderline flexible, seeking to protect the woman's status, as well as that of any children of the union.

8–09   There is broad agreement that, in modern times, polygamy has been decreasing, due less to legal restrictions than economic constraints and, as Hinchcliffe (1970, p. 19) argues, more significantly the spread of education, "which has made women less willing to accept a polygamous marriage and husbands less inclined to think such an arrangement desirable".

8–10   As to whether polygamy is a practice unsuitable to the twentieth/twenty-first century, opinions continue to differ. Emphasising that Islam as a world religion "had to look into the requirements of all ages, circumstances, countries and civilizations" (Bharatiya (1996), p. 75), the same author nevertheless claims that "there are certain factors under which polygamy becomes inevitable" (*id.*). These were historically portrayed as a consequence of wars and the presence of many widows and orphans, but also biological and psychological characteristics relating to "certain individuals who have a more active sexual impulse than others" (*id.*) have been adduced to justify polygamy. Similarly, Doi (1984, p. 146) lists eight situations in which polygamy would be "the best solution", including lastly, "if the man feels that he cannot do without a second wife in order to satisfy his natural desire which is very strong and when he has enough means to support her, he should take another wife". The same writer, at page 149, criticises the so-called modernists as 'misguided', a word that appears rather often in this discussion and has also been used against the so-called 'apologists' of limited polygamy.[14] Hinchcliffe (1970, p. 19) also refers to eloquent pleas by eminent Islamic scholars in defence of polygamy.

8–11   There are essentially two factors which have made the issue of polygamy so contentious. First, it is the view of many women's groups, for instance in Pakistan and in Egypt, that the existence in law of the right to take a second wife severely hinders the progress towards the emancipation of Muslim women. Secondly, and as a contrary factor, the orthodox and more conservative sections of the community have been challenged into issuing a continuous stream of

---

[14] For a recent debate on polygamy with an Indian focus see Khan (1989) (1) K.L.T. 47–58; Menski (1990a), Haq [1990] (2) K.L.T. 14–18 and Menski (1991).

apologetics and polemics directed against the antagonism of some Western Orientalists (Hinchcliffe (1970), p. 19). The controversy is all the more unfortunate bearing in mind, as we have seen, that polygamy has been decreasing in all Muslim countries. Indeed, it may well be argued that the introduction of external checks on the system of polygamy in many Muslim countries coincides with a general trend towards monogamy.

8–12   It is also true that restrictions on polygamy which are not accompanied by similar restrictions on the power of a husband to divorce his wife unilaterally can actually work to the disadvantage of women. Is it better to be a discarded and divorced elderly woman, or a respected first wife in a polygamous household?[15] However, those who would wish to reject legislative amendments to the law of polygamy are today in a minority. Indeed, only India, for apparent political reasons, together with Saudi Arabia and Jordan,[16] stand outside the move towards legislative restrictions.

Legal reforms of polygamy

8–13   During the colonial era, many Muslim countries changed their law of personal status and imposed some legal restrictions on polygamy. It is not clear to what extent such legal reforms have actually contributed in restricting the social practice of polygamy. It is certainly correct to argue, however, that such legislative provisions are a step towards abolition of polygamy (Mahmudunnasir (1968), p. 66).

8–14   Several countries, prominently Turkey and Tunisia, appear to have abolished the capacity to contract a second polygamous marriage.[17] Still, whether polygamy has really been outlawed completely may be doubted, since this depends on the approach to marriages contracted in contravention of the relevant provisions.[18] In many other jurisdictions, including Syria, Morocco, Iraq, Iran, Egypt, Algeria, Yemen, Pakistan and Singapore, various restrictions have been introduced by statute.[19] The following extracts from the relevant legislative provisions are in no way complete; they merely serve to illustrate the differing ways in which the problem has been tackled and provide a basis for discussion about the scope for further reforms.[20]

8–15   The Syrian Law of Personal Status of 1953 (Decree No. 59 of 1953) was an early attempt to restrict polygamy.[21] Article 17 of the Code empowered the judge (*qadi*) to refuse permission to a man who is already married to marry another woman, if it is established that he is not in a position to support two wives. It seems therefore that "financial ability appears to be the only criterion in Syria for polygamous marriage" (Hinchcliffe (1970), p. 20).

---

[15] Interesting fieldwork on this question was conducted in Pakistan and is reported in the undated study by Firdous Khanam, discussed in para. 8–50, below.

[16] On the debates in Jordan see Welchman (1988), pp. 883–884.

[17] Turkey did so in 1926. On Tunisia see Hinchcliffe (1970), pp. 26–27.

[18] In Turkey, it appears, polygamous Muslim marriages entered into in violation of the state law remain nevertheless valid in law. See, however, the article by Adnan Guriz in Ansay and Wallace, *Introduction to Turkish law* (1996), which only talks about the official legal position, according to which such a marriage is not valid. For Tunisia, which changed its law in this respect in (1964), see further below.

[19] For relevant details see earlier Anderson (1968b), (1971), pp. 8–9 and (1976), as well as Hinchcliffe (1970). Comprehensive up-to-date coverage is now provided by El Alami and Hinchcliffe (1996). On Morocco and Iran, see Mir Hosseini (1993). In Bangladesh, Rabbani J. in *Jesmin Sultana v. Mohammad Elias* (1997) 17 B.L.D. 4 has very recently called for the total prohibition of polygamy.

[20] Appendix IV in Pearl (1979c) reproduced a selection of relevant legislation, much of which is still in place.

[21] For details see Anderson [1955b] Vol. XVIII B.S.O.A.S. 34–49; Hinchcliffe (1970), pp. 20–21; Doi (1984), pp. 149–150.

8–16 Despite their training in Western law, however, as emphasised by Doi ((1984), p. 150), the Syrian jurists did not declare such a marriage invalid if a man simply ignored the law and entered a *nikah* with another woman. Evidently, the *sharia* continues to override state law in this respect. While a second marrriage in contravention of the legal provisions was deemed valid, defaulting men were made liable to penalties. The law also made further provisions to safeguard the legitimacy of the children from such marriages (Hinchcliffe (1970), p. 21).

8–17 The Tunisian Code of Personal Status of 1956 took the Qur'anic provisions in Sura IV, verse 3 as a legal condition precedent to polygamy but went one step further, prohibiting polygamy outright.[22] The Code provided:

> "18. Plurality of wives is prohibited.
>
> Any person who, being already married and before the marriage is lawfully dissolved, marries again, shall be liable to imprisonment for one year or for a fine of 240,000 francs, or to both, even if the second marriage is in violation of any requirements of this law."

Doi (1984, p. 150) discusses this particular reform at some length, reiterating that polygamy is forbidden in Tunisian law and constitutes a criminal offence. The Tunisian jurists, too, took economic criteria as a key element, arguing in essence that since in modern socio-economic conditions impartial treatment of several wives was a practical impossibility, the essential Islamic condition of polygamy was impossible to fulfil. Hinchcliffe (1970, pp. 26–27) explains that public policy arguments were strongly in evidence, with President Bourgiba making declarations to that effect. Here was a country, therefore, which wanted to be modern, while staying within an Islamic framework. The nature of this legal provision has continued to be controversial. Significantly, Tunisia experienced a lively debate about whether to make polygamous marriages invalid, and indeed this was achieved by a legal reform in 1964, which makes Tunisia stand out even more from other Muslim countries.

8–18 The Moroccan Code of Personal Status of 1958,[23] according to Doi (1984, p. 150) took a middle course between Syria and Tunisia and prohibited polygamy when there was any apprehension of unequal treatment. In other words, the initiative for challenging a polygamous arrangement comes not primarily from the court or any other official body, but from the wife or wives concerned. This form of regulation is related to the fact that the Moroccan Law of Personal Status allows a wife to stipulate in her marriage contract that the husband shall not take a second wife and allows her to demand divorce if he violates this condition. This example shows, again, the importance of stipulations in the marriage contract for protecting the position of a Muslim wife against unwanted changes of circumstance at a later date. The relevant earlier law provided as follows:

> "30. Impediments to Marriage
>> (1) If any injustice between the wives is feared, plurality of wives is not permitted.
>> (2) Where a husband contracts a second marriage, and the wife had not stipulated against such an act in the marriage contract, the *Qadi* may consider whether the second marriage has caused any injury to the first wife; marriage with a second wife shall not be contracted unless she is informed that the husband is already married to another woman.

---

[22] For details see Anderson (1958b); Hinchcliffe (1970), pp. 26–27.
[23] For details see Anderson (1958a).

31. A wife may stipulate in the marriage contract that her husband shall not marry a second woman along with her, and if the husband violates such a stipulation she will have a right to seek dissolution of her marriage."

In Moroccan law, there is a provision that a marriage contract for the second or subsequent marriage shall not be drawn up until the new wife has been informed that the husband is already married. This is obviously a legal attempt to ensure that women are provided information about the polygamous arrangement *before* they enter the marriage. The existing wife was further sought to be protected, in accordance with principles of traditional Maliki law, which allowed such a wife to claim divorce, if she was not given proper maintenance. The courts of Morocco could therefore grant a polygamously married woman a divorce on grounds of unequal treatment, perhaps also based on the argument that entering a polygamous marriage constituted injury to the wife (Hinchcliffe (1970), p. 29).

8–19 In 1993, this area of the law was slightly reformed, adding the requirement that the existing wife should be informed that her husband is intending to take another wife.[24] In addition, the courts appear to have been given a larger role in assessing when a polygamous union should not be permitted.

8–20 The Iraqi Law of Personal Status, 1959 also did not prohibit polygamy but imposed some restrictions, similar to Syrian law.[25] The law provided in Article 3, in essence, that it is not permissible for a man to marry more than one woman without authorisation from a judge, who will not grant such permission unless he is satisfied that the husband can fulfil three conditions. These are, first, that he is financially capable of supporting an additional wife and secondly that some lawful benefit is found for the husband in such a marriage. Thirdly, the Qadi will also not give permission unless he was satisfied that there was no fear of any unequal treatment of the wives. The relevant provisions are found in Article 3, clauses 4–6 of the Law:

"(4) Marriage with more than one wife is not permissible except with the permission of the Qadi and the granting of such permission shall depend on the following conditions:
  (a) the husband's financial position should be sound enough to have more than one wife, and
  (b) any lawful interest . . . should be involved.
(5) Where injustice between the wives is feared, plurality is not permissible, and determination of this fact is left to the *Qadi*.
(6) All those who enter into a contract of marriage with more than one woman in contravention of clauses (4) and (5) shall be liable to imprisonment for a period not exceeding one year, or to a fine not exceeding hundred dinars, or to both."

Clause 6 details the penalties for men who fail to comply with these legal provisions. Hinchcliffe (1970, p. 21) outlines details of the procedures to be followed and highlights that no detailed guidance is provided for how to construe 'lawful benefit' or how to assess unequal treatment. In Iraq, it is possible to argue that the presence of a sick or barren first wife is a valid ground. Similar requirements exist in Algeria by virtue of the Family Code of 1984, under which a

---

[24] This, for example, is also the rule in Pakistan, under s.6, M.F.L.O. 1961 (see para. 8–50, below). Whether such provisions will be vigorously enforced in Morocco remains to be seen. Examination of material from two Moroccan courts, produced by Mir Hosseini (1993), seems to suggest that the protective provisions of the earlier law have not been rigorously implemented.
[25] For details see Anderson (1960a) and (1963); Hinchcliffe (1970), pp. 21–23.

man who wishes to take a second wife must establish a clear and genuine need. The court will grant him such permission if it is satisfied of such need, and further if there is evidence that the man is able and willing to treat the wives and children with equality. The first wife may obtain a divorce on the sole ground of the husband's second marriage.[26]

8-21 When it comes to determining whether a wife would have a case for claiming unequal treatment, Hinchcliffe (1970, p. 22) points out that the testimony of the husband usually goes unchallenged. This does not, then, constitute a very effective safeguard against chauvinistic male discretion in simply choosing another wife. It appears to be difficult for women who become party to a polygamous marriage against their will to get out of this arrangement.[27] The legal validity of polygamous marriages contracted in violation of the law has also been a matter of concern in Iraq. Hinchcliffe (1970, p. 23) points to important evidence in this regard which goes the other way than in Tunisia:

> "The 1959 Law took the radical step of declaring such marriages invalid. However, the 1963 Amendment expunged the clause "marriage with more than one wife without permission of the court" from the list of temporary impediments to a valid marriage. The result is that a polygamous marriage without the *qadi's* permission is no longer invalid *per se*, although . . . it gives rise to penal sanctions."

Regarding *muta* marriages among Shias in Iraq, the play with words about legal validity is equally interesting. Instead of *batil* or *fasid*, the term 'without validity' (*gahyr sahih*) has been used, obviously protecting the offspring of such unions against total loss of status.

8-22 The Jordanian Law of Family Rights 1951, amended in 1976, now called the Jordanian Law of Personal Status, did not provide Muslim wives any other remedy against polygamy than to rely on stipulations in the marriage contract.[28] The Jordanians adopted the prevalent Hanbali doctrine that a stipulation in the marriage contract restricting the husband to one wife is valid and if the husband violates the stipulation the wife has a right to seek a judicial dissolution. The relevant Article 21 is now Article 19(1) and is self-explanatory:

> "If a stipulation is made in the marriage contract for the benefit of either party, it must be complied with, e.g. a stipulation that the wife should have the power to divorce herself in specified circumstances or should live in a specified place or that the husband should not have a co-wife. But such a stipulation can be enforced only if it is incorporated in the registered marriage-deed and also in the certificate by the Qadi. Violation of such a stipulation shall give to the wife a right to seek dissolution of marriage."

The Family Protection Act 1967 in Iranian law was seen as a most radical reform in family law in the Muslim world.[29] While its key provision was to take away the husband's right to unilateral repudiation, the Act also placed restrictions on polygamy. The relevant section provided:

---

[26] For information on Algeria see Hinchcliffe (1970), p. 34; Mahmood (1983–1984).

[27] For details see Hinchcliffe (1970), p. 23.

[28] *ibid.*, p. 32. For details on Jordanian law see now Welchman (1988), (1992) and (1994) and El Alami and Hinchcliffe (1996).

[29] For details see Hinchcliffe (1968b) and (1970), pp. 25–26. The (1967) Act, later consolidated into the Family Protection Act 1975, was repealed under the new regime. On more recent developments see Ibrahim and Bakar (1980); El Alami and Hinchcliffe (1996).

"14. If a husband wishes to marry another woman, he must seek permission of the Court to do so. The Court shall give such permission after it satisfies itself, through all necessary measures including examination of the existing wife, regarding the financial capability of the husband and his capacity to do justice. If a person, without obtaining the Court's permission, contracts a second marriage, he shall be punishable with the penalty laid down in Article 5 of the Marriage Law of 1310–1316 (1931–1937)."

Again, if a man contracted a second marriage without permission from the court, the marriage would be valid, but the man would be liable to a sentence of imprisonment not exceeding two years. Hinchcliffe (1970, pp. 25–26) noted that a wife who had not consented to the marriage could ask for divorce.

8–23 In Egypt, there have been fierce debates about the need for reform of polygamy since the 1920s, with unsuccessful attempts to legislate on the matter in 1929, then in the 1940s and the early 1950s.[30] Egyptian law still does not support the complaining polygamously married wife, unless she can establish ill-treatment. Hinchcliffe (1970, p. 33) argued that failure to treat a wife on a par with a co-wife could be construed as ill-treatment but emphasised that Egyptian law has not adopted the Maliki doctrine which supports polygamously married wives in their claims for divorce.

8–24 Later Egyptian reforms in 1979 and again in 1985 (Act No. 100 of 1985) on the lines of Moroccan law also remained limited, but appear to be focused on the complaining wife.[31] Evidence of capacity to support the wives has to be provided as well, and the registrar was made responsible for notifying both the first wife and the second wife of each other's existence. The registrar cannot prevent the second marriage, although the first wife has a ground for divorce. This indicates some progress in assisting wives but does not constitute an effective control system.

8–25 Readers are also referred to Article 13 of the Somali Family Law of 1975 and the interesting reforms in Indonesia of the same year.[32] Under the Indonesian legislation, a man may receive permission from a court to contract a second marriage if, and only, if:

"(i)   his wife cannot carry out her conjugal duties, or
(ii)   his wife becomes crippled or terminally ill, or
(iii) his wife cannot give him children, and
    (a) his present wife or wives give him permission,
    (b) his ability to support all his wives and children is certain, and
    (c) his ability to be fair to all his wives and children is certain."

The Somali law also requires prior permission of the court before a second and polygamous marriage can be contracted. Such permission can be contracted on the grounds of (i) medically certified sterility of the wife; (ii) her contagious or chronic ailment which is incurable; (iii) her imprisonment for over two years; and (iv) desertion by the first wife for more than a year. The court can, in addition to these specific grounds, grant permission on the ground of 'social necessity'. Again, this shows that the legal system provided a plethora of grounds for men to argue that they should be allowed to have more than one wife.[33]

---

[30] For some details see Hinchcliffe (1970), p. 20 and 33; Nasir (1990a), p. 67; Nasir (1990b), p. 25–26.
[31] For relevant details see also Nasir (1990b), pp. 25–26; Nasir (1990a), pp. 67–68.
[32] On Somalia see Mahmood (1982b), p. 253–254. On Indonesia Katz and Katz (1975). Reforms in several other countries are discussed by Hinchcliffe (1970) and Anderson (1968b).
[33] The Somalian Law 23 of January 11, 1975 was reproduced in Pearl (1979b), pp. 256–305.

8-26 It is apparent that the various reforms in the Muslim world do not amount to a complete ban on polygamy. They are educative reforms, measures of social engineering rather than social control. They are also incomplete since husbands continue to benefit from the discretionary elements in the respective laws and women are not protected from men who simply wish to 'enjoy' several women by rotation. It could, of course, be argued that no legal system can achieve that aim anyway, and that this has nothing to do with Muslim law. It is a fact, though, that Muslim husbands justify their choice in favour of polygamy by arguments phrased in terms of *shari'a*.

8-27 Hinchcliffe (1970, p. 35) emphasised that giving polygamously married women a right to divorce is not really that helpful and seems to suggest that curbs on the husband's unilateral power to divorce would be more useful. This is a difficult issue. Would a husband, faced with a law which seriously and fully outlaws and invalidates any polygamous marriage and does not permit easy divorce really stick to his existing wife? The argument advanced by many Muslim scholars has been that such men, if not allowed to be polygamous, would start extra-marital relationships, so it is better to avoid *zina* and to allow for limited polygamy. Another way to look at this problem, less male-centred, is to emphasise that easy divorce rules without a legal right to polygamy would lead to a large pool of divorced women, many of whom are presumably either infertile, ill, or in some form unsuited to full marital life. Muslim writers appear to have deep fears about such a scenario. These are rarely voiced directly, but come out in phantasising criticisms of Western societies with roaming millions of abandoned women and deviant children.[34]

8-28 Much of the existing older writing on polygamy lacks clarity and depth. Some Muslim writing simply emphasises the charitable nature of Muslim polygamy.[35] Doi (1984, pp. 151–153) considers the conflict between Qur'anic injunctions and the legal reforms in various countries and argues that the countries which have prohibited polygamy by law have actually gone against the injunctions of the Qur'an, Sunna and other authoritative sources. In his view, it is a violation of the *shari'a* provisions on polygamy that a husband in several countries has to justify his decision before an official body (Doi (1984), p. 153). An Indian Muslim author, Siddiqi (1980, p. 117), takes a more balanced view:

"... the permission given by the Qur'an for polygamy arose out of particular circumstances. Since these circumstances are likely to recur now and then in the life of the Muslim community and since there will always be individual cases where polygamy may become necessary in order to avoid more serious moral and social evils, it is not right to prohibit polygamy by legislation. But since the Qur'an has made it conditional on a just and equal treatment of the wives, it is open to the State to prescribe conditions under which polygamy will be allowed. For example, it may be laid down that polygamy will be allowed only if a person shows sufficient cause for it and satisfies the authorities that he will be able to bear the additional economic burden and will not thereby injure his health."

---

[34] For examples see Khan [1972] P.L.D. 6, and Haq (1990). See also Khan, *Women between Islam and Western society* (1995) p. 190 in the context of one of the most recent attempts to justify Islamic polygamy.

[35] This relates first of all to the example of the Prophet, early battle scenarios and the need to take care of war widows and orphans. For a detailed analysis and examples of the Prophet's life see Khan (1972). For a recent discussion about polygamy as a social welfare institution in India see Haq (1990) and Menski (1991) (2) K.L.T. 20–24.

As for the effects of the legal abolition of polygamy, Doi (1984, p. 153) confirms that there is a dearth of empirical evidence about whether the prohibition of polygamy has actually served as a deterrent. He argues that the reforms have not been useful, driving men into secret extra-marital relations instead of allowing them the peaceful enjoyment of polygamy. There is clearly not enough academic legal writing which emphasises the voices of women in this context.

Muslim polygamy in South Asia

8–29 Some Indian Muslim writers have come out in open, vocal defence of polygamy (see Khan (1989); Haq (1990); Khan (1995)). Several South Asian and British Muslim writers criticise the hypocrisy of outlawing polygamy while tolerating extramarital relationships or living together outside wedlock.[36]

8–30 The modern South Asian, secular view of the law considers polygamy, at best, as an institution 'to be tolerated but not encouraged' (Malik (1988), p. 57), a phrase borrowed from the leading Indian case on the subject, *Itwari v. Asghari*, A.I.R. 1960 Al. 684. The three major South Asian jurisdictions covered here have taken quite different paths towards getting that basic message across, so the legal systems of India, Pakistan and Bangladesh look quite different in formal terms, especially as regards case law. In social reality, however, South Asian women anywhere are not well-protected today against men who use polygamy as a convenient arrangement that suits them, rather than the women concerned. The test will be whether a woman who objects to becoming part of a polygamous arrangement will be given any support by the respective official legal system. As we saw with regard to classical Muslim law, academic writing on polygamy is somewhat undeveloped, legal analysis sparse, up-to-date statistics are not really available,[37] and even the case law on this subject does not have much to say, for the simple basic message is that polygamous Muslim marriages in the subcontinent continue to remain legally valid marital unions under Muslim law as well as the respective state law.

Indian law

8–31 There has been no direct legislative reform of Muslim personal law in India on the subject of polygamy. Within the framework of a secular law, some middle-class Muslims in the large urban areas have got used to marrying, or rather to registering their existing Muslim marriages, under the procedure laid down by the Special Marriage Act 1954 (as amended in 1976), thereby invoking a monogamous regime on the union.[38] However, the majority of Muslims still solemnise their marriages in the classical religious form, prepare documentation like a *nikahnama*, but are not subjecting their marriages to the modern state law, which in turn has accepted the *shariat* rules as the basis for the operative Indian law. Muslim marriages in India are, therefore, potentially polygamous, and the husband may, subject to conditions stipulated by the wife, make arrangements for polygamy

---

[36] See in particular Mahmood (1986), pp. 115–117; for Britain see Ahsan (1995), p. 26. Doi (1984), p. 148, quotes Billy Graham to the effect that Christian countries make a great show of monogamy but actually practise polygamy, which makes Islam a fundamentally honest religion in this respect.

[37] In line with several earlier reports, an article in the *Hindustan Times* of October 14, 1997, claims that a substantial number of Indian men get around the law to practise polygamy. Interestingly, the sample figures given show a much lower rate of polygamy for Muslims (15 per 1000 men) than for non-Muslims (72 per 1000 men).

[38] See Hinchcliffe (1970), p. 29, indicating the growth of this practice among Muslims in Bombay.

over which the wife has, legally, very little control, unless she has put relevant stipulations into her marriage contract.

8–32 In one curious case, a Muslim husband had registered his second marriage under the provisions of the Special Marriage Act 1954. He had thus become subject to criminal penalties as a bigamist and his defence was not accepted.[39] This case is useful for the insight it provides into the approach which Indian Muslims take to secular law; it also illustrates current judicial and popular attitudes towards polygamy.

8–33 Malik (1988, p. 58) points to some early Indian case law on the question whether the Muslim husband's right to polygamy is a fundamental right. This became, during the late 1940s and early 1950s, an important issue in Indian law, since the reformers of modern Hindu law at that time abolished the Hindu male's right to polygamy and outlawed and criminalised it completely.[40] Up to the present day, there is implied and often explicit resentment among Hindus and others, including judges,[41] that Indian Muslims continue to have the right to arrange polygamous unions, while other Indians in the same situation would be criminalised.[42]

8–34 In *Badruddin v. Aisha Begum*, 1957 A.L.J. 300, a Muslim wife's suit for separate maintenance after her husband had contracted a second marriage, the husband challenged the wife's right under section 488 of the Criminal Procedure Code 1898 on the ground that it violated his freedom of religion, *i.e.* his basic right to be polygamous. This, so his argument, was guaranteed under Article 25 of the Indian Constitution of 1950. The husband relied on an earlier Supreme Court judgment which had held that not only religious opinion, *i.e.* belief, but also acts done in pursuance of religion were protected by that Article of the Constitution. Oak J. was quick to repel that argument and held, at page 301:

> "I do not agree. It may be that under the Personal Law of Muslims a Muslim may have as many as four wives. But I do not think that, having more than one wife is a part of religion. No authority was cited to show that it is obligatory upon a Musalman to have more than one wife. So any legislative requirement to the effect that a Musalman may not have more than one wife does not amount to interference with freedom of conscience or interference with the right to profess, practise and propagate religion. I, therefore, do not think that any provision of law in favour of monogamy involves violation of Art. 25 of the Constitution."

In the absence of any legislative provision in Indian law which completely bans polygamy among Muslims, the only real protection against subsequent polygamy for Indian Muslim women at the time of their marriage would appear to be a stipulation in the marriage contract that the husband shall not take a second wife.[43]

---

[39] For details see *Anwar Ahmed v.State of Uttar Pradesh*, 1991 Cri.L.J. 717 and the comments in Menski (1993b).

[40] Details are not relevant here. For background material see Derrett (1968b).

[41] See Derrett [1970] 72 Bom.L.R. 61–63, and, for the most recent example, *Sarla Mudgal v. Union of India*, A.I.R. (1995) S.C. 1531, with detailed comments in Mahmood (1995), pp. 35–68.

[42] This argument comes up in constitutional petitions in India, claiming that allowing Muslims to indulge in polygamy is a violation of the human rights of Indian Muslim women and an infringement of the equality principles under the Constitution. It is not of central concern here to analyse how effective the legal control of Hindu polygamy has been in India. The statute law is well-phrased and clear but the case law points to problems of implementation and thus the absence of fully effective legal control.

[43] The technique of such a stipulation was originally introduced into the Muslim law as applied in India from Hanbali law, since this is not a Hanafi concept.

As Hinchcliffe (1970, p. 29) confirms, such stipulations would be enforceable, in that the wife should be entitled to claim divorce from the husband or a judicial dissolution of the marriage under section 2(viii)(f) of the DMMA 1939 if the husband does indeed marry a second wife in contravention of the stipulation. This section provides that a woman married under Muslim law shall be entitled to obtain a decree for the dissolution of her marriage on the ground:

(viii) that the husband treats her with cruelty, that is to say –
. . .

(f) if he has more wives than one and does not treat her equitably in accordance with the injunctions of the Quran;

It was held in an early case from Sindh, a distressed wife's suit for divorce on the ground of non-maintenance, that violation of the requirement to treat a wife equitably entitled her to a decree for judicial divorce. A case in which the husband made no real attempt to treat the wife equitably fell squarely within the purview of section 2(viii)(f).[44] In another case, involving a Muslim man who had migrated to East Africa, leaving two wives in the Panjab, the second one with a home and maintenance and the first one without provisions, it was held that the husband had not treated the first wife equitably in accordance with the injunctions of the Qur'an and she was therefore entitled to divorce.[45]

8–35 In post-Independence India, the much-noted decision by Dhavan J. in *Itwari v. Asghari*, A.I.R. 1960 Al. 684 went much beyond technical interpretations.[46] It defined the Muslim husband's unilateral action of taking another wife not only as inequitable treatment in Qur'anic terms but also as cruelty to the first wife for the purposes of the 1939 Act.[47] This was a husband's suit for restitution of conjugal rights against the first wife, who had refused to live with the husband after he had taken a second wife. The learned judge found that Muslim law permits polygamy but does not encourage it, since the Qur'anic injunction showed that achieving perfect equality in the treatment of co-wives is practically impossible. It was held, at page 686:

"... Muslim law as enforced in India has considered polygamy as an institution to be tolerated but not encouraged, and has not conferred upon the husband any fundamental right to compel the first wife to share his consortium with another woman in all circumstances. A Muslim husband has the legal right to take a second wife even while the first marriage subsists, but if he does so, and then seeks the assistance of the Civil Court to compel the first wife to live with him against her wishes on pain of severe penalties including attachment of property, she is entitled to raise the question whether the court, as a court of equity, ought to compel her to submit to co-habitation with such a husband. In that case the circumstances in which his second marriage took place are relevant and material in deciding whether his conduct in taking a second wife was in itself an act of cruelty to the first."

---

[44] *Asmabai v. Umer Mahomed Sidik Mirza*, A.I.R. 1941 Sindh 23.
[45] *Zubaida Begum v. Sardar Shah*, A.I.R. 1943 Lah. 310, discussed in detail by Shabbir (1988), pp. 31–33, where further case references are found.
[46] For a detailed discussion see *ibid.*, 39–47. Key passages from the judgment are reproduced in Hodkinson (1984), pp. 172–179. See also *ibid.*, pp. 179–182, the case of *Syed Ahmad Khan v. Imrat Jahan Begum*, A.I.R. 1982 Al. 155.
[47] In modern Indian law, divorce on the ground of cruelty became common, to such an extent that the judges have, more recently, warned that the – judicially determined – definition of cruelty has become too liberal. These debates did not concern cases involving Muslim spouses.

The phrase that polygamy is merely to be tolerated appears to be borrowed from the early leading case of *Moonshee Buzloor Raheem v. Shumsoonnissa Begum* [1867] 11 M.I.A. 551, also a restitution case, in which it had been held that a Muslim husband undoubtedly had the legal right to take a second wife during the subsistence of his first marriage. However, if such a Muslim husband then went to court to compel his first wife, who objected to the polygamous arrangement, to submit to cohabitation, the question arose whether such a wife could treat the husband's action as cruelty and thus as a valid defence to his claim for restitution. It had been held in the 1867 case, in a thoroughly modern-sounding judgment, that the concept and understanding of cruelty was based on universal and humanitarian standards. There was no such thing as 'Muslim cruelty', 'Christian cruelty' or 'Hindu cruelty'. Any conduct of the husband that caused bodily or mental pain to the wife would fall under this concept.[48] In *Itwari v. Asghari*, it was held at page 687:

> "In deciding what constitutes cruelty, the Courts have always taken into consideration the prevailing social conditions, and the same test will apply in a case where the parties are Mohammedans. Muslim society has never remained static and to contend otherwise is to ignore the achievements of Muslim civilisation and the rich development of Mohammedan jurisprudence in different countries. Muslim jurisprudence has always taken into account changes in social conditions in administering Mohammedan Law . . .
>
> Formerly, a Muslim husband could bring a second wife into the household without necessarily meaning any insult or cruelty to the wife. Occasionally, a second marriage took place with the consent or even at the suggestion of the first wife.
>
> But social conditions and habits among Indian Mussalmans have changed considerably, and with it the conscience of the Muslim community. Today the importing of a second wife into the household ordinarily means a stinging insult to the first. It leads to the asking of awkward questions . . .
>
> A husband who takes a second wife in these days will not be permitted to pretend that he did not realise the likely effect of his actions on the feelings and health of the first wife. Under the law, the husband will be presumed to intend the natural consequences of his own conduct . . . Under the prevailing conditions the very act of taking a second wife, in the absence of a weighty and convincing explanation, raises a presumption of cruelty to the first."

In the absence of any convincing explanation, it was apparent that the husband in this case was not entitled to restitution of conjugal rights. Indian law had a new leading judgment, which was bound to become famous for its strong language. Academic comment has been conservative,[49] taking the view that the underlying assumptions in this "exceptional case" (Diwan (1977), p. 42) may not be widely acceptable to other judges,[50] and that this case should not be seen as a precedent for stating that cruelty as a ground for divorce under the 1939 Act may be established simply by proving a polygamous marriage (Hinchcliffe (1970), p. 30). However, the same author has also suggested that it is not unlikely that such a view would be taken by an Indian court in a future case.

8–36   Notably, in *Syed Ahmad Khan v. Imrat Jahan Begum*, A.I.R. 1982 Al. 155,

---

[48] This was also applied in *Hamid Hussain v. Kubra Begum*, A.I.R. 1916 Al. 235.

[49] For scathing comments in the context of a debate about the future of Muslim law in India see Derrett (1968b), p. 538, n.2.

[50] See also Diwan and Diwan (1991), p. 44 n.11.

Deoki Nandan J. refused to accept evidence of a Muslim husband's plural marriages as cruelty *per se*. However, this is to a large extent due to the peculiar facts of this case. Here the husband had married three women and the respondent was the second wife of the husband. She had been complaining of non-payment of her prompt dower as well as rough treatment from the first wife. She had therefore withdrawn herself from the company of the husband and had sought employment as a teacher in a different place against the husband's wishes. Resisting the husband's petition for restitution of conjugal rights and still claiming her prompt *mahr*, she combined various arguments, obviously aiming to retain her job, her married status as well as claiming her dower.

8–37   This case must be read in the context of many similar Indian High Court cases at the time, very few of which involved Muslim spouses, about the right of a wife (whether polygamously married or not) to have an independent career and to choose to live in a place convenient to her, rather than her husband.[51] While that case law remained inconclusive and has lost its prominence today, it established the voice of wives in the context of making proper arrangements for a couple's married life.[52] In *Syed Ahmad Khan*, Deoki Nandan J. looked through these interlocking issues and harmonised his decision with those about the wife's entitlement to dower if she refused to cohabit with the husband after having, at some point in the past, consummated the marriage. Referring in this regard to *Rabia Khatoon v. Mohd Mukhtar Ahmad*, A.I.R. 1966 Al. 548, and distinguishing that case,[53] it was held that the proper course would be to refuse the husband's petition for restitution of conjugal rights unless he paid the wife the outstanding dower.

8–38   There is ample evidence that various courts in India have taken a serious view of polygamous arrangements while accepting that the Muslim husband retains a legal right, on certain conditions, to marry polygamously.[54] The Calcutta High Court, in particular, took a strong stance against polygamous marriages and treated them, from early on, as a 'continuing wrong' to the first wife.[55] One further example must suffice here to indicate latent judicial awareness of the need to protect those women who are unwilling parties to such arrangements. In *Shahulameedu v. Subaida Beevi*, 1970 K.L.T. 4, a Muslim wife had refused to live with her husband after he had married another woman and the husband had then failed to maintain her and the four children, so this was a criminal case regarding maintenance under section 488 of the Criminal Procedure Code 1898. Krishna Iyer J. referred during the course of his judgment in strong terms to the duty of the Indian state to enforce maintenance provisions for women and children in such a predicament. Referring to a number of earlier cases which discussed the position of Muslim wives in a polygamous marriage and their entitlement to separate residence and maintenance, the learned judge, in his usual forthright manner, doubted whether Muslim law actually permitted "multi-marriages", as he called them (page 9) and said, at page 10 that "those who quote the sacred Koran or cite the holy prophet as sanctioning for a male the rather unholy practice of a conjugal quadrangle are sinning against their religion itself". Citing Ameer Ali in support of his views and considering the relevant Qur'anic verses, the learned judge found, at page 10:

---

[51] The links with para. 7–03 and para. 7–38, above, on the husband's control of the wife are obvious but cannot be explored further here.

[52] The case law remained inconclusive because all the courts could say was that a sensible couple should agree such matters, otherwise the marriage would probably break up.

[53] For details see above, para. 7–50.

[54] The extensive discussion in Shabbir (1988), pp. 31–65 contains many further case references.

[55] *Ayat-un-Nissa v. Karam Ali*, I.L.R. [1908] 36 Cal. 23, discussed by Shabbir (1988), pp. 33–34 and 41.

"In short, the Koran enjoined monogamy upon Muslims and departure therefrom as an exception. That is why, in the true spirit of the Koran, a number of Muslim countries have codified the personal law wherein the practice of polygamy has been either totally prohibited or severely restricted."

Thus, there was no doubt in the judge's mind that the Muslim wife in this situation was entitled to maintenance, and the husband's appeal failed. The strong wording of this judgment in terms of the need to legislate against polygamy and to provide a uniform civil code for all Indians does not concern us here directly. Like *Itwari v. Asghari*, A.I.R. 1960 Al. 684, this decision is well in line with general Indian legal developments, making cruel treatment a more widely available ground for divorce,[56] and protecting the maintenance rights of women and children.

8–39 More recently, *Subanu v. A. M. Abdul Gafoor*, A.I.R. 1987 S.C. 1103, raised the interesting point whether a Muslim wife whose husband has married another woman is worse off under the law in terms of maintenance entitlements than a wife whose husband has merely taken a mistress. This issue arose in relation to the interpretation of the Explanation in section 125(3) of the Criminal Procedure Code 1973, which provides as follows:

"If a husband has contracted marriage with another woman or keeps a mistress, it shall be considered to be just ground for his wife's refusal to live with him."

Natarajan J. provided a detailed review of the case law on the rights of such a wife in terms of separate residence and maintenance. He clearly viewed the husband's action of taking another woman, whether as wife or mistress, as a matrimonial injury to the existing wife but, it seems, carefully avoided the critical term 'cruelty'. The judge concluded, at page 1108:

"From the point of view of the neglected wife . . . it will make no difference whether the woman intruding into her matrimonial life and taking her place in the matrimonial bed is another wife permitted under law and not a mistress. The legal status of the woman to whom a husband has transferred his affections cannot lessen her distress or her feelings of neglect . . . It will undoubtedly lead to a strange situation if it were to be held that a wife will be entitled to refuse to live with her husband if he has taken a mistress but she cannot refuse likewise if he has married a second wife. The Explanation has to be construed from the point of view of the injury to the matrimonial rights of the wife and not with reference to the husband's right to marry again."

Finding in addition that the husband had not made a genuine offer to take the wife back and to maintain her, the Supreme Court severely criticised the lower courts for finding in favour of the husband and proceeded to award maintenance at a reasonable rate for the appellant and her child. This case says little about polygamy, but it confirms the willingness of the Indian Supreme Court to come to the aid of Muslim women whose legitimate matrimonial rights have been denied by an unscrupulous husband.

8–40 The current position in Indian law is therefore clearly that a wife who is an unwilling party to a polygamous Muslim marriage can approach the courts for various remedies, but she cannot legally challenge the basic right of the husband to make polygamous arrangements, whether with another wife or with a mistress.

---

[56] This has now also led to significant reforms (through case law) to the outdated Christian divorce law of India, under which cruelty is now a ground for divorce. See *A. v. B.*, 1996(1) K.L.T. 275.

Today, such a woman can expect to be maintained by the husband indefinitely if she can show inequitable treatment, which does not appear to be too onerous a requirement. In the alternative she can ask for divorce, but there is much evidence to confirm that this is hardly attractive to most women (see Anjum 1992). If the husband divorced her, taking advantage of his own wrong, the maintenance problem has now to some extent been taken care of by the Muslim Women (Protection of Rights on Divorce) Act 1986 (see paragraph 7–75, above). It remains of course a fact, disagreeable to many, that Muslim wives cannot question the husband's superior discretion with respect to polygamy.

8–41 There is considerable evidence of public policy intervention in India to the effect that government employees, male or female, are not allowed to become party to a polygamous marriage.[57] This is a healthy trend, but monitoring and implementation of such rules will remain difficult and, in terms of a different public policy, any activism directed against polygamous Muslim men would immediately be treated as evidence of religious discrimination.

8–42 The communally charged nature of Indian debates on polygamy can be further illustrated by reference to the issue of religious conversion for the sake of being able to enjoy a legally valid polygamous marriage. This argument can be used to the effect that an Indian Hindu husband who wants to maintain his marriage with his first wife while he takes another wife has, since 1955, had to become a Muslim in order to avoid prosecution for bigamy. However, in reality, in most cases the conversion to Islam appears to be a device allowing the husband to take a second wife and to avoid prosecution for bigamy under section 494 of the Indian Penal Code with little concern for the position of the first wife.[58]

8–43 This sensitive issue flared up in the case of *Sarla Mudgal v. Union of India*, A.I.R. 1995 S.C. 1531, which has become as well-known for its robust call for a uniform civil code as for the firm views expressed on the consequences of conversion to Islam for married persons. *Sarla Mudgal* is a cluster of petitions, mainly by Hindu wives claiming that their husbands, after conversion to Islam, should be restrained from marrying other ladies under Muslim law and if they disobeyed they would be guilty of bigamy under section 494 of the Indian Penal Code.[59] Kuldip Singh J., giving the main judgment, considered in detail the older case law on the subject and concluded firmly, at page 1536:

> "It is, thus, obvious from the catena of case-law that a marriage celebrated under a particular personal law cannot be dissolved by the application of another personal law to which one of the spouses converts and the other refuses to do so."

Examining the effects of traditional Hindu law and modern Hindu law in this regard, the learned judge found little difference. Even under modern Hindu law, a convert to Islam remained a party to the Hindu marriage. Thus, a second marriage by such a convert would be illegal and void under the Hindu law and would be a crime under section 494 of the Indian Penal Code. Probably to avoid charges of

---

[57] See Hinchcliffe (1970), p. 30 and in detail Derrett (1968b), p. 445–446.

[58] One must suspect that the pattern of informal desertion of the first wife is related to the advanced state of modern Indian law on maintenance, since a divorcing husband would now be held liable for post-divorce maintenance. The complainant wives, therefore, are in effect bringing petitions for restitution of conjugal rights against the erring husband. They may of course also be seeking to have the husband punished for his bigamous escapade.

[59] Significantly, it is not quite clear what remedies the petitioners expected from the court, nor does the court specify any remedies. This makes the political nature of the petition all the more apparent.

communalism, but also reflecting the fact that this litigation had become a matter of interpersonal conflicts of law (see paragraph 4–88, above), the learned judge also tested his conclusions in terms of 'justice, equity and good conscience' and came in effect to the same conclusion. It was held, at page 1537:

> "Looked at from another angle, the second marriage of an apostate-husband would be in violation of the rules of natural justice. Assuming that a Hindu husband has a right to embrace Islam as his religion, he has no right under the Act to marry again without getting his earlier marriage under the Act dissolved . . . .We, therefore, hold that the second marriage of a Hindu husband after his conversion to Islam is a void marriage in terms of Section 494 I.P.C."

Sahai J., concurring with his senior colleague, neatly summarised the issue of polygamy before he, too, at page 1540, called for the government to enact legislation which would provide that irrespective of religion "every citizen who changes his religion cannot marry another wife unless he divorces his first wife". It was stated *id.*:

> "The problem with which these appeals are concerned is that many Hindus have changed their religion and have become convert to Islam only for purpose of escaping the consequences of bigamy . . . Obviously because Muslim Law permits more than one wife and to the extent of four. But no religion permits deliberate distortions. Much misapprehension prevails about bigamy in Islam. To check the misuse many Islamic countries have codified the personal law, wherein the practice of polygamy has been either totally prohibited or severely restricted . . . The Government would be well advised to . . . examine the matter and bring about the comprehensive legislation in keeping with modern day concept of human rights for women."

Predictably, this judgment has given rise to many comments. It is relevant to note that it has been welcomed by Professor Tahir Mahmood, now the Chairman of the Minorities Commission of India, in a long discussion of fraudulent conversions to Islam for the sake of bigamy (Mahmood (1995), pp. 57–68), which also contains many details of other recent cases on the subject decided by various Indian courts.

8–44   In some of the secondary literature, the issues aired above are being brought out, but rarely in depth and detail. A good discussion of the issues and cases is provided by Arora (1986). Hodkinson (1984, pp. 151–152) briefly summarised the obligations of the polygamous husband, the main issue being that he should be treating his co-wives impartially. In this context, Indian textbooks do not emphasise as the first duty of the husband to provide a separate residence for each wife.[60]

8–45   Some writers refer to the fact that only very few Indian Muslims actually practise polygamy and challenge the consequent arguments that, therefore, the existence of the institution should be ignored by the law and reforms should come from within the community, ideally with the consent of the *ulema*.[61] It is manifestly too simple to demand the total prohibition of Muslim polygamy in India on grounds of gender equality and to overlook the political dimensions of such a step for the Indian state. Disregarding basic principles of Muslim law as they are currently perceived is simply not an option in view of the communalised scenario of

---

[60] Compare, *e.g.* Hinchliffe (1970), p. 15 and Malik (1988), p. 58.
[61] On this see briefly Diwan (1977), p. 42; Diwan and Diwan (1991), p. 41. Instructive debates are also found in Bharatiya (1996), pp. 79–81 and Shabbir (1988), pp. 51–65.

Indian law making. Opting for the minority view within the rich field of Muslim jurisprudence is risky. Islamisation, in the sense of introducing liberalising reforms based on re-interpretation of the Qur'anic foundations, is not only an option in Muslim countries, as the *Shah Bano* case and the 1986 Act (see paragraphs 7–75— 7–125) show, but in India any openly debated legal reform of Muslim law is bound to be challenged with extra vigour by some spokespersons of Muslims as a violation of the religious freedom of all Indian Muslims. This is a dilemma which Indian law-making has always had to live with.

8–46 Moreover, a detailed analysis of the legislative controls of polygamy in the various Muslim countries, even in Tunisia with its boldly attempted abolition and criminalisation of polygamy, would probably show that these reforms can still not effectively override the continuing discretion of any Muslim male, claimed as a Muslim rather than a citizen, to enter a polygamous union. This is a complex issue concerning conflicts of law and religion. For, any Muslim who argued to himself that he would be a sinner if he were to commit *zina* could still rely on his conscience today, anywhere in the world, and feel a better Muslim if he took the woman he desires as a Muslim wife rather than a mistress or a lover. We have seen in Chapter 6 above how very simple it is to contract oneself into a Muslim marriage. Our discussion of Muslim polygamy in Britain in paragraph 8–91, below will further illustrate this particular point. It may be correct, historically, to view polygamy as an anachronism. Sexual promiscuity, on the other hand, is simply not of the same category and is, moreover, decidedly 'modern' as well as ancient. So any form of state law has inherent limits when it comes to controlling polygamous arrangements. As we saw, classical Muslim law itself relied, in its typical idealistic fashion, on the conscience of the Muslim individual and the question of state control did not arise then.

8–47 Today, it appears therefore that neither engaging in communal politics nor challenging the advocates of limited polygamy and simply demanding instant legislative abolition of polygamy can actually address the key points in a meaningful debate on how to control Muslim polygamy.[62] By retreating into gender polemics and refusing to address the central issues that arise for polygamously married Indian women in their daily life, rather than for a small elitist class, the academic debate has missed important points about the fact that modern Indian law has actually progressed some considerable way in controlling Muslim polygamy in an indirect manner, mainly by strengthening the power of women to challenge this male discretion, which cannot be entirely taken away in legal proceedings of various kinds.

8–48 Therefore, it is submitted here that the common view that Indian law has developed no legal control of Muslim polygamy is in need of considerable modification. While it is correct to say that there is no direct legislative control of Muslim polygamy, the judicial supervision of Muslim polygamy in India has already shown the potential to be just as effective, in terms of remedies, as the impressive legislative provisions in various Muslim countries. If states like Morocco leave it to the wife or wives to complain and will then assist them in finding appropriate remedies through the courts, why do we refuse to see that Indian law has exactly the same remedies without providing this in a specific statute? After all, Indian law is to some extent a common law system and relies less on legislative activity. Secondly, it appears that the combination, in Indian law, of Muslim personal law and secular general law has been a reasonably effective mechanism for protecting disadvantaged individuals, including polygamously married wives.[63]

---

[62] But see, in strong terms Diwan (1977), p. 42 and Diwan and Diwan (1991), p. 41, and n.13.
[63] An early indication of this is reflected in Fyzee (1974), pp. 212–213.

8–49   Of course, in Muslim countries as well as in India, many barriers exist for women to go to court to voice their grievances. However, that in itself cannot be a valid reason for claiming that Indian law has no protective mechanisms and has simply left Muslim wives alone in their opposition to victimisation through polygamy. As the comparison with Pakistan and Bangladesh below confirms, what difference does it really make for the average woman that in Muslim countries there are some statutory hurdles for Muslim polygamists which everyone knows to be no real barriers against arranging polygamous unions? If we look at it this way, Indian women do not appear to be worse off than other women subjected to Muslim polygamy.

Pakistani law

8–50   It appears that the expressly pro-women position, taken by Dhavan J. in *Itwari v. Asghari*, A.I.R. 1960 Al. 684, has not been accepted in Pakistan, as the case of *Resham Bibi v. Muhammad Shafi*, P.L.D. 1967 A.J.K. 32, confirms. It was held in that case, at page 39, that the mere fact that a husband takes a second wife is not sufficient to prove cruelty to the first wife, since Muslim law allows him to have four wives at the same time. The apparent lack of judicial enterprise in protecting the position of the polygamously married wife in this case must, however, be seen against the factual background of this case. The wife had lived with the husband and the second wife for several years and had allegedly not complained. Since polygamy was only a minor issue in this particular case, it is not possible to determine the general policy of the Pakistani courts from *Resham Bibi*.

8–51   In *Muhammad Khan v. Zarina Begum*, P.L.D. 1975 A.J.K. 27, the same High Court dissented from the strict view taken in *Resham Bibi*, as discussed immediately above, and granted a young second wife a *khul* divorce under the principle of the well-known case of *Khurshid Bibi v. Muhammad Amin*.[64] This case did not consider whether taking a second wife was an act of cruelty, but it is noteworthy that the judges, based on the facts, took a dim view of the husband's reasons for marrying an unwilling orphan girl as a second wife when he already had a wife, four sons and a daughter, and he was not a rich man. Evidently, the husband's sheepish response was merely that "a Muslim is allowed to have even four wives" (page 31), which convinced the learned judges that he had some ulterior motives for marrying the girl and no *bona fide* reason at all.

8–52   The Pakistani law on Muslim polygamy was the subject of reform in the context of the MFLO 1961 (for the text see below, page 259). Section 6(1) of the Ordinance appears to restrict polygamy by controlling the husband's discretion to take a second or further wife. It must be noted, however, that this provision appears to be something like a dead letter, since it provides little effective help for wives who see themselves victimised by a man's polygamous arrangements and want to oppose them before the marriage takes place. It is therefore misleading to state, simply and without any further comment, that "in Pakistan it is not possible to practise polygamy without permission from the Arbitration Council" (Verma (1988), p. 57). Rubya Mehdi (1994, p. 166) has correctly summed up her study by stating:

> "All this shows that, though Pakistan has put academically impressive restrictions on man's unrestricted and arbitrary right to polygamy, in practice

---

[64] P.L.D. (1967) S.C. 97. For details see para. 9–82, below.

the requirement that prior permission for a polygamous marriage be obtained from an Arbitration Council appears to be a formality rather than an effective deterrent."

Rahman (1966, p. 415) confirms that, in Pakistan, the attempted legislative restriction on polygamy "has aroused the most vigorous protests on the part of the conservatives". But it was not a simple struggle between 'modernists' and 'traditionalists', for even traditionalists asked for state interference, seeing that the idealised model of Islamic polygamy is beyond the reach of the average Pakistani Muslim. Tanzil-ur-Rahman, who later became an important judicial figure in Pakistan, pushing for islamisation of the legal system, called in one of his earliest writings for state interference to put a stop to polygamy (Rahman (1967), pp. 38–39). The extent of the debate in Pakistan is well-documented in the Report of the Pakistani Commission on Marriage and Family Laws,[65] which asked five questions on polygamy and suggested, above all, that it should be made obligatory for a person who intends to marry a second wife during the subsistence of his marriage to obtain a court order. It was argued that this requirement "would be absolutely in the interest of justice and in conformity with the spirit of the Holy *Qur'an*" (page 1216). For, as stated *id*.:

"There may be some cases in which there may be rational justification and in such rare cases, the court could permit a man to take a second wife only on the condition that in the matter of maintenance and other treatment no injustice is done to the wife and her children . . . In such matters the court shall also see whether a man desiring to have a second wife and a second family is capable financially of supporting two families, satisfying their basic needs of life and guaranteeing the standard of living to which his first wife and her children have been accustomed."

The Pakistani plans for legal intervention, therefore, were broadly in line with the early reforms in Syria, as discussed in paragraph 8–13, above. Apart from the requirement of financial probity of the husband, they also focused on the issue of equitable distribution of resources between the two women, stressing that this, too, was enjoined by the Qur'an (page 1217).

8–53   The dissenting report by Maulana Thanvi reflects the contentious nature of the proposed legal intervention.[66] This long note is interspersed with a series of polemical comments, typical of modern juristic discourse.[67] It appears that any control of polygamy is opposed as a sign of "inferiority complex against the West and the desire to copy it blindly" (page 1591). On the other hand, it is argued that "the practice of unnecessarily keeping more than one wife at a time, as was in vogue about 50 years ago, is fast dying out" (page 1591). A third argument is that nature allows polygamy, but of course only to men.[68] The Maulana thus opposed any legal reform and warned of dangerous political consequences, an argument familiar from the Indian discourse:

---

[65] For details see *Gazette of Pakistan*, "Extraordinary," June 20, 1956, pp. 1215–1218.
[66] The relevant portions of the dissenting note are found in the *Gazette of Pakistan*, "Extraordinary," August 30, 1956, pp. 1590–1601.
[67] For more recent Middle Eastern examples of juristic debates, *inter alia*, about termination of pregnancy, see Lohlker (1996).
[68] At pp. 1593–1594. The author uses, *inter alia*, an agricultural simile of field and seed, which is typically South Asian, to justify the male prerogative.

". . . it would be an interference in the revealed religion, if the plurality of marriages is declared to be unlawful or any restriction is imposed on it. The Quranic injunction must remain general and unrestricted in its application. If the Government impose any legal restrictions in accordance with the Commission's recommendations and the Muslim public protest against it by taking second or third wife, as they violated the provisions of Sharda Bill by resorting to practical demonstrations, a great social disruption in the country may result from it."[69]

Other arguments advanced are that moral education of the public, rather than legal reform, would be a suitable remedy to fulfil the Islamic injunctions. Therefore, "the proper course would be to give the people suitable mental training" (page 1598). It was also argued that any restrictive legal intervention would actually damage the interests of women (page 1599) and that the financial criteria, in particular, would discriminate in favour of a small, self-interested rich class.

8-54 Probably the most interesting aspect raised in this dissenting note relates to the issue of equity between the wives (*adl*), discussed at pages 1599–1600. The Maulana's key argument is that a violation of the equity principle can in practice only be maintained once there is evidence of actual inequity, *i.e.* after the polygamous marriage has been experienced or lived, so to say. Instead, his conclusion is that "the Court has no right to intervene unless the woman appears before it as a complainant" (page 1600). This suggestion is obviously based on the rationale that arranging polygamy should not be perceived as inequity *per se*, not to speak of cruelty, but that any subsequent complaint by a female party to a polygamous marriage should be taken seriously. The Maulana therefore objected to the process of initial scrutiny of a polygamous marriage proposal but did argue in favour of giving access to courts for women who felt aggrieved about being party to a polygamous marriage.

8-55 It appears that precisely this rationale has become the foundation of the relevant provisions in section 6 of the MFLO, 1961, which cannot be read in isolation, but must be understood in conjunction with a number of legal provisions relating to dower, restitution of conjugal rights, maintenance and divorce. Read by itself, section 6 is indeed a paper tiger, a set of legal formalities which many Pakistanis simply ignore and whose violation carries minimal legal sanctions. Pakistani law has maintained a soft approach to checking the husband's motives and credentials before the polygamous marriage is entered. Hinchcliffe (1970, pp. 24–25) has emphasised in this respect that the provisions regarding polygamy in the MFLO are rarely invoked and appear to be largely ignored in practice. We need to ask whether this picture is different three decades later.

8-56 In a pilot study of Quetta, the capital of the Province of Baluchistan, then a town of 100,000 people, it was found that in the period 1966–1968, 32 applications for permission to contract polygamous marriages were forwarded to 10 different Union Councils, the relevant administrative bodies (Pearl (1971b)). In these 32 applications, permission to take a second wife was granted in all but one case.[70] The Union Committee is responsible for setting up an Arbitration Council, made up of a representative of the existing wife, a representative of the husband, and the

---

[69] At p. 1597. The reference to the Sharda Bill relates to the legislative control of child marriages in the Child Marriage Restraint Act 1929 which was widely opposed by the public at the time and led to deliberate violations of the law.

[70] For details see Pearl (1971b), p. 564; Pearl (1969a), p. 188 and Hinchliffe (1970), pp. 24–25 refer to 31 cases.

Chairman of the Union Committee. If the Arbitration Council is satisfied that the proposed marriage is 'necessary and just' under section 6(3) of the 1961 Ordinance, it may grant permission to contract the second union. Rule 14 of the Rules under the MFLO, cited below, lists the criteria which the Arbitration Council may take into account in making a judgment on what is 'just and necessary'. If a second marriage is solemnised without the approval of the Arbitration Council, the husband runs the risk that criminal proceedings may be instituted against him, but the second marriage is clearly valid. We shall test below, studying the case law, to what extent Pakistani women can expect any meaningful assistance from courts of law if they complain about polygamy. Turning first to the statutory provisions, we see that section 6 of the MFLO provides as follows:

"6. Polygamy.–

(1) No man, during the subsistence of an existing marriage, shall, except with the previous permission in writing of the Arbitration Council, contract another marriage, nor shall any such marriage contracted without such permission be registered under this Ordinance.

(2) An application for permission under sub-section (1) shall be submitted to the Chairman in the prescribed manner, together with the prescribed fee and shall state the reasons for the proposed marriage, and whether the consent of existing wife or wives has been obtained thereto.

(3) On receipt of the application under sub-section (2) the Chairman shall ask the applicant and his existing wife or wives each to nominate a representative, and the Arbitration Council so constituted may, if satisfied that the proposed marriage is necessary and just, grant subject to such conditions, if any, as may be deemed fit, the permission applied for.

(4) In deciding the application the Arbitration Council shall record its reasons for the decision and any party may, in the prescribed manner, within the prescribed period, and on payment of the prescribed fee, prefer an application for revision to the Collector concerned and his decision shall be final and shall not be called in question in any Court.[71]

(5) Any man who contracts another marriage without the permission of the Arbitration Council shall:-

(a) Pay immediately the entire amount of the dower, whether prompt or deferred, due to the existing wife or wives, which amount, if not so paid shall be recoverable as arrears of land revenue: and

(b) On conviction upon complaint be punishable with simple imprisonment which may extend to one year, or with fine which may extend to five thousand rupees, or with both."

8–57 This section shows that the position in Pakistan (and Bangladesh) is similar to that in other countries, except that here the permission granting authority is an administrative body which, under the MFLO 1961, is provided with certain quasi-judicial functions. The provisions of the MFLO have been

---

[71] The word 'Collector' was introduced by the Federal Adaptation of Laws Order 1975 and replaced 'Sub-Divisional Officer'.

supplemented by the West Pakistan Rules under the Muslim Family Laws Ordinance 1961.[72] These rules are of a procedural nature, with rules 14–15 specifically concerned about polygamy:

> "14. In considering whether another proposed marriage is just and necessary during the continuance of an existing marriage, the Arbitration Council may, without prejudice to its general powers to consider what is just and necessary, have regard to such circumstances, as the following amongst others: –
>
> Sterility, physical infirmity, physical unfitness for the conjugal relation, wilful avoidance of a decree for restitution of conjugal rights, or insanity on the part of an existing wife.
>
> > 15. An application under sub-section (1) of section 6 for permission to contract another marriage during the subsistence of an existing marriage shall be in writing, shall state whether the consent of the existing wife or wives has been obtained thereto, shall contain a brief statement of the grounds on which the new marriage is alleged to be just and necessary, shall bear the signature of the applicant, and shall be accompanied by a fee of 100 rupees."

Significantly, the efficacy of these rules has been affected by an amendment in the province of Panjab to rule 21 about complaints. The unamended rule, which is operative in the rest of Pakistan, provides:

> "21. No Court shall take cognizance of any offence under the Ordinance or these rules save on a complaint in writing by the Union Council stating the fact constituting the offence."[73]

The Panjab Amendment of November 26, 1976 substitutes the following wording for rule 21:

> "21. No Court shall take cognizance of any offence under the Ordinance or these rules save on a complaint in writing by the aggrieved party, stating the facts constituting the offence."

8–58 Not surprisingly, this rule gave rise to litigation, seeking to clarify the meaning of 'aggrieved party'.[74] It is apparent that a complaint by a wife is competent under this rule. This also includes a wife who originally gave her permission for a co-wife but later finds that she has reason to complain.

8–59 *Fauzia Hussain v. Khadim Hussain*, P.L.D. 1985 Lah. 165, is an interesting case on the question of standing, because it also involves questions about the nature of a marriage solemnised between two Muslims in England. The husband had married the wife in Birmingham, England in a civil ceremony and presumably also in a *nikah*. Both parties were dual nationals of Pakistan and the United Kingdom. The husband had then married a second wife in Pakistan without the permission of his first wife or of the Arbitration Council but had been acquitted by the lower court of an offence under section 6(5) of the MFLO. The wife, who apparently

---

[72] Dated July 20, 1961. These are reprinted in Ch. M. Mahmood (1991), pp. 217–225 and Abid (1993), pp. 62–73.

[73] An early case on procedural questions under this rule is *Muhammad Islam v. The State* P.L.D. 1967 Pesh. 201. As the Union Committees were abolished for a time in 1971–1972, it was decided in one case that no organisation had *locus standi* and that proceedings against a polygamous husband were to be quashed. See *Fateh Muhammad v. Chairman. Union Committee, Ward No. 14/15*, P.L.D. 1975 Lah. 951.

[74] For details, including case references, see Abid (1993), p. 71.

wanted him punished, appealed to the High Court of Lahore, which rejected the argument of the husband that no complaint could be brought against him for the reason that the first marriage had been contracted in the United Kingdom. Muhammad Munir Khan J. clearly held, at pages 172–173, that "such marriage conforms to requirements of Muslim marriage and would be recognized as a valid marriage under Muslim law". The wife was an aggrieved party, and she could therefore file a complaint directly in a court of competent jurisdiction. The husband would face another criminal trial.

8–60 Rule 21 also protects a second wife who did not know that the husband was already married, since she is also an aggrieved person.[75] In *Ejaz Mahmood v. Humaira*, P.L.D. 1983 Lah. 615, the husband had duped the second wife by not disclosing to her that he was already married and had not sought prior permission. Sardar Muhammad J. had no difficulty in finding that, if the second wife had come to know of the existence of the first marriage, she might not have married the man. In the circumstances, she was clearly an aggrieved person. However, a second element in this case before the Lahore High Court is that, after the Panjab amendment of rule 21 in 1976, it was held (at page 619) that a complaint filed by the Chairman of a Union Council had not been filed by an 'aggrieved person'. This could be interpreted as a definite restriction of standing, shutting out social activism and reformist interference, but perhaps also seeking to control local abuses of basic power structures. In *Sher Muhammad v. The State*, 1986 P.Cr.L.J. 1510, it was held that in Baluchistan, at any rate, a private person is not entitled to initiate proceedings on behalf of a Union Council. Such judgments indicate that in Pakistani law, the criminal offence of contracting a polygamous marriage in contravention of the MFLO is not a cognisable offence.[76] The onus for initiating and filing complaints falls, therefore, more or less exclusively on the women who feel that the polygamous arrangements are inequitable towards them. There may be many reasons why such women do not come forward as an 'aggrieved person'.

8–61 Regarding punishment for violating the rules of the MFLO with respect to polygamy, the evidence from the case law indicates that the courts are not very interested in the deterrent force of either imprisonment or financial penalties. In the few cases in which there is evidence of erring husbands being punished under section 6(5) of the MFLO, the husband almost always tries to appeal for reduction of sentence. Farani (1992, pp. 13–14) refers to several relevant cases. In one of these judicial sympathy with the offender shines through when it was held that if the husband has to pay dower on demand, that is in itself sufficient punishment.[77] It is not possible to say, therefore, that the Pakistani courts have adopted a tough criminal law approach towards polygamous husbands. The legal provision in section 6(5)(a) that the man must repay the entire dower and that it can be collected as arrears of land revenue is certainly helpful, since it expedites the payment and avoids the need for lengthy court proceedings. In practice, though, even such beneficial provisions will probably not help the majority of affected women because recourse to legal remedies remains limited.

8–62 It appears to be a reflection of this lack of enthusiasm in pursuing polygamists that the Pakistani case law on polygamy is not very extensive.[78] Its

---

[75] On this point see especially *Faheemuddin v. Sabeeha Begum*, P.L.D. 1991 S.C. 1074, discussed further below.

[76] See also *Zakir Hussain Siddiqui v. Nasim Bano*, (1989) CLC 1062; *Muhammad Hanif v. The State*, 1990 P.Cr.L.J. 975.

[77] *Manzoor Bibi v. Muhammad Afzal Haq*, (1989) P.Cr.L.J. 749.

[78] A good collection of comments is found at Abid (1993), pp. 21–26; see also Farani, *Manual of family laws in Pakistan* (1992), pp. 13–17.

basic message is clear, at any rate: Failure of the husband to seek permission of the wife or wives and/or the Arbitration Council does not render the polygamous marriage invalid or void, while it gives rise to criminal as well as civil consequences. A useful early case explaining this basic position is *Muhammad Aslam v. Ghulam Muhammad Tasleem*, P.L.D. 1971 Lah. 139.

8–63 Balchin (1994, p. 77) confirms that there are very few reported cases where a complaint has been made against the husband for contracting a subsequent marriage in contravention of the MFLO. It is evident that all petitions by wives to have the polygamous marriage declared void and illegal have not succeeded. In *Abdul Basit v. Union Council, Ward No. 3, Peshawar Cantt.*, 1970 S.C.M.R. 753, a bench of five judges heard a case in which a husband had earlier divorced his wife and had given notice to the Union Council. On exploring the potential for reconciliation between the spouses, it transpired that the wife was complaining about the husband's unilateral act of marrying another woman, apparently in Germany. The Chairman of the Union Council filed a complaint against the husband under section 6(5) of the MFLO but the husband's appeal before the High Court of Peshawar was successful. The very brief case report indicates judicial doubts over the fides of the wife and the Union Council in bringing those proceedings in the first place but the validity of the marriage is never in doubt.

8–64 In *Inayat Khan v. District Magistrate, Sialkot*, 1986 P.Cr.L.J. 2023, the wife had filed a suit for divorce, while the husband sought restitution of conjugal rights. The wife alleged that the husband had entered a further marriage without permission from the Arbitration Council and the District Magistrate had therefore registered a case under section 6 of the MFLO. It was held that this had been done without lawful authority and, at any rate, neither the wife nor her family wished to pursue the matter. The woman was not even in court and her father deposed on her behalf that the marriage had been dissolved. The case against the husband was therefore dropped.

8–65 *Ghulam Fatima v. Anwar*, 1981 C.L.C. 1651 is a typical inheritance suit involving two widows of the deceased, with the first wife and her children trying to oust the second wife by alleging that she was not party to a valid marriage. This petition had been unsuccessful throughout. On second appeal before the High Court of Lahore, it was first of all alleged that the marriage document, the *kabinnama*, had been drawn up before the marriage actually took place and was therefore invalid. The learned judge held this did not render the document invalid, for "it is not uncommon that marriage documents are drafted before the marriage ceremonies take place but they are usually signed at the time when the ceremonies are held or thereafter" (page 1652). As to the plea that this marriage was not valid because it had been entered into without agreement of the first wife and therefore in violation of section 6 of the MFLO, the judicial response, at page 1652, was as follows:

> "Contravention of the said provisions of law can be visited with punishments provided therein but it has not been laid down anywhere in the said Ordinance that a marriage which is not registered under section 5 . . . or is contracted in contravention of the provisions of section 6 thereof would be invalid."

Balchin (1994, p. 77) comments that this decision strengthens "the argument that the MFLO fails to act as an effective deterrent to polygamy". Mehdi (1994, p. 163) argues that "even though the practice of polygamy is not common in Pakistan, the very fact that polygamy is lawful has a negative effect on women's position within the family because it enables emotional pressures to be used as a constant threat to women". Anjum (1992, pp. 58–59) and the excellent research report by Khanam (n.y.) refer to field studies showing that this still is a real threat for women in Pakistan.

8–66 Whether the total abolition of polygamy would make a difference in this respect must be questioned, however. If polygamy was no longer an option, men and mothers-in-law would threaten women with divorce, as they already do, anyway. The remedy, in either case, would appear to lie more in the field of social negotiation and informal dispute settlement than in recourse to state law.

8–67 Notwithstanding the justified social criticisms by a number of authors, and doubts about the efficacy of state law in this field, there are some signs that the Pakistani Supreme Court has recently taken a firmer view of the rights of women in polygamous marriages and has, in particular, defended the rights of second wives to complain about a husband's polygamous arrangement. *Faheemuddin v. Sabeeha Begum*, P.L.D. 1991 S.C. 1074 is a case on the interpretation of section 21 in the West Pakistan Rules under the Muslim Family Laws Ordinance, 1976.[79] Muhammad Afzal Zullah C.J. had before him an appeal by a polygamous husband, who had responded to his second wife's complaint against his actions under section 6(5) of the MFLO by alleging that this amounted to an abuse of the process of law (page 1077). The technical point falling for decision was whether the second wife in a polygamous marriage had *locus standi* to complain about polygamy. The husband claimed that the provisions of section 6 of the MFLO were intended only for the protection of the rights of the first wife.[80]

8–68 Zullah C.J. agreed that perhaps, initially, the statutory protection had been intended for the benefit of the first wife. However, in view of the "recent trend of authority by this Court . . . towards expansion of the connotation of the word "aggrieved" rather than restricting it" (page 1078), it was held that a second wife was undoubtedly an 'aggrieved person' if, as in the present case, she had not been told about the husband's first marriage. The learned Chief Justice then launched, at page 1079, into a small lecture on some socio-legal aspects of polygamy in Pakistan today, indicating that the criminalisation of polygamy by the law would by now have had important social consequences:

". . . the appellant had made mis-representation about his first marriage. This would shatter the faith of a loving wife in her husband. His esteem may dwindle considerably in her view. This besides causing unhappiness to the husband would also cause serious grievance to the second wife whose expectations of a harmonious married life would suffer. Secondly, . . . the act or omission of the husband in such a case in her view would amount to an offence as it is punishable as an offence. A respectable lady might feel a shock that she had been married to a criminal. Thirdly, . . . if the husband would have obtained requisite permission there can be visualised a possibility that she might have married him notwithstanding there being a first wife. But without such a permission she might not have married him for an obvious common place reason that she might also be treated as a criminal – at least by extending of vicarious liability as an accessory in crime through abetment or otherwise . . . In our society marriage by young unmarried girls with widowers or with [a] man having another wife under a subsisting marriage, to a considerable extent carries a stigma also for the second wife. It is so important in our society

---

[79] This case is also reported at 1990 S.C.M.R. 612. Here, Nasim Hasan Shah J. emphasised, at p. 613, that the question raised requires further consideration and therefore granted leave for a full hearing.
[80] In view of *Ejaz Mahmood v. Humaira*, P.L.D. 1983 Lah. 615, this was a questionable contention. However, that case does not appear to have been cited in *Faheemuddin*.

that some social workers and organizations try to influence and prevail upon the second would-be wives not to go through such a marriage as acccording to them it might prove harmful for both the wives or one of them on account of the nature of a husband in not being observant of limits of God in doing justice between them in accordance with Islamic principles. And above all the ladies before solemnizing the contract of marriage do look at the qualification of the would-be husband and amongst which an important one is that he should be bachelor and unattached."

The husband was, therefore, not able to save himself from a criminal trial and his dilatory tactics had not worked at all. It is not known, however, what kind of punishment he was given.

8–69 Case law on polygamy has also arisen under two provisions of the Dissolution of Muslim Marriages Act 1939. Unique to Pakistani law, and Bangladeshi law, is that the husband's polygamy has become a ground for divorce under the 1939 Act if the marriage was contracted in contravention of the MFLO. This new ground was created when section 13 of the MFLO, as promulgated in 1961, added the husband's polygamy to the existing grounds for divorce under section 2 of the 1939 Act.[81] The resulting section 2(ii-a) provided that a woman married under Muslim law shall be entitled to obtain a decree for dissolution of her marriage on the ground:

"(ii-a) that the husband has taken an additional wife in contravention of the provisions of the Muslim Family Laws Ordinance, 1961."

Abid (1993, p. 178) states correctly that "the fact that the husband has married another woman is not a ground for dissolution of marriage". Dissolution can only be claimed where the polygamous mariage was in contravention of the provisions of the MFLO, and where this is the case, a wife is entitled to dissolution of her marriage. Abid (1993, p. 178) cites only one reported case on this point. Balchin (1994, p. 78) reports that in the 30 years since the MFLO was promulgated, section 2(ii-a) has only been invoked in about half a dozen cases, which have invariably also involved a claim under section 2(viii)(f) relating to inequitable treatment of the wife.

8–70 In the reported cases, it has been held that the onus to prove that the second marriage was contracted with the consent of the wife lies heavily on the husband; where consent is not proved, the wife is entitled to a decree for divorce.[82] In *Aurangzeb v. Ejazul Hassan Khan*, P.L.D. 1984 Pesh. 49, the first wife had at first instance not succeeded in proving that the husband's subsequent marriage had been contracted without her consent and that the husband had been cruel towards her, so her petition for divorce had been rejected. She succeeded on appeal to the District Court. The husband then appealed to the High Court of Peshawar but it was found that he had no case and it was affirmed, at page 50, that the fact that the husband had taken the second wife without the consent of the first wife, and thus in contravention of the provisions of the MFLO, entitled her to seek dissolution of the marriage under section 2(ii-a) of the 1939 Act. One wonders how useful such a judgment ultimately is for a woman in Pakistan. Being given a right to divorce is only meaningful if the woman actually wants to take up that offer, and she may have many reasons not to do so.

---

[81] Mannan (1990) indicates in the Appendix, at pp. 26–27, that this section has been omitted by the Federal Laws (Revision and Declaration) Ordinance (XXVII of 1981), Second Schedule, Part I, item 18, but other textbooks and the case law treat s.2(ii-a) as operative law.

[82] *Nadir Khan v. Zeenat Bibi*, (1990), C.L.C. 293.

8–71 This may explain why we find more cases regarding the rights to maintenance of polygamously married wives. As in Indian law, a Muslim wife in Pakistan can petition for divorce under section 2(viii)(f) of the 1939 Act, arguing that her polygamous husband has not treated her equitably in accordance with the injunctions of the Qur'an. Balchin (1994, p. 79) refers only to one case of 1989, which held that a polygamously married wife is entitled to separate living quarters and maintenance, and that failure to provide this is a ground for dissolution of the marriage under the 1939 Act. Abid (1993, p. 176) discusses only the old pre-independence cases and does not cite a single recent case.

8–72 It would appear, therefore, that this particular ground for dissolution of a polygamous marriage has not been found helpful in Pakistani law. It is likely that local Pakistani views on how a woman who is party to a broken marriage should be maintained are of relevance in this context. In paragraph 7–75, above, our argument was that Pakistanis seem to expect the wife's family to take care of her in case the marriage runs into difficulties. Implementation of that family-based strategy, coupled with the absence of Indian-style judicial activism in the area of maintenance law, which puts financial pressure on husbands, or ex-husbands as the case may be, appears to explain the low profile of case law in this area. Change could only be expected if the husband's liability to maintain the wife was extended to the ex-wife, as was done under Indian law in section 125 of the Criminal Procedure Code 1973 which is of course not part of the law of Pakistan and Bangladesh.

8–73 However, the enforcement of conditions stipulated in the marriage contract has been relevant in a number of cases. Where the marriage contract or a subsequent agreement between husband and wife specifies that in case the husband takes a second wife, the first wife shall be entitled to separate residence and maintenance, the husband is bound by such an agreement. Pakistani courts have firmly upheld that principle and therefore confirm the practical usefulness of such stipulations. In *Muhammad Zaman v. Irshad Begum*, P.L.D. 1967 Lah. 1104, the husband eventually took a second wife but did not honour the maintenance agreement with his first wife, nor had he paid the prompt dower. When the wife decided to reside in her parental home rather than with the husband, and filed a suit for maintenance, the husband responded in typical fashion with a suit for restitution of conjugal rights. The Lahore High Court undertook a detailed review of the case law and held, at page 1109, that an agreement between husband and wife, allowing her to live away from him in case he took another wife, cannot in any way be termed as opposed to public policy either under the Muslim law or within the meaning of section 23 of the Contract Act 1872.[83] Thus, the husband's petition for restitution of conjugal rights was rejected. The fact that the wife was not even represented in court may be taken to indicate that she and her family had no financial interest in the case. They were probably simply concerned to preserve the status of the woman as a wife, albeit a polygamously married wife, rather than a divorcee.

8–74 Where a woman is subjected to polygamy against her will and asks the court to grant her the right of separate residence and maintenance, the courts in Pakistan have sometimes been helpful. This could be tested with particular reference to cases on restitution of conjugal rights. For instance, in *Zulaikhan v.*

---

[83] This is to the effect that contracts are to be enforced unless they are contrary to public policy We see here again, in contrast to the Middle Eastern countries, which rely upon reforming legislation, often hidden behind the concept of restatement through codification, that the subcontinental law adheres to the common law tradition of judicial developments within the context of a loose enabling statute.

Noor Muhammad, P.L.D. 1986 Quetta 290, it was held that a polygamous marriage is valid in law, but it was also stated, in no uncertain terms, that a husband in such a situation had no legitimate expectation of total condonation of his unilateral act. It was held, at page 296:

> "It may be observed that woman in Islam is not bound in all circumstances to live with her husband. Of course, predominance of a Muslim husband in matrimonial matters [is] . . . recognized, but this in no way means that the husband enjoys unfettered right to compel his wife to live with him in all circumstances. The right of the husband is not free from conditions or limitations. The Islamic injunctions lay down conditions, which if not fulfilled, would absolve the woman from obligation to accompany the husband or to live with him."

We have already stated that where a husband has taken permission of the first wife and later he, or the new wife, mistreat the first wife, the latter does not lose the right to complain about unequal treatment. However, women who wish to complain through court actions have only few options. Hinchcliffe (1970, p. 25) rightly pointed out that they would only claim their dower in extreme cases, namely if they really wanted to leave the husband, and this was their only security. Observation in Pakistan today would suggest that women who can fall back on the support of their natal families will probably prefer to return to the parental home. Even if that means a loss of financial provision from the husband, at least the status of a married woman may be preserved in this way. The current Pakistani system thus encourages married women in marital relationships that are damaged by polygamy to remain officially married to the polygamist, while relying for maintenance and necessities on their natal family or their own resources. That this obviously suits husbands, too, is unwittingly confirmed by Khanam (n.y.: 5) who notes with some surprise that the number of deserted women in her sample was much greater than the number of divorced women.

8–75 Contemporary Pakistani society, therefore, does not conform to the ideal Muslim pattern of the intact family unit, whether potentially or actually polygamous, but allows rather wide scope for a range of convenient arrangements which suit men who wish to 'enjoy' wives by rotation or in serial monogamy, but are unwilling to face the legal and financial consequences for the women and children involved in such relationships. This scenario was highlighted by Kamila Tyabji in Mahmood (1972b, p. 142) with reference to Indian Muslims, but the issue is clearly relevant for the whole of South Asia:

> ". . . according to most observers, the largest number of bigamous marriages found among Indian Muslims today are not cases where the husband lives with and supports two wives, which few can afford to do. In most cases of bigamy, the husband abandons his first wife (and frequently children as well) and goes off to marry another woman. Most of these people cannot be bothered with a divorce, and think nothing of leaving their wife legally bound to them . . . This is nothing but simple desertion, followed by bigamy. And yet, the present law of polygamy upholds it."

This confirms that it may suit both men and women to ignore the state law *and* the Muslim law and to make convenient arrangements in line with local concepts of appropriateness, seeking to preserve status and honour (*izzat*) as best possible. While monogamy is undoubtedly the ideal, polygamous arrangements may be preferred to divorce, as many of the respondents in Khanam's study confirmed. We have already seen that in Pakistan, the current understanding about the onus of providing for divorced and deserted women falls on their natal families, or the women simply have to look after themselves.[84] In view of the Indian experience regarding the enforcement of maintenance obligations against husbands during marriage and after divorce, it may be asked whether a similar activist social welfare strategy in Pakistan could perhaps have beneficial side-effects for the control of polygamy. If husbands in Pakistan knew that taking a wife meant accepting life-long responsibility for her welfare, would polygamists think again? Further, as the important decision in *Subanu v. A. M. Abdul Gafoor*, A.I.R. 1987 S.C. 1103, confirmed for India, if the state law recognises cohabitation for several related purposes and makes no distinction between a legally married wife and a mistress, would intending polygamists rather stick to their existing marriage than risk financial penalties? Interestingly, the point of view of a man interviewed by Khanam (n.y.: 40) highlighted one possible strategy of females living with the threat of polygamy when it was stated that "some ladies would not mind if their husbands keep extra marital relations with other women, so long as they remain their sole wives in their homes".

8–76 In summary, it is evident that the legal reforms in Pakistani law have not seriously attempted to control polygamy. Thus, it is quite obviously misleading if authors simply list the relevant legal provisions in Pakistan as though they form an effective control mechanism against polygamy (see *e.g.* Doi (1984, pp. 151, and 153). Hinchcliffe (1970, p. 25) suggested earlier that section 6 of the MFLO is largely ignored in practice and that some husbands are contracting polygamous marriages contrary to its provisions. Pearl (1969a, p. 188) also observed that the law was not very effective and that many men were ignoring the MFLO procedures. Thirty years later, we still do not know much about the extent of polygamy, but we understand better now that it is not just a singular, easily identifiable and isolated phenomenon.

Bangladeshi law

8–77 Bangladesh has of course inherited the provisions in sections 6 and 13 of the MFLO, 1961 from Pakistan. Some pre-independence case law from the Dacca High Court concerns polygamy,[85] with an emphasis on cases of polyandry.[86] There are many indications that the legal regulation of polygamy in Bangladesh today is no longer identical to that in Pakistan, if indeed it ever was.

8–78 For a start, a married man wishing to obtain permission for a second or further marriage has to approach different local bodies than in Pakistan. The

---

[84] We shall see in Chap. 9, below, how easily this has given rise to allegations of *zina*, especially after the islamisation of relevant laws in Pakistan in 1979.

[85] See *Abu Sufian v. Nurjahan Begum*, 18 D.L.R. (1966) 230, where a jurisdictional point arose. In *Amena Khatoon v. Sherajuddin Sardar*, 17 D.L.R. (1965) 687, a second wife complained that the husband continued to live with the first wife and thus sought a decree of divorce on the ground of unequal treatment. In *Md. Ebrahim Hossain Sarkar v. Solemanessa*, 19 D.L.R. (1967) 751, a second wife complained about the third wife and sought separate maintenance. She was successful in her claim that the husband's attempts to bring her back to the marital home were not bona fide.

[86] *Ainuddin Karikar v. Salatennessa Bibi*, P.L.D. 1953 Dacca 216 confirms that polyandry is reprehensible and void, and that the children from such a marriage are illegitimate. *Amena Khatun v. Munshi Miah*, P.L.D. 1960 Dacca 723, states that polyandry is also punishable under s. 494 of the Penal Code, 1860. In *Jahanara Khatun v. The State*, P.L.D. 1967 Dacca 704, a Muslim woman had been accused of bigamy under s.494 of the Penal Code of 1860, together with her father and a person who solemnised the alleged marriage. The woman's defence was that she had given a delegated *talaq* to her first husband and therefore contracted the second marriage in the bona fide belief that she was free to do so. Her evidence was accepted and the convictions and sentences were set aside.

necessary administrative amendments to section 6 of the MFLO and related provisions were made in Bangladesh in various Orders, in the Muslim Marriages and Divorces (Registration) Act 1974 and in three smaller changes to the MFLO at later dates. Section 15 of the 1974 Act amended three provisions of the 1961 MFLO for Bangladesh. Relevant here is that section 5 of the MFLO, the provision on registration of marriages, was altogether omitted and that section 6 on polygamy was consequently reworded to provide for registration facilities for Muslim marriages in accordance with the 1974 Act rather than under the MFLO. Section 6(1) in the Bangladeshi MFLO now reads as follows:

> "6. Polygamy – (1) No man, during the subsistence of an existing marriage, shall except with the previous permission in writing of the Arbitration Council, contract another marriage, nor shall any such marriage contracted without such permission be registered under the Muslim Marriages and Divorces (Registration) Act 1974 (LII of 1974)."

Bangladeshi law has therefore initially sought to focus on registration of marriages to effect a better control of polygamy. Further amendments to this part of the Ordinance have been of an administrative nature. By Ordinance No. 14 of 1985, the word 'Munsif' was introduced in section 6(4), replacing the words 'Sub-Divisional Officer' in the original section. Earlier, Ordinance No. 21 of 1982 had replaced the words 'five thousand rupees' in section 6(5)(b) with 'ten thousand taka'.[87] It should be noted that this does not represent an increase of punishment for polygamists, merely an adjustment to the new currency.

8–79   The Bangladesh Muslim Family Laws Rules differ in many respects from the equivalent rules in Pakistan. For our present purposes, it is sufficient to confirm that rules 14 and 15 are *verbatim* the same as in Pakistan (cited above, pages 259–260), with the exception of the prescribed fee for an application to the Arbitration Council, which at the end of rule 15 is given as 25 takas, rather than 100 rupees. This probably indicates that Bangladesh tried to make registration procedures as cheap as possible so as to facilitate maximum acceptance of the new rules. Significantly, the Bangladeshi rules do not contain an equivalent of rule 21 as in Pakistan about complaints. This indicates that the infringement of any provision under the Rules or the Ordinance is treated like a cognisable offence. Consequently, there has been no debate in Bangladeshi law about who is an 'aggrieved person' under the MFLO and related provisions.[88]

8–80   Bangladeshi law also makes explicit allowances for Muslim polygamy in certain situations and on specific conditions, operating on the basic principle that an intending polygamist has to seek permission for a further marriage. The man must submit an application to the Chairman of the Union Parishad, Pourashava or Administrator of the Municipal Corporation, as the case may be, stating his reasons and certifying whether consent of the existing wife or wives has been obtained. If it is found that he has proper reasons, permission will be granted. The relevant procedure was outlined in some detail in *Makbul Ali v. Manwara Begum*, 39 D.L.R. (1987) 181. In this case, the first wife, the mother of two small children, had complained that the husband, who worked in London and came home occasionally, had taken another wife in 1984, during one of his visits. The husband claimed that he had divorced the first wife before that and had sent her a letter to that effect, so

---

[87] A third Ordinance in 1986 introduced s.11A into the MFLO relating to place of trial.
[88] A very recent constitutional law case asserts categorically that Bangladesh has always operated a liberal approach to granting standing in court, see *Dr Mohiuddin Farooque v. Bangladesh* (1997) 17 B.L.D. 1.

his defence was that he had not committed any offence under section 6 of the MFLO. This case is more focused on the extent of culpability of the second wife and the case report does not clearly state what the legal position of the husband is. It appears that the court took the view that the first wife's case was devoid of fides.

8–81 Not surprisingly, polygamous marriages in contravention of the MFLO remain fully valid marriages also in Bangladesh. The couple is not allowed to register the marriage under the Muslim Marriages and Divorces (Registration) Act 1974 but it may be doubted whether this is in fact a real punishment, since the registration system is not as effective as was perhaps hoped. Unregistered marriages in Bangladesh remain clearly valid marriages and can be proved in various ways. As in Pakistan, the husband has to pay the full dower, whether prompt or deferred, to his existing wife or wives. Finally the husband, but not the second or subsequent wife, as we already saw,[89] is subject to the stipulated penalties of simple imprisonment for up to a year, a monetary fine of up to ten thousand takas, or both.

8–82 In one of the first reported cases on the subject, *Ahmed Mia Shaha v. Kazi Abdul Motaleb*, 23 D.L.R. (1971) 118, criminal proceedings had been filed against a polygamous husband and several persons who were alleged to have abetted the crime, including the second wife. These were proceedings under section 109 of the Penal Code 1860 as well as section 6(5) of the MFLO, brought by the father of a first wife, obviously designed to criminalise the husband's family for the injury to his daughter. Section 109 is a general provision which concerns punishment for abetment. At first instance, the father's case was successful, but the Additional Sessions Judge found that section 6(5) of the MFLO read with section 109 of the 1860 Code did not warrant such action and set aside the Magistrate's order. The first wife's father then appealed to the High Court, persisting in his strategy of seeking to punish the alleged offenders. Ahsanuddin Choudhury J. appeared concerned to cool down tempers when he emphasised that the proceedings were still at a very early stage and that proper evidence had not even been taken. While it was held that a husband who violated the provisions of section 6(1) of the MFLO was liable to be prosecuted, the judge commented about the position of the second wife, a young girl who, in his view, should not and could not be prosecuted at all. At page 120 it was held:

"Before we part with the matter we like to point out that so far as petitioner Bulbuli Begum (the second wife) is concerned her case stands on a different footing and deserves some consideration. It is difficult to say if Bulbuli Begum had any knowledge that her husband had another wife when the husband contracted his second marriage with her. A Muslim girl living particularly in rural areas mostly acts according to the dictates of her superior relations, including the father. In almost all cases she surrenders to the will of the superiors in the characteristic shyness that prevails upon her at the time of marriage and mechanically gives her consent thereto. Moreover, it is difficult to believe that a girl would readily accept a husband in whose dominion she will have to face a co-wife."

The Magistrate was therefore directed to drop the proceedings against this young second wife.[90] As indicated above, in *Makbul Ali v. Manwara Begum*, 39 D.L.R.

---

[89] This was clarified by the Sylhet Bench in *Makbul Ali v. Manwara Begum*, 39 D.L.R. (1987) 181.
[90] Sobhan, *Legal Status of women in Bangladesh* (1978), p. 9 criticised the decision in *Ahmed Mia*, arguing that if the law was serious about controlling polygamy, it should also make the second wife subject to punishment.

(1987) 181, the second wife was also a co-accused, but it was held by this court that the second wife is exempt from any penalty under the MFLO, even as an abettor of a crime. This is undoubtedly a correct interpretation of the Ordinance and it seems appropriate that such attempts to criminalise women who may be entirely innocent should be soundly rebuffed. It is less certain that anyone aiding and abetting a polygamous husband should be let off without penalty, but this was decided in the earlier case of *Abdul Halim Pattader v. M. Rahmat Ali* (1981) B.L.D. 377, where the co-accused were a marriage registrar and several other persons participating in the polygamous marriage.

8–83   *Tahera Begum v. Farukh Meah*, 35 D.L.R. (1983) A.D. 170 reflects considerable confusion over the new administrative and local government structures in Bangladesh after Independence in 1971 and their relation to the control of polygamy under section 6 of the MFLO as amended. This case arose as a complaint by a first wife about the husband's unilateral action of marrying again some time in 1975 without seeking permission of the Arbitration Council. The husband had been sentenced by the Magistrate at first instance to five months of rigorous imprisonment and a fine of 200/- takas or further imprisonment for one month. Three co-accused persons had also been sentenced to pay a fine of 130/- takas each. On appeal, the co-accused persons had been acquitted but the husband's sentence had been upheld. On a further appeal, the husband had also been acquitted on the ground that there was no competent authority at the relevant time to whom he could have applied for permission to contract a further marriage. The wife, who obviously wanted the polygamist punished, went before the Appellate Division of the Bangladeshi Supreme Court but her appeal did not succeed. The case report goes mainly through details of local government legislation which do not concern us here. It was held that since there was a hiatus in the law (page 173) at the relevant time, there had been no competent authority from whom permission for a second marriage could have been obtained, hence no offence had been committed.[91]

8–84   A few years later, it was found that there had not been such a gap in the law and that the Government had in fact duly appointed local authorities to perform all necessary functions under the MFLO. This came to light in the case of *Ayesha Sultana v. Shahjahan Ali*, 38 D.L.R. (1986) 140, which is also a first wife's complaint about the husband's illegal second marriage in violation of the provisions of section 6 of the MFLO. The husband had at first instance been convicted but had been acquitted on appeal, on the ground that there had been no competent authorities to whom he could have made his application for permission to remarry. The wife appealed further because she wanted the husband to be punished and, in this case, succeeded. The facts of this case indicate that the wife had borne a dead child in 1976, some two years after the marriage, and that the husband had married another wife some time in 1978. When it came to sentencing the husband, Amin-Ur-Rahman Khan J. held, at page 145:

> "Regarding the sentence having regard to the facts and circumstances of the case and the possible ignorance of the accused respondent we are of the view that imposition of a fine of Tk. 1,000/- (taka one thousand) only in default to suffer simple imprisonment of three months will meet the ends of justice."

---

[91] It must be noted that this point was also carried into English case law, strengthening the misguided view of some English judges that a Muslim wife in this situation had no legal right at all to object to the husband's polygamy. See *Quoraishi v. Quoraishi* [1985] F.L.R. 780 at 783 and again, more clearly, at 786.

This appears to strike an equitable balance between punishing the offence and taking account of the possible ignorance of the husband, but it is a penalty on the lenient side, without any attempt at social activism on the part of the judges. More recent cases support the conclusion that Bangladeshi law is becoming more strict on polygamous husbands who continue to violate the law with impunity. In *Abul Basher v. Nurun Nabi*, 39 D.L.R. (1987) 333, a man who worked in the Gulf had borrowed money from his wife's brother for obtaining that employment, but had later fallen out with his wife and had refused to maintain her and the youngest of four daughters. He then married another woman and his brother-in-law filed a complaint. It transpired that a Magistrate had ascertained the husband's failure to obtain permission for the second marriage but had acquitted the husband nevertheless. This was strongly deprecated on appeal. When considering the provisions of section 6 of the MFLO, it was confirmed, at page 335, that "the legislative intent of section 6 of the Muslim Family Laws Ordinance, 1961 is to restrict the practice of polygamy and to permit it only in cases where it appears to be reasonable to the Arbitration Council". Since the husband in the present case had failed to obtain permission in writing from the Arbitration Council, the case was remanded for fresh and expeditious trial.

8–85 The most recent case of *Jesmin Sultana v. Mohammad Elias* (1997) 17 B.L.D. 4, probably represents a turning point in the legal treatment of polygamy in Bangladesh. This case is first of all a suit for payment of dower and maintenance, arising in a family of prosperous circumstances. The husband's claim that the wife should not be entitled to any maintenance because she left his company without good reason gave rise to an investigation into the wife's motives. It transpired that the husband had, some time in 1996, made an application for permission to marry another woman, claiming that his wife was sickly and unable to perform conjugal relations. Rabbani J. had no difficulty in finding, as a result, that the wife was compelled to leave her husband and was therefore entitled to maintenance. It appears that such cases arise frequently in Bangladeshi law, but few cases are reported.[92]

8–86 In *Jesmin Sultana*, Rabbani J. was not satisfied to do justice merely in terms of dower and maintenance. The learned judge considered section 6 of the MFLO and produced, at page 5, an authoritative restatement of Bangladeshi law, to the effect that such marriages remain valid but carry certain punishments. The judge then, *suo moto*, ventured to reconsider the foundations of Bangladeshi Muslim law on polygamy, saying at page 5 that he found it necessary to examine the issue as to whether Islam truly approved of polygamy. Finding that, "since long . . . there had been great difference of opinion regarding this issue" (*id.*), the judge turned to the relevant Qur'anic verses and learned commentaries, concluding that the narrow view of the meaning of the expression 'to be able to deal justly' had to be rejected, so that polygamy was in fact not allowed under Muslim law. Rabbani J. supports his view and interpretation with a brief reference to the Tunisian Law of Personal Status of 1957 and concludes, at page 6:

> "So we find that section 6 of the Muslim Family Laws Ordinance is against the principle of Islamic law. We recommend that this section be deleted and be substituted with a section prohibiting polygamy. Let a copy of this judgment be sent to the Ministry of Law."

It is too early to suggest that this case heralds a total change in the legal approach to Muslim polygamy in Bangladesh. However, this judgment fits in well with other

---

[92] Monsoor (1994), p. 255 confirms this and discusses several unreported cases from Dacca.

recent judicial verdicts from Bangladesh which provide evidence of a re-assessment of existing legal foundations in the light of current socio-economic pronouncements conditions. Given the population pressures in South Asia and the unwillingness and inability of the modern states to provide social welfare payments, adopting the traditional minority view from within Muslim jurisprudence is clearly a viable strategy to give desirable socio-legal messages to the effect that polygamy is not acceptable, except perhaps in very few controlled situations. We must wait to see how this particular discussion in Bangladeshi law proceeds. It will have important implications on the whole of South Asia.

8-87   The secondary literature on the legal position of women in Bangladesh has much to say about polygamy as an indicator of the disadvantaged legal status of women. Sobhan (1978, p. 23) took the view that the provisions of the MFLO "are not really sufficient to stamp out the evil of polygamy", since "the real sanction is not applied, that of invalidity". However, few authors call for this particular remedy, probably well aware that it clashes with basic principles of Muslim law about the contractual nature of *nikah* and mindful of the negative social consequences for women and children if all polygamous marriages were suddenly invalidated. Concern for the welfare of women is also reflected in the observation by Sobhan (1978, p. 23) that "the courts have long been liberal towards the wife who left the family home on grounds that her husband had married again and were not averse to granting maintenance in such a situation".[93]

8-88   Chaudhury and Ahmed (1981) frequently refer to polygamy during their study and argue, at page 22, that the existing laws are perceived as "inadequate in providing protection against the abuses of polygamy and therefore its vices continue to cause hardship and misery for wives and children". A decade later, Alia Ahmad (1991, p. 96) confirms that the enforcement of the anti-polygamy law has been poor and argues that the insecure economic position of women and their lack of education prevent them from exercising their rights, which aids the already inefficient functioning of the law. Bhuiyan (1985, pp. 237–238) as well as Chaudhury and Ahmed (1981, pp. 21–22) usefully summarise the law on polygamy in Bangladesh. Bhuiyan (1985, p. 238) confirms that "unfortunately, even educated women are not aware of the existence of such legal rights" and "even if women know about such rights they are unable to implement these because of socio-economic conditions". The same author argues that while very often the legal remedy remains out of the reach of women, "in most cases the consent of the existing wife is exacted who settles with her husband at the cost of her feelings for fear of becoming destitute" (page 238).

8-89   Chaudhury and Ahmed (1981, p. 14) emphasise that even husbands with several children may marry another wife to have a son, which seems a typical South Asian phenomenon. At pages 28–29, they refer to fieldwork studies of 1968 showing that the absolute majority of husbands (80 per cent) did not even bother to make an application to an Arbitration Council. Of those 20 per cent who did, 70 per cent were granted permission, 13 per cent were refused, and the remaining 17 per cent were fined for contracting a further marriage without permission. The authors conclude from this, at page 29, that "the existing law is not adequate to provide protection against the abuse of polygamy in the society". It is recommended in this study that "polygamy should be prohibited" (page 32), and that "such a marriage will be declared void" (*id.*). But the authors apparently cannot envisage the total abolition of polygamy either, for they suggest a scheme for ensuring that men do

---

[93] See *Md. Ebrahim Hossain Sarkar v. Solemannessa*, 19 D.L.R. (1967) 751; *Begum Hamida v. Abdul Hamid*, 26 D.L.R. (1974) S.C. 26.

not abuse their discretion to marry again "if circumstances require a man to contract a second marriage". These conditions are not specified, but the details of the proposed scheme look remarkably like the control mechanisms which already exist under the MFLO 1961 and the DMMA 1939.

8-90 It appears that the conclusion one must draw is that very few people in Bangladesh argue in favour of polygamy. The existing law is clearly seeking to restrict it, but the legal mechanisms for controlling polygamy are not as effective as they could be, being defeated by a combination of social forces and awareness of the Muslim justifications of polygamy in cases where husbands simply exercise their discretion. If the recent judicial decisions discussed above are a reliable indication, Bangladesh may be heading for a more vigorous system of legal control of polygamy, but total prohibition remains elusive in view of South Asian social and religious realities. However, in Bangladesh, too, the current judicial activism concerning maintenance laws and post-divorce maintenance rights for divorced Muslim wives may as yet have the side-effect of curbing polygamous tendencies.

Polygamy in Britain

8-91 In contrast to the reluctant South Asian acceptance of limited polygamy among Muslims, English law has taken an openly hostile, negative and restrictive approach to polygamy, which has long been prohibited and more or less totally outlawed, with strict consequences in terms of legal validity and punishment. The underlying reason for this can be found in Christian teaching, although recent research doubts this.[94] At any rate, the long maintenance of a strictly negative approach to polygamy confirms that modern Western state law, divorced from religion, has developed other grounds for opposing polygamy, now prominently arguing in favour of gender equality and human rights. Any Muslim individual, or indeed anyone else, putting forward any of the traditional justifications for polygamy would elicit the response that such arguments are irrelevant in a secular setting where state law prevails and where polygamy is simply not acceptable.

8-92 The strict prohibition on polygamy in English law has had many consequences, only some of which concern us here. In English law, a Muslim marriage in the form of the *nikah* can only be recognised as legally valid if it was entered into outside the United Kingdom (see already Chapter 4). Under conflict of laws rules, English law remains constrained to recognise the legal validity of polygamous marriages validly solemnised abroad where both parties have capacity to contract such plural marriages. In this way, the legal validity of South Asian plural Muslim marriages will of necessity continue to be recognised by English law.

8-93 However, for the purposes of immigration law, United Kingdom law has been refusing to give recognition to the consequences of such marriages and the law now allows the polygamously married foreign husband to bring only one wife to the United Kingdom, rather than his entire family.[95] This demonstrates the public policy objections of English law against the practice of polygamy, which are also brought out very strongly in decisions of courts and tribunals relating to social security and pension matters.[96] The very recent case of *Bibi v. Chief Adjudication*

---

[94] For details see Poulter (1986), p. 45, with reference to an ongoing re-assessment of Christian doctrines in view of African pressures for the recognition of local customary practices.

[95] The relevant legal rules are found in Immigration Rules, HC 395, paras 278–280.

[96] For details see Poulter (1986), pp. 64–65, indicating at p. 64 that some of these decisions may be unduly harsh.

Officer,[97] confirms this harsh approach, denying the wife of an actually polygamously married man entitlement to the widow's pension on the husband's death. In this case, a Bangladeshi Muslim man arrived in the United Kingdom in 1958, registered as a citizen and married his first wife in a Muslim ceremony in Bangladesh in 1966. In 1969, he married a second wife under Bangladeshi Muslim law. In 1970, he returned to the United Kingdom to work and in 1986, he settled here with his first wife, while the second wife remained in Bangladesh. After his death in 1988, the first wife's application for a widowed mother's allowance was refused. On appeal it was held by the Court of Appeal on June 25, 1997 that in view of the hallowed definition of monogamous marriage in English law as in *Hyde v. Hyde* (see below), the absence of a power to divide a widow's benefit, and the fact that only one allowance was payable, the widow's case could not succeed. The narrow interpretation of 'wife' in this case excludes both surviving widows. Obviously, this case raises important policy issues and quite a few questions about the scope for arrangements between two widows.[98]

8–94 Historically, the English domestic law has been opposed to legal recognition of all Muslim forms of marriage, mainly on the ground that they lead to what has been called 'potentially polygamous marriages' (see already Pearl (1972b), p. 127). Such negative presuppositions also apply where the facts of the case obviously show that a particular marriage is monogamous. The point is that it was assumed that such a marriage could, at any time, be turned into an actually polygamous marriage.[99]

8–95 An important early effect of the strict approach against polygamy, based on the old Mormon case of *Hyde v. Hyde*,[1] was to deny any form of matrimonial relief to spouses even in a 'potentially polygamous' marriage. It became important for a time to ascertain precisely what was the status of a particular overseas marriage.[2] Poulter (1986, p. 50) has written that the decision in *Hyde v. Hyde* "seemed to reflect an outmoded Victorian attitude towards foreign customs and was obviously capable of operating extremely harshly on the individuals concerned". Finally, in the Matrimonial Proceedings (Polygamous Marriages) Act 1972, soon re-enacted in the Matrimonial Causes Act 1973, the jurisdictional barriers against potentially polygamous marriages were removed. It was suggested by the Law Commission that this reform was designed to encourage parties to polygamous marriages to conform to English standards of behaviour, while at the same time "increased recognition was being given to an essentially alien custom" (Poulter (1986), p. 51). After 1972, therefore, cases came up in which the English courts accepted jurisdiction even if there was a polygamous marriage. Not many such cases involving Muslims have been reported.[3] The case of *Chaudhry v. Chaudhry* [1976] Fam. 148, illustrates the beneficial effects of the new law for wives, since

---

[97] Reported in the *Gazette* 94/27, July 9, 1997, p. 22.

[98] It also gives added arguments to Muslim proponents of extra-legal arrangements for polygamy, on which see further below.

[99] On the legal position of Muslim marriages solemnised in Pakistan see the important and instructive case of *Hussain v. Hussain* [1983] Fam 26; [1982] 3 All E.R. 369; [1982] 3 W.L.R. 679 and the comments in Pearl (1986a), pp. 46–48. See now ss.5 and 6 of the Private International Law (Miscellaneous Provisions) Act 1995.

[1] For details see Poulter (1986), pp. 47 *et seq.*

[2] See in detail Pearl (1972b), Poulter (1986), pp. 44–65.

[3] *Radwan v. Radwan (No. 2)* [1973] Fam. 35, was the first case in which an English court had to decide whether an English wife had capacity to enter a potentially polygamous marriage abroad. The important later case of *Hussain v. Hussain* [1982] 3 All E.R. 369; [1982] 3 W.L.R. 679; [1983] Fam 1; [1983] 4 F.L.R. 339, concerned Muslim marriages in Pakistan and complex questions of domicile rather than Muslim jurisprudence.

polygamous husbands could now no longer rely on the convenient argument that the English courts had no jurisdiction to grant any form of matrimonial relief.

8–96 *Quoraishi v. Quoraishi* is one case of some interest here.[4] The spouses were Bangladeshi Muslims who married in Karachi in 1964 and came to the United Kingdom as medical practitioners in the early 1970s. The couple remained childless and the husband discussed with the wife the possibility of taking a second wife. Although the wife had refused to consent to this, the husband married again in May 1979, by proxy, and this time in Bangladesh, where he was then domiciled. The second marriage was valid according to Bangladeshi law. By June 1979, the husband returned to the United Kingdom and his first wife demanded that he should terminate the second marriage, which he refused to do, whereupon the wife left the matrimonial home. The husband, in turn, left for Bangladesh, consummated the marriage with his second wife, and then brought her to the United Kingdom in early 1980. The first wife brought a complaint about the husband's desertion, which was dismissed.[5]

8–97 Here, then, was a Muslim husband living in England with two wives whom he had validly married under an overseas law. When the husband subsequently petitioned for divorce from the first wife under section 1(2)(c) of the Matrimonial Causes Act 1973, *i.e.* on the ground of desertion, the question arose whether the wife had just cause to leave the husband. It was held by Butler-Sloss J. in the High Court that, in modern circumstances, the taking of a second wife without consent even in Muslim societies could amount to cruelty.[6] The husband appealed on the ground that the judge had failed to take into account evidence of Muslim law tendered to her. Before the Court of Appeal, the husband's case was dismissed again and it was concluded that the wife had just cause for leaving the husband.[7] This judgment is interesting because of its manifest unwillingness to address the questions that would arise under Muslim law. Ewbank J., at page 785, even stated that it was not necessary to consider the Muslim law in any detail because it was a marginal matter. This is only partly explained by the fact that the learned judge seemed to have formed the misguided view that a first wife in a polygamous South Asian Muslim marriage had no legal right.[8] There is, in addition, much emphasis on asserting the role of English law and English principles. The underlying argument appears to be that individuals who have lived in England for a long time are to be judged by reference to standards applicable in English law, rather than any other legal system. One could see this case as a missed opportunity to clarify the extent of the first wife's rights under Muslim law on polygamy.

8–98 As in South Asian countries, the protective mechanism of stipulations in the marriage contract could be of some assistance to Muslim wives in Britain. Pearl (1986a, p. 35) emphasised the role of such conditions in the marriage contract:

---

[4] [1983] 4 F.L.R. 706; [1983] 3 Fam. Law 86 and [1985] F.L.R. 780; [1985] Fam. Law 308, CA.

[5] Note the explanation in Pearl (1986a), p. 59 to the effect that the 'expert evidence' in that case was faulty. It is the case that under s.2(ii-a) of the DMMA, as amended by the MFLO 1961, Bangladeshi law allowed a wife to seek divorce from a husband who had married again without permission from the Arbitration Council.

[6] It appears that *Itwari v. Asghari*, A.I.R. 1960 Al. 684 with its strong emphasis on 'cruelty' influenced the decision in this case to some extent.

[7] It has been mooted whether a wife in this situation has a case for divorce on the ground of adultery under s.1(2)(b) of the Matrimonial Causes Act 1973. The response appears to be negative. See Pearl (1986a), pp. 60–61; Poulter (1986), pp. 48–49.

[8] See p. 786 of the learned judge's decision. Pearl (1986a), p. 59, has pointed out that the expert evidence was deficient, and there are several references to this in the case report itself.

". . . if the husband does marry a second wife then a restriction imposed upon him in the marriage contract will be highly significant in a petition for divorce based on unreasonable behaviour."

We have already stated that such stipulations will probably be upheld by English courts, more so with reference to polygamy, in view of the strong public policy stance against it. However, as paragraph 8–29 indicated in several ways, this public policy approach is not replicated in the modern South Asian jurisdictions, so that some legal insecurities are bound to remain over the precise status of Muslim marriages which involve migrant spouses from different countries and possibly with different domiciles. It appears, in fact, that English law has remained somewhat purposely unclear, avoiding a head-on conflict.[9]

8–99 The Pakistani case of *Fauzia Hussain v. Khadim Hussain*, P.L.D. 1985 Lah. 165, discussed briefly in paragraph 8–50, above, illustrates this continuing potential for conflicts from a Pakistani Muslim perspective. In this case, the parties had married in a register office in Birmingham, United Kingdom and the husband had later taken a second wife in Pakistan. One of the husband's arguments in resisting the wife's complaint about his polygamous arrangement was that the first marriage had been entered into in England and was registered under the provisions of the relevant English law. Therefore, the courts in Pakistan had no jurisdiction in the matter. The lower court had accepted that argument when acquitting the husband, but in the High Court, Muhammad Munir Khan J. took a different view and held, at pages 172–173:

"Even if the earlier marriage of the parties was performed in Birmingham, then also that was a valid marriage between the two Muslims and as such, Mian Khadim Hussain could not have entered into second marriage without permission of his first wife under the Muslim Family Laws Ordinance. The marriage before a Registrar in Birmingham does not necessarily import the essential of monogamy. Such marriage conforms to requirements of Muslim marriage and would be recognized as a valid marriage under Muslim law."

This judgment does not take explicit notice of the fact that the spouses also contracted a Muslim marriage in England at about the same time as they registered their marriage there. We have already seen in paragraph 6–92, that under *angrezi shariat* this is exactly what normally happens. The Pakistani courts clearly take the view that a Muslim marriage entered into in the United Kingdom is still a potentially polygamous marriage. This would be in opposition to the English legal position, as stated, *e.g.* by Poulter (1986, p. 46).

8–100 Faced with the outright legal prohibition of polygamy under English law, British Muslims have not, however, abandoned all thoughts of polygamy. We have seen that upon migration to the United Kingdom, Muslims did not give up their Muslim identity, nor did they drop their customary conceptualisations of what is right and wrong. With regard to polygamy, there is much potential for a head-on conflict of rules, about which very little has been written. While the official viewpoint is that Muslims in Britain must adapt to the local law, this is clearly not going to be achieved at the cost of abandoning all facets of Muslim identity. While Muslim identity certainly does not depend on the practice of polygamy, it has been tempting for Muslim husbands, and sometimes wives, to argue that Islam allows limited polygamy in certain situations.[10] Ahsan (1995, p. 26) indicates that, from a

---

[9] This is indicated subtly by Poulter (1986), p. 46.
[10] Some unpublished fieldwork material produced by students at SOAS, University of London, shows that, even in Britain, some Muslim wives suggest polygamous arrangements to their husbands to retain married status for themselves.

Muslim perspective, English law's prohibition of polygamy appears hypocritical but avoids the real issue: How do Muslims in Britain today handle polygamy in those admittedly few situations when it is considered necessary or preferable?

8–101 In Britain today, there are many Muslim families with polygamous arrangements which were made abroad prior to migration to Britain. We are not concerned with those cases. In addition, there are some Muslim husbands who wish to make polygamous arrangements in Britain without falling foul of English law. In those cases, with reference to polygamy, too, *angrezi shariat* represents again an expedient combination of Muslim and English law. It is really a rather simple expedient device to avoid criminalisation and yet have two, if not more, wives at the same time.[11] A Muslim husband in England would marry the first wife under *angrezi shariat*, as outlined in paragraph 6–92, above, fulfilling all legal requirements under the English legal system as well as in Muslim law. While such a marriage under English law is certainly monogamous, we saw that it can be treated as potentially polygamous under *angrezi shariat* and, as *Fauzia Hussain* confirmed, will be so perceived in Pakistan as well. The man may thereafter choose to marry a second wife under *shariat* only, contracting the *nikah* with her, but not any form of official registration. This, in a nutshell, is *angrezi shariat* on polygamy. As we saw, the official legal position of the second woman in English law would rather be like a concubine. In other words, she would be a cohabitant in the technical language of modern English family law. While the notion of a polygamous cohabitation is certainly not acceptable to English law, this very real issue has remained hidden, since the domestic law has only concerned itself with the official processes of solemnisation and registration. The contract of the Muslim marriage is simply not perceived and treated as a legal fact, as far as English law is concerned.

8–102 Unpublished fieldwork by several students at SOAS, University of London, has unearthed a variant of the above pattern of polygamous arrangement without infringement of the official law which has the same social and legal effects. In this case, the husband and the first wife would divorce under English law. This is very simple if both spouses agree, which happens in some cases because the wife knows (or at least hopes) that she will remain a respected Muslim wife for all intents and purposes. The official divorce accomplished, the husband is then free to remarry in English law, *i.e.* under *angrezi shariat*. This second union is, of course, also a polygamous marriage in the eyes of Muslim law but English law treats it as a monogamous union. The fact that Muslim law does not outrightly and totally prohibit polygamy allows the husband sufficient room for polygamous discretion. This confirms that unless interpretations of Muslim law take the stance that polygamy is not allowed, convenient arrangements can be made, not only in Muslim countries but anywhere in the world.

8–103 Both polygamous patterns within *angrezi shariat* appear to depend at least to some extent on the agreement of the wives, but it is not possible to be certain, as in South Asia and elsewhere, that this is always a matter of free consent. Because the polygamous arrangements are invisible to the official English law, and most Muslims are aware of this, it is unlikely that a polygamously married Muslim wife will approach an English court today. It is rather more likely that organisations like the Muslim Law (Shariah) Council (U.K.) will become involved in dispute resolution. Until fieldwork is undertaken to ascertain how such cases would be and are handled, it is not possible to say much about Muslim perceptions of the stipulated need for equal treatment among co-wives in Britain.

---

[11] Fieldwork evidence from Britain suggests strongly that taking more than two wives is seen as virtually unmanageable.

8–104 Individuals and families making such arrangements appear to be well aware of the risks in terms of disharmony in the family and, especially, problems over succession and other property matters. Polygamy is of necessity a grey area but it is no co-incidence that, apart from immigration, the legal problems most closely linked with polygamy arise in relation to various aspects of social security law and matrimonial litigation.[12] The practical problems in these areas of law will continue to exercise writers and lawyers, certainly leaders of the Muslim communities in Britain, perhaps also judges. While Muslim polygamy is a minority phenomenon in Britain today, it presents nevertheless an intractable problem (Poulter (1995), p. 85) which has defied any attempts at legal solutions which please everyone.

8–105 As *Quoraishi v. Quoraishi* showed, unless detailed specialist knowledge of relevant aspects of Muslim law is placed before the courts, a full examination of the undoubted rights of Muslim wives to oppose polygamous arrangements cannot be made within the parameters of English law. While we are not saying that this should necessarily be done in all cases, it is not an option for English law, in the long run, to assume that the ban on polygamous marriages is sufficient by itself to control the phenomenon. As in South Asian jurisdictions, the key test in English law, too, must be whether a Muslim woman who complains about the husband's polygamy will be heard and will be given a meaningful remedy. If, as we must assume at present, Muslim wives take their grievances to Muslim organisations rather than English courts, the solutions are only found in the realm of the so-called extra-legal sphere.

---

[12] Pearl (1986a), p. 40. On social security aspects and taxation, see *ibid.*, 49–50, Pearl [1978b] *Journal of Social Welfare Law* 24–35, and various articles by the same author in *New Community*. See now *Bibi v. Chief Adjudication Officer Gazette* 94/27, July 9, 1997, p. 22.

Chapter 9

Dissolution of marriage

9–01 Muslim law knows various forms of dissolution of a marriage, at the initiative of the husband, the wife, by mutual agreement, or by judicial process.[1] On Muslim law of divorce in general and the Hanafi law in particular, it can be said that divorce at the instance of the husband is prominent and rather simple. However, this does not mean that divorce is treated as desirable. In fact, there is a much-quoted saying of the Prophet to the effect that, of all permitted things, divorce is the most reprehensible.[2]

9–02 Divorce at the instigation of the wife has often been portrayed as particularly difficult, and this is certainly true for Hanafi Muslim law, which is most restrictive in this regard. But the issue should not be overstated, since the basic principle of Muslim divorce law is that a marital bond which does not function any more should be terminated to avoid further problems (see Doi (1984), pp. 168–169). Underlying this principle is the unstated major concern that forcing unwilling or unhappy spouses to stay together will lead to various forms of extra-marital relations (*zina*). As in our discussion of polygamy, we see therefore that unspoken but powerful apprehensions about sexual morality have influenced the way in which Muslim divorce rules have developed over time. In addition to various kinds of divorce initiated by the husband or the wife, there are forms of divorce which involve an agreement between husband and wife, often linked to the right to divorce at a future point of time, or in case of some eventuality. The two modes of judicial dissolution of marriage are *lian* and *faskh*.

9–03 The pre-Islamic law, treating women as chattels, allowed husbands absolute discretion to divorce and gave wives virtually no right in this regard.[3] The trend for reforms in Muslim law, therefore, has been towards making divorce by the husband more difficult and less instant and harsh, whereas women's rights to divorce have been strengthened and expanded by reforms in various countries, notably in the South Asian jurisdictions. In this chapter we briefly discuss first the classical position and then outline some legislative reforms in the Muslim world. The bulk of the chapter is taken up by a detailed discussion of South Asian Muslim divorce laws, which have recently witnessed much new development, particularly in Pakistan. Muslim divorce law has also become a very important topic because, in Pakistan as well as now in Bangladesh, the modern state's claim to control the husband's unilateral right to divorce has led to an important new conflict of laws scenario within the Muslim personal law itself. Finally, the entirely new section on Muslim divorce in Britain today also focuses on a new conflicts scenario and produces evidence of divorce arrangements among British Muslims which deserve further discussion.

---

[1] For a convenient overview see now F. Ahmad (1994), p. 15.
[2] Tayyibji (1968), p. 143; Doi (1984), p. 169; Bharatiya (1996), p. 98.
[3] A good overview is found in Fyzee (1974), pp. 146–148; see also F. Ahmad (1994), p. 3.

The classical Muslim law on divorce

Traditional forms of Muslim divorce

9–04 It is useful to summarise at the outset the most important aspects of the institution of the Muslim divorce given by the husband, the *talaq*, which appears in different forms.[4] In essence, the *talaq* is the unilateral repudiation or cutting off of the marital tie.[5] Use of the *talaq* is a power available exclusively to the husband, although it is possible for the husband to delegate the power to pronounce the *talaq* to some other person, or indeed the wife, who then uses the so-called 'delegated *talaq*' (*talaq-i-tafwid*) to free herself from the marital bond (Carroll (1982a)). In the classical Muslim law on *talaq*, the consent of the wife is not required and the pronouncement or declaration of the *talaq* is extra-judicial and in no way subject to any external check.[6] Muslim law is evidently not happy with limping marriages. Doi ((1984), pp. 169, 173) and other authors repeatedly emphasise that the husband should not leave the wife 'hanging in the air'. Such concerns may reflect human rights awareness, but they focus much more on sexual morality.

9–05 In classical Hanafi law, a *talaq* can be pronounced in one of a number of forms. The more meritorious forms (*talaq as-sunna*) are clearly those which offer the opportunity of revocation. In contrast, the least meritorious forms (the *al-bida* forms) are the irrevocable modes which are more or less instantly effective, *i.e.* immediately final from the moment of pronouncement. The *talaq al-bida* can be instituted either as a triple pronouncement (commonly called the 'triple *talaq*') or as a single *talaq*, which will then be accompanied by some expression of finality. In Hanafi law, this *talaq* can be either pronounced orally or it can be reduced to writing, while the Shia law does not accept it as a valid form at all.

9–06 *Talaq as-sunna* in the *ahsan* form is the most approved method of repudiation.[7] At a time when the wife is not menstruating, in what is known as the *tuhr* period, the husband pronounces a single *talaq*. If he wishes the divorce to be final, he must then refrain from sexual intercourse with the wife he has divorced during the *iddat* period of three menstrual cycles.[8] At the end of this *iddat* period, the marriage is terminated. The dissolution of the marital tie arises directly from the unilateral *talaq* pronounced three months earlier. This form of repudiation provides an opportunity for revocation, as the husband can take back his wife at any time during this period. The *ahsan* formula is therefore categorised as revocable (*raji*). Revocation can be implied by conduct; resumption of intercourse clearly constitutes sufficient evidence of an intention to revoke. The *ahsan talaq*, provided it is not the third of such *ahsan talaqs*, is referred to as having smaller or lesser finality and is called the 'little method' (*sughra*), compared to the greater finality of three divorces, the 'great method' (*kubra*).[9] The practical impact of this distinction is very important and explains the stress laid on the difference between the two categories. Where only one pronouncement of *talaq* has taken place, and the divorce

---

[4] Tayyibji (1968), p. 144, lists and distinguishes twelve different forms of Muslim divorce altogether. *Talaq* is clearly the leading phenomenon.

[5] Doi (1984), p. 168 says it "literally means to set an animal free", see in more detail Fyzee (1974), p. 150.

[6] This parallels the situation in polygamy (see Chap. 8, above), where the absolute discretion of the husband was also the basic element.

[7] For details see Tayyibji (1968), pp. 157–159; Fyzee (1974), pp. 152–153; Nasir (1990a), p. 119; Doi (1984), pp. 175–178; F. Ahmad (1994), p. 17.

[8] If the wife is beyond the age for menstruation, or if she does not menstruate, or if her periods are irregular, then three lunar months form the *iddat* period. Several textbooks provide separate chapters on *iddat*.

[9] Nasir (1990a), p. 121 calls these the 'minor' and 'major' methods of repudiation.

becomes final simply through the expiry of the *iddat* period and non-resumption of cohabitation, lesser finality results and the man has the capacity to remarry his wife by contracting another marriage with her after the expiry of the *iddat* period without an intervening marriage (Nasir (1990a), p. 121). In general, the practical implications of the 'greater finality' are so much more serious that it is to be avoided.

9–07 The *talaq as-sunna* in the *hasan* form, like the *ahsan*, is classified as an approved or good method of repudiation, accepted by all schools. However, this form is not considered as acceptable as the *ahsan* form, mainly because the *hasan* form leads to 'greater finality'.[10] The procedure is that the husband repudiates his wife three times. The first *talaq* is given during a *tuhr* period and the husband then pronounces two subsequent *talaqs* during the following two *tuhr* periods. As soon as the husband pronounces the third *talaq*, this divorce becomes irrevocable. This form of *talaq* is also revocable, but only until the third pronouncement. In other words, in the *hasan* form the marriage does not come to an end until the pronouncement of the third *talaq*. The third pronouncement, however, ends the marriage immediately and by 'greater finality', because this was the third of three *talaqs*. The wife then has to observe an *iddat* period after the third pronouncement; but the husband cannot revoke his decision to divorce the wife and if he wishes to remarry her, he can only do so if she concludes a contract of marriage with another man which is consummated and is itself validly dissolved.[11]

9–08 In Hanafi law, the 'triple *talaq*' or *talaq al-bida* may be used by the husband.[12] Although disapproved by classical jurisprudence, it has the advantage, for the husband at least, of simplicity and finality. Doi (1984, p. 179) says it "is usually done by ignorant Muslims to satisfy their selfish motives" and emphasises that it involves a heinous sin against the precepts of the *shari'a*. However, such a divorce is legally valid, except for Shi'ites and the moral disapproval of this form has not stopped it from becoming popular in many parts of the Muslim world, for the obvious reason that it suits men. The most common method of *talaq al-bida* is for the triple pronouncement of *talaq al-hasan* to be brought together into a single sitting. Such a divorce creates an instant irrevocable termination of the marriage. As the divorce pronouncement has been effected three times, there is no scope for reconciliation and it is not possible for the parties to remarry each other unless and until the wife has gone through another marriage which has itself been consummated and dissolved. A *talaq al-bida* can be effected also when a husband repudiates his wife during her menstrual flow, in which case it is still revocable, or when he accompanies a single *talaq* with some expression of finality, in which case it is a final divorce[13] If the marriage has not been consummated, a single *talaq* without any additional words will also constitute a completed and immediate divorce.

9–09 Regarding the effect of a *talaq*, an important point is the exact moment in time when the divorce takes effect. This moment differs depending on the form of *talaq*. In the *ahsan* form, the *talaq* is effective at the expiry of the *iddat* period. In the *hasan* form, it is effective on the third pronouncement, while in the *al-bida* form, it

---

[10] For details see Tayyibji (1968), pp. 159–160; Fyzee (1974), pp. 153–154; Nasir (1990a), p. 119; very briefly Doi (1984), pp. 178–179; F. Ahmad (1994), pp. 19–20.

[11] For this reason, this form of *talaq* is referred to as a 'big *talaq*' or *kubra*. For details see Nasir (1990a), p. 121.

[12] It is also called *talaq-i-bain*. For some details see Tayyibji (1968), p. 160. *ibid.*, p. 163 says it is even favoured by the law, despite being the most disapproved form. An excellent new study on this subject is F. Ahmad (1994), esp. pp. 20–22, see also Pirzada, *Triple talaq in the light of Qur'an and Sunna* (1996).

[13] Illustrations of such pronouncements are found in Tayyibji (1968), p. 168.

is effective at once.[14] As soon as the divorce is irrevocable, the marital relationship is over. Indeed, any intercourse at this stage will be viewed as *zina*. A revocable divorce, of course, is subject to the *iddat* period. One important effect which arises as a result is that if either party dies during this period of *iddat*, the rights of inheritance are preserved. Inheritance rights *inter se* do not exist after the pronouncement of *talaq al-bida*, even if one of the parties dies during the *iddat* period following such a divorce. The *iddat* period following the *talaq al-bida* and the third pronouncement of the *talaq as-sunna* in the *hasan* form enables the wife to obtain maintenance from her former husband.[15] A woman has no capacity to contract herself in marriage to another man during the *'idda* period.

9–10   There are no fixed formalities in the classical Sunni law, laying down the manner in which the repudiation is to be pronounced. There is no requirement of witnesses and the wife need not even be present. The *talaq* can be either oral or in writing and any words can be used. In one old Indian case, the husband said to his wife, "Thou art my cousin, and daughter of my uncle, if thou goest".[16] Evidence was presented to the court, and accepted, that this statement meant that if or when the wife left the house, she would be no other relation to the man than a cousin, which she was, indicating clearly that she would no longer be regarded as his wife. In this case, therefore, effect was given to the intention of the husband to pronounce a *talaq al-bida*.[17]

9–11   There are a number of important differences between the Sunni and Shia law of divorce. The most significant of these is the legal disability which accompanies an *al-bida* divorce in Shia law. As stated, the Shia law does not accept the *talaq al-bida* and only the *talaq as-sunna* divorces are recognised.[18] In India, this has now given rise to the argument that through the use of eclectic choice of the rule of another school (*takhayyur*) the Shia principle should be adopted to outlaw *al-bida* divorces for all Indian Muslims.[19] In Egypt and elsewhere, the legislatures have relied on the views of certain individual Sunni jurists for this. In Sunni law, the difference between the approved divorce forms (the *as-sunna*) and the disapproved (the *al-bida*) is simply based on the spurious morality of divorcing one's wife by an instant pronouncement. In Shia law, the *talaq* pronouncement must be declared orally in the presence of two witnesses with the exact term itself being used and there has to be a definite intention to repudiate. In contrast with this position, in the Hanafi law a divorce pronounced by way of jest is valid.[20] Indeed, in this law even a divorce pronounced when drunk, or by mistake, or under duress is valid. The justification for this rule in Hanafi law is that this law looks to the act rather than the intent.

9–12   Two other forms of repudiation, the *ila* and the *zihar*, may be briefly mentioned.[21] They are not of much importance today. The *ila* is really a variant

---

[14] The *al-bida* form has been declared ineffective by a recent *fatwa* of the Ahl-i-Hadith in India, which was published on May 21, 1993. For details see F. Ahmad (1994), esp. pp. 140–141. Such attempted reforms reflect growing disquiet over the husband's unilateral power to divorce if it is not matched with obligations on him to consider the welfare of the wife and, in particular, any children of the marriage.

[15] We have seen in para. 7–75, above that this may be denied in practice.

[16] *Hamid Ali v. Imtiazan* I.L.R. [1872] 2 Al. 71.

[17] For evidence of different *talaq* pronouncements which came to the notice of English courts, see para. 9–206, below.

[18] This position was also confirmed in the important Pakistani case of *Ali Nawaz Gardezi v. Muhammad Yusuf* P.L.D. 1963 S.C. 51.

[19] See in detail F. Ahmad (1994), pp. 82–84. The argument is a good one, but in view of sectarian Sunni/Shia troubles this will probably be ignored and sidelined.

[20] For details on this see Nasir (1990a), p. 115–116; Bharatiya (1996), pp. 102–103. This is also being challenged in modern India, see F. Ahmad (1994), pp. 95 *et seq.*

[21] On these see Tayyibji (1968), pp. 174–175 and 182–184; Nasir (1990a), pp. 112–113; Nasir (1990b), pp. 69–70.

form of the husband's unilateral repudiation of the wife. The husband swears on oath to abstain from marital relations for four months. If he keeps his oath, in Hanafi law this declaration is treated as equivalent to one irrevocable pronouncement of divorce. However, it can be withdrawn against the performance of a self-imposed penalty. The *zihar* is a pre-Islamic practice, an 'injurious assimilation' (Nasir (1990a), p. 112), in effect a declaration by the husband that his wife is to him like a relative in a prohibited degree. The most common example, often cited, is a phrase like "You are for me as the back of my mother". *Zihar* requires a particularly heavy expiation but, by itself, it is not a divorce.

9–13 In the extra-judicial forms of Muslim divorce, the husband's right of *talaq* can be either suspended or delegated. In the suspended or conditional *talaq*, the repudiation occurs automatically after a particular event. The most common example of this form of delegated *talaq* occurs when the husband contracts a marriage with a second wife, in which case the second marriage will activate a suspended *talaq*. Stipulations generally are not very common, however. Interestingly, they have changed in nature, as detailed recent research confirms.[22] If any particular condition is agreed upon, then to that extent the wife will have some protection, in that she can be sure to be released from a disagreeable marriage. The right of *talaq* in this situation is no longer the right of the husband, since it was the woman who inserted the stipulation.

9–14 The delegated *talaq* (the *talaq-i-tafwid*) is also well-recognised by the schools of law.[23] In this form of divorce, the husband has delegated to the wife the power to pronounce a *talaq*, *i.e.* to free herself from the marital bond when a certain event occurs. This is a 'suspended' or 'conditional' divorce, which thereby also delegates, in such cases, the power of *talaq* to the wife. The agreement about this power to pronounce a *talaq* can be made either at the time of the marriage, and may be inserted in the marriage contract, or after the marriage.[24]

9–15 As we have seen in paragraph 6–02, above, a marriage in classical Muslim law is a contract which, depending on the various school traditions, can be terminated by either party, by the agreement of both parties or by a court. The classical law made a general distinction between *talaq*, which necessitates some form of compensation from the husband, *khul*, involving an element of compensation from the wife, and *mubaraat*, a mutual agreement which led to the waiving of existing rights. In classical Hanafi law, the wife cannot insist on a *khul*, the husband must actually pronounce the *talaq* and therefore it is an agreement by mutual consent, but commonly known as *khul*.[25] Not surprisingly, there has been some confusion of terminology, especially as far as Middle Eastern and South Asian usage of the terms *khul* and *mubaraat* is concerned.[26]

9–16 It is important to emphasise that both of these forms are extra-judicial methods (see now also F. Ahmad (1994), p. 2 and 15). This means that the term

---

[22] For a detailed study on marriage stipulations, with particular reference to Muslims in the occupied West Bank, see Welchman (1994).

[23] This is often spelled *talaq-e-tafwiz* or, in Arabic, *tafwid at-talaq*, delegation of divorce. Nasir (1990a), gives it little attention. For details see Fyzee (1974), pp. 158–160; Bharatiya (1996), p. 105; F. Ahmad (1994), pp. 26 27.

[24] For details see also Tayyibji (1968), p. 165.

[25] On *khul*, see Nasir (1990a), pp. 122–125; Nasir (1990b), pp. 78–81; Fyzee (1974), pp. 163–166; Chap. 12 in Doi (1984), pp. 192–197; Bharatiya (1996), pp. 105–107.

[26] For some details see Fyzee (1974), pp. 163–164. Specifically in South Asia, there has been some confusion about terminology since *khul* was treated by Mulla as a divorce by mutual consent (see Bharatiya (1996), p. 106). This shows reluctance to give a voice to the wife which, of course, accurately reflects Hanafi law. Most authors try to make a clear distinction. See in detail Tayyibji (1968), pp. 176–182; Bharatiya (1996), pp. 106–107.

khul has been used for the extra-judicial method as well as for judicial dissolution of the marriage, which is strictly speaking called *faskh*. That term, in turn, has been used to denote annulment of a marriage rather than divorce, so these categories themselves are obviously not as clearly distinct as most writers assume.

9–17 Usually the wife will offer to pay a certain sum, normally the amount of the dower either given to her or promised to her, in return for the agreement of the husband to release her from the marriage tie. It is sometimes argued that this mirrors the husband's *talaq*. However, where the husband's consent is needed for a *khul*, there is no precise parity for the wife since the husband's right to *talaq* remains unconditional. Under Hanafi law, there is no need to pronounce *talaq* when there is a *khul* or *mubaraat*, but the Shias, in particular, expect a *talaq* pronouncement. The jurists and school traditions also differ on the rights relating to *mahr* and on the interpretation of Qur'an, Sura IV, verse 128 and some other verses (see Doi (1984), p. 193) to the effect that if a couple fear they would be unable to 'keep the limits ordained by Allah' (a much-used phrase which refers to extra-marital relations), there is no blame on them if they make an agreement to divorce. Some suggest that a husband can demand a sum larger than the *mahr* given by him to his wife. Other jurists forbid the taking by the husband of more than the *mahr*. All the debts which exist between the parties are cancelled by a divorce agreement.

9–18 If the husband is the one who makes the initial offer of a mutually agreed divorce (*mubaraat*), his offer may not be retracted before the wife has given an answer. This is the case primarily because the offer by the husband is deemed equivalent to an oath of repudiation. This oath becomes effective immediately when the wife signifies her consent and acceptance of the offer. However, if the wife initiates this process, she may retract her offer at any time before the acceptance by the husband. Thus in the classical Hanafi law, the *mubaraat* is treated as equivalent to one irrevocable pronouncement of *talaq* and it is necessary for the parties to contract a fresh marriage with each other if they wish to resume a marital relationship. In a consensual divorce, it could be argued that the agreement is voidable if it can be illustrated that either of the parties lacked the necessary consent or was induced into accepting the agreement by fraud or duress of sufficient gravity. Duress (*ikrah*) in Muslim law envisages a threat, which is recognised only if one party is in a position to carry out the threat and the other party fears that it might actually happen. A threat based on death, physical injury or deprivation of liberty makes the agreement voidable, at the option (*khiyar*) of the person subjected to the threat. Old Indian decisions suggest that a *khul* (rather, of course, a *mubaraat*) obtained by duress creates a valid divorce, but that the compensation payable by the wife cannot be enforced by the husband. Perhaps a more appropriate way of looking at this matter would be to say that in such circumstances, unless there is clear evidence of a repudiation by the husband so as to constitute a *talaq*, the decision whether to acquiesce in a divorce should be that of the party subjected to the fraud or duress. As the *mubaraat* may be the only effective method in the classical Hanafi law for a wife to obtain a divorce, the law relating to it, often discussed under *khul*, as we noted already, has frequently been abused by husbands who demand very large sums in return for consenting to divorce the wife, rather than giving a *talaq*, which would give rise to the wife's entitlements to *mahr* and *iddat* maintenance, if not some form of additional compensation, as we saw in paragraph 7–75, above.

9–19 Doi (1984, p. 193) briefly mentions that *mubaraat* does not involve the payment of compensation by the wife, since this is truly a divorce by mutual

consent. In practice, however, given that the Muslim husband can always exercise his right of *talaq*, the wife may be put to considerable trouble in obtaining the husband's consent, since he may simply pretend that he is still interested in the marriage, whereas in fact he wants to save money. In such a situation, it may be part of the *mubaraat* that the wife has to give up some entitlements and/or pay some compensation. This confirms that the borderlines between the two concepts have remained somewhat fluid.

9-20 Divorce by judicial authority is not unknown to Muslim law and appears in two forms, under the headings of *lian* and *faskh*. The form of divorce by *lian* or mutual imprecation is perhaps not strictly a judicial termination of the marriage but is generally classified under this category.[27] It arises where a husband challenges the legitimacy of a child of the wife by an affirmation that the wife was adulterous.[28] The wife may or may not respond and in fact the husband may be unable to prove the allegation. In classical Islamic law, the Prophet terminated such a marriage (Fyzee (1974), p. 166). This precedent led to a rule in Hanafi law that a *Qadi* must intervene. The factual matrix of a *lian* more or less inevitably leads to a permanent divorce and the parties cannot remarry. This law is not entirely obsolete (F. Ahmad (1994), p. 33).

9-21 Formal judicial rescission of a Muslim marriage is called *faskh*.[29] Significantly, Nasir (1990a, p. 125) indicates that divorce by judicial intervention, literally 'separation' (*tafriq*) is "a subject of controversy among jurists". Bharatiya (1996, p. 109) characterises it as "annulment" with reference to Indian law. In classical Hanafi law, the only ground on which a woman was permitted to obtain a judicial termination of her marital status occurs when she can prove to the court that her husband is incapable of consummating the marriage.[30] This looks like a classic case of annulment, known from other legal systems. However, the other classical schools of Muslim law, besides acknowledging this ground, provide additional bases for judicial dissolution. Thus the Ithna Ashari school enables the *Qadi* to grant a judicial decree where the husband is suffering from insanity, leprosy or venereal disease.[31] The Shafi'i school, in addition to these grounds, considers wilful refusal to maintain as a sufficient reason for a judicial divorce. The Hanbali school recognises various physical and mental defects, as well as the following: failure to maintain, desertion for more than six months without just cause, and failure to comply with a condition in the marriage contract. Even more liberal than the Hanbali school is the Maliki school. Physical and mental defects, failure to maintain, desertion, absence for more than one year for whatever reason, and ill-treatment (*darar*) are all acknowledged as grounds for dissolution in this school. Maliki law, therefore, is the only classical school which permits a divorce on the basis of cruelty or ill-treatment by the husband. The important point to make, however, is that when the Maliki *Qadi* grants the wife a decree, he does so by way of exercising the right of *talaq* on behalf of the husband, thereby continuing the legal fiction of the exclusive right of the husband to repudiate his wife. The reason for

---

[27] For details see Tayyibji (1968), pp. 184–188; Fyzee (1974), pp. 166–168; Nasir (1990a), p. 113; Nasir (1990b), p. 70. A procedure relating to defamation of the spouse was introduced into Pakistani law by the Offence of Qazf (Enforcement of Hadd) Ordinance 1979 (VIII of 1979).
[28] See also para. 10–05, below and the instructive case of *Nurjahan v. Md. Kajim Ali*, A.I.R. (1977) Cal. 90.
[29] Nasir (1990a), p. 112 and Nasir (1990b), p. 69 use the modern term *tafriq* for a judicial order of separation.
[30] Tayyibji (1968), p. 144; Nasir (1990a), p. 126. *ibid.*, pp. 131–136, discusses defects of the husband as a ground for divorce in great detail.
[31] Nasir (1990a), p. 125, notes that the Shia Ithna Asharis allow divorce by the court only in the event of the husband's impotence, "provided that the wife shall apply for divorce, and that she has not known about it at the time of the marriage".

the difference in approach is the emphasis placed by the Maliki school on Qur'an, Sura IV, verse 35, which reads as follows:

> "If ye fear a breach between them twain,
> Appoint two arbitrators,
> One from his family
> And the other from hers."

In Shafi'i, Hanbali and Hanafi law, the arbitrator's role is no more than conciliatory and, if possible, reconciliatory. In Maliki law, however, the arbitrators are representatives of the court. Thus, according to Maliki law, if the arbitrators fail to reconcile the parties, they can decide that the marriage should be terminated, which they can do by way of ordering the husband to divorce his wife by *talaq*.

9–22 In summary, we see clearly that the traditional Muslim law of divorce remained a matter of extra-judicial arrangement between the spouses and their families, with minimal involvement of official agents and generally no need for a court or other state functionary to play a legal role in the dissolution of a Muslim marriage. Two important trends towards reform were, in this way, programmed into traditional Muslim divorce law in its encounter with modern developments. First, state legal systems would seek to exercise at least some control over the sphere of divorce law and its consequences. Secondly, as indicated, legal reforms, especially of Hanafi Muslim divorce law, would attempt to restrict the unilateral powers of the husband and to enlarge the supposedly limited rights of Muslim wives to bring about or negotiate a divorce.

Divorce reforms in the Muslim world

9–23 As indicated, the institution of the unilateral *talaq* has been subjected to severe criticism. One Western observer has commented that "without doubt it is the institution of talaq which stands out in the whole range of the family law as occasioning the gravest prejudice to the status of Muslim women" (Coulson (1964), p. 209). The 'triple *talaq*' has become a particular target of adverse criticism (F. Ahmad (1994), p. 125). It is apparent that the typically idealistic *shari'a* framework of restrictions and reservations has provided only limited checks on the husband's unilateral powers. In all Muslim countries there has been pressure to introduce reforms to safeguard the wife's rights and to facilitate an attempt as at reconciliation. While in traditional law the most common procedure has been the *talaq*, "modern personal law status legislators show an increasing tendency to curb such a power of the man to the extent that, under some legislation, no divorce shall be effective, or even allowed, outside the court". (Nasir (1990a), p. 113).

9–24 This indicates a shift from extra-judicial regulation of Muslim divorces towards judicial intervention. However, this does not mean that the extra-judicial modes will vanish. In fact, our analysis of South Asian divorce laws in paragraph 9–39, below shows that the extra-judicial sphere has constantly been re-asserting itself.

9–25 Given the limited facilities for divorce available to women under traditional Hanafi law, it is not surprising that most of the legislation in the Muslim world in this area in the last 80 years or so has been in Hanafi countries.[32] It appears

---

[32] It is impossible to provide a full survey here. For detailed coverage, not structured by country but by topic, see Nasir (1990a), pp. 112–145; Nasir (1990b), pp. 70–98. An updated country survey is now provided in El Alami and Hinchcliffe (1996). Among the older literature, much of the writing by Professor Sir Norman Anderson remains relevant, see especially Anderson [1970] 31 *Studia Islamica* 41–52. With specific reference to *talaq al-bida*, F. Ahmad (1994), pp. 118–122 gives a useful overview.

that the Ottoman Law of Family Rights 1917 opened the floodgates of legal reform. This law was enacted in the aftermath of the first World War in a spirit of reformism. In addition, reforms were introduced particularly to alleviate the difficulties created by foreign husbands marrying Turkish girls and then deserting them. Since the traditional law did not allow such women to divorce, the 1917 Law provided for judicial dissolution in cases where the husband was suffering from a serious disease and in cases where the husband had failed to provide maintenance and had deserted the wife. This law (Articles 119, 121 and 126) is applicable today amongst the Muslim communities both in Israel and in the Lebanon.

9–26   The first major reforms after the Ottoman Law of Family Rights 1917 were introduced in Egypt in the 1920s. The early Egyptian reforms of Law No. 25 of 1920 (regarding judicial separations on grounds of defects) and Law No. 25 of 1929 (on conditions of validity of divorces and further grounds for separation) introduced provisions from Maliki law in place of the predominant Hanafi doctrine. Article 4 of the 1920 Act stated:

> "Where a wife demands dissolution of the marriage with the husband who fails to support her and who has no known property from which a maintenance order could be executed, her demand shall be granted forthwith unless the husband proves by evidence that he is destitute, in which case he may be given a respite not exceeding one month."

Article 1 of Law No. 25 of 1929 repealed the Hanafi doctrine which had looked to the act of the *talaq* and had ignored its intent. Article 1 stated: "Any divorce uttered in intoxication or under compulsion is henceforth invalid". The dominant Hanbali view was therefore adopted. Article 4 had a similar emphasis, providing that "ambiguous expressions which might or might not imply divorce shall only have the effect which the speaker actually intended". Article 5 of the 1929 Law was of considerable importance, for it restated the circumstances where a *talaq al-bida* will be acceptable, providing that:

> "Every repudiation is revocable except a repudiation pronounced for the third time, a repudiation pronounced before consummation of the marriage, a repudiation in exchange for compensation, and repudiations considered irrevocable by the 1929 Law and the 1920 Law."

Moreover, by Article 3 it was provided that "a repudiation coupled with words or gestures indicating a number is equivalent to a single repudiation". Thus the Egyptian reformers adopted the *hasan* and *ahsan* methods of *talaq* and effectively sought to abolish the instant effect of the triple *talaq al-bida*.

9–27   Articles 12 and 13 of the 1929 Law enabled the wife to obtain a divorce in the case of desertion by her husband for a continuous period of one year. Affliction of a serious disease "making the continuance of marriage injurious to the wife" (1929 Law, Article 9) constituted a ground for a single irrevocable divorce granted by the court. Failure to maintain and desertion, in contrast, constituted grounds for a revocable divorce in that the situation could be saved by a husband who proved during the *iddat* that he was able and willing to maintain the wife.

9–28   An important reform of the Egyptian legislation was contained in Article 6 of the 1929 law, which introduced the Maliki law of ill-treatment or harm (*darar*) in relation to cases where the husband was missing or had been jailed. In such a case, a wife could now obtain divorce on the ground of the husband's impeachability. The Maliki law which enables the wife to obtain a judicial divorce even in cases where she is herself at fault was not, however, introduced. The explanatory memorandum accompanying the law stated:

> "It was, therefore, considered in the interest of general welfare to adopt the doctrine of Imam Ibn Malik concerning disagreement between spouses except in the case where the arbitrator finds that the fault was exclusively with the wife."

The procedure under the 1929 Law was as follows. The wife alleged that her husband was guilty of cruelty in a way which made the continuance of the marital relationship impossible for people of their class. If the allegation was proved, the Qadi granted a dissolution by way of an irrevocable divorce. If she was unable to provide proof of the allegation, an arbitration procedure was established to attempt a reconciliation. The arbitrators were able to make recommendations involving a dissolution of the marriage, although such a recommendation could be made only if it was found that the fault for the discord lay with the husband.

9–29 The Egyptian reforms were themselves subjected to further changes in that country in 1979, but the general scheme of the law as laid down in 1920/29 remained unchanged.[33] Law No. 44 of 1979 added in this area only the requirement to register the *talaq*, and the requirement on the husband to give notice of the *talaq* to the wife.[34] This also had the effect that a *talaq* divorce did not take effect if the notice did not reach the wife. Further, Article 10 of the 1929 Law was amended to state that if the arbitrators determine that the fault is that of the wife, then the court can dissolve the marriage on payment of compensation by the wife. Thus the Egyptian law as we shall see was brought more into line with Jordanian law and moved closer to the Maliki law in this regard. The 1979 reforms were challenged and, in April 1985, the Supreme Court of Egypt held these 1979 reforms to be unconstitutional. The Egyptian law has since been amended by Act No. 100 of 1985, replacing the 1979 law, with two major omissions.[35]

9–30 The 1920/1929 reforms in Egypt were influential in other Islamic countries and formed the basis for change elsewhere, especially in countries which are predominantly Hanafi. Similar provisions to the earlier Egyptian reforms were introduced in Jordan (1951) and in Syria (1953). The Jordanians, however, have gone further than the 1929 Egyptian law by enabling a termination to be decreed in the event of an allegation of ill-treatment, even if the fault for the breakdown is determined to be that of the wife. F. Ahmad (1994, p. 119) writes that the Jordanian Code of Personal Status (Law 61 of 1976), as amended by Law 25 of 1977, with effect from June 1, 1977, derecognises a *talaq* which is not intended, as well as a *talaq al-bida* or 'triple *talaq*', but these reforms were already introduced in the Jordanian Law of Family Rights 1951.[36]

9–31 Article 92 of the Syrian Law of Personal Status of 1953, in contrast to the Jordanian law, provided that if a divorce is coupled with a number, expressly or impliedly, still not more than one divorce shall be deemed to have taken place (see also F. Ahmad (1994), p. 120). Article 117 of the Syrian law introduced a novel and highly significant concept into Sunni Muslim law.[37] This Article stated that where

---

[33] For details of the 1979 reforms introduced in Egypt see in detail Ibrahim and Bakar (1980).

[34] In addition, the debate about polygamy as a ground for a claim for dissolution of marriage by the wife was reflected in the new law. For details see *id*.

[35] For details see El Alami and Hinchcliffe (1996).

[36] For details see Welchman (1988) and now El Alami and Hinchcliffe (1996).

[37] This relates, as we have seen in para. 7–75, above, to the very significant reforms in Indian and Bangladeshi law concerning post-divorce maintenance rights for Muslim wives.

the *Qadi* considers that a husband has repudiated his wife without reasonable cause, and the wife has suffered material damage, the *Qadi* may ask the husband to pay the wife compensation, limited to the equivalent of one year's maintenance and support. Professor Coulson (1964, p. 209) emphasised that this provision represented the first real attempt in Muslim law to control the husband's unilateral power of repudiation in that his motive for exercising this power was subjected to scrutiny and the wife's position was at least to some extent protected in the event of abuse of this power.

9–32   The reform, of course, did not affect the man's right to repudiate his wife. Notwithstanding its limited nature, however, this reform does serve as a valuable expedient in discouraging men from unilaterally and unjustly divorcing their wives. The justification for the provision can be found in the Qur'an, Sura II, verse 241, "For divorced women, maintenance on a reasonable scale", although the juristic consensus (*ijma*) has been that this verse was abrogated by later revelations. In effect the Syrian reformers have exercised *ijtihad* by justifying the new law with reference to the concept of 'compensation' (*muta*). Section 18 of the 1979 reforms in Egypt extended the same principle just a little further by stating that where the wife is divorced by the husband without any fault on her part, she shall be entitled to compensation (*muta*) which should be an amount equivalent to not less than two years' maintenance, which can be paid by instalments. Again, this provision was subject to the 1985 ruling of the Supreme Court on its constitutionality and was held to be unconstitutional. However, these provisions were subsequently reintroduced in Law 100 of 1985.

9–33   A more dramatic reform was the Tunisian Law of Personal Status 1956. Articles 25–33 state that a divorce can be obtained only by judicial means. The grounds are as wide as in any country in the world: on the demands of the husband or the wife on grounds specified in the Code; when agreed upon by both spouses; when insisted upon by either spouse. In the last situation, the court shall determine the indemnity due to the wife as compensation for injuries suffered or the indemnity she shall pay to the husband. Article 30 states categorically that extra-judicial divorces are no longer to be effective, "Any divorce outside a court of law is without legal effect".[38] It is important to make clear, however, that the Tunisian legislation did not completely remove the right of the individual to obtain a divorce on his own volition,[39] for the court must still issue a decree of divorce if the husband, or indeed the wife, remains obdurate. In these circumstances, the court can order the husband to pay compensation to the wife, no limit being laid down in the law. The transference to judicial decrees is justified by the Qur'an, Sura IV, verse 37, "Where discord arises between spouses, then appoint arbitrators". The verse, however, has been reinterpreted by the Tunisians, for the consensus has been that the verse relates to an 'optional obligation' prior to a consensual divorce and whether 'arbitrators' need to be judges is yet another contentious matter.

9–34   Article 32 introduces an arbitral process, laying down that "the court shall not grant a decree of divorce until it has exhausted all means of establishing the causes of conflict between the spouses and has failed to reconcile them". The Tunisian law is clearly an example of social engineering. It has been justified by Tunisians themselves as being within the spirit of the Islamic jurisprudential process. Indeed, the modern formal law makes important concessions to the traditional law.

---

[38] Nasir (1990a), pp. 114–115, shows that this is also the case for Druzes in Lebanon and Syria and reiterates this at p. 125.

[39] Also, if a man were to pronounce a *talaq* in court, it would be of full legal effect.

9–35 In Iraq, the *shari'a* remained the general law of the land until the Provisional Sharia Procedures Act of 1917 (Nasir (1990a), p. 33). The Iraqi reforms in the Personal Status Act of 1959 require the husband who seeks a divorce from his wife to obtain a judgment in the court.[40] If the domestic dispute is not brought before the court, the repudiation must be registered during the wife's *iddat* period. If this is done, the *talaq* is valid and effective. It is not explicitly stated what will be the position if the repudiation is not registered. The same is true also of Algeria as a result of reforms in 1959 and again in 1984. The Algerians appear to require not only recording of the husband's divorce by a local court but the court also has the duty of attempting to arrange a reconciliation.[41]

9–36 One Muslim country which at some point took a position similar to the Tunisian law was Iran, where the right of the husband to repudiate his wife without any judicial intervention was abolished by statute in 1967. As indicated earlier, this was hailed as a major legal reform. Under Article 11 of the Act, the party to a dispute had to apply to the court for arbitrators to be appointed on one or more of a number of grounds based primarily on the culpability of the other party. The arbitrators were to attempt reconciliation and, in the event of failure, had to submit a report to the court. The court issued what was referred to as a 'certificate of impossibility of reconciliation'. The certificate was to remain valid for a three-month period, and during this time it could be produced before a notary who was responsible for registering the certificate and effecting the divorce. The usual procedure was, therefore, for the man to pronounce a *talaq* in a notary's office.

9–37 An interesting aspect of the Iranian legislation was Article 17 which stated that the provisions of Article 11 were inserted by mandatory provision into all marriage documents drawn up in Iran. This factor enabled the Iranians to say that a divorce is still the right of the husband who, in his marriage contract, has delegated his right, first to the court, and second to the wife, in the event that she can prove one of the grounds of culpability. This law has been repealed by the current regime in Iran.

9–38 No other Arab Muslim country except perhaps South Yemen in 1974 has gone quite as far as the Tunisians in reforming the Muslim divorce law. Interestingly, the Family Law of North Yemen of 1978 also turned a triple *talaq* into a single pronouncement (F. Ahmad (1994), p. 120). In Africa, the Somali Family Law No. 23 of 1975 required the man to obtain the permission of the court to divorce his wife by *talaq*.[42] This permission would be granted only after the failure of a conciliation body to reconcile the parties. In the case of failure in the attempted reconciliation, the committee was to transmit its findings to the court within 60 days of its appointment. The Somali law by Article 36(4) expressly stated that the court shall not authorise more than one *talaq* at a time. Moreover, by Article 44, the court was empowered to award maintenance from a husband to a former wife, in all cases where the *talaq* resulted through the fault of the husband, for a period not less than three months and not more than one year. In the current situation in Somalia, these legal reforms are not being implemented, but the relevant portions of the Somali Code deserve citation in full because they constitute a typical example of aborted modernist legislative attempts to reform the traditional extra-judicial Muslim law by requiring state intervention.

---

[40] F. Ahmad (1994), p. 119; for details on subsequent reforms see Nasir (1990a), pp. 33–34.
[41] For details see F. Ahmad (1994), p. 119, and in particular El Alami and Hinchcliffe (1996). South Yemen introduced similar reforms in 1974, but they are no longer in force.
[42] Note also that Algeria reformed its divorce law in 1984 along similar lines. For details on Somalian law see Mahmood [1982b] 2 *Islamic and Comparative Law Quarterly* 256–259.

"Article 42. Dissolution (faskh)

    (1) Dissolution (faskh) means the rescission of the marriage contract brought about by the court.

    (2) Dissolution has the same legal effects as revocable divorce.

    (3) A suit for dissolution of the marriage shall deprive the husband of his right of divorce.

Article 43. Cases for Dissolution

    (1) Both the husband and wife are entitled to file a petition in any of the following cases for dissolution of the marriage:

        (a) If one of the spouses is suffering from an incurable disease which does not allow consultation or even if possible, it causes harm, on condition that the fact is proved by a medical practitioner.

        (b) If the whereabouts of one of the spouses are not known for more than four consecutive years; but if the missing person reappears before the dissolution judgment is delivered, the dissolution petition shall be rejected.

        (c) If one of the spouses, though able to provide maintenance, habitually fails to provide maintenance where the petitioner is actually in need of such maintenance.

        (d) If both husband and wife do not own anything and therefore none of them is able to meet the maintenance obligations, the Court shall decide the case only after six months from the date the dissolution was filed.

        (e) If disagreement between the spouses has become so serious as to make conjugal life impossible. In this instance the court shall follow the procedure laid down in Article 36.

        (f) Perpetual impotency or sterility of one of the spouses.

        (g) If one of the spouses is sentenced to imprisonment for a period exceeding four years, provided the petition of dissolution is submitted after the imprisoned spouse has completed his sentence.

    (2) The wife is entitled to apply for dissolution of her marriage if her husband has been authorised, according to Article 13, to contract another marriage and on condition that no children were born.

Article 44. Maintenance

Where divorce (talaq) or dissolution (faskh) results through the fault of the husband, the Court shall order him to maintain the former wife for a period not less than three months and not more than one year. If the divorce or dissolution results through a fault on the part of the wife the Court shall order her to pay to the husband a sum not less than her dower."

It is with this background of reform in mind that we now turn our attention to the important recent changes which have occurred on the Indian subcontinent. As we shall see, the debates about legal reforms of Muslim law in South Asia bring out the inherent conflicts and tensions between different interpretations of traditional Muslim law, as well as clashes between the modern state-sponsored forms of Muslim personal law and its unreformed, shari'a-based rule systems. The developments in South Asia are, therefore, of tremendous importance for the analysis of Muslim jurisprudence anywhere in the modern world.

Muslim divorce law in South Asia

9–39   This subject is extremely complex and divorce law is, in South Asia, the largest aspect of Muslim matrimonial law (Diwan and Diwan (1991), p. 76). We shall proceed here by analysing briefly the legal position under the Anglo-Muslim law and will then turn to the major legislative reforms in this area and the important case law. The DMMA 1939 and relevant provisions of the MFLO 1961 are the major enactments of relevance to this debate, which covers again Indian, Pakistani and Bangladeshi law.

Anglo-Muslim divorce law in South Asia

9–40   As we saw in Chapter 2 above, the major effect of British interference in the legal development of South Asian Muslim law has been the creation of a case law, misleadingly called Anglo-Mohammedan law,[43] which builds on Muslim law principles but is not free from misunderstanding. In the area of divorce law, the *talaq* was soon well-known to the British judicial personnel and probably posed no official problems for adjudication.[44] Another apparent reason for the low profile of the *talaq* divorce is that the *talaq* is, of course, an extra-judicial process, so courts would not be involved in this subject.[45] Whether Muslim wives in those times were actually given their *mahr* and proper *iddat* maintenance would be of historical interest but cannot detain us here.

9–41   F. Ahmad (1994, p. 28) has been critical of the fact that the case law of the British period undervalued the Muslim wife's right to seek a divorce. However, that case law was built on classical Hanafi doctrine, according to which a Muslim wife could not obtain a *khul* divorce from the court and a wife could not get out of a violent or otherwise unbearable marriage unless she gave up all her financial rights. We shall see in paragraph 9–57, below that this highly unsatisfactory situation led, during the early twentieth century, to the frequent conversion of Muslim wives to other religions, which terminated the marriage. This, in turn, led to the reformist provisions in the DMMA 1939. F. Ahmad (1994, pp. 27–28) states what he considers to be the appropriate position:

> "Irrespective of incorporation of a clause in the marriage deed, to every Muslim wife is available the right of *khula*, the attributes of which are, *mutatis mutandis* the same as of the man's right of *talaq*. The right of divorce which Islam confers on women, if understood in its true perspective, will indeed [be] found dazzling. A wife having subjective satisfaction that it is no more possible for her to live with her husband, may simply tell him that she wants a divorce. He can, thereupon, attempt persuasion and reconciliation, but cannot force the wife to cohabit. The only thing he can demand is that [the] wife forgo her *mahr* . . . If the wife agrees to it and the husband peacefully relents, there follows a *khula* which means a divorce at the instance of the wife. A woman who is forced to go to the court for a degree of *khula* where the man is trying to maintain the marital bond against the wife's wishes need not even give the court the reasons why she wants it like the man pronouncing *talaq*.

---

[43] This appears in various spellings and the term itself has been much criticised by Professor Tahir Mahmood and others. On the nomenclature see Mahmood (1982a), pp. 5–8. For historical details see, *e.g.* Mahmood (1977).

[44] A good overview of early cases on Muslim divorce in Indian law is found in *Ahmad Kasim Molla v. Khatun Bibi*, I.L.R. [1932] 59 Cal. 833.

[45] This is reflected in modern India today, where the *shariat* law on *talaq* still applies and there are hardly any reported cases on *talaq* itself.

Unfortunately, the courts in India have ignored the extremely liberal and pro-woman law of *khula* in Islam as if it were totally non-existent . . . this form of divorce at the instance of [the] wife has remained eclipsed by the judicial ignorance of and juristic prejudice against Islamic law. In Pakistan and Bangladesh the true law of *khula* has now been restored by the Supreme Court of Pakistan in a famous case. But in this country, very unfortunately for Muslim women, it is still lying in the dustbin of misconceptions."

These are very appropriate comments in the context of current debates on Muslim divorce law, to which we shall return at several points in the present chapter. The author does not attempt to restate authoritatively the classical position of any one school, he speaks for himself. Such comments should not be read simply as Muslim apologetics, or yet another criticism of the distortions brought about by Anglo-Muhammadan law. We shall see, however, that the reported cases depict less harmonious scenarios than the above quote, which relates mainly to the extra-judicial *khul*.

9–42   Early judicial involvement in British India is recorded in cases of divorce by consent of both parties, under the misleading label of *khul*.[46] The focus of concern in such cases tends to be on the financial arrangements, rather than discussions about concepts of Muslim law. Already at that time, Muslim husbands were trying to deny the fact that they had divorced their wife, arguing instead that the wife had divorced them, so that she should lose any financial benefits she may have obtained, and should in fact have to pay for the 'privilege' of release from the marital bond. This factual matrix appears to have led to an early misunderstanding to the effect that Muslim wives have less than equal say in the process of dissolution of a marriage. The early leading case on this subject is the Privy Council decision in *Moonshee Buzul-ul Raheem v. Luteefut-oon-Nissa* [1859–1861] 8 L.R. I.A. 379. The facts of this case, which really concerned dower money rather than divorce concepts, were that in 1842 the husband had married the respondent and a dower had been fixed at Rs. 10,000/- and 1,000 gold pieces, worth Rs. 16,000/-, a huge sum of money at that time. In 1847, the husband married a second wife, a lady referred to in the judgment (at page 380) as a "rich widow". The judgment continues the story at page 380:

"From that time, the Appellant did everything he could to get rid of the Respondent; treating her with great harshness, refusing to permit her to see her mother, denying her food and clothing adequate to her station, in the hope of inducing her to ask for a divorce, by which she would forfeit her right in respect of her dower, and to force her to return the marriage settlement, which was at this time deposited with her mother for safe custody."

The facts of the case indicate that financial considerations were uppermost in everyone's mind. There was a dispute on the facts as to what happened next. It was claimed that on account of the ill-treatment meted out to her, the wife had complained to her mother and had begged her to arrange for the termination of the marriage. The mother filed various petitions, seeking the interference of the court, although it was not quite clear what the court was supposed to do. The husband at some point allegedly claimed that he had divorced the wife and that the mother should take her away after giving the husband a deed of some kind, referred to in

---

[46] The more appropriate term would appear to be *mubaraat*, although the borderlines between *khul* and *mubaraat* are in practice often not so clear.

the judgment merely as "the paper" (page 381), which turns out to be the marriage deed (*kabinnama*). When the mother finally agreed to hand over this document, the husband allegedly forced the wife to execute a deed of divorce and promptly threw her out of his house at midnight and in miserable circumstances.

9–43   The wife turned to the courts for help and filed a suit for recovery of her *mahr*, alleging that the husband had divorced her and that he had fraudulently and by force obtained from her a deed of divorce. The husband claimed that he had not divorced her by *talaq* but that, on her initiative, there had been a *khul* agreement amounting to a consensual divorce.[47] Furthermore, declared the husband, as consideration for this *khul* agreement, the payment of dower was waived. The wife claimed that she was forced into this agreement. Such situations arise frequently. The court clearly saw that the issues required a consideration of Muslim law principles.

9–44   In that situation, the judges asked for an expert opinion from a Muslim Law Officer, a *Moulvi*, who gave a convoluted opinion, stating the basic principles of Muslim law on the subject.[48] Evidently, much in this case depended on the evidence before the court. The lower court, well aware of the factual circumstances in this polygamous marriage, decided that no divorce other than a *khul* had been proved by the evidence, in fact the appellant husband admitted divorce by *khul*. The lower court held further that the documents put in evidence by the husband purporting to show that the wife had released him from the duty to pay a dower were fraudulent and therefore of no effect. As the marriage was admittedly dissolved, the wife was not required to prove that she had been divorced by *talaq* and was therefore entitled to recovery of the sums claimed, with interest.

9–45   On the husband's appeal before the equivalent of the High Court of Calcutta, another *fatwa* was commissioned by that court, asking whether an alleged *khul* divorce, as pleaded by the husband, was to be treated as a divorce under Muslim law. The very brief *fatwa* was to the effect that the allegation of *khul* made by the husband established the factum of divorce, entitling the wife to demand the *mahr*. The Calcutta Court, therefore, concluded that the factum of divorce was proved, while the genuineness of the two documents allegedly executed by the wife was questioned and it was found that the execution of the *khoolanama* "was not a voluntary unrestrained act" (page 391).

9–46   On the husband's final appeal to the Privy Council, it was indicated that the *talaq* and *khul* forms of divorce are well-known in India (page 391). It was found that the decision of the courts below should not be disturbed. Lord Kingsdown confirmed that the question before the Court was one of Muslim law and that "we should not lightly in such a case disturb the concurrent decision of two Courts" (page 395). Declaring himself satisfied that the decision was "conformable both to law and to justice" (page 395), the learned judge said, at page 395:

> "A divorce by *Khoola* is a divorce with the consent, and at the instance of the wife, in which she gives or agrees to give a consideration to the husband for her release from the marriage tie. In such a case the terms of the bargain are [a] matter of arrangement between the husband and wife, and the wife may, as the consideration, release her *dyn-mohr* and other rights, or make any other agreement for the benefit of the husband."

---

[47] The terms used here are *ibranamah* and *khoolanama*.
[48] The term used for this opinion is *futwa*, an anglicised spelling of *fatwa*, the authoritative statement of a jurist on a point of law.

It was also observed (*id.*) that, according to existing usage:

".... a divorce by *Talak* is not complete and irrevocable by a single declaration of the husband; but a divorce by *Khoola* is at once complete and irrevocable from the moment when the husband repudiates the wife and the separation takes place. In these particulars the two modes of divorce differ."

Thus, the husband's case was found to be implausible and based on a misconception of the nature of Muslim divorce. In this regard, it was held, at page 396:

"The divorce is the sole act of the husband, though granted at the instance of the wife, and purchased by her. The *Khoolanamah* is a deed securing to the husband the stipulated consideration, but it does not constitute the divorce. It assumes it, and is founded upon it. The divorce is created by the husband's repudiation of the wife, and the consequent separation."[49]

Since the husband in the present case, while denying a *talaq* divorce, had set up a divorce by *khul*, he could not argue that there was no divorce under Muslim law. On the other hand, he could not prove that the alleged deeds were validly executed, so his claim had to fail and the wife was entitled to the *mahr*.

9–47   Fyzee (1936, p. 113) refers to a decision of the Calcutta High Court of 1935, which established that a Muslim wife can, in certain situations, sue for the dissolution of her marriage.[50] This shows that, well before the liberating judgments in Pakistan during the late 1950s and early 1960s, awareness of the potential for *khul* and/or *mubaraat* divorces was well-developed. Fyzee welcomed the Calcutta decision, provided a detailed discussion of relevant classical sources and recommended two remedies to protect women's rights. First, the adoption of Maliki rules and the use of 'equity, justice and good conscience', secondly the wide use of delegated *talaq*. Fyzee (1936, p. 123) concluded with a very useful comment about the predicament of Muslim wives when it came to divorce:

"It is sometimes suggested that the greatest defect of the Islamic system is the absolute power given to the husband to divorce his wife without cause. Dower to some extent restricts the use of this power. But experience shows that greater suffering is engendered by the husband's withholding divorce than by his irresponsible exercise of this right. Under such conditions the power to release herself is the surest safeguard for the wife. No system of law can produce marital happiness, but human laws may at least alleviate suffering. And when marital life is wrecked, the home utterly broken up by misunderstanding, jealousy, cruelty or infidelity, what greater boon can a wife have than the power to secure her liberty? The unfortunate position of the women of India is due to the fact that women, being illiterate, are ignorant of their rights; and men, being callous, choose to remain ignorant."

An instructive leading case on *talaq* in the Indian subcontinent is *Ahmad Kasim Molla v. Khatun Bibi*, I.L.R. [1932] 59 Cal. 833. This decision has been criticised for assuming too readily that a Muslim husband has unfettered discretion in terminating a marriage. The marriage had only lasted a month and a few days. The

---

[49] F. Ahmad (1994), p. 28, rightly criticises this statement as an example of judicial blindness to the wife's right to ask for divorce.
[50] *Kadir v. Koleman Bibi*, I.L.R. [1935] 62 Cal. 1088.

husband claimed to have divorced the wife by *talaq* in accordance with Muslim law and to have sent information of this to the wife. She denied that the husband had validly divorced her and claimed, in the alternative, that if she was divorced, she had no knowledge of it. The wife's claim related to very small amounts of maintenance and *mahr*. The sum of Rs. 232.14 had been deposited in court by the husband but, relying on her *kabinnama*, the wife also claimed maintenance for life for herself and some support for her grandmother.

9–48   Costello J. rightly identified that his first task was to decide whether the wife was validly divorced by a *talaq* under Muslim law. He found before him a husband of mature age, in his late thirties, who already had two wives and six children, some of them older than the third wife. He found that the husband had married the young girl "solely in order to satisfy his carnal desires" (page 838), while the girl's grandmother "saw an opportunity of what can only be described as "selling" her granddaughter to the plaintiff" (pages 838–839). The girl was never treated as a wife, but rather as a concubine, and she was simply abandoned by the man, which the judge clearly found disagreeable.[51]

9–49   As to whether the husband had validly divorced the wife, it was argued on behalf of the wife that there was no valid ground for divorcing her. The husband was, in effect, taking advantage of his own wrong because he had treated her with cruelty. However, by this time the law on *talaq* appeared to be crystal-clear and the judge's comments at page 840 are telling:

> "I regret that I have to come to the conclusion that, as the law stands at present, any Mahomedan may divorce his wife at his mere whim and caprice."

This decision reiterates the common perception of the rule in Hanafi law that, no matter how disapproving Islam may be of a man who divorces his wife without cause, nonetheless a Muslim may repudiate his wife as he pleases.[52] Referring to a phrase used in an earlier judgment, Costello J. reiterated that this kind of repudiation is "good in law, though bad in theology".[53] Going through various authoritative texts and judgments, the judge did find evidence that a Muslim wife could seek to protect herself against such capriciousness by stipulating adequate provision of dower, but in the present case the stipulation was for what the judge found the "extremely trivial" sum of Rs. 201/- (page 841). Regarding the second point, whether absence of notice of *talaq* given to the wife made any difference to the legal validity of the divorce, Costello J. decided that the divorce was effective, having considered the facts of this case as well as a number of earlier reported cases in which this matter had been at issue. He said, at pages 846–847:

> "It seems to be clear, therefore, that not only can a Mahomedan divorce his wife without assigning any reasons, but also that a *talak* is valid, where it is made by a written instrument, notwithstanding that it is not brought to the knowledge of the wife; and the only question which can arise is with regard to the wife's maintenance during such period as may elapse until the fact of the execution of the *talaknama* actually comes to the knowledge of the wife."

---

[51] The learned judge added, at p. 839: "But I have to administer the law as it stands", a telling reflection of the difficulties caused when judges from one particular background have to administer the personal status laws of another community.

[52] F. Ahmad (1994), p. 9, identified this brief judicial statement as an example of a decision which is "totally inconsistent with [the] true Islamic law of divorce". Such comments raise the question, of course, to what extent the idealised statements of the 'true' Islamic law should and can be treated as divorced from social realities. What is immoral, *i.e.* bad to do, is not necessarily illegal, but often still legally valid, in the doctrines of the classical jurists.

[53] See Batchelor J. in *Sarabai v. Rabiabai*, I.L.R. [1906] 30 Bom. 537.

9–50 There are a number of Indian cases which discuss this topic, which continues to be debated.[54] *Abdul Khader v. Azeeza Bee*, A.I.R. 1944 Mad. 227 is a very short older case, making reference to two earlier leading cases. This was a typical case of a wife seeking maintenance from her husband under section 488 of the Criminal Procedure Code 1898, answered by the husband's claim that he had divorced her. It was found that the woman had come to know of the divorce. Ayyar J. held, at page 227:

> ". . . there could be a valid thalak in the absence of the wife but it would come into operation only from the date on which the wife comes to know of it . . . all that has been stated is that it must be communicated to the wife before it could be acted upon."

Thus, a *talaq* itself may be valid and irrevocable, but to determine the entitlements of the wife, it remains important to know when precisely she had knowledge of it. Later cases, discussed in the section below, assume for the purposes of calculating maintenance and *iddat* payments that the divorce becomes effective when the wife obtains information about it, in whatever form. This appears to be also the view taken today. While witnesses to the act of divorcing are not strictly essential, it may well be impossible to prove a *talaq* in the absence of such witnesses. This has led to practical problems also more recently, documented by Latifi (1983, pp. 335–336), who criticises judicial leniency towards an offending husband and calls for legal reforms in India to bring the Muslim law in line with Qur'anic injunctions.

The unreformed 'triple *talaq*' in Indian law

9–51 The first comment to make about the dissolution of Muslim marriages in India at the initiative of the husband is that *talaq* divorces have remained a matter of extra-judicial practice. Hence the difficulties faced in English law and elsewhere over the 'bare *talaq*' are likely to persist. However, this does not mean that such forms of divorce are devoid of procedure, it simply means that the procedure involved in such divorces remains flexible, open to much male discretion, and of course, that there is hardly any case law on the subject in India. There is, however, a modicum of judicial supervision in that a wronged wife could approach the courts for ancillary relief, although no Muslim wife could question the unilateral right of the husband to terminate the marriage by *talaq*. The few reported cases raise some interesting questions and confirm that Indian law has by no means left the field entirely to the divorcing Muslim husband. Judicial supervision extends not only to checking compliance with Muslim law but covers particularly the acceptability of a husband's arrangements regarding the maintenance rights of divorced women and their children (see paragraph 10–85, below). In the context of current Indian social and legal policies, emphasising public interest over private interest, powerful disincentives for facile male discretion to divorce have developed. As paragraph 7–75 showed in great detail, the Indian Muslim ex-husband's liability for the welfare of his divorced wife or wives has now become a lifelong burden. This, rather than procedural hurdles, will in the long run prove to be a most effective catalyst for developing a less capricious system of unilateral divorce. Some of the case law is beginning to reflect this.

9–52 In *Dilshada Masood v. Gh. Mustaffa*, A.I.R. 1986 J.&K. 80, a *talaq* divorce was held invalid because the individuals concerned were Shia Muslims and

---

[54] For details see F. Ahmad (1994), pp. 91–94.

according to Shia law, the pronouncement must be made in a specific form and ideally in Arabic. Rizvi J. restated the established principle of Shia law that pronouncement of *talaq* "must be uttered orally in the presence and hearing of two male witnesses who are Muslims and of approved probity" (page 82). It was held that it had not been provided anywhere that such a pronouncement had to take place before an *imam*, nor, interestingly, was the pronouncement before two lawyers as witnesses acceptable, since they could "by no stretch of imagination" (page 83) be considered as suitably qualified witnesses. The learned judge made it quite clear why he took this hard line, since here was a Muslim husband deliberately and mischievously divorcing his wife "in a unique way which is unknown to Shia Law" (page 83) as well as refusing to maintain her. It was held, at page 83:

> "No Shia Muslim will marry the petitioner unless she gets a proper divorce as provided under Shia Law as she continues to be the wife of the respondent. The order of maintenance has been passed as far back as on 30th June, 1973 and since then the respondent has with impunity defied the said order."

Latifi (1986, pp. 631–632) comments that this is a correct decision but does not mention the social dimensions of the case and its maintenance angle. Instead, he takes this as an occasion to argue for reforms in Indian Muslim divorce law, pointing out that Pakistan and Bangladesh appear to have devised an appropriate system.[55] At page 632 he argues:

> "In the present age the consensus among all schools of Muslim lawyers, throughout the world, is that restrictions should be placed on the man's right to pronounce divorce . . . Such restraints are implicit in the text of the Holy Quran. It is only in India that the *talaq* mongers, firmly entrenched in the male chauvinist so-called "Personal Law Board" unfortunately treated by the politicians as a sort of Papacy of Indian Islam, are holding up all reforms."

A lone recent case reported from Kerala considers whether in Muslim law a divorce can be effected by addressing the *talaq* to a person other than the wife. In *Pareed v. Aysha*, 1988(1) K.L.T. 27, an extremely brief, one-page case report reflecting the deprived economic condition of the litigants, the wife of a daily wage labourer claimed maintenance for herself and an infant daughter. The husband tried to argue, rather feebly, that he had divorced the wife and that he had no money to spare. It was held that "the suggestion put by counsel for the husband to the wife in the box is not communication of divorce, nor can the statement of the husband in the box addressed to the Court be communication of divorce to the wife, or someone on her behalf". Reliance was placed on *Mohammed Haneefa v. Pathummal Beevi*, 1972 K.L.T. 512, a maintenance petition under section 488 of the Criminal Procedure Code 1898. In that case, the husband had divorced the wife without proper notice, so that it became necessary for the court to determine the precise date from which the wife would be entitled to *iddat* money. By 1988, of course, the Indian law on maintenance for divorced wives had been changed dramatically. In *Pareed*, the husband's appeal was dismissed without any further explanation. The social welfare objective is apparent and the child and the wife were awarded Rs. 100/- monthly maintenance each. This case represents the tip of an iceberg, indicating that many Muslim husbands in India, as elsewhere in South Asia, are simply abandoning their wives and children, who may rarely go to court to obtain

---

[55] We shall see in para. 9–82, below, that this is a fallacy and that, contrary to Latifi's assertion, the *talaq al-bida* is not really outlawed in Pakistani law.

an official order for maintenance. Without saying a word about the Act, *Pareed* implies that the Muslim Women (Protection of Rights on Divorce) Act 1986 does have beneficial effects for deserted women and their children.

9–53 A more recent case, also from Kerala, contributes to the debate about the point at which a *talaq* divorce which is not communicated to the wife becomes effective for the purposes of maintenance. In *Ummulkulus v. Executive Magistrate*, 1990(2) K.L.T. 524, the facts point to an unhappy marriage, an illiterate wife with three small children, and a husband who divorced his wife without giving her notice. Nayar J. applied the law to these facts and could do little else than noting that the wife had now come to know of the divorce through the court proceedings and that she could no longer stay in the husband's home since she was divorced.

9–54 However, this became a constitutional law case, through the husband's petition for police protection after he had taken out an injunction against her trespassing on his property, while the wife claimed a fundamental right to stay in the house of the husband. The politicised nature of the dispute is apparent and need not distract us here. The wife had apparently made a public show of occupying the husband's property, which was only a small hut used as a reading room for an 'Islamic Study Circle'. There was evidence before the court of a well-known custom that the wife lives in the maternal house, so these were matrilocal Muslims. The wife therefore had no lawful right to live in that property. The learned judge severely criticised her for taking the law into her own hands and creating a public order problem, while praising the local Magistrate for his astute action. As regards the validity of the *talaq* divorce, it was not even in question. Nayar J. relied on standard judicial knowledge and *Pathayi v. Moideen*, 1968 K.L.T. 763, reiterating at page 529:

> ". . . a major husband of sound mind can effect divorce in Muslim Law, whenever he desires. No special form is required. Even the presence of the wife is not necessary. Husband can effect the dissolution by conveying his intention to the wife. No direct communication is necessary and it is effective when the wife knows about it. Therefore when the wife knew from the counter-affidavit in any case the divorce has become effective and dissolution has taken place."

Therefore it was held, at page 529, that the petitioner had no right to live with the husband, and her misguided case collapsed miserably. This litigation confirms that it does not help a Muslim wife to protest against the unilateral divorce inflicted on her; she would have been better advised to ask for appropriate maintenance for herself and the children.

9–55 As far as the law on *talaq* is concerned, an important recent study (F. Ahmad 1994) focuses on the triple *talaq*, providing in Chapter 7 a useful analysis of the judicial trends in the case law on *talaq al-bida*. We have already reflected on criticism of this institution. *Ahmad Kasim Molla v. Khatun Bibi*, I.L.R. [1932] 59 Cal. 833 (see paragraph 9–40, above) showed that Indian judges have been constrained to hold such a *talaq* legally valid, but there have been strong judicial reactions against this. In other words, the *talaq* has had a rather hostile reception in Indian courtrooms and it is no surprise that on this account, too, disputes concerning the husband's right to divorce are not brought before the official courts. A pertinent example of vocal judicial criticism is found in *Mohammed Haneefa v. Pathummal Beevi*, 1972 K.L.T. 512, which refers to an earlier Kerala case, *Pathayi v. Moideen*, 1968 K.L.T. 763, also a maintenance case, with a clear restatement of the principles of Muslim divorce law, as quoted above, and reference to a number of earlier cases. A Muslim judge, Khalid J., concluded his judgment in *Mohammed Haneefa* at page 514 in strong terms, criticising the existing state of affairs:

"Should Muslim wives suffer this tyranny for all times? Should their personal law remain so cruel towards these unfortunate wives? Can it not be amended suitably to alleviate their sufferings? My judicial conscience is disturbed at this monstrosity. The question is whether the conscience of the leaders of public opinion of the community will also be disturbed."

F. Ahmad concludes his recent analysis of judicial trends in Indian law with a comment focused on what he calls 'misunderstandings of true Islamic laws', manifestly not the classical *shari'a* as found in the authoritative texts, confirming in essence that nothing has been done in the past 20 years to improve our understanding of the law. Ahmad (1994, p. 109) wrote:

"The true nature of Islamic law of divorce is that neither a husband nor a wife has an unbridled right to do away with an existing marriage unilaterally and arbitrarily. But if either has a reasonably tenable ground to seek separation, there is no compulsion on him or her to remain united and in that case the alliance can be dissolved in a just and equitable manner. In this case [the] Supreme Court of India might have to consider the fallacy of old judicial opinion regarding [the] true nature of the Islamic law of divorce. . . . However we wish that instead of leaving this to the Supreme Court our *ulamaa* perform the important task of presenting Islamic law in its true perspective. So long as they do not act the judiciary will have to step in."

It appears that the Indian Supreme Court has simply not been given a chance to pronounce on the matter, while the Muslim Personal Law Board has been widely criticised for inaction. To break this stalemate, three *maulanas* of the Ahl-e-Hadith, an Indian Hanbali organisation, took the initiative in 1993 and issued a *fatwa* to the effect that the notorious 'bare *talaq*' or *talaq al-bida* was against the injunctions of the Qur'an, in other words, this practice was not Islamic. Predictably, this caused heated debates.[56] In a long discussion of the triple *talaq* and its potentially obnoxious consequences, Latifi (1993, pp. 174–180) criticises the Privy Council case of *Rashid Ahmad v. Aniisa Khatun* [1931] 59 L.R. I.A. 21, as a faulty precedent establishing that three *talaq* pronouncements in the same breath irrevocably terminate a marriage. He also explains, quite correctly, that the three *maulanas* said nothing new at all, since the Shias and some of the Hanbalis had always taken the position that a *talaq al-bida* was not acceptable. Latifi (1993, p. 176) was fully in favour of this, declaring that "needless to say this is a healthy rule and should be encouraged for all. None should object to it except moth eaten minds". His final recommendations (at pages 179–180) are to the effect that women should use their marriage contracts to stipulate better conditions on divorce, that the Supreme Court should review the old faulty Privy Council precedent, that legislation might be used to the same effect, that the DMMA 1939 should be amended to require divorcing men to pronounce their *talaq* before a Qadi, that Hanafi Muslims should in effect switch schools and finally that the procedure of remarrying one's divorced wife should be outlawed and ruthlessly repressed.

9–56 F. Ahmad (1994) emphasises in his detailed study the scope for balancing the husband's unilateral power with similar powers for the wife. Reporting on the *fatwa* by the three learned men, he also highlights an important but regrettably unreported judicial decision of H. N. Tilhari J. of the Allahabad High Court to the effect that "the practice of uttering the word 'talaq' at one go to effect an irrevocable

---

[56] For details see also Bharatiya (1996), pp. 122–124.

divorce was both unconstitutional and illegal".[57] While the author emphasises that this judgment caused a big stir and increased the intensity of the debate, from an outside perspective it appears that nothing has changed in the Indian law on *talaq*. The low profile of case law reflects the extra-judicial nature of the *talaq* procedure and also points to conscious efforts on the part of local Muslim leaders to keep disputes about Muslim divorce, including the 'triple *talaq*' issue, out of the legal limelight. The experience of the Shah Bano controversy and its aftermath (see in detail paragraph 7–75, above) evidently taught the Indian Muslim leadership that using test cases is, in modern Indian law, not going to favour male-dominated interests. So it appears to suit the Indian state as well as substantial sections of the Muslim leadership to maintain the status quo on *talaq*. The parallels with the scenario of partial invisibility of *talaq* divorces in England today (see paragraph 9–205, below) are remarkable.

The Dissolution of Muslim Marriages Act 1939 and Indian law

9–57 While the *talaq* has almost entirely remained an extra-judicial phenomenon, the opposite is true for divorce at the initiative of the wife. Here the – undoubtedly wrong – assumption has often been that the official law governs the entire field and that extra-judicial divorce at the behest of the wife does not occur. Legislative reforms to Muslim divorce law on the Indian subcontinent started to operate on March 17, 1939 with the promulgation of the Dissolution of Muslim Marriages Act 1939 (Act 8 of 1939) which concerns women's rights to divorce. This Act is still in force in all three countries on the subcontinent, albeit with minor variations.[58] We discuss here briefly the origins of this Act in the colonial period and then analyse its present low-key position in modern Indian law, which is partly related to the fact that Muslim wives in India can also use various extra-judicial mechanisms to bring about termination of their marriage.

9–58 The Statement of the Objects and Reasons of the Act makes it clear that there was a clearly-felt social need for this legislation and that there were two major aims, which appear to represent a sophisticated trade-off between the colonial state and the Muslim leadership.[59] The first stated aim was to consolidate and clarify the Muslim law regarding suits for dissolution of marriage by women married under Muslim law. This turned out to be a liberating reformative measure, allowing Muslim women several grounds for divorce on demand. The second stated aim was to remove doubts about the effect of renunciation of Islam by married women, a concession to those Muslims who were worried that many women at that time were abandoning Islam merely to obtain a divorce. This is a conservative concern, protecting Islam rather than women.

9–59 Fulfilling the first aim meant that in South Asia, mainly a Hanafi territory, a reform of the divorce entitlements for all Muslim women was to be introduced through the 1939 Act by borrowing concepts from Maliki law, which was more liberal in this respect, though not in others.[60] The classical Hanafi law of

---

[57] F. Ahmad (1994), p.x and elsewhere. For further details of the politicised moves to challenge the triple *talaq* in 1993, see Bharatiya (1996), pp. 123–124.

[58] In India, s.1(2) of the (1939) Act indicates that "it extends to the whole of India (except the State of Jammu and Kashmir)". This wording was introduced by the Miscellaneous Personal Laws (Extension) Act 1959 (Act 48 of 1959). The state of Jammu and Kashmir has had its own statute along the same lines as the DMMA since 1942. Kashmiri Muslims, whether from India or Pakistan, pose specific legal issues. For details see Pearl (1986b).

[59] See in detail Bharatiya (1996), pp. 109–110; Ahmad (1994), pp. 78–80 and especially Malik (1988), pp. 1–5. Malik's book is the leading specialist study from India of the DMMA 1939.

[60] See also Hinchcliffe (1968a), p. 17.

divorce had been causing great hardship, making no provisions for divorce in cases where the husband had disappeared, had been imprisoned for a long time or had failed to maintain the wife.[61] V. Malik (1988, p. 1) suggests that denying the Muslim wife any right to divorce where the husband refused to release her "was undoubtedly the fundamental concept of divorce as laid down by the Mahomedan law" but indicates in the very next sentence that this was not universally accepted. So we find here again a long-standing disagreement among Muslim jurists which has, in this century, opened the door for legislative reforms. Malik (1988, pp. 2–3) shows very clearly that the language chosen in the 1939 Act carefully avoided the impression that any real reform was being introduced through the Act, recognising the conservative agenda, so the legal provisions are classed as 'consolidating' rather than 'reforming' the Muslim law. These were and are matters of great sensitivity (see in detail Anderson (1972)). At the same time, Malik (1988, pp. 2–3) states that "the rights of a Mohammedan wife have been greatly enlarged" by the DMMA 1939 and that the Act "has made a distinct endeavour to ameliorate the lot of Muslim wives" (Malik (1988), p. 3). The reluctance to admit that this is a reforming statute is of course politically motivated, based on fear of all-too-familiar allegations that the divine Muslim law was being tampered with.

9–60 The second aim arises from the related problem that Muslim wives who either could not obtain a divorce from a husband who was unwilling to set them free, or who could not obtain divorce because classical Hanafi law offered them no grounds for a divorce, had to resort to apostasy from Islam to get rid of their marital tie.[62] The 1939 Act clarifies in this regard, in section 4, that the conversion of a Muslim woman to another faith shall not by itself have the effect that her marriage is automatically dissolved. This obvious concession to Muslim sentiments still allows women, based on section 2 of the Act, to approach a court with a petition for divorce when the husband's support is no longer available or, so it seems, when she simply wants a divorce against his will. The full wording of section 4 is as follows:

> "4. Effect of conversion to other faith. –
> The renunciation of Islam by a married Muslim woman or her conversion to a faith other than Islam shall not by itself operate to dissolve her marriage.
> Provided that after such renunciation, or conversion, the woman shall be entitled to obtain a decree for the dissolution of her marriage on any of the grounds mentioned in section 2;
> Provided further that the provisions of this section shall not apply to a woman converted to Islam from some other faith who re-embraces her former faith."[63]

For our present discussion, the most important provision is clearly section 2, the key section of the 1939 Act, enabling a woman married under Muslim law to obtain a decree for the dissolution of her marriage on any one or more of a number of grounds. The section in its original form provided as follows:

> "2. Grounds for decree for dissolution of marriage. –
> A woman married under Muslim law shall be entitled to obtain a decree for the dissolution of her marriage on any one or more of the following grounds, namely: –

---

[61] See also *K. C. Moyin v. Nafeesa*, A.I.R. (1973) Ker. 176 at 177.
[62] For details see Malik (1988), pp. 4–5. Several writers confirm that this was an extremely sensitive matter.
[63] On Pakistani case law see succinctly Abid (1993), p.196.

    (i) that the whereabouts of the husband have not been known for a period of four years;

    (ii) that the husband has neglected or has failed to provide for her maintenance for a period of two years;

    (iii) that the husband has been sentenced to imprisonment for a period of seven years or upwards;

    (iv) that the husband has failed to perform, without reasonable cause, his marital obligations for a period of three years;

    (v) that the husband was impotent at the time of the marriage and continues to be so;

    (vi) that the husband has been insane for a period of two years or is suffering from leprosy or a virulent venereal disease;

    (vii) that she, having been given in marriage by her father or other guardian before she attained the age of fifteen years, repudiated the marriage before attaining the age of eighteen years;

        Provided that the marriage has not been consummated;

    (viii) that the husband treats her with cruelty, that is to say,

        (a) habitually assaults her or makes her life miserable by cruelty of conduct even if such conduct does not amount to physical ill-treatment, or

        (b) associates with women of evil repute or leads an infamous life, or

        (c) attempts to force her to lead an immoral life, or

        (d) disposes of her property or prevents her exercising her legal rights over it, or

        (e) obstructs her in the observance of her religious profession or practice, or

        (f) if he has more wives than one, does not treat her equitably in accordance with the injunctions of the Quran;

    (ix) on any other ground which is recognised as valid for the dissolution of marriages under Muslim law;

        Provided that –

        (a) no decree shall be passed on ground (iii) until the sentence has become final;

        (b) a decree passed on ground (i) shall not take effect for a period of six months from the date of such decree, and if the husband appears either in person or through an authorised agent within that period and satisfies the Court that he is prepared to perform his conjugal duties, the court shall set aside the said decree; and

        (c) before passing a decree on ground (v) the Court shall, on application by the husband, make an order requiring the husband to satisfy the Court within a period of one year from the date of such order that he has ceased to be impotent, and if the husband so satisfies the court within such period, no decree shall be passed on the said ground.

There is a considerable amount of reported early case law under this section, especially during the 1940s. Details on this jurisprudence can be found in Tayyibji

(1968) and Malik (1988).[64] The North Indian High Courts decided the bulk of these early cases, so that Pakistan, too, had an immediate corpus of relevant case law in 1947. Most of the cases, in one form or another, concerned maintenance matters; some of them we have already discussed.[65]

9–61 Another focal point for case law became the grounds of cruelty and incompatibility of temperament. The 1939 Act as cited above provided, in section 2(viii), six illustrations of cruelty. Section 2(ix) was much wider in its ambit, as later cases established. Initially, the legal position was quite restrictive. It was held in *Umar Bibi v. Mohammad Din*, A.I.R. 1945 Lah. 51, that a wife could not claim divorce on account of incompatibility of temperament, dislike or hatred.[66] As we saw in paragraph 8–31, in the leading Indian case of *Itwari v. Asghari*, A.I.R. 1960 All 684 at 687, where a husband had taken a second wife against the wishes of his first wife, cruel conduct was defined as "conduct of the husband which would cause such bodily or mental pain as to endanger the wife's safety or health" and the court supported the wife's case.

9–62 More recent reported cases in India are not that numerous, but some of them raise interesting points. A case from Rajasthan on cruelty confirms that Indian courts today no longer grant divorce based on any kind of pleading of cruelty. This has little to do with Muslim law but is a matter of wider social policy, designed to prevent a situation where the modern law facilitates marital breakdown. *Mohd. Sharif v. Nasrine*, A.I.R. 1996 Raj. 23, is a husband's appeal against the decree of divorce granted by the Family Court to the wife under section 2(viii)(a) and (b) of the DMMA 1939. The facts are rather typical of confused modern Indian conditions, depicting a young wife who expected to live separately with her husband after the marriage but, due to the man's modest means, was forced to share her accommodation with several other family members. Seeing her expectations of post-marital bliss shattered, the wife made unsubstantiated allegations of adultery against the husband and refused to consider any form of reconciliation. The judges found her stubborn, "somewhat arrogant and temperamental" (page 26) and were not convinced of her claims. Allowing the husband's appeal, it was finally held, at page 27:

> "Cruelty in order to be a ground for dissolution of marriage or divorce has to be of such a type which should satisfy the conscience of the Court and further the Courts should have reason to believe that the relations between the parties have deteriorated to an extent that it would be impossible for them to live together."

It was not even raised as an issue whether this decision would mean forcing the wife into a hateful union in which she could not live within the limits of God. This confirms that this decision was concerned about Indian social policy, not the application of Muslim law principles. In a secular framework, this is an obvious outcome, but one must wonder how the wife's case would have developed if she had pleaded inability to live with the husband in accordance with Muslim principles.

9–63 In *Ghulam Mohammad Khan v. Hasina*, A.I.R. 1988 J.&K. 62, a Muslim

---

[64] See Tayyibji (1968), pp. 195–198 and Malik (1988), pp. 2–5, 13–19 and 21 *et seq*. *Said Ahmad v. Sultan Bibi*, A.I.R. (1943) Pesh. 73, is a relevant case on the right of a Muslim wife to claim divorce and the position of a rich Muslim woman in terms of maintenance.

[65] See para. 7–75, above. For example, in *Asmabai v. Umer Mahomed Sidik Mirza*, A.I.R. (1941) Sind. 23, it was held that inadequate maintenance was a ground for divorce.

[66] This case served as an important negative precedent in Pakistan; see further below, para. 9–82.

wife had petitioned for dissolution of her marriage on the ground of the husband's impotence. The husband was directed by the lower court to seek an examination by the Medical Board, but due to procedural difficulties had then been told to undergo a fresh examination. The main issue in this case appears to be whether an individual can be ordered to get himself medically examined. It was found that the lower court had acted without lawful authority and the case was remitted to the trial court.

9–64 Not surprisingly, under section 2(ii) of the DMMA, much early litigation had centred on the issue of disobedience of the wife and, related to this, the husband's obligation to maintain the wife.[67] The traditional consensus view had been that the husband of a 'disobedient' wife is entitled to refrain from maintaining his recalcitrant wife without laying himself open to divorce proceedings. Otherwise, however, a Muslim husband had a duty to provide maintenance. Malik (1988, p. 14) indicates that the Indian judges have been sharply divided on the woman's right to divorce in this context as well as her entitlement to maintenance.

9–65 Krishna Iyer J., then in the High Court of Kerala, decided in two important cases that a divorce may be granted to a Muslim wife on the ground of non-maintenance even where the husband is under no legal duty to support his wife. In *A. Yousuf Rawther v. Sowramma*, A.I.R. 1971 Ker. 261,[68] the learned judge heard a husband's appeal against his wife's claim for divorce based on non-maintenance. By that time, both spouses had already remarried and there was obviously no prospect of reconciliation. The facts were that after an extremely brief marriage, the very young wife had obtained a decree for dissolution of marriage on the ground that the husband had failed to maintain her. Krishna Iyer J., who had keenly researched the traditional Muslim law, reviewed the legal position regarding the Muslim wife's right to divorce and produced a most interesting judgment which emphasised that "it is a popular fallacy that a Muslim male enjoys, under the Quaranic law, unbridled authority to liquidate the marriage" (page 264). Noting that the Prophet himself had declared divorce detestable, the learned judge reproduced *hadith* evidence of the Muslim wife's right to divorce and also referred to the leading Pakistani case of *Khurshid Bibi v. Muhammad Amin*, P.L.D. 1967 S.C. 97 (see paragraph 9–57, above) to show that a Muslim wife is entitled to *khul* "as of right, if she satisfies the conscience of the Court that it will otherwise mean forcing her into a hateful union" (page 266). Indian law, however, has been less clear on this point. Krishna Iyer J. found, at page 266:

> "The Indian Judges have been sharply divided on the woman's right to divorce. Is she eligible only if she has not violated her conjugal duties? Or can she ask for it on mere failure of the husband to provide maintenance for her for two years, the wife's delinquency being irrelevant? If the latter view be the law, judges fear that women, with vicious appetite, may with impunity desert their men and yet demand divorce – forgetting, firstly that even under the present law, as administered in India, the Muslim husband has the right to walk out of the wedlock at his whim and secondly, that such an irreparably marred married life was not worth keeping alive."

Dividing the case law into 'moralist' and 'realist' decisions, and finding that the Supreme Court of India had not spoken on the issue, the learned judge held at page 266 that,

---

[67] See para. 7–35, above. On case references see in detail V. Malik (1988), pp. 12–21
[68] The same case is reported as *Yusuf Rowthan v. Sowramma*, (1970) K.L.T. 477.

"the Islamic law's serious realism on divorce, when regarded as the correct perspective, excludes blameworthy conduct as a factor and reads the failure to provide maintenance for two years as an index of irreconcilable breach, so that the mere fact of non-maintenance for the statutory period entitles the wife for dissolution."

The learned judge cited a large number of judicial and scholarly authorities in support of his view to hold finally, at page 270, that the wife was entitled to a divorce:

"For all these reasons, I hold that a Muslim woman, under Section 2(ii) of the Act, can sue for dissolution on the score that she has not as a fact been maintained even if there is good cause for it – the voice of the law, echoing public policy is often that of the realist, not of the moralist."

This bold judgment has not been given the importance it deserves, in fact it has been criticised in various ways, mainly because of its decision regarding the wife's right to maintenance.[69] Professor Anderson (1972, p. 41) welcomed what he called "a notable extension of the grounds on which an unhappy wife may obtain a judicial divorce" but was also critical of the maintenance part of the judgment. With explicit reference to the learned judge's decision in *Aboobacker Haji v. Mamu Koya*, 1971 K.L.T. 663, Professor Anderson (1972, p. 41) stated that the interpretation of the Muslim wife's entitlement to maintenance irrespective of her behaviour appeared to him as a "wholly unjustifiable interpretation of the statute". In *Aboobacker Haji*, Krishna Iyer J. had heard another case of a Muslim wife who sought divorce under sections 2(ii), (viii) and (ix) of the DMMA 1939 and reiterated his view as stated in *A. Yousuf Rawther v. Sowramma*, A.I.R. 1971 Ker. 261. More recent cases affirm that the words "failed to provide" in section 2(ii) of the DMMA 1939 must be understood as "failed to provide without reasonable cause".[70]

9–66 In the context of modern Indian legal developments in maintenance (see paragraph 7–75, above), we must again briefly mention *Zohara Khatoon v. Mohd. Ibrahim*,[71] a maintenance case under section 125 of the Criminal Procedure Code 1973. The wife had obtained a divorce under section 2 of the DMMA 1939. Her claim for continuing maintenance under the 1973 Code was that as a divorced Muslim wife, she was still a 'wife' for the purposes of the 1973 Code. The husband's defence, which not surprisingly turned out to be unsuccessful, was in essence that since she had divorced him, rather than him divorcing her, she did not fall under the expanded statutory definition of 'wife' for the purposes of maintenance. This case is also useful because it contains a good summary of the Muslim law of divorce at pages 1248–1250. Another unsuccessful plea by a Muslim husband that he should be exempt from maintenance liabilities, this time in a case involving polygamy, is found in *Subanu v. A. M. Abdul Gafoor*, A.I.R. 1987 S.C. 1103.

9–67 The focus of judicial and scholarly attention on the wife's maintenance rights has somewhat distracted from the fact that the Indian case law under section 2(ix) of the DMMA 1939 has produced a position rather similar to that in Pakistan, which has been much noted and commented on in detail (see paragraph 9–82, below). The two Kerala cases of 1970–1971, discussed above, were criticised because of the points they made regarding maintenance, but commentators have overlooked the factual dimension in these two cases and the important points they raise about dissolution of Muslim marriages at the behest of the wife.

---

[69] See, *e.g.* Fyzee (1974), p. 172, saying that this part of the decision is "open to serious doubt".
[70] See *Ahmed Abdul Qadeer v. Raffat Banu*, A.I.R. (1978) A.P. 417, a case which discusses many of the older authorities.
[71] A.I.R. (1981) S.C. 1243; [1981] 2 S.C.C. 509.

9–68 The debate on this in India has been strangely restrained. It is probably considered politically too sensitive by most Indian commentators to say openly that Pakistani law could provide useful guidance, but the important case of *Khurshid Bibi v. Muhammad Amin*, P.L.D. 1967 S.C. 97, has certainly not remained without impact in Indian law.[72] In *A. Yousuf Rawther v. Sowramma*, A.I.R. 1971 Ker. 261 at page 270, Krishna Iyer J. finally concluded with some comments on the equality of the right to divorce, which are relevant to the present discussion:

> "The view that I have accepted has one other great advantage in that the Muslim woman (like any other woman) comes back into her own when the Prophet's words are fulfilled, when roughly equal rights are enjoyed by both spouses, when the talaq technique of instant divorce is matched somewhat by the Khulaa device of delayed dissolution operated under judicial supervision. The social imbalance between the sexes will thus be removed . . ."

This pertinent comment about gender justice in Muslim law hides the fact that, at the same time, the learned judge was engaged in the important and contentious debate in Indian law about whether the manifest breakdown of a marital relationship should in itself be a ground for dissolution of the marriage. This point comes out more clearly in *Aboobacker Haji v. Mamu Koya*, 1971 K.L.T. 663, which we also discussed briefly above. In this case, the wife had refused to accept the husband's offer to maintain her and thus laid herself open to challenge. Her story of cruelty did not impress the judge either, so these two grounds failed. There was, however, the matter of breakdown of the marital relationship. It was found that "the Islamic ethos accepts irreconcilable breach as a ground for dissolution" (page 670). Remanding the case to the lower court for determination of the extent of marital breakdown, the judge stated finally, at page 671:

> "Let me again emphasise the correct approach on the point I am asking the lower appellate court to decide. Not some stresses and strains marring the matrimonial broadsheet, inevitable anywhere in the world, but deeper incompatibility which threatens to burn up the bond altogether – that is the test. The Prophet has placed profound emphasis on divorce being the last reluctant step of law and religion, and the court must act in that spirit."

This was manifestly not an instruction to the lower court to dissolve this particular marriage on the ground of irretrievable breakdown, but a re-appraisal of the facts would probably lead to just that outcome. Regarding irretrievable breakdown of marriage as a ground for divorce, readers need to be aware that during the 1970s and 1980s modern India has witnessed a vigorous debate about the relevance of the breakdown principle as a ground for divorce. Details are not pertinent here since, curiously, this debate did not prominently include Muslim law cases and concerns. So it appears again, from the outside, as though no progress has been made in Indian Muslim law.

9–69 There are some reported cases, however, which indicate that Indian Muslim women have successfully petitioned for divorce on the ground that the marriage has broken down irretrievably. This sheds some light on the current position in Indian law, which is not, then, so different from Pakistani law today, where the breakdown principle is also applied. The only difference appears to be that in Pakistani law wives have to plead Islamic grounds, whereas in India the

---

[72] The case was cited with approval by Krishna Iyer J. in *A. Yousuf Rawther v. Sowramma*, A.I.R. (1971) Ker. 261 at 266.

wife's claim that the husband was cruel to her and failed to maintain her,[73] or an explicit reference to the breakdown principle, has the same effect. This is clearly confirmed by *Mohammed v. Sainaba Umma*, 1987(1) K.L.T. 712, where a petition had been brought under section 2(ix) of the DMMA alleging irretrievable breakdown of the marriage. The wife had successfully complained of cruelty and non-payment of maintenance and the husband appealed to the High Court. The facts showed that the husband was a habitual drunkard and that the couple had not lived together since 1981. Varghese Kalliath J. found that section 2(ix) of the Act was "in the form of a residuary ground where the courts have an area of discretion and freedom" (page 713). Since the spouses had been living separately for so long and the wife had clearly expressed her great hatred and aversion towards the husband, there was no possibility of reconciliation. The judge, at page 713, makes some pertinent policy comments about the importance of the family and of an intact family life, but clearly sees that this couple's marriage cannot be revived. The judge himself, rather than the pleading of the spouses, reinforces Islamic arguments for the decision when he holds, at page 713:

> "When the wife verily detests the husband and he reciprocates it in the same measure and the spouses keep rigidly a fixed and morbid aversion and abhorrence to each other, life becomes a hell upon earth and a harrowing torture for both. In such circumstances, Islam concedes the right to the wife to seek dissolution of marriage on the ground of Khul."

Quoting a Pakistani case on the subject, reported at [1986] 1 *Current Civil Cases* 241, which had been referred to by the District Judge, it was held that there was no reason to interfere in the finding of the lower court that there was clear evidence of irretrievable breakdown of the marriage. This single case should probably not be taken as an exception since it appears that, unnoticed by a wider public, many Indian Muslim wives have been successful in demanding divorce from unwilling husbands. The fact that such cases are neither reported nor discussed does not prove that they do not exist. Muslim divorce law in India is, as other cases confirm, not necessarily located in the official sphere.

9–70   In fact, this is such an important issue in relation to Indian Muslim divorce law that we must discuss it here more fully. It has wide implications beyond Muslim divorce law and touches on all aspects of modern Muslim law in the world today. It has rightly been emphasised that, in Indian law, *faskh* now comes under section 2 of the DMMA 1939 as a variant form of divorce or judicial annulment (see Bharatiya (1996, p. 109), with several grounds having been made available to a wife. But does a Muslim wife have a right to divorce the husband without the intervention of a court?

9–71   Scholarship on traditional Muslim law has largely restricted itself to stating generally that the husband enjoys larger rights when it comes to divorce than the wife. We have seen already that these larger rights have been reinforced by juristic interpretation, coloured by patriarchal concepts and strengthened by local notions about the superior social standing of men. The traditional position, the view of the matter according to jurists, has been authoritatively stated by Doreen Hinchcliffe (1968a, p. 13) as follows:

---

[73] An interesting case in this respect, coming also from the Kerala High Court, is discussed in some detail by Latifi, "Muslim Law", in *Annual Survey of Indian Law 1983* (1983), pp. 334–335, who calls for urgent attention to this problem from the Indian Supreme Court, when in fact the High Courts seem perfectly capable of handling such questions with authority and sensitivity.

"Islamic law has never required that a matrimonial offence should be proved before a divorce can be effected. The law has always recognised that the parties to a marriage may dissolve their union by mutual agreement. In addition the husband, if he wants a divorce, has always been free to repudiate his wife without alleging any matrimonial offence on her part. A divorce of this type is known as *talaq*."

Asking about the position of the wife, Hinchcliffe points to the Qur'an, Sura II, verse 228 and confirms that the early jurists, as it were, interpreted away the wife's right to demand a divorce. Hinchcliffe (1968a, p. 14) found that:

"It was never suggested by the jurists that men and women had an equal right to divorce. On the contrary, it was firmly established that it was the husband who had the power of divorce, and for more than twelve centuries the majority of Muslim women lived not only under the constant threat of repudiation by their husbands, however blameless they might have been, but were themselves unable to obtain a divorce no matter how harshly they were treated or how desperate their situation."

The discussion in this important article of 1968 then moves towards analysing the reforms in Muslim family law regarding the wife's enlarged right to divorce, with particular reference to Pakistan and the famous *Khurshid Bibi* case. Here, we need to attempt a wider analysis of the Muslim wife's right to divorce which we will take up again in the section below on Pakistan.

9–72   In Indian law, there is a simmering tension between state law and the rule systems that Muslims recognise as *shariat*. An innocuous case from Kerala illustrates these tensions very well. In *K. C. Moyin v. Nafeesa*, A.I.R. 1973 Ker. 176, the question was whether a Muslim wife can repudiate her marriage outside the provisions of the DMMA 1939. Khalid J. firmly answered this question in the negative but this matter is not as simple as it appears at first sight. In this case, a Muslim couple had married in 1950 and a child was born. After that, the wife did not return to the husband, who filed a petition for restitution of conjugal rights in 1959. The wife responded, originally with a suit for *mahr* and return of ornaments, three years later with a petition for divorce on the grounds of non-maintenance and cruelty. The husband was granted a decree for restitution subject to payment of *mahr* and the wife's divorce petition was dismissed in 1963. By that time, the marriage had clearly broken down for a long time and it is evident that the court decrees did not match the social reality on the ground. Indeed, Khalid J. found, at page 176, that the wife,

"thereafter adopted an ingenious device to avoid the decree of Court by taking the advice of . . . who is said to be well-versed in Islamic theology and on the strength of that advice unilaterally divorced her husband, apparently by means of 'Faskh' without the husband's presence or his consent. Thereafter she entered into another marriage . . ."

The husband then filed a criminal complaint under section 494 of the Indian Penal Code 1860 alleging bigamy.[74] The District Magistrate acquitted the wife and the co-accused persons of the charge, hence the husband's appeal to the High Court of Kerala. Khalid J. assumed that "the grounds on which a Muslim wife can seek divorce are now codified in the Act mentioned above" (page 177). This is no doubt

---

[74] A Pakistani husband would in that situation, after 1979, probably have filed a case under the Zina Ordinance. For cases of that kind see below, para. 9–126.

correct, but were these the only grounds for divorce? The judge first went into the legislative history, reiterating that under strict Hanafi law, Muslim women had no right to initiate divorce from their husbands, which caused untold hardship. He cited in detail the work of Tahir Mahmood and quoted Professor Anderson (1959, p. 26) to the effect that this was an intolerable position. He also noted, at page 177, citing the Qur'an, Sura II, verses 228–229, that:

"It has to be remembered in this connection that the Muslim jurists did not recognise the rights of wives to claim divorce although the Quran had clearly recognised such rights in them."

The learned judge then noted that among Shafi'is, repudiation of the marriage by *faskh* was known and practised, without the intervention of courts. Relying on his knowledge of local society, and undoubtedly in view of the facts before him, the judge said that there had been serious abuses of this particular right by fathers-in-law and other near relatives. He then held, at page 177, that after the DMMA 1939,

"divorce can be effected only by taking recourse to its provisions and under no circumstances can a marriage be dissolved at the instance of the wife except under one or other of the provisions of the Act."

9–73   Turning to the 1939 Act itself, Khalid J. considered the effect of section 2(ix) of the Act and saw this provision clearly as "a statutory preservation of prior Islamic rights" (page 178). Having considered other relevant provisions, he concluded at page 178:

"Thus it is clear that the scheme of the Act is elaborate and conclusive and a dissolution outside the provisions of the Act cannot be held to be valid; nor can a Court countenance such a dissolution."

The learned judge also said that the 1939 Act "held that dissolution of Muslim marriage at the instance of the wife can be effected only under its provisions" (page 178), but this does not appear to be correct on scrutiny of the wording of the Act itself. It is also not correct, as suggested by the judge, that after the 1939 Act divorce at the instance of the wife must inevitably be processed by a civil court. In fact, the example of the *talaq-i-tafwiz* is referred to by the judge himself as an exception from this general rule (page 178). One could also refer to the concept of *mubaraat*, the mutual agreement to divorce, which does not require court intervention (Diwan and Diwan (1991), p. 87). One could think of several other modes of dissolving a marriage, including rights under local customary laws. Significantly, Khalid J. assumed that because the law had been codified, it now covered every scenario of a Muslim wife seeking a divorce. This appears to be a wrong interpretation, since the rationale of the 1939 Act was to enlarge the right of Muslim wives to seek divorce, not to restrict pre-existing local or customary rights, including the processes in Shafi law which the learned judge referred to.

9–74   Turning to the facts of the case, Khalid J. noted that the second marriage had been registered, "which is unusual for a Muslim marriage" (page 178). He then proceeded to discuss the concept of *faskh* and merely reiterated that "to repudiate the marriage by 'Faskh' without the intervention of a court is opposed to the law of the land" (page 178). The learned judge then launched into a revealing explanation of why, according to him, Muslim women must not be allowed to act as this lady did. He said, at page 179:

"It was to prevent such abuses that the Act has been enacted. If, without intervention of Courts, marriage can be dissolved by the unilateral repudiation by the wife calamitous results will follow. There have been instances in the past where unscrupulous fathers-in-law or other near relatives of the wife resorted to "free advice" from "agreeable men" learned in theology to get rid of recalcitrant or poor sons-in-law but loving husbands. It is the duty of Courts to guard against any such encroachment in its domain by unscrupulous persons. No person, however great or learned, should be allowed to usurp the functions of a Court. The advice given by a person, no matter however learned or great, can hardly be a substitute for a decree of Court. It is therefore clear that the unilateral repudiation of the marriage by the wife in this case does not have the sanction of law."

With respect, this socio-legal consideration, as valid as it may be in its own right, goes too far in its claim that the state law controls the entire socio-legal field. With reference to Muslim divorces at the initiative of the wife, Khalid J. is clearly mistaken to assume that the 1939 Act prohibited any form of extra-judicial dissolution of a marriage. The judge should have reflected more deeply on the fact that the state law created additional grounds for Muslim wives to seek a divorce. This is very different from assuming that it took away rights which Muslim wives already had in this regard. In fact, Khalid J. himself noted that Shafi wives (and many South Indian Muslims are Shafis) enjoyed larger rights in this respect. It is therefore submitted that the judge was a little too concerned about the disadvantaged position of the son-in-law before him.[75] A proper course of action for the judge would perhaps have been to enquire whether the wife in the present case had been forced out of the marriage.

9–75   As it were, the facts of the case are clearly taken into account by the judge when it comes to sentencing. Having found the wife and her new husband guilty of what the judge himself refers to as the serious crime of bigamy, he sentences them "till the rising of the Court" (page 181), obviously taking account of the fact that the impugned acts took place many years before, thus implicitly recognising but not officially condoning a customary practice that does not appear to be out of line with Muslim jurisprudence if we accept what F. Ahmad (1994, pp. 27–28), as cited above at pages 292–293, had to say on this topic.

9–76   While the above case gives rise to a wide-ranging debate about the interaction of modern state law, Muslim law and customary laws, one particular case confirms that smaller issues in the study of Muslim law also come up in Indian Muslim law today. In *Nurjahan Bibi v. Md. Kajim Ali*, A.I.R. 1977 Cal. 90, it was held that the doctrine of *lian* has not become obsolete under Muslim law and that under section 2(ix) of the DMMA a Muslim wife can bring a suit for divorce against the husband on the ground that he had falsely charged her with adultery. In this case, the wife had brought a suit for dissolution of her marriage in 1964. At that time the husband had claimed in defence that his wife was of bad character and that she had committed adultery with another Muslim male, in fact a cousin. At first instance, the wife had been granted divorce, but the husband appealed and won his case before the Additional District Judge. Bhattacharya J. referred to a number of textbooks and judicial authorities and found that *lian* was well-known, that pleadings to the effect that it was obsolete had been rejected in earlier cases, and that there was no authority to the contrary. Thus it was held, at page 92:

---

[75] It is relevant to point out that the appellant in this case was a *gharjamai*, a son-in-law who moves to his wife's residence, and thus has less authority than the husband who brings his wife home.

"My attention has not been drawn to any authority which has declared that the doctrine of . . . Li'an has become obsolete. I am, therefore, of the view that a Mahommedan wife can bring a suit for a divorce against her husband on the ground that her husband has charged her with adultery falsely."

In view of the peculiar facts of the case, however, the learned judge raised the technical question whether the husband's allegation of the wife's adultery had not been made in self-defence rather than as an aggressive and voluntary charge. In a roundabout way, this indicates that the judge did not believe the wife's story and saw that the husband's allegation was not false. In fact, it transpired that the 'wife' had been married to her cousin in the meantime, which raises the presumption that she must have been divorced by the husband through a *talaq*, or there must have been a *khul* or *mubaraat* in the meantime, or the marriage had been dissolved in some other form. Again, as in *K. C. Moyin v. Nafeesa*, A.I.R. 1973 Ker. 176, the extra-legal sphere of Muslim family law regulation raises its head. None of this was discussed in this case, in which the wife's appeal is simply dismissed without further explanations.[76]

9–77 The wife's position with regard to a 'delegated *talaq*' or *talaq-i-tafwiz* is well-recognised in Indian law.[77] This has been referred to as "perhaps the most potent weapon in the hands of a Muslim wife to obtain her freedom without the intervention of any court" (Fyzee (1974), p. 159) and has gradually become more common in practice.[78] Some earlier case law established that a wife can exercise her right as and when she pleases.[79] Diwan and Diwan (1991, pp. 80–81) emphasise that in the eyes of the law, it is still the husband who divorces, so this is indeed a form of *talaq*.

9–78 In India, there are some reported cases but the extra-judicial nature of this form of divorce has the effect that few instances will come to official notice.[80] In *Mohd. Khan v. Shahmali*, A.I.R. 1972 J.&K. 8, there was a pre-nuptial agreement, according to which the husband would have to pay Rs. 700/- to the wife, to compensate her father for the marriage expenses, if he left the matrimonial home, which was the wife's paternal home. There was some dispute about the validity of this particular agreement, but it was confirmed that this was neither opposed to public policy nor to Islam. Jalaluddin J. held, at pages 9–10:

"In my opinion a pre-nuptial agreement according to which the husband undertakes to pay the amount of marriage expenses incurred by his father-in-law in case he leaves the parental house of his wife is not opposed to the policy of the village folk who usually bring Khana Damads for their daughters and keep son-in-laws in their houses . . . [A]ccording to the institution of Khanadamadi which is prevalent in the valley of Kashmir a Khanadamad puts himself voluntarily under a customary obligation to live in his father-in-law's house permanently, for that solves many of the problems of the family . . . So if in the pre-nuptial agreement the son-in-law binds himself to pay a specified

---

[76] The discussion of *lian* in Bharatiya (1996), pp. 108–109, helps to clarify the problem and points to further debates. See also Ch. M. Mahmood (1991), pp. 66–67 and Mannan (1990), pp. 460–461.

[77] For details see Tayyibji (1968), pp. 154–157; Fyzee (1974), pp. 158–160; Diwan and Diwan (1991), pp. 80–81; Carroll (1982a).

[78] See Fyzee (1974), p. 159, with further details and Diwan and Diwan (1991), pp. 99–102, in the wider context of enforcement of agreements between spouses.

[79] For details and case references see Fyzee (1974), pp. 158–160; Diwan and Diwan (1991), p. 80.

[80] An early leading case is *Buffatan Bibi v. Sheikh Abdul Salim*, A.I.R. (1950) Cal. 304. The court made clear that an ante-nuptial agreement giving the wife power to exercise the *talaq* in the event of failure to pay maintenance for a certain period is not against public policy and is clearly enforceable. See also *Sufuddin v. Sureka*, A.I.R. (1955) Assam 153.

sum . . . on his running away from the house and deserting his wife . . . if he is called to pay the specified sum that in my opinion would not constitute a doctrine opposed to Muslim Law."

Having briefly considered a number of earlier judicial decisions, it was therefore concluded, at page 10, that this kind of agreement "is not opposed to the Muslim Law or public policy and the violation of this condition would entitle the wife to claim separation from her husband". Interestingly, as the judge noted without disapproval, the wife had already taken another husband.

9–79 In *Mangila Bibi v. Noor Hossain*, A.I.R. 1992 Cal. 92, a case under the Muslim Women (Protection of Rights on Divorce) Act 1986, we find confirmation that the delegated *talaq* remains an accepted feature of Indian law.[81] In this case, the wife had been falsely led to believe that the husband was a medical doctor and the marriage ran into various difficulties. The wife, based on her *kabinnama*, executed a divorce deed before a Muslim Marriage and Divorce Kazi in February 1988. The divorce was communicated to the husband but he failed to provide maintenance and dower to the wife, hence her application under the 1986 Act. The husband tried to argue that the entries in the *kabinnama* were made against his will or were even fraudulently added later, but the High Court, finding that according to Muslim law the power to give divorce may be delegated to the wife either absolutely or unconditionally, firmly concluded that in this case the wife was entitled to exercise her power of divorce on behalf of the husband.

9–80 Cases such as this confirm that Muslim wives in India, where the husband obstructs them in seeking divorce and the consequent ancillary reliefs, can expect strong judicial support for their claims. We do not appear to know much about the procedures followed when Muslim wives do not approach a state forum and seek to establish their entitlement to matrimonial relief with the help of Muslim organisations. Anecdotal evidence is to the effect that in such cases pressure may be put on the wife to give up any financial entitlements and property which, under the official law, the woman may be entitled to.

9–81 Financial considerations will not always be the main concern, however. As some of the cases discussed above indicate, the freedom of a woman to marry another husband, or the decision to remain unmarried, however much this may be socially disapproved, are also important considerations which some Indian Muslim women are prepared to fight for through the courts. Our analysis shows that the Indian law on Muslim divorce, within the context of a secular framework, has the potential to assist Muslim women, either in obtaining relief from an unwanted marriage, or in securing ancillary support after they were subjected to a unilateral divorce. While the Indian state law does not openly espouse Islamic key concerns such as the avoidance of extra-marital relations (*zina*), the effects of general public policy developments, especially when it comes to maintenance entitlements for divorced and abandoned wives, have also benefited Muslim women.

The DMMA and women's rights to divorce in Pakistan

9–82 The Pakistani law on *talaq* is discussed in paragraphs 9–119—9–188, below. Regarding divorce at the initiative of the wife, as indicated, on independence in 1947 Pakistan immediately had a body of case law under the DMMA on which further decisions could be built.[82] This happened early on, during the 1950s and

---

[81] The case is also very briefly referred to, with approval, by Latifi (1992), p. 179.
[82] Details of the old case law can be found in Fyzee (1974), pp. 171–176; Hidayatullah (1977), pp. 339–348; Verma (1988), pp. 281–327; Malik (1988); Mannan (1990), pp. 433–467.

1960s, when a vigorously debated body of case law developed under this Act, securing Muslim wives a larger right to demand divorce from a husband who was unwilling to release the wife. After the pro-women position had become well-established since *Balqis Fatima v. Najm-Ul-Ikram Qureshi*, P.L.D. 1959 (W.P.) Lah. 566, reiterated in the leading case of *Khurshid Bibi v. Muhammad Amin*, P.L.D. 1967 S.C. 97, little attention seems to have been paid to this area of the law during the 1980s and 1990s. This is one reason, it seems, why the parallel liberal position built up in the surprisingly voluminous litigation under section 8 of the MFLO 1961 has not been widely noticed so far.[83] This avenue for Muslim wives to dissolve their marriage will need to be discussed here in some detail. The current law is much more supportive to women's claims than has been assumed but this does not mean that any woman going to court to ask for divorce will find this easy.[84]

9–83   Turning first to the DMMA, we see that in Pakistan, after 1947, a limited Administrative Order in 1949 had the effect that section 1(2) of the DMMA 1939 was amended to say that the Act extends to all the Provinces and the Capital of the Federation.[85] For all intents and purposes, this would appear to include the territory of Azad Jammu & Kashmir.[86]

9–84   Later, section 13 of the MFLO 1961 made two amendments to section 2 of the DMMA with effect from 15 July 1961. As we saw in paragraph 8–29, above, the Pakistani and Bangladeshi versions of the DMMA have an additional sub-section 2(ii-a), providing as a further ground for divorce "that the husband has taken an additional wife in contravention of the provisions of the Muslim Family Laws Ordinance, 1961".[87] The only other amendment in Pakistan is that in section 2(vii) the age limit of 15 years old has been raised to 16 years old (see also Balchin (1994), p. 33). This was obviously required to harmonise the provision in section 12(1) of the MFLO 1961 regarding minimum age of a woman for marriage, which is 16 years old, amending section 2(a) of the Child Marriage Restraint Act 1929 for Pakistan to that effect.[88]

9–85   The 1939 Act did not introduce an arbitration procedure, such as is available in classical Maliki law, and introduced, for example, in Egypt, Jordan and Syria. However, by Order XXXIIA of 1976, the Code of Criminal Procedure has been amended so far as Pakistan is concerned to make it the responsibility of the Court wherever it is possible to do so, consistent with the nature and circumstances of the case, to assist the parties in arriving at a settlement in respect of the subject-matter of the suit. The court has power to adjourn the proceedings for such period as it thinks fit to enable attempts to be made to effect such a settlement. In addition, as we shall see, the effect of section 8 of the MFLO is to introduce the arbitral

---

[83] That the provisions of the MFLO have overshadowed s.2 DMMA is also indicated by Balchin (1994), p. 56.

[84] Impressive details, depicting the lively debates in Pakistan, are found in Balchin (1994), pp. 56–64.

[85] Abid (1993), p. 170 indicates that this was re-enacted in Ordinance 21 of 1960, with retrospective effect from October 14, 1955.

[86] We quote below, at p. 327, an authoritative statement from the High Court of A.J.K. to that effect, made in the case of *Muhammad Khan v. Zarina Begum* P.L.D. 1975 A.J.K. 27.

[87] It is further evidence of Pakistan's low-key approach to controlling polygamy that there is no prominent case law under this section.

[88] While most textbooks and statute collections assume that this is the current situation, Mannan (1990), pp. 26–27 indicates that the Federal Laws (Revision and Declaration) Ordinance 1981 (27 of 1981) omitted these two amendments, deleting s.2(ii-a) and restoring the minimum age of 15 years in s.2(vii). It appears that the constitutional validity of that Ordinance was challenged, so the position was confused.

procedures of the Pakistan Code in all circumstances, except the exercise of the option of puberty and possibly the consensual *mubaraat*.[89]

9–86 Regarding the case law under section 2 DMMA, disputes over maintenance arose early on and have continued without any clear trend. It is important to note that the legal development in this area is quite different from India since in Pakistan, a husband faced with a recalcitrant or 'disobedient' wife may simply divorce her and give her only the *mahr* and *iddat* maintenance – or not even that. As we saw in paragraph 7–75, above, the protective social welfare provisions of the Indian general law and the Indian Muslim law in this regard have not been adopted in Pakistan. As highlighted already, Pakistani society and law continue to assume that the wife's family should bear the burden of maintaining a divorced woman. With regard to cruelty, too, the important debates in Indian law about the nature of matrimonial cruelty and appropriate relief in cases of cruel behaviour have not been absorbed in Pakistan, although there are parallel debates about the breakdown principle. One major reason for this lack of cross-fertilisation is that such debates in India have been taking place with reference to Hindu law and secular legal regulation rather than Muslim law.

9–87 Therefore, most attention in Pakistani divorce law has been focused on those provisions which enable women to seek a divorce where the husband was either cruel or unreasonable but refused to agree to a divorce. In other words, disputes arose where the marriage had broken down irretrievably as far as the wife was concerned, but the husband refused to accept this. Reliance on traditional Hanafi principles, coupled with male chauvinism, therefore imprisoned women in unwanted marital relations. If in such a situation the husband agreed to a divorce, the classical concepts of *khul* or rather *mubaraat* would come into operation and an extra-judicial arrangement could be finalised. We must presume that this happens regularly in Pakistani society, but such cases are not officially reported anywhere because they require no court intervention.

9–88 Inevitably, the question for legal intervention in Pakistan revolved around whether a Muslim wife could seek divorce against the wishes of the husband. Petitions brought under section 2(ix) DMMA often allege that the marriage has broken down irretrievably and that it would be a violation of Islamic principles to force the spouses (in effect, of course, the wife) to endure a married life that could not be continued, as the standard phrase has developed, 'within the limits of Allah'.

9–89 In the early 1950s, it looked at first as though Pakistani law would not assist women in this kind of predicament. *Sayeeda Khanam v. Muhammad Sami*, P.L.D. 1952 Lah. 113, provides a long, exhaustive discussion of the problems posed by incompatibility of temperament and the resultant lack of adaptation between husband and wife. In this case, the wife had petitioned for divorce "almost on all the grounds recognized by law as adequate" (page 116). The wife had stated that it was impossible for the couple to live together because of differences of temperament and that she hated her husband. The district judge had taken the view that as long as the husband "does not give her an excuse for seeking the cancellation of her marriage with him, the ill-fated union must continue" (page 117). The husband had successfully relied on *Umar Bibi v. Mohammad Din*, A.I.R. 1945 Lah. 51 to the effect that incompatibility of temperament, dislike or hatred were not sufficient grounds to terminate a marriage.

---

[89] *Muhammad Ishaque v. Ahsan Ahmad*, P.L.D. 1975 Lah. 1118; *Muhammad Amin v. Surraya Begum*, P.L.D. 1970 Lah. 475. This may be a mere formality, however, not affecting the legal validity of the divorce itself. See further below our discussion of *Aiysha Yasmien Abbasi v. Maqbool Hussain Qureshi*, P.L.D. (1979) Lah. 241, and the debate in Balchin (1994), pp. 56–64.

9–90 Cornelius J., then the Acting Chief Justice, found that 'incompatibility of temperaments' was not a term of art. He defined it as "a total lack of sympathy between them, such as induces a resistance to mutual adaptation . . . basically hatred or aversion on the part of one or both of the parties to the marriage" (page 120). Surprisingly, it was found that the evidence on record was insufficient to support such a conclusion in the present case and it was therefore held, at pages 131–132, that:

> "under Muslim Law, such matters as incompatibility of temperaments, aversion or dislike cannot form a ground for a wife to seek dissolution of her marriage, at the hands of a Qazi or a Court, but they fall to be dealt with under the powers possessed by the husband as well as the wife under Muslim Law, as parties to the marriage contract."

One could interpret this as a gentle judicial reminder to the couple that, in the first instance, Muslim law allows for extra-judicial divorce on the basis of an agreement between the two spouses, perhaps with the assistance of arbitrators, whose potential role is discussed at some length in this judgment. Thus, this comment could be read as a judicial plea not to waste precious court time and to make use instead of the well-known Islamic extra-judicial processes of dispute settlement. However, there is another reason for the judicial unwillingness to accept the wife's pleading. This comes out in a statement by Muhammad Jan J. at page 137:

> "If wives were allowed to dissolve their marriages, without the consent of their husbands, by merely giving up their dowers, paid or promised to be paid, the institution of marriage would be meaningless as there would be no stability attached to it. No authority has been cited before us to show that this is allowed in Islam and the position appears to be wholly untenable . . . There are many people who, in spite of serious differences, do not resort to divorce."

The judge himself indicated that, if everything else has failed, a Muslim wife who hates her husband but cannot persuade him to agree to a divorce may go to court with a petition under the DMMA. Somehow, however, the court's duty under the Act towards such a woman in the case before them was not realised. Instead, the judges hid behind precedent and their own barely concealed social views of the matter rather than addressing the relevant basic principles of Muslim law. Acknowledging that the wife hated the husband, but at the same time refusing to accept the wife's petition, the judges upheld the traditional Hanafi law rather than the provisions of the 1939 Act.

9–91 Not surprisingly, the same question was soon raised again for judicial consideration. In *Balqis Fatima v. Najm-Ul-Ikram Qureshi*, P.L.D. 1959 (W.P.) Lah. 566, the court came to the opposite conclusion, albeit not without some important reservations. It was held in this case that a Muslim wife may demand a *khul* as of right, provided the court is satisfied that the marriage has broken down and provided she is willing to return the benefits she has received from the marriage. In *Balqis Fatima*, the facts were slightly different from *Sayeeda Khanam* in that there had been a *nikah* but no *rukhsati*, so that the marriage had never been consummated.[90] The lower courts had found no evidence to blame the husband for this, so the case could easily

---

[90] There were some allegations of pre-marital connection between the spouses, but the wife had, after the *nikah*, resided in her parental home. The concept of *rukhsati*, which refers to the physical transfer of the bride from her natal family to the husband's family, is closely linked to consummation of the marriage, which is, however, not a prerequisite for legal validity. For details see also Chap. 6, above.

have been decided in favour of the husband. However, the wife's lawyer raised what was treated as a "new point" (page 569), and a point of pure law, namely that a *khul* is the right of a wife, so that "the wife can at any time come to Court and demand a divorce on abandonment and restitution of any benefit which she may have received from her husband" (page 569). Reliance was placed on the writing of Maulana Maududi, to the effect that a Muslim wife was entitled to relief on payment of a kind of compensation to the husband. Kaikaus J. referred the case to a full bench, including himself, and launched into a full discussion about whether, under Muslim law, a wife is entitled to *khul* as of right. Naturally, the first task was to consider what *khul* means and involves. It was clarified immediately that the kind of *khul* discussed here was not an agreement between the spouses or *mubaraat*, although that term itself was not used. Relying on the Qur'an, Sura II, verse 229, it was found that the role of the judge was crucial in this context. Kaikaus J. boldly grasped the nettle of this judicial task and said, at page 573:

> "All jurists agree that if parties agree, no such finding is needed. If without agreement there could be no termination of marriage and if in case of agreement nothing further was needed, the determination by the Judge would become meaningless. The reference to the Judge can only mean that he is entitled to pass an order even though the husband does not agree."

9–92 Finding that the Prophet himself had never asked for consent of the husband in cases decided by him, locating support for the wife's right to *khul* in the writings of Maulana Maududi, a distinguished religious scholar of the orthodox school, "not a person against whom a charge of heresy or schism can be brought" (page 575), and having consulted a large number of other authorities, the learned judge began to discuss the attitude of Islam towards a discord between husband and wife. Thus, as the issue was phrased at page 579: "If a husband and wife cannot live together in peace and harmony, does Islam allow them to separate or does it force them to continue?". In this context, there was a notable discrepancy between the position of the husband and the wife. It was noted at pages 581–582:

> "To the husband the law grants full power of divorce. He can put an end to the marital tie at will whether he has a ground or not. It would be reprehensible that he should divorce one wife and take another just for sexual enjoyment, yet the law places no restrictions on his power of divorce and leaves the matter to his good sense. If such power be granted to the husband, why should there be a great disparity between the rights of the wife and the husband? One can understand that the husband having paid or taken on himself the responsibility of payment of dower, the wife should not be allowed to put an end to the contract so as to appropriate that which is paid or promised by the husband and she should be forced to restore the benefit she has taken. It is also sometimes argued that the female is fickle-minded and may on a passing fancy or a sudden impulse effect a separation. But assuming without conceding that in this respect the male is better than the female, the objection can be met with by giving the right to pronounce a divorce in a case where the wife wants it to the Qazi and not to the wife herself. The Qazi will in that case be able to see whether there is really any dispute between the parties and whether the wife is serious in her demand for dissolution. But it does not seem reasonable that while to one of the two contracting parties has been granted a plenary power to put an end to the contract, there should be no power given to the other party and the wife must in order to get a release prove some such misconduct on the

part of the husband as will disentitle him to the continuance of the marriage. The wife ought, in reason, to have a right similar to that of the husband subject only to the order of the Court. She should approach the Qazi who may advise and make an effort to effect a reconciliation, but if she is adamant and the Qazi apprehends that the limits imposed by God will not be observed, she can only be ordered to restore all the benefits she has received. The rights of the contracting parties should as far as the circumstances permit be at par."

It was further held, at page 582:

"Islam does not force on the spouses a life devoid of harmony and happiness and if the parties cannot live together as they should, it permits a separation. If the dissolution is due to some default on the part of the husband, there is no need of any restitution. If the husband is not in any way at fault, there has to be restoration of property received by the wife and ordinarily it will be of the whole of the property but the judge may take into consideration reciprocal benefits received by the husband and continuous living together also may be a benefit received."

9–93   It seems that the judge was concerned about being challenged for granting a wife this right for the first time, but he found a number of grounds to counter any objections. His strongest point, in fact, was that the question before the court was a matter of interpretation of the very basis of Muslim law. Kaikaus J. said, at page 584, in a way which an Indian judge, of whatever religious background, would not find quite so simple because of the politics of the personal law system in that country:

". . . we are really dealing with the interpretation of the Holy Qur'an and on a question of interpretation we are not bound by the opinions of jurists. If we be clear as to what the meaning of a verse in the Qur'an is, it will be our duty to give effect to that interpretation irrespective of what has been stated by jurists. "*Atiullah-ha-wa Ati-ur-Rasul*" is the duty cast on the Muslim and it will not be obedience to God or to the Prophet if we fail to decide in accordance with it."

This kind of judicial statement would probably have led to stormy protests in India. Indeed, we noted in paragraph 9–57, above the marked absence of such evidence of judicial intervention. Here it led to some praise for the pathbreaking boldness of this judgment.[91] Kaikaus J. turned next to the earlier cases which opposed the right of wives to seek divorce against the wishes of the husband. He found *Umar Bibi v. Mohammad Din*, A.I.R. 1945 Lah. 51 based on several misinterpretations and *Sayeeda Khanam v. Muhammad Sami*, P.L.D. 1952 (W.P.) Lah. 113 was, in his view, decided on the basis of an incomplete analysis of the relevant sources and in particular a failure to appreciate the role of the arbitrator (*hakam*) in Muslim law. The learned judge was rather critical of the way in which that case dealt with the statute itself and said, at page 592:

"The law provides that in matters of marriage and divorce Muslim Law shall apply to the Muslims. If the Muslim Law provides a particular procedure for the enforcement of a right of dissolution either we regard that as a substantive provision and apply it as such or we regard that as a mere matter of procedure

---

[91] This case has of course been overshadowed by the subsequent Supreme Court verdict in *Khurshid Bibi v. Mohammad Amin*, P.L.D. 1967 S.C. 97. The reserved reaction in Mehdi (1994), pp. 177–178, seems too negative. See similarly Hinchcliffe (1968a), p. 19.

and having regard only to the substance of the right enforce it by whatever procedure is available. But the right of the wife cannot be defeated. Either we should appoint Hakams or we should ourselves assume the jurisdiction of the Hakam in so far as it relates to dissolution for that is a judicial function . . .

I would regard the word 'Hakam' in its ordinary sense of judge or arbiter. One who is only a conciliator is neither a judge nor an arbiter and I am unable to accept that the jurisdiction of the Qazi is exhausted by the appointment of the arbiter, that if the effort at reconciliation fails, there is nothing further to be done and that the wife must be forced to live with the husband even though she be unhappy and may be in no way to blame and though the result would be that the spouses "do not observe the limits of God" . . . Is this what Islam contemplates? Is it possible that the husband and wife can under the circumstances live happily? . . . Why should there be such a disparity between the rights of the spouses?"

9–94   There is not one word here referring explicitly to the now so fashionable human rights discourse, but Kaikaus J. was certainly concerned about protecting the basic human rights of Muslim wives in this respect. However, he immediately emphasised the limits of the freedom of the individual which he had just so vigorously defended and held, at page 593:

"Let it not be understood that our answer to the question referred grants a right to [the] wife to come to the Court at any time and obtain *khula* if she is prepared to restore the benefit she has received. There is an important limitation on her right of *khula*. It is only if the judge apprehends that the limits of God will not be observed, that is, in their relations towards one another, the spouses will not obey God, that a harmonious married state, as envisaged by Islam, will not be possible that he will grant a dissolution. The wife cannot have a decree for every passing impulse. The judge will consider whether the rift between parties is a serious one though he may not consider the reasons for the rift. That the wife may go wrong if dissolution is not ordered is rather a reason for grant of dissolution for Islam prefers divorce to adultery.

The rights of the spouses as regards dissolution may be summed up by saying that the husband can effect a dissolution himself by pronouncing a divorce, while the wife has to approach the Court and she is to get a dissolution only if the Court regards further continuance of the marriage as not proper. But if it does regard continuance of the marriage as improper, there is no further limitation on its jurisdiction to dissolve the marriage."

While this express reservation led to critical comments by female writers, it was apparent that the court's decision was a huge victory for women. It was held, at page 593:

"The answer to the question referred is that the wife is entitled to a dissolution of marriage on restoration of what she received in consideration of marriage if the judge apprehends that parties will not observe the limits of God."

9–95   Although *Balqis Fatima* was a Full Bench decision, the conflict between the above High Court cases was said to have created legal uncertainty in Pakistan for some time. Hinchcliffe (1968a, p. 19) wrote that it appeared extremely doubtful at the time if *Balqis Fatima* would be followed. In *Ghulam Sakina v. Umar Baksh*, P.L.D. 1964 S.C. 456, Cornelius C.J. heard another case of this kind together with

Hamoodur Rahman J. The latter delivered the judgment of the Court without making reference to the simmering controversy and to *Balqis Fatima*. This is a technical decision, partly a preemption suit, giving rise to a discussion on the distinction between *khul* and *mubaraat*. The husband had taken a second wife, whereupon the first wife went away to live with her father. The husband's suit for restitution of conjugal rights was decreed and the wife's suit for divorce was dismissed. Subsequently, an unregistered compromise between the parties had been effected, involving an agreement to divorce and the wife's renunciation of her share in the disputed property. However, this agreement broke down. Finally, before the Supreme Court, the legal position of the unregistered compromise decree was at issue in relation to the preemption suit and the question was raised whether this agreement was a *khula* or a *mubaraat*. It was held, at page 459:

> "The main distinction between a *khula* and a *mubaraat* is that in the former the aversion is on the side of the wife and she desires a separation but in the latter the aversion is mutual and both sides desire separation. Secondly, in a divorce by *khula* some consideration must be given by the wife to the husband for her release from the marital tie. It is in effect an offer from the wife for her release on payment of a compensation."

On the basis of the facts, it was found that the agreement to divorce was a *khul*, *i.e.* an agreement demanded by the wife. This decision strengthens the view that if a woman asks for divorce, she has to bear the financial penalties. Remarkably, though, this case did not make any reference to the ongoing debate at that time about the wife's right to demand a divorce. This is probably so because in the present property dispute, it would not have made a difference to the outcome of the case, unless one could assume the unlikely argument that a wife who was subjected to polygamy had a proper case for demanding divorce without any financial penalty. Pakistani law was clearly not prepared to support such an argument.

9–96 The conflict was finally resolved in favour of the liberal interpretation of Muslim law and the pro-women position when the Supreme Court of Pakistan came to examine this issue in the leading case of *Khurshid Bibi v. Muhammad Amin*, P.L.D. 1967 S.C. 97.[92] Khurshid Bibi had been contracted in marriage at a very young age to Muhammad Amin, whilst at the same time her brother had married Muhammad Amin's sister. No children were born to Khurshid Bibi and Muhammad Amin took a second wife. After this, the relationship between the spouses became very strained. Khurshid Bibi demanded a separate house which her husband promised to provide. He did not actually take positive steps to implement this promise. After complaining of ill-treatment by her husband and after her brother had her removed from the matrimonial home through a warrant under section 100 of the Criminal Procedure Code of Pakistan, the wife petitioned for divorce under section 2(ix) DMMA. The husband, at the same time, instituted a successful suit for restitution of conjugal rights. The wife finally appealed to the Supreme Court, asking for a *khul* divorce on consideration of giving up her dower, claiming that it was impossible for the spouses to live together. The wife relied on the Full Bench decision in *Balqis Fatima*; the husband was unwilling to release the wife, even if she returned her dower (page 108). While the lower court at second instance appears to have found the wife somewhat obstinate (page 108) and went as far as claiming that a wife's opposition to the husband's polygamy was not a proper

---

[92] The case has been excerpted at length in Hodkinson (1984), pp. 271–296. For discussions of the case see, *e.g.* Hinchcliffe (1968a); S. S. Ali (1985).

ground for divorce,[93] S. A. Rahman J. noted the determined efforts of the wife to get release from the matrimonial bond and found the husband less than sincere. He put the issue before the court as follows (page 111):

"This being the state of relations between the parties, the question arises whether the wife is entitled, as of right, to claim *khula*, despite the unwillingness of the husband to release her from the matrimonial tie, if she satisfies the Court that there is no possibility of their living together, consistently with their conjugal duties and obligations."

The learned judges proceeded to examine the question in the light of relevant Qur'anic verses, the *hadith* literature and other sources and found a number of controversial issues which required determination.[94] It was noted that "the question whether *khula* is to be equated with *talaq*, or it is a form of dissolution of marriage in a category of its own, has been the subject of controversy among the jurists" (page 116). It was soon found that *khul* and *talaq* were different, as the right of the husband to take back the wife after *khul* does not exist, as it does in the case of a revocable *talaq* (*id.*). This case also makes reference to reforms in various Muslim countries (page 119). S. A. Rahman J. finally held, at page 121 that the view of Kaikaus J. in *Balqis Fatima*, to the effect that the relevant verse of the Qur'an gives the wife the right of *khul* subject to certain limitations, was correct. In view of the facts, he found that there was no possibility left of the spouses living together in amity and goodwill. There had been protracted litigation, the wife had shown intense dislike of the husband after he took a second wife, had refused to cohabit ever since, and it was idle to consider reconciliation, which had been tried and had failed. The wife was, therefore, entitled to separation from the husband by *khul*.

9–97 S. A. Mahmood J. produced another long judgment in this case, from page 129 onwards, which goes over the same ground, emphasises that the Qur'anic verse of prime importance for understanding the judicial role in this context is Sura II, verse 229 (pages 134–135) and interprets this as clear authorisation for judicial intervention. Finding that *khul* is a right conferred on the wife by the Qur'an itself (page 136), and that it is different from *talaq* (page 136–37), it was concluded, at page 137:

"Obviously, therefore, the dissolution cannot rest on the consent of the husband, but must depend on the order of the Qazi . . . The verse is thus, in particular, a rule of decision in cases where reference to the Qazi is necessitated by the refusal of the husband to divorce his wife and in such cases dissolution is by the order of the Qazi and is not dependent on the consent of the husband or on his pronouncing a *talaq*. There are no words in the verse indicating that the consent of or *talaq* by the husband is necessary for *khula*."

9–98 It was further clarified by S. A. Mahmood J., at page 140, that "there are thus two classes of cases of *khula*: (1) by mutual agreement, and (2) by order of the Qazi or Court, where dissolution of marriage takes place by the husband's pronouncing a *talaq* in the first class of cases, and by the order of the Qazi or the Court in the second". At page 141, the judge added that, where *khul* takes place as a result of mutual consent of the spouses, technically called *mubaraat*, no reference to a Qazi is necessary. However,

"where the husband disputes the right of the wife to obtain separation by *khula*, a third party must decide the matter, and it will have to be adjudicated

---

[93] See p. 109; at p. 131 it is indicated that the High Court took a similar view.

[94] The judgment contains an appendix at pp. 122–129 with relevant extracts from Islamic sources.

upon by the Qazi, and any other interpretation of the Qur'anic verse would deprive it of all efficacy as a charter granted to the wife" (page 141).

The judge also explicitly stated that in view of the hierarchy of sources of Muslim law, where a Qur'anic verse provided a rule, subsequent juristic interpretations would not be binding on courts. Thus, accepting the view taken in *Balqis Fatima*, it was held, at page 141:

"The opinions of Jurists and Commentators stand on no higher footing than that of reasoning of men falling in the category of secondary sources of Muslim Law, and cannot, therefore, compare in weight or authority with, nor alter the Qur'anic law or the Ahadith. If the opinions of the Jurists conflict with the Qur'an and the Sunnah, they are not binding on courts, and it is our duty, as true Muslims, to obey the word of God and the Holy Prophet."

S. A. Mahmood J., at page 143, further clarified the concept of *khul* by holding that "*Khula* by judicial decree, is thus a dissolution of marriage by the Qazi at the demand of the wife". It was not the same as *talaq*, and the husband's role was in fact limited, as stated at page 143:

"The pronouncement of *talaq* by the husband even in case of *khula* by mutual agreement is not essential in every case, because it has been held by the Courts that for the purpose of dissolving a marriage under *khula* or *mubarat*, which is dissolution of the marriage by mutual agreement for a consideration to be paid by the wife, when there is mutual aversion, it is sufficient that the husband should propose to pronounce a *talaq* or otherwise to dissolve the marriage for a consideration, and that the wife should accept the proposal, in which case it is not necessary that *talaq* should be pronounced by him, because the contract itself dissolves the marriage."

The decision to grant divorce to the wife in the present case was explicitly presented as in accordance with Qur'an, Sura II, verse 229 (page 148). This was probably done to avoid the argument that this judicial decision lacked a basis in *shariat* and was violative of the injunctions of Muslim law. It appears that S. A. Mahmood J. was conscious of such possible objections when he held, at page 144:

"There are no basic ideological reasons militating against the view that the Holy Qur'an in conferring a right on woman to seek dissolution of marriage and providing the forum and rule of decision, authorised the Qazi to dissolve a marriage by *khula*. In Islam, marriage is a contract and not a sacrament, and whatever sanctity attaches to it, it remains basically a contractual relationship between the parties. Islam, recognising the weaknesses of human nature, has permitted the dissolution of marriage, and does not make it an unseverable tie, condemning the spouses to a life of helpless despair. The Qur'anic legislation makes it clear that it has raised the status of women. The Holy Qur'an declares in Verse 2:228 that women have rights against men similar to those that men have against them. It conferred the right of *khula* on women as against the right of *talaq* in men."

9–99 The Pakistani Supreme Court in *Khurshid Bibi v. Muhammad Amin*, P.L.D. 1967 S.C. 97, therefore, in what would today be called a judgment marked by 'social activism', decided that *khul* could be effected without the consent of the husband, so that a wife can demand from the court as of right a termination by *khul*, provided she can show that married life has, in effect, irretrievably broken down. It has been argued, notably by Hinchcliffe (1968a, p. 19), that the Supreme Court interpreted Sura II, verse 229 in a fashion which derives no authority from any school. In Maliki law, the court can order a *khul* on certain occasions, but Maliki jurisprudence is firmly based on the judicial *talaq*, whereby if the husband is to blame, the court exercises the *talaq* on behalf of the husband, and the wife keeps her dower. If the wife is to blame, the court, in its discretion, exercises the *talaq* conditional on the wife giving up her rights to the dower. In Pakistan, as pointed out by Hinchcliffe (1968a, p. 24), the Supreme Court's decision made the wife more equal in relation to demanding a divorce, which was to be welcomed. But the court also held (at pages 148–149) that the wife would have to return the benefits of the marriage, so that it became necessary for the court in a case of *khul* to ascertain "what benefits have been conferred on the wife by the husband as a consideration for the marriage, and it is in the discretion of the Court to fix the amount of compensation" (page 149). Hinchcliffe (1968a, p. 24) warned of a hidden risk, in that husbands would now use the new law to obtain financial advantages by switching tactics, forcing the wife to ask for a *khul* rather than giving a *talaq*. It was commented with much foresight at page 25:

> "The law of Pakistan, therefore, still favours husbands. It is not difficult to visualise the case of a husband who might wish to get rid of his wife but not want to repudiate her and thus become liable to pay her deferred dower. Such a husband could make life extremely unpleasant for his wife, while taking care not to commit an offence under the Dissolution of Muslim Marriages Act. He could then suggest divorce by agreement, in return for the relinquishment of her dower debt by the wife, and possibly some further compensation. Or the wife might be provoked into going to court and asking for a *Khul'* as of right, relying on the decision in *Khurshid v. Muhammad Amin*. In this case also the husband would not only be freed from the dower debt, but would also receive back anything he might have given to his wife during the marriage."

This prediction has been borne out, to some extent, by more recent evidence of case law, which has developed under section 8 of the MFLO rather than under the DMMA.[95] We discuss this further below. Hinchcliffe's call for further legislation, however, has been ignored. As we shall see in the rest of this section, Pakistani women are not absolutely equal to men when it comes to bringing about a divorce, but it may be doubted whether any further legislation would be beneficial. Divorce is clearly available to Muslim men and women in Pakistan, extra-judicially as well as through the courts. While the husband's power of the unilateral *talaq* has not really been curbed by Pakistani law, as we shall show in detail in paragraphs 9–119—9–188, below, women have simultaneously been assisted in their claim to have a right to divorce and to exercise it when they cannot live with the husband. We have seen that this is supported by statute and case law. From *Balqis Fatima* in 1959 onwards, and certainly after *Khurshid Bibi* in 1967, Pakistani wives have been able to free themselves from an unwanted marriage, but they have had to face the financial consequences of that right.[96]

9–100 Related to the financial arrangements on divorce, the question of culpability under Pakistani law has clearly remained a vexed problem. In *Siddiq v.*

---

[95] It will be necessary to conduct detailed research on this case law. There is, at present, remarkably little writing on this important subject.
[96] Difficulties of access to courts and the negative financial consequences of divorce are not peculiar to Pakistan, of course. The case law indicates that cultural factors make it more difficult for wives to assert themselves.

Sharfan, P.L.D. 1968 Lah. 411, the wife had asked for divorce on various grounds under the DMMA but it was found that the wife was wholly to blame for the break-up of the marriage because she had committed adultery. The court was aware of the recent case law, finding at page 412–413:

> "The wife is entitled to the dissolution of marriage on the restoration of what she received in consideration of marriage if the Judge apprehends that the parties will not observe the limits of God. It was so held in *Balqis Fatima* . . ."

However, the decision of the lower court was found unacceptable in view of the evidence of the wife's adultery. It was thought that to underwrite a wife's right to divorce in that situation would lead to an unacceptable situation in society. The comments of Sardar Muhammad Iqbal J. on this, at page 413, are very instructive.

> "If this view is accepted, a woman by her self-confessed guilt of adultery will become entitled to the dissolution of marriage. An unwilling wife, who otherwise is not able to make out a case for dissolution on marriage . . . will ask the Court for *khula'* by making an admission of adultery with someone, whom she may be interested to marry. To concede that marriage can be dissolved on this ground will run counter to the concept of the marriage as a sacred tie. It will disrupt the family life which will have serious repercussions on the creation of a happy and healthy Islamic society. The wife to satisfy her lust, will succeed in getting divorce, but it would expose the children of the spouses to the ridicule of society and will also be a cause of invisible suspicion of the character of the children of such a lady, whether from the first or from the second husband. It is for this reason that an absolute right is not conceded to a wife to claim *khula'* on the restoration of the benefits which she may have received from her husband."

The judge then quoted the concluding comment by Kaikaus J. in *Balqis Fatima* (cited above, page 319). Thus, the court refused the wife a *khul* divorce, providing at pages 414–415 an elaborate explanation of the court's decision which demonstrates how Pakistani Muslim divorce law operates in its socio-legal context:

> "If it is established before him that the wife was seeking the divorce to have a sexual enjoyment, the judge will not dissolve the marriage because it will amount to placing a premium on an immoral life. Such a course is not permitted in Islam. Islam aims at doing right and sets examples for others to do right and it emphasises that the wrong and injustice should be defeated. A great sanctity is attached to a marriage in Islam. It is a most intimate communion and the mystery of sex finds its highest fulfilment when intimate spiritual harmony is combined with the physical link. Islam tries to maintain the married state as far as possible. It does not countenance anything which may imperil such a life and the future of the wife and children. The Judge in considering the claim of the wife for *khula'* has to do justice. Islam strictly enjoins that he is to stand firm for justice and has to act as in the presence of God. Therefore, if a separation is inevitable the parties should not throw mud at each other. Such a prohibition is in the interests of good and honourable lives for both sides, and in the interests of a clean and honourable social life which is possible only if it is without public or private scandals."

Finally, it was firmly held that it would be anomalous to dissolve this marriage on the basis of the wife's self-confessed adultery (page 415) and this case was brought to a swift end. Emphasising that the above comments omit any mention of the Muslim husband's continuing freedom to seek sexual pleasure outside the marital bond, and to use the power of *talaq* without judicial supervision, we simply reiterate the fact that the case looks like another example of concern about controlling female sexuality rather than about limiting male discretion.

9–101 In *Hakimzadi v. Nawaz Ali*, P.L.D. 1972 Kar. 540, we find evidence that lower courts in Pakistan at the time were actually unwilling to implement the *Khurshid Bibi* decision.[97] The wife had been driven out of the house within a month of the marriage, had been drugged and accused of adultery. Repeated efforts at settlement between the families had failed. The lower courts had refused to grant the wife a divorce, evidently assuming that a wife in Pakistan has to put up with the kind of treatment meted out to this young girl. On appeal to the High Court of Karachi, it was strenuously argued that the view taken by the lower courts was perverse (page 542). Dorab Patel J. held, at page 547, that where admittedly the wife was not at fault, and had been insulted and hurt by the husband's actions, she was not required to prove that each and every allegation was true. It was sufficient to show that her marriage had completely broken down and that there was no hope of reconciliation. The appeal was allowed, therefore, and the case was remanded to the trial court for determining whether the wife would have to return any benefits she might have received from the husband.

9–102 *Rashidan Bibi v. Bashir Ahmad*, P.L.D. 1983 Lah. 549, confirms that the lower courts were, in the 1980s, still unwilling to accept a wife's claim that she could not live any more with her husband. The wife in this case, forced to live separately from the husband for more than two years, had asked for divorce based on *khul*, saying that she could not live with the husband within the limits prescribed by God and that she would rather be shot dead than having to go back to her husband. The Judge of the Family Court had apparently been impressed by the reasoning in *Siddiq v. Sharfan*, P.L.D. 1968 Lah. 411, quoted above, had not applied his mind to the facts before him and had instead broken into an unwarranted religious sermon (page 551), moralising against women living by themselves. On appeal, the Additional District Judge had simply taken the view that the wife had not proved that there was hatred between the parties to such an extent that they cannot live within the limits prescribed by God.

9–103 The Lahore High Court found this failure to appreciate the wife's evidence "strange" (page 551) and decided that there was certainly sufficient material to satisfy the conscience of the Court. Javid Iqbal J. asked what other evidence the lower courts could have wanted and held, at page 552:

> "In my view, if a woman had stated that she would rather prefer to be shot dead than to go and live with her husband, it obviously means that she is determined not to live with her husband and the hatred was so deep that not to dissolve such a marriage would amount to compelling her or rather pushing her in a hateful union with the husband which certainly is not contemplated by the law in the present case."

The case was remitted to the Additional District Judge to consider the facts anew in the light of observations made by Iqbal J. This case is clear authority that the restrictive approach taken in *Siddiq v. Sharfan* should no longer be followed in

---

[97] A similar case is *Bilqees Fatima v. Noor Muhammad*, P.L.D. 1978 Lah. 1109, in which the judge held, at p. 1116, that not to appreciate the wife's claims and to resolve the dispute speedily was "disobedience of the command of God".

Pakistan.[98] In *Akhlaq Ahmad v. Kishwar Sultana*, P.L.D. 1983 S.C. 169, a well-placed husband's appeal against the wife's successful petition for *khul* was thrown out on the ground that there was really nothing to argue about. The Supreme Court established two important points in this case. First, that conduct of the parties subsequent to the institution of the proceedings was relevant, especially their behaviour during reconciliation proceedings (page 171). Secondly, based on the old case of *Moonshee Buzul-ul Raheem v. Luteefut-oon-Nissa* [1859/61] 8 L.R. I.A. 379, cited earlier, it was confirmed that non-payment of the stipulated consideration for *khul* does not invalidate the dissolution of the marriage. Thus, it was held at page 172:

> "Once the Family Court came to the conclusion that the parties cannot remain within the limits of God and the dissolution of marriage by Khula' must take place, the inquiry into the terms on which such dissolution shall take place does not affect the conclusion but only creates civil liabilities with regard to the benefits to be returned by the wife to the husband and does not affect the dissolution itself."

The case of *Muhammad Siddique v. Kalsoom Bibi*, 1984 S.C.M.R. 523, demonstrates that, by this time, the Supreme Court was getting impatient with litigious husbands who would not give up their wives. Nasim Hasan Shah J., in the tersest terms possible, refused to entertain any further arguments by the husband since the wife had clearly said that she could not live with the husband "within the limits prescribed by God Almighty" (page 523). Even during the 1980s, however, Pakistani women could not be sure that their husbands had understood the implications of *Khurshid Bibi* and the wife's right to *khul*. In *Abdul Rahim v. Shahida Khan*, P.L.D. 1984 S.C. 329, it transpires that a husband pursued his wife through the entire court system, challenging her right to divorce him by *khul*. The two lower courts had refused the woman's case but the High Court had decreed divorce, against which the husband appealed to the Supreme Court. The lower courts had refused a *khul* on two grounds. First, the wife was said not to have proved cruelty of the husband or maltreatment. Secondly, the husband used the argument that the couple had three children, the oldest a teenage girl, and that breaking up the marital home was not desirable (page 331). It appears, therefore, that the best interests of the children had been used as an argument to impress on the mother that she should try harder to live with the family within the limits of God (page 331). The High Court had basically taken the view that a broken home was not a healthy place for children to grow up (page 331), found that the marriage had broken down irretrievably, and had therefore allowed the petition for *khul*.

9–104   Nasim Hasan Shah J. in the Supreme Court expressed astonishment and indignation that the lower courts of the country should not be familiar with the law on *khul* as laid down in *Balqis Fatima* and *Khurshid Bibi* decades ago. It should not make a difference, of course, and was not even noted in the judgment, that the older cases are decided under section 2(ix) of the DMMA, while the bulk of the recent case law appears under section 8 of the MFLO. The precise wording of the learned judge's final verdict is indicative of the liberality which the highest judiciary of Pakistan, but manifestly not the entire judiciary of the country, is willing to apply to divorce petitions brought by women. It was held, at page 333:

> "In the present case, in view of the aversion, which the wife had developed towards the husband whether it is justified or not, it is quite evident that the

---

[98] Strong judicial condemnation of the continuing abuse of the Muslim divorce system by men is found in *Mohammad Rafique v. Ahmad Yar*, P.L.D. 1982 Lah. 825, at p. 831 (cited below, p. 356). The discussion in Balchin (1994), pp. 56–64, supports this view and provides further case references.

husband and the wife cannot live a life of *sukoon* and harmony in conformity with their obligations."

The deliberate emphasis on "whether it is justified or not" in this dictum approximates the Muslim wife's right to divorce in Pakistan with that of the husband. This application of the breakdown principle has been in operation under section 8 of the MFLO also during the 1990s, and a large number of cases could be cited.[99] As the final judgment in *Abdul Rahim* above confirms, Pakistani law has gradually been approaching a scenario of 'equality of misery', since it remains of course a fact that a Muslim husband can use his right of *talaq* at any time.

9-105   This 'equality of misery' also extends to financial provisions. As we have seen in Chapter 7 above, Muslim husbands may simply choose to withold any payments due to the wife after the divorce. Wives, as we shall see, can now actually do the same, provided they are prepared to burden their conscience with a deliberate infringement of *shariat* injunctions, as their male counterparts still do in abundance.[1]

9-106   In this context it is significant that many decisions on *khul* deal explicitly with the question of compensation. In *Muhammad Khan v. Zarina Begum*, P.L.D. 1975 A.J.K. 27, the court was first of all critical of litigious husbands who, "especially when decrees are passed against them, try to prolong litigation simply to wreak vengeance on the poor women" (page 29). Further, this High Court brought itself in line with the Pakistani law on the matter, as laid down in *Khurshid Bibi*, thus dissenting from the earlier authority in *Resham Bibi v. Muhammad Shafi*, P.L.D. 1967 A.J.K. 32. This gave rise to an authoritative restatement of the legal position of Azad Jammu & Kashmir within the context of Pakistani law. It was held by M. Y. Saraf J., at pages 30–31:

> "Apart from being in agreement with the view lately taken in Pakistan, another reason for us to depart from the view of the Division Bench of this Court is that in our considered opinion, the decisions of the Pakistan Supreme Court should have the same force in Azad Kashmir as they have in Pakistan. Although Azad Kashmir is not constitutionally a part of Pakistan as yet, it is practically as good as Pakistan . . . legal systems in force are identical and what is more, both have the same ultimate goal, namely, creation of a socio-economic order wherein Muslims can order their lives in accordance with the basic tenets of Islam. Besides, the Movement which brought Azad Kashmir into being aims at bringing about the State's accession to Pakistan. It is, therefore, only in the fitness of things that the Supreme Court decision reported as P.L.D. 1967 S.C. 97 be henceforth followed by all Courts in Azad Kashmir . . . We may also point out that in a sitting of the Islamic Laws Committee set up by the Azad Kashmir Government and attended by us, all its Ulema members who belonged to various schools of the Hanafi Sect, such as Deobandis, Barelvis and Ahl-Hadis, were of the unanimous opinion that *khula'* was not dependent upon the consent of the husband and that the Judge could, in exercise of his own powers dissolve a marriage by *khula'*."

The facts of the case show that this was a polygamous marriage. The respondent wife was the second wife, very young and apparently not agreeable to this marriage, which was arranged against her will. The court found that "to expect them to live

---

[99] Lack of space prohibits further detail. We refer to Balchin (1994), pp. 56–64 for much evidence of recent cases.
[1] This is confirmed *ibid.*, 62–63.

happily as man and wife is beyond expectation" (page 32). The issue of compensation was easy to decide. The wife was held to be entitled to *khul* on payment of the Rs. 500/- which she had received as *mahr*.

9–107   Abuses of the *mahr* payment are recorded in some cases. In *Shamshad Begum v. Abdul Haque*, P.L.D. 1977 Kar. 855, the wife had been granted a *khul* on condition that she should pay Rs. 5,000/- to the husband, which was challenged by the wife. Channa J. ascertained from authorities on Muslim law that the amount of consideration paid should not normally be more than the *mahr* or any other property given by the husband. It was also found that if the divorce was due to the wife's ill-treatment by the husband, no consideration was to be paid. Re-examining how the amount of Rs 5,000/- was arrived at in the present case, the court found that the wife claimed to have received a *mahr* of Rs. 50/-, while the husband argued it was more but did not say how much. It was also found that the husband had promised to give gold ornaments but had not done so. The lower court had obviously been too concerned about the welfare of the husband, who would have to buy himself, as it was stated, another wife (page 857). Channa J. was swift in his criticism and held, at page 858:

> "In our view, this factor cannot at all be considered for the purposes of determining the amount of consideration for *khula'*. None of the grounds on the basis of which the learned Judge has determined the amount of consideration of *khula'* are thus valid in law and this part of the judgment, fixing the amount of consideration therefore suffers from a patent illegality."

It was also held, finally, that "the failure of the wife to pay the consideration does not cancel the *khula'* but the husband shall be entitled to recover the same from the wife under the law or he may set off the same against any claim that she may have against him" (page 858).

9–108   *Parveen Begum v. Muhammad Ali*, P.L.D. 1981 Lah. 116, allows a glimpse of local customary traditions which are not in line with Muslim law, but typical of Panjabi Muslims, particularly in and around Lahore, where the so-called 'dowry problem' has been judicially noted.[2] In this case, the husband had not actually paid any *mahr*, but the wife had brought with her what was referred to as 'dowry', all kinds of goods and property provided by her parents for the wife's use in the new home. The wife had been granted *khul* but had also been directed to give up her dowry in favour of the husband. She challenged this decision as a violation of Muslim law. The court went through a large number of sources on the quantum of compensation payable by the wife. During this discussion, Zaidi J. emphasised the court's duty of vigilance and said:

> "Resultantly there is always a likelihood of fleecing and robbing of helpless and poor wives by some revengeful husbands, if we detach our adherence from the traditions and teachings of the Holy Prophet . . .
>
> I . . . am of the opinion that taking back more than what the husband has given to his wife as a quantum of ransom of *khula'* though not expressly prohibited in the Holy Qur'an, is a sheer deviation from the established traditions of the Holy Prophet."

Thus, in view of the evidence in this case, the Family Court judge ought to have allowed *khul* in consideration of the wife giving up her right to the recovery of

---

[2] See *The State v. Senior Superintendent of Police, Lahore*, P.L.D. 1991 Lah. 224, a judicial investigation of the notorious 'stove blast' cases, which have turned out to be a form of dowry murder which still continues unabated today.

dower money, which she had never received. Zakiuddin Pal J. added an elaborate treatise on the subject and came to the same conclusion, namely that the marriage stood dissolved without the wife having to return anything, since she was not given a *mahr*. It is not indicated how the wife should recover her dowry from the husband's illegal possession, so this case did not go as far in the protection of women's legitimate claims as it could have done.

9–109 As indicated, since about the mid-1980s, the case law under section 2(ix) has been taking a distinctly lower profile and attention has shifted to another provision in Pakistani Muslim law which has turned out to be equally relevant for protecting the rights to divorce of Muslim wives. This provision is section 8 of the MFLO, which provides as follows:

"8. Dissolution of marriage otherwise than by talaq. –
   Where the right to divorce has been duly delegated to the wife and she wishes to exercise that right, or where any of the parties to a marriage wishes to dissolve the marriage otherwise than by talaq, the provisions of section 7 shall, *mutatis mutandis* and so far as applicable, apply."

This section, first of all, concerns the delegated *talaq*, but it is apparent from more recent case law that it also covers all forms of *khul* divorces. Cases under this section have raised a number of interesting questions. The main issue became very soon whether in divorces under section 8 of the MFLO there is a need to give notice of the divorce to any Chairman or other local authority. Typically, this pleading was used by husbands to drag their estranged wives' cases back into the local fora, away from the courts. Some judges were quick to notice this abuse, but it took time for the law to settle down. The case law under section 8 of the MFLO therefore interlinks with the tremendously complicated litigation under section 7 of the MFLO regarding *talaq* and the requirement to give notice, which is discussed in paragraphs 9–119—9–188, below. In one respect, the development of the law in this area is different from that under section 7, since the *talaq* could at best be deferred for 90 days by the interference of section 7 of the MFLO, while Muslim husbands were actually trying to use referral to local bodies under section 8 of the MFLO to annul *khul* divorces granted by courts. By the late 1970s, as we shall see below, that strategy had been blocked by judicial vigilance in cases which have confirmed the traditional Muslim law position that a *khul* is an irrevocable divorce. Thus, the basic Muslim position that men and women have roughly equal rights of divorce was actually confirmed and it has become increasingly apparent in Pakistan that the notice requirements under section 7 and under section 8 of the MFLO are really mere procedural provisions which cannot modify the substance of a decision to divorce. Since that is so, as we shall show in detail below, the question today is what is the point of following the registration requirements of the MFLO if one wants to protect the interests of women?

9–110 Evidently, the legal position in Pakistan was quite confused for a long time, and these confusions still reverberate in the United Kingdom today.[3] Turning to the case law under section 8 of the MFLO, we see that *Mumtaz Mai v. Ghulam Nabi*, P.L.D. 1969 B.J. 5, is one of the earliest cases, instituted in March 1961, a few months before the MFLO came into operation on July 15, 1961. The wife had been

---

[3] Thus, in a recent action under English law, a *mubaraat* entered into in Pakistan and evidenced by a deed was challenged as ineffective in Pakistani law because there had not been any notice of the agreement to any Chairman. The case was settled out of court when it transpired that, in Pakistani law, notice of a *mubaraat* need not be given to any Chairman or other body to bring about legal validity and that the divorce settlement had been effective from the date of the agreement. Significantly, this was a woman's case, claiming that she was not divorced, so as to achieve a better financial settlement.

granted a *khul* divorce and the husband had successfully appealed on the ground that the procedure for reconciliation laid down under the MFLO had not been followed. This shows at once that Pakistani husbands were now using the new provisions and procedural requirements of the MFLO to put further hurdles in the paths of their divorcing wives. In other words, they were abusing the provisions as a means to protract *mala fide* litigation.

9–111 In *Mumtaz Mai*, the only question before the High Court was whether it was now essential for a divorcing wife to seek the appointment and involvement of an Arbitration Council. It was held, first of all, that the Ordinance is not retrospective in nature (page 8). The Court looked in detail at *Balqis Fatima* and *Khurshid Bibi*, which had both discussed the role of the *hakam* or arbitrator at some length, and concluded that if a judge took up the role of the *hakam* himself, this would not invalidate a dissolution of marriage ordered by him (page 9). It was also held, at page 9:

> "The question of reconciliation in the case of Khula' does not arise for how can a wife who has a 'fixed aversion' for her husband be reconciled with him. A reference of such a case to *Hakams* would be a useless pastime."

On the other hand, where there was evidence of discord between the spouses, there was a case for appointing arbitrators. It was held, at page 10:

> "It is, therefore, incorrect to say that, under the pure Muslim Law, *Khula'* cannot be finalised without first referring the matter to *Hakams*. The enforcement of the Muslim Family Laws Ordinance, 1961, has, however, made it incumbent and in cases arising after its promulgation reference to an Arbitration Council in cases covered by section 8 is a precondition to recourse to the Courts of law."

This early decision is in line with early cases on *talaq*, as we shall see, in that Pakistani courts assumed in the first decade or so of the operation of the MFLO that its provisions had more or less completely overridden the traditional Muslim law. As we know today, that is not what actually happened. Instead, the MFLO created new conflicts of law between the traditional extra-judicial Muslim law and the procedure-focused requirements of the MFLO. An interesting controversy was therefore beginning to develop. With the benefit of hindsight, we can see that a number of confused judgments were being produced at this early stage. It took a while for the courts to cut through this thicket of conflicting arguments. Of course the politics of islamisation have intervened in this debate as well, making it yet more complex.

9–112 *Muhammad Amin v. Surraya Begum*, P.L.D. 1870 Lah. 475,[4] is a case involving the option of puberty. This was now covered by section 2(vii) of the DMMA as well as section 8 of the MFLO. The husband was resisting the wife's attempts to free herself from the marriage and used the new provisions in sections 7 and 8 of the MFLO to argue that the jurisdiction of the courts had been ousted and an Arbitration Council should have been involved. It was firmly held by M. A. Cheema J. that there had been no ouster of the jurisdiction of the civil courts (page 479) and that the subsequent promulgation of section 21 of the Family Courts Act 1964 had clearly confirmed this (page 480). As for the option of puberty, once it had been exercised, the marriage simply came to an end and a court could only recognise and officially declare the termination of the marriage (page 481). It was therefore thought that section 8 of the MFLO also covered a declaratory suit in a case of option

---

[4] Significantly, the previous edition treated this as a "rogue decision". See Pearl (1987a), p. 127, n.52.

of puberty (page 482), which probably meant that a young person could seek a declaration under section 8 of the MFLO as well as section 2(vii) of the DMMA. For, Cheema J. went on to say that a suit for dissolution of marriage based on the option of puberty was not hit by section 8 of the MFLO, since the traditional Muslim law on the subject was still in operation. It was held at pages 483–484:

> "Having once repudiated the marriage by a proper exercise of her option of puberty a Muslim woman is under no obligation to wait for the decree of the Court for contracting a second marriage and instances are not wanting where the matter has come up before the Court the woman has already gone in for a second marriage and has even born children in the subsequent wedlock as is stated to have happened in the instant case."

The judge realised that the relevant provision of traditional Muslim law had not been overridden by the statute. It was clearly stated by Cheema J. that the husband's recourse to sections 7 and 8 of the MFLO was merely a tactical move to drag her through the courts, so the appeal had to fail.

9–113 *Muhammad Ishaque v. Ahsan Ahmad*, P.L.D. 1975 Lah. 1118, arose from several cases of *khul* instituted before Family Courts under the West Pakistan Family Courts Act 1964. Section 5 of that Act seemed to indicate that Family Courts should have exclusive jurisdiction over a large number of matters. Zullah J. (as he then was) reviewed four earlier decisions on this matter, including *Mumtaz Mai* (discussed above), which was taken to have held that reference to an Arbitration Council was now a precondition for applying to a Family Court under the MFLO for dissolution of marriage on ground of *khul* and *Muhammad Amin* (see above), which had held that section 8 of the MFLO did not oust the jurisdiction of courts to deal with divorce cases. This case contains an immensely complex discussion of procedural matters which does not concern us here directly. Zullah J. concluded, at page 1130, that any proceedings under section 8 of the MFLO can only be resorted to *after* the decree of dissolution of marriage was passed by a court. It was also held, at p.1132, that after the decree of dissolution had been made by the Family Court, the court should continue to follow the then current practice of sending a copy of the decree to the Chairman concerned. At the same time it was also necessary for the wife herself to inform the Chairman about the decree, as also to send a notice thereof to the husband. Thus the assumption underlying this decision is that the procedures of section 7 of the MFLO apply to section 8 cases like the *Khurshid Bibi* type of *khul*.

9–114 Regrettably, the complex discussion in this case did not take account of the fact that many divorcing husbands in Pakistan never resorted to the proceedings under section 7 of the MFLO. In 1975 it was perhaps still assumed that they did, or at least that they ought to do so in accordance with the law. On the other hand, the learned judge was probably only concerned with those situations where the court was involved in divorce arrangements. Based on the assumption that section 8 of the MFLO had introduced the arbitral provisions of section 7 of the MFLO into the *khul* procedure, a formalistic approach appears to have been followed during the 1970s, apparent from several of the cases discussed here.

9–115 There has of course been a view that the truly consensual divorce, which today should be called *mubaraat* rather than *khul*, does not require any judicial involvement nor judicial investigation under section 2(ix) of the DMMA or section 8 of the MFLO.[5] Zullah J. was evidently not concerned with that kind of case in his

---

[5] See *Ghulam Sakina v. Umar Bakhsh*, P.L.D. 1964 S.C. 456 at 459.

discussion in *Muhammad Ishaque*. However, in legal practice, this simmering conflict would have to come up sooner or later. Indeed, already in *Muhammad Nawaz v. Faiz Elahi*, P.L.D. 1978 Lah. 38, Zullah J. himself was confronted with this problem and it is very instructive how he reacted to this challenge. In this case, a Family Court Judge had held that a marriage stood dissolved through *khul* and upon subsequent notice to the Chairman, the divorce was withdrawn and a certificate issued to that effect. In other words, male-dominated Pakistani society had, once again, asserted itself over the pro-women provisions of Muslim law and the legislated Muslim law. It appears from the facts that the husband had engineered a consensual *khul*, really therefore a *mubaraat*, had not allowed his wife to take her ornaments with her, and now expected her to pay him Rs. 1,200/- as consideration for the divorce. In court, he was behaving as though he had been forced out of the marriage, but Zullah J. looked through that false pleading and confirmed that there was what he called a *khul* divorce.

9–116 The main question in this case was whether the husband could have the dissolution of the marriage cancelled or revoked. Having found that the *khul* was a divorce by agreement (page 330), Zullah J. stated that the consensual *khul* did not fall within the requirement to inform the Chairman, and that section 8 of the MFLO could not be applicable. He arrived at this decision because of the irrevocable nature of the *khul* and said, at page 330:

> "Islamic Law does not permit revocation of dissolution of marriage effected through *khula'* or *mubara'at*. Subsection (3) of section 7 has not changed the Islamic Law. The expression "unless revoked earlier" used therein carries the implication that the revocation should be lawful. In this case it is not denied that under Islamic Law, revocation is not permissible."

Thus, it was held that the action of the Chairman was without lawful authority and the divorce was confirmed as effective, presumably from the time of the agreement. Obviously, this put the standard interpretation for the purpose of the procedural requirements in sections 7 and 8 of the MFLO into confusion, and into sharp conflict with the position taken in this case. Zullah J. also made reference at the end of *Muhammad Nawaz*, at page 330, to the important case of *Haji Nizam Khan v. Additional District Judge, Lyallpur*, P.L.D. 1976 Lah. 930, which he described as in accord with Islamic law and philosophy.[6]

9–117 Some cases focused on the fact that there was an additional problem concerning extra-judicial divorces. Assuming that the truly consensual divorce does not require judicial investigation under section 2(ix) of the DMMA, or section 8 of the MFLO, as the case may be, is a successful wife still required to give notice to the chairman of the Union Council under section 8 of the MFLO? The question was discussed in the case of a Princess, *Aiysha Yasmien Abbasi v. Maqbool Hussain Qureshi*, P.L.D. 1979 Lah. 241. Here, after a short marriage, the spouses had signed an agreement to divorce, which was notified to the Chairman of a Union Committee, who then arranged an Arbitration Council and began proceedings under sections 7 and 8 of the MFLO. It transpired that this was not a *khul* but rather a *mubaraat*, so that the matter could not be treated as a notice under section 7 of the MFLO, since there had been no *talaq*. Zullah J. was prepared to recognise the finality of an agreement, but this time only within limits. It was held, at page 245:

---

[6] This case, which concerns maintenance of minors by a grandfather, contains an elaborate discussion of the Islamic nature of Pakistani family law and a re-assessment of the role of 'justice, equity and good conscience', moving towards islamisation of the entire legal system.

"I agree with the learned counsel that dissolution of marriage by way of Khula' and Mubara'at is irrevocable in so far as the authority of the husband to revoke the same is concerned; but the ancillary argument that on account of the stated position of law the proceedings before the Arbitration Council would either be unnecessary or without lawful authority is not acceptable."

The judgment in *Muhammad Nawaz* was distinguished on the basis that the Chairman in that case had sought to interfere in the validity of that divorce and had given a certificate of cancellation. That was against the spirit of Muslim law and those proceedings were without lawful authority. Zullah J. then went on to state, at page 245:

"The spirit of the law would be satisfied if a notice of dissolution of marriage in the form of Khula'/Mubara'at is sent to the Chairman by virtue of the provisions contained in section 8 read with section 7 of the Ordinance."

This statement needs to be analysed. What the learned judge says here, in veiled form, is that formal notice is required under sections 7 and 8 of the MFLO. The spirit of that law would be satisfied, as he indicates, by the mere act of giving notice. This is an implied admission that otherwise this process is an empty formality, a symbolic action designed to show formal compliance with the MFLO. As we knew from the earlier case, nothing can change the legal validity of the divorce itself and there is no scope for arguing that the agreement between the spouses does not amount to a legally valid divorce. The only remaining question, then, was when precisely the divorce had become effective. We have seen earlier that this may become important if one wants to determine the wife's ancillary entitlements, if any. It is relevant to note how Zullah J., in 1978, handled this issue with utmost delicacy. It almost appears as though the judge was glad that nobody started arguing over this point. It was held, at page 246:

"The question as to when exactly the dissolution of this case became effective is in the circumstances of this case, more academic than real. The respondent has not contested the writ petition. There is no reason to dispute the fact that the dissolution became effective in accordance with the provisions of the Muslim Family Laws Ordinance on expiry of 90 days, i.e. on September 26, 1978. It cannot be seriously questioned."

9–118 Readers will be aware that this is not in line with the provisions of traditional Muslim law, according to which a divorce agreement becomes instantly effective. However, at this point of time, everyone concerned let the obvious conflict between the two types of Muslim law in Pakistan, the classical *shariat* and the law of the MFLO, pass unnoticed. The learned judge, obviously keen to finish with this case,[7] merely restated, at page 246, that the Chairman had extremely limited room for action in a case such as this. However, only a few years later, the entire discourse about the relevance and impact of sections 7 and 8 of the MFLO changed in the light of a fresh debate about islamisation. As we shall see in paragraphs 9–119—9–188, below, since the 1980s the mandatory requirement of section 7 of the MFLO for notice of the *talaq* to be given to the appropriate Chairman is no longer as strictly interpreted as some years ago. This had obviously parallel implications on the

---

[7] Zullah J. went on to become Chief Justice of Pakistan and became known for his judicial activism and his concern to protect the human rights of the disadvantaged within an Islamic framework of reference. In other cases he did not hesitate, *suo moto*, to discuss a contentious issue at great length.

procedures under section 8 of the MFLO. Even in the mid-1980s, it was not clear whether the consensual divorce operated within the framework of sections 7 and 8 of the MFLO. *Aiysha Yasmien Abbasi* indicates, as subtly as can be at the time, that the notice requirements under the MFLO are mere formalities which cannot take away the legal effects under Muslim law. If a *mubaraat, khul* or *talaq* had occurred, all the modern state law could do was to take official notice of it, without affecting the legal validity of the action. This confirms that modern Pakistani Muslim law will protect a wife's claim to divorce and that the state law has not allowed itself to be abused to defeat the right to ask for divorce which the Qur'anic law so clearly gave to Muslim women. It is significant but not surprising at all (because in section 7 cases we are dealing with the man's right), that our discussion below will produce the same result, albeit through a different route. In effect, then, one major impact of the MFLO has been to affirm the traditional right of Muslim spouses, male and female, to terminate the marital contract without prior sanction of the modern state.

Talaq divorces under the MFLO in Pakistan

The debate about reforms and the statutory basis

9-119 In Pakistan, the Commission on Marriage and Family Laws recommended in its report in 1956 that there was a need to regulate divorce by the husband in several respects.[8] It was stated that the protection of happiness and security in family life required that easy divorces should be prevented (page 1212). To achieve this, the instant 'triple *talaq*' should be made equivalent in law to one single pronouncement and the better form of the *talaq as-sunna, i.e. talaq al-ahsan*, should become obligatory (pages 1212–1213). The opponents of the report's recommendation, like the proponents, accepted that the Prophet regarded the *talaq as-sunna* as the favoured method of divorce but opposed the abolition of the 'triple *talaq*', simply on the ground that Islamic law allowed for it (page 1583) and that "the innovation of declaring three pronouncements of *talaq* as one in effect is contrary to all the tenets of the Holy Quran, Hadith, *Ijma* and *Qiyas* and entirely unacceptable" (page 1585). The dissenting report, written by Maulana Thanvi, accepted the need for control of the unfettered right of the Muslim husband, but sought to achieve this by suggesting that a *talaq* in whatever form "should not be permitted without compelling reasons" (page 1585) and that there should be mass education rather than court intervention, which was declared to be "repugnant to *Shariat*" (page 1586). The dissenting report concluded, at page 1586, that "it is necessary to take effective measures to keep the practice of *talaq* in proper check and within the bounds of *Shariat*; but it would be inviting ruin in both the worlds to declare three pronouncements of *talaq* at one sitting as one".

9-120 The main report also argued, at page 1213, for the compulsory registration of divorces, supporting this by evidence that in cases of alleged abduction husbands often claimed that they had not divorced their wife, while the so-called abductor claimed to be the lawful husband of a divorced woman.[9] To avoid such turmoil in society, and to prevent waste of time and money in litigation, the Commission recommended the introduction of a standard divorce deed (*talaqnama*), which should be made available widely and cheaply, and which should

---

[8] For relevant details see *Gazette of Pakistan*, "Extraordinary", June 20, 1956, pp. 1211–1215. The relevant portions of the dissenting report are found in *Gazette of Pakistan*, "Extraordinary," August 30, 1956, pp. 1581–1589.

[9] Precisely this scenario was to resurface in so-called *zina* cases a few decades later, when the Offence of Zina (Enforcement of Hodood) Ordinance 1979 began to make its presence felt.

contain all the necessary information to ascertain the status of a divorced person (pages 1213–1214). In fact the Commission realised that this would not be effective and went further. Noting the wide abuse of the husband's discretion to remarry at once, it linked the right to divorce to making appropriate financial arrangements for the divorced woman with the involvement of a court (page 1214):

> "It was suggested that it should be enacted that no one can divorce his wife without recourse to a Matrimonial and Family Laws Court. When a court is approached, it should not permit the person to pronounce divorce until he has paid the entire dower and made suitable provision for the maintenance of his first wife and her children."

Apparently, the dissenting member of the Commission vigorously opposed this suggestion. The printed version of the dissenting report contains a very far-sighted criticism of the proposed involvement of courts which is worth reproducing here. It was said, at page 1587:

> "If a man pronounces *talaq* in these circumstances in the presence of his relatives, his marriage would stand dissolved from the point of view of *Shariat* but, if he subsequently avoid to seek the intervention of the Court with a view to evading the incidence of maintenance or dower payable to the wife or discharging any other liability, and, if the Court, on a reference being made to it, refuses to permit *talaq* on the ground of non-fulfilment of certain conditions of *talaq* by the husband, the pair would be constrained by this technicality of the law to live a life of immorality, giving birth to illegitimate children."

Notwithstanding the confusing syntax and the fixation on immorality, this objection contains a sound message, borne out by subsequent developments in the operation of section 7 of the MFLO. In the light of knowledge of local Pakistani society, it was predicted here that Pakistani men would ignore a new law that expected them to register their divorces. It appears that this argument was underplayed in the subsequent debates over the necessity of giving notice after a *talaq*. For, it remains a basic principle of *shariat*, the Muslim personal law, that a Muslim husband has the right to divorce his wife as and when he pleases. How would any legal reform of the Muslim personal law in modern Pakistan, while desiring to construct an Islamic environment, handle this particular conflict?

9–121   President Ayub Khan proved sufficiently strong to discount the orthodox protagonists and pushed through reforms in the MFLO 1961 which look progressive and modern, but clearly represent a compromise solution. In various ways, the new law allowed space for the continued application of the unreformed Muslim personal law as found in the *shariat*. With regard to *talaq* divorce, registration of divorces was required by section 7(1) of the MFLO, which seemed to postpone the legal validity of a *talaq* for at least 90 days and penalised non-compliance with the provisions of the Ordinance. However, what section 7 of the MFLO did not say is equally important for understanding the Pakistani law on *talaq* divorces during the past few decades. Crucially, the statute did not provide for the eventuality that the husband might simply not give any notice of the *talaq* at all, as was predicted by Maulana Thanvi in the dissenting Report of the Commission in 1956 (above). The silence of section 7 of the MFLO in this respect gave rise to the assumption that non-compliance with the statutory provisions must have negative consequences, so that a *talaq* without subsequent notification would be invalid. Under *shariat*, however, this divorce would undoubtedly be valid and effective, so that a limping marriage situation had been created. It took Pakistani judges and foreign commentators some time to work out that strict legalistic interpretation of these provisions would ultimately operate to the disadvantage of women and children. It did not help to clear the ensuing confusions that the islamisation debates intervened in this scenario during the 1980s. By now, as we show in detail in the sections below, it seems certain that the provisions of section 7 of the MFLO, while not unconstitutional, are more in the nature of procedural provisions which may be used if parties so desire, but non-compliance has few consequences in social reality.

9–122 This conflict needs to be discussed at some length because it also has important implications on legal practice in the United Kingdom.[10] We proceed by analysing first how the Pakistani law on *talaq* has developed. The relevant provisions in section 7 of the MFLO are as follows[11]:

> "7. Talaq. –
> (1) Any man who wishes to divorce his wife shall, as soon as may be after the pronouncement of talaq in any form whatsoever, give the Chairman notice in writing of his having done so, and shall supply a copy thereof to the wife.
> (2) Whoever contravenes the provisions of sub-section (1) shall be punishable with simple imprisonment for a term which may extend to one year or with fine which may extend to five thousand rupees or with both.
> (3) Save as provided in sub-section (5), a talaq unless revoked earlier expressly or otherwise, shall not be effective until the expiration of 90 days from the day on which notice under sub-section (1) is delivered to the Chairman.
> (4) Within 30 days of the receipt of notice under sub-section (1) the Chairman shall constitute an Arbitration Council for the purpose of bringing about a reconciliation between the parties, and the Arbitration Council shall take all steps necessary to bring about such reconciliation.
> (5) If the wife be pregnant at the time talaq is pronounced, talaq shall not be effective until the period mentioned in sub-section (3) or the pregnancy, whichever be later, ends.
> (6) Nothing shall debar a wife whose marriage has been terminated by talaq effective under this section from remarrying the same husband, without an intervening marriage with a third person, unless such termination is for the third time so effective."

The wording of section 7 assumes that Muslim husbands in Pakistan would henceforth notify an official body of the fact that they had pronounced *talaq*. The section is silent on the consequences of non-compliance, other than threatening such husbands with punishments. The section does not say how its provisions are supposed to be harmonised with the pre-existing Muslim law on the subject, under which a *talaq al-bida*, in particular, would be instantly valid and effective, while the new law suspended the effectiveness, if not the validity, of the husband's unilateral action as though he had given a *talaq al-ahsan*. Since the mechanism for enforcing

---

[10] For further details see para. 9–205, below. The position in Azad Jammu and Kashmir is complicated, to say the least, since it would appear that officially the Ordinance does not apply in that territory, but it is widely applied in practice. Officially, the traditional law of *talaq* is therefore still in force. On this see in detail Pearl (1986b), and the judicial comments in *Muhammad Khan* P.L.D. (1975) A.J.K. 27, cited above, p. 327.

[11] This is also found in Hodkinson (1984), p. 223.

the letter of this law is not clearly spelt out – for who would complain if a husband did not give notice of a *talaq*? – section 7 was always in danger of being little more than an elaborate legal fiction. The presumed effect of the notice is to 'freeze' the *talaq* for 90 days, so that section 7 of the MFLO has converted the *talaq al-bida* into a revocable *al-ahsan* divorce. During this period of 90 days, the Chairman should constitute an Arbitration Council for the purpose of bringing about a reconciliation. After the expiry of 90 days, the *talaq* takes effect. But could anybody challenge the *talaq* itself and render it ineffective? There are no clear answers in the statute itself, so court intervention was obviously required.

9–123 No time limits are laid down by the Pakistani law about when notice is to be given under sections 7 and 8 of the MFLO. If we follow section 7(1) of the MFLO, which indicates that notice should be given "as soon as may be after the pronouncement of *talaq*", the question arises how long one can wait before the lack of registration will be considered as revocation of the divorce. There is no easy answer to this question and the case law has offered no reliable clues.

9–124 In *Inamul Islam v. Hussain Bano*, P.L.D. 1976 Lah. 1466, the pleadings were confused since both parties haggled over maintenance payments for the wife and her young daughter. The couple separated in 1970. The husband claimed that he had sent a notice of *talaq* on September 10, 1971 but this had not been received. The wife, on the other hand, seemed to have obtained some support from a local administrator and, in March 1973, she filed a suit for maintenance, claiming to have been divorced on May 12, 1972, and asking for backdated maintenance from December 1970. She won this case and the husband appealed. In the High Court, Zullah J. seemed to indicate that notice under section 7(1) of the MFLO is essential to make a divorce effective and held, at page 1468:

> "There are three important requirements under subsection (i) of section 7: (i) pronouncement of *Talaq* in accordance with Muslim law; (ii) service of the notice on the Chairman; and (iii) service of copy of notice on the wife. If any one of these conditions is not satisfied, the *Talaq* would not become effective even after 90 days. The supply of copy to the wife is a necessary part of the requirement of service of notice on the Chairman. Similarly, the provision is clear that the notice to the Chairman shall have to follow a pronouncement of *Talaq*. Thus, that is also a mandatory requirement."

Zullah J. criticised the lower courts for ignoring the wife's claim that she had been divorced on May 12, 1972 and held that she was entitled to maintenance from the date of separation until the date of divorce, plus three months of *iddat* maintenance. This decision seems to assume that without notice, there cannot be any valid divorce among Muslims in Pakistan. If this had been made explicit, it would have been seen as a bold assertion which entirely overlooks the traditional Muslim law. If we speculate, however, what would have been the consequence if the learned judge had decided that notice of divorce was not essential, we see that this would have yielded a lesser amount of maintenance for the wife. It is possible, therefore, that justice-focused concern to support the divorced wife's maintenance claim sparked off the above comments about notice requirements.[12] In terms of the relevant period, the case offers no guidance. In later cases, where it transpired after more than a decade that notice of divorce had never been given, all the courts could do was to take account of

---

[12] The case also concerned maintenance for a small child. It is significant that the judge, at p. 1469, also made explicit comments about this, quoted in para. 10–85, below.

the fact that the parties concerned had been entirely ignorant of the notice requirements.[13] We pursue this issue further in paragraph 9–155, below.

9–125 Neither is there anything in the MFLO which unambiguously changes the classical law as regards a *talaq* being pronounced under compulsion or by way of a jest. A good example of this position is found in a case decided by Changez J. before the enactment of the MFLO, *Muhammad Azam Khan v. Akhtar-Un-Nisa Begum*, P.L.D. 1957 (W.P.) Lah. 195. This position is still not challenged.

Requirement of notice of talaq

9–126 Given the confusing statutory foundations, and in view of the obvious, yet hidden conflict between traditional Muslim law and section 7 of the MFLO, it is not surprising that the Pakistani courts have had to consider many cases about the implications of section 7 of the MFLO. In the first phase of case law, which is discussed in the present section and extends from the early 1960s into the early 1980s, it could be said that a kind of reformist euphoria prevailed, certainly initially. This was assisted by the fact that, already in 1963, the Pakistani Supreme Court decided a famous case, a high society scandal involving senior army personnel, which appeared to lay down the law on the subject with a firm hand. This case involved Shia Muslims, so the formal requirements of marriage and divorce dealt with in this case were rather stricter than in the Hanafi law, which added to the firmness of the rules laid down in this early precedent. However, there was also a strong moral element to this case, which many commentators have overlooked.

9–127 As the early leading case on the subject of *talaq* and notice requirements, *Ali Nawaz Gardezi v. Muhammad Yusuf*, P.L.D. 1963 S.C. 51, is important for various reasons. The facts were, briefly, that Ali Nawaz Gardezi, a Shia Muslim domiciled in Pakistan, married a German woman at a register office in Kingston-upon-Hull in England on July 21, 1951. There were three young children of the marriage. The couple came to Pakistan in 1953, where the husband took up employment as manager of the Lahore office of a large German company. In August 1961, returning to Pakistan from one of their frequent visits abroad, the couple broke their journey at Quetta, Baluchistan, where they met Lt. Col. Muhammad Yusuf. Soon a relationship developed between the wife and the Lt. Colonel. One of his love letters was intercepted, to be later produced as evidence in court. In November 1961, when the husband returned from a business trip to the matrimonial home in Lahore, he found that his wife had gone to Quetta. Although she soon returned, she left her husband for good at the end of 1961 and got married to the Lt. Colonel on January 2, 1962 at Quetta according to Muslim law. The wife declared that she had become a Muslim already in October 1961 and had changed her name. In quick succession, Mr Gardezi filed a complaint under sections 497 and 498 of the Pakistan Penal Code 1860 for enticement and connivance and a prosecution for bigamy under section 494 of the Code.

9–128 The question arose, naturally, whether the woman in this triangle had been validly divorced. Mr Gardezi managed to have the Lt. Colonel convicted by a lower court, but he was eventually acquitted by the High Court. The Lt. Colonel's main defence had been that the wife had been divorced by her husband on December 29, 1961. It was alleged that on that day the wife had produced two copies of a draft document of divorce for her husband to sign. The document, reproduced on page 56 of the judgment, read:

---

[13] See, *e.g. Noor Khan v. Haq Nawaz*, P.L.D. 1982 F.S.C. 825; *Chuhar v. Ghulam Fatima*, P.L.D. 1984 Lah. 234.

"While in full possession of my senses and having considered the matter objectively, I . . . son of . . . hereby divorce my wife . . . d/o . . . of my own free will and set her at liberty to marry whomsoever she likes. I shall have no case for any complaint or litigation against her or the person whom she may marry."

The complainant husband claimed that he had refused to sign this document, while the defence claimed that the husband had signed this document which, in effect, amounted to a *talaq* pronouncement. A key issue in this case concerned the validity and effectiveness of this divorce document. The trial judge had held that it was a fabricated document. The Appellate Bench of the High Court had disagreed. The Supreme Court, on examining the evidence, held that the matter was inconclusive and that the court was thus unable to arrive at a positive finding about the genuineness or otherwise of the divorce document. The Supreme Court found that the alleged *talaq* was at best a *talaq al-bida*, which is not recognised as valid by Shia law (page 72). A lot of private correspondence was produced in court to support the conflicting accounts of events. There was a weak attempt to challenge the validity of the first marriage on the ground that it involved a Shia male and a non-Muslim woman, but this issue was not pressed (page 59). The court spent a long time considering evidence of the wife's conversion to Islam and it was eventually held, at page 71, that it was not possible to accept the assertion that she had become a Muslim on October 26, 1961. This also led to the conclusion that she had not been properly divorced by the complainant, as she was not a Muslim on the relevant date (page 72).

9–129 Regarding the impact of section 7 of the MFLO and its requirements, it was common ground between the parties that Mr Gardezi had not given notice to the Chairman of the Union Council concerned. The lower courts had come to conflicting conclusions, to some extent because it was not clear whether the provisions of the MFLO would also apply if one of the parties was not a Muslim. On section 7 of the MFLO, the comments of S. A. Rahman J. at page 74 are relevant to the present discussion:

"... it seems to us that the Legislature had attempted to incorporate the Islamic Law provisions with regard to the two forms of "*Talaq-us-Sunnat*", viz. "*Talaq Ahsan*" and "*Talaq Hasan*", as far as may be, in this section. ... Whether the result achieved is in strict conformity with Islamic Law is a question which does not fall within the province of this Court to determine ... The section clearly contemplates a machinery of conciliation whereby a husband wishing to divorce his wife unilaterally, may be enabled to think better of it, if the mediation of others can resolve the differences between the spouses. The *talaq* pronounced is to be ineffective for a period of 90 days from the date on which notice under subsection (1) of this section is delivered to the Chairman and this period is to be utilized for the attempt at reconciliation ... All that the section requires is that the marriage in question should be dissolvable by means of a *talaq*."

This shows that, first of all, the judge did not see it as a task of the court to get involved in questions of the Islamic nature of the MFLO and that the judicial task was perceived to be one of statutory interpretation. The comments of the judge indicate how he viewed the operation of the legal fiction established by section 7 of the MFLO regarding effectiveness and validity of a *talaq* divorce. Apparently, it had been put to the court that if a husband failed to give the required notice to the Chairman, the *talaq* would be effective at once. The judicial response to this, at page 75, is revealing:

"This interpretation would make the section itself wholly nugatory. All that the husband has to do then is that he should refrain from giving the requisite notice and the *talaq* would automatically take effect. This is exactly the mischief which the section seems designed to remedy. The alternative contention raised by the learned counsel that *Talaq Bidat* is altogether outside the purview of the section is plainly untenable as it takes no account of the words "*talaq* in any form whatsoever" occurring in subsection (1) of section 7."

This statement clearly defends the MFLO as a piece of legislation with a social purpose. It was held at page 75:

". . . the object of section 7 is to prevent hasty dissolution of marriages by *talaq*, pronounced by the husband, unilaterally, without an attempt being made to prevent disruption of the matrimonial status. If the husband himself thinks better of the pronouncement of *talaq* and abstains from giving a notice to the Chairman, he should perhaps be deemed, in view of section 7, to have revoked the pronouncement and that would be to the advantage of the wife. Subsection (3) of this section precludes the *talaq* from being effective as such, for a certain period and within that period, consequently, it could not be said that the marital status of the parties had in any way been changed. They would still in law continue to be husband and wife. The result in the present case, so far as the question of legality of the subsequent marriage . . . is concerned, would not be in any way different, even if the period envisaged by this section is deemed to start from the time of the pronouncement of *talaq* or as soon as may be thereafter, instead of postponing the start to the date of receipt of the notice by the Chairman, in order to avoid giving the benefit of his own default to the husband. Ninety days had not yet elapsed from the date of alleged pronouncement of *talaq*, when the respondent went through his marriage with the lady."[14]

We see here how the judge moves, without explicitly saying so, between the two forms of conflicting Muslim personal law. It appears that the decision in this case was crucially influenced by the fact that the second marriage followed so soon after the alleged divorce.[15] Thus, in a sense, there was no need to consider the question of notice in depth, because of the speed with which the second marriage had been contracted, which meant that the offence complained of had been committed anyway. Had the case involved Hanafi Muslims, the court's discussion might have developed differently.

9–130 Elsewhere in this long judgment, the Court's understanding of the reformatory character of the MFLO is reiterated. At page 76, strongly refuting the claim that the Ordinance should only apply to Muslim spouses, S. A. Rahman J. said that "the policy of the Ordinance seems to be to provide some curbs on too facile pronouncements of divorce and unnecessary or unjustified plural marriages". The culpability of the Lt. Colonel was therefore established and it was held, at page 76, that on January 2, 1962 the wife was still the wife of the first husband:

". . . she was still the wife of the complainant as the divorce, even if granted by the latter, could not have become effective, without recourse to the provisions

[14] In the paragraph immediately following this quote, the judge takes a brief look at s.8 of the MFLO but decides that it "would be idle to speculate what alternative forms of dissolution are contemplated by this section" (p. 75).
[15] We shall see in para. 9–155, below, how the courts were later forced to recognise that the *Gardezi* principle could not be maintained when abandoned wives married another man years after the event. A very instructive case is *Noor Khan v. Haq Nawaz*, P.L.D. 1982 F.S.C. 265, discussed in detail below.

of section 7 of the Muslim Family Laws Ordinance, 1961. It is also fairly clear that by the 2nd of January 1962, even the *iddat* period prescribed by Islamic Law for a divorced wife, had not yet expired."

The learned judge also found convincing evidence that the Lt. Colonel was guilty of enticing away the other man's wife and was highly critical of his conduct. At page 79 it was said, restoring the order of conviction:

"The circumstances clearly point to the inference that he knew her to be the wife of Mr Gardezi at the relevant time. The intention to "marry" her, had no genuine basis as he must have known that there was no legal separation between her and her first husband and no marriage ceremony, even if gone through, could wipe out that fact from his consciousness. The subsequent marriage, in the circumstances, must be regarded merely as a disingenuous device to put up a facade of respectability over an illegal union."

These strong words must be seen in their social context at the time. As indicated, this was a well-publicised high society scandal; the nation was watching.[16] The judges could hardly have come to a finding that the facts of this case were morally acceptable in a society where many men treat women as property and where allowing women to make their own choices was widely perceived as underwriting immorality.

9–131 *Ali Nawaz Gardezi* has been treated as an important precedent but it has also frequently been distinguished on facts. The statement about the mandatory nature of the notice to the Chairman has been followed in a number of cases, thus maintaining the image of *Ali Nawaz Gardezi* as an operative precedent. As we shall see even in the present section, however, many cases subscribed to the position that notice was essential in order to achieve a social objective, most often protection of the interests of the women and children involved in such cases.

9–132 In *The State v. Tauqir Fatima*, P.L.D. 1964 (W.P.) Kar. 306, it transpires that a married woman had originally been claiming maintenance from her husband under section 488 of the Criminal Procedure Code 1898. She had obtained an order granting her maintenance of Rs. 50/- p.m. in 1960. Subsequently, the husband claimed to have divorced her on December 6, 1962, after about 17 years of marriage. The wife had refused to accept notice of the divorce on the advice of her lawyer and was now claiming arrears of maintenance as well as *iddat* money. The husband, in desperation, tried to claim that he had divorced his wife 15 years earlier, but nobody took that seriously and in fact he was punished by an order granting the wife Rs. 100/- p.m. On appeal before the High Court, Khan J. criticised the lower court for overlooking that the husband had failed to give notice of the divorce to the Chairman of the Union Council concerned. The husband claimed to have given notice, but there was nothing on record to prove this. Khan J. referred to section 7(3) of the MFLO and held at page 308 that, as no notice had been given, the *talaq* could not have become effective. This decision, therefore, is typical of the cases which appear to hold that notice is essential, in that it protects and in a sense enlarges the maintenance rights of a troubled woman, without saying this in so many words.

---

[16] This is evident from pp. 80 *et seq.* of the judgment, which are strictly speaking not part of the decision but deal with internal disciplinary matters of the judiciary. They reflect concern and unease about the "undue publicity" given to this case by the press and the consequent embarrassment for the individuals involved in this case, which was at one stage heard for a whole month. It is in addition suggested, at p. 84, that the public grilling of an Army official who took away a civilian's wife was particularly appropriate during a period of Martial Law.

9-133   *Fahmida Bibi v. Mukhtar Ahmad*, P.L.D. 1972 Lah. 694, is a useful case for understanding how the role of the Chairman of a Union Council was perceived, once notice had been given. The facts of the case are strange and not very material here. Briefly, a husband's petition for restitution of conjugal rights was resisted by the wife on the ground that she had already been divorced by the husband. The wife produced evidence of an order from a Chairman, purporting to make her divorce effective, while the husband denied having given notice. The case reeks of bogus documents and the wife's pleading was not accepted, so she was basically treated as a recalcitrant wife. In view of the wife's pleading, the Court considered section 7 of the MFLO and found, at page 697:

> "A divorce thus does not become effective unless the notice is served on the Chairman of the Union Committee or Council and 90 days expire from the date of receipt of the notice by him. The Chairman is required to bring about reconciliation between the parties for which purpose he is to give notice to them to nominate their representatives in order to constitute the Arbitration Council. If any of the parties fails to appear before him, he cannot enforce his attendance . . . The divorce, notwithstanding the conduct or attitude of any of the parties, shall become effective after the expiry of 90 days unless the divorce is revoked earlier by the husband. In the event, the parties appear before the Chairman and an Arbitration Council is constituted, but reconciliation does not succeed, the only thing the Council or the Chairman may do, is to record in writing that reconciliation has failed. There is no other function which a Chairman or an Arbitration Council is competent to perform in this behalf. If reconciliation does not succeed or the husband does not revoke *talaq* before expiry of 90 days, it becomes automatically operative and effective. There is no provision either in the Ordinance or the Rules requiring the Chairman or the Arbitration Council to give a decision or to issue a certificate to make the divorce effective."

This detailed description of the Chairman's function is supplemented by further pertinent comments. At page 697, it is pointed out that there is no provision in law "under which the husband is to inform the Chairman of his decision that he has revoked the *talaq*". Thus, another argument is advanced for why the Chairman has no right to issue a certificate of validity making a divorce effective:

> "A husband who pronounces divorce on his wife and has served the Chairman with the notice under section 7 of the Ordinance may simply revoke it and inform his wife of his decision. What will in such a case be the value of a certificate which the Chairman may have issued in his ignorance of the factum of revocation of the divorce? The certificate, therefore, cannot at all be a proof, let alone a conclusive proof, of the divorce, as is alleged in the present case. If the certificate is used as a proof of divorce, it will be inconsistent with the statutory right of the husband to revoke *talaq* before the expiry of 90 days either "expressly or otherwise". It may be one of the reasons for the Legislature in not providing for the issuance of the certificate of divorce by the Chairman of a Council."

This judicial reasoning allows freedom to the Muslim husband to revoke a *talaq* as and when he pleases during the 90 day period stipulated by the MFLO.[17] Pitted

---

[17] The discussion in this case itself indicates that such discretion may be abused by husbands. Other case reports, too, indicate that husbands do use this weapon to harass the wife and leave her 'hanging in the air'. The most obvious examples are of course those cases in which a husband then also abuses this limbo situation to launch a *zina* prosecution. For details see numerous cases in paras 9–155—9–166, below.

against this was the pleading that if the Chairman or the Arbitration Council does not have the right to issue a certificate, the entire purpose of section 7 of the MFLO would be frustrated (page 698). Iqbal J. defended the MFLO and said at pages 698–699, with pointed reference to the facts before him:

> "We are not called upon to adjudicate on the propriety or expediency of the legislation, our functions being limited only to the interpretation and enforcement of the law. Nonetheless, we have no doubt in our mind that the provisions are in the public interest. They have obviated a lot of complications which have been experienced in the past. The provisions of section 7 are meant to prevent hasty dissolution of marriages by *talaq* pronounced by the husband unilaterally. Similarly, a recalcitrant husband or wife cannot now successfully raise the plea of divorce in the event a dispute arises between the spouses about their marital rights and obligations, unless it is substantiated by proving that notice as required by section 7 of the Ordinance had been served. There is now no possibility of any dispute about the status of a woman after the death of her husband that she had been divorced during his lifetime . . . The Ordinance has, doubtless, ensured certainty about marital status."

9–134 With respect, this is perhaps a too positive assessment of the beneficial effects of section 7 of the MFLO, but the learned judge was certainly right to say, in view of the wife's fraudulent plea before him, that the new law had helped to clarify the position in this particular case. That section 7 of the MFLO has not at all brought about certainty of marital status is demonstrated by *Rashida v. Ghulam Raza*, P.L.D. 1977 Lah. 363, a case involving Shia Muslims. This was a wife's appeal against a decree for restitution of conjugal rights in favour of the husband. The couple had made a divorce agreement on October 15, 1969 and the wife produced a certificate of effectiveness of that divorce, dated January 17, 1970, from the Chairman of her locality. The husband claimed to have revoked the divorce on December 9, 1969. The wife had apparently married again, but the court did not want to take notice of this (page 365). Zullah J. in the Lahore High Court made it clear, at page 367, that section 7 of the MFLO covers any form of *talaq*; thus it could not be argued that the notice of divorce could not become effective. Another relevant point made in this case is that the sending of the *talaq* notice has to be made after the pronouncement of divorce, but how the *talaq* is to be pronounced has not been covered by the Ordinance (pages 368). Similarly, the form of revocation has not been prescribed by the Ordinance. Zullah J. held, therefore, at page 368, that the general Muslim law would still govern all aspects of pronouncement and revocation. It is submitted that this is quite correct and should be read as an indication that the pre-MFLO Muslim law was not in fact entirely superseded by the Ordinance. The learned judge refused to go further into the question whether the divorce agreement before him was in fact a *khul* divorce, or rather a *mubaraat*, allowed the wife's appeal without a further word about her second marriage and remitted the case to the Family Court for decision. This case could hardly serve as an authority for the proposition that notice is essential. Rather, it illustrates that judges were struggling hard, at that time, to harmonise disparate social facts with the new rules of the state law, without getting too involved in the obvious conflict between *shariat* law and the provisions of the MFLO.

9–135 Another early case in which a court made clear statements to the effect that notice of divorce was considered essential in all kinds of situations is *Manzoor v. Allah Wasaya*, P.L.D. 1973 B.J. 36. A wife had filed a suit for divorce on the grounds of cruelty and maltreatment, the husband's polygamy and incompatibility of temperament resulting in mutual hatred. She had offered to relinquish her *mahr* as consideration for a *khul* divorce but the husband had successfully resisted the suit, forcing the wife to appeal to the High Court. Examining the requirements of notice, Aftab Hussain J. referred to *Ali Nawaz Gardezi* and said, at page 39:

> "The procedure provided by section 7 can be invoked when the husband wishes to exercise his right of divorcing the wife, or the wife wishes to exercise the right of divorce delegated to her or where any of the parties to the marriage wishes to dissolve the marriage otherwise than by Talaq and in all these cases notice must be given to the Chairman. The stage at which such notice is required to be given is expressly stated in section 7. It provides for the notice to be given after the pronouncement of Talaq. The apparent inconsistency between the provision that notice should be given to [the] Chairman when a man wishes to divorce his wife (i.e. at the stage when he has an unfulfilled desire) and the latter provision fixing the time when notice is to be given (i.e. at the stage when he has pronounced the divorce and has thus fulfilled his desire at least in part) is resolved by the provisions of subsection (4) that the divorce will not be effective for 90 days from the date when notice is given. The pronouncement of divorce, therefore, does not operate as divorce. It is merely a manifestation of [a] wish to divorce."

It was also held at page 39 that the provisions of section 7 apply *mutatis mutandis* to cases under section 8 of the MFLO, so that notice of a *talaq-i-tafwiz* would be required under this section where a wife had pronounced the delegated *talaq*, which would also be valid only 90 days after receipt of notice. The learned judge went further in stating his view of court involvement in divorces and said, at pages 39–40:

> "For dissolving marriage between the spouses, ordinarily the order of the Qazi or decree of the Court is essential. If the wish to dissolve marriage emanates from the wife she has to seek the assistance of the Court, in case the husband does not agree to the severance of marital ties. In such a case the decree for dissolution of marriage will be a substitute for divorce or pronouncement of divorce ... such decree or dissolution of marriage will not be effective for a period of 90 days from the date when notice ... is given to the Chairman. In the case of divorce, notice is required to be given to the Chairman after pronouncement of the divorce."

The learned judge also pointed to relevant provisions in section 21 of the West Pakistan Family Courts Act 1964 which supported his view that court involvement was essential. Since the wife in the present proceedings had obtained a decree of dissolution from a court, and the husband was manifestly not interested in reconciliation, the divorce must have been presumed to become final, so the wife's appeal was allowed and the case was sent back to the lower court.

9–136   The line of cases indicating that notice under section 7 of the MFLO is essential to bringing about effectiveness of a divorce has been continued in decisions both by the Supreme Court and the High Courts into the early 1980s.[18] In *Muhammad Latif v. Hanifan Bibi*, 1980 P.Cr.L.J. 122, a polygamously married husband appealed against being charged under section 6(5) of the MFLO for

---

[18] As we shall see in paras 9–206—9–225, below, it has therefore been assumed in English law, despite warning signs, *e.g.* in Pearl (1987a), pp. 111–119, that the notice requirements are treated as absolutely essential in all cases. That, given the continued existence of various forms of extra-judicial divorce arrangements between spouses, was clearly not the case.

contracting another marriage without permission. He had divorced his first wife in October 1977 by written *talaq*, which was notified to the wife and a local authority Chairman and had married another woman only eight days later. The divorced wife had filed a complaint about the husband's polygamy, arguing that the divorce became effective only three months after it was given. The husband's main argument was that the *talaq*, notwithstanding the provisions of section 7(3) of the MFLO, became effective under Muslim personal law on the day when it was given. It was contended, at page 124, that "though section 7(3) of the Muslim Family Laws Ordinance had the effect of suspending the effectiveness of the divorce for 90 days for collateral purposes . . . it could not destroy the irrevocability of the Talaq-ul-Bida'at" and reliance was placed on some of the cases we discussed in the present section. The wife's case was in essence that the *talaq* remained ineffective for 90 days and that "the marital status of the parties did not, in any way change" (page 125). Sidhwa J. in the Lahore High Court found that the wife was an 'aggrieved party' and held, at page 126, that on the principle laid down in *Ali Nawaz Gardezi*, the present *talaq* had remained ineffective for three months, which meant that the husband should have sought the permission of the Arbitration Council before he married another woman. The charge against him would stand.

9–137   The important Supreme Court case of *Ghulam Fatima v. Abdul Qayyum*, P.L.D. 1981 S.C. 460, confirms again that the courts' insistence on notice of *talaq* as essential was used when it helped the woman's case. In *Ghulam Fatima*, the wife had sued for divorce in 1970 and the husband had responded with a suit for restitution of conjugal rights. Soon afterwards, the wife filed another suit, alleging that the husband had divorced her by *talaq*, which was disputed by the husband, who claimed to have revoked any *talaq* he may have given. The husband then died on December 3, 1971 and the husband's family joined the case, claiming that the wife had been divorced before the date of the husband's death, so that she was not entitled to any succession rights.

9–138   Both lower courts had held that there was no valid divorce because the husband had not given notice of it and, in addition, he had claimed to have revoked his divorce. Significantly, the High Court came to a different conclusion, finding that there had been a *mubaraat* divorce between the spouses, which was irrevocably effective. It had also been held by the High Court that, in a situation where both parties agreed, there was no need for notice under section 8 of the MFLO, since "Muslim Law does not contemplate revocation in such cases nor is there any purpose to efforts at conciliation" (page 462). Examining the evidence on record, the Supreme Court considered suggestions that the husband had given a triple *talaq* to the wife in front of a committee of elders (a *jirga*) and that the wife had executed documents regarding return of her belongings and withdrawal of her suit in the court. The document of the husband's divorce had not been produced on record, however. The Supreme Court found, in the light of other evidence in this case, that the husband had not agreed to a divorce of the wife, and thus there was neither a *khul* nor a *mubaraat*. Since there was no evidence of mutual consent of the parties, the wife was not divorced and therefore entitled to a share of the property. It was held by Muhammad Haleem J. that the purported *talaq* "had not become effective but stood revoked as no notice under subsection (1) of section 7 was given" (page 464). Again, this clearly helped the wife, who was now a widow.

9–139   By 1982, the Federal Shariat Court entered the debate on the notice requirements in the case of *Aziz Khan v. Muhammad Zarif*, P.L.D. 1982 F.S.C. 156. In this very brief case report, it transpires that a man had complained about the abduction of his wife by another man, who had subsequently married her. The first marriage had lasted less than a month during 1980 and had not been consummated. The Federal Shariat Court dismissed the appeal of the second husband and relied on *Ali Nawaz Gardezi* to the effect that the notice requirements of section 7 of the MFLO also applied to divorce in an unconsummated marriage. The judgment gives a very brief indication of the inability of the F.S.C. to declare section 7 of the MFLO repugnant to the Holy Qur'an (page 157). This shows a glimpse of the beginning of a fresh debate about the nature and role of section 7 of the MFLO in the light of Pakistan's islamisation policies.

9-140   This debate was propelled by the newly emerging case law under section 10 of the Offences of Zina (Enforcement of Hudood) Ordinance 1979. A typical case on *zina* from that period is *Shera v. The State*, P.L.D. 1982 F.S.C. 229. A man and a woman had both been convicted to seven years of imprisonment and 30 lashes because of illicit relations (*zina*). The couple had admitted to having lived as husband and wife after the wife had been divorced by her first husband. Actually, the two men were brothers and the complaint had been lodged by the first husband himself, complaining that his brother had enticed away his wife. The defence of the convicted couple was throughout that the first husband had pronounced an oral *talaq* about two years earlier and had also executed a divorce deed a year later. The Federal Shariat Court considered the evidence on record and refused to accept the evidence of an earlier divorce in whatever form, dismissing it as "absolutely false" (page 232). Aftab Hussain C.J. then referred to the impact of section 7 of the MFLO, holding at page 232 that:

> "Non-compliance with section 7 makes a divorce ineffective. It has been held in a number of cases that the relationship of the husband and wife in spite of divorce does not cease to exist in case of non-compliance with the provisions of section 7 . . . The alleged divorce is ineffective and does not put an end to the relationship . . . They are even now husband and wife. There can be no doubt that by living apparently as husband and wife and by having sexual intercourse with one another in that capacity the appellants are committing Zina with one another and both of them have been rightly convicted."

It was briefly considered by the judge whether ignorance of the law as found in section 7 of the MFLO should be taken into account, but this issue was not pursued. This strict decision, no doubt, propelled realisation among the judiciary, if not among the public, that there was an irreconcilable conflict between those judgments which hold that notice is essential and those judicial decisions, which had appeared in the meantime (see paragraphs 9–155—9–166, below) and held that notice was not essential. Here, we conclude our analysis with one particular case, decided during 1983–1984, which confirms that the conflict over notice requirements had by then been brought fully into the judicial arena, but was not resolved.

9-141   In *Muhammad Nasir Siddique v. Muhammad Salahuddin Khan*, 1984 C.L.C. 879, it had been held by the High Court of Lahore that once the execution of a divorce deed was proved, it became effective after 90 days, even if notice had not been served on the Chairman concerned. In this case, the facts were that a woman had been divorced by her husband by a deed executed on March 30, 1975. She had then died on October 17, 1975 and the former husband claimed a half share in her property, which was resisted by her natal family. It had been held by the lower appellate court that in the absence of notice the divorce had remained ineffective, so the husband had a rightful claim as one of the heirs. On appeal before the Lahore High Court, it was successfully argued that a duly executed divorce deed had the effect, even without notice to a Chairman, that the *talaq* became effective after the expiry of 90 days from the date of pronouncement of *talaq*.[19]

9–142 The husband immediately filed a petition for leave to appeal to the Supreme Court. In *Muhammad Salahuddin Khan v. Muhammad Nazir Siddiqi*, 1984 S.C.M.R. 583, Nasim Hasan Shah J. (as he then was) dismissed this petition "in view of the peculiar facts and circumstances of this case" (page 586), but not without having made some observations which thoroughly confused commentators, leading to the conclusion that the Supreme Court of Pakistan was still insisting on the notice requirements under section 7 of the MFLO.

9–143 A brief analysis of this failed petition is instructive because it transpires from this report that the case involved polygamy, Pakistanis working abroad, and apparent abuse of a Muslim husband's decision not to give notice of the divorce. The couple was working in Libya at the time of the divorce, the dead woman had been a second wife, and the husband had apparently used his second marriage to secure a good job in Libya.[20] These carefully recorded facts must have demonstrated to the learned judge that the husband was taking advantage of his own wrong when claiming that his failure to give notice should not have any effect.

9–144 Patently, the judge did not say that the Lahore High Court had decided the case before him wrongly, otherwise he would have had to allow the petition. It was observed, however, that the case of *Mohammad Rafique v. Ahmad Yar*, P.L.D. 1982 Lah. 825, decided in June 1982 by the same High Court, appeared to have overlooked the leading Supreme Court case of *Ali Nawaz Gardezi* and another case along the same lines.[21] The judge therefore suggested that the view expressed in *Mohammad Rafique* "cannot be supported and is, in fact, erroneous" (page 585). The matter was simply left there, however, and this case can be read either way.

9–145 There are several cases in which the procedures for giving notice to the wife are at issue. Such cases arise when a woman tries to claim that she has not been notified of the divorce. Most such cases tend to be evidence of litigiousness rather than a desire to clarify the law. The Ordinance states in section 7(1) that the husband shall also serve a copy of the *talaq* notice on the wife. Is the notice to the wife mandatory or optional? In a Lahore decision, *Inamul Islam v. Hussain Bano*, P.L.D. 1976 Lah. 1466, the court appeared to give mandatory force to the need to inform the wife, holding at page 1468 that "the supply of copy to the wife is a necessary part of the requirement of service of notice on the Chairman". The Karachi High Court, in an obiter remark in *Parveen Chaudhry v. VIth Senior Civil Judge 1st Class, Karachi*, P.L.D. 1976 Kar. 416, appears to have taken the opposite view. In this case a wife challenged the order of a Chairman of an Arbitration Council to the effect that her husband's *talaq* was confirmed. The husband was a doctor working in the United States of America, the *talaq* had been attested in New Jersey, and the document had been forwarded, by a complex route, to a District Judge in Karachi who at the time had jurisdiction as Chairman of a Union Council under the MFLO.[22] The wife objected to this order on the ground that the divorce had not been communicated to her by the husband before he had given notice to the Chairman. Regarding the law of divorce in Pakistan it was stated at page 419:

> "In regard to the validity of the divorce we have no hesitation in expressing our confirmed opinion that under the Muslim Personal Law as well as the

---

[19] Reliance was placed on the Lahore High Court case of *Muhammad Rafique v. Ahmad Yar*, P.L.D. 1982 Lah. 825, which we discuss in the next sub-chapter below.

[20] The man's first marriage had been to a cousin and he declared himself unable to leave her.

[21] This is *Abdul Mannan v. Safuran Nessa* (1970) S.C.M.R. 845, which we discuss in para. 9–199, below.

[22] The dispute was subject to judicial proceedings both in Pakistan and in New Jersey. Apparently, the New Jersey court recognised the *talaq* as effectively terminating the marriage.

Ordinance no mode is prescribed for pronouncement of divorce. It is established law that a Muslim can pronounce a divorce orally or make the divorce in writing. In fact, under the Muslim Personal Law a divorce in writing became irrevocable as soon as the same was written but the Ordinance has made inroads into the Muslim Personal Law by providing a machinery and procedure for confirmation of the divorce and postponement of its effect for 90 days."

It was found as a fact, however, that the divorce had been communicated to the wife. It was then stated, at page 420, that:

". . . the only impediment to immediate effectiveness of the divorce is information to the Chairman and the forming of the Arbitration Council. To such extent it is very clear to us that the mere fact of absence of communication of the divorce before moving the Chairman under subsection (1) of section 7 of the Ordinance does not invalidate the divorce."

It is not clear whether this means that notice to the wife is not required, but it seems that in this case the wife had merely insisted that she should have notice of the divorce *before* the Chairman was notified. That subtle point was not accepted as a serious matter. There was obviously no prospect of reconciliation between the spouses and the judge criticised this petition as "hardly purposeful" (page 421) before he dismissed it.

9–146 In *M. Zikria Khan v. Aftab Ali Khan*, P.L.D. 1985 Lah. 319, the husband had pronounced *talaq*, had duly dispatched notice to a Chairman and the Chairman began to constitute an Arbitration Council. The wife contested the validity of the proceedings on the ground that notice had not been given to her by the husband, and that in the absence of such notice the proceedings were a nullity. In separate proceedings, she had also applied for a handsome sum of backdated maintenance and wanted to prolong the validity of her marriage for that purpose. The Chairman of the Union Council had awarded the wife maintenance of Rs. 1500/- p.m. and suspended the effectiveness of the *talaq* on the ground that the husband had not appeared for reconciliation. Taking a constitutional petition, the husband appealed to the Lahore High Court.

9–147 The main question before the court was whether the Chairman of a Union Council has authority to annul a divorce once given by the husband and/or to suspend its operation. It was noted, at page 322, that notice must be given to the Chairman and to the wife. According to the MFLO, the period of 90 days started from the day notice was received[23]:

"This period is available to the parties to reconsider and retrace their steps if they are so minded. Legal effects of non-supply of a divorce notice to the wife are not provided in express terms in section 7 of the Ordinance *qua* the effectiveness of divorce."

Referring to *Fahmida Bibi v. Mukhtar Ahmad*, P.L.D. 1972 Lah. 694 (see above, pages 341–342) and citing some points from that case, it was highlighted at page 322 that:

"The divorce, notwithstanding the conduct or attitude of any of the parties, shall become effective after the expiry of ninety days unless the divorce is

---

[23] The statement cited here is reiterated at p. 325 of the judgment, where it is correctly said that the whole emphasis in the MFLO is on the date of receipt of the notice.

revoked earlier by the husband . . . If reconciliation does not succeed or the husband does not revoke Talak before expiry of ninety days, it becomes automatically operative and effective."

Since there was no provision in the MFLO or the Rules requiring the Chairman to give a decision or to issue a certificate to make the divorce effective, the order passed by the Chairman in favour of the wife was without lawful authority (page 323). The court decided that the argument of the wife was without foundation. There was evidence that the husband had sent a copy of the notice to the wife who had refused to receive it, and in any event she was informed of the pronouncement when she was summoned to send a representative to the proceedings initiated by the Chairman of the Union Council. The case confirms again that a wife cannot refuse to accept a husband's divorce once he has given the *talaq*. Negotiation has to occur during the marriage, rather than after its breakdown. It is possible, therefore, that one of the side-effects of the operation of section 7 of the MFLO is to put pressure on spouses in Pakistan to settle the terms of the divorce among themselves. If that happens, we may find a growing trend towards *mubaraat* rather than simply use of the *talaq*.

9–148 From the above decision, and earlier cases which we cited, it appears that courts in Pakistan would be likely to uphold a *talaq* even where the wife had not actually been supplied with a copy of the notice. It is entirely clear that the provisions of the Ordinance relating to the formation of the Arbitration Council and the functions of the Chairman are directory only. Thus, if the Chairman does not summon the Council, or if the parties fail to turn up, the *talaq* is still valid 90 days after notice has been received.

9–149 This was not the position taken by some judgments in 1986–1987, however. In *Ghulam Nabi v. Farrukh Latif*, 1986 S.C.M.R. 1350, it transpires that the husband had given *talaq* to the wife less than one month after the marriage in 1982. Apparently, the husband did not give notice of the divorce, although there were some proceedings before the Chairman. The wife, claiming to be still married, filed a claim for maintenance and was successful throughout because the husband could not prove that he had served proper notice of the divorce. The desperate husband appealed to the Supreme Court, where he was reminded of the leading cases on the subject and the need to give proper notice to the wife. Dismissing the appeal, the Supreme Court gave the husband a clear message to the effect that proper notice procedures should be followed. This looks very much like a stern lesson in legal literacy for this particular husband, who had not even bothered to appear in court for this hearing. One could therefore read this decision also as an indication of judicial indignation that precious court time should be spent on somewhat superfluous litigation.

9–150 In *Javid Ali v. Abdul Kadir*, 1987 S.C.M.R. 518, we see how the untidy facts of life in Pakistani society create complex legal issues which demand considerable judicial skills in promoting justice. A husband had divorced his wife by *talaq* in November 1974 but the couple had resumed cohabitation and the wife gave birth to a further child in February 1977. In December 1978, she contracted a marriage with another man and was subsequently accused of polygamy and of *zina*. While the *zina* prosecutions had failed for lack of evidence, the first husband's prosecution case for bigamy under section 494 of the Pakistan Penal Code was successful against the wife, as the Court assumed that she knew herself not to be validly divorced when she married the second husband. The second husband was acquitted of all charges, while the wife's sentence was reduced, taking account of her position as the mother of young children. This case is significant in that it proceeds on the assumption that proper notice of divorce remains essential, but condones the absence of notice in view of the particular circumstances of the parties.

9–151 Some of the cases point to a difficult procedural problem in identifying which is the appropriate Chairman for giving notice. The West Pakistan Rules under the Muslim Family Laws Ordinance 1961, amended in 1965, contain complex provisions on this subject.[24] In essence, according to rule 3(b), notice should be given to the Chairman of the district where the wife is residing at the time of the pronouncement of the *talaq*. If the wife has left Pakistan, notice is to be given to the Union Council where the wife last resided with the man under rule 3(b)(i), or where the person pronouncing the *talaq* permanently resides under rule 3(b)(ii). There are a number of problems relating to the interpretation of these rules. For instance, what is the meaning of the words 'residence' and 'permanent residence'? In addition, it is not entirely clear from a reading of the rules whether a man can serve notice on a Chairman in a place where he and his wife resided together in Pakistan, if in fact their last place of residence was in another country. When both husband and wife reside out of Pakistan, there are enormous difficulties. The MFLO, as section 1(2) provides by saying that the Ordinance extends to the whole of Pakistan and "applies to all Muslim citizens of Pakistan, wherever they may be", is clearly extraterritorial in scope. Pakistani missions abroad were at some time given authority to act as Chairmen of Union Councils, but their exact constitutional status is far from clear.[25]

9–152 The rules were considered by the Lahore High Court in *Masood Khan v. Chairman, Arbitration Council, Wah*, P.L.D. 1982 Lah. 532. This case also confirms the assumption that notice under section 7 of the MFLO is essential to make a divorce effective. The husband and the wife married at Wah, District Campbellpur (now called Attock) in 1975. The husband was employed in the United States of America and soon returned there. The wife joined the husband in August 1975 until November 1977, when she returned to her parental home in Wah, apparently in connection with the birth of their first son. The husband visited Pakistan thereafter and claimed to have resided with his wife at Wah until March 1978. Another son was born. On November 4, 1979, the husband pronounced a *talaq* in the United States. He sent a notice of it to the Chairman, Arbitration Council, Wah and posted a copy of this notice to the wife at her address in Wah as well as in the United States of America, where she had by then moved. The secretary of the Union Council of Wah returned the husband's notice with the endorsement that under rule 3(b) of the rules framed under the MFLO, the notice could not be registered in that Union Council as the wife did not reside within its territorial limits (page 533). The husband appears to have sent off two further notices which met with the same fate, and the wife also returned the notice sent to her. The husband then sought a directive from the Lahore High Court under Article 199 of the Constitution of 1973 for an order directing the Chairman to constitute an Arbitration Council and to declare his *talaq* absolute. The wife contested this petition on jurisdictional grounds, a typical case of a recalcitrant Muslim divorcee, seeking to stop the husband from divorcing her. However, it transpired that the wife had herself instituted divorce proceedings in America, probably hoping to achieve a better divorce settlement there.

9–153 The case report brings out that "service of notice on the Chairman of the Union Council . . . is a condition precedent for assumption of jurisdiction by him for constituting an arbitration council" (page 534). The wife vehemently denied ever

---

[24] For details on the Rules and their status see Abid (1993), pp. 62–73; Ch. M. Mahmood (1991), pp. 217–225.
[25] S.R.0.1086(K) 61 dated November 8, 1961, stated that "in exercise of the powers conferred by clause (b) of s.2 of the Muslim Family Laws Ordinance 1961 (VIII of 1961), the Central Government is pleased to authorise the Director General (Administration), Ministry of External Affairs to appoint officers of Pakistan missions abroad to discharge the functions of Chairman under the aforesaid Ordinance".

having resided with the petitioner anywhere in Pakistan and thus sought to argue that no Chairman in Pakistan could have jurisdiction. Before the court, both parties agreed that rule 3(b) could not apply since at the time of pronouncement of *talaq*, the wife was residing in the United States of America. Thus the court concerned itself with whether either rule 3(b)(i) or rule 3(b)(ii), or both, were applicable. The judgment goes into much detail on the definition of 'residence'. M. A. Lone J. adopted a very wide interpretation of the words 'last resided' and held, at page 536:

" It is but natural to presume, that after her marriage, the third respondent, must have lived together with the petitioner presumably, in his house, for sometimes, may be for a couple of days only, before he left for U.S.A. In our view, where a person has a permanent or quasi-permanent abode, howsoever short his stay therein may be, that would constitute residence for the purposes of sub-clause (i) of rule 3, but where a person is obliged to leave his place of residence and goes to some other place on an occasional visit, the place of such visit, cannot be considered as his residence."

Thus it did not matter that the parties had last resided together outside Pakistan. The judge also noted explicitly that the MFLO had extra-territorial application (page 537) and that the impact of section 7 of the MFLO was relevant. It was stated at page 537:

"The provisions of this section are not only mandatory, but their contravention has also been made punishable . . . Furthermore, it is now well settled that a divorce not routed through the procedure contemplated by section 7 of the Ordinance, does not become effective. Thus, if the argument of the respondent's learned counsel is accepted that the parties never resided together in Pakistan, its consequences will be very serious. Despite the pronouncement of divorce by the petitioner, the respondent would continue to remain clothed with the status of his wife and entitled to the rights attached to such status. The construction put on rule 3 by the respondent's learned counsel would thus defeat the intention of the Legislature and lead to unjust result. Such an interpretation has got to be avoided. The words 'last resided' therefore, should receive liberal construction."

Therefore, even though the parties had only stayed together in Pakistan for brief periods, they had been 'resident' there (page 537). Regarding rule 3(b)(ii), the court decided that even if the husband had established himself in the United States, and at present was permanently residing there, he still had a strong attachment to his birthplace, and he had not abandoned his home in District Attock (page 538). The court accepted that it was possible for a man to have two permanent residences at the same time. As to where both parties to this dispute 'last resided', the material on record was considered insufficient and the case was to be decided by a collector, since the relevant Chairman had been challenged by the petitioner husband. The approach taken by the court in this case makes it almost certain that a Chairman will have jurisdiction even if the parties have left the country a considerable time before. If the marriage was solemnised in Pakistan, it is likely that the parties stayed together in Pakistan prior to one or both of them leaving for abroad. Even if the marriage was solemnised abroad, the husband is likely to have retained an 'attachment' to his ancestral home, and, according to the judgment, he may well have two permanent residences.

9–154 Apart from a large number of decisions to the effect that notice under section 7 of the MFLO was essential,[26] Pakistani courts also produced a growing

---

[26] It appears that during the 1980s the number of such decisions declined markedly also as a result of the increasingly prominent islamisation debates, on which see paras 9–167—9–188, below.

number of decisions in which it was effectively held that notice was not essential. We now turn to those cases in the next section.

Notice of talaq not essential: Recent case law

9–155 Despite the presence of the leading case of *Ali Nawaz Gardezi*, P.L.D. 1963 S.C. 51, and other cases discussed in the previous section, the argument that notice of *talaq* may not be essential to achieve legal validity has grown in strength, especially over the past decade. Some of the cases in the previous section already provided much evidence of indications that notice under section 7 of the MFLO may not in fact be essential in all cases. There is no doubt that many courts, especially lower courts, did adopt this line. We are able to demonstrate here that this particular position was regularly taken by Pakistani courts in three situations. First, where the facts were obviously showing that the persons involved in the litigation had been unaware of the registration provisions of the MFLO. Secondly, as noted already, in cases where women would otherwise have been disadvantaged, mostly in terms of property rights and maintenance, but also social and moral status (*izzat*). Thirdly, where a woman was trying to argue that she was not divorced and the courts found her evidence not credible, the judges have supported the man's position. In many of these decisions, Pakistani judges have made statements showing their awareness about the simmering conflict between *shariat* law and the letter of the MFLO in terms of notice requirements and legal validity of a *talaq* divorce. These comments are of much interest to the study of modern Muslim law in the world today and are very relevant beyond the South Asian legal context.

9–156 It seems that the underlying conflicts were not brought out into the open until, more recently, the islamisation debates in Pakistan forced the issue (see paragraphs 9–167—9–188, below). The position today would appear to be that compliance with the notice requirements under section 7 or section 8 of the MFLO is still desirable and expected, but if it does not occur, the divorce can still be valid. This confirms that it is not possible to read the rules of Pakistani law like those of a Western legal system, as a uniformly binding set of prescriptions for everyone.[27]

9–157 *Farida Parwin v. Qadeeruddin Ahmad Siddiqi*, P.L.D. 1971 Kar. 118, appears to be the first reported case which holds that the notice requirements of the MFLO are not essential for legal validity of the divorce. In this case, a wife had successfully petitioned for divorce from a Family Court on the ground of cruelty and had also asked for payment of her *mahr* of Rs. 5,000/-. The husband resisted the suit, arguing that he had not been given proper notice, so the divorce was not valid. The Karachi High Court, much concerned with procedure on account of the pleadings in this case, held that the notice requirements relating to conciliation were not essential and that the divorce had become legally effective on the expiry of 90 days after the receipt of notice by the Chairman. This case is, therefore, no real authority for the proposition that notice of the husband's *talaq* is not essential, but it prepares the ground for that argument.

9–158 *Fahmida Bibi v. Mukhtar Ahmad*, P.L.D. 1972 Lah. 694 (see above, pages 341–342) was cited extensively and with approval with reference to procedure under the MFLO in *Maqbool Jan v. Arshad Hassan*, P.L.D. 1975 Lah. 147.[28] However this case also accepts that notice may be a mere formality which is not essential for legal validity. A divorced Shia Muslim wife challenged the certificate of a Chairman to

---

[27] We shall need to return to this issue at the end of paras 9–167—9–188.
[28] In *Akhtar Hussain v. Collector, Lahore*, P.L.J. (1974) Lah. 419, too, the inability of a Chairman to annul a divorce was emphasised with reference to the absence of any rules in that respect.

the effect that her marriage was dissolved and claimed to be still the wife of her husband. The suit had been dismissed by the lower courts on the basis that, once a *talaq* has been pronounced, if not revoked within 90 days after delivery of notice to the Chairman, it becomes automatically effective. Before Zullah J. in the Lahore High Court, it was noted that section 7 of the MFLO postulates a *talaq al-ahsan* (page 148). The wife could not prove that the Shia method of divorce had not been followed by the husband and, at any rate, section 7(1) of the MFLO spoke of *talaq* "in any form whatsoever", which was a comprehensive provision (page 149). Interestingly, Zullah J. held, at pages 151–152:

> "In view of the facts and circumstances of the present case . . . if the *talaq* is otherwise valid (*i.e.* if under the Personal Law of the parties the Talaq is valid) it would become effective under that law; but the only clog thereon is that the effectiveness would be postponed for 90 days under subsection (3) of section 7 of the Ordinance."

It was apparent from the facts of the case that the wife in this case was simply refusing to acknowledge the legal validity of the husband's *talaq* and that her case could not succeed. Significantly, Zullah J., at page 152, noted finally that:

> "If the prayer is read in continuation . . . it becomes absolutely clear that the entire case was fought on the question as to the legality/validity or otherwise of the certificate . . . by the Chairman and that the validity/legality of the *talaq* under the Personal Law of the parties was not made [the] subject of contest."

This statement indicates that a *talaq* which has not been notified to a Chairman within 90 days and which has not been revoked, may be presumed to have become legally valid for all intents and purposes.

9-159 The argument that notice under section 7(1) of the MFLO cannot be essential to bringing about legal validity of a divorce received an important boost when cases began to appear in the early 1980s under the Offence of Zina (Enforcement of Houdood) Ordinance 1979. In those cases, as became only too obvious, husbands who had divorced their wives earlier but had not given proper notice were now taking advantage of their own wrong by claiming, often many years afterwards, that the woman before the court was still their wife and was therefore guilty of *zina*, together with the new husband. Judicial alertness had the obvious effect that in such cases it could not be held that notice of the divorce was an essential element to make a *talaq* divorce legally effective. It is an additional element in those cases that the Islamic dimension of the problem was beginning to be explored.

9-160 The earliest relevant case on this matter was not reported in the P.L.D. and has therefore escaped notice. It is also significant in that it so very clearly distinguished the presumed precedent of *Ali Nawaz Gardezi*. In *Amanullah Khan v. Eidat Shah*, N.L.R. 1981 Criminal 164, a Muslim marriage had broken down, the husband had executed a written divorce deed in September 1979, and the wife had been married to another man in January 1980. The first husband then filed a complaint under the Zina Ordinance. In the Lahore High Court, Aftab Farrukh J. made it clear that the facts of this case spoke for themselves when he said, at page 166:

> "I am quite satisfied that the parents would have married their daughter only on obtaining the divorce deed, i.e. the divorce, and on the expiry of the *iddat* period . . . Taking the broad facts into consideration and the normal pattern of our society, I am of the view that the parents, howsoever low or high in social

standing, would not marry their daughter during the subsistence of the first marriage and the girl is always remarried after obtaining a divorce through the intervention of the elders and the respectables who enjoy esteem and respect with both the families."

The first husband sought to rely on *Ali Nawaz Gardezi* and the requirement of notice, but that case was clearly distinguished (page 167). Having examined the wording of section 7 of the MFLO, the judge showed that he had looked through the husband's scheme for blackmailing his former wife. It was finally held, at pages 168–169:

"The failure of the husband to send notice u/s. 7(1) makes him punishable with simple imprisonment for a term which may extend to three months or with fine upto one thousand rupees, or with both, and this section does not enjoin upon the wife to issue any such notice to the Chairman or any such information to the Chairman, regarding the receipt of divorce, and therefore, if the proposition canvassed by the . . . complainant was to be accepted it could lead to many mischiefs, i.e. to say that the husband by handing over a written divorce deed could make his wife believe that she had been divorced and then kept quiet about the matter and when the other spouse remarries, . . . the husband could blackmail the new couple. Could it be possible to say that a wife will have to wait for the rest of her life for her husband who sends her a written divorce and thereafter does not contact her or she does not hear from the Chairman for a reasonable period? Could it be possible to challenge the legal and social status of the children of the couple whose marriage was duly solemnized under the Muslim rites and who married honestly believing and having been led to believe that they were legally free and competent to contract marriage . . .? Therefore, a careful analysis of the above-quoted observations . . . in *Ali Nawaz Gardezi's* case do leave a room open for a conclusion that mere failure to give notice to the Chairman would not render ineffective a talaq which has been pronounced in accordance with the tenets of Islam and which has otherwise become effective, or that non-compliance with the provisions regarding the registration of the marriage, etc. would not invalidate the marriage itself. The failure to comply with the provision of section 7 in the case of talaq and the contravention of the provisions of the above-referred Ordinance in the case of marriage would render the offender, i.e. the husband in the former case liable to imprisonment or fine or both."

The proceedings instituted by the first husband were therefore quashed and it was found that the *zina* prosecution was clearly not maintainable. The court also took specific notice of the fact that the first husband's complaint about the wife's remarriage had been made with a delay of three months. It was therefore clearly not a genuine case but a malicious and mala fide action, in the concluding words of Aftab Farrukh J., at page 169, "a clear abuse of the process of law". As indicated, the fact that this early strong and instructive judgment is not reported in the P.L.D. gave it a low profile, thus delaying the process of public recognition that notice of divorce may not be essential in all cases.

9–161 More well-known and equally instructive on this subject is *Noor Khan v. Haq Nawaz*, P.L.D. 1982 F.S.C. 265. This was a prosecution for *zina* in which an Additional Sessions Judge had acquitted the couple in question. On appeal before the Federal Shariat Court, significantly at the behest of an army major exercising martial law functions, it transpired that the woman concerned had been married about 30 years ago and had given birth to eight children from her husband. She had had to leave her husband about 10 years ago and had since then given birth to another four children from the co-accused. The first husband alleged that his wife had been abducted by the second man and asserted that he had not divorced his wife, while the accused couple claimed to be validly married and therefore innocent of any offence under the 1979 Ordinance.

9–162 This case offers much insight into the psychology of Pakistani Muslim society. It appears that the first husband had been shunned by the local community and was not able to remarry because he had treated his wife so badly. The accused woman deposed that her first husband had cruelly maltreated her some 12 years before, after she had complained about a male relative's advances to her,[29] and that he had divorced her on the spot. The wife had sought refuge with her mother and, after some time, had taken steps to ascertain that she was divorced. When this was confirmed, she married her second husband with the involvement of her extended family, referred to as "brotherhood" (page 272). It was noted with much disapproval, and turned out to be fatal to the prosecution case, that the first husband had not taken any steps for about 10 years or so to oppose this marriage or to prosecute the woman.[30]

9–163 Zahoorul Haq J. briefly considered *Ali Nawaz Gardezi*,[31] pointing out, as we have done above, that this case was decided on the basis of its peculiar facts, especially since the second marriage had followed so very soon after the alleged divorce, during the *iddat* period. The present case was therefore clearly distinguishable. On the role of section 7 of the MFLO, the following comments were made by the judge at page 275:

> "In the particular circumstances of this case, it is not necessary to notice the arguments . . . on the point that since notice under section 7 of Muslim Family Laws Ordinance is not alleged to have been given . . . therefore, the marriage . . . should be held to be subsisting.
>
> . . . the challenge in respect of lack of notice . . . is really of academic importance and the trial Judge should have ignored the same as the factum of lack of notice as such was not a fact in respect of which any question had been asked . . . The case had been fought on the question of divorce which had been denied by one party and asserted by the defence. None of the parties was conscious of the requirement of notice under section 7 and therefore no one had considered it as material for the purposes of a criminal case."

Significantly, Aftab Hussain J., the Chairman of the F.S.C., was also readily prepared to acquit the accused couple, giving them the benefit of doubt because of their evident lack of knowledge of the provisions of the MFLO (page 276). He spoke in this context of the "mere technical nature of section 7 of the Muslim Family Laws Ordinance and its applicability to criminal cases" (page 276). However, at page 281, it was also said by the same judge that "not much discussion is necessary" on section 7 of the MFLO:

> "It clearly lays down that Talaq not followed by the procedure provided by the section is not complete which means that the marriage would subsist."

---

[29] In fact, this was the very same man who pursued the appeal against the couple.
[30] See pp. 272–275 of the judgment, as well as an extended discussion of delay in prosecution and the principle of an 'old offence' (*taqadum*) at pp. 276–281 and again at pp. 283–284.
[31] P.L.D. 1963 S.C. 51. A civil case briefly considered at p. 275 of the judgment is *Manzoor v. Allah Wasaya*, P.L.D. 1973 B.J. 36.

Referring to *Ali Nawaz Gardezi* and a number of other cases interpreting section 7 of the MFLO,[32] it was asserted at page 281 that the Supreme Court "categorically gave a finding about the Talaq being ineffective on account of non-compliance with the provisions of section 7". Further, a number of comments are made on page 282, showing that the judge understood the leading case to mean that "failure of the husband to give notice to the Chairman about the divorce amounts to revocation about the pronouncement of the divorce". These comments appear to be consciously made with a view to educating the public and especially the accused persons before the court, undoubtedly a well-meaning attempt on the part of the judge to publicise the formal message of the MFLO. This lecture was given to the accused, and people like them, "so that any conscious persistence on their part to flout the law may not land them in the difficulty of another prosecution".[33] The assumption of the learned judge clearly was that *Ali Nawaz Gardezi* had laid down the law under section 7 of the MFLO and that the legally illiterate population of Pakistan would need some guidance on how to avoid unwarranted *zina* prosecution. One senses some judicial concern here about the ease with which mala fide prosecutions could be brought, since undoubtedly many Pakistanis would not be aware of the notification requirements under the MFLO.

9–164 While it could, therefore, be argued that *Noor Khan* still underwrites the position that notice of *talaq* is essential, the leading case of *Mohammad Rafique v. Ahmad Yar*, P.L.D. 1982 Lah. 825, took a very clear stand on the issue, holding in essence that a *talaq al-bida*, once pronounced, could not be held to be ineffective simply because no notice was given. This case, at page 831, also called for a determination regarding the Islamic nature of section 7 of the MFLO by the Federal Shariat Court. In this case, a husband was pressing charges of *zina* against his wife and a man with whom she was allegedly living in sin. He claimed that a forged notice of *talaq* had been sent to the Union Council concerned and that he had not divorced his wife nor did he intend to do so (page 826). The alleged lover asserted that the lady had been divorced by her husband and that after 90 days she did not remain the wife of her first husband and married him. There was much evidence that the woman's family members wanted her to marry another man and were unhappy about the new alliance, but the woman had insisted on her own choice of partner. The first husband not only claimed that he had not divorced his wife, he also argued that the alleged divorce could not become effective unless the prescribed notice under section 7(1) of the MFLO had been given by him to the Chairman (page 828). S. H. Kadri, the Acting Chief Justice, gave a separate judgment in which he criticised the continuing abuse of the Muslim divorce system by men. He stated, at page 831:

> "Suffice it to say that the objective of this Ordinance was to provide protection to the weaker sex from the tyranny, high-handedness and upper hand of the man, surely it did not extend to keep a woman hanging in matrimony. This is not the only case. I have come across several cases of great hardship where the life of a woman is made miserable and she seeks even *khula*, yet a District Judge despite the statement of the girl that she will prefer to jump into the well than to go with the callous husband, did not allow the dissolution of marriage and a direction was issued that she be beaten and confined in the house by the

---

[32] The other cases mentioned here are *Fahmida Bibi v. Mukhtar Ahmad*, P.L.D. 1972 Lah. 694; *Maqbool Jan v. Arshad Hassan*, P.L.D. 1975 Lah. 147; *Muhammad Latif v. Hanifan Bibi*, 1980 P.Cr.L.J. 122 and *Ghulam Fatima v. Abdul Qayyum*, P.L.D. 1981 S.C. 460.

[33] At p. 282. The suggestion that the couple could be prosecuted again for the same alleged crime was, however, explicitly rejected by Muhammad Siddique J. at p. 284.

husband. Obviously this is nothing but height of ignorance . . . The most simple and practicable religion is being exploited by the 'heroin' man by misinterpretation of the commands of God. The weaker sex is not treated according to the status which was conferred upon her by the Prophet."

9-165 The final statement in this case, at page 831, with reference to *Ghulam Fatima v. Abdul Qayyum*, P.L.D. 1981 S.C. 460 (see above, page 345) where a distinction between revocation and taking effect of a *talaq* was made, has since become well-known in Pakistan:

"It is thus clear that the absence of notice would obviously be a violation of section 7 of the Ordinance only, the crime punishable under the Ordinance. By no stretch of imagination Talak, if pronounced, can be claimed to be ineffective."

This has been interpreted to mean that non-giving of notice is clearly punishable under the MFLO, but the divorce itself cannot be held to be invalid. In *Chuhar v. Ghulam Fatima*, P.L.D. 1984 Lah. 234, a succession case involving validity of a divorce as well as legitimacy of a child, the High Court of Lahore again decided that a notice of *talaq* was not essential for legal validity of the divorce. Over reliance on the technicality of section 7 would have damaged the best interests of the child in this case. Here, a woman and her son were faced with a suit for possession of the deceased husband's property on the ground that there had been no valid marriage. The facts were complicated because the lady had been married to another man earlier and there had been no notice of divorce from him. This case illustrates the potential difficulties for women in a legal system where written documentation is not routinely prepared, whether for marriages, divorces or other transactions. M. M. Khan J. was not convinced by the greedy cousin's case and seemed to be acutely aware of public opinion when he held, at page 236:

"Since in our country there is no concept of adultery and illegitimacy and a woman living in adultery and an illegitimate child are looked upon with great disapproval and resentment and the findings given by the courts have important bearing on the feelings of the people, . . . I am of the view that in cases relating to the validity of marriage and legitimacy of a child, the evidence should be appreciated, assessed and weighed very carefully. A heavy onus would lie on the party pleading invalidity of the marriage and illegitimacy of a child to prove the same through unambiguous and convincing evidence. In this case in the larger interest of justice, I have reappraised the evidence."

9-166 The judge found that the woman had been living with the deceased till his death and declared himself fully convinced that she had been his wife and that the son was a legitimate child of that union. Taking the view that each case should be decided on its own facts (page 237), the judge found much evidence that the wife's case was genuine. There had been no notice of the divorce from her first husband, nor evidence of the revocation of that divorce. Relying on *Ghulam Fatima*, P.L.D. 1981 S.C. 460, it was explicitly noted at page 239 that in that case the judge "had not declared Talaq ineffective for want of notice but in his wisdom has stated that Talaq had not become effective but stood revoked. The words "stood revoked" are of great significance." The present case could be clearly distinguished because it was a case of determined *talaq* or separation by mutual consent where the question of revocation did not arise. It was emphasised that the *talaq* was pronounced some 15 to 18 years back, and that the husband had never revoked it in any form. It was therefore held in favour of the wife and son, at page 239:

"In these circumstances, I am convinced that the main object of section 7 of the Ordinance to prevent hasty dissolution of marriage by Talaq pronounced by the husband unilaterally, has not been defeated by non-giving of the notice. Section 7 of the Ordinance is obviously for the benefit of the female and if section 7(1) . . . is interpreted in a manner as desired by the learned counsel, it may create many mischiefs and ruin [the] lives of the respondents. To my mind, in the case in hand, the non-giving of notice under section 7(1) of the Ordinance does not render Talaq ineffective. The decisions relied on . . . are quite distinguishable . . . in those cases either Talaq was revoked expressly/impliedly/otherwise or the factum of Talaq was denied/disputed whereas the situation herein is altogether different . . . as the Talaq was given with full determination and mutual consent and the same was never revoked expressly/impliedly or otherwise by [the] first husband."

Even before the input of the islamisation arguments, therefore, social considerations and a realistic assessment of the facts and circumstances of particular cases rather than religious or political ideology led to the conclusion, in many cases, that a strict legal requirement of notice could not be maintained. The case law took a different development during the 1980s, in particular, following the explicit reminder that under *shariat* a Muslim husband can continue to divorce his wife unilaterally, and that this is in line with the Pakistani constitutional requirements to follow the dictates of the Qur'an and Sunna.

The islamisation debate and its impact on the talaq

9–167 It appears that there are two phases of this important debate with reference to section 7 of the MFLO. The first stage represents a constructive approach, based on the assumption that the notice requirements in section 7 of the MFLO are beneficial to women and can be harmonised with the injunctions of Islam. The result of this avoidance of open conflict, as we have seen in the sections above, was the eventual co-existence of two lines of cases which clearly contradicted each other. Was notice of divorce required for legal validity or not? No clear answer emerged, but the view that notice was essential became dominant and became, so to say, the official law.

9–168 The second phase of the debate is confrontational, seeking to assert the supremacy of *shariat* over the modern state law. It now looks as though this was largely due to the activities and decisions of one particular scholar-judge, Tanzil-ur-Rahman, in his various capacities, who sought to challenge the notice requirements of section 7 of the MFLO on the ground that they were un-Islamic and violated the injunctions of Islam. The current and third phase is again marked by flexibility, as clearly expressed in the leading case of *Kaneez Fatima*, P.L.D. 1993 S.C. 901. This puts the focus back on consideration of the facts and circumstances of individual cases, emphasising the requirement to do justice to the parties, especially women and children.

9–169 The first stage of the debate, endorsing the reforms in section 7 of the MFLO as Islamic is first reflected in *Muhammad Latif v. Hanifan Bibi*, 1980 P.Cr.L.J. 122 (see above, page 344), where a polygamous husband argued unsuccessfully that he could lawfully marry again a few days after he had divorced his wife by *talaq*. Doing so, he relied on the Muslim personal law, in opposition to section 7 of the MFLO. Sidhwa J., referring to *Ali Nawaz Gardezi*, P.L.D. 1963 S.C. 51, and other cases following that decision, held that a *talaq* given by the husband now remained ineffective, notwithstanding the obsolete principle of Hanafi Muslim personal law, "which recognised the heretical Talaq-ul-Bidaat or Talaq-i-Badai (introduced by the Omeyad Monarchs) as irrevocable and taking effect immediately on its execution if given in writing" (page 126). It was held in this case, at page 126:

> "Section 7(3) of the Muslim Family Laws Ordinance 1961, by providing a period of 90 days for purposes of bringing about a reconciliation introduces into the Talaq-ul-Bidat or Talaq-i-Badai the provisions of Talaq Ahsan referred to in Sura Al-Talaq of the Holy Qur'an. Section 7(3) of the 1961 Ordinance is therefore, not repugnant to the injunctions of Islam as laid down in the Holy Qur'an or the Sunnah of the Holy Prophet so as to invite any special examination under Article 203-B of the Constitution of Pakistan. Even otherwise, under the Explanation to Article 203-B of the Constitution, Muslim Personal Law is exempt from any such examination and a provision which makes a material amendment to any particular branch of Muslim Personal Law is as much a part of the personal law itself to earn the exemption as provided by the Explanation. The amendment is a beneficial amendment and brings the provisions of *talaq* more in conformity with the principle of Talaq Ahsan and therefore, deserves the greatest respect. Being nearest to the Injunctions of the Qur'an and the Sunnah of the Holy Prophet, its sanctity is all the more enhanced."

This elaborate defence of section 7 of the MFLO and its reforms reflects the constructive judicial approach at the time, to the effect that this beneficial reform ought to be known to a wider public. In *Noor Khan v. Haq Nawaz*, P.L.D. 1982 F.S.C. 265, apart from the manifestly concocted *zina* prosecution, the judges were concerned with the Islamic dimension of the case because a lower court judge had suggested in this case that the provisions of section 7 of the MFLO were against the injunctions of Islam with regard to giving of notice of *talaq* to the Chairman and in respect of the notice becoming effective only after 90 days (page 272). Zahoorul Haq J. repelled that proposition and held, at page 273:

> "The learned Additional Sessions Judge has not been able to correctly construe the provisions of the Constitution and his view that section 7 . . . is against Muslim Personal Law or against the Constitution is evidently unjustified. The jurisdiction for declaring any law to be repugnant to the Injunctions of Qur'an and Sunnah rests with the Federal Shariat Court under Article 203-D of the Constitution as provided in the Provisional Constitution Order of 1981 and appeal from that judgment can be taken to the Supreme Court. No other Court has the power to declare any law un-Islamic."

At page 276 of the same case, Aftab Hussain J. also raised this issue and expressed his agreement with the above-stated position. Of course, the judges in this particular case were not asked to decide whether these provisions were un-Islamic or not. Early attempts to attack the validity of section 7 of the MFLO on the ground that it is contrary to the Quran and Sunna had failed. In *Aziz Khan v. Muhammad Zarif*, P.L.D. 1982 F.S.C. 156, Aftab Hussain J. merely said, at page 157, that it was not within the jurisdiction of the Federal Shariat Court to declare section 7 MFLO as repugnant to the Holy Quran "in view of the embargo placed on our jurisdiction in this respect by Article 203(B) of the Constitution".[34] In *Mohammad Rafique v. Ahmad Yar*, P.L.D. 1982 Lah. 825, at page 831, it was stated,

---

[34] This 'embargo' is explained in *Mirza Qamar Raza v. Tahira Begum*, P.L.D. 1988 Kar. 169 at 191.

regarding the question whether section 7 of the MFLO is repugnant to the Quran and Sunna, that "it is for the Federal Shariat Court to look into this aspect of the case as it is the domain of that Court".

9–170 The second phase of the debate about the Islamic nature of the notice provisions in section 7 of the MFLO began with some vigour in the High Court of Karachi during January/February 1988. The key case for retracing this debate and understanding the more recent position of Pakistani law on notice requirements under the MFLO appears to be *Mirza Qamar Raza v. Tahira Begum*, P.L.D. 1988 Kar. 169. In this case a learned Islamic scholar, Tanzil-ur-Rahman J., sat as a single judge and grasped the nettle of re-examining the provisions of section 7 of the MFLO in the light of important constitutional changes in Pakistan. This was a constitutional petition under Article 199 of the Constitution of 1973, seeking a declaration that the *talaq* pronounced by a husband on February 10, 1982 and re-affirmed in a written deed on March 8, 1982 was valid in the eyes of the law and that the wife had ceased to be the legally wedded wife on February 10, 1982. This suit, brought by a husband whose wife purported not to accept the divorce, therefore pinpoints exactly the key question in the simmering conflict between unreformed *shariat* law and the provisions in section 7 of the MFLO. The husband had duly sent notices of the divorce to the wife and the Chairman, but the wife had responded by asking the Family Court for a declaration that the divorce was invalid and contrary to the injunctions of Islam. This had been successful and the husband appealed. In the Karachi High Court, the husband raised, *inter alia*, the following pleas at page 183:

"(ii) The provisions of the Muslim Family Laws Ordinance 1961 are applicable to all Muslim citizens of Pakistan and override the tenets of Muslim Personal Law which are in conflict with the provisions of the said Ordinance and the Personal Law of any Muslim sect stands impliedly repealed by overriding provisions of the said Ordinance to the extent of such conflict.

(iii) The provisions of section 7 of the Muslim Family Laws Ordinance have dispensed with the requirement and necessity of pronouncement of Talaq in any particular form.

(iv) Under the scheme of law as envisaged by section 7 of the Muslim Family Laws Ordinance, a pronouncement of Talaq becomes automatically effective after the expiry of 90 days from the receipt of intimation of Talaq by the Chairman of the Union Committee and such effectiveness cannot be hampered by any other law."

9–171 The wife, on the other hand, pleaded jactitation (the continued existence of the marriage) of marriage.[35] In addition, she sought to argue that the provisions of the MFLO cannot override the substantive Muslim personal law and that these provisions are in conflict with the injunctions of Islam, more particularly after the incorporation of Article 2-A in the Constitution on March 2, 1985 (see further below). Turning to the question of overriding effect of the MFLO at page 190, the judge examined section 3(1) of the MFLO which implies that any pre-existing law, custom or usage is repealed by the relevant provisions of the MFLO. The judgment explains (at pages 190–191) the protected position of the MFLO after the promulgation of the West Pakistan Muslim Personal Law (Shariat) Application Act 1962 and outlines the background to the promulgation of the MFLO by a Martial Law Administrator rather than Parliament (page 191). Reference was also made to

---

[35] After a long discussion (pp. 184–187), it was found that this was a suit of jactitation of divorce rather than of marriage.

the revival of the Pakistani Constitution of 1973 in 1985 by the Revival of the Constitution Order (P.O. 14) 1985. This constitutional amendment, with effect from March 2, 1985, had the consequence that the original Objectives Resolution of 1949, which had become the Preamble of the Pakistani Constitution, was made a substantive provision of the Constitution in Article 2-A. It was assumed that after this, it could now be argued that the MFLO could be challenged if it came into conflict with the injunctions of Islam.[36] In essence, the position was, as stated at page 201:

> "In this scheme and order of things it becomes evident that all laws prevailing in Pakistan are firstly to conform to the Constitution whereas the Constitution and all such laws are then amenable to be tested on the touchstone of the Qur'an and Sunnah, if sovereignty of Allah really prevails and the law of the Qur'an and Sunnah is really supreme."

Thus, having found that the provisions of the MFLO were not immune from challenge (page 202), Tanzil-ur-Rahman J. immediately declared his opposition to section 7 of the MFLO at page 202:

> "Testing section 7 of the Muslim Family Laws Ordinance, in particular, on the touchstone of Article 2-A (read with the Objectives Resolution), it appears that, for detailed reasons which will follow shortly, it violates the limits prescribed by Allah Almighty . . . and is 'in conflict with clauses (2) and (3) of the said Resolution' inasmuch as it violates the principles of social justice enunciated by the Qur'an and Sunnah, and disables the Muslims to order their lives, in accordance with the teachings and requirement of Islam, as set out in the Holy Qur'an and Sunnah. It may be mentioned that the Holy Qur'an gives special place and treatment to family relations and greater number of injunctions are to be found in the Holy Qur'an than on any other subject. The reason is obvious. 'The family' is a basic social institution and cornerstone of the development of human society."

Restricting his challenge to the MFLO to section 7 of the Ordinance, the judge then examined the provisions of that section, relating them to the case law. He found, at page 203, that the impact of Article 2-A in the Constitution makes a difference to the legal position as stated by the Supreme Court in *Ali Nawaz Gardezi*, P.L.D. 1963 S.C. 51. The judge summarised the practical effects of the provisions of section 7 of the MFLO (at pages 203–204) and outlined the different forms of *talaq* under Muslim law (pages 204–206). Regarding requirement of written notice, the judge cited a large number of Qur'anic verses (pages 206–214) and held at page 207 that:

> ". . . the effectiveness of Talaq pronounced by him, cannot in any case, be made dependent on the receipt of notice by the Chairman as provided in section 7 of the Ordinance. The waiting period ('Iddat) begins to run immediately on pronouncing a valid Talaq by [the] husband. In fact, the verse . . . [Sura II, verse 237] clearly shows that it is the husband in whose hand is the marriage-tie. It is thus evident that the right of divorce granted to the husband is in no way tied with or made conditional or contingent upon giving notice of the said Talaq to any council or a Court of law or getting its confirmation from any such council or the Court."

---

[36] Details of this part of the extensive and erudite judgment, concerning the process of islamisation, are omitted here since they would distract from our main topic.

9-172   Interpreting the various sources quoted by him, the judge focused on the right of the husband to terminate the marriage unilaterally but distinguished it from other forms of divorce which might involve a judge. It was found, at page 214, that the cited verses:

> ". . . are clear manifestation of the power of the husband to pronounce talaq, without an intervention of any Court or tribunal. Had it been dependent on the decision of any Court or tribunal, there, at least, would have been an indication to it in the Qur'an or Sunnah. (The authority of the Court to dissolve marriage on the causes recognized by Shari'ah is quite distinct)."

Tanzil-ur-Rahman J. was also critical of the usurpation of judicial functions by Chairmen of Union Councils (at page 214) and found, as others before him, that the arbitrators themselves had no power to effect separation between the spouses. To the learned judge, an arbitrator (*hakam*) was different from a judge (page 215). More contentious, potentially, was his conclusion about keeping the effectiveness of a divorce in abeyance for 90 days from the date of receipt of notice by the Chairman. It was held, at page 215, that "it seems to be against the Injunctions of Islam". With particular reference to *The State v. Tauqir Fatima*, P.L.D. 1964 Kar. 306, the practical problem of legal validity was considered (*id.*):

> "Suppose, the husband after pronouncing divorce to his wife does not give the written intimation to the Chairman. The divorce pronounced, according to the Qur'an and Sunnah, becomes operative on pronouncement, whereas under section 7 above the said divorce will not take effect at all."

The judge then went through a number of judgments, which we have discussed already and cited, at pages 217–218, what Coulson (1971, p. 21) had written about the validity of an unnotified *talaq* in Pakistani law:

> ". . . where a husband does not give the requisite notice of his talaq, or the spouses do not give notice of 'divorce by agreement', the divorce will apparently be valid and effective under the terms of traditional Shari'ah law, since the sanction for failure to comply with the provisions of the Ordinance is purely punitive."

9-173   His conclusion was, basically, that after the introduction of Article 2-A into the Constitution of Pakistan, a re-assessment of the Islamic nature of section 7 of the MFLO was required. Judicial concern about implications on the *iddat* period is evidenced on pages 218–220 and on page 220 it is emphasised that section 7 of the MFLO appears to make all forms of *talaq* revocable, which cannot be in harmony with the injunctions of the Qur'an. The judge then produced six points to sum up his discussion (pages 221–222), holding section 7 of the MFLO as against the injunctions of Islam. The major points for our present purposes are:

> "(i) Providing for the effectiveness of talaq, on the receipt of notice by the Chairman is against the Injunctions of the Qur'an and Sunnah. Mere non-receipt of the notice will not render the talaq as ineffective or void. Suspending the effect of Talaq for 90 days from the date of the receipt of notice is also against the Injunctions of the Holy Qur'an and Sunnah. A talaq, if otherwise valid under Qur'an and Sunnah, takes effect immediately on its pronouncement.
>
> (ii) The Arbitration Council or its Chairman are not talaq-enforcing agencies. They are not supposed to give any decision on the question of validity or

otherwise, of the Talaq, under the substantive law of talaq, applicable to the parties, or even issue a certificate to make the divorce effective or declare the same as ineffective . . .

. . .

(iv) Prescribing 90 days period for effectiveness of all kinds of divorces, including a wife, who has been divorced by her husband without consummation of marriage, is against the manifest injunction of the Qur'an and Sunnah."

At page 222, Tanzil-ur-Rahman J. therefore refused to recognize section 7 of the MFLO to the extent that receipt of the husband's notice of *talaq* and the expiry of 90 days from the receipt of notice had made the divorce effective. The judge discussed what he saw as the proper procedures for *talaq* in accordance with Muslim law, making reference to a large number of cases and other sources (pages 223 *et seq.*). Much of this debate concerns the presence of the wife and of witnesses in the Shia system, since the parties in this case were Shia Muslims. It was therefore held, finally, at page 237, that the husband had not validly divorced the wife and that she continued to be his wife until he chose to divorce her in a proper form.

9–174 This extremely long and complex judgment was immediately noted and applied in subsequent decisions in 1988 and 1989. In *Muhammad Sarwar v. The State*, P.L.D. 1988 F.S.C. 42, a husband had complained that a family friend had abducted his wife and had taken some property as well. The absconding couple were located in Lahore and had been sentenced by a lower court in Karachi for *zina* to be stoned to death. On appeal to the Federal Shariat Court, the appellants denied having committed *zina* or to have taken away property. They claimed to be husband and wife, having married after the first husband validly divorced his wife (page 46). The F.S.C. swiftly set aside the conviction for stoning, which was manifestly not maintainable in law because there was no *hadd* offence (page 47).

It was further noted, at page 47, that in the then still unreported case of *Mirza Qamar Raza v. Tahira Begum*, P.L.D. 1988 Kar. 169, it had been held that section 7 of the MFLO was repugnant to the Qur'an and the Sunna, for a *talaq* pronounced orally or in writing becomes effective even without a notice given to the Chairman. It was therefore submitted at pages 47–48, in line with the arguments in *Mirza Qamar Raza*, that in view of Article 2-A of the Constitution the law of Pakistan had now changed, and notice was no longer essential. It was said, at pages 48–49, that the earlier leading judgments had missed an important fact[37]:

"The view taken practically in all the above cases is that if no notice is sent to the Chairman the pronouncement of Talaq shall stand revoked. No time for sending the notice is stipulated. On the other hand the violation of this provision attracts criminal liability. But if the husband changes his mind immediately after the pronouncement of the Talaq and so omits to send notice to the Chairman there should be no offence committed. It means that the view that the revocation of the pronouncement is automatic in effect defeats the penal clause, for it may either be presumed or represented by the husband that he never intended to press the pronouncement right from the very beginning."

Our analysis of the case law above has already shown that Pakistani judges, in the late 1960s and during the 1970s and 1980s, were not unaware of this problem. However, they rarely chose to voice their concerns over this conflict of legal rules

[37] The cases referred to here are *Ali Nawaz Gardezi*, *Abdul Mannan* and *Muhammad Salahuddin Khan*.

before them. Suddenly, in the late 1980s, a fresh impetus for legal debate arose and is reflected here with instant effect. In the present case, reference was made to *Noor Khan v. Haq Nawaz*, P.L.D. 1982 F.S.C. 265, claiming now openly that the F.S.C. had since 1982 held that notice was not essential. It was said, at page 49:

> "Thus, the view of this Court from 1982 has been that if two persons were living as husband and wife for a long time and it is proved that there was a pronouncement of Talaq but no notice to the Chairman, they may not be punished for zina. In the same case of Noor Khan this Court did not attach much importance to the objection that no notice had been given to the Chairman and thought it only of academic interest. The Court observed 'None of the parties was conscious of the requirements of notice under section 7 and, therefore, no one had considered it as material for the purposes of a criminal case'."

It was noted by Gul Muhammad Khan C.J., at page 49, in the light of *Mirza Qamar Raza*, that the established position following *Ali Nawaz Gardezi* stood now radically challenged. It is significant how the learned judge reacted to this, given that the jurisdiction of the F.S.C., over which he presided, did not permit "to declare a statutory law or a custom or usage having the force of law as repugnant to Qur'an and Sunnah if it inter alia pertains to Muslim Personal Law" (page 50). It was said, at page 50:

> "We have gone through the judgment in Mirza Qamar Raza and appreciate that the effectiveness of the 'Talaq' cannot be subjected to the service of notice to the Chairman. The observations of the learned Judge that the reconciliation efforts ordained in Qur'an pertain to a period before the pronouncement of 'Talaq' or that an official or other person cannot be designated in a man-made law to enforce and oversee the reconciliation proceedings in obedience to the dictates of Allah, are mere obiter dicta as these questions never fell to be decided."

9–175   Thus, as stated by the Chief Justice at page 51, "this Court is obliged to follow the statutory law as interpreted by the Supreme Court and in its absence that of the High Court in whose jurisdiction the matter would otherwise fall". However, the situation had changed after Article 2-A had been made a substantive provision and now that the F.S.C. could claim larger jurisdiction, it was held, at page 51:

> "We may, however, make it clear that it is the right of every citizen in a Muslim State to get his grievances redressed and no law can refuse such a remedy. Even no Government or legislature can reserve to itself the right to exclude from the jurisdiction of the Courts any subject though it has the right to confer such a jurisdiction on a special Court horizontally or vertically. Thus, a matter may be excluded from the jurisdiction of some Courts, but it must be included in the authority of some other Courts. Consequently, the exclusion of certain subjects from the jurisdiction of the Federal Shariat Court was valid but the moment Article 2-A was introduced in the Constitution the excluded subjects stood included in the jurisdiction of the general Courts of the country."

In consequence, it was said, High Courts now had the authority to declare any provision of Muslim personal law repugnant to Qur'an and Sunna, and the F.S.C. was obliged to follow that decision (page 51). Therefore, applying this new situation to the facts of the case before him, the Chief Justice held that, since the Sindh High Court had declared section 7 of the MFLO repugnant to Qur'an and Sunna, the F.S.C. was bound by the conclusion:

"So, in that situation, the pronouncement of written 'Talaq' could not be held invalid just for the reason that no notice had been served on the Chairman (page 52)."

The order of the lower court was therefore set aside, the accused couple were freed on bail, and the case was sent back to the Sessions Judge for disposal. This decision confirms the immediate adoption of the position taken by Tanzil-ur-Rahman J. in the Karachi High Court by the F.S.C.

9–176   A number of important cases were reported in 1989, all focused on the interrelation between the Objectives Resolution and sections 7 and 8 of the MFLO. We discuss them in the order in which they were decided. In *Aijaz Haroon v. Inam Durrani*, P.L.D. 1989 Kar. 304, a number of issues arose which do not concern us here.[38] During a review of the then recent case law on the Objectives Resolution, reference was made to *Mirza Qamar Raza* by Wajihuddin Ahmad J., who sought to clarify the import of that particular judgment. He commented on the ambit of section 7 of the MFLO, saying at page 325:

"While I am in respectful agreement with the view of the learned judge that every statute in Pakistan has not only to satisfy the test whether it is in consonance with the constitutional mandates generally but has also to further fulfil the additional or inclusive qualification that it does not contravene the principles and provisions of the Objectives Resolution, as now also mandated by Article 2-A of the Constitution, I respectfully, in adherence to the Supreme Court dictum in Syed Ali Nawaz Gardezi's case (PLD 1963 SC 51), tend to think that all that the legislature, in codifying section 7 ibid, intended to do, was to abolish "Talaq-e-Bidat" and to legislate the Islamic Law provisions pertaining to two forms of "Talaq-us-Sunnat" viz. "Talaq Ahsan" and "Talaq Hasan", as far as may be. As rightly pointed out by my learned brother Tanzilur Rehman, J., the legislative machinery does not appear to have fully succeeded in doing so and Ordinance VIII of 1961, being an "existing law" in terms of Article 260 of the Constitution read with Article 268(7), adaptations can be construed therein."

9–177   This statement by a High Court judge, is significant in that it indicates that the legislative aim in section 7 of the MFLO was not fully reached and that new interpretations of the ambit of section 7 of the MFLO may be permitted and could be expected. The effects were soon noticeable. In *Kaniz Fatima v. Wali Muhammad*, P.L.D. 1989 Lah. 490, a couple had entered a divorce agreement with effect from November 1, 1977. The wife received Rs. 10,000/- as prompt dower, as well as some gold, and she was to have no further claims against the husband. However, in March 1978 the wife filed a suit for recovery of her remaining dower and for maintenance, claiming, *inter alia*, that her marriage was subsisting because there had been no notice of the divorce to any Chairman. The lower appellate court took the view that the divorce had become effective on November 1, 1977. The wife appealed to the Lahore High Court, her main contention being that since no notice had been given under section 7 of the MFLO, her marriage subsisted and she remained entitled to maintenance. She also placed reliance on the corresponding provisions in section 8 of the MFLO. The husband submitted that section 7 was

---

[38] This includes the very important topic of interest (*riba*) and its status *vis-à-vis* Islamic law. The judgment is also full of citations about the Islamic foundations of Pakistan as a state and reviews the case law on the Objectives Resolution.

only applicable where the marriage was dissolved by the husband alone. Further, as noted on page 493:

> "It was contended with vehemence that the provisions of Section 7 ibid were un-Islamic as it provided fetters on the absolute right of [the] husband to annul the marriage. It was contended that by virtue of Article 2-A of the Constitution . . . the Courts were competent not to enforce any law which was against the basic principles of Islam."

Allah Nawaz J. found, at page 493–494, that the questions before him were whether sections 7 and 8 of the MFLO offend the basic principles of Islam as laid down in the Holy Qur'an and Sunna, whether he had jurisdiction to declare these sections un-Islamic and therefore ineffective, and whether the marriage was still subsisting. To answer the first question, the judge examined in detail (pages 494–502) the history of the MFLO, the involvement of the F.S.C. and the Council of Islamic Ideology, as well as the genesis of Article 203 and the importance of Article 2-A in the Constitution of Pakistan. The judge concluded from this analysis that changes in the Constitution are the prerogative of the legislature and not the court. It was held, at page 502 that "the Court, therefore, has no jurisdiction under Article 199 of the Constitution of the Islamic Republic of Pakistan to declare any constitutionally protected law to be invalid being repugnant to the Injunctions of Islam". The inevitable consequence of that was a basic disagreement with the views expressed earlier by Tanzil-ur-Rahman J., so that it was held here, at page 503, that the MFLO is a valid subsisting law.

9–178   Regarding the question whether the marriage between the parties was still subsisting, Nawaz J. turned to the case law on the subject and relied in particular on *Muhammad Salah-Ud-Din Khan*, 1984 S.C.M.R. 583, a case in which a mischievous, greedy husband had unsuccessfully claimed that his marriage was subsisting because of failure to provide notice. Applying the principle laid down in that case, and in view of the facts of the case before him, Nawaz J. held, at page 505, that the wife's case stood dismissed:

> "From the resume of the facts of the case it is clear that both the parties contracted out of the provisions of section 7 of the Act and agreed not to have a recourse to arbitration proceedings before the Chairman Union Council, therefore, both of them waived the compulsory proceedings aimed at to restore the marriage. Therefore, the petitioner cannot claim the benefit of section 7 of the Act for the purpose of claiming maintenance."

This was a case, therefore, which protected a husband against a wife who was seeking an unfair advantage. This interesting case confirms that the provisions of section 7 of the MFLO were still portrayed as essential and more or less compulsory in 1989, but one must interpret the court's statement as a diplomatic gesture. For, it is evident from this case, and not for the first time in Pakistani case law, that where a couple had entered a *mubaraat*, the provisions of the MFLO would not necessarily be triggered off.[39] This means that the assumptions made earlier by Coulson (1971, p. 21) about the application of registration procedures for all forms of Muslim divorce in Pakistan may have been too sweeping. They appear today as a typical

---

[39] But see Carroll [1987a] P.L.D. 121–127 to the contrary. This case went on appeal to the Supreme Court and is reported as *Kaneez Fatima v. Wali Muhammad* P.L.D. 1993 S.C. 901. It is discussed further below, pp. 370–372. The wife's appeal was dismissed again, but on completely different grounds, as we shall see.

manifestation of the reformist spirit of the 1960s. By the end of the 1980s, it was increasingly apparent that despite *Ali Nawaz Gardezi* and other precedents, the requirements of notice under sections 7 and 8 of the MFLO were not as strict as had been assumed earlier.[40]

9–179 In *Shaukat Hussain v. Rubina*, P.L.D. 1989 Kar. 513, we find another case decided by Tanzil-ur-Rahman J. in the High Court of Karachi. In this case, a young couple with two very young children had suffered marital breakdown because of the alleged cruelty of the husband's parents.[41] In a fit of anger, the husband pronounced an oral divorce on March 18, 1987. In subsequent proceedings the Family Court confirmed the dissolution of the marriage, ordered dower and maintenance to be paid to the wife and refused the husband's petition for restitution of conjugal rights. The husband appealed to the High Court in a constitutional petition, purportedly "since no appeal is provided against the decree of dissolution of marriage" (page 519). It was argued on behalf of the husband, at page 520:

> "No notice having been sent by the petitioner to the Union Council, the Talaq did not become effective. In any case, absence of notice amounted to revocation of divorce."

Tanzil-ur-Rahman J. made a swift response to this plea at page 522. The precise wording of this response is relevant for our present debate:

> "The contention that no notice of the pronouncement of Talaq was given by the petitioner to the Chairman, and as such no Talaq became effective has no force. It has already been held in the case of Qamar Raza . . . that Talaq becomes operative soon after it is pronounced and no notice to be served on the Chairman, Union Council is necessary, for the divorce to become effective on the expiry of 90 days from the date of the delivery of such notice."[42]

The judge could have left the matter there, dismissing the husband's appeal. Instead, the case report contains a history of the promulgation of the MFLO and a detailed re-examination of the case law. This part of the judgment highlights the resentment against the MFLO on the part of the *ulema* (page 524) and emphasises the view of Tanzil-ur-Rahman J. himself that the MFLO "prevents Muslims to practise their religion according to their belief and faith".[43] Following a brief discussion of the ultimately aborted Enforcement of Shari'ah Ordinance 1988,[44] the judge emphasises that various Qur'anic verses "are absolutely clear that the right of [the] husband to divorce his wife is absolute and unqualified" (page 536) and challenges the statutory provisions of the MFLO as "derived and borrowed from the most defective laws of marriage and divorce of the West", copied in blind imitation (page 537). Finally, the argument is raised that the Ordinance itself was never subjected to the basic and fundamental process of legislation in a democracy (page 539).

---

[40] Note that Carroll (1997b), p. 98 writes now of "some minimal restrictions on the Muslim husband's rights of easy extra-judicial divorce".

[41] The husband worked in Oman and the wife complained that she had been treated by his parents like a maid servant.

[42] Note the wording "soon after it is pronounced", which avoids a clear statement on when an unnotified *talaq* becomes effective.

[43] At p. 525. Reference is here made to the academic writing of the judge; see Rehman [1989a] P.L.D. 17–20; Rehman [1989b] P.L.D. 20–28. It became a notable pattern at this time for the judge to rely on his own writing and/or judgments.

[44] The full text of that Ordinance is given at pp. 529–530 of the judgment. The Ordinance, promulgated on June 15, 1988, lapsed on February 15, 1989, as it was not placed before the newly elected National Assembly (p. 531).

9–180   This renewed full challenge to the constitutionality of the MFLO was supplemented by a detailed analysis of the entire case law under section 7 of the MFLO (pages 539–561). In this context, reference was made to *Bashiran v. Muhammad Hussain*, P.L.D. 1988 S.C. 186, a case in which Nasim Hasan Shah J., sitting in the Shariat Appellate Bench of the Supreme Court, had accepted an appeal against an earlier confirmation of conviction for *zina* by the Federal Shariat Court. In this case, a couple had been married in 1961. This was the husband's second wife, their relations soon became strained, and she moved back to her parents' home. In February 1979, the husband was prevailed upon to pronounce an oral divorce and to produce a *talaqnama*. The wife then married another man in March 1980. When the former husband came to know of this, he filed criminal proceedings and succeeded in having the woman and her new husband convicted for *zina*. Nasim Hasan Shah J. found that in order to determine whether the couple had committed *zina*, it was necessary to ascertain whether they had done so wilfully (page 189). In the present case, it was found that the wife had entered into the second marriage believing that she could validly do so, and the convictions were therefore set aside. Without explicitly saying so, this case therefore confirms the position taken since *Noor Khan v. Haq Nawaz*, P.L.D. 1982 F.S.C. 265, that formal notice of divorce in cases of this kind is not at all essential to bring about legal validity of a *talaq* divorce.

9–181   Significantly, in *Shaukat Hussain*, P.L.D. 1989 Kar. 513, the judge concludes from this analysis that the judges of the Pakistani Supreme Court have been anxious "to adhere to the norms of justice and not to sacrifice it at the altar of the precedent established in Gardezi's case" (page 560). It was found, at page 561:

> "The question of the validity of talaq or its revocation for want of notice to Chairman has arisen in innumerable cases, but only few criminal cases and two cases involving the question of inheritance have been mentioned above. The question has also been [the] subject-matter of cases relating to [the] wife's maintenance under Islamic Laws . . . Besides, there are many cases that the parties have been dragged in Courts of law for sending notices to wrong Union Committees or for non-receipt of notices by them. Such proceedings have been continued for number of years and the matters of talaq have remained undecided, just on technical grounds of service of such notices . . ."

Finally, the law on *talaq* was reiterated by the judge at pages 562–563:

> "To sum up, if the Talaq by a Hanafi Muslim has been pronounced to his wife thrice, it becomes . . . Ba'in. The husband has no right of its revocation according to the interpretation of the relevant Injunctions laid down in the Holy Qur'an and Sunnah, relating to the divorce and its revocation as put in by the Hanafis and to that extent the provision of section 7 of the Family Laws Ordinance will give its way to those injunctions as enshrined in the Constitution of Pakistan."

The third stage in the development of the recent Pakistani case law on notice requirements starts around this period of time. The judges clearly see that the *shariat* rules on *talaq* co-exist with the provisions of section 7 of the MFLO and that in their task to do justice they have to consider both provisions. Later cases exemplify the new spirit of compromise and appear to have adopted the position outlined in *Shaukat Hussain* without explicitly challenging the Islamic standing of section 7 of the MFLO.

9–182 In *Allah Banda v. Khurshid Bibi*, 1990 C.L.C. 1683, it was held by the Lahore High Court that a *talaq* pronounced thrice in one sitting becomes effective immediately and that the question of revocation does not arise. Here, the couple had married in 1985, with a *mahr* agreed at Rs. 32/-. The husband was said to have divorced the wife on October 9, 1987 but on October 10, he filed a suit for restitution of conjugal rights and he later claimed to have revoked his *talaq*. The wife's counsel submitted that the divorce became effective either immediately "or at the most on the expiry of 90 days from the date of the Talaqnama" (page 1685). It was found as a matter of fact that the husband had issued a written divorce deed on the date in question. Thus it was concluded that the husband had willingly and voluntarily divorced the wife (page 1686). It is significant how Akhtar J. then proceeded to determine the relevant law, almost as though the MFLO did not exist any more. It was held at page 1686:

> "As mentioned above, the parties are Sunni Muslims and governed by the Hanafi Fiqa as expounded by Imam Abu Hanifa. Hence, the reply to the question as to whether the Talaq . . . dissolves the marriage at once would be replied in the light of the interpretation of the Qur'an and Sunnah of the said sect. This would be in consonance with the letter and spirit of the explanation given under Article 227 of the Constitution."

At page 1689, it was argued by the husband that the provisions of section 7 of the MFLO were violative of the limits prescribed by Allah and the court was asked to strike this provision down as opposed to Islam. Relying on *Mirza Qamar Raza*, in fact reproducing the discussion from that case almost *verbatim* (for key portions of the text see above, pages 360–362), the judge followed the views expressed in that case and held, at page 1692, without attempting to strike down section 7 MFLO, that in the present case the *talaq* pronounced by the husband became effective immediately and could not be legally revoked.

9–183 In *Ashique Hussain v. 1st Additional District Judge and Family Appellate Court, Karachi East*, P.L.D. 1991 Kar. 174, a wife sought to claim Rs. 3,000/- p.m. maintenance for herself and a small son after she had been divorced by her husband, a doctor, who vigorously opposed the wife's action. He had sent her a notice of divorce in April 1985 but the Family Court ordered him to pay Rs. 1,400/- p.m. maintenance until he had sent proper notice of *talaq* to the Union Council. The husband went on appeal to the Sindh High Court, where the wife did not even appear. Junejo J. relied on a textbook of Islamic law by Tanzil-ur-Rahman J. to the effect that any adult Muslim male can divorce his wife directly or indirectly (pages 176–177). Falling back on an old case,[45] it had been suggested in that study that a divorce would take effect from the date on which it was acknowledged. It was held, accordingly, that the husband was deemed to have divorced the wife in February 1987, when he had made a statement to that effect in court. Regarding notice of divorce, Junejo J. referred to *Mirza Qamar Raza*, P.L.D. 1988 Kar. 169, and *Muhammad Sarwar*, P.L.D. 1988 F.S.C. 42 and held that omission of the husband to send notice of *talaq* under section 7 of the MFLO "would not operate to make the

---

[45] In *Asmat Ullah v. Khatun Unnisa*, A.I.R. (1939) Al. 592, a Muslim widow claimed a one-eighth share in the property of her deceased husband. It was alleged that she had been divorced during the husband's lifetime. Relying on an old textbook of Muslim law, Syed Ameer Ali, *Mohamedan law* (5th ed.), it was held that if a husband states that he divorced his wife and then denies that she has been divorced, the divorce should be held to take effect from the date on which the statement was made. The widow's case therefore failed. The obvious negative implications of this kind of reasoning for women cannot be explored here further.

Talaq inoperative if the applicant had pronounced Talaq with an intention to dissolve the marriage . . ." (page 177). Thus, even if the husband's notice in April 1985 did not constitute *talaq*, his admission in court in February 1987 that he had divorced the wife and had sent her and a Chairman notices had brought about an effective divorce. This decision does not make the legal position as clear as one might wish, but it follows the line of cases in the late 1980s which clearly confirm that formal notice is desirable but by no means essential. If we assume that the wife in *Ashique Hussain* did not have a bona fide case, the decision is correct, but the potential for abuse – in denying divorced Muslim wives proper ancillary remedies – should not remain unnoticed here.

9–184   In *Allah Dad v. Mukhtar*, 1992 S.C.M.R. 1273, the Shariat Appellate Bench of the Supreme Court of Pakistan decided a *zina* case, an appeal brought by a vindictive ex-husband who was obviously intent on punishing his former wife and her new husband for alleged *zina*, a fact which did not escape judicial notice (see page 1280). The husband's case was that his wife had been abducted, whereas she claimed to have been divorced by him in May 1981. There was also evidence of the wife's earlier suit for divorce in 1979, withdrawn in June 1981 after the husband had divorced her. The husband had lost his case throughout the appellate process but continued to press for charges against his former wife. Maulana Muhammad Taqi Usmani J. saw clearly that the husband's arguments about the need for notice to the Chairman were concocted and had not been accepted by three earlier judicial fora, including the FSC. The Maulana's response, at pages 1278–1279, is a remarkable recognition of the fact that the notice requirements as found in section 7 are not in fact compulsory:

". . . a deeper study of the relevant law as has developed during [the] last few years brings out a picture totally different from what appears from the perusal of section 7 of the Family Laws Ordinance."

Relying on the position taken in *Mirza Qamar Raza*, which had been applied and strengthened in *Muhammad Sarwar*, it was held that the acquittal of the couple in the present case was entirely justified. Thus, it was held, at page 1281:

"It is now evident that a notice of Talaq to the Chairman is not mandatory under the Injunctions of Islam and any divorce pronounced or given by a husband cannot be ineffective or invalid in Shariah merely because a notice has not been given to the Chairman, therefore, if a woman after obtaining a divorce from her husband and after the necessary period of 'Iddat' contracts a marriage with a third person, their marriage cannot be held as [an] invalid marriage, at least for the purpose of the Ordinance."

While this unambiguous statement clarified the picture, a further issue was brought up by the complainant, namely that the second marriage had been contracted only 79 days after the alleged divorce, so that the *iddat* had not been completed. Maulana Usmani J. considered this question in the light of Qur'anic sources and found that the *iddat* period laid down by the Qur'an is not 90 days, as stipulated in section 7 of the MFLO, but three periods of menstruation. He then produced evidence that, according to Hanafi jurists, the minimum period of *iddat* may be as little as 39 days (page 1282). Thus, the complainant's case failed also on that ground and the petition was firmly dismissed. This typical case of a malicious *zina* prosecution confirms the picture, from *Noor Khan v. Haq Nawaz*, P.L.D. 1982 F.S.C. 265, onwards, that Pakistani courts will not blindly follow pseudo-Islamic arguments but will carefully examine the Islamic nature of particular rules, whether it be the absence of a requirement to register or the minimum length of the *iddat* period, as in the present case.

9–185 Finally, in *Kaneez Fatima v. Wali Muhammad*, P.L.D. 1993 S.C. 901, we find the Pakistani Supreme Court confirming that there can be no crystal-clear position as regards the interpretation of the notice requirements in section 7 of the MFLO because of the co-existence of the classical and the modern law. We have considered this case at the High Court stage (see above, page 365). Evidently, the wife in that case was unwilling to give up her claim that she was still married, and the corresponding entitlements. The Supreme Court, faced with a constitutional petition involving, *inter alia*, Articles 2A and 203 of the Constitution of 1973, as well as section 7 of the MFLO, noted that at the time of granting leave to appeal, there had been a conflict between *Kaniz Fatima*, P.L.D. 1989 Lah. 490, and *Mirza Qamar Raza*, P.L.D. 1988 Kar. 169, regarding the jurisdiction of the Court to strike down any law which was perceived as inconsistent with the Injunctions of Islam.[46]

9–186 Saleem Akhtar J. examined the purpose of Article 2A and found that it must be read as an integral part of the Constitution rather than a controlling part of the entire Constitution, for that would undermine the Constitution as a whole (page 907). In other words, it would otherwise render the entire political and legal system of Pakistan dysfunctional. This part of the judgment (pages 906–914) offers an extended discussion of the constitutional role of the Objectives Resolution which does not concern us here. However, the comments of the learned judge on the complex process of islamisation are relevant to our present debate, showing that the Court was not willing to rush into speedy action. It was said, at page 913, that:

". . . a proper scrutiny of the provisions of law by the Federal Shariat Court and the Shariat Appellate Bench of the Supreme Court with an interregnum period has been provided to enable the President and the Governor, as the case may be, to move the Legislature to bring the law in conformity with the injunctions of Islam. The intervening period has been provided to enable the Legislature to legislate proper laws and there may not be a vacuum of lawlessness which may create complications and confusion. The process of Islamisation of the laws is an important and difficult subject. The lead given by Pakistan in this regard is being watched with interest by all the Muslim countries who are anxious to bring their laws in conformity with the injunctions of Islam and by the non-Muslim countries as well. Any hasty action without the process of Ijma' at Ummah level may lead to difficulties and confusion, which may prove irreversible. Furthermore, due to sudden change, complex problems in economic, commercial and financial fields may arise creating difficulties. However, it does not mean that in the fear of such new controversies and problems the process of Islamisation may be retarded or stopped. It is an ongoing process. It has to take effect with utmost despatch, vision and regularity."

Coming to the case in hand, Saleem Akhtar J. emphasised, at page 915, that the MFLO had not as yet been declared in conflict with the injunctions of Islam by the F.S.C. or the Shariat Appellate Bench of the Supreme Court. The learned judge was made aware of *Allah Dad*, 1992 S.C.M.R. 1273, which had held that in the absence of notice under section 7 of the MFLO a divorce becomes effective, but it was

---

[46] The hectic activity over islamisation of laws at that time can be gauged by the fact that a total of 39 judgments on this matter had been decided by 1992 (p. 906).

reiterated that the jurisdiction of the F.S.C. and the Shariat Appellate Bench of the Supreme Court does not extend to the Constitution and the MFLO (page 915). The Supreme Court was therefore supporting the continued operation of section 7 of the MFLO, but this did not mean that notice of divorce was, in every case, an absolutely essential element. It was held, in this respect, at pages 915–916:

". . . it may be observed that failure to send notice of Talaq to the Chairman of the Union Council does not by itself lead to the conclusion that Talaq has been revoked. It may only be ineffective but not revoked. This controversy should be considered from practical and purposive point of view taking into consideration the facts and circumstances of each case."

Akhtar J. applied this principle to the facts of the case before him and found that it would not make sense to insist on a strict interpretation of the notice requirements in section 7 of the MFLO. It was finally held by the learned judge, at pages 916–917, dismissing the wife's appeal:

"The provisions of section 7 of the Ordinance have remained controversial from the very beginning and there are conflicting views in general about it. In view of the Constitutional restraints the Courts cannot give any verdict on the conflicting claims challenging or justifying the provisions of section 7 of the Ordinance. However, keeping in view the facts of each case the applicability and interpretation of section 7 has to be construed in that light. In a case where with the consent of both the parties divorce is effected and confirmed in writing under their undisputed signatures section 7 should not be strictly construed particularly in cases where [the] penal provision of section 7(2) is to be enforced because in such cases the parties do not wilfully commit breach and bona fide believe that they have been divorced with the consent of each other and sending of notice to the Chairman, Union Council, is merely a formality. The notice can be sent at any time thereafter to comply with the provisions of section 7. Where such view has been taken but its validity has been challenged, the Court would be justified to refuse to issue writ and exercise its jurisdiction."

9–187   Today, therefore, the Pakistani law on notification of a *talaq* divorce is clearly limited in its effect. There is no strict requirement to notify a divorce; we find instead an expectation on the part of the modern state law that notice should be given. The notice requirements under the MFLO are therefore, in effect, optional and not compulsory. It remains an evident fact that many Pakistanis do not use the provisions of section 7 of the MFLO and order their lives in accordance with *shariat* norms which involve no recourse to formal bodies like Chairmen of Union Councils, Arbitration Councils or courts.[47] The courts have firmly accepted, time and again, in the last decade, that notice is not essential. Some cases have emphasised that arbitration needs to occur before the divorce, rather than after it. If no notice of the divorce is ever given, as the Supreme Court has confirmed in *Kaneez Fatima*, the divorce would still appear to become fully effective either at once or after the 90 days stipulated by the MFLO. Significantly, the argument that unnotified divorces must be deemed to be revoked is declared not maintainable by Saleem Akhtar J. in *Kaneez Fatima* (pages 915–916, quoted above). This position is evidently justified in the light of manifest social facts in Pakistani society today.

---

[47] The parallels with how Muslims in Britain organise their lives in the presence of an unquestionably dominant state law and *shariat* norms are remarkable.

Since arbitration is not compulsory, the system under section 7 of the MFLO appears no more than equivalent to a form of voluntary registration of divorces. It does not prevent a man from divorcing his wife unilaterally, nor does it introduce universal judicial divorce, as English law, for example, has purported to do.

9–188 In summary, today we can see very clearly that notice is not essential to bring about legal validity under Pakistani law, it is merely desirable. In terms of reformist strategies, the provisions of section 7 and 8 of the MFLO therefore represent no more than another halfway house, as we also saw with regard to registration of marriages and official permission for polygamous marriages. The legal developments under section 7 of the MFLO illustrate and typify the South Asian method of harmonising legal and social norms, using statute and precedent as aids towards achieving justice, not as universally binding inviolable legal rules.

Bangladeshi Muslim divorce law

9–189 The legal developments in Pakistan can hardly have remained without repercussions on developments in Bangladesh; after all both countries share a large core of common legislation and leading older case law. On the other hand, Pakistan's Zina Ordinance 1979 is of course not part of the law of Bangladesh. Dividing our discussion on Bangladeshi divorce law into a section on divorce at the initiative of the wife and divorce by the husband, we see first of all that the DMMA 1939 is in full operation in Bangladesh and that the leading case of *Khurshid Bibi v. Muhammad Amin*, P.L.D. 1967 S.C. 97, is also treated as a precedent by Bangladeshi courts, which have reiterated the position that the consent of the husband is not a required criterion to bring about a divorce.

9–190 Earlier case law from the Dacca High Court focused much on the husband's failure to maintain the wife and/or children (see also paragraph 7–75, above). In *Amena Khatun v. Sherajuddin Sardar*, 17 D.L.R. (1965) 687, a number of issues arose. In essence, the wife sought dissolution of her marriage since the husband had failed to honour the various obligations arising out of the marriage contract. The Munsif's court had dissolved the marriage and asked the wife to pay Rs. 200/- to the husband and to give up her claims for dower. The husband appealed successfully, forcing the wife to appeal further to the High Court. It was found that the lower appellate court had not properly considered the wife's evidence, so Murshed C.J. proceeded *de novo*. He considered relevant parts of section 2 of the DMMA, examined the *kabinnama* and found that the husband had entered into a "marriage of convenience" (page 690) with this very young wife because he was already married. Since the husband had failed to maintain the wife for more than two years, and more importantly since the marital relationship had ceased a long time ago, the judge found that this marriage fell within the ambit of *Balquis Fatima*, P.L.D. 1959 (W.P.) Lah. 566. It was held, dissolving the marriage, at pages 691–692:

> "I would prefer to base my decision on the ground that defendant has failed to provide for plaintiff's maintenance for a period of two years in breach of the terms of the Kabinnama. The plain fact is that on a total assessment of the relationship between the parties it would amount to cruelty to the plaintiff to continue the marital tie. Another important factor in this case is that if the marital tie is not dissolved it would be impossible for the wife to live within the limits of the shariat. Islam does not ignore the propensities of human nature."

An important but somewhat confused early case under section 2(viii) of the DMMA 1939 is *Md. Kutubuddin Jaigirdar v. Nurjahan Begum*, 25 D.L.R. (1973) 21. This was originally a wife's suit for dissolution of marriage on the basis of delegated divorce, in the alternative asking for dissolution of the marriage by the court. This appears to have been a 'love marriage' but the very young wife alleged cruelty soon after the marriage in July 1965 and claimed that the husband had agreed to divorce her in May 1966 on condition that she relinquished her dower claims. Her father's hand may be suspected also behind a *talaqnama*, which had been prepared in that connection. However in 1967 the husband brought a suit for restitution of conjugal rights, allegedly to restrain the wife from taking another husband. Interestingly, the lower court had decreed that suit, based on the finding that no notice of the divorce had been served under sections 7 or 8 of the MFLO, so that the marriage was still subsisting.[48] The wife's appeal against this decision was dismissed, coupled with an order restraining her from marrying again until a valid divorce had been obtained. The wife then divorced the husband in July 1967 by a *talaq-e-tawfiz* and served notice upon the husband as well as the Chairman of the local Union Committee. The case report, at page 24, notes that this was done as required under the provisions of the MFLO, thus reflecting the early view – as in Pakistani law – that notice of the divorce is an essential element for bringing about legal validity. The Additional District Court had then granted the wife a *khul* divorce. The husband, who still pleaded love, appealed and blamed his wife's father for this litigation. His counsel claimed that the divorce decree was illegal, as the wife had not even asked for *khul*. Bhattacharya J. criticised the lower court for getting carried away by the *Khurshid Bibi* precedent and simply giving the wife a *khul* (page 26). It transpired that the wife had said that she wanted to retain her right of dower (page 28). In the end, Bhattacharya J. held that the wife was entitled to a divorce by delegated *talaq*. This, obviously, had the advantage that there was no financial penalty for the wife.

9–191 It appears that in the Bangladeshi case law this is a matter of considerable concern. Monsoor ((1994) pp. 267–273) has argued that courts in Bangladesh have been rushing to grant women *khul* divorces, which could be interpreted as an attempt to grant distressed women freedom from an oppressive marriage, but may also be seen as a male-focused strategy to deprive women of dower and other financial entitlements.[49] If the latter is correct, earlier warnings by scholars about this issue apply with equal force to Bangladesh as to Pakistan.[50] In addition, the delays in court proceedings have been a matter of concern, but the Family Courts Ordinance 1985 has been of some help in reducing the anguish over excessive delays. Growing judicial awareness of the need to protect the financial entitlements of women is reflected in the very recent case of *Jesmin Sultana v. Mohammad Elias* (1997) 17 B.L.D. 4, which reiterates that unless a wife voluntarily remits any part of her dower, the husband remains under an obligation to pay it, and the court has no right to reduce the amount.

9–192 As in Pakistan and India, lower courts in Bangladesh have required assistance from higher courts regarding the rights of Muslim women to demand divorce against the husband's wishes. *Hasina Ahmed v. Syed Abul Fazal*, 32 D.L.R. (1980) 294, is a wife's appeal in a divorce petition under section 2(viii)(a) of the DMMA 1939, claiming cruelty. The husband had alleged that his wife was maintaining adulterous relations with a cousin. This allegation had caused great mental agony, but she had been refused a decree of divorce by the lower courts.

---

[48] This point is also reiterated at pp. 36 and 38 in this convoluted judgment, expressing the assumption that non-notice of the divorce would operate as a revocation.
[49] Another early case of this type is *Muhammad Siddiq v. Ghafuran Bibi*, 25 D.L.R. (1973) 1.
[50] See already Hinchcliffe [1968a] 2 *Journal of Islamic and Comparative Law*, 24, also Carroll [1985a] 27 No. 3 J.I.L.I. 494.

Rather than just mechanically applying the precedent of *Khurshid Bibi*, in allowing the wife's appeal, S. M. Husain J. went into some detail, perhaps seeking to establish a Bangladeshi position in this area of the law.[51] He clearly defined the husband's allegation as cruelty (page 296) and pointed out the link with divorce by imprecation (*lian*).[52] In addition, the judge highlighted that the wife was willing to part with her dower money of Takas 14,000/- in consideration of the divorce (page 296) and took this as an occasion to reiterate the basic position on Muslim divorce law as applicable in Bangladesh, saying at pages 296–297:

> "It is a well-known principle in Muslim Personal Law that apart from the unilateral right of 'Talaq' at the instance of the husband, the wife can claim divorce by consent or agreement with her husband which is known as 'Khula' in Muslim Personal Law. This is of course as against a consideration and that consideration includes the wife's surrender of the dower money and other claims against her husband. This divorce by way of 'Khula' if not obtained with the consent and agreement between the parties, can, by analogy, be obtained from a Court of law before whom the case of dissolution of marriage is pending."

Referring to the rationale of the decision in *Khurshid Bibi*, it was said, at page 297, that this case "is a classic and monumental example where the principle of Muslim Law on divorce by consent by way of 'Khula' has by analogy been made a rule of the court, so that an unwilling wife is not forced to live with her husband against her expressed will". The judge also emphasised that the social dynamics in a changing society demand legal change. For, as was said at page 297, "with the changing society women are coming of their own and their independence of mind and will must be respected while considering the legal and contractual obligation in marriage between man and woman as such". This was hardly a new point, but an obvious attempt to restate a familiar principle for the benefit of the lower courts of a new country which is torn between adherence to norms coming from local traditions as well as Islamic foundations.

9–193 Regarding the delegated *talaq*, it has been seen as one of the most potent weapons in the hands of a Muslim woman – provided the woman has been given this right in the first place through her marriage contract, which in Bangladesh is normally called the *kabinnama*, and provided the wife was not in some form taking advantage of her own wrong. Earlier cases tended to focus on the male perspective. In *Ahmed Ali v. Sabha Khatun Bibi*, P.L.D. 1952 Dacca 385, the marriage was contracted in 1938 with a stipulation that on certain conditions the wife was entitled to divorce the husband. The couple split up after some time and in April 1945 the husband received a notice telling him that the wife had divorced him and was proposing to marry someone else. The husband challenged the validity of the *talaq*. Ultimately, in the Dacca High Court, he persisted in his claim that the wife had no right to divorce herself. Afzal J. examined the relevant clauses of the *kabinnama* and found, at pages 387–388:

> "It was no doubt quite in the power of the parties to impose the conditions upon which the marriage took place. If the wife acting upon a condition exercised the power of divorce delegated by the husband to her upon the contingencies which occurred, there is no reason why the reason should not be given effect to provided the condition appears to be reasonable . . .

---

[51] This is suggested by Monsoor (1994), p. 267.
[52] An earlier case on *lian* is *Saleha Khatun v. Siddikulla*, P.L.D. 1958 Dacca 62, holding that a valid retraction of a charge of adultery must be unconditional. This case confirms that *lian* remains a divorce ground under the Muslim personal law.

When such an agreement is made, the wife may, after the happening of any of the contingencies, repudiate herself in the exercise of the power, and a divorce will then take effect to the same extent as if a talak had been pronounced by the husband. The power so delegated to the wife is not revocable, and she may exercise it even after the institution of a suit against her for restitution of conjugal rights."

However, the judge also emphasised the obligations of the wife and introduced the argument that the circumstances of the wife's refusal to live with her husband needed to be examined. This leads to a familiar argument, found at page 388:

"In other words, it has to be tested whether the condition exercised in the circumstances of the case is one which is reasonable and not opposed to the policy of the Muhammadan Law. It is no doubt true that the husband is bound to maintain his wife so long as she is faithful to him and obeys his reasonable orders. But he is not bound to maintain her if she refuses herself to him or is otherwise disobedient unless the refusal or disobedience is justified."

In the present case, it was found that the wife had been under the influence of her father who had even prevented the husband from meeting his wife. It was held, therefore, at page 389, that "a husband's duty to maintain his wife is conditional upon her obedience and the performance of her marital duties". The wife's father was entirely to blame for the breakdown of the relationship; the wife had no right to obtain a divorce in this case.

9–194 In *Nur-Ud-Din Ahmad v. Masuda Khanam*, P.L.D. 1957 Dacca 242, the wife had asked for dissolution of the marriage and recovery of her dower. The *kabinnama* contained a clause that the husband's failure to pay the monthly maintenance allowance would entitle her to payment of the entire dower and would give her the right to divorce the husband. In the High Court, Rahman J. found, at page 247, that since the DMMA does not prescribe what the duty of a Muslim husband in terms of maintenance payments is, the extent of this duty is to be ascertained from the Muslim personal law. Thus, non-payment of maintenance *per se* did not constitute a failure within section 2(ii) of the DMMA. However, the husband's case being that the wife had wilfully refused her company to him, the judge turned next to the right of a Muslim wife to refuse herself to the husband unless and until the prompt dower is paid. Various authorities were cited on this point (pages 248–249), and it was held, at page 250, that a wife in that situation has a lawful excuse to refuse to live with her husband. The husband's appeal was therefore dismissed and the marriage stood dissolved.

9–195 In *Aklima Khatun v. Mahibur Rahman*, P.L.D. 1963 Dacca 602, a husband had agreed to execute a *kabinnama* in favour of the wife, giving her an unconditional right of divorce. Later, it was alleged that the wife had begun an illicit relationship with a cousin and the husband asked successfully for restitution of conjugal rights. The husband had also pleaded that the unconditional delegation of the right of divorce was illegal, while the wife's case was, in essence, that her marriage had been dissolved by the *talaq-e-tafwiz*. On the wife's appeal before the High Court, it was argued that unconditional delegation of the right to divorce is legal and that the wife had other grounds for divorce, in particular *lian*. Idris J. agreed, at page 603, relying on a detailed discussion of various authorities, that the delegation of the right of divorce can be conditional or unconditional. However, based on the evidence, he did not find that the wife had exercised her right of divorce, and he did not accept the argument that in the present case *lian* could be used as a ground for divorce. The wife's appeal was therefore dismissed, which confirms that during the early 1960s courts were not actively supporting women in claiming the right to a delegated divorce. However, several cases from the late 1960s indicate that this view has changed.

9–196 In *Gul Nawaz Khan v. Maherunnessa Begum*, 17 D.L.R. (1965) 199, the husband had executed a *kabinnama* delegating to the wife the right to repudiate the marriage on certain grounds. Less than a year later, the wife used that right and the husband contested her action, denying the various allegations of the wife and claiming, therefore, that she did not have the right to exercise the delegated *talaq*. Based mainly on the non-payment of dower, the lower courts had supported the wife's case. In the High Court, the husband pressed only one ground, namely that after consummation of the marriage, a wife did not have a right to refuse further cohabitation if there was non-payment of *mahr*. M. R. Khan J. was not impressed with this argument and cited a number of authorities to the effect that payment of prompt dower on demand is an essential condition of a Muslim marriage contract. It was held at page 201 that giving the wife the right to exercise her delegated power of divorce for the husband's failure to pay the prompt dower on demand "does not appear to be against public policy or the principles of Muslim Law". Since the wife had clearly established the fact of her repudiation, the husband's appeal was dismissed. A similar point was made by Idris J. in *Tahazzad Hossain Sikdar v. Hossneara Begum*, P.L.D. 1967 Dacca 421, and it was further held in this case, at page 425, that the wife's pronouncement of *talaq* did not have to be made in the presence of the husband or witnesses.

9–197 The leading case on the subject in Bangladesh is *Nelly Zaman v. Giasuddin Khan*, 34 D.L.R. (1982) 221, which is also the most important case in Bangladeshi law on restitution of conjugal rights. Both lower courts had refused the wife's case for recognition of her right to delegated *talaq* and had granted the husband a decree for restitution of conjugal rights. This was a 'love marriage', but when the husband was transferred to a job out of the capital city, the wife refused to follow him and the husband filed a suit for restitution of conjugal rights. The wife responded by exercising her right to a delegated *talaq*, registering the divorce and sending a notice of it to the Mayor of Dacca as well as the husband. The husband amended his legal action, now opposing the exercise of the wife's delegated *talaq* rather than asking for restitution. The response of S. M. Hussain J. to the various pleadings is interesting because it reflects the changing social conditions in Bangladeshi Muslim society. At pages 223–224 it was held:

> ". . . it clearly appears that the wife while freely entering into the marriage bond with her husband had subsequently freely exercised her right of divorce . . . and such exercise of the right of divorce by the wife cannot be said to be illegal in terms of the Kabinnama and the Muslim Personal Law with reference to [the] Family Laws Ordinance itself.
>
> . . . it may be observed that when the petitioner wife could marry against the wishes of her family members while entering into the marriage bond by appearing at the marriage registration office without any social formality, it cannot be accepted that she could not exercise her right of divorce granted in the Kabinnama freely and willingly, particularly when she appeared in court as the only witness for the defendant and deposed in the case wherein she had denied any undue influence and asserted her right to divorce her husband by way of delegated power given in the registered deed of divorce."

The husband had also tried to argue that proper notice of the divorce had not been given, but this contention was found without force in view of the facts. This judgment represents an enlightened statement of modern marriage law with particular reference to a decree for restitution of conjugal rights. The judge tackled this question *suo moto*, in terms of constitutionality, and held at pages 224–225:

"In this connection it may be specially mentioned that by lapse of time and social development the very concept of the husband's unilateral plea for forcible restitution of conjugal rights as against a wife unwilling to live with her husband has become outmoded and does not fit in with the accepted State and Public Principle and Policy of equality of all men and women being citizens equal before law being entitled to equal protection of law and to be treated only in accordance with law as guaranteed in Articles 27 and 31 of the Constitution of Bangladesh. In the husband's unilateral plea for forcible restitution of conjugal rights as against a wife unwilling to live with her husband, there is no mutuality and reciprocity between the respective rights of the husband and the wife, since such plea for restitution of conjugal rights is not available to a wife as against her husband apart from claiming maintenance and alimony. A reference to Article 28(2) of the Constitution of Bangladesh guaranteeing equal rights of women and men in all spheres of the state and public life would clearly indicate that any unilateral plea of a husband for forcible restitution of conjugal rights as against a wife unwilling to live with her husband is violative of the accepted State and Public Principle and Policy."

9–198 This would appear to be a statement reflecting a modern, secular understanding of marital relationships, without explicit reference to Muslim law. In the context of the present case, it appears that it served mainly to underpin the judicial strategy of upholding the wife's right to exercise her delegated right of *talaq* as and when she saw fit to do so. This is undoubtedly to the advantage of women, particularly since it does not involve financial penalties. It appears that these comments must be read in the light of fierce Indian discussions about the constitutionality of the remedy of restitution of conjugal rights at that time, details of which do not concern us here. While it is noteworthy that no attempt was made by the learned judge to give his arguments an Islamic dimension, this was done in the more recent case of *Hosne Ara Begum v. Md. Rezaul Karim*, 43 D.L.R. (1991) 543, at 545, where Hoque J. held, allowing the wife's appeal:

". . . the learned Court of appeal below forgot that even under the Muslim Law several rights have been recognised to the wife and she can refuse to subject to the conjugal domain of the husband if the husband treats her with cruelty."

The husband's right to repudiate the marriage has not been questioned in Bangladeshi law. When it comes to notice of divorce under sections 7 and 8 of the MFLO, we have already seen a reflection, in *Md. Kutubuddin Jaigirdar v. Nurjahan Begum*, 25 D.L.R. (1973) 21, at 24, 36 and 38, of the official legal assumption that notice of divorce is an essential element. This clearly relied on the leading case of *Ali Nawaz Gardezi*, P.L.D. 1963 S.C. 51. However, *Md. Kutubuddin Jaigirdar* also contains evidence that the popular understanding of procedures regarding a *talaq* divorce, in Bangladesh, too, is to the effect that notice of a divorce is not essential to make it valid. It was observed by Bhattacharya J., at pages 36–37:

"Whatever might have been the circumstances under which the defendant pronounced Talaq, it does not appear on an examination . . . that either the plaintiff or her father had ever any doubt as to the effectiveness of the said divorce, as will appear from the fact that the father admittedly arranged a second marriage for his daughter to be solemnised . . . and also from the fact that the plaintiff made a statement . . . that she was unwilling to go with her former husband as she had already been divorced by him . . . In this context, it is most improbable that a Muslim girl would desire to live with a person who was no longer her husband because of the Talaq given by him and in the absence of any positive evidence it cannot be presumed that the defendant was desirous of committing an illegal act."

An early case in East Pakistan to the effect that notice may not be essential is *Abdul Aziz v. Razia Khatoon* [1969] D.L.C. 586, which was later cited with approval in *Maqbool Jan v. Arshad Hassan*, P.L.D. 1975 Lah. 147, where Zullah J. held with reference to the Dacca case, at pages 151–152, "that if the *talaq* is otherwise valid (*i.e.* if under the Personal Law of the parties the Talaq is valid) it would become effective under that law; but the only clog thereon is that the effectiveness would be postponed for 90 days under subsection (3) of section 7 of the Ordinance". This is a somewhat ambiguous case, which must be read in light of the Pakistani decisions on this question at the time.

9–199 An often-cited pre-Independence Pakistani Supreme Court case which originated from the then East Pakistan is *Abdul Mannan v. Safuran Nessa*, 1970 S.C.M.R. 845. This was a maintenance application by a wife for herself and a young child under section 488 of the Code of Criminal Procedure 1898. The magistrate had allowed Rs. 40/- p.m. for the wife and a further Rs. 20/- p.m. for the child. The husband had twice appealed unsuccessfully against this order and was now approaching the Supreme Court of Pakistan, pleading that he had divorced the wife with her consent. However, the High Court at Dacca had found that no notice of the alleged divorce had been given to the Chairman of the local Union Council. In an extremely brief order, the judgment of the Dacca High Court was confirmed at page 846:

"The learned counsel for the petitioner concedes that no notice of the alleged divorce was given to the Chairman as required by section 7(1) of the Muslim Family Laws Ordinance. That being so the alleged divorce, in view of the express provision of subsection (3) of section 7 of the said Ordinance, is yet to become effective."

In *Abdus Sobhan Sarkar v. Md. Abdul Ghani*, 25 D.L.R. (1973) 227, a case decided in June 1971, the functions of the Arbitration Councils and their scope under the MFLO are explained in some detail, probably for the benefit of lower court judges in the newly created Bangladeshi legal system. This is a familiar case scenario, a husband's complaint about the fact that his wife was married by another man during the subsistence of his marriage. Apparently, there was evidence that the wife had exercised her right to a delegated divorce and had this officially approved by an Arbitration Council, permitting the wife to take a second husband. The court examined sections 6, 7 and 8 of the MFLO and found a number of inconsistencies. It was held by A. M. Sayem J., at page 229, regarding section 7:

". . . nothing has been said in the section or anywhere else in the Act providing as to what will happen if upon receipt of such a written notice of the talaq the Chairman does not constitute an Arbitration Council or if the Arbitration Council so constituted does not take any steps to bring about reconciliation between the parties. Failure of the Chairman to constitute an Arbitration Council or that of a duly constituted Arbitration Council to take necessary steps to bring about reconciliation is thus inconsequential. Once written notice of the pronouncement of a talaq in terms of sub-section (1) is delivered to the Chairman, the talaq, if otherwise valid, will be effective on the expiry of 90 days of the delivery of such notice . . . Thus, so far as talaqs are concerned the Arbitration Council has no function except to take steps to bring about reconciliation between the parties. Beyond this the Arbitration Council has nothing to do in this matter."

The appeal was therefore dismissed, but this case did not express clearly enough what the key issues in this context are, so that Bangladeshi law on this point remained somewhat unclear. There is also hardly any academic writing on this topic with reference to Bangladesh and the existing studies are too descriptive and technical. S. S. Rahman (1988) briefly discussed the requirements under section 7 of the MFLO, remarking that the Chairmen of Union Parishads seldom perform their functions under the Ordinance. He was much more concerned about the financial implications of divorce and suggested that notice of the divorce must have been received or refused by the wife and that a notice of *talaq* should be accompanied by a bank draft for dower and three months' maintenance at the rate of Takas 300/- p.m. (Rahman (1988), p. 25).

9–200 However, important clarification was given in a 1996 case, *Sirajul Islam v. Helana Begum*, 48 D.L.R. (1996) 48. This was a husband's appeal against his wife's substantial and successful claim for dower money, maintenance, medical expenses and the value of gold ornaments. The parties married in November 1983 and the *kabinnama* fixed the dower at Takas 39,999, half of it as prompt dower. The bride's father also gave gold ornaments and other presents, apparently in the form of dowry, to the value of at least Takas 39,000. It appears that the husband ignored the wife's demands for her dower, misappropriated the dowry items, and took a loan from her father which he never returned. The husband had angrily denied this and it was alleged that he had been cruel to the wife, hence her additional claims for medical expenses. The wife also claimed that the husband had forced her and the two minor daughters to leave the matrimonial home, and they had sought refuge with her father.

9–201 The lower courts had found in favour of the wife throughout. Before the High Court Division, the husband vigorously contested the financial claims of the wife. A new limb of his arguments, however, was the claim that the couple was still married in the eyes of the law, so that the wife could not claim the various financial entitlements. The husband claimed that he had pronounced *talaq* and had sworn an affidavit to that effect on April 11, 1990 but that this was not valid and effective since no notice of this had been given to the Chairman of the Union Council, nor indeed to the wife. As such, it was claimed at page 49, "the said talaq has not been made effective and the decree for entire dower money is unwarranted and it is liable to be set aside".

9–202 This desperate pleading, however, was shown to be entirely false and concocted. It was found as a matter of fact that the court below had already considered this matter and that a copy of the sworn affidavit had been sent to the Nikah Registrar in accordance with the provisions of section 6 of the Muslim Marriage and Divorce (Registration) Act 1974. Syed J. R. Mudassir Hussain J. turned to the provisions of section 7 of the MFLO and section 6 of the 1974 Act and found that the husband had indeed not followed the letter of section 7 of the MFLO, but he had instead followed the procedure under section 6 of the 1974 Bangladesh Act. In fact, the husband himself had disclosed his action in January 1992. In this context it was argued on behalf of the wife, at page 51:

". . . mere non-service of notice upon the Chairman under the Ordinance of 1961 will not render the talaq ineffective and, as such, the decree for the entire amount of dower is valid in law."

The judge found this a convincing argument and, in view of the facts of the case, considered the legislative intent of the MFLO, which was clearly said to be a beneficial legislation with the object of supporting the vast majority of a particular class of people, namely women and children (page 51). Turning to section 7 of the MFLO, it was held at page 51:

"On plain reading of section 7 of the Ordinance 1961 it can be said that it was never the intention of the legislature that a husband exercising his independent act pronouncing talaq cannot be given effect to until and unless such notice is given to the Chairman, and it means if a husband divorces his wife but does not give notice purposely to the Chairman then the divorce will not be effective till eternity. The intention of the legislature while enacting the said Ordinance 1961 was to prevent hasty dissolution of marriage and a duty is cast upon the husband to give notice under section 7 of the said Ordinance. If he failed to do so intentionally, the very object of the said section becomes redundant."

9–203   In the light of the facts of this case, it was evident that the petitioner had assaulted his wife, had driven her out of the house along with two minor daughters and he had not bothered about their maintenance. This man, in effect, was taking advantage of his own wrong. The judge stated, at page 51:

"It shows that he purposely avoided to give notice to the Chairman of the Union Council under section 7 of the Ordinance 1961 and with an intention not to revoke it again, otherwise he would have given notice to the Chairman and would have tried for reconciliation but he did not. Be that as it may, we are however, of opinion that mere non-service of notice upon the Chairman of the Union Council under section 7 of the Muslim Family Laws Ordinance cannot render the divorce ineffective if the conduct of the husband appears to be so."

While this decision was apparently reached on the basis of the particular facts of the case, the judge was not content to let the issue rest there and provided important clarifications for our understanding of the notice requirements under Bangladeshi law today. Making explicit reference to Pakistani law and to the fact that his view was supported by judicial authority from that jurisdiction, the judge cited two cases from Pakistan, significantly not *Ali Nawaz Gardezi*, P.L.D. 1963 S.C. 51, nor indeed the more recent and helpful *Kaneez Fatima*, P.L.D. 1993 S.C. 901, but instead *Chuhar v. Ghulam Fatima*, P.L.D. 1984 Lah. 124,[53] as well as *Parveen Chowdhury v. 6th Senior Civil Judge, 1st Class, Karachi*, P.L.D. 1976 Kar. 416 (see above, page 347). The judge quoted detailed key excerpts from these two cases and finally held, at page 52, that in view of these High Court decisions from Pakistan the divorce given the husband was "valid and effective".[54]

9–204   It appears, therefore, that the long-lasting insecurity over the legal status of a Bangladeshi divorce which is not notified under section 7 of the MFLO is now more or less resolved. It is not surprising that the recent Supreme Court case of

---

[53] We have already discussed this case at p. 357, above. In the present case report, the case name is strangely mis-spelt as *Ganhar v. Ghulam Fating*, which is evidently a plain mistake.
[54] This decision, at pp. 52–55, also provides a detailed discussion regarding arrears of maintenance, which is not relevant here, but should not be overlooked.

Kaneez Fatima, P.L.D. 1993 S.C. 901 in Pakistan was not cited in *Sirajul Islam*, since judgment in the latter was already given on July 27, 1994. However, as the law stands at present, both Pakistani and Bangladeshi law on the subject, with slight variations, agree that non-compliance with the formal requirement to give notice of a Muslim divorce is not fatal to the legal recognition of that divorce. The latent conflict between traditional Muslim law and the modern legislated Muslim law of Pakistan and Bangladesh has therefore been resolved in a compromise of mutual accommodation. We shall see below that in the same scenario the interaction of traditional Muslim law and English legal rules produces a quite different result.

Muslims and divorce in Britain

9–205 The presence of large transnational communities of Muslims in Britain has, over time, given rise to many complex divorce issues.[55] Questions relating to Muslim divorce law have come before English courts and tribunals on many occasions and in various contexts. It is important to note at the outset that both the English law on recognition of Muslim divorces, and Muslim practice on divorce itself, have undergone significant development in Britain over the past few decades. The former remains confused and has developed quite restrictively, within the framework of the official law, through legislation and case law, while the latter has invisibly grown within the unofficial sphere and within the context of *angrezi shariat*, as discussed in Chapter 3, above. Our present discussion centres first on the much-contested problem of recognition of overseas Muslim divorces (see already Chapter 4, above) and the legal de-recognition of Muslim divorces effected in the United Kingdom itself. In addition, we briefly outline the development of *angrezi shariat* on divorce in Britain and discuss the growing role of informal Muslim agencies involved in the divorce process among Muslims resident in the United Kingdom.

The recognition of Muslim divorces by English law

9–206 Emphasising that "the legal effect of religious divorces has in the past raised many problems in the conflict of laws", Maidment (1974, p. 618) highlighted that the English courts were particularly vexed by the fact that such divorces tend to be "non-judicial". Poulter (1986, p. 98) reiterated the principal difference between divorces in the English legal system and in Muslim law, writing that in the former "a divorce always involves obtaining a decree of dissolution from a competent court of law", while in the latter extra-judicial divorces may be the norm. Gordon (1988, p. 1) emphasised that the increasingly multicultural nature of the United Kingdom population has brought with it new practical legal problems. It is evident, as Gordon (1988, p. 10) emphasises, that more contentious issues will arise in litigation with regard to divorce. Gordon (1988, p. 1) saw the potential for conflicts between recognition of 'the other' and preservation of one's own rules and value system:

> "English law has responded to this change in society by enacting rules that recognize foreign law and customs but which also seek to balance the interests of English public policy, as perceived by Parliament and the judiciary, against

---

[55] For details see Poulter (1986), pp. 98–131; Pearl (1986a), pp. 67–81; Hamilton (1995), pp. 82–139. Gordon (1988) is a very detailed specialist study of divorce law. Other European countries are beginning to develop a literature on Muslim divorces in Europe, too, *e.g.* Meron [1995] 4 *Revue Internationale de Droit Comparé* 921–939 for France, Rutten (1988) for the Netherlands, Foblets (1994b) for Belgium, Foblets (1996).

the desire, and the necessity, to promote international comity and certainty of status."

This statement indicates the depth of underlying tensions, which remain unresolved today. Even recent writing in Britain points to the continuing unhappy state of affairs. Conway (1995, p. 1618) confirms that "at present the civil system pays insufficient attention to the role which religious beliefs should play in divorce". It has also been argued that the continuing failure of the legal system to allow religious laws influence in the dissolution of marriages "has the potential to cause injustice to members of religious minorities" (Conway (1995), p. 1618) and that "a civil system in a growing multi-faith society ought to be able to reflect justice for all sections of the populace.[56]

9–207 It is impossible for any one state or legal system to insist that its own rules alone shall prevail. International norms, on the other hand, are constantly challenged by the fact that different legal systems use a variety of concepts, such as different connecting factors (nationality or domicile or residence) rather than agreeing on first principles. Under the rules of English private international law, as we have seen in Chapter 4, overseas Muslim divorces may be recognised as valid for all intents and purposes. This will often involve a judicial determination, but it need not be so at all if sufficient documentary evidence is available and there is no dispute over the legal status in question. Sometimes, however, an English official or a court or tribunal decision will achieve a result which is different from the respective overseas law, so that we find 'limping marriages' again. Most obviously, this situation arises when an English court or tribunal refuses to recognise a divorce brought about in a non-judicial manner overseas[57] A divorce might, thus, be treated as valid only according to traditional Muslim law. It might also be valid by Pakistani law, for example, assuming its effectiveness there, especially when notice was given or other procedural steps have been followed. However, legal recognition by English law may still be refused in many cases.

9–208 Under the old common law rules, based on the connecting factor of domicile, it was possible for a divorce to be obtained in a non-judicial form in England and to be recognised as valid here so long as the parties were domiciled in a foreign country, such as Pakistan.[58] This was the situation up to January 1, 1972, when the Recognition of Divorces and Legal Separations Act 1971 came into effect. Under the common law rules, a foreign divorce would be recognised if it was obtained in the country of the husband's domicile. If it had been obtained in a different country, the test was whether it would be recognised by the law of the husband's domicile.[59] For many Muslims in Britain, during the 1950s and 1960s, this became a critical issue. A Muslim husband wishing to divorce his wife could of course go back to his country of domicile and use the divorce procedures there, but could a Muslim husband validly divorce his wife by recourse to Muslim law while he, or normally both spouses, lived in England? To give an affirmative answer to this question would have meant, ultimately, to recognise the Muslim personal law system in Britain itself. We have seen in Chapters 3 and 4, above, that this policy

---

[56] Conway [1995] *New Law Journal*, November 3, 1995, p. 1619. Such concerns are also reflected in the detailed studies by Bradney (1993) and Hamilton (1995).

[57] Mole (1987), p. 39, indicated that problems were most likely to arise where local customs were involved and there was no official documentation.

[58] In English law, prior to January 1, 1974, a wife's domicile was dependent on that of her husband. For a good discussion on the older legal position see Maidment [1974] 37 *The Modern Law Review* 611–626.

[59] On the complexities of the earlier law see, *e.g.* Pearl (1974-1975) 4 No. 1 *New Community* 119–121; Carroll (1981a).

has not been found acceptable and that English law has tried to resist the recognition of personal law elements.

9–209 Significantly, many of the earlier cases concerned Jewish couples. It appears that Muslim divorces and their peculiarities did not become an issue until the *Hammersmith* case in 1917.[60] While under common law, overseas Muslim divorces would be endorsed if the divorce was recognised by the respective overseas legal system, the facts in the *Hammersmith* case raised policy issues which were soon to become more prominent. Here was a monogamous English marriage involving an English woman and a Muslim husband, domiciled in India, who sought English legal recognition for a *talaqnama* executed in London. Not surprisingly, legal recognition of this divorce was refused on public policy grounds, although there was awareness that the divorce would be legally valid under Indian law. It appears that the unilateral nature of this divorce was an important factor, but this was certainly not the only consideration. In two other early cases of Muslim divorce in 1957–1958, the wife had played an active part in the divorce proceedings and legal recognition was granted.[61] The focus shifted therefore, at first imperceptibly, towards public policy arguments which assessed Muslim divorce procedures, compared them to the domestic proceedings, and found them wanting on grounds of procedure as well as protective potential for the position of the wife. In other words, the currently dominant argument, to the effect that the male-centred unilateral Muslim divorce regime amounts virtually to a human rights violation,[62] began to gain prominence.

9–210 Earlier, however, in *Qureshi v. Qureshi*,[63] we find the high water mark of liberality, when legal recognition was granted to a Muslim divorce effected in England. Sir Jocelyn Simon P. considered in detail the provisions of the MFLO in Pakistan, saw clearly that this short marriage between two Muslim spouses had irretrievably broken down anyway and that the husband's *talaq* divorce would be recognised as fully valid under Pakistani law (page 536). He also found, at page 540, that the wife was probably better off with an order granting her financial rights than with a practically meaningless court order which declared the husband's *talaq* invalid for the purposes of English law, given that the divorce was manifestly valid in Muslim law and in Pakistani law. This approach was very much in line with the Government's attitude towards divorces pronounced abroad by English domiciliaries,[64] namely that limping marriages should be avoided.

9–211 However, the enactment of section 16 of the Domicile and Matrimonial Proceedings Act 1973, now section 44(2) of the Family Law Act 1986, regressed from the flexibility in *Qureshi v. Qureshi*, applying as it did both to English and foreign domiciliaries habitually resident in England. It appears that the decision in *Qureshi v. Qureshi* was the reason for parliamentary action in this field. Judges felt that women were being thrown out of their homes with no financial provisions, since the English

---

[60] *R. v. The Superintendent Registrar of Marriages, Hammersmith, ex p. Mir-Anwaruddin* [1917] 1 K.B. 634.
[61] These are *Yousef v. Yousef* and *El-Riyami v. El-Riyami*, for details see Gordon (1988), p. 59.
[62] See esp. Poulter (1986), p. 101, portraying the *talaq* as "clearly discriminatory on the grounds of sex". Poulter (1995), p. 85 discusses *talaq* as one of three "points of absolutely irreducible conflict". Significantly, the same writer had taken a more positive stance earlier. Thus, Poulter (1977), p. 9, argued that in view of changes to English divorce law in the early 1970s, "the actual form of the Moslem *talaq* can hardly be regarded as especially objectionable".
[63] [1972] Fam. 173; [1971] 2 W.L.R. 518, following *Har-Shefi v. Har-Shefi (No. 2)* [1953] P.220, a case involving Jews. For a good discussion of this case see Poulter (1977).
[64] See ss.2 and 3 of the Recognition of Divorces and Legal Separations Act 1971, now ss.46(1) and (2) of the Family Law Act 1986.

laws of maintenance at the time did not provide for such cases.[65] There were other considerations, however, relating first of all to the rules of private international law. With effect from January 1, 1972, the Recognition of Divorces and Legal Separations Act 1971 was enacted, partly to enable the United Kingdom to ratify the 1970 Hague Convention on the Recognition of Divorces and Legal Separations, which was concerned to control and reduce problems over 'limping marriages'.[66] Another important concern of the international activity over recognition of divorces, which proved to some extent counterproductive to the efforts regarding avoidance of 'limping marriages', was the attempt to protect the defendant spouse, normally the woman, in extra-judicial divorces. It is for this reason that the phrase 'judicial or other proceedings' became so central in the subsequent legal debates. The Hague Conference had confirmed that there was much opposition to the recognition of informal, extra-judicial divorces, especially of the unilateral and instantly effective type like the 'triple *talaq*' of Muslim law. Gordon (1988, p. 62) explains that the intervention of public or religious authorities in the state in question should be regarded as 'proceedings' and records differing views on the matter at the time, indicating clearly that the controversy has carried on.

9–212 The provisions of the Recognition of Divorce and Legal Separations Act 1971 were solely concerned with the recognition of foreign divorces. In essence, the Act required that a divorce seeking the recognition of English law should have been obtained "by means of judicial or other proceedings" and should be effective under the laws of the country in which these proceedings took place. A number of public policy grounds under section 8 of the 1971 Act allowed courts to refuse legal recognition to a foreign divorce.[67] In the meantime, it became apparent through the decision in *Qureshi v. Qureshi* in 1971 that Muslims in Britain itself could still divorce their wives through a *talaq* divorce. In evident reaction to that decision, virtually overruling it, section 16(1) of the Domicile and Matrimonial Proceedings Act 1973 outlawed this practice, requiring that henceforth no extra-judicial divorce taking place in England should have legal effect. Poulter (1986, p. 114) noted that there may well be now "a complete and outright prohibition of extra-judicial divorces occurring in this country". In a sense, this could be seen as a similar intended effect to that of section 7 of the MFLO in Pakistan, if we assume for a moment that the law makers in Pakistan actually wanted to ban all unregistered divorces.

9–213 In English law, the manifest intention of the legislature has been put into legal practice, uninhibited by religious concerns about the supervening authority of Muslim law in its *shariat* form. It is significant to emphasise here that the subsequent English case law has not focused, as Pakistani law undoubtedly has, on the status of the unregistered *talaq* and its socio-cultural significance in the context of the legal system as a whole, but rather on procedural aspects. In other words, the muffled Pakistani debate about the precise role and place of the *talaq* without notice in Pakistani law has not been replicated in English law, adding therefore to the apparent difficulties of cross-cultural legal communication. For a number of reasons, it was simply assumed that the Pakistani law demanded notice of a *talaq* and could therefore be treated as a 'proceeding', while any unnotified *talaq* must be denied recognition. Given the key phrase of 'judicial or other proceedings', which also appears in section 54(1) of the Family Law Act 1986 (while section 46(1) of the

---

[65] However, the Matrimonial and Family Proceedings Act 1984 has offered some remedies in this respect. For details see Gordon (1988), pp. 165–195; Schuz, "Divorce and ethnic minorities", in *Divorce: Where next?* (1996), pp. 141–143.
[66] Since that Convention was not ratified by many states, its effectiveness remained limited. For details see Gordon (1988), p. 61.
[67] For details see Gordon (1988), pp. 63–66.

same Act only speaks of 'proceedings') and the disagreements over its precise ambit, the apparent consequence has been that English law has been willing to recognise 'procedural' *talaqs*, but not the so-called 'bare *talaq*', except if obtained in the country of domicile while neither spouse is habitually resident in the United Kingdom. It is evident, therefore, that the confusions over the position of the *talaq* in Pakistani law have also been transported into the legal debates in English law. This is a further reason why the present position in English law over the recognition of Muslim divorces remains quite confused and unsatisfactory (see also Gordon (1986)). We shall need to come back to this issue further below.

9–214 If we briefly consider the relevant English case law of the past two decades, we can conveniently focus on a few leading cases which would appear to require re-assessment in the light of our earlier discussions in the present chapter. The leading case of *Quazi v. Quazi*,[68] much-debated in its time,[69] held that a *talaq* which was validly and effectively obtained in Pakistan in accordance with the provisions of the MFLO was a divorce obtained within the meaning of section 2 of the Recognition of Divorces and Legal Separations Act 1971. In this case, a Pakistani Muslim wife challenged the legal validity of the husband's *talaq*, which had been given to her in Pakistan, with the husband following the notice procedures required under section 7 of the MFLO. The question was whether such an overseas divorce was entitled to legal recognition by English law. In the House of Lords, Lord Diplock explicitly recognised that this was a matter of considerable relevance to modern English law, saying at page 898: "This is of general importance in view of the number of Pakistani nationals who are settled in the United Kingdom either accompanied or unaccompanied by their wives". Lord Diplock also indicated, at page 901, that the English courts were by now familiar with *talaq* divorces:

> "The concept of divorce by talaq under the classic religious law of Islam is one with which English courts have become familiar. It is effected by the husband solemnly pronouncing the word 'talaq' either once or thrice in the presence of witnesses. Neither the presence of the wife nor even any notice to her is required by the classic religious law of Islam. The absence of any requirement of notice or publicity in this classic or 'bare' form of talaq, has led certain Muslim states, of which Pakistan is one, to pass legislation requiring additional formalities to be complied with in order to make a bare talaq effective to dissolve the marriage."

At page 909, Lord Fraser put the same issue as follows:

> "Under classical Muslim law all that a husband had to do in order to divorce his wife was to pronounce talaq before witnesses three times either orally or in writing and the divorce was immediately effective. But modern legislation in Pakistan has imposed further requirements in addition to the mere pronouncement of talaq."

This latter statement, as well as Lord Diplock's discussion of the changes brought about by the MFLO at page 902 and again at page 903, show clear judicial awareness of the fact that the 'bare *talaq*' becomes effective immediately and is irrevocable. The key issue in this case was whether the proceedings followed by the husband in Pakistan were such as to fall within the phrase 'judicial or other

---

[68] [1979] 3 All E.R. 897; [1979] 3 W.L.R. 833; [1980] A.C. 744; 10 Fam. Law 148.
[69] For details see Sylvester [1980] *Journal of Social Welfare Law* 282–292; Canton [1983] *New Law Journal*, October 21, 1983, pp. 928–930; Forsyth [1985] 34 I.C.L.Q. 398–402; Poulter (1986), p. 117 *et seq.*; Gordon (1986a); Gordon (1988), p. 91 and elsewhere.

proceedings' in the 1971 Act. There was no disagreement that the proceedings followed had not been of a judicial nature, even though the Chairman of the Union Council involved had happened to be a judge. While the wife's case was, in essence, that the proceedings needed to be of a quasi-judicial nature to qualify for recognition, the husband's argument was that any form of proceedings should satisfy the English legal criteria for recognition of the divorce. This argument prevailed in the House of Lords.

9–215 While *Quazi v. Quazi* is undoubtedly an important case, it did not settle the controversy over the ambit of 'other proceedings'.[70] It is a correct decision on the basis of its facts, but what if the facts are not so clear? For example, where notice has not been given in accordance with the provisions of section 7 of the MFLO, but everyone involved assumed for years that the divorce had been legally effective, as we saw in so many Pakistani cases, what would be the approach of English law? And what of cases where there had been an agreed divorce of the *mubaraat* type, or a *khul*, and there had been no notice to a Chairman? By establishing that a Pakistani *talaq* which was accompanied by formal notification under section 7 of the MFLO was to be recognised as a valid divorce under English law, so long as the connecting factor was complied with, *Quazi v. Quazi* did not conclusively answer all other questions about the legal validity of the various forms of Muslim divorce, including the 'bare *talaq*'. This is so because the House of Lords assumed, inaccurately, as we have shown in the concluding sections of paragraphs 9–167—9–188, above, that all Pakistani divorces would follow the factual pattern of *Quazi*, involving official notice.[71] In other words, like the superior Pakistani courts, until *Kaneez Fatima*, P.L.D. 1993 S.C. 901, finally clarified the matter, English judicial decisions have been based on the general assumption that notice under section 7 of the MFLO is essential, whereas it is a fact, well-recognised even in *Quazi v. Quazi* itself, that a *talaq* divorce becomes irrevocably effective at once under the classical Muslim personal law. In this respect, Lord Scarman's assumption, voiced at page 917, that the MFLO "overrides even the classic law of Islam", is also open to question.

9–216 It was noted by Lord Fraser at page 910 of *Quazi v. Quazi* that the High Court, in the 1976 case of *Minhas*,[72] had overlooked the leading Pakistani case of *Ali Nawaz Gardezi*, P.L.D. 1963 S.C. 51, and it was held that that case "was evidently based on a misunderstanding of the ordinance".[73] With respect, it appears now that that case was based on a realistic assessment of the practical operation of the MFLO and was decided correctly. However, in the light of our discussion of the Pakistani law on *talaq* divorces, we must emphasise here that the decision in *Quazi v. Quazi*, in view of subsequent developments in Pakistani law and the consequent re-interpretation of the 1961 Ordinance, may be questioned as a general precedent for this whole area of the law. It remains undoubtedly a correct decision as far as this case was concerned, but it does not solve the conundrum of 'other proceedings' and

---

[70] Sylvester (1980), p. 291, predicted that it would cause more litigation.

[71] This misguided assumption has also been used by legal writers. Poulter (1986), p. 117 wrongly assumes that notice under s.7 "must immediately be given", while s.7(1) of the Ordinance provides merely that "any man who wishes to divorce his wife shall, as soon as may be after the pronouncement of talaq in any form whatsoever, give . . . notice". We have shown above that the appropriate interpretation of 'shall' in s.7(1) of the MFLO must be 'ought to'.

[72] The full citation is *R. v. Registrar General of Births, Deaths and Marriages, ex p. Minhas* [1976] 2 All E.R. 246; [1977] Q.B. 1. For comments on the case see Gravells [1976] 92 *The Law Quarterly Review* 347–353; Canton [1976] 25 I.C.L.Q. 909–912. Poulter (1977), p. 8 called this a "bizarre case" but provides a useful discussion.

[73] At p. 910. This view was subsequently also reflected in the academic writing, see Forsyth (1985), p. 399.

does not lead the way out of the labyrinth, as perceived by Lord Scarman at page 912 of *Quazi v. Quazi*. Poulter (1986, pp. 116–117) had outlined the problem prior to his discussion of *Quazi v. Quazi*, indicating that even the most informal divorce could well be entitled to legal recognition if one took a broad view of 'other proceedings'. He returned to this issue at page 119, emphasising its relevance:

> "There has been a serious division of judicial and academic opinion as to whether or not a 'bare *talaq*', *i.e.* a simple pronouncement of divorce without notification to the wife or to an arbitral council, qualifies for recognition here as an 'overseas divorce'. Does a purely informal divorce by means of unilateral repudiation without the need for any official involvement fall within the expression 'other proceedings . . .?'"

At page 916 of *Quazi v. Quazi*, Lord Scarman had explicitly referred to the purpose of the recognition rule and said in that context, in a much-quoted obiter dictum that he construed 'other proceedings' in section 2 of the 1971 Act,

> "as applying to any divorce which has been obtained by means of any proceeding, ie any act or acts, officially recognised as leading to divorce in the country where the divorce was obtained, and which itself is recognised by the law of the country as an effective divorce. Specifically, 'other proceedings' will include an act or sequence of acts other than a proceeding instituted in a court of law . . ."

Apparently in reliance of this statement, it was held in *Zaal v. Zaal* [1983] 4 F.L.R. 284, that a unilateral 'bare *talaq*' pronounced in Dubai was a recognised divorce obtained by 'other proceedings'. This was despite the fact that the wife was an English woman. Bush J., at pages 286–287, made reference to *Quazi v. Quazi* and found that Lord Fraser had, in that case, "declined to express an opinion whether a bare talaq pronounced in some countries where . . . it would be effective without any further procedure, would be recognized . . . as a valid divorce" (page 287). Lord Fraser himself had said, at page 814 of the judgment, that "anything that can properly be regarded as proceedings will qualify so long as it is legally effective" and referred further to the statement of Lord Scarman, as quoted above, to support his view that a 'bare *talaq*' would be entitled to recognition. It was held, at page 288:

> ". . . for centuries, it has been part of the law of Islam that a man may divorce his wife by a ceremony of religious significance which involves a pronouncing of the talaq three times. If he does this, with or without witnesses, and with or without a document to support it, then he and she are divorced and his State, or community, recognizes it as a divorce. In my view these are proceedings in Dubai effective as divorce under the law of the country and are 'other proceedings' within the meaning of the English Act so permitting recognition."

9–217   This judgment also contains an instructive discussion on public policy considerations in this context. The judge comments explicitly on the fact that the wife knew that she was entering into "a marriage governed by Islamic religious laws and customs and . . . clearly knew of the dangers which might arise as a result of the ease with which a talaq could be pronounced" (page 289). Significantly, Bush J. held that it would not be right to lay down a general rule, but instead one should consider the facts and circumstances of the case. This is, of course, precisely what the Pakistani courts have been saying in so many words and what *Kaneez Fatima*, P.L.D. 1993 S.C. 901, has now authoritatively enshrined as the appropriate approach. This attitude also explains the final outcome of *Zaal v. Zaal* for, although Bush J. had held that a Dubai *talaq* could qualify as 'other proceedings', legal recognition to this particular *talaq* was still refused on public policy grounds. It was held, at page 289:

> "I have come to this conclusion on the restricted ground that what was done, though properly done according to the husband's own customary laws, was done in secrecy so far as the wife was concerned. The first this wife knew of it the deed was done and she was divorced in fact and in law and it was irrevocable and binding according to the law of the husband's state. No opportunity was given to enlist the aid of her's or the husband's relatives in repairing the breach. Common justice requires that some notice other than a casual threat ought to be given for so solemn a proceeding. It is this that in this case offends one's sense of justice and jars upon the conscience . . ."

The added benefit of this approach, of course, was that the court could then proceed to grant ancillary relief to the wife under English law, given that it had been noted explicitly at page 286 that "orders by this court for ancillary relief are not enforceable in the Arab Emirate State of Dubai". Some other cases were decided at this time, notably *Sharif v. Sharif* [1980] 10 Fam. Law 216, involving an Iraqi divorce by *talaq* which was held not to fall within the phrase 'judicial or other proceedings'. There was, thus, a conflict of judicial decisions, as noted at page 479 in *Chaudhary v. Chaudhary*,[74] which involved a 'bare *talaq*' from Kashmir.[75] Here again, the consideration of the facts and circumstances of the case as a basic principle of adjudication is evident. The Court of Appeal was clearly aware that holding in favour of the husband would deprive the wife of ancillary relief. Regarding the legal position of a 'bare *talaq*' as 'judicial or other proceeding, it was held in this case, at page 481:

> "In our judgment, the phrase must be intended to exclude those divorces which depend for their legal efficacy solely on the act or acts of the parties to the marriage or of one of them. In such cases, although certain formalities or procedures have to be complied with, there is nothing which can properly be regarded as "proceedings". We think that, given the apposition of the words "other proceedings" to the word "judicial", "proceedings" here means that the efficacy of the divorce depends in some way on the authority of the State expressed in a formal manner, as provided for by the law of the State. To put it in other words, the State or some official organization recognized by the State must play some part in the divorce process at least to the extent that, in proper cases, it can prevent the wishes of the parties or one of them, as the case may be, from dissolving the marriage tie as of right. It, therefore, includes some "extra-judicial" divorces, but, as it seems to us, it is impossible to be more precise. Individual examination by the court of the divorce process in each case seems to be unavoidable."

9–218 There is much evidence, in fact, that this court was outrightly hostile to the husband's claims that he could use legal or other processes outside the English

---

[74] [1985] F.L.R. 476. There are numerous other citations for this case, at Court of Appeal level see: [1984] 3 All E.R. 1017; [1985] Fam. 19; [1985] 2 W.L.R. 350; [1985] Fam. Law 26.
[75] On the understanding of the English courts about the applicability of the MFLO in Kashmir, see the Court of Appeal decision in *Chaudhary v. Chaudhary*. In *R. v. Immigration Appeal Tribunal ex p. Secretary of State for the Home Department* [1984] 2 W.L.R. 36, later known as the *Ghulam Fatima* case, the assumption was that the MFLO applied in Kashmir because the point was conceded by counsel for the Secretary of State in the pleadings.

jurisdiction to bring about the dissolution of the marriage.[76] This is also evident from the statement of Oliver L.J., at page 488, in the context of public policy, refusing the husband recognition of his *talaq*:

> "In my judgment, it must plainly be contrary to the policy of the law in a case where both parties to a marriage are domiciled in this country to permit one of them, whilst continuing his English domicile, to avoid the incidents of his domiciliary law and to deprive the other party to the marriage of her rights under that law by the simple process of taking advantage of the financial ability to travel to a country whose laws appear temporarily to be more favourable to him. This, as it seems to me, is precisely the sort of situation which the legislature must have had in mind . . ."

This particular decision seems concerned, therefore, to plug the perceived loophole of recourse to the respective foreign law. This was a negative decision, in hostile terms and tone,[77] and the message was probably not lost on British Muslims. It is significant that during the last 10 years the English courts have not had a chance to adjudicate further on this question. This may be not merely because the law was now clearly laid down, and Pakistani Muslims would follow the notice requirements of the MFLO, but rather because South Asian Muslims (and others) felt offended by the approach taken in *Chaudhary v. Chaudhary* and turned increasingly either to overseas fora or to particular extra-judicial forms of dispute settlement, thus bypassing English courts, as we shall see further below. No matter what the law says, it would appear to remain open to individuals with strong foreign connections, especially those with the means to travel, to resort to overseas legal provisions rather than to English law. On the other hand, as Poulter (1977, p. 8) pointed out in a detailed discussion of *Minhas*, the strong assimilationist message from that case has been that Muslims in Britain should obtain their divorces through the processes available under English domestic law.

9–219   Complicated questions about Muslim divorces often arise in immigration contexts. Here again, the situational context would tend to operate in favour of non-recognition of a foreign divorce, as clearly happened in the leading House of Lords case of *Ghulam Fatima*.[78] This case involved a Pakistani fiancee who was refused entry clearance to Britain because the immigration officer could not be sure that her proposed husband had validly divorced his first wife. This divorce had been a transnational divorce, in which the husband had pronounced the *talaq* in England and had then "perfected" (page 661) it by sending notification of this to the relevant Chairman in Pakistan. Slade L.J. in the Court of Appeal emphasised that in Pakistan, "a bare talaq is no longer recognised as effective by itself to dissolve a marriage" (page 661), took a close look at section 7 of the MFLO, but refused recognition of this divorce on public policy grounds. Despite judicial recognition that it was somewhat undesirable to create limping marriages, it was held at page 667:

---

[76] This hostility is particularly obvious in the judgment of Cumming-Bruce L.J. at [1985] F.L.R. 476, at pp. 482–483. Oliver L.J., at p. 488, castigates the strategy of avoiding the incidents of the domiciliary law. The Immigration Appeal Tribunal has applied the approach in *Chaudhary v. Chaudhary* even in cases where a *talaq* pronounced in Kashmir has been communicated to a Chairman of the Union Council. See *Nahid Akhtar v. E.C.O. Islamabad* (April 24, 1998) (17071).

[77] Several writers discuss this, see especially Smart (1985).

[78] See *R. v. Secretary of State for the Home Department, ex p. Ghulam Fatima*, under numerous references, the Court of Appeal decision being reported at [1984] 2 All E.R. 458; [1984] 3 W.L.R. 659; [1985] Q.B. 190 *et al.*; for detailed comments see Gordon (1986b); Gordon (1988), pp. 159–161 emphasises the impact of immigration considerations. See also Pearl (1986b).

". . . we are far from certain that it would be the policy of the legislature to encourage the obtaining of "divorces by post" by Pakistani nationals resident in this country by means of the talaq procedure. Section 16 of the Act of 1973 seems to us to suggest otherwise. We can therefore see no obvious reasons of legislative policy sufficient to justify giving section 2(a) of the Recognition Act a meaning other than that which the wording of the subsection in its context appears to require."

It is therefore evident, again, that English courts have been concerned to stop Muslim migrants from using overseas legal provisions for divorce. Slade L.J., speaking for the Court of Appeal, evidently saw this kind of transnational divorce as an abuse of legal procedures rather than a genuine reflection of the transnational nature of Muslim communities in Britain. This decision, therefore, must also be read as intended legal education for Muslim migrants in the United Kingdom, to the effect that they must use the provisions of domestic English law, rather than any overseas legal system or indeed their own personal law, which carries no legal validity in Britain.

9–220   One can imagine other scenarios, involving for example a divorced wife from Pakistan who remarried a United Kingdom-based man there and then applied for an entry certificate to the United Kingdom to join her second husband. It is very likely that questions would be asked about the precise legal status of her previous marriage. In practice, many such women face great difficulties because of the informal nature of Muslim marriages and divorces and the lack of official documentation.

9–221   One obvious solution would be for the English courts to decide that the validity of a person's second marriage depends upon the validity of the earlier divorce. However, in cases where the earlier divorce cannot be recognised because it was actually arranged in the United Kingdom itself and is thus hit by provisions preventing the legal recognition of Muslim divorces given in the United Kingdom itself,[79] the Pakistani woman would not be allowed to enter the United Kingdom for settlement purposes because her marriage would not be considered valid. There is no reported English case directly in point, although the views expressed by the House of Lords, as found in *R v. Secretary of State for the Home Department ex p. Ghulam Fatima*,[80] suggest that English courts would not be unduly worried by the fact that non-recognition of the *talaq* divorce would lead to a limping marriage situation. It was authoritatively confirmed in that case that a *talaq* pronounced in England and then sent abroad for the initiation of proceedings under the MFLO in Pakistan could not be recognised as a foreign divorce in terms of sections 2 and 3 of the 1971 Act because it could not be regarded as wholly obtained in an overseas country. Neither could it be regarded as a divorce obtained in England, since in view of section 16(1) of the 1973 Act, it was not granted by a United Kingdom court of civil jurisdiction.

9–222   The unhappy state of the law relating to the recognition of foreign non-judicial divorces was highlighted in a number of Articles during the late 1970s and early 1980s.[81] Despite much discussion, many useful suggestions and a call for more flexibility as regards extra-judicial divorces from the Law Commission itself, the legislature has pursued a strict line. The Family Law Act 1986 has not remedied this problem at all and its provisions still result in serious practical problems arising from

---

[79] These provisions were earlier introduced in s.16(1) of the Divorce and Matrimonial Proceedings Act 1973 and are now found in s.44(1) of the Family Law Act 1986. For details see Gordon (1988), pp. 72 *et seq.*

[80] [1986] 2 W.L.R. 693; [1986] A.C. 527. On this case see Berkovits (1988); Berkovits (1990).

[81] See especially Sylvester (1980); Forsyth (1985); earlier North [1975] 91 *The Law Quarterly Review* 36–67; Canton (1976); Gravells (1976); Poulter (1977).

limping marriages, particularly in cases of transnational divorces, where the divorce is partly obtained in England and partly elsewhere. More recently, in the important test case on Jewish law of *Berkovits v. Grinberg* [1995] 2 All E.R. 681, the strict approach of English law to questions of recognition of overseas divorces was confirmed.[82] The policy of the law inherent in section 16 of the Divorce and Matrimonial Proceedings Act 1973 has clearly been continued and has been declared paramount.

9–223 Undoubtedly, Muslims and other ethnic minority groups in Britain are aware of the strict legal approach and have been drawing their own conclusions, to the effect that a divorce which is perfectly valid by the law of countries like Pakistan, India or Bangladesh would probably be treated as void by English law, so it is better to avoid recourse to English law in the first place. Among the many Muslims settled in the United Kingdom with close family connections in South Asia, non-recognition in England of a status which is patently recognised in the subcontinent is not perceived as a light matter. The absence of visible public protest does not mean that the perceived injustice is not noticed.

9–224 Berkovits (1988, p. 77) questions whether it is really acceptable for English courts to impose concepts of family law on persons who have married under a different system and confirms that eliminating limping marriages appears to be treated as less important than subordinating all residents of England to a uniform municipal jurisdiction. One of the main underlying reasons for the strict approach to overseas and transnational divorces appears to be fear of possible infringement of the right to sexual equality. One leading writer has throughout portrayed the *talaq* as a discriminatory practice, a wholly unregulated act entirely at the whim of the husband (see still Poulter (1995), p. 85). While this may be the case in the 'bare *talaq*' form, it should be acknowledged, as emphasised in our detailed discussion of Muslim divorce law in paragraphs 9–04—9–38, above, that there are various forms of Muslim divorce, that Muslim women also have the right to divorce, and that important reforms have been introduced in a number of Muslim jurisdictions to protect the position of women with regard to divorce, not to speak of social safeguards. By not making reference to such factors and not mentioning that Muslim fora in Britain have been debating and actively tackling such questions, too, one maintains the image of a backward community resistant to change and unwilling to uphold modern human rights standards. Hamilton (1995, p. 97) politely speaks in this context of "a general dislike of unilateral repudiation" and contends that if English law is prepared to accept the validity of certain religious marriages, then there is little logic in refusing to accept the validity of religious divorces.[83] She makes the more general point, however, that "the courts in both England and the United States have shown great reluctance to cede any of their authority over domestic divorces to religious courts" (Hamilton (1995), p. 83), which suggests a different kind of power struggle, no less important and certainly very tangible for courts. Hamilton (1995, p. 97) mentions the possibility of a dual system for divorce, separating the legal termination from its practical consequences, so that the state would perhaps recognise the religious ceremony as ending the divorce, but all ancillary matters relating to property, maintenance and children would have to be dealt with by the secular civil system.[84] However, she foresees several practical problems with such a system (see Hamilton (1995), pp. 98–99).

9–225 One particular problem concerns what Schuz (1996, p. 134) has called the 'chained spouse', giving a compelling reason to courts to be prepared to do

---

[82] We discussed this case and its implications in paras 4–44—4–67, above.
[83] See Hamilton (1995), p. 105, with examples from cases.
[84] *ibid.*, p. 97; see also Berkovits (1990), for a similar solution. In a sense, the Matrimonial and Family Proceedings Act 1984 has at least taken care of the latter.

everything to help such a victim of a 'limping marriage'. Taking her cue from an Australian judge, Schuz (1996, p. 135) observes that "it is the duty of the court to ensure that appropriate orders are made fully effective not only in theory, but in fact". In our present scenario of international divorces, it means that the law should assist spouses to get rid of 'limping marriages'. In the purely domestic context, where the duality of state-sponsored official marriage or divorce and of religious marriage and divorce becomes an issue, it means that until the religious divorce is obtained, the civil divorce cannot be fully effective because, in reality, one party (normally the wife) is unable to remarry. Significantly, this problem was first discussed in English law with reference to Jewish spouses, in *Brett v. Brett* [1969] 1 All E.R. 1007. This very helpful decision forced the husband to grant the wife a Jewish divorce (a *get*) or to face progressively more severe financial penalties. No decision on this matter involving Muslim spouses has been reported. Part of the reason for this is that Muslims are generally wary of bringing problems to courts and that, in fact, such cases are being dealt with by informal Muslim dispute settlement fora.[85] In the United States of America,[86] but not in England, the state has been willing to introduce further legal protection by statute, although it can be argued that sections 9 and 10 of the Family Law Act 1996 may as yet prove beneficial (see paragraph 4–68, above). New developments have not included explicit concern for Muslim wives in such predicaments. Hamilton (1995, p. 134) has correctly pointed out that the *Brett* solution would be effective only where the husband has reasonably substantial financial assets and can be threatened with their loss. Jewish and Muslim organisations would prefer a rather firmer footing from which the courts could encourage and assist parties to obtain a religious divorce, but how this is to be achieved has not been worked out.

Muslim divorces and *angrezi shariat*

9–226 In the meantime Muslims in Britain appear to have chosen a path of self-help. Various forms of self-organisation can be discussed under the wider umbrella of *angrezi shariat* on divorce. As in the area of marriage, it is becoming increasingly apparent that the traditional patterns of divorce have not been completely abandoned in Britain, despite the strictures of the law. Just as *angrezi shariat* on marriage was developed by the Muslim communities themselves rather than by jurists or the state law, we see a similarly semi-planned development when it comes to divorce. Here, too, the superiority and dominance of Muslim law over English law are re-asserted. Hamilton (1995, p. 50) has pointed to what she calls anecdotal evidence in the context of marriage that many Muslims appear to be marrying outside the official English system. The same is true for divorce. Unless detailed research work on such topics is produced, our evidence will remain 'anecdotal'. It is well-known, however, that Muslim husbands in Britain can and do still divorce their wives by *talaq*, although English law has laid down explicitly, since 1973, as we saw, that no extra-judicial divorce shall be recognised in English law. So, having married the same person twice, as it were, most British Muslims have also learnt that it would be necessary to divorce twice.

---

[85] See further below for Britain. In the U.S.A., there has been a stream of such cases. For details see Hamilton (1995), pp. 118–120 and 122–129. The U.S. courts, despite the Establishment Clause of the Constitution (see Hamilton (1995), pp. 9–14), have been ready to enforce a religious divorce to achieve a clear secular purpose, namely completing the process of dissolution, so that spouses can remarry, which the state wishes to encourage.

[86] There has even been an enactment, the New York Get Statute, which reflects the approach taken in *Brett v. Brett* and shows that despite apprehensions about interfering in religious matters, the state must take account of empirical reality and deal with the problems referred to courts. For details on this see Hamilton (1995), pp. 129–133.

9-227 This realisation has very important implications which have not been discussed in detail anywhere. An inkling of the issue is found in a recent article about the Muslim family in Britain, written by a very experienced Muslim scholar. Having outlined the traditionally liberal Muslim approach to divorces, albeit in rather idealistic terms, Ahsan (1995, p. 24) writes:

> "Since Muslim law of divorce is not recognized by British justice, Muslims cannot simply follow the law as given by Islam. Should a Muslim couple decide to divorce, the matter must go through an English court. Muslims in Britain have been asking for the application of Muslim personal law for their community; but so far with no success ... As Islam gives the right to non-Muslim communities which exist in Muslim countries to apply their own personal law in all matters of family life, one might expect Muslims living in non-Muslim countries to be offered reciprocal rights."

This does not give us the whole picture of Muslim divorce in Britain because the author was more concerned to raise the politics of the personal law issue than to talk about the realities of *angrezi shariat* on divorce. Unfortunately, it is very often a fact that a couple does not amicably decide to divorce, but one spouse unilaterally seeks to terminate the marital bond, frequently in dramatic circumstances. While it appears, indeed, that the presence of English law in the social field of Muslim divorce in Britain exercises pressure in the direction of conciliation and mutual agreement, and thus of *mubaraat*, this is by no means the norm.

9-228 In social reality this means that if a Muslim husband in Britain wishes to divorce his wife, he could still pronounce *talaq* and could then behave as though the couple was instantly and effectively divorced. Of course, this does not mean that the couple is divorced under English law. However, once a Muslim husband has given *talaq* to his wife, she, as a good Muslim, would be under considerable pressure to sign the special procedure affidavit in English law to the effect that her marriage had broken down irretrievably and that she agreed to be divorced. As a Muslim wife, she really has no other option. In this way, the latent conflict between English law and *shariat* would not become known. If, as we have seen in previous sections of this Chapter, it is not possible for a Muslim wife to refuse to accept the husband's divorce, how could English law help her to maintain the marriage? We do not know the answer, since such cases, if they have arisen, have not been reported. However, going by the case law under the hardship provisions of section 5 of the Matrimonial Causes Act 1973, which has mainly involved Hindu spouses,[87] a Muslim wife in this situation would probably find no help from English law at all.

9-229 Thus, after the divorcing couple have sorted out their affairs according to *shariat*, they may very well follow the procedure for English divorces, although by that time there is, in a social sense, no marriage left to dissolve. In other words, *angrezi shariat* on divorce actually uses the formal English divorce proceedings to rubberstamp the more informal *shariat* procedures. The proceedings of English law are being used, therefore, to legalise and formalise, in a sense to 'perfect' the Muslim process of divorce. Recourse to this strategy has been facilitated by the increasingly informal nature of English divorce law itself. To save money, court hearings for divorce cases exist now only in contested cases, which are not even 2 per cent of the total any more. Almost 99 per cent of all divorces in English law now go through what is called the 'special procedure' or a 'quickie divorce', which counts as 'judicial proceedings' but is in fact almost entirely an administrative process. If both spouses

---

[87] On this see, for example, Poulter (1986), pp. 105–106.

file affidavits to the effect that their marriage has irretrievably broken down, and if all matters of custody and finances are certified to have been sorted out, then a judge will, without any hearing, pronounce decree *nisi* and ultimately decree absolute in open court. Even this is no longer necessary today, as English law has developed methods to further decrease judicial involvement to save resources.

9–230 It is today fairly easy and probably more convenient for a divorcing Muslim couple in Britain to behave as though their divorce was agreed or uncontested, so that it can be officially processed as a 'quickie' divorce. This may well be the case irrespective of whether a Muslim husband has given or is planning to give the *talaq*, or whether a Muslim wife asks for a divorce through the courts. Most Muslim spouses seem well aware now that English law is not interested in taking cognisance of the 'foreign' element, and it suits English law, too, to retain an outwardly colour-blind and religiously neutral position.

9–231 The problem remains, of course, that the official legal process of an English divorce is not perceived to be able to dissolve the Muslim marriage as well. If a Muslim husband has already pronounced the *talaq*, then there will be no need for any further action after the English divorce decree. But if the husband has not given the talaq, and is in fact withholding it, and it was the wife who asked for the divorce, as seems to be increasingly the case, then there are two ways, under *angrezi shariat*, to handle this. In the simpler of the two scenarios, the husband gives the *talaq* at some point during the process of the English divorce. English law does not really show any concern about this and would not take any notice of the parallel divorce. However, when the husband refuses to give a *talaq*, although he may have agreed to an English divorce, the wife may well be in some difficulty. A jealous or simply mischievous Muslim man might wish to withhold the *talaq* to prevent his wife from marrying somebody else. We have seen earlier in this chapter that such cases have arisen in Pakistan and have given rise there to *zina* prosecutions under the Hudood Ordinance 1979. As we saw, the English courts have reacted to this scenario, in Jewish cases of this kind, by issuing a decree that the husband must give the religious divorce to the wife, or he will be punished financially.[88] This has proved to be a viable strategy but it is not known at the moment how widely this is applied in divorce negotiations.

9–232 The invisibility of Muslim divorce cases under English law in this field is remarkable, given that divorce is such an important legal issue. While there was earlier a rich case law on recognition of overseas and/or extra-judicial divorces (Pearl (1986a), p. 67), it is highly significant that since the mid-1980s there does not appear to have been any reported case in English law involving Muslim spouses in either of these scenarios. Two reasons may be given for this. The official view is probably that the application of statute and precedent by English lawyers makes prolonged recourse to courts and complex legal arguments unnecessary.[89] This view is to the effect, therefore, that British Muslims have learnt the law, have assimilated to the domestic legal rules and probably welcome the simple procedures for divorce in English law. In the absence of ethnic monitoring, it is impossible to quantify such assumptions.

9–233 Equally powerful, however, and more convincing in view of social realities, is the second explanation for the invisibility of Muslim divorces in England, confirming that the negative approach of English law to *talaq* divorces generally and to the recognition of Muslim divorces executed in Britain, in particular, appears to have led to a gradual distancing, even a withdrawal of British Muslims from the

---

[88] See again *Brett v. Brett* [1969] 1 All E.R. 1007.
[89] It also seems unlikely that legal aid would be granted to pursue such matters.

official legal fora.[90] While there are no figures available, it is of course a fact that many Muslim couples living in the United Kingdom were not married under English law, either because they got married abroad, or because they simply had a Muslim *nikah* in Britain, but no official legal registration. Whatever the size of those populations, the apparent effect, over time, has been to render Muslim divorce in the United Kingdom more invisible because couples who are only married through a *nikah* will not need to, in fact cannot, go through the English system when it comes to divorce and couples with strong overseas connections, as we saw, can continue to use overseas laws for the purposes of divorce.

9-234   There is, however, growing evidence that unofficial Muslim dispute settlement fora in Britain have been getting busier with sorting out the loose ends of Muslim divorces in the United Kingdom itself. An important area of concern in this regard, as for Jewish couples, is the position of the 'chained spouse'. A Muslim wife may have managed to obtain a divorce from the English court by means of the uncontested procedures, but is still not considered divorced under Muslim law.[91] Thus, she feels that she cannot remarry under Muslim law, although she would be entitled to remarry under English law. We must turn, therefore, to the emerging evidence of such divorce arrangements among Muslims in Britain.

Informal Muslim dispute settlement of divorce

9-235   The official non-recognition of religious divorces has long been a matter of concern for religious minority leaders (see Ahsan (1995), p. 24). It appears, on the other hand, that there is less concern about the conflicts with Pakistani law, which have engaged the minds of so many English judges, lawyers and writers. We have already suggested that there is pressure towards the consensual *mubaraat* form of Muslim divorce in Britain, given that the mere presence of English law strengthens the hands of women in the bargaining over divorce settlements. However, where a Muslim husband remains unwilling to grant divorce to the wife, we return again to the concept of the *khul* divorce, given at the behest of the wife, who will need to seek some form of official support for her action if the husband proves unwilling to negotiate.

9-236   Given that in Britain the state would not tolerate the official presence of Muslim dispute settlement fora, the development of support mechanisms for 'chained' Muslim wives has taken place within the extra-legal sphere. It has been known for a long time that the effects of religious divorces performed in Britain by persons domiciled in England would need to be considered. Maidment (1974, p. 616) clearly emphasised in this regard:

> "The problem has unknown dimensions. Certainly religious Jews require a religious divorce in addition to a civil divorce granted by the English courts. It is possible that Moslems in immigrant communities from Pakistan and other countries would insist on religious rites to dissolve a marriage in the eyes of Islam. These religious divorces in this country are supervised by the relevant religious bodies. The question therefore is: what legal effect does English law give to these religious divorces performed in this country by persons domiciled here?"

[90] On the phenomenon of Muslim withdrawal from various state institutions, see Wahab (1989), pp. 19–20.
[91] Research on this particular issue is currently being conducted. The preliminary evidence is to the effect that many Muslim women feel very strongly bound in conscience to seek effective termination of their Muslim marriage before they remarry. Fear of accusations of *zina* may be a factor in this context.

A decade later, Pearl (1986a, p. 32) emphasised that conciliation within the family and the community is well understood amongst South Asian families and that a satisfactory solution achieved through these channels will often ensure that the wounds resulting from broken marriages will heal relatively quickly. However, where a Muslim husband continues to be uncooperative despite pressures from family, clan or community, or where a woman cannot rely on such informal support, recourse to formal dispute settlement processes outside the family or clan, but still within the Muslim community, may be necessary. Since, as Pearl (1986a, p. 32) emphasised, "proceedings in the English court will exacerbate the difficulties, and an imposed solution will be unacceptable to the cultural expectations of the parties," religious leaders faced considerable pressure to act and some enlightened leaders and active organisations appear to have taken up the challenge.

9–237   At present, there is not much published material on this topic, but the need to undertake specific research has begun to be recognised.[92] Nielsen (1992c, pp. 110–111) reported briefly on unpublished research in 1983–84 which appeared to indicate merely that the divorce rate among British Muslims may be very low. More recently, one particular organisation, the Muslim Law (Shariah) Council (U.K.), has received some scholarly attention and appears open to debate about the role of the Council, its functions, and its place in the construction of *angrezi shariat*. It has been said that conflict resolution is "an area in which we have made some progress" (Badawi (1995), p. 77), and it has transpired that assisting Muslim women in obtaining a divorce from an obstinate husband, apart from inheritance issues, has become a major focal point of concern:

> "A common problem was that you get a woman seeking a divorce in the courts and obtaining it. She becomes therefore eligible for marriage in accordance with the civil law, but her husband has not given her a *talaq* which is the prerogative of the husband within an ordinary contract of marriage, so the woman becomes unmarried according to the civil law but still married according to the Sharia law. The man could remarry according to the civil law and according to Sharia law as well, since it is open to him to have a polygamous marriage and he is quite happy. He leaves the woman hanging there, unable to remarry, because in conscience she does not want to challenge the law of Islam because she is a committed Muslim or because she is frightened as a Muslim from doing so. Also socially, she does not want to lose face and honour in her community by marrying someone else when she is still married in the eyes of God." (Badawi (1995), pp. 77–78.)

Dr Badawi recounts how he and other leaders sought to devise a resolution to such problems "without breaking either the Sharia or the law" (Badawi (1995), p. 78). The strategy chosen, namely to constitute a kind of Arbitration Council, an informal body of 'arbiters' who can negotiate a way out of this impasse without any official legal sanction but clearly with the backing of traditional Muslim concepts of extra-judicial dispute settlement, seems to have worked well and has attracted a steady flow of applications from women seeking to extricate themselves from a broken marriage with the help of the Council. By now, the Council has standard procedures, forms and certificates to fill in, a fixed fee of £50 and a take-up rate of well over 50 cases a year.[93] There are apparently several other organisations of this kind involved in divorce matters.

---

[92] As indicated in the previous note above, important research in this field is currently being conducted, supported by the Nuffield Foundation.
[93] This figure comes from a document produced by the Council itself which simply gives statistics of the number of divorce cases per year. Carroll (1997a), p. 115, reports that the Council has dealt with as many as 1,150 cases since 1982.

9–238 Dr Badawi also reports that the Council has become established as an expert body of consultants for courts and other organisations and refers in this context to the case of a man seeking to withhold *mahr* from his wife who was prevailed upon to recognise this right of the wife under Muslim law.[94] Other commentators have not been so positive. Carroll (1997, p. 98) perceives what she calls "a disturbing reaction on the part of what might best be termed the spokesmen of Muslim male interests" and goes on to claim that Muslim women in England appear to be blackmailed into giving up financial entitlements as a result of the intervention of informal Muslim bodies. Carroll (1997a, pp. 105–106) suggests that a Pakistani woman wishing to ensure that she is also divorced in accordance with Islamic concepts should merely send relevant documents to Pakistan and register the divorce under the provisions of section 8 of the MFLO. However, there are two problems to this approach. First, just as men (and women) in Pakistan do not appreciate the need for formal registration of divorces, as we clearly saw in the various sections of paragraphs 9–39—9–204, above, British Muslims are not at ease with paperwork and formal court procedures when it comes to divorce and prefer to make informal extra-judicial arrangements. Secondly, English law has maintained its negative approach to any form of transnational divorce arrangement.

9–239 This explains to some extent why and how the various Islamic Councils in Britain appear to have come into the picture as helpful intermediaries, fulfilling a socio-legal need within a large and important community which the official state law and modernity-focused scholars remain unwilling to recognise. If the Beth-Din, on which some of the Muslim organisations appear to be modelled, has been functioning for so long and has achieved such a well-recognised position, there is no need for hostility to informal Muslim groupings along similar lines. It is a fact that Muslim religious leaders themselves have recognised that there are certain legal problems arising in the various Muslim communities which require action. It does not seem a useful starting point for a discussion of Muslim divorce in Britain to make allegations of heavy-handed attitudes to Muslim wives (see however Carroll (1997a)). That there will be struggles over financial entitlements and economic resources is almost inevitable at the point of divorce. As we have seen, the English legal approach to Muslim divorces is not beyond criticism either and it would appear to be eminently desirable that new research should be conducted.

---

[94] Badawi (1995), p. 79. The reference to "dowry" here instead of "dower" is unfortunate and confusing.

Chapter 10

Parents and children

10–01 In this chapter we turn to various issues concerning the parent-child relationship. In particular, we consider questions of legitimacy (including brief coverage of adoption), custody and guardianship, as well as maintenance. Some of these are growth areas of legal concern today but it is important to mention at the outset that the problems arising out of the legal relationships of parent and child in Muslim law have historically been treated subsidiary, by and large, to the major issue of inheritance. Indeed, the law relating to parental rights over children and the legitimacy of children becomes a feature of litigation in many situations because of the overwhelming importance of inheritance (see below Chapter 11).

Legitimacy

10–02 Illegitimate birth is severely stigmatised in Muslim law, *inter alia*, because it threatens a dominant principle in traditional Muslim law, that of purity of the blood line through males.[1] Concern over legitimacy, as the institution of the *'idda* period confirms,[2] seeks to avoid confusion over paternity, but also reflects a desire to uphold proper sexual mores in society and to avoid illicit sexual relations (*zina*).

10–03 In Muslim law, the illegitimate child has no right to inherit property through the father and in the classical law, as well as in some 'Islamised' modern jurisdictions, the mother of an illegitimate child may well find herself subject to draconian punishments imposed or inflicted on those found guilty of *zina*. Thus, the difficult status of legitimacy in Islamic law has very important consequences for children and their parents, especially mothers.[3]

10–04 Legitimacy is established either by the birth of a child in a marriage which is valid (*sahih*) or irregular (*fasid*), but not in a void (*batil*) marriage or, alternatively, through the application of the doctrine of acknowledgement (*iqrar*).

Traditional law

10–05 Nasir (1990a, p. 156; 1990b, p. 107) emphasises that "the child's first right is to establish parentage, a right both of the child and the father" and also points out that regarding rights of inheritance, guardianship and maintenance, the interest of the child is deemed paramount to any other consideration (*id.*). This goes hand in hand with general provisions in Muslim law suggesting that "care of a foundling is a religious duty if there is any risk that the baby might otherwise die" (Nasir (1990a), p. 168; (1990b), p. 117).

10–06 In Muslim law, legitimacy by birth has been the main technique of confirming a child's legitimate status. The principle that marriage is the basis of relationship in the family has been reiterated in recent scholarly writing.[4] The

---

[1] Bharatiya (1996), p. 126 emphasises that "Muslim law is very harsh on illegitimacy, yet fairly liberal in the rules on legitimacy" and refers to concerns of sexual morality.
[2] See paras 6–02—6–40, above.
[3] For some details see Hodkinson (1984), pp. 308–309.
[4] See Ibrahim and Bakar (1980), p. 65 with reference to Qur'anic verses and modern Egyptian law.

general rule is therefore that a child born into a valid marriage is a legitimate child for all intents and purposes. Thus, "when the paternity of a child is established, its legitimacy is also established".[5] This right may commence *in utero* (Nasir (1990a), p. 156; (1990b), p. 107). Perhaps in order to escape the drastic consequences for individuals of being stigmatised as illegitimate, all the Sunni schools recognise gestation periods well beyond the medically proved maximum.[6] Thus Hanafi law concedes that there can be a gestation period of up to two years between the conception of the child and its birth. Hanbali, Shafi'i and the consensus of the Maliki jurists extend this period to four years, and there is a divergent opinion in Maliki law that would even extend this period to five years. Nasir (1990a, p. 158; 1990b, p. 109) confirms the existence of such divergent opinions but concludes that "in practice it has been laid down as one lunar year".

10–07 Conversely, there is also a minimum period of gestation, which in this case is accepted by all the schools, that a child born less than six months from the date of the marriage will be illegitimate.[7] If the child is born after six months from the marriage, the legitimacy of the child cannot be rebutted either by proof that there was no physical access between the parties or indeed even by proof that the marriage had never been consummated. Interesting questions can arise with regard to whether one calculates the pregnancy term from the time of the contract of marriage, or of its consummation.[8]

10–08 Bharatiya (1996, p. 128) draws a distinction between 'legitimacy' and 'legitimation' and argues, specifically in view of the disapproval of adoption, that "there is no *legitimation* in Islam". However, confirmation of paternity by a child's father is possible under Muslim law in certain circumstances and the doctrine of acknowledgement (*iqrar*) can be used to establish legitimacy, but only when real paternity is possible.[9] Thus the acknowledged child must be at least 12 years and six months younger than the acknowledgor (Bharatiya (1996), p. 138). This represents the minimum period of gestation added to the minimum age at puberty. A father can acknowledge paternity if the following three conditions are met: First, the child is of unknown paternity; secondly, there is no definite proof that the child is the offspring of an illicit liaison (*zina*); and thirdly, there can be no rebuttal of the presumption of paternity of another by this acknowledgement. These principles are clearly rules of substance, which led to interesting debates in Indian and Pakistani law (see paragraph 10–11, below).

10–09 Apart from denial (see Nasir (1990a), p. 159; (1990b), p. 110) there is only one method available to a husband to challenge the legitimacy of a child born to his wife and to disown his own paternity, namely the doctrine of imprecation, leading to divorce through *lian*, which involves a judicial procedure.[10] Where the husband challenges the legitimacy of a child of the wife by an affirmation that the wife was adulterous, this amounts in Hanafi law to a permanent divorce.[11] The husband swears four oaths that the child is not his child. He then invokes the curse of Allah if he has sworn falsely. After the oath-taking by the husband, the wife can confess to the adultery or deny her guilt, herself swearing four oaths as to her

---

[5] Mannan (1990), p. 469. *ibid.*, pp. 468–480 contains a useful chapter on this subject.
[6] Hodkinson (1984), p. 307 wrote that ". . . the Muslim law has been extremely generous in its presumptions as to the duration of gestation".
[7] See also Nasir (1990a), p. 157; (1990b), p. 108.
[8] For details see Nasir (1990a), pp. 158–159; (1990b), pp. 109–110.
[9] For details on this see Nasir (1990a), p. 163; (1990b), p. 113 and Mannan (1990), pp. 473–475.
[10] On this see, with examples from several modern jurisdictions, Nasir (1990a), pp. 159–161; (1990b), pp. 110–111. For modern Pakistan, see Mannan (1990), pp. 460–462.
[11] For details see also Tayyibji (1968), pp. 184–188; Nasir (1990a), p. 113; Nasir (1990b), p. 70.

innocence and calling upon herself the curse of Allah if she is guilty. The procedure amounts to an irrevocable divorce.

10–10 In Egypt, in 1929, this procedure was placed on one side and modern notions of the proof of non-access were introduced in its place. Thus, the child will be illegitimate if it can be established that the union had never been consummated or that there was no access for more than one year from the last act of intercourse.[12] Nasir (1990a, pp. 159–161; 1990b, pp. 109–111) provides some detail of relevant legal provisions about legitimacy in several Middle Eastern and North African jurisdictions today.

South Asian law

10–11 The position on the Indian subcontinent is somewhat confusing, and the case law has been a little inconclusive, with clear distinctions today between Indian law on the one hand, and Pakistani and Bangladeshi law on the other. This is partly due to an old conflict between 'general law' and 'personal law' in this area (see already paragraphs 2–48—2–51, above). In brief, there has been a long-standing dispute over whether the relevant Muslim law rules relating to presumptions of legitimacy fall under the substantive law or under general rules of evidence. The early British law makers took the latter view and section 112 of the Indian Evidence Act 1872, which relates to presumptions of legitimacy when a child's birth takes place during a marriage, introduced the English law rule, providing:

> "The fact that any person was born during the continuance of a valid marriage between his mother and any man, or within 280 days after its dissolution, the mother remaining unmarried, shall be conclusive proof that he is the legitimate son of that man, unless it can be shown that the parties to the marriage had no access to each other at any time when he could have been begotten."

In Anglo-Indian law, the general position was therefore that section 112 abolished the Hanafi law relating to the presumption of legitimacy.[13] The opinion that the old Muslim law has been replaced clearly rests on the view that the Hanafi law in this area is an aspect of the procedural law of evidence, rather than of substantive Muslim law, and therefore it has been superseded by the secular, general law as codified in the Indian Evidence Act 1872.

10–12 However, this view has not been accepted in post-Independence Pakistani law, where further difficulties have arisen in relation to the Punjab Muslim Personal Law (Shariat) Application (Amendment) Act 1951.[14] Section 2 of that Act lists "legitimacy, or bastardy" among the matters to be governed by the

---

[12] Art. 15 of Law No. 25 of 1929 states that no disputed claim of paternity shall be heard regarding the child of a divorced or widowed woman who gave birth more than a year after her divorce or widowhood. Art. 17 of the same Law states that no claim of maintenance shall be heard in respect of an *'idda* period in excess of one year from the date of divorce, nor shall any disputed claim of inheritance on the grounds of marriage be heard regarding a divorced woman whose husband died more than a year after the date of the divorce. For details on modern Egyptian law see Ibrahim and Bakar (1980).

[13] In *Muhammad Allahdad Khan v. Muhammad Ismail Khan*, I.L.R. [1888] 10 Al. 289, the question whether s.112 supersedes the rules of Muslim law was left open. Other old Indian cases on this point held that s.112 supersedes the Muslim law. See *Sibt Muhammad v. Muhammad Hameed*, I.L.R. [1926] 48 Al. 625; *Rahim Bibi v. Chiragh Din*, A.I.R. 1930 Lah. 97; *Ghulam Mohy-Ud-Din Khan v. Khizar Hussain*, I.L.R. [1929] 10 Lah. 470; *Ismail Ahmed Peepadi v. Momin Bibi*, A.I.R. 1941 H.P.C. 11.

[14] Punjab Act 11 of 1951. This Act amends the Punjab Muslim Personal Law (Shariat) Application Act 1948, reinforcing the message that Muslims should be governed by the Muslim personal law rather than local customary laws.

Muslim personal law. Notwithstanding the provision in that Act, the general academic view was that the relevant Muslim law had not been reactivated by this provision, for the simple reason that it had earlier been classified as evidential rather than substantive (see the cases cited in note 13, above).

10–13   The Lahore High Court, in the important case of *Abdul Ghani v. Taleh Bibi*, 1962 P.L.D. (W.P.) Lah. 531, disagreed with this view. In this case, the central question before the court was whether the claimant was the legitimate child of Allah Bakhsh. If so, then she would be entitled to inherit. On the other hand, if she were illegitimate, she would have no claim to the inheritance. The claimant in this case was born within the first six months of her mother's marriage to Allah Bakhsh. The following table is reproduced from page 532 of the judgment:

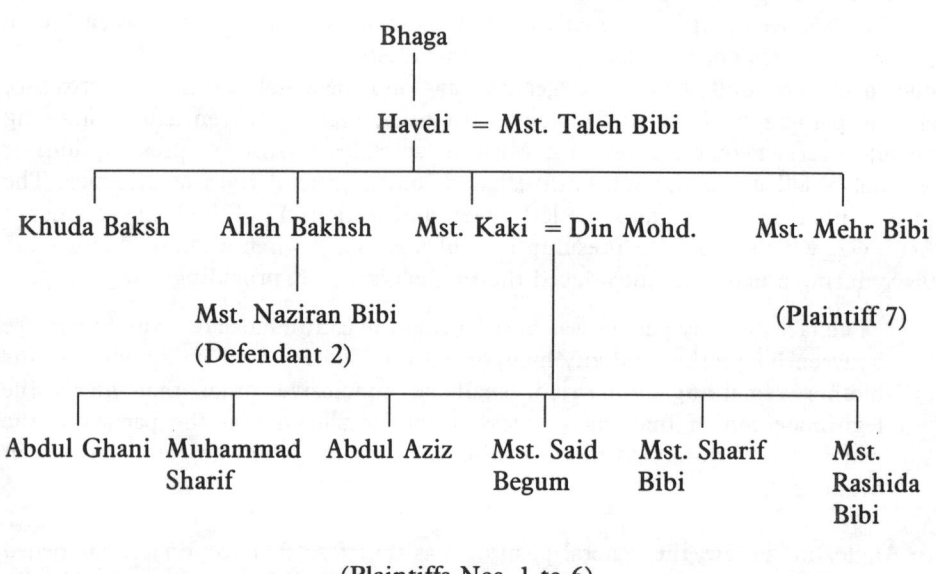

(Plaintiffs Nos. 1 to 6)

Taleh Bibi was the first defendant and Naziran Bibi was the second defendant in an action brought by Mehr Bibi and Abdul Ghani and the other five children of Mst. Kaki and Din Mohammed. The facts of the case were as follows. The land in dispute was owned by Allah Bakhsh who died in 1936 leaving his mother, Taleh Bibi, and a daughter, Naziran Bibi (who at that time was four years old) as his surviving heirs. The entire property was mutated into the name of the daughter as requested by Taleh Bibi, although the old lady continued to manage the land on behalf of her granddaughter. Some time afterwards, Taleh Bibi gave the land on lease to Din Mohammad, her son-in-law and the father of the first six plaintiffs. In 1953, the plaintiffs filed a suit to seek a declaration that they were the owners of the land in dispute. They alleged that Taleh Bibi was solely entitled to the land on the death of Allah Bakhsh, and that she had relinquished her right in their favour. They alleged further that Naziran Bibi was disentitled to any share in the property because she was born within six months of the date of marriage of her mother, Aishan Bibi, with Allah Bakhsh. Therefore, according to Muslim law, she was not the legitimate daughter of Allah Bakhsh. The suit was contested by Naziran Bibi, who claimed, *inter alia*, that she was the legitimate daughter of Allah Bakhsh and was therefore entitled to the land in dispute.

10–14 The trial judge at first instance had found that as Naziran Bibi was born during the marriage between her mother Aishan Bibi with Allah Bakhsh, albeit within six months of the marriage. Therefore, in accordance with the provisions of section 112 of the Evidence Act, she was presumed to be the legitimate daughter of Allah Bakhsh. The plaintiffs appealed against this, claiming that the trial judge was wrong in law to apply section 112 of the Evidence Act.

10–15 The complex argument accepted by the Lahore High Court in this case is as follows. First the rule of Muslim law in question is a rule of substantive law (see above). In Muslim law, as held by Masud Ahmad J. at page 541:

". . . if a child is born six months after the marriage of its parents, or within two years of the dissolution of the marriage, by death or divorce, it is considered to be the legitimate child of its father, unlike the rule of evidence in section 112 of the Evidence Act, under which only a presumption of legitimacy can be raised under certain circumstances."

The court went further and advanced the view that the decisions to the contrary in *Sibt Muhammad v. Muhammad, Hameed* I.L.R. [1926] 48 All 625, and other cases which state that the Muslim law is a rule of evidence, had been materially altered by the repeal of section 2 of the Evidence Act 1872.[15] This argument had found favour with, for instance, Kayani J., in *Ghulam Bhik v. Hussain Begum*,[16] but was not accepted by this court. In the opinion of the court in *Abdul Ghani v. Taleh Bibi*, even if the relevant Muslim law was a rule of evidence as opposed to substantive law, it was reactivated by the repeal of section 2 of the 1872 Act. Having held that the rule of Muslim law regarding legitimacy is a rule of substantive law, it was open for the court to apply Muslim law. It must be recalled that, according to Muslim law, if a child is born within the first six months of the date of the marriage of its mother, the child is deemed to be an illegitimate child, unless the man claims it to be legitimate. The court held, therefore, that Naziran Bibi could not be the legitimate daughter of Allah Bakhsh because she was born within six months of the marriage of her mother Aishan Bibi with Allah Bakhsh. She was not entitled, therefore, to the property in dispute, although at the end of the day the court concluded that because she had been in possession of the land for more than 12 years, she had become owner of the property in dispute by reason of adverse possession. The main interest of this complex case lies in the way in which the court classified the Muslim rule relating to legitimacy as a rule of substantive law.[17]

10–16 If the facts of this case were to come before an Indian court, the Indian court would certainly apply the Indian Evidence Act 1872 on the basis of the old argument that the rule of Muslim law is a rule of evidence and thus has been superseded by the codified Indian evidence law.

10–17 In *Abdul Rahimankutty v. Aysha Beevi*, A.I.R. 1960 Ker. 101, the facts were such that intricate legal argument was not necessary. A child had been born within four months of the marriage and the husband had driven the wife out of the home very soon after the marriage. It was held that concealment of pregnancy at the time of the marriage clearly amounted to fraud. No presumption under section 112 of the Evidence Act could be drawn that there was a valid marriage in this case.

---

[15] This is a highly technical argument, found at pp. 541–543 of the judgment.
[16] P.L.D. (1957) (W.P.) Lah. 998. This case does not appear to have been cited before the court in *Abdul Ghani*.
[17] The case was discussed by the Pakistani Supreme Court in *Hamida Begum v. Murad Begum* P.L.D. 1975 S.C. 624.

10–18   More recently, in the process of islamisation of laws, the Pakistani *Qanun-e-Shahadat Order* 1984 has modified section 112 of the old Evidence Act, which is now section 128 of the 1984 Ordinance.[18] This provides as follows:

> "128.   Birth during marriage is conclusive proof of legitimacy.
>
> (1)   The fact that any person was born during the continuance of a valid marriage between his mother and any man and not earlier than the expiration of six lunar months from the date of the marriage, or within two years after its dissolution, the mother remaining unmarried, shall be conclusive proof that he is the legitimate child of that man, unless –
>
> > (a)   the husband had refused, or refuses, to own the child; or
> >
> > (b)   the child was born after the expiration of six lunar months from the date on which the woman had accepted that the period of iddat had come to an end.
>
> (2)   Nothing contained in clause (1) shall apply to a non-Muslim if it is inconsistent with his faith.

These significant changes, part of the process of Pakistan's islamisation, re-introduce Muslim law rules of evidence, apply the position developed in the case law, as well as making an appropriate saving clause for the non-Muslim citizens of Pakistan.

10–19   In the Indian and Pakistani context, the rules on acknowledgement (*iqrar*) have not been affected by the Indian Evidence Act 1872.[19] The leading case on this matter is *Muhammad Allahdad Khan v. Muhammad Ismail Khan*, I.L.R. [1888] 10 Al. 289.[20] The parties in this case were Sunni Muslims. Muhammad Allahdad Khan and his alienee Mst. Hakim-un-Nissa brought a suit against Muhammad Ismail Khan, his three sisters, and others, for a declaration of right to and possession of two shares in villages left by one Ghulam Ghaus Khan, who was the father of Muhammad Ismail Khan and his three sisters. Muhammad Allahdad Khan asserted that he was the eldest son of Ghulam Ghaus Khan; thus he was entitled to shares in the estate in accordance with the Islamic laws of inheritance. In reply, Ismail Khan and the three sisters contended that Allahdad Khan was no more than a step-son of Ghulam Ghaus. According to Muhammad Allahdad Khan, even if he failed to prove that he was the full son of Ghulam Ghaus, nonetheless Ghulam Ghaus had *acknowledged* him as his child, which gave him the status of a legitimate child. The latter argument found favour with Mahmood J. who decided this case. A child born of illicit sexual relations (*zina*) can never be legitimated and is barred from inheriting from the father. Illegitimacy, in those circumstances, is a proved and established fact, and no amount of acknowledgement of the child can change the situation. Put the other way round, there must be "a reasonable presumption of paternity" (page 294), so that "the essential condition of this mode of filiation is that the person to be filiated must not be known to be the son of a person other than the acknowledgor" (page 293). Mahmood J., at page 328, came to the firm conclusion that "acknowledgement of parentage . . . is in effect a rule of *personal status* in the eye of Muhammadan law" and expressed the rule on acknowledgement in the following manner at page 335:

---

[18] For some detail see Mehdi (1994), p. 148.

[19] For Indian law, see in detail Mahmood (1982a), pp. 150–158; Diwan and Diwan (1991), pp. 106–114.

[20] Mannan (1990), p. 475, confirms that this case was followed throughout the subcontinent and was later approved by the Privy Council in *Sadik Husain Khan v. Hashim Ali Khan* [1916] 43 L.R. I.A. 212.

". . . the doctrine applies only to cases of uncertainty as to legitimacy, and in such cases acknowledgment has its effect, but that effect always proceeds upon the assumption of a lawful union between the parents of an acknowledged child. This is abundantly clear from the authorities . . ."

On the basis of the facts in *Muhammad Allahdad Khan*, Mahmood J. was able to hold that the case presented all the conditions to which the law of acknowledgement is most appropriately applicable. Thus, Allahdad Khan could inherit together with his brother and three sisters.

10–20 Another important case on this subject is *Habibur Rahman Chowdhury v. Altaf Ali Chowdhury*, [1920–1921] 48 L.R. I.A. 114. In this case, the plaintiff submitted before the court that he was the son of one Nawab Sobhan of Bagba by the second wife, a Mozelle Cohen. He said that his mother was a Jewess who had converted to Islam. The respondent, the Nawab's grandson, denied the claim of Habibur to any share in the Nawab's estate and argued that Habibur was the illegitimate son of the Nawab and Mozelle Cohen. There were therefore three interlinked questions. First, did Mozelle Cohen marry the Nawab? Secondly, if so, was Habibur the legitimate son of the Nawab and Mozelle? Thirdly, was there an acknowledgement? The Judicial Committee of the Privy Council discussed the plaintiff's contentions but found that there was no proof whatsoever of a marriage between Mozelle and the Nawab. Thus, Habibur was held to be illegitimate and no amount of acknowledgement could make him legitimate.

10–21 Pakistani cases reflect the negative attitude of *shari'a* law to illegitimacy and demonstrate that the courts have generally been very reluctant to stigmatise children as illegitimate.[21] In the important Pakistani case of *Hamida Begum v. Murad Begum*, P.L.D. 1975 S.C. 624, it was common ground that Hamida Begum had been born during the subsistence of the marriage between her mother and Mehar Din. The reasoning of the court was as follows: The shortest period of gestation is six months. If therefore a child is born within six lunar months of the marriage, then no affiliation is permitted unless the husband acknowledges the child to be his. The case suggests that it is the right of the husband to legitimate a child born within the first six months of the marriage. Anwarul Haq J. summarised the legal position under Muslim law at pages 651–652 as follows:

"Under the Muhammadan law, as in all civilised systems of law, the child follows the bed (*firash*), that is, the paternity of the child born in lawful wedlock is presumed to be in the husband of the mother without any acknowledgement or affirmation of parentage on his part and such child follows the status of the father. According to the Sunni schools the presumption of legitimacy is so strong that in cases where a child is born after six months from the date of marriage and within two years after dissolution of the marital contract, either by the death of the husband or by divorce, a simple denial of paternity on the part of the husband would not take away the status of legitimacy from the child. Of course, presumption based on the bed is subject to the right of disavowal on the part of the husband for want of access. This right has to be exercised in accordance with the custom of the locality either on the day of the child's birth or at the time of purchasing articles necessary in view of its birth or during the period of rejoicing. If the husband is absent, he must disown the child immediately he is informed of its birth."

---

[21] For details, with case references, see Mannan (1990), p. 476. In *Kausar Iqbal v. Mahmooda Akhtar*, 1989 S.C.M.R. 674, Saad Saood Jan J. granted leave to appeal to the Supreme Court because in the case before him there was a risk of four children becoming illegitimate.

Accordingly, following lengthy examination of evidence, the court held that the plaintiff would be presumed to be a legitimate child. This judgment adopts a different approach from that taken in *Abdul Ghani*, P.L.D. 1962 (W.P.) Lah. 531. More recent decisions in Pakistan, too, show that courts are protective of the interests of children and are therefore increasingly willing to take social objectives into account rather than emphasising the more technical aspects arising from the substantive/procedural debates of earlier cases. The decision in *Chuhar v. Ghulam Fatima*, P.L.D. 1984 Lah. 234, a succession case concerning validity of an unnotified divorce as well as legitimacy of a child, confirms that modern Pakistani law leans in favour of legitimacy to achieve desirable social welfare objectives. In Indian law, too, cases on legitimacy among Muslims arise from time to time because of the temptation to challenge the legitimacy of a rival claimant for succession.[22]

10–22   We indicated briefly above that the challenge to the legitimacy of a child by a husband's imprecation (*lian*) amounts to a permanent divorce. This procedure has been introduced into Pakistani law by section 14 of the Offence of Qazf (Enforcement of Hudood) Ordinance 1979 which provides as follows:

"14. Lian.
   (1) When a husband accuses before a Court his wife who is 'muhsan'[23] within the meaning of section 5, of 'zina' and the wife does not accept the accusation as true, the following procedure of 'lian' shall apply, namely:
      (a) the husband shall say upon oath before the Court: "I swear by Allah the Almighty and say I am surely truthful in my accusation of 'zina' against my wife (name of wife)" and, after he has said so four times, he shall say: "Allah's curse be upon me if I am a 'liar' in my accusation of 'zina' against my wife (name of wife)"; and
      (b) the wife shall, in reply to the husband's statement made in accordance with clause (a) say upon oath before the Court: "I swear by Allah the Almighty that my husband is surely a 'liar' in his accusation of 'zina' against me", and after she has said so four times, she shall say: "Allah's wrath be upon me if he is truthful in his accusation of 'zina' against me".
   (2) When the procedure specified in sub-section (1) has been completed, the Court shall pass an order dissolving the marriage between the husband and wife, which shall operate as a decree for dissolution of marriage and no appeal shall lie against it.
   (3) Where the husband or the wife refuses to go through the procedure specified in sub-section (1), he or, as the case may be, she shall be imprisoned until:
      (a) in the case of the husband, he has agreed to go through the aforesaid procedure; or
      (b) in the case of the wife, she has either agreed to go through the aforesaid procedure or accepted the husband's accusation as true.

---

[22] For some examples of cases see Mahmood (1982a), p. 155. A good illustration is provided in *Syed Amanullah Hussain v. Rajamma*, A.I.R. 1977 A.P. 152.
[23] A *muhsan* in this context is a woman who has consummated a marriage.

(4) A wife who has accepted the husband's accusation as true shall be awarded the punishment for the offence of 'zina' liable to 'hadd' under the imposition of 'hudood' for the Offence of Zina Ordinance 1979."

Subject to a number of conditions, the punishment laid down in sections 5, 6 and 17 of the Ordinance is stoning to death in a public place.[24] It should be noted that no such punishment has been carried out to date on the orders of a court in Pakistan, however, the threat of such drastic penalties looms over all Pakistani women who may be accused of having given birth to an illegitimate child (see in detail Mehdi (1994)). Only recently has a sensible and enlightened decision by Dr Ghous Mohammed J. in the Sindh High Court voiced powerful reservations about the tendency to criminalise women in such situations.[25]

Muslim legitimacy in English law today

10–23 Interestingly, threats to the physical safety of women in Pakistan in connection with accusations of unchastity and the birth of illegitimate children have recently become a matter of considerable concern in English asylum cases. In *R. v. IAT and Secretary of State for the Home Department ex p. Syeda Khatoon Shah* [1997] Imm.A.R. 145, the basic facts were stated at page 146:

"The applicant, a citizen of Pakistan, was a battered wife. She had been brought up partly in the United Kingdom but had returned to Pakistan at 17 in order to marry. She and her husband had six children, all of whom are being brought up by the extended family. Her husband, after years of violence, had finally driven her out of her home. On arrival in the United Kingdom she found that she was pregnant. She had given birth and now credibly fears that if she has to return she will be accused by him of conceiving the child adulterously, exposing her to the operation of the Shariah statute which prescribes stoning to death as the punishment for adultery. If returned to Pakistan she would have nowhere but her husband's house to go."

The special adjudicator had dismissed the woman's claim for asylum, giving as one of the reasons, as stated at page 147, "that since 1988 no individual has been punished by the authorities by the use of the death penalty for adultery". The woman herself had claimed (*id.*):

"I will face problems in Pakistan and may be arrested under Sharia Laws of Pakistan on the charge of giving birth to a child which my former husband would deny the legitimacy."

Accordingly, Mrs Shah's case had been first that she was a battered Pakistani wife, then that she belonged to the group of Pakistani women "who are perceived to have transgressed Islamic mores" (page 148) and finally that her relevant group was "women rejected by their husbands on the ground of alleged adultery" (*id.*). While the severity of the threat to Mrs Shah's physical safety was almost self-evident, the case ultimately turned on the technical point of the definition of 'social group' under the 1951 Refugee Convention. Sedley J. in the High Court decided that

---

[24] A similar procedure to that in Pakistan was earlier introduced into Libyan law by Art. VIII of Law No. 52 of 1973. For details see Mayer [1980] 28 *The American Journal of Comparative Law* 287 at p. 311.
[25] See *Rani v. The State*, P.L.D. 1996 Kar. 316.

Mrs Shah's case fell under the Convention, but the Court of Appeal later came to the opposite conclusion.[26] In various forms, this scenario has repeated itself in a number of unreported cases.

10–24   Apart from such matters of asylum law, it would be surprising if there was no concern among Muslims living in Western countries about questions of legitimacy and illegitimacy. However, in common with other sex-related topics, there are powerful taboos about discussing such topics publicly and litigation will be kept to a minimum for reasons of confidentiality and status (*izzat*). This does not mean that within the community, and in the more secluded realm of extended families, such conflicts are not dealt with. One recent study of Pakistanis in Britain (Choudry (1996)) emphasises the ambivalent role of status and honour (*izzat*) for Pakistani women and shows links between the suspicions of husbands about chastity, or unchastity, as the case may be, to the level of domestic violence. Neither the recent collection of Articles by writers concerned about Muslims in Britain (King (1995)) nor earlier law-related studies (Pearl (1986a)) discuss questions regarding legitimacy in any detail.[27] Concern about such issues is generally subsumed under the rubric of 'conflicts of values and traditions'. It may well be that bodies like the Shariat Council have some experience in deciding or settling complex questions, but only further research will enlighten us on this point.

Adoption

10–25   Traditional Muslim law does not appear to allow formal adoption because it refuses to accept the legal fiction which an adoption creates, namely that an adopted child can become equal to a blood relative of the adopting father. On the other hand, in view of social facts and circumstances, various devices have been used in Muslim law to take account of the welfare of orphaned or otherwise destitute children, and of the interests of childless couples, who may seek to treat such a child as their own.

10–26   Nasir ((1990a), p. 166; (1990b), p. 115) emphasises that "adoption was widespread among the Arabs before Islam, and remained valid during the early days of Islam until it was prohibited". Bharatiya (1996, p. 125) writes to the same effect and suggests that the Prophet himself adopted a young man but was later criticised for this. This episode is also referred to by Hodkinson (1984, p. 309), with further details about why adoption is not permissible in Muslim law. Sura XXXIII, verses 4–5 and 37 of the Qur'an oppose the pre-Islamic custom of adoption whereby an adopted child could be assimilated in a legal sense into another family.[28] The legal fiction of adoption, in the sense that it creates paternity where no actual bloodlink exists, is therefore not allowed in Muslim law. It can be suggested, however, that the acknowledgement of paternity of a person of unknown origin amounts, in a way, to a form of adoption (Schacht (1964), p. 166). There are some Muslim scholars who argue that the relevant verses of Sura XXXIII do not actually prohibit adoption, but merely classify it into the category of acts known as *mubah* – acts towards which religion is indifferent.

10–27   Such arguments have not found favour with the legislators in most Muslim countries and, by and large, there is no law of adoption in the Muslim

---

[26] *Secretary of State for the Home Department v. Syeda Khatoon Shah* [1997] Imm.A.R. 584. The case is, at the time of writing, awaiting a hearing before the House of Lords.

[27] Pearl (1986a), pp. 48–49 briefly considers the status of the child in a polygamous marriage.

[28] For details see Nasir (1990a), p. 157; (1990b), p. 107–108.

world.[29] This is also a major reason why many Muslim countries have made reservations regarding various Articles in the International Convention on the Rights of the Child of 1989.[30] As far as domestic Muslim law in North Africa and the Middle East is concerned, Nasir (1990a, p. 157) refers specifically to Moroccan law which declares adoption null and void but recognises that a person may treat another as his child for the purposes of passing on property. Adoption has, however, been introduced into Somalia's codified Muslim law by Articles 110–116 of the Family Law 1975. Under this typically reformist law, adoption is however restricted to cases where the parents are unknown, which appears to be a social welfare measure serving the interests of abandoned children.[31] As several authors confirm, adoption has also become part of Tunisian law as a result of legal reforms brought about by Act No. 28 in 1958, and with clear social objectives in mind.[32] Undoubtedly, reformers in many Muslim countries feel that a legal transfer of responsibility for children in certain cases through a process similar to adoption serves an essential social function for destitute children and often also for childless couples. *De facto* arrangements exist as a result of custom across the Muslim world, and such cases may give rise to legal disputes. Whether legislative changes in this area can be expected in the future remains a matter of speculation.

10–28 In South Asian laws, as Bharatiya (1996, pp. 138–139) outlines, adoptions among Muslims have been legally possible in certain circumstances.[33] Hodkinson (1984, p. 309) rightly points out that attempts in India to introduce a statutory regime for adoptions have failed.[34]

10–29 In Pakistan, the official view, strengthened by Islamisation ideology, is of course that adoptions are not permitted in Islam.[35] The law of adoption was discussed by the Pakistani Supreme Court in *Sher Afzal v. Shamim Firdaus*, P.L.D. 1980 S.C. 228, where in the context of a dispute relating to the validity of a marriage and the legitimacy of the offspring, the Supreme Court, at page 266, found that "the plea of adoption is totally misconceived because it is well known that there is no institution of adoption in Islamic Law". However, as Mannan (1990, p. 480) and other writers confirm, a special family or tribal custom of adoption, if proved, will prevail in certain circumstances.

10–30 In the United Kingdom, lack of detailed knowledge about Muslim law has underpinned the stereotype that Muslims do not know any form of adoption. Certainly, statements by the Pakistani Ministry of Foreign Affairs to the effect "that adoption is not known under Muslim law" have been accepted by immigration

---

[29] For examples of legislation prohibiting adoption see Nasir (1990a), p. 166–167; (1990b), p. 116.

[30] This was adopted by the U.N. General Assembly on November 20, 1989 and came into force on September 2, 1990. Over 150 countries are parties to this Convention. Many Muslim countries have entered general reservations regarding all provisions of the Convention that are seen as incompatible with the Islamic *shari'a* and, often, relevant local legislation. Several countries, *e.g.* Bangladesh, Egypt, Indonesia, Jordan and Kuwait have expressed reservations regarding Art. 21 on adoption. See pearl (1998.)

[31] For details see Mahmood (1982b), esp. p. 263, where the author describes the Somali provisions for adoption as "the most remarkable provisions found in the family-law chapter".

[32] See *id.* and Nasir (1990a), pp. 166–167; (1990b), p. 116.

[33] *Mohd. Ismail v. Noor-ud-Din*, A.I.R. 1986 J. & K. 14 treats adoption as a matter of fact and confirms that it is recognised among certain groups of Muslims by custom.

[34] See also Mahmood (1982a), p. 148. It must be emphasised here that this failure relates to creating a uniform adoption law for all citizens. For details see in particular Dhagamwar, *Towards the uniform civil code* (1989). Indian adoption laws, especially for Hindus and Sikhs, are quite well-developed under the Hindu personal law and through some important recent cases, several of which concerned overseas adoptions of Indian children.

[35] Thus, Mannan (1990), p. 480 comments merely that "the Mahomedan law does not recognize adoption as a mode of filiation" and refers to a number of cases, including *Muhammad Allahdad Khan v. Muhammad Ismail Khan*, I.L.R. [1888] 10 Al. 289, at 340.

adjudicators and tribunals in England to deny entry to young persons who were alleged to have been adopted under Pakistani law by their sponsors settled in the United Kingdom.[36] A recent British study on immigration and adoption refers specifically to *de facto* adoptions.[37]

10-31 For Canada, it has been reported that immigration visas for adopted children are being turned down on the ground that Muslim law does not permit adoption. In this context, S. M. Ali ((1994), pp. 203–204) explains that,

> "as far as the *true spirit*, charitable purpose and humanitarianism of adoption in the Muslim and Canadian legal context is concerned, the *de facto* practice of Muslim adoption is the same as Canadian adoption. In effect, the only main difference between the Muslim and Canadian system of adoption concerns the adopted child's legal capacity to inherit from the intestate adopting parents. The Canadian law allows the adopted child to inherit from his adoptive parents and not from his biological parents, whereas the Muslim would permit the adopted child, even after adoption, to inherit from his biological parents but not from automatically the adoptive parents or guardian."

Regarding Muslims in Britain, not much can be said about adoptions at this stage and research is needed to ascertain details in this particular field. Given that social services departments in the United Kingdom have developed specific policies, mainly directed against inter-racial adoptions, one finds indications, mainly through relevant advertisements in the ethnic minority press, that Muslim adopters are actively being sought for children who have a Muslim background or one of whose birth parents is a Muslim.[38] From the perspective of the Muslim community, too, helping such children to grow up as Muslims and in agreeable circumstances will be seen as desirable, so that there is growing pressure to find Muslim adoptive parents, or at least foster parents who are Muslims. It is evident, however, that not enough Muslim couples are coming forward to satisfy the considerable demand, undoubtedly a reflection of traditional and religious reservations against adoption among Muslims living in the West today.

Custody

The traditional concerns and provisions

10-32 Muslim law makes a basic distinction between custody and guardianship. Custody has more to do with practical matters, such as care and control of the child and therefore the rights and obligations of mothers and persons who might take their place, while guardianship centres on the legal rights and obligations of the child's father and his representatives. Bharatiya (1996, p. 141) sees it as an element of "foresightedness that in an essentially patriarchal society, they could lay down

---

[36] For details see Pearl (1986a), pp. 92–93 with reference to the earlier Immigration Appeal Tribunal cases of *Rafiq v. Secretary of State for the Home Department* [1972] Imm.A.R. 167, *Malik v. Secretary of State for the Home Department* [1972] Imm.A.R. 37 and *Tohur Ali v. Entry Clearance Officer, Dacca* [1985] Imm.A.R. 33. For more recent developments in this field, leading to the legal recognition of *de facto* adoptions among Bangladeshi Muslims, see *R. v. Immigration Appeal Tribunal, ex p. Tohur Ali* [1987] Imm.A.R. 189 and especially *Immigration Appeal Tribunal v. Tohur Ali* [1988] Imm.A.R. 237, which contains a detailed discussion of adoption.

[37] For details see Mortimore, Claudia (1994): *Immigration and adoption*, esp. pp. 48–51.

[38] Thus the *Asian Times*, a weekly paper from London, regularly publishes local authority advertisements offering young children for adoption, including Muslim children, for whom Muslim foster parents or adoptive parents are sought.

that the custody of children of tender years belonged to the mother". Hodkinson (1984, p. 311) summed up the position by saying that "in the classical Hanafi law the custody of the child is first vested in the mother as the person best fitted to administering to the child's needs and to release the father for work".

10–33 At the same time, while there is much concern about the respective legal position of the adults, within the context of a patriarchal society, the best interests of the child are an important matter of concern in such rules. Indeed, Nasir (1990a, p. 173; 1990b, p. 121) emphasises that in Muslim law "custody is an established right for the baby from the time of its birth" and differentiates three different types of guardianship, confirming thereby that the terms 'custody' and 'guardianship' are not neatly distinguished at all times.[39]

10–34 Nasir (1990b, p. 170) also emphasises that in Muslim law a child has a right to be brought up, "which imposes a duty on the father, namely maintenance, and another on the mother, namely fosterage and custody until the end of infancy".[40] Custody is defined as the caring for the infant during the period when it is in many ways dependent on women and their services for the child (Nasir (1990a), p. 173; (1990b), p. 122). From that follows the agreement of all school traditions, Sunni and Shia alike, "that the mother, whether she is separated or living with her husband, has the first claim to the custody of her infant" (Nasir (1990a), pp. 173–174; (1990b), p. 122). If a mother is unable or unwilling to take custody of the young child, the general principle is either that a close female relative of the mother, first of all the mother's mother, takes charge, or this obligation passes to the child's paternal female relatives, or indeed the father, who would then need to identify a suitable female carer for the child. It appears that the different schools of Muslim jurisprudence differ widely on the person to whom custody of the child should pass when the mother is dead or disqualified in some form.[41]

10–35 Not surprisingly, there are also different opinions about when the period of a child's custody comes to an end.[42] In all schools of traditional Islamic law, the mother of a child has the primary responsibility for care and control of the child for the first few years of the child's life. In Hanafi law, the prevailing opinion is that the mother retains the right of custody until age seven for boys and age nine for girls (Nasir (1990a) p. 188). The ages in Maliki law when mothers lose the right of care and control are puberty for boys and marriage for girls (Nasir (1990a), p. 187; (1990b), p. 134). In Hanbali law, the relevant ages are seven years for both boys and girls and, interestingly, the child is then given a choice between either parent (*id.*). Shafi'i law lays down no fixed limits; on the attainment of discretion, the child is given the opportunity to decide which parent to live with (*id.*). In Ithna 'Ashari law, however, the period of custody is only two years for boys and seven years for girls.

10–36 The traditional rules about age limits in custody cases are unimportant in an undivided family where the husband and wife live together. In a divided family, however, problems are bound to occur. In cases of conflict, the general rule is

---

[39] Nasir (1990a), p. 173; (1990b), p. 122 distinguishes in essence (a) guardianship during the early years of the infant's life, in other words custody, then (b) guardianship of education and (c) guardianship of property.

[40] The same quote in Nasir (1990b), p. 119 emphasises the mother's duty to suckle the child, a topic to which the author gives considerable attention. A balanced outline of the various competing considerations is given by Schleifer (1986), pp. 75–81.

[41] See in detail Nasir (1990a), pp. 174–178; (1990b), pp. 122–126, with many examples from modern jurisdictions in the Middle East and North Africa. In the Shi'i law of the Ithna Ashari school, in the mother's absence, priority in custody is given to the father, and failing him, to the paternal grandfather.

[42] On this topic see in detail Nasir (1990a), pp. 187–189; (1990b), pp. 133–136.

clearly that the father, who has rights over the child as the guardian (*wali*), retains the overall rights and indeed powers of guardianship. However, this right of the father must be seen in perspective, since especially the older child has been given a voice in such matters. As we saw, this is a principle coming from the Hanbali and Shafi'i school traditions, matching closely with the concept of the 'best interests of the child'.

10–37 At the same time, there are certain situations in a Muslim state where the *Qadi* may well consider it necessary to remove the child from the care of the mother. In particular the carer must be sane, trustworthy and of good morals. The classical law based upon *hadith* is that the right to custody will be lost when the mother or other custodian marries a man who is not related to the child within the prohibited degrees. While remarriage of the mother is one critical point, there is also much evidence of concern over female carers who are not Muslim.[43]

10–38 The Shafi'i rule, with its in-built flexibility, has been adopted as part of the reform movements in some Muslim countries. For instance, Egyptian law now provides:

> "The female's right to custody of the child shall come to an end on the boy reaching the age of 10 and the girl reaching the end of 12 years. The judge may grant females the custody of the boy who has reached seven years of age until he is nine, and of the girl who has reached nine years of age until she is 11, should their interests so require."[44]

Sudanese law extended this departure from Hanafi law, in 1932, to enable the mother to keep custody up to puberty for boys, or marriage for girls. In 1953, Syrian law provided the general rule that "custody shall come to an end for the boy on completing nine and for the girl on completing eleven years of age" (Nasir (1990a), p. 188) but also ruled that "if a wife deserts her husband, and her children are more than five years old, the Qadi may place them with whichever of the spouses he sees fit, provided he has regard to the welfare of the children". Similar provisions have been enacted in Tunisia (1957), Iraq (1961) and Algeria (1984).[45] Several articles of the Somali Family Law of 1975 also illustrate the flexible Shafi'i approach in statutory form (Mahmood (1982b), pp. 260–261).

Custody law in South Asia

10–39 There are some indications that the fine distinctions between custody and guardianship in traditional Muslim law were not appreciated by the early colonial administrators in the subcontinent (Bharatiya (1996), p. 141). This lack of clarity seems also reflected in the fact that many textbooks do not contain separate sections on 'custody' and cover the subject under 'guardianship'.[46] Mannan (1990, p. 485) confirms that Pakistani law follows the traditional position but makes a notable comment at pages 485–486:

> "The mother's custody is subordinate custody and is subject to the control of the father, who is deemed to have the real 'custody' within the meaning of the Guardians and Wards Act."

---

[43] For some details see Nasir (1990a), pp 180–181. The non-Muslim mother is also a prominent theme in Schleifer (1986).

[44] This is Art. 20 of Act No. 25 of (1929), as amended by Act No. 100 of 1985 and cited in Nasir (1990a), pp. 189; (1990b), p. 135. For details on Egyptian law see also Ibrahim and Bakar (1980).

[45] Details of these provisions are cited in Nasir (1990a), pp. 188–189; (1990b), pp. 135–136.

[46] For Pakistan, the most detailed coverage of the subject is now found in Balchin (1994), pp. 137–252, with an immensely useful long section summarising the recent case law.

Notwithstanding such indications of the overriding claims of male guardians, a general observation about custody law for Muslim children in India and Pakistan is that the age limits of custody for young children, especially girls, appear to have been gradually extended, for girls to the onset of puberty – which may well be later than the traditional limit of nine years. The father who retains rights as guardian (*wali*) of the child will then assume custodial powers, a subject especially relevant in South Asia with regard to guardianship in marriage.

10–40 The most important development in this field, for academic analysis as well as legal practice, is the way in which traditional Muslim assumptions about the respective rights and duties of the parents and the principle of the best interests of the child have interacted in the South Asian social field.[47] As we saw in paragraph 10–32, above, this interaction itself is not new, and is now also observed in Middle Eastern laws, as Nasir's study illustrates in many ways. However, in certain cases it appears necessary to assert the principle of the best interests of a child against powerful assertions of patriarchal and religious interests.[48] In this respect, children continue to have a weak lobby in South Asian laws, although this appears to be changing gradually.

10–41 South Asian textbooks and courts have upheld the principle that the welfare of a young child is best taken care of by giving custody to the mother, unless she is unsuitable (see in detail Balchin (1994), pp. 158–162). The nature and extent of the mother's right to custody were authoritatively discussed by the Privy Council in *Imambandi v. Mutsaddi*.[49] If a mother ceases to be the wife of the child's father, she does not thereby automatically lose custody.[50] However, if such a woman then remarries, it is likely that she will lose custody of her children to the former husband, based on the argument that the child's father remains the guardian of the person of the child.[51] Some writers suggest that such a rule remains subject to the principle of the best interests of the child.[52] Abid (1993, p. 259) confirms this and seems to go further:

> "The Islamic law, however, does not lay down that a woman who has married a stranger to the minor is disqualified from being appointed a guardian under any circumstances. It merely lays down that such a woman loses any preferential right which she had by virtue of her relationship to the minor, but if no other suitable guardian is forthcoming, the Court is not bound to follow the personal law, and she can be appointed."

This is well in line with the same author's argument, at page 258, that "it is the personal Law that should guide, subject only to the welfare of the minor". This key issue, again a matter of the relationship between personal law and general law, is raised in a very interesting way by the Guardians and Wards Act 1890 which appears to preserve the personal law despite being a family law enactment which applies to all religious communities in South Asia. In all three jurisdictions of the Indian subcontinent with which we are concerned here, section 17 of the Guardians

---

[47] For a good overview on the various factors influencing courts see *ibid.*, pp. 145–146.

[48] In this respect, *ibid.*, p. 155, highlights the fact that local patriarchal notions operate in favour of male claims and tend to override the general Islamic rules in practice.

[49] [1918] 45 L.R. I.A. 73. For details see also Fyzee (1974), pp. 198–199; Bharatiya (1996), p. 144.

[50] This was held in *Rashida Begum v. Shahab Din*, P.L.D. 1960 (W.P.) Lah. 1142.

[51] Of course, the basic principle of Muslim law, stated above, that the woman will lose custody if her new husband is not within the prohibited degrees is also applied here. This relates to prohibitions connected to incest. For details see Fyzee (1974), pp. 199–200 and in particular Bharatiya (1996), p. 145.

[52] For details see Bharatiya (1996), p. 145; Balchin (1994), pp. 168–169.

and Wards Act 1890 sets out the procedure for applications for appointments of guardians,[53] providing as follows:

> "17. Matters to be considered by the Court in appointing guardian.
>
> (1) In appointing or declaring the guardian of a minor, the court shall, subject to the provisions of this section, be guided by what, consistently with the law to which the minor is subject, appears in the circumstances to be for the welfare of the minor.
>
> (2) In considering what will be for the welfare of the minor, the Court shall have regard to the age, sex and religion of the minor, the character and capacity of the proposed guardian and his nearness of kin to the minor, the wishes, if any, of a deceased parent, and any existing or previous relations of the proposed guardian with the minor or his property.
>
> (3) If a minor is old enough to form an intelligent preference, the Court may consider that preference.
>
> (4) As between the parents who are European British subjects adversely claiming the guardianship of the person, neither parent is entitled to it as of right, but other things being equal, if the minor is a male of tender years or a female, the minor should be given to the mother, and if the minor is a male of an age to require education and preparation for labour and business, then to the father.
>
> (5) The Court shall not appoint or declare any person to be a guardian against his will."

10–42 A distinction must be drawn between the provisions of section 17 and of section 7 of the same Act, which regulates the power of the Court to make an order as to guardianship and provides explicitly in section 7(1) that the court must be satisfied "that it is for the welfare of the minor" that an order should be made. In this section, therefore, all that the court has to take account of is the welfare of the minor, while the respective personal law of the parties does not appear to be relevant. In section 17 cases, however, where an adult is being removed or appointed as guardian, the personal law is clearly of considerable importance. The distinction between the two provisions is apparent from *Rashida Begum v. Shahab Din*, P.L.D. 1960 (W.P.) Lah. 1142.[54]

10–43 In Pakistan the courts have, to some extent, developed a presumption that the minor's welfare lies in granting custody in accordance with the personal laws of the minor. Mahmud J. said in *Atia Waris v. Sultan Ahmad Khan*, P.L.D. 1959 (W.P.) Lah. 205, at page 214:

> "In considering the welfare the Court must presume initially that the minor's welfare lies in giving custody according to the dictates of the rules of personal law, but if circumstances clearly point that his or her welfare dominantly lies elsewhere or that it would be against his or her interest, the Court must act according to the demand of the welfare of the minor, keeping in mind any positive prohibitions of personal law."

---

[53] It will be noted that the language of the Act does not draw a neat distinction between 'custody' and 'guardianship' either. This observation is confirmed by Kaikaus J. in *Niaz Bi v. Fazal Ilahi*, P.L.D. 1953 Lah. 442 at 444.

[54] This case has been criticised by Fyzee (1974), p. 199 for introducing what he calls "irrelevant considerations regarding the Koran and traditions".

In this case, following the death of her husband, a widow wanted to leave her parents-in-law and wanted to take the young child with her. This was refused by the family, and ultimately by the court. Custody was given to the paternal grandparents to ensure that the minor child was brought up as a Muslim, despite the positive rule of Muslim law which states that if the mother is found unsuitable to have the custody of her female child, the right of custody devolves on the maternal grandmother.

10–44 Sometimes it is difficult to decide which law is the personal law and this may be raised as a preliminary question. An example of this problem is found in *Mosselle Gubbay v. Ahmad Said*, P.L.D. 1957 (W.P.) Kar. 50. Two children were born to Mosselle and her husband Ahmad when they lived together in Calcutta. It appears that the parties contracted a Muslim marriage in Calcutta in 1943 at a time when both parties were Muslim, although Mosselle's parents were both Jewish. In 1954, the marriage was terminated as a result of a petition brought by Mosselle, presumably under the provisions of the DMMA 1939. Custody of the young children was given to the mother. The husband, however, kidnapped the children and took them to Karachi in Pakistan. Following this early case of international child abduction, contempt proceedings against Ahmad were drawn up in the Calcutta High Court and he was sentenced *in absentia* and committed to prison. Mosselle then travelled to Pakistan, instituted a criminal prosecution under section 368 of the Pakistan Penal Code and, in addition, filed a petition for a writ of *habeas corpus* praying that the two children be brought before the court and dealt with according to law. Although the petition was not filed under the Guardians and Wards Act 1890, the principles applied by the court relate to the jurisdiction under that Act. The court held, at page 52, that it was "improper to give the custody of the two Muslim children to a Jewess mother who is an Indian national and is residing in India" and thus swiftly dismissed the mother's petition.

10–45 The preliminary problem regarding the personal law was not actually raised by the court, probably because this case involved an Indian national only 10 years after the painful separation of British India. In Jewish law, children are presumed to follow the religion of the mother. In Muslim law, the children are presumed to follow the religion of the father.[55] In Pakistan, the personal law governing the father is certainly applied on grounds of public policy. In the present case, the Pakistani court simply claimed jurisdiction over the future of the children and did not consider the possible views from the perspective of Indian law.

10–46 Another Pakistani case, *Grace Abdul Hadi Haqani v. Abdul Hadi Haqani*, P.L.D. 1961 (W.P.) Kar. 296, illustrates the problem of the selection of the personal law of the child for the purposes of the Guardians and Wards Act. The father of the child in question had married Grace Rodrigues, a Muslim convert, according to Muslim rites. Notwithstanding her conversion to Islam, however, the mother continued to attend church. In 1955, a female child was born to the couple. Soon afterwards, the father was court-martialled for an offence under the Official Secrets Act and was convicted and sentenced to three years of rigorous imprisonment. Before the conviction, the parents signed a joint statement whereby they gave an undertaking that they would provide a Catholic education for their child. After the undertaking was signed, the child was baptised. While the husband was in prison, the wife commenced an affair with another man and left the matrimonial home to

---

[55] On this see also *Atia Waris v. Sultan Ahmad Khan*, P.L.D. 1959 (W.P.) Lah. 205 at 215: "Under the law, the minor must be presumed to have the father's religion and corresponding civil and social status". This principle has also given rise to many reservations by Muslim states regarding the International Convention on the Rights of the Child of 1989.

live with this man. As soon as Mr Haqani was released from prison, he filed an application, with his mother as co-petitioner, under the terms of the Guardians and Wards Act 1890 for custody of the child. The first question was to ascertain the personal law of the child. Faruqui J. held that despite the baptism the child was a Muslim governed by the Muslim law and stated, at page 300: "The minor was born a Muslim and the fact of her baptisement, particularly in the circumstances in which it took place, does not change her religion unless after coming of age she chooses to do so".[56]

10–47   In the result, the judge held that it was in the interests of the welfare of the child and consistent with her personal law, to be brought up as a Muslim. Custody was given, therefore, jointly to the father and the paternal grandmother. If the personal law of the child had been applied exclusively, the mother would have had custody until the child attained puberty. If she were unsuitable, the right of custody would have devolved on the maternal grandmother.

10–48   Substantive Muslim law, as applied in the subcontinent, lays down that apostasy from Islam is a sufficient ground for taking custody of infant children away from the mother, or of depriving a father of custody.[57] The Caste Disabilities Removal Act 1850, which refers to deprivation of "right or property", established the statutory choice of law rule which ensures that apostasy itself is not a sufficient reason for denying the rights of the mother or of the father.[58] The three cases discussed above, *Atia Waris v. Sultan Ahmad Khan*, *Mosselle Gubbay v. Ahmad Said* and *Grace Abdul Hadi Haqani v. Abdul Hadi Haqani*, however, illustrate that in Pakistan the principle of the Caste Disabilities Removal Act 1850 is treated as subsidiary to the overriding rule of the general welfare of the child.[59]

10–49   As we saw in paragraph 10–32, above, the classical law based upon *hadith* is that the right to custody will be lost when the mother or other custodian marries a man who is not related to the child within the prohibited degrees. This rule was followed in Pakistan in *Muhammad Bashir v. Ghulam Fatima*, P.L.D. 1953 Lah. 73, where, in response to the suggestion that the case before him should be decided without reference to the rules of Muslim law, Kaikaus J. said, at page 78:

> "This argument is based on a misconception of the provisions of Muhammadan Law. All rules of Muhammadan Law relating to the guardianship and custody of the minor are merely the application of the principle of benefit of the minor to diverse circumstances. Welfare of the minor remains the dominant consideration and the rules only try to give effect to what is [the] minor's welfare from the Muslim point of view."

In this case, the father had not paid any maintenance for the child but claimed her custody as soon as the mother married another man. Kaikaus J. found that this was his right and proceeded, comparing the financial means of the parents, to argue that the best interests of this child lay with her father. The judge said, at page 82 : "If

---

[56] On a similar question with reference to Indian Christians, see *Emperor v. Maha Ram*, I.L.R. [1918] 40 Al. 393.

[57] For some details see Bharatiya (1996), p. 149; Balchin (1994), pp. 172–175.

[58] See *Muchoo v. Arzoon Sahoo* [1866] 5 W.R. 235 and *In Re Muhammad Alam Md. Ibrahim*, A.I.R. 1939 Sindh 311. But *In the Matter of Mahin Bibi* [1874] 13 *Bengal Law Reports* 160, where the father's consent as guardian to his daughter's marriage was considered, it was held that because the father had renounced Islam and re-embraced his former faith, Judaism, consent by him to the marriage of his minor daughter was not necessary; the consent of the Muslim mother was sufficient.

[59] In Pakistan, the 1850 Act was a little later amended by the Caste Disabilities Removal (West Pakistan Amendment) Act 1963 to the effect that nothing in the 1850 Act shall apply to the rights of inheritance to the property of a Muslim. While this is not directly relevant to questions of custody and guardianship, this is further evidence for the weakened status of this old and peripheral 1850 Act.

the minor lives with her father there is a far better chance of her getting a suitable husband than if she stays with her mother". Accordingly, the judge ruled that the father must deposit Rs. 10,000/- in the name of the minor, and allow all reasonable facilities to the mother for seeing the child. As stated at page 82, "this is necessary not only on account of the right of the mother but in the minor's interest for she should not be absolutely deprived of the company of her mother". The judgment was concluded by saying that if the husband did not abide by the conditions or acted in any way to the detriment of the child, then it would be open to the mother to reapply to the court. The judge certainly envisaged cases when the classical law would be departed from.

10-50 The rationale for the departure from the strict letter of the traditional law is contained in another case from Lahore, *Fahmida Begum v. Habib Ahmad*, P.L.D. 1968 Lah. 1112. Here, the father of the three children in question had married another woman and had several children with her. He had not maintained his children from the first marriage, who had been brought up exclusively by their mother and were well-educated young people by the time this matter went on appeal. The judge was well aware of the custody rules of the personal law but, having taken statements from the three young people concerned, who all confirmed their desire to stay with their mother, he proceeded to act in the best interests of the children rather than to adhere to the personal law rules. The judge in that case summarised the conclusion of a Full Bench in the earlier decision of *Zohra Begum v. Latif Ahmad Munawwar*, P.L.D. 1965 (W.P.) Lah. 695 and stated, at page 1115:

> ". . . it is permissible for Courts of law to differ from the rules of Hizanat stated in the text-books of Muslim Law since there was no Quranic or Traditional Text on the point and Courts which have taken the place of Qazis can, therefore, come to their own conclusions by process of Ijtihad . . . Therefore it would be permissible to depart from the rules stated therein if on the facts of a given case its application is against the welfare of the minor."

In the present case, the judge did not doubt where the best interests of the minors lay. An earlier example of a case where the rule of personal law was departed from is found in *Amar Ilahi v. Rashida Akhtar*, P.L.D. 1955 Lah. 412. In this case, it appears that the husband, in order to avoid his liability to maintain his minor daughter, and also to avoid paying the dower debt to his wife, gave up all claims to the custody of his daughter when she was very young and took no further interest in her until the time came to arrange for her marriage to someone of his choice. The court rejected the subsequent application made by the husband under the Guardians and Wards Act 1890 for an order that the child be returned to his custody. It was firmly held that the remarriage of the mother in this case did not prohibit her from being appointed both as the daughter's carer and as her guardian. This case, therefore, also confirms that a Muslim father who defaults on maintenance arrangements for a minor child runs the risk of forfeiting his traditional right to exercise guardianship functions.

10-51 The very recent case of *Shahzad Muhammad Siddiq v. Shahnaz Farzana*, 1997 M.L.D. 1026, concerned a fierce battle over custody of three young children, conducted under Article 199 of the Constitution of Pakistan 1973 as well as the relevant guardianship law. The father had lost his claim for custody of a young daughter (the other two children were already with the mother) but continued to appeal, bringing in complex constitutional arguments. In the Karachi High Court, Dr Ghous Muhammad J. stated, at page 1028, that the courts acting as parental court in guardianship matters "should avoid technicalities in administering justice". The learned judge saw that this was a case without merit and merely mentioned the Muslim law arguments of the father in passing (page 1028). Instead, attention was focused on contact arrangements for the young daughter, rather than disturbing her present living conditions. Without explicitly saying so, this case, too, is centrally concerned about the best interests of the child.

10–52 The above cases show that, depending on the facts and circumstances of the case, classical law rules have not been followed in Pakistani case law if this is seen not to operate in the best interests of the minor concerned. This can work both ways for the parents, therefore, and makes for interesting case law. In *Niaz Bi v. Fazal Ilahi*, P.L.D. 1953 Lah. 442, the judge very reluctantly gave custody of minor children to the father because of the mother's poor health, but ordered the man to afford the mother reasonable facilities for seeing the children once every 15 days. It was held, at page 446, that "ordinarily a female's right to custody cannot be defeated on the ground of want of funds to maintain the child", but in this case there were exceptional circumstances. In *Hurbai v. Usman*, P.L.D. 1963 (W.P.) Kar. 888, the dispute concerned, *inter alia*, custody of a young daughter. The wife in this case had been divorced and was forced to work in menial jobs, despite the fact that the girl's father was well-off. Anwarul Haq J. held, at page 890:

> "There is no doubt that compared to the father, the appellant is poor, and because of that very poverty she has to work. It is, however, clear to me that the mere fact that a mother is poor and has to work for her living can never be allowed to operate to deprive her of her right of custody of her minor children, to which she is entitled under the personal law applicable in the case. The rule of Muslim Law that the custody of a boy under seven years of age and of a girl under the age of puberty should remain with the mother is based on certain fundamental human considerations, namely that it is only a woman and a mother who can look after the needs of the child under the ages specified, and who can give that love, affection and guidance which are necessary for the proper development of the child. A mother can do all this even though she be poor. As regards the question of providing proper education for the girl, the responsibility clearly lies on the father who has to provide maintenance for his minor children, irrespective of the fact whether they stay with him or with the mother."

It was held, therefore, that the mother was entitled to custody of her young daughter and that it went to her credit that she was prepared to work even in menial jobs to make a living.

10–53 In *Tahera Begum v. Saleem Ahmed Siddiqui*, P.L.D. 1970 Kar. 619, the court refused to implement that part of a private compromise settlement between a divorcing husband and wife which related to the mother's agreement to give up custody of a young daughter. Here, too, the fact that the mother had no financial means of her own was noted, but the duty of the father to maintain his child was highlighted and custody was given to the mother.

10–54 In Indian cases on the same subject, it is quite evident that the secular basis of the Guardians and Wards Act 1890 and the general secular framework of modern legal adjudication in Indian law have contributed to an approach which favours the best interests of the child over any consideration of the personal law.[60]

---

[60] On the relevant Indian Muslim law, see in detail Mahmood (1982a), pp. 147–186. For Indian child law generally, see Jain and Loghani, *Child and the law* (1979); Diwan and Diwan, *Children and legal protection* (1994).

In *Hassan Bhat v. Ghulam Mohamad Bhat*, A.I.R. 1961 J.&K. 5, it was held that although section 17 of the 1890 Act provides that the court is to be guided by personal law, the words "subject to the provisions of this section" in sub-section (1) clearly indicate that the consideration of the welfare of the minor should be the paramount factor and cannot be subordinated to the personal law of the minor. Where the Court finds that due to a conflict of interests between the minor and the guardian, the interests of the minor cannot be looked after properly by a person who is a preferential guardian under the personal law, such a person cannot be appointed as a guardian under the Guardians and Wards Act. The court also commented on the value of the minor's opinion and held that, where a minor is not old enough to form an intelligent opinion of the matter, the court cannot take into consideration the stated preference of the minor herself.

10–55 *Imtiaz Bano v. Masood Ahmad Jafri*, A.I.R. 1979 Al. 25, was a constitutional petition involving a writ of habeas corpus and the custody of two minor sons. The husband had divorced the wife and had remarried, but tried to deny this. The judge noted, at page 26, that the parties are governed by the Hanafi Muslim law and that the mother had therefore a right to custody of her infant sons up to the age of seven years. Finding that the immediate welfare of the children is of primary consideration (page 28), custody of the children was given to the mother with immediate effect. It is interesting that the judge tried, without success, to ascertain the wishes of these two young boys. This judgment also makes pertinent comments on delays in judicial proceedings, very relevant when definite age limits for custody come into play. Further, Hussain J. referred to the risks for young children in being exposed to a step-mother (page 26).

10–56 In *Mohammad Shafi v. Shamin Banoo*, A.I.R. 1979 Bom. 156, a couple had three young children. When the marriage broke up and the husband married another woman, the wife was driven out and was allowed to keep only the third child, a small baby. The wife filed a petition under sections 7 and 25 of the Guardians and Wards Act 1890 for the return of the other two children to her. The husband's response was that the mother was unsuitable as a custodian and that he therefore had the right to custody under the Muslim personal law. Tulpule J. held, at page 163, that "even during the marriage the custody of the minor children in case of a boy until he attains the age of seven years, and in the case of a female until she attains puberty is with the wife". It was observed, in addition, that under the personal law, "the right of the father to the custody of the child is deferred, and the primary right is in the mother and in the absence of the mother in other female heirs" (*id.*). Therefore it was held, at page 165, that "the provisions of the personal law applicable to the parties stand superseded to the extent to which a provision is made and which is inconsistent or contrary to that personal law in the Guardians and Wards Act". Since the Muslim personal law itself accepted that a mother was the best person to take care of young children, there was no scope for arguing the technical point that the father's superior right to guardianship had the effect of ousting the mother from custody.

10–57 In *Khurshid Gauhar v. Siddiqunnisa*, A.I.R. 1986 All 314, the court examined the relevant Muslim personal law in detail and reiterated the principle that the mother is best suited for rearing small children.[61] This right is not lost by the mere fact that she has been divorced by the husband and is living away from the husband. In this respect it was held, at pages 318–319:

---

[61] This case is discussed approvingly and in some detail by Latifi, "Muslim Law", in *Annual Survey of Indian Law 1986* (1986), pp. 632–633. The author also raises the argument that mothers in such cases should be protected from character assassinations by the award of exemplary or punitive damages, in addition to costs.

> "We are here dealing with the case of a divorced wife. It is normal and natural for a divorced wife to reside separately and away from the husband and so long as it is not demonstrated that general supervision of the child to which the father is entitled as the natural guardian has not become impossible, in my opinion, the mother cannot be deprived of the right of Hizanat. Moreover, as has been repeatedly stressed in the conflict of rival claims put forward by the father and the mother in regard to the custody of a child of tender age based on their respective rights under the personal law, the interest of the child cannot be sacrificed. The overriding consideration in all such cases and in all circumstances is the interest of the child and all other claims of rival parents must be subordinated to it."

In *Abul Kalam v. Akhtari Bibi*, A.I.R. 1988 Ori. 279, a husband had divorced his wife and drove her away, keeping the very young son in his custody. He relied on the personal law argument that his former wife was of loose morals and thus unsuitable as a carer for the young child. The court made short thrift of the man's submission that the Guardians and Wards Act 1890 did not apply to Muslims (page 280). Relying on several Supreme Court cases, this High Court confirmed the general position in modern Indian law, holding at pages 280–281 that "it has been the consistent view of all courts that in respect of a child of tender age, the mother is more suitable to have the custody". In *Farjanabi v. Sk. Ayub Dadamiya*, A.I.R. 1989 Bom. 357, the Muslim law rule that the father is entitled to the custody of a son over seven years of age was noted and applied. However, this was done not in obedience to the personal law, but on consideration of the best interests of the two young boys concerned, who had actually expressed a preference for staying with the mother. It was held, at page 358:

> "There is, therefore, no good reason why the ordinary rule of Mohammedan Law should not be adhered to in the present case and it must, in the circumstances, prevail over the desire of the children."

It is not obvious from this very brief judgment why exactly the single judge felt that the best interests of the children were served by returning to their father against their expressed wish. The court might at least have explored the question whether a higher maintenance payment for the children could have taken better care of their needs. On the other hand, this is a judgment marked by social realism in a situation where the divorced mother could not even afford a home, let alone any formal education for the children, as the case report indicates.

10–58   Cases over custody continue to arise before Indian courts. In *Abdulsattar Husen Kudachikar v. Shahina Abdulsattar Kudachikar*, A.I.R. 1996 Bom. 134, there was actually no dispute over the principles of Muslim law or their applicability. The father had forcibly snatched the young son from the mother and she went to court seeking custody of the child. Both parents were earning well, which led the judge to comment, at page 136:

> "But for children of tender years, it is not money alone which matters. It is the natural love and affection and particularly, the care which the mother can take which is more important and which has no substitute."

The judge in this case made detailed reference to a number of recent Indian Supreme Court cases which all involved Hindu or Christian parties and reiterated the basic principle of the best interests of the child. The father had remarried, but the proposed arrangements for the care of the young boy were not found satisfactory by the court. It was held by Savant J., at page 138:

"Having regard to the above guidelines laid down by the Supreme Court, there is no doubt in my mind that in the facts of the present case the welfare of the child Mohd. Wasim is safer with the mother. The father has admitted that he has married a second wife. He has a touring job, leaving his only son from his first wife to the care of his second wife, in preference to the natural mother of the child, would not be in the best interest of the child. The child certainly needs the love and affection of his natural mother, who is anxious to bestow it upon her child."

Even the most recent cases show, however, that the principle of the best interests of the child can work either way and does not necessarily lead to an award of custody of a minor child to the mother. In *Rahima Khatoon v. Saburjanessa*, A.I.R. 1996 Gau. 33, a widowed mother of a young girl and her mother-in-law were contesting each other's claim to custody. The Assam High Court referred back to the old leading case of *Imambandi v. Mutsaddi*,[62] which had laid down the principle, *inter alia*, that a remarrying Muslim mother loses the right to custody of a minor child. Apparently, the court had also ascertained the wishes of the young girl concerned and must have found reasons, which are not discussed in this brief judgment, for coming to the conclusion that her welfare lay in staying with the deceased father's mother.

10–59 In Bangladesh, the same issues have been debated and the law has developed along similar lines. The leading case on how Bangladeshi law views custody matters is *Md. Abu Baker Siddique v. S. M. A. Bakar* [1986] B.L.D. 245 A.D.,[63] where the custody of a minor son with health problems was at issue. Here, too, the Court had no hesitation to state that the welfare of the minor child should be of paramount importance. The father alleged that the child's mother had been cruel, irresponsible and neglectful, but it was found as a fact that this lady, a doctor, had given up a well-paid job in Saudi Arabia to look after her son who required some medical treatment. Considering a number of earlier cases from the 1950s and 1960s, it was found, at page 248:

"Courts in all these cases, seem reluctant to give automatic effect to the rules of Hizanat enunciated by Islamic jurists. If circumstances existed which justified the deprivation of a party of the custody of his child to whose custody he was entitled under Muslim Law, courts did not hesitate to do so. Nevertheless [the] court's power to determine the entitlement of a party to the Hizanat is not limited to mere observance of [the] age rule so as to exclude the consideration of the interest of the child which would, however, depend on the facts and circumstances of a given case."

Fazle Munim C.J. also noted, at page 250, that the rules of custody differ from school to school and stated:

"This shows that there was no consensus among the jurists of these schools on the question of guardianship of minor children leaving scope for difference of opinion, there being no definite rule in the Quran or Sunnah on the matter."

---

[62] The citation given in the case is A.I.R. 1918 P.C. 11. We have earlier cited this case as reported in [1918] 45 L.R. I.A. 73.
[63] The case is also reported at 38 D.L.R. (1986) 106. This is an appeal to the Appellate Division of the Supreme Court of Bangladesh, the highest court in the land.

Taking the welfare of the minor as the overriding criterion, it was therefore held that custody of this young boy should be given to his mother.

10–60 A topic of relatively new provenance,[64] on which more research needs to be undertaken, concerns international child abduction. All South Asian jurisdictions have had to deal with this problem due to the large number of South Asians living overseas.[65] It appears that especially in cases where non-Muslim foreign mothers claim custody of children born to them from Pakistani Muslim men, the courts have earlier tended to favour the father.[66] Courts are thereby probably asserting the traditional principle that the child, irrespective of the religion of the mother, is subject to the same personal law and religion as the father.[67] More recently, however, there is evidence that foreign mothers have at least been able to get temporary custody of their children, pending the decision of the guardian court.[68]

10–61 In *Christine Brass v. Javed Iqbal*, P.L.D. 1981 Pesh. 110, a Canadian mother and a Pakistani father who was a medical practitioner fought over the custody of four young children, whom the father had abducted to Pakistan in February 1979. The mother had obtained a court order from a United States court and sought enforcement of that order in Pakistan through her petition to the High Court of Peshawar. It was held, in line with domestic cases, that the welfare of the child was the paramount consideration. Emphasising the father's rights under Muslim law, it was held that since the father was a Muslim and the children were now living with him in Pakistan, it would be in the best interests of the children that they should remain in the custody of the father.

10–62 *Sara Palmer v. Muhammad Aslam*, 1992 M.L.D. 520, involved a British mother and a Pakistani father with dual nationality. Three of the couple's five children were the subject of this custody dispute. The couple had been divorced in 1983 and the mother had custody of all the children, while the father had been given contact but had been told not to remove the children from England and Wales without the leave of the court. The father subsequently removed three of the children to Pakistan and the mother filed a habeas corpus petition in Pakistan under section 491 of the Criminal Procedure Code 1898 for the recovery and return of the three children. The court stated that Pakistan was a "non-convention country" and therefore there was no presumption of an automatic return (see below para. 10–68) and that the welfare of the minors was the main consideration. Relying on *Christine Brass*, it was held that full custody of the minors could not be given to the mother, since this would entitle her to remove the children from the jurisdiction of the Pakistani courts. While it was held that the father's removal of the children had been illegal, the mother was given temporary custody, but only within Pakistan.

10–63 In Bangladesh, two cases deserve some attention. In *Akter Jahan Tanzia alias Bab v. The State* [1986] B.L.D. 281, the mother of a girl of 10 years had remarried but had abducted her daughter from school and was now facing criminal proceedings. The court stated, at pages 282–283:

---

[64] But see *Mosselle Gubbay v. Ahmad Said* P.L.D. 1957 (W.P.) Kar. 50, discussed at p. 415, above.

[65] Indian cases have mainly concerned non-Muslim children and are not discussed here.

[66] This was the case in *Mosselle Gubbay v. Ahmad Said*, P.L.D. 1957 (W.P.) Kar. 50. More recent cases are *Christine Brass v. Javed Iqbal*, P.L.D. 1981 Pesh. 110 and *Sara Palmer v. Mohammad Aslam*, 1992 M.L.D. 520 discussed below.

[67] For details see Balchin (1994), pp. 153, 172–176. However, the author also points out that there are different views on this subject.

[68] *ibid.*, 174 refers in this context to the beneficial effect of s.491 of the Criminal Procedure Code 1898 in Pakistan, under which more child custody cases have recently been brought by foreign mothers. In such cases, temporary custody may be restored to the mother, but only within Pakistan.

"According to Mohammadan Law a mother is the legal guardian of her minor daughter until the girl attains the age of puberty and this legal guardianship of the mother continues even if she is divorced by the husband; but the guardianship is lost by operation of law as soon as she marries another person who is not related to the minor girl within the prohibited degree."

It was therefore held, at page 283, that the mother had no legal right to take away the daughter in the capacity of her guardian and her action had therefore been illegal and unauthorised. Concerning the question of punishment for the act of kidnapping under section 363 of the Penal Code, the court referred to the exception provided under section 361 of the Code. This is to the effect that if a person acted in good faith and believed to be entitled to the lawful custody of such a child, and no immoral purpose was contemplated, then no offence shall be deemed to have been committed. The proceedings against the mother were therefore quashed but custody of the minor girl was given to the father.

10–64 The more recent kidnapping case of *Sharon Laily Begum Jalil v. Abdul Jalil*, 48 D.L.R. (1996) 460 involved a young Bangladeshi mother born in Britain, who was married to a Bangladeshi man in England in 1984. The couple had four children, one of whom was still very young. Due to various complications, the husband turned violent and, in November 1993, he brought the wife and children to Bangladesh and left them there without passports. However, after some time, the father divorced the mother and the children were abducted from the mother's residence and taken to the father's paternal home. When the mother found that her local efforts to recover the children could not succeed, she returned to England and filed a suit for the recovery of the children in the Family Division of the High Court. In July 1995, the High Court made the children wards of the court and directed that they should be returned to the jurisdiction of the court. The mother then served a notice for return of the children in Bangladesh, but to no avail. Finally she filed a habeas corpus petition in Dhaka under Article 102(2)(b)(i) of the Constitution of Bangladesh. The father responded by pleading that it had not been considered to be in the best interests of the children to grow up in Britain and that the family had planned a future for them in Bangladesh. It was stated at page 462:

"Seeing the life style of the teen-aged children in London, specially their free mixing, immoral social life, spending time at night clubs, the petitioner, in consideration of the future welfare of the minors proposed to respondent No. 1 to take her and their children to Bangladesh to rear up them [*sic*] in Bangladeshi culture and education."

The father alleged, however, that the mother had been leading an immoral life in Dhaka while he was working in Britain and he therefore claimed custody of all the children. The court refused to go into details of the various pleadings and focused on the constitutional element of the case. It was held, at page 464, that under Muslim law it is abundantly clear that the mother is the custodian of young children up to a certain age. Custody of the three younger children was therefore given to the mother, while custody of the oldest child, a boy above the age of seven years, was given to the father. This decision clearly avoids a consideration of the international dimension of the case, which has been possible because the custody battle between the parents was ultimately centred on dispute settlement fora in Dhaka itself, despite the mother's earlier attempt to involve an English court. It remains to be seen how Bangladeshi courts would react if the mother was a non-Bangladeshi foreign citizen who is not a Muslim.

Custody law in Britain

10–65 There is little knowledge about issues affecting Muslim parents and children in relation to British courts and it does not appear that the courts have much experience of custody cases involving Muslim litigants. Pearl (1986a, pp. 87–88) refers in some detail to the somewhat unique case of *Alhaji Mohamed v. Knott* [1969] 1 Q.B. 1, much-discussed in its time. This concerned a young Muslim woman of Nigerian origin who had been married in Nigeria at the age of 13 and who was allegedly in danger of moral corruption. It was held, in a judgment reflecting Britain's liberal approach to ethnic minority legal issues at that time, that there was nothing abhorrent for Nigerians in that situation to be married at such an early age, and thus there was no reason for legal intervention, in terms of protecting the best interests of such a young girl, since she was a married woman.

10–66 Pearl (1986a, pp. 88–91) also refers to a few cases and some evidence of academic discussion relating to disputes involving custody of young Muslim children before English courts. It appears that a key issue in such cases is often the question of religious upbringing of the child, especially where the mother (as is often the case) is not a Muslim. In at least one case, *Jussa v. Jussa* [1972] 1 W.L.R. 881, the judge showed much awareness of the need for the children to grow up fully aware of their mixed inheritance. In this case, the father was a Muslim and the mother Christian. There were three young children, two boys and a girl. The mother had left the matrimonial home with the children and had obtained an order granting her sole custody. The father appealed against this. He admitted that the children should remain in the care and control of the mother but argued that either custody of the three children should have been given to him or no order for custody to the mother alone should have been made. In other words, he contended, as stated at page 883, "that there was no reason why a wholly unimpeachable father should be cut out from any form of guardianship of his children at all". The Family Court was happy to note that both parents admitted freely that the other was a good parent. In addition, the mixed inheritance of the children was highlighted at pages 885–886:

> ". . . this was a mixed marriage between a man of Oriental origin and a woman of European origin. The children, therefore, have a mixed inheritance . . . it is much in their interest to get the full value of that mixed inheritance. The father can contribute to them something which no European could do; the mother can contribute something that no Oriental could do. I feel myself it would be a great advantage to them that they should retain the closest possible contact with their father while remaining, of course, in the care and control of their mother."

In this spirit of multicultural tolerance, the father's appeal was therefore allowed and a joint custody order for both parents was made, with care and control given to the mother. Sir George Baker P. added at page 886 that for him, the most important question was what order would best promote the welfare of the infants. With reference to modern English child law, the overriding welfare principle as found earlier in section 1 of the Guardianship of Infants Act 1925 is now restated in section 1 of the Children Act 1989.[69] Another relevant provision in English law is likely to be section 11 of the new Family Law Act 1996, which requires divorcing parents to make sure that any arrangements regarding their children are agreed and are acceptable in terms of the Children Act 1989.

---

[69] For some relevant details see, *e.g.* Hoggett *et al.*, *The family, law and society. Cases and materials* (1996), pp. 532–551.

10–67 We have already seen that in situations of custody disputes, cases of international child abduction do occur, reflecting elements of self-help rather than adherence to the letter of a particular national law. This is also an area of the law in which research with specific reference to Muslims is needed. In *Re S (minors (abduction)* [1994] 1 F.L.R. 297, is an interesting Court of Appeal case which involved Pakistani Muslim parents.[70] The couple were both born in Pakistan, had married in Britain but had then moved to Pakistan. There were three children and at some point, without the father's knowledge or consent, the mother brought the two younger children to Britain. The father applied for an order for their return to Pakistan, which was granted. The mother's appeal in the Court of Appeal was not successful and it was held that in view of the facts, it was in the best interests of these children to be returned to Pakistan, to allow the courts of their own country to decide what would be in their best interests.

10–68 In the international field, the 1983 Hague Convention on the Civil Aspects of International Child Abduction and the European Convention on Recognition and Enforcement of Decisions Concerning Custody of Children, signed in Luxembourg in May 1980, are designed to enable contracting states ('convention countries') to work together to bring about the speedy return of abducted children.[71] However, by January 1, 1997, no Muslim country had become party to either of the two Conventions. This means that in cases of abduction to a 'non-convention' country, the home country of the child concerned has to rely on its domestic law alone and the remedies are extremely limited. We have already seen that in such cases a parent may need to take legal action in the respective overseas courts to secure return of the children. As far as Britain is concerned, there is some evidence, especially from advice agencies such as Reunite, that a large number of child abductions involve Muslim children. The Child Abduction Act 1984 makes child abduction a criminal offence, while the Child Abduction and Custody Act 1985 brought the two international conventions mentioned above into force for English law.

Guardianship

The traditional position

10–69 We have already seen that although the mother is the custodian of young children, the supervisory right of guardianship remains with the father. Apart from guardianship over the young person, which somewhat coincides with custody, there are two types of guardianship, guardianship over property and guardianship in marriage, which is also sometimes referred to as guardianship of the person.[72]

10–70 Nasir (1990a, pp. 205–217) treats guardianship of property quite briefly, with useful references to a number of Muslim jurisdictions in the Middle East and North Africa.[73] Again, this author stresses the element of duty (at page 205). Discussing the concept of guardianship in Muslim law, Bharatiya (1996b, p. 140 *et seq.*) points out that the Qur'an itself is replete with statements about the topic,

---

[70] For some excerpts, see also *ibid.*, pp. 696–698.

[71] See in detail Evans, *International families and the law* (1988). Hoggett *et al.* (1996), pp. 688–700 gives a useful brief summary.

[72] The latter continues to be of relevance in a patriarchal setting where local customs and Islamic concepts work together to strengthen male claims for authority over the movements of women. See in this regard the recent *Saima* case in Lahore, on which, see now Lau (1997).

[73] The subject is not covered in Nasir (1990b), confirming that guardianship of property falls to some extent under property law rather than family law.

reflecting much concern about corrupt pre-Islamic practices, which led to the detriment of orphaned children, in particular.[74] Muslim law, therefore, seeks to protect the interests of the minor against the guardian and places many restrictions on the guardian's authority and powers, especially with regard to the minor's property (Bharatiya (1996), p. 141). This confirms again that becoming a guardian is treated in Muslim law more as a duty towards the ward than as a right.

10–71   The father is the natural guardian of his legitimate children. No formal appointment by any authority is necessary for a competent person to act as guardian (Bharatiya (1996), p. 141). Next to the father, an executor appointed by the father's will is to act as guardian, before the father's father.[75] If the father is dead and there is no appointed testator, guardianship of the minor's person and property shifts to the grandfather, and in his absence to the brother.[76] This shows that, in contrast to custody, guardianship rights have been given to the agnatic line. A testamentary guardian is someone appointed as guardian by the natural father through a testament or will. Bharatiya (1996, p. 143) affirms in this context that the mother can become a testamentary guardian on certain conditions.

10–72   Hodkinson (1984, p. 313) emphasises that "the Muslim law severely restricts the guardian's powers over the property of the child" and gives several examples.[77] Nasir (1990a, p. 214) comments on the strict rules regarding qualifications of the guardian, highlighting for example that a spendthrift father should not be acting as a guardian of his ward's property. Such rules clearly serve the major purpose of safeguarding the financial interest of the minor, protecting it from misappropriation. Accordingly, various modern Muslim laws are, as Nasir (1990a, pp. 214–217) shows, quite strict in their treatment of the rights of guardians. Court-appointed guardians may act in situations where no natural guardian is available and no testamentary guardian has been appointed. In Muslim law, this power of appointment rested with the *Qadi*, but that power has been abrogated in South Asian laws by the Guardians and Wards Act 1890.

South Asian laws on guardianship

10–73   South Asian legal textbooks reiterate the Muslim law principles regarding the rights of guardians and the restrictions on their powers. For example, Balchin (1994, p. 182) summarises the conditions under which a guardian may alienate the minor's immovable property.

10–74   South Asian courts have upheld the principle that after the father's death, guardianship falls on the father's executor, next the paternal grandfather, and then the paternal grandfather's executor. The guardian stands in a fiduciary relationship to his ward. Only in the most exceptional circumstances, when it is in the best interests of the child, will the court allow a guardian to buy or sell a ward's property.[78] On guardianship over property, the leading case is *Imambandi v. Mutsaddi*, [1917–1918] 45 L.R. I.A. 73, where it was held by the Privy Council that the legal powers of a guardian are subject to strict conditions as to immovable property. While a mother, as *de facto* guardian, had the power to incur debts or to pledge the minor's goods and chattels for the minor's imperative necessities, such as food or clothing, she had no power at all to deal with the minor's immovable property.

---

[74] See also Doi (1984), p. 209.
[75] For further details on who can act as a guardian see Bharatiya (1996), pp. 150–151;
[76] Detailed tables as to who could act as a guardian are found in Nasir (1990a), p. 174. See also Balchin (1994), pp. 150–151; Abid (1993), pp. 262–263; Bharatiya (1996), pp. 147–148.
[77] For details see also Mannan (1990), pp. 497–498.
[78] See *Rahimuddin v. Abdul Malik Bhuyia*, P.L.D. 1968 Dacca 801.

10-75 In this case, the facts were that a Muslim male, Ismail Ali Khan, had died in March 1906 leaving three widows and numerous children. The third wife had two children from Ismail Ali Khan. In June 1906 this wife conveyed to purchasers the property which not only she, but also the children, had inherited. The purchaser then applied for mutation (substitution) of the names in the local land register. The first two wives and the children of the first two wives successfully opposed this mutation. This case is important not only regarding the rights of alienation of a minor's property but also with reference to the powers of *de facto* guardians, especially when they are women. It was held, at page 83:

> "It is perfectly clear that under the Mahomedan law the mother is entitled only to the custody of the person of her minor child up to a certain age according to the sex of the child. But she is not the natural guardian; the father alone, or, if he be dead, his executor (under the Sunni law), is the legal guardian. The mother has no larger powers to deal with her minor child's property than any outsider or non-relative who happens to have charge for the time being of the infant. The term "de facto guardian" that has been applied to these persons is misleading; it connotes the idea that people in charge of a child are by virtue of that fact invested with certain powers over the infant's property. This idea is quite erroneous . . ."

With particular reference to a mother's powers of alienation, the court explored in some detail the various restrictions on such powers (pages 84–86) and voiced criticism about equating the powers of a *de facto* guardian with those of a legal guardian. To do so, it was held at page 88, "would wipe out one of the most important safeguards provided by the Mahomedan law for the protection of the interests of infants". Thus, it was finally held, at pages 92–93:

> "For the foregoing considerations their Lordships are of opinion that under the Mahomedan law a person who has charge of the person or property of a minor without being his legal guardian, and who may, therefore, be conveniently called a "de facto guardian," has no power to convey to another any right or interest in immovable property which the transferee can enforce against the infant; nor can such transferee, if let into possession of the property under such unauthorized transfer, resist an action in ejectment on behalf of the infant as a trespasser."

Based on this decision, Bharatiya (1996, pp. 142–143) claims that the *de facto* guardian is "out of vogue in the modern Muslim law". In addition to *Imambandi*, two other leading decisions clearly establish that the minor's benefit is the paramount consideration.[79]

10-76 In Indian cases involving Muslim litigants, these principles have been applied and further developed in a fairly large number of cases, often involving custody as well as guardianship issues, and very often focusing on the legal position of *de facto* guardians. We can only provide a brief overview here. *Mohamad Amin Shah v. Ateeka Banu*, A.I.R. 1963 J.&K. 32, concerned guardianship of two girls above the age of puberty whose father had died and whose mother had remarried. Faced with various options, Murtaza Fazl Ali J. carefully considered what would be best for these two girls in view of the family circumstances and awarded guardianship of the person to an elderly male step-cousin, while joint guardianship

---

[79] These are the earlier Privy Council decision in *Mata Din v. Ahmad Ali* [1912] 39 L.R. I.A. 49 and *Mohd. Amin v. Vakil Ahmad*, 1952 S.C.J. 539.

of the property was given to the same person and the girls' father's sister, whom the court did not feel able to trust as sole guardian because she had an unmarried grown-up son.

10–77 *Rafiq v. Bashiran*, A.I.R. 1963 Raj. 239, was a father's successful appeal against award of custody to a female relative of his divorced wife. This case applied the proposition that where the rules of the personal law are in conflict with the provisions of the Guardians and Wards Act 1890, the latter shall prevail over the former. In fact, under section 19 of the 1890 Act, the court had power to award custody to a minor's father if he was not found to be unsuitable. Since there was nothing on record to show that this particular father was unfit, it was held that the father was entitled to the custody of his minor daughter. However, this position was dissented from in *Khatija Begum v. Gulam Dastagir*, A.I.R. 1976 A.P. 128, where the father of a minor girl, whose mother had died at her birth, contested the claim to the girl's custody by the deceased woman's mother. It was held that under Muslim law the father is the natural guardian when he is living and not unfit to be guardian, while the maternal grandmother of a Hanafi Muslim girl aged six years old, while not entitled to be appointed a guardian, is entitled to custody of the female child until she attains puberty.

10–78 In *Ali Mohammad v. Ramniwas*, A.I.R. 1967 Raj. 258, a *de facto* guardian had signed a mortgage deed, but it was held that such guardian has no power to transfer any right or interest in immovable property of the minor and such transfer is void. In *S. S. Gulam Ghouse Mohiuddin v. S. S. Ahmad Mohiuddin Kamisul Qadri*, A.I.R. 1971 S.C. 2184, it was similarly held, relying on *Imambandi v. Mutsaddi*, that a minor's brother is not entitled as of right to be appointed as guardian of a minor's property. In *Fathima Bivi v. Sadhakatalla*, A.I.R. 1977 Mad. 215, it was confirmed that a mother, not being a *de jure* guardian under Muslim law, has no right to sell the interest of her minor children in an immovable property. Such transactions are not merely voidable, but void.[80] *Rugia Begum v. Iqbal Ali Khan*, A.I.R. 1989 A.P. 30, held that a minor can challenge the alienation of property by a *de facto* guardian, while it is not open to third parties to challenge such alienations. *Mammad v. Nabeesa*, 1989(1) K.L.T. 489 revisits the role of the *de facto* guardian in relation to alienations. It was held, at page 490:

> "Mohammedan Law does not recognise a de facto guardian and views such a person as a rank outsider with no authority to deal with the minor's property under any circumstance whatsoever. He is merely a custodian of the person and property of the minor."

Noting that even a legal guardian has no power to sell the immovable property of the minor except in a case where he can obtain double its value or where the minor has no other property and the sale is necessary for his maintenance or in certain other situations of necessity, it was held that a mother as a *de facto* guardian had no power to alienate or lease the immovable property of a minor. However, this general proposition has been circumscribed in another case from the same year, which lays down the proposition that only the minor himself, and not a third party, can impugn a sale made by a *de facto* guardian.[81]

10–79 *Ahmadellah v. Mafizuddin Ahmad*, A.I.R. 1973 Gau. 56, concerned the extent of the guardian's powers to sell the minor's immovable property for

---

[80] See similarly *Gurubax Singh Gorowara v. Begum Rafiya Khurshid*, A.I.R. (1979) M.P. 66.
[81] See *Rugia Begum v. Iqbal Ali Khan*, A.I.R. (1989) A.P. 30. For a brief comment see Mahmood (1989), p. 234.

necessity. It was reiterated that under Muslim law a legal guardian of the property of a minor can sell the immovable property of the minor when the sale is necessary for his maintenance and when the minor has no other property. Interestingly, this case discusses the question whether education forms part of a minor's 'maintenance'. It was held, at page 59, that "in the present state of our society, which is rapidly advancing in all directions, education up to the Higher Secondary Stage cannot be said to be extravagant, so as to be excluded from maintenance".

10–80 *Noohu Pathuammal v. Ummathu Ameena*, A.I.R. 1980 Mad. 66, focused on the appointment of a guardian *ad litem*. It was held that under the rules of the Civil Procedure Code 1908 and irrespective of the personal law, a court had the power to appoint such a guardian despite the presence of the natural guardian. It was held at page 70 that "the essential requirements are that the person who is appointed as the guardian must be major, of sound mind and must have no interest adverse to that of the minor". This again re-affirms the overriding importance of the principle of the best interests of the child. This case reverts to a number of older decisions on relevant points such as the rights of widows to be appointed guardian *ad litem* and legal controls on a child's father once he has been appointed by the court as guardian *ad litem*.

10–81 Recently, the Indian Supreme Court has pronounced on a number of relevant issues. *Mahboob Sahab v. Syed Ismail*, A.I.R. 1995 S.C. 1205, concerned a question of gift as well as the guardian's right to alienate the minor sons' property. It was noted, in an *obiter dictum*, that "in Mohammadan Law mother cannot act nor be appointed as property guardian of the minor. She equally cannot act as legal guardian". The case is of little interest otherwise. In *Meethiyan Sidhiqu v. Muhammed Kunju Pareeth Kutty*, A.I.R. 1996 S.C. 1003, the facts were that a minor's father had died and no property guardian had been appointed by the court. A sale of property by the minor's mother, acting as *de facto* guardian, had been questioned and was ultimately held to be void by the Supreme Court. In this case, the sale had been effected in 1949. Counsel for the appellant sought to argue that since the minor's father had died, the mother is the natural guardian and therefore the sale made by her should not be void. This submission was rejected by the court. The Supreme Court, referring to the 19th edition of Mulla's *Principles of Mahomedan law* (Hidayatullah and Hidayatullah (1990)), and a number of other authoritative sources, re-stated the traditional position, at page 1003:

> ". . . only father, executor appointed by the father's Will, father's father and the executor appointed by the Will of the father's father, are legal guardians of property. No other relation is entitled to be the guardian of the property of a minor as of right; not even the mother, brother or uncle but the father or the paternal grand-father of the minor may appoint the mother, brother or uncle or any other person as his executor or executrix of his Will in which case they become legal guardian and have all the powers of the legal guardian . . . The Court may also appoint any one of them as guardian of the property of the minor in which case they will have all the powers of a guardian appointed by the Court . . ."

Noting that, in this case, after the demise of the father no property guardian had been appointed, it was found that "the mother, therefore, is not guardian for the alienation of the property of the minor. The sale made by the mother, therefore, is void" (page 1004). In this case, the Supreme Court also refused to recognise the appellant alienee's argument that he had perfected his title by adverse possession and thus showed an almost aggressive concern for protecting the property interests of minors. This activist approach must be understood not only as implementation of the principle of the welfare of the child, but also in the wider context of current Indian legal developments, which are very much focused on protecting the rights of weaker sections of the population, among whom children have a definite place.[82]

Guardianship of minor's property in English law

10–82   As we have already seen concerning custody matters, Muslims in Britain may occasionally litigate before English courts on matters relating to guardianship of property. However, there is no readily available evidence of such cases, and the matter requires further research.

Maintenance of children

The traditional Muslim law on paternal responsibility

10–83   We have already considered maintenance rights as one of the consequences of a Muslim marriage in paragraphs 7–23, 7–75 and 7–145, above. In that context, we did not discuss the legal position of children, which is more closely linked to the subjects discussed in the present chapter.

10–84   Traditional Muslim law clearly recognises the father's liability to maintain his legitimate children and draws a distinction between this liability and the husband's obligations towards the wife (Hodkinson (1984), p. 310). Doi ((1984), p. 204) treats the two together and writes that maintenance is an essential right of one's wife and children, relating to food, clothing, residence, some other essential services and medicine, even if the wife happens to be a rich lady. Further, "it will be the responsibility of a father to maintain his daughters until they are married, and sons until the age of puberty".[83] Nasir points out in the very beginning of his discussion of the child's rights during infancy that, once parentage is established, "it is followed by the child's right to be brought up, a right which imposes a duty on the father, namely maintenance".[84] Nasir also shows in considerable detail how this right has been incorporated into modern Middle Eastern and North African jurisdictions.

Maintenance rights of Muslim children in South Asian laws

10–85   Failure by a father to maintain a minor child means that he stands to lose any claim to custody.[85] Guardianship (*jabr*) includes the duty to maintain the ward. It has been held, however, that this duty is not an absolute one. An indication of the way in which maintenance rights may be restricted is found in the Pakistani case of *Ghulam Fatima v. Muhammad Bashir*, P.L.D. 1958 (W.P.) Lah. 596. This was a father's case for custody of his minor daughter, following the remarriage of his divorced wife. The lower court had held that it would be in the interests of the minor to live with her mother until the age of 13 and the father appealed to the High Court of Lahore, ultimately with limited success.

---

[82] See, *e.g.* article 15(3) of the Indian Constitution, which explicitly empowers the state to make any special provision for women and children.
[83] Doi (1984), p. 204. The author also discusses the duties of every Muslim to maintain aged parents and other needy relatives. Mahmood (1982a), pp. 178–179 reiterates the basic responsibility of the Muslim father to his various children and emphasises that the extent of this liability depends on the facts and circumstances. At pp. 178–184, this author provides an excellent, detailed overview of the subject.
[84] Nasir (1990a), p. 170; (1990b), p. 119. See also Nasir (1990a), p. 156; (1990b), p. 107. Schleifer (1986), pp. 67–74) emphasises and explains the extent of the financial obligations of the father towards the mother of his children and his minor children.
[85] See above, p. 417. For further details see Abid (1993), p. 257.

10–86 One issue in this case concerned the mother's claim for recovery of maintenance expenses for the young girl from the father. The court considered a number of earlier decisions on related points and found that while a Muslim father is bound to maintain an indigent child himself, his duty does not necessarily extend to providing maintenance for that child through another person. Akhlaque Husain J. held in this regard, at page 599:

"A father's liability to maintain his children, excepting of course those who have not been weaned, extends only to such of them as are really in need of maintenance . . . A child having means of its own is by common consent not entitled to any maintenance from his father. It follows from these premises that a child, who is being already voluntarily maintained by another and therefore does not stand in need of his food, clothing or lodging, cannot require its father to pay maintenance. Similarly, a person maintaining the child of another voluntarily without reference to its father would not be entitled to claim its maintenance from the father."

These statements were backed up by reference to the *Hedaya* and other sources, giving an impression that when a father manages to avoid payment of maintenance for some time, he can later take advantage of his own wrong, so to say, and will be free from any further liability. Laying down, at page 600, that "even decreed maintenance, if allowed to remain in arrears for some time, cannot be recovered from a non-absentee father, on the grounds that maintenance is due only when the claimant, other than a wife, is in actual need of it", the court clearly took the father's side, with no recognition of the fact that this rule may be abused in social reality. Finding that "an examination of the authorities leaves no room for doubt that past maintenance . . . cannot be recovered from the father by the mother who has maintained a child" (page 600), it was held that the wife in this case was not entitled to any payment. This case seems to indicate that where a mother never claims maintenance for some time, the child loses this potential source of support. In the particular facts and circumstances of this case, the judge appears to have taken the view that the mother's claim for recovery of expenses was not bona fide. It is therefore doubtful whether this case establishes a general proposition that the liabilities of men *vis-à-vis* their children are limited.

10–87 In South Asian laws today while there has been much focus on the maintenance rights of Muslim wives, and divorced wives, in particular,[86] there is now increasing emphasis on children's rights to maintenance. This is an obvious consequence of social problems linked to impoverishment and destitution, particularly in modern states which cannot afford a welfare system which would take care of destitute children. This concern is apparent in all three South Asian jurisdictions covered here.

10–88 As regards Pakistan, we have already discussed the case of *Amar Ilahi v. Rashida Akhtar*, P.L.D. 1955 Lah. 413, where a father who refused to pay for the maintenance of his minor daughter was later held to have no right to act as her marriage guardian (see paragraph 10–50, above). In *Inamul Islam v. Hussain Bano*, P.L.D. 1976 Lah. 1466, the facts were somewhat similar. The husband had abandoned his wife and young daughter. The mother had managed to obtain a decree of maintenance for herself at Rs. 50/- per month, plus Rs. 40/- for the daughter. The husband appealed, no doubt hoping to save money. Zullah J. concluded the judgment with a comment about the treatment of this young child, who was less than five years old at the time, holding at page 1469:

---

[86] See in detail paras. 7–75—7–125, above.

"Since the time of her birth, it is common knowledge and has not been denied by the learned counsel for the petitioner that cost of living in Pakistan has gone high. Rs. 40 p.m. is not such a sum which can be considered as excessive. The petitioner is an able-bodied person and there is no reason why he should not be able to maintain his daughter by paying Rs. 40 p.m. as her maintenance."

Recent studies confirm that the child's right to maintenance from the father has been protected by Pakistani law. Balchin (1994, p. 87) writes:

". . . the courts have consistently upheld the right of children living with their separated/divorced mother to maintenance from their father. Minor children cannot and should not be deprived of their right to maintenance on the grounds that they were not living with their father."

Thus, when it comes to determining a wife's quantum of maintenance, the courts take into account the burden of taking care of a child.[87] The same principle has been followed in numerous Indian cases.[88] In Bangladeshi law, too, the important case of *Hefzur Rahman v. Shamsun Nahar Begum* (1995) 15 B.L.D. 34, while focusing on the divorced wife's right to maintenance beyond the *iddat* period, firmly protects the rights to maintenance of the small child of the appellant until the age of puberty.

10–89 It appears that maintenance of children has become an important matter of policy concern in all South Asian countries today, since the welfare state finds itself unable to provide for such children and legal means are therefore devised to ensure that such children are taken care of at the level of the family rather than in state institutions. As in cases concerning destitute former wives, the underlying purpose of protecting the maintenance rights of children is, therefore, to protect the state from expenses of a social welfare nature.

10–90 Recent Indian cases have therefore been particularly vigilant about protecting the maintenance rights of children and will not listen to the pleas of men pleading poverty. In *Pareed v. Aysha*, 1988(1) K.L.T. 27, a labourer on daily wages was trying to argue that the court had awarded excessive maintenance to his former wife and his minor daughter. Shankaran Nair J. was willing to reduce the monthly maintenance awarded to the wife from Rs. 150/- to Rs. 100/-, but refused to disturb the maintenance award of Rs. 100/- per month for the young daughter. In *Kadeeja v. Aboobacker*, 1995(1) K.L.T. 563, a Muslim man who used to work in a Gulf country but had had an accident and was now unable to work pleaded impecunious circumstances. M. M. Pareed Pillay C.J. held the father liable for the children's maintenance and said, at page 564:

"Under Islamic law father has to maintain his sons till they attain puberty and daughters till they are married. He cannot take the stand that he is in impecunious circumstances and so unable to maintain them."

A particularly good earlier example of a case on Muslim children's maintenance is *Ibrahim Fathima v. Mohamed Saleem*, A.I.R. 1980 Mad. 82.[89] More specifically, the

---

[87] See, *e.g. Abdul Latif v. Surat Khatoon*, 1989 S.C.M.R. 456.
[88] Most such cases concerned Hindu wives. A prominent example of a Muslim wife's claim is found in *Bai Tahira v. Ali Hussain Fissalli Chothia*, A.I.R. 1979 S.C. 362, discussed in para. 7–89, above.
[89] On this case see F. Ahmad (1994), p. 10, praising this case for discovering "the true principles of Islamic law relating to minor children's right of maintenance".

question was whether the father's obligation to maintain is purely personal or whether it attaches to his property in such a way that it could even be enforced against an alienee. The father had two wives, a childless first wife, and a second wife with four children. For some reason, he fell out with the second wife and settled all his properties on the first wife, thus impairing the maintenance rights of his four children. The first wife, who had been made a party to the suit, claimed that the children could not question the settlement of properties on her by a claim for maintenance against their father.

10–91 The lower court had directed the father to pay maintenance totalling Rs. 140/- per month for the four children and made this a charge on the properties and the lower appellate court had agreed. On second appeal before the Madras High Court, it was apparent that the children's claim to maintenance from their father itself could not really be questioned (page 83). However, the first wife challenged the fact that the maintenance payment had been made a charge over her properties and argued that this was in violation of principles of Muslim law. The case of *Mahomed Jusab Haji Adam Nurani v. Haji Adam Haji Usman Nurani*, I.L.R. [1913] 37 Bom. 71, was cited as authority for the proposition that a father's obligation to maintain his children was entirely personal and was separate from any consideration of whether he owned property or not.

10–92 It was agreed that there was only this one reported earlier case on the subject, and it went against the children's claim. A lively discussion followed, concerning also the role of the judge in interpreting Muslim law rules today. Counsel for the appellant cautioned against "reading ancient Arabic texts too astutely and too liberally for mouthing new-fangled legal principles" (page 85) and said that "courts of law should not attempt to put their own construction on the Quran nor give any effect to new rules of law, however logically they may be deducible from ancient texts, when they have not been dealt with earlier by authoritative commentators" (*id.*). However, the judge in this case was well aware of other principles laid down in various authoritative textbooks of Muslim law and refused to be bound by the decision cited before him. It was held, at page 86:

> "I conceive that this court and other courts in this land must administer the personal law for Muslims on this difficult question only on the basis of the ancient textual authorities, whose validity as sources of law can hardly be questioned. Having regard to the tradition handed down from the Prophet himself in the two anecdotal references I have earlier cited, there seems to me to be every judicial compulsion to follow the injunction which the Prophet administered to his followers as the only rule of law bearing on the subject of maintenance. Without attempting to discover exact parallels between one system of personal law and another, I may make bold to assert that it would be quite purposeless and self-stultifying for any system of family law or jurisprudence worth the name to confer a right on minor children to maintenance, while allowing the parent, at the same time, the liberty of sapping the substance of that right."

The judge therefore concluded, at page 86:

> "At the end of the discussion I am quite satisfied that under the Mohammedan Law, minor children are entitled to have a decree for their maintenance made a proper charge on the property of the father. I hold that the children's right to maintenance in a Muslim household always attaches to the father's property in such a way and in such measure that it is not effected by any subsequent

alienation by the father with notice of the charge or by an alienation which is gratuitous."

More recently in Indian law, a number of new cases under section 125 of the Criminal Procedure Code 1973 and now under the Muslim Women (Protection of Rights on Divorce) Act 1986 focus on the maintenance rights of Muslim children. Following the very important new developments concerning divorced Muslim wives' rights to maintenance after the promulgation and judicial interpretation of the 1986 Act, the established position is that the maintenance rights of children continue to be governed by the provisions of the Criminal Procedure Code 1973, since the Act of 1986 relates to divorced women only.[90]

10–93 This position was confirmed in *Siraj Sahebji Mujawar v. Roshan Siraj Mujawar*, A.I.R. 1990 Bom. 344, which also reiterated the absolute nature of the Muslim father's obligation to provide maintenance to his minor children. In this case, a Muslim father had argued unsuccessfully that, in view of section 3(1)(b) of the Muslim Women (Protection of Rights on Divorce) Act 1986 he should not be required to pay maintenance to his children beyond two years. The relevant portions of section 3 provide as follows:

"(1) Notwithstanding anything contained in any other law for the time being in force, a divorced woman shall be entitled to –

   . . .

    (b) where she herself maintains the children born to her before or after her divorce, a reasonable and fair provision and maintenance to be made and paid by her former husband for a period of two years from the respective dates of birth of such children;

This provision was interpreted by Sugla J. as follows at page 347:

"The new Act deals with the obligation of the husband *vis-à-vis* his divorcee wife. For two years from the date of their respective births, the children are supposed to be ordinarily if not necessarily in the custody of the mother. In other words she has necessarily to maintain them. That is why a provision is made under Section 3(1)(b) of the new Act that the husband shall pay to the divorcee wife for a period of two years from the date of their respective births in respect of their maintenance and will have no right to claim custody as that may not be in the interest of the children."

With reference to the traditional Muslim law, the judge continued (*id.*):

"The obligation of the father to maintain his children under Section 370 of the Mahomedan law is absolute. Under this section it may be open to the father to contend that he is prepared to maintain them if they stay with him and not otherwise. In other words, a Muslim husband/father may claim the custody of the children to fulfil his obligations to maintain them. But having not claimed the custody of the children, he cannot certainly refuse to maintain them because the children are in the custody of their mother *i.e.* divorcee wife or somebody else."

---

[90] See Mahmood (1989), p. 232. In *Abdul Gafoor Kunju v. Pathumma Beevi*, 1989(1) K.L.T. 337, it was held that a divorced Muslim wife is no longer entitled to invoke the provisions of s.127 of the 1973 Code after the 1986 Act came into force. The maintenance right of the daughter, however, was unaffected.

10–94 It was held, therefore, that the right of the children to maintenance from their father is a separate right, independent from the rights of their divorced mother, and the father's claim failed.[91] The same position was established in *Abdul Majid v. Kamrunnisa*, 1990 Cri.L.J. 2799 (M.P.), where an award in favour of two minor daughters, who were above the age of two, was upheld by the High Court despite objections by the father under section 3(1)(b) of the 1986 Act. This decision, which cites a number of other recent cases, also shows that the courts are not willing to be swayed by procedural technicalities when the welfare of minor children is at stake. In *Rupsan Begum v. Md. Abdus, Sattar* 1990 Cri.L.J. 2391 (Gau.), it was similarly held that orders for the maintenance of children above two years could be made against a Muslim father after he divorced his wife and she was unable to maintain the children who are living with her. It was said, at page 2393:

> "Proper maintenance of child is imperative. In the paramount interest of the child, laws compelling a parent to maintain his child/children are to be construed liberally so as to embrace all beneficial legislation in favour of the child."

Very recently, the Supreme Court of India has finally had an occasion to pronounce on the extent of the obligations of divorced Muslim fathers to provide for the maintenance of their children who stay with their former wives. In *Noor Sabha Khatoon v. Mohd. Quasim* (1997) 6 S.C.C. 233, a case which was widely reported and welcomed in the Indian press, the Supreme Court has come down firmly in favour of the protection of children's rights, irrespective of community and religion. The case confirms the position established in *Siraj Sahebji Mujawar v. Roshan Siraj Mujawar*, A.I.R. 1990 Bom. 344, and other cases discussed above. In the words of Dr A. S. Anand J., at page 235, the question before the court was,

> ". . . whether the children of Muslim parents are entitled to grant of maintenance under Section 125 CrPC for the period till they attain majority or are able to maintain themselves whichever date is earlier or in the case of female children till they get married or is their right restricted to the grant of maintenance only for a period of two years prescribed under Section 3(1)(b) of the Muslim Women (Protection of Rights on Divorce) Act 1986 notwithstanding Section 125 CrPC."

The couple had married in 1980 and there were three children. The husband turned the wife out of the house when the children were only six, three and one and a half years old and took a second wife. In 1992, the wife filed a suit for monthly maintenance of Rs. 400/- for herself and Rs. 300/- each for the children. In 1993, the trial court awarded Rs. 200/- per month to the wife and Rs. 150/- for each of the children till the age of majority. The husband then divorced the wife and the maintenance order of the court was modified, significantly because the trial court held, as stated at page 236, "that in view of the provisions of the 1986 Act the appellant-wife after her divorce was entitled to maintenance only for a period of three months i.e. for the period of *iddat*".[92] The maintenance awards for the children were not disturbed, on the ground that the rights of children were not affected by the 1986 Act. This was successfully challenged by the husband on

---

[91] See to the same effect *Abdul Sathar v. Arifa Beevi*, 1991(1) K.L.T. S.N. 17 [Case No. 22].

[92] This confirms that even in 1993, significantly in North India, lower courts were holding that the 1986 Act only entitled divorced Muslim wives to maintenance for the duration of the *iddat*, rather than following the various High Court decisions which we discussed in detail in paras 7–75—7–125, above.

appeal to the High Court of Patna, in which a single judge decided that a divorced Muslim wife is entitled to claim maintenance from her previous husband for her minor children only for a period of two years from the birth of the child (page 236). The mother appealed to the Supreme Court.

10–95 Dr A. S. Anand J. considered the provisions of the 1986 Act and stated, at page 237, that "the 1986 Act was enacted as a sequel to the judgment in *Mohd. Ahmed Khan v. Shah Bano Begum*",[93] noting in addition that the 1986 Act was not enacted to regulate the maintenance obligations of a Muslim father towards his minor children, a subject matter which continued to be governed by section 125 of the Criminal Procedure Code 1973. Regarding the interpretation of section 3 of the 1986 Act it was held, at pages 238–239:

> "Clause (b) of Section 3(1) . . . provides for grant of *additional* maintenance to her for the fosterage period of two years from the date of birth of the child of [the] marriage for maintaining that child during the fosterage. Maintenance for the prescribed period referred to in clause (b) of Section 3(1) is granted on the *claim* of the divorced mother *on her own behalf* for maintaining the infant/ infants for a period of two years from the date of the birth of the child concerned who is/are living with her and presumably is aimed at providing some extra amount to the mother for *her* nourishment for nursing or taking care of the infant/infants up to a period of two years. It has nothing to do with the right of the child/children to claim maintenance under Section 125 CrPC So long as the conditions for the grant of maintenance under Section 125 CrPC are satisfied, the rights of the minor children, unable to maintain themselves, are not affected by Section 3(1)(b) of the 1986 Act. Under Section 125 CrPC the maintenance of the children is obligatory on the father (irrespective of his religion) and as long as he is in a position to do so and the children have no independent means of their own, it remains his *absolute obligation* to provide for them. Insofar as children born of Muslim parents are concerned, there is nothing in Section 125 CrPC which exempts a Muslim father from his obligation to maintain the children. These provisions are not affected by clause (b) of Section 3(1) of the 1986 Act and indeed it would be unreasonable, unfair, inequitable and even preposterous to deny the benefit of Section 125 CrPC to the children only on the ground that they are born of Muslim parents . . . . A Muslim father's obligation, like that of a Hindu father, to maintain his minor children as contained in Section 125 CrPC is *absolute* and is not at all affected by Section 3(1)(b) of the 1986 Act."

The learned judge immediately continued, at page 239, linking his decision on maintenance law with specific reference to custody law:

> "Indeed a Muslim father can claim custody of the children born through the divorced wife to fulfil his obligation to maintain them and if he succeeds, he need not suffer an order or direction under Section 125 CrPC but where such custody has not been claimed by him, he cannot refuse and neglect to maintain his minor children on the ground that he has divorced their mother. The right of the children to claim maintenance under Section 125 CrPC is separate, distinct and independent of the right of their divorcee mother to claim maintenance for herself for maintaining the infant children up to the age of 2

---

[93] The precise choice of words here is highly significant, since the learned judge did not say that this Act was enacted to overrule, nullify or modify the *Shah Bano* judgment.

years from the date of birth of the child concerned under Section 3(1) of the Act. There is nothing in the 1986 Act which in any manner affects the application of the provisions of Sections 125–128 of the CrPC relating to grant of maintenance insofar as minor children of Muslim parents, unable to maintain themselves, are concerned."

10–96   The judge also explicitly addressed the question of compatibility with the Muslim personal law and stated, at page 239:

"Apart from the statutory provisions referred to above, even under the Muslim Personal Law, the right of minor children to receive maintenance from their father, till they are able to maintain themselves, is absolute."

This position was confirmed by reference to the writing of Professor Tahir Mahmood (pages 239–240) and it was held, at page 240:

"Thus, both under the personal law and the statutory law (Section 125 CrPC) the obligation of a Muslim father, having sufficient means, to maintain his minor children, unable to maintain themselves, till they attain majority and in the case of females till they get married, is absolute, notwithstanding the fact that the minor children are living with the divorced wife."

This most recent decision on the subject confirms authoritatively that the modern Indian law on maintenance seeks to harmonise the modern secular law and the personal laws for the sake of protecting the financial interests of women and children. This may also be designed to protect the state itself from any social welfare claims, but it is ultimately a strategy that seeks to safeguard the best interests of the child, which are placed above all other considerations. In that respect, indeed, there is no conflict between the modern secular law and the Muslim personal law on this subject.

Maintenance of children under English law

10–97   It would be surprising if the arguments advanced by Muslim fathers in South Asian courts of law were not reflected in English courts. However, there are a number of reasons why legal problems of this kind appear not to have attracted attention. Two main reasons for this lack of official recognition of the very tangible problems in this field can be advanced. First, the presence of a welfare state in Britain has allowed Muslim men who divorce their wives not only to exonerate themselves from maintenance payments for wives, but also for their children. In other words, some Muslim fathers have simply, and successfully, sought to rely on the state to provide maintenance for their children. Secondly, the extent to which divorcing Muslim men in Britain make use of concepts in traditional Muslim law which expect the former wife's family to shoulder the burden of the maintenance not only of the divorced woman, but also her children, should be a matter of concern.[94]

10–98   Officially, of course, the Child Support Act 1991 and the Child Support Act 1995 place the responsibility for a child's maintenance under English law firmly on the father. Disputes over child support are now dealt with by the Child Support Agency.

---

[94] See an indication of this strategy in *Ghulam Fatima v. Muhammad Bashir* P.L.D. 1958 (W.P.) Lah. 596.

10–99 According to the concepts of traditional Muslim law, discussed in paragraphs 10–83—10–84, above, and reiterated in modern South Asian laws, as we have seen, there should be no doubt that Muslim fathers have definite obligations towards their offspring, whether in marriage or after it. However, in real life, such principles do not appear to be implemented to the fullest possible extent and in the process of undoing marriage arrangements, the children may suffer not only emotionally but also financially. As we have argued with regard to divorce and other aspects of Muslim family law in Britain, the invisibility of the unofficial Muslim law in Britain may not help children of Muslim fathers to safeguard their rightful claims to the fullest possible extent.

Chapter 11

Inheritance, gifts and endowments (*waqf*)

11–01 This chapter discusses the basic rules of the Muslim law of succession, as well as the law relating to gifts and religious endowments (*waqf*). Emphasis is given to the Hanafi Sunni law of succession, although some details of the Shi'i system will be covered. For details of the law of succession, readers are referred to the excellent, detailed study by Professor Coulson.[1]

11–02 Doi (1984, p. 271) emphasises that the laws of inheritance form one of the most important branches of Muslim family law. Nasir (1990a. 218 *et seq.*) provides a succinct treatment of the transition from the pre-Islamic to the Islamic system of inheritance. Coulson (1971, p. 1) began his study with explicit reference to the inherent conflict between the interests and claims of the family and the freedom of the individual to dispose of property. Muslim law responded to the conflicts between various group interests and individual discretion by imposing compulsory rules of succession, designed to protect the interests of close relatives of the deceased, while still allowing the individual limited discretion to dispose of some property by will or in other forms.

11–03 In Islamic law, succession is therefore of two kinds, namely optional and compulsory. Optional succession (testamentary succession) is limited to one-third of the property owned by the *propositus* (the deceased). This principle is based firmly on *sunna*. The remaining two thirds of the property, together with any property which has not been bequeathed, is distributed according to a fixed and compulsory set of rules which represent the synthesis of the Qur'anic verses with the pre-Islamic customary law, and the interpretation of these verses as accepted by consensus (*ijma*).

11–04 We proceed in this chapter by first considering some questions relating to the administration of estates and the important topic of 'death sickness', which brings out the limitations on individual discretion of giving property away in one's lifetime. We then move on to testamentary succession before we consider in some detail the position of the various heirs in the Muslim law of inheritance. On gifts and endowments (*waqf*), this study can only provide a brief overview but we felt that this should remain included in the book to allow readers to see the many links between the various issues treated in the separate sub-sections of this Chapter.

Administration of the estate and death sickness

The traditional law

11–05 An important general point to make is that the Muslim law of inheritance does not draw any distinction between movable and immovable

---

[1] See Coulson, *Succession in the Muslim family* (1971). This pioneering study has long been out of print. For the forthcoming new edition see Edge (1999, forthcoming). A major analysis of the Islamic law of inheritance, which includes a detailed commentary on certain aspects of Coulson's work appears in Powers (1986).

property or between ancestral and self-acquired property.[2] Before any bequests can be paid to the beneficiaries the debts of the deceased must be accounted for. The order of priority of debts, more or less irrelevant in a fully solvent estate, takes on considerable importance in an insolvent estate. Most jurists will give priority to the burial expenses.[3] After these expenses have been paid, the next charges on the estate are the secured debts, such as a pledge which is secured to a part of the property, followed by the unsecured debts.[4]

11–06 According to Hanafi law, the unsecured debts which are incurred during sound health prior to the deceased entering what is referred to as the 'disease of death' take priority over debts where the only evidence for their existence is an admission by the deceased whilst suffering from the 'disease of death', as expressed in the doctrine of death-sickness (*mard al-maut*).[5] At the point in time when the *propositus* enters this 'death sickness', the personal debts and the claims of the compulsory heirs attach to the property. The *propositus*, therefore, cannot defeat the expectations of the claimants by donating, or selling below value, parts of the estate which amount to more than one-third of the net estate. Such a donation, like bequests, is *ultra vires* and depends for its efficacy on the consent of the heirs. The limitations imposed upon bequests are thus extended to cover gifts made by dying persons and "the purpose of the law is primarily to control the acts of dying persons" (Coulson (1971), p. 260).

11–07 These kinds of rules raise very important questions about when succession actually begins. In the classical system, there was no administration of the estate as such, merely distribution of the estate in accordance with the principles of Muslim law, "by the state if not by the heirs themselves".[6] Ultimately, responsibility for administering the estate lay with the state, with the *Qadi* acting as the agent (Fyzee (1974), p. 375). Bharatiya (1996, p. 288) explains the basic position as follows:

> "According to the Muslim legal theory, the property of a deceased Muslim vests in his heirs immediately after his death. But it is subject to the injunction that the heirs are entitled only to take that residue which is left after the payment of a legacy or debt. Since the payment of legacies and debts necessarily involves the administration of the estate, such administration may be said to be implied in the very spirit of Muslim law itself."[7]

In fact, the classical doctrine is that the deceased fictitiously survives and remains the owner of the estate until all obligations have been discharged. Thus in an insolvent estate, the property does not pass to the heirs unless and until the debts have been paid. This rule, in particular, has been modified in South Asian law.

---

[2] See, *e.g.* Mannan (1990), p. 59. The second set of criteria is of special relevance in South Asian laws because of the influence of Hindu legal concepts.
[3] See, *e.g.* Fyzee (1974), p. 375; Doi (1984), p. 272; Mahmood (1982a), p. 220. Bharatiya (1996), pp. 287–289, provides a succinct overview of the main rules relating to administration.
[4] It will be recalled that the widow's unpaid *mahr* ranks as an unsecured debt. See also Mahmood (1982a), p. 220.
[5] See in detail Coulson (1971), pp. 259–279.
[6] Fyzee (1974), p. 376, compares the process to dividing up a cake in accordance with pre-ordained rules, so that all that remains to be done is to hand over the particular pieces to the various beneficiaries.
[7] This point is also discussed *ibid.*, p. 378.

South Asian concepts

11-08 Two important complications in the Muslim law of inheritance and related subjects need to be noted for the Indian subcontinent. First, the relevant South Asian laws are to some extent influenced by local customs relating to property law, in particular South Asian concepts of joint family property, in some cases based on matrilineal principles. While these are not part of Muslim law, and in fact there have been many attempts to exclude them by statute, they have influenced the operation of the law.[8] Balchin (1994, p. 262) argues with reference to Pakistani law that the dominant role of custom has had a negative impact on women's rights in that the shares in inheritance given to women under Muslim law used to be denied to them in practice. Commenting on the general trends in the case law since independence, Balchin (1994, p. 287) writes that "at first glance, Pakistani case law on inheritance and succession rights of women is very encouraging". However, she also notes the extremely small number of cases in this field, which reflects on the obstacles women face in bringing an inheritance dispute to the courts, in the first place.

11-09 Secondly, various statutory enactments have interfered in the Muslim system of inheritance, but these are really in addition to, not in supersession of, the Muslim rules on inheritance.[9] Mahmood (1982a, p. 219) outlines that in India all questions related to succession of Muslims,

> "are not governed wholly and exclusively by the Muslim law. These are determined by a heterogenous body of rules drawn partly from the law of Islam and partly from Indian legislation. In this body of legal rules, Islamic principles, of course, still constitute the dominant element."

This particular combination of legal sources has given rise to some interesting questions and developments. Influenced by equity considerations and English concepts, the British Indian courts held, after a long period of insecurity, that the deceased Muslim's estate devolved at death on his heirs irrespective of whether the estate was solvent or insolvent. In British India, therefore, in contrast to the Muslim world, the heir's ownership was acquired immediately on death and was subject to a personal liability to pay the debts of the deceased in proportion to the respective shares in the estate. While this position has been adopted in modern Indian law, too, it is not surprising that in Pakistani legal textbooks this rule has been criticised as not correct in view of clear provisions of Islamic law.[10]

11-10 The leading authority on the subcontinent for the proposition that an inheritance vests in the heir immediately after the deceased's death is *Jafri Begam v. Amir Muhammad Khan*, I.L.R. [1885] 7 Al. 822.[11] The facts of this case were as follows: One Ali Muhammad Khan left considerable wealth when he died in 1878, leaving behind him as his heirs his parents, his widow, two sons, three daughters and a brother, Amir Muhammad Khan. The family tree in graphic form looks as follows:

---

[8] See in some detail Mahmood (1982a), pp. 219 222 and 237 240.

[9] Bharatiya (1996), pp. 288–289, emphasises that much of the relevant Muslim law is replaced by the Indian Succession Act 1925 while Mahmood (1982a), p. 219 explains that "though the substantive law of intestate and testamentary succession laid down in the Central Act 1925 does not apply to Muslims, many of its remaining provisions do apply to them and thereby restrict the scope of the Islamic law of succession in this country".

[10] See in detail Mannan (1990), p. 43. *ibid.* pp. 39–58, provides a detailed analysis of succession and administration with reference to Pakistani law.

[11] On this case see also Fyzee (1974), pp. 376–378.

Table 1

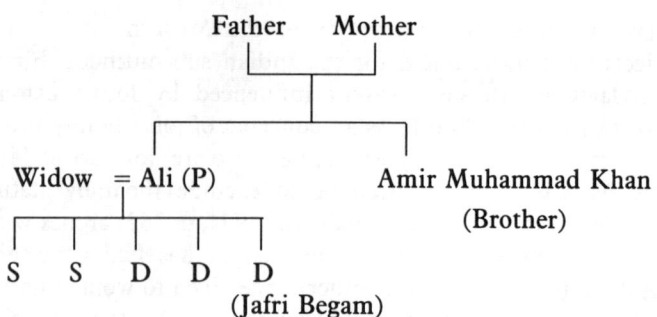

The husband of the third daughter originally started court proceedings, securing a court decree in his favour against the widow, two sons, and the three daughters for a debt which was due to him from the deceased. This decree was executed, and a part of a village which had originally belonged to the deceased was sold to this man as a result. The brother of the deceased was not involved in that dispute. However, following the death of the two parents soon afterwards, he brought an action to recover what he considered himself entitled to out of their estate, claiming a portion of the estate which he inherited on the death of his mother and his father, who of course had earlier been heirs of Ali Muhammad Khan. The defendants in the action were Ali Muhammad Khan's widow, the two sons, and the three daughters.

11–11   This case raised three important, interlinked questions. The first one was whether upon the death of an intestate Muslim, who had left unpaid debts, ownership of the estate devolved immediately on the heirs of the deceased, or whether such devolution was contingent upon payment of the debts. Mahmood J., speaking for the Full Bench of the Allahabad High Court, initially deplored the paucity of accurate textbooks on Muslim law in English (page 826) and then reserved his judgment, citing as a major reason "the long conflict of decisions which exists in the Reports upon the subject to which this reference relates" (page 827). In his full judgment, Mahmood J. examined in detail the various sources of Muslim law, citing provisions of the Qur'an itself, noting that the various heirs take, in every case, after various legacies and debts have been paid (pages 831–832). The learned judge interpreted such provisions as directions about the administration of the estate, with "no bearing upon the question of the exact point of time when inheritance *devolves* upon the heirs" (page 823). This situation was compared with the inheritance of property subject to prior charges, as known to the judges at the time from Hindu cases. Applying the equitable principles developed by the courts in such contexts, the learned judge could find no reason not to hold that inheritance should operate immediately on death. Thus it was held, at page 834:

> "These authorities leave no doubt in my mind that the devolution of inheritance takes place *immediately* upon the death of the ancestor from whom the property is inherited."

The second issue in that case, discussed at pages 840–845, concerned the question whether a decree for a debt passed against those heirs who are in possession of the deceased's estate binds the other heirs. The learned judge, considering various rules of Muslim law in this respect, found that this was not a matter of substantive law but of procedure. Rephrasing the first proposition, it was stated, at page 842:

> "Upon the death of a Muhammadan owner, his property, as I have already shown, immediately devolves upon his heirs, in specific shares; and if there are

any claims against the estate, and they are litigated, the matter passes into the region of *procedure*, and must be regulated according to the law which governs the action of the Court. The plaintiff must go to the court having jurisdiction, and institute his suit within limitation, impleading all the heirs against whose shares he seeks to enforce his claim; and if he omits to implead any of the heirs, the decree would be ineffective as regards the share of those who were not parties to the litigation."

Noting, at page 843, that "Muhammadan heirs are independent owners of their specific shares, and if they take their shares subject to the charge of the debts of the deceased, their liability is in proportion to the extent of their shares", it was then stated, at page 844, that the Muslim rules of procedure no longer applied, since "the law of British India has framed its own rules of procedure". It was therefore held, at page 845, that a decree for a debt passed against such of the heirs as are in possession of the estate does not bind the other heirs.

11–12 The third question, discussed at pages 845–847, was immediately stated to depend on rules of equity. Applying those principles, it was held, at page 847,

"that the plaintiff cannot obtain a decree for possession of his share of the property in suit without such decree being rendered contingent upon payment by him of such proportion of the purchase-money as would represent his proportionate share of the liability to the ancestor's debts liquidated by the proceeds of the auction-sale."

It will be seen, of course, that the first decided point is directly opposed to the principle of Muslim law relating to the fictitious survival of the *propositus*.[12] The essential difference between classical doctrine and the *Jafri Begam* rule is that under the latter, an heir who alienates the property of which he has taken possession can pass a valid title, which would debar the claims of the creditor of the estate. Two earlier cases, *Wahidunnisa v. Shubrattun* [1870] 6 Bengal L.R. 54, and *Bazayet Hossein v. Dooli Chund* [1877–1878] 5 L.R. I.A. 211, illustrate this proposition very clearly. The facts in the latter case were as follows. A Muslim died, survived by his widow and a son. The widow's dower had not been paid during the husband's lifetime. The son, in debt, mortgaged his share of the estate to M without paying the dower debt. Thus the widow applied for, and obtained a decree against the son in possession for her dower debt. The estate was attached in execution of the decree. The mortgagor, M, then in his turn obtained a decree against the son on the basis of the mortgage in order to sell the son's property to recoup the mortgage amount. In execution of this decree, the property was sold to a third party. The question before the court, therefore, was who had the better right to the property, the third party purchaser or the widow? It was held that the widow could not trace the property into the hands of the purchaser. The son had absolute capacity to dispose of his share of the inheritance; it was vested in him immediately on death, and there was no condition imposed that the debts must be paid prior to the property passing to the heirs. The decision in *Wahidunnisa v. Shubrattun* was to the same effect.

11–13 Since all Muslim heirs take individual shares, one of several heirs, though he may be in possession of the whole estate, has no power to alienate the share of co-heirs.[13] However, certain decrees of a court will nonetheless bind heirs

---

[12] These propositions are restated and discussed in Mannan (1990), pp. 42 *et seq.*
[13] *Jan Mohammed v. Karam Chand*, A.I.R. 1947 P.C. 93.

not in possession. The Supreme Court of India considered this last issue in the case of *N. K. Mohammad Sulaiman v. N. C. Mohammad Ismail* [1966] 1 S.C.R. 937. The facts of this case were as follows. M, K and L mortgaged a certain property in 1933 in favour of NR to secure payment of Rs. 20,000/-. M died in 1937. In 1940, NR commenced proceedings for the enforcement of the mortgage against K, L, and the three widows and one daughter of M. A decree was obtained in 1941 and, in execution of this decree, the properties were sold at a court auction. The properties were purchased by NR with leave of the court. NR thereafter transferred the properties to P, who in turn alienated the properties to others. Subsequently, Muhammad Sulaiman, the plaintiff, claiming that he was the son of M, instituted a suit for a decree for partition of the mortgaged properties or, in the alternative, for a declaration that he was entitled to redeem the mortgage or portion thereof equal to his share in the mortgaged properties. The suit was resisted by NR and the alienees on two grounds. First, it was submitted that the plaintiff was not the son of M. Secondly, that NR had made a full enquiry and he was instructed that only the three widows and one daughter were the surviving members of the family of M. Shah J., in the Indian Supreme Court, set out at page 940 what he referred to as accepted, well-settled principles:

> "The estate of a Muslim dying intestate devolves under the Islamic law upon his heirs at the moment of his death, i.e. the estate vests immediately in each heir in proportion to the shares ordained by the personal law and the interest of each heir is separate and distinct. Each heir is under the personal law liable to satisfy the debts of the deceased only to the extent of the share of the debt proportionate to his share in the estate. A creditor of a Muslim dying intestate may sue all the heirs of the deceased, and where the estate of the deceased has not been distributed between the heirs, he may execute the decree against the property as a whole without regard to the extent of the liability of the heirs *inter se*. The creditor is however not bound to sue all the heirs: the creditor may sue some only of the heirs and obtain a decree against those heirs, and liability for satisfaction of the decree may be enforced against individual heirs in the property held by them proportionate to their share in the estate."

The judge continued, at page 940, with reference to the situation where a defendant dies during the pendency of the suit:

> "It is also settled that where the defendant in an action dies after institution of the suit, the creditor after diligent and *bona fide* enquiry impleads some but not all the heirs as legal representatives, the heirs so impleaded represent the estate of the deceased and a decree against them binds not only those heirs who are impleaded in the action but the entire estate including the interest of those not brought on the record."

Necessarily, therefore, the appeal by the son to the Supreme Court failed. The Supreme Court held that the son, on the assumption that he was a bona fide heir, was sufficiently represented in the 1940 suit and was bound by the decree of the court arising out of the suit. Bona fide enquiry had been made and, in any event, the defendant had no defence to put forward which had not been presented in 1940.

11-14 At the beginning of this section, we referred to the role of local customary concepts and their potential clash with Muslim principles. The Shariat Act 1937, as stated above, was designed to destroy the application of large areas of customary law. One of the areas in which the Shariat Act was of much significance is intestate succession on death. In many parts of the Indian subcontinent, customary law operated to the effect that women could not inherit land. With the enactment of the Shariat Act, Muslim women became entitled to inherit the shares given to them in accordance with Muslim law. However, despite their right in law to inherit, many women were in practice deprived of their rightful shares by distant male kinsmen.

11–15 In Pakistan, this situation was reviewed by the Supreme Court in *Ghulam Ali v. Ghulam Sarwar Naqvi*, P.L.D. 1990 S.C. 1. The three petitioners were the three sons of Ghulam Ahmed Shah and the respondent admittedly was his daughter. Ghulam Ahmed Shah died in about 1963 leaving land in several estates, all of which had been divided amongst the heirs, including the daughter, with the exception of one estate. This estate had also been divided but the daughter of the deceased had evidently been excluded by her name not being entered in the pedigree table.

11–16 The petitioners' case was that they had spent large sums of money on the two marriages of the respondent and in legal actions following her divorce. They also argued that they had maintained her for a period of about five years. Accordingly, they claimed that because of the funds expended on her behalf, the respondent had relinquished her claim to inheritance in this estate.

11–17 The brothers had been unsuccessful throughout. On appeal before the Supreme Court, they persisted in using "a strong moral claim to the suit property" (page 8) because of their expenditure for the sister and argued that on account of adverse possession, time bars and the fact that she had not challenged the arrangement for a long time, the sister's suit should have been dismissed. Muhammad Afzal Zullah J. referred in detail to a number of recent cases on the point of adverse possession and held that in such cases, different considerations apply where Muslim women are involved. It was stated, at page 11:

> "As the question involved in this case relates to the claim of adverse possession and ouster by brothers against a sister, some more features of the legal controversy are to be examined, vis-a-vis, Islamic Law. Holy Prophet . . . declared some important rights of female, vis-a-vis, male. It is against the spirit of those rights, to hold that a brother can legally claim "adverse possession" against his sister and much less "ouster". Under the new dispensation in Pakistan such a claim may not be entertainable at all without encountering jurisprudential hurdles."

Finding that this was not really a new legal issue, the judge made reference to a number of older cases and then returned in detail to Muslim jurisprudence, stating at page 12:

> "The main points of the controversy in this behalf get resolved on the touchstone of Islamic law of inheritance. As soon as the owner dies, succession to his property opens. There is no State intervention or clergy's intervention needed for the passing of the title immediately, to the heirs. Thus it is obvious that a Muslim's estates [*sic*] legally and juridically vests immediately on his death in his or her heirs and their rights respectively come into separate existence forthwith. The theory of representation of the estate by an intermediary is unknown to Islamic Law of inheritance as compared to other systems. Thus there being no vesting of the estate of the deceased for an interregnum in any one like an executor or administrator, it devolves on the heirs automatically, and immediately in definite shares and fractions. It is so

notwithstanding whether they (the heirs) like it, want it, abhor it or shun it. It is the public policy of Islamic law. It is only when the property has thus vested in the heir after the succession opens, that he or she can alienate it in a lawful manner. There is enough comment and case-law on this point which stands accepted."

Accordingly the judge held, at page 12, in strong terms and focused on the legal protection of women and their interests under Muslim law:

"Thus the brother, the father, the husband, son or vice versa, does not or cannot intervenue [*sic*] as an intermediary. Here we are dealing with the brothers trying though illegally, as if a guardian-in-inheritance-so-called, of a sui juris sister, on allegedly "moral" basis, to oust her. It is clearly prohibited by Islam. The females cannot be treated so in our system. And we cannot in the present constitutional and legal system import or apply any foreign system or so-called common law, or law of nature in preference to our own."

11–18   The remainder of this important judgment is taken up with a detailed analysis of the Muslim law of inheritance and the position of females in this respect. The judge ventured into a comparative analysis of the position of females in Roman, English, Hindu and Muslim law (pages 12–17) and then reiterated the leading principles of Muslim law on the subject. Interestingly, he compared the position of many women in Pakistan today with those prevailing before the advent of Islam (pages 19, 20–21) and held, at page 20:

"The combined effect of all this, amongst others, lead us to assume that in case of need a woman can claim as of right, her maintenance and protection by her menfolk. But more important than this is the guarantee and enforcement of all the rights of women including that of inheritance which, as demonstrated find special place in the injunctions of Islam. This part of Islamic law from its background and nature is a matter of public policy of high importance. This amongst others is one field wherein a Muslim woman has more rights than man. Her treatment, status, rights and enforcement thereof, under Islam was a complete departure from what existed earlier or elsewhere. Unless it was given State protection, the change could not have been effective."

In several other recent cases, the Supreme Court of Pakistan has reinforced and extended its protection to women in *pardah*. In *Janat Bibi v. Sikandar Ali*, P.L.D. 1990 S.C. 642, the facts were that a woman had been cheated out of her property rights by a cunning neighbour, a police officer, who had persuaded the illiterate lady to affix her thumb impression on certain documents which she was not in a position to check. The Supreme Court held, at page 646, that as this case concerned an illiterate *pardanashin* lady, the burden of proof regarding any document executed by her or on her behalf and affecting her right or interest in immovable property is on the person who claims a right under the document. This was a well-settled position in law and the court went through a number of relevant cases on the subject. It was further noted, at page 648, that "the above rule applicable to pardanashin ladies has been extended to ignorant and illiterate women". Since there was no scope for dispute over the *pardanashin* status of the appellant, the court proceeded to examine the relevant documents and found, at page 651, that "it could not be said that these documents were read over or explained to the appellant or . . . to her mother". This finding was reiterated at the conclusion of the judgment and the illiterate lady won her case.

11-19 Some three years later, the Supreme Court reviewed the position as stated in *Janat Bibi* regarding the special protection for *pardanashin* and illiterate women in Pakistan in *Irshad Hussain v. Ijaz Hussain*, P.L.D. 1994 S.C. 326. In this case, however, it was found as a matter of fact that the old lady had not been illiterate. The court held that while the protective principles did extend to all illiterate women, when a woman was educated, not in *pardah* and capable of understanding the execution of a deed with a full and proper understanding of its implications, the principle was not attracted.

11-20 On the topic of 'death sickness', a few examples must suffice. In one Indian case,[14] a man was attacked by paralysis of the lower limbs and became a helpless invalid. He was a very old man and, as a result of his illness, he could no longer leave his bed either to say his prayers or to perform 'the ordinary offices of nature'. He executed a charitable endowment (*waqf*) in March. He was bedridden for nine months and finally died in November. It was held by the court that he executed the *waqf* during his death sickness, thus the endowment was valid only to the extent of one-third of the estate. A contrasting case is *Muhammad Gulshere Khan v. Mariam Begam*, I.L.R. [1881] 3 Al. 731. In this case a donor suffered an attack of boils and carbuncles. At the time of the donation, this illness had lasted for over a year, and there was no evidence to suggest that he apprehended death. It was held that the gift was not made during death sickness. It is interesting to note that in Shi'i law, an illness which has lasted for over a year can never constitute death sickness.

11-21 In Pakistan, the emphasis has been placed firmly on the subjective element of the law. Indeed, in one case, *Shamshad Ali Shah v. Hassan Shah*,[15] Kaikaus J. observed obiter that the rules must apply so long as the donor believes he was dying even if, in fact, he does not in the event actually die. This is perhaps an extreme view, although the proof of the subjective apprehension of death in the mind of the donor is clearly the crucial test in India as well as Pakistan. In *Asmat Begum v. Hussain Jan*, P.L.D. 1956 (W.P.) Pesh. 5, at page 8, it was stated that the law was settled "pretty accurately". In this case a daughter challenged the gift of his entire property by her father to his mother. The donor suffered an advanced stage of tuberculosis, and the court found that this was a case of 'death sickness'. Consequently, as held at page 11, the gift of the property "had no other value but that of a will, and since the mother is an heir the will in her favour would be completely invalid".

11-22 In *Abdul Hafiz Beg v. Sahebbi*, A.I.R. 1975 Bom. 165, when referring to previous cases,[16] Masodkar J. said, at pages 167–168:

". . . it may be taken as settled that [the] crucial test of marz-ul-maut is the (proof of the subjective apprehension of death in the) mind of the donor, that is to say, the apprehension derived from his own consciousness, as distinguished from the apprehension caused in the minds of others, and the other symptoms like physical incapacities are only the indicia, but not infallible signs or a sine qua non of marz-ul-maut . . . Thus as far as the decisions of Indian Courts are concerned, the law of marz-ul-maut is answered if it is proved that the ailing donor was apprehending death and in that condition had proceeded to effect disposition."

---

[14] *Karimanissa Bibi v. Hamedulla* [1925–1926] 30 Cal. W.N. 129.
[15] P.L.D. 1964 S.C. 143. *Jahan Khan v. Feroze*, P.L.D. 1951 Lah. 433, apply a strict test for death sickness. See also *Safia Begum v. Abdul Rajak*, A.I.R. 1945 Bom. 438, which is referred to in later cases.
[16] At p. 168, the judgment also refers to Pakistani case law as taking the same view.

In this case, one Abdul Kadar, a man of 80 years old, had been taken seriously ill and never recovered from this illness. In somewhat poetic language, the principle was further enunciated at page 169:

> "The apprehension that the curtain is wringing down on the life in such a state would easily grasp all the consciousness as the physical malady surely affects every faculty clouding the will and reason of human being ... The light of reason at such moment is not expected to burn bright as the flame of life itself flickers drawing ghastly shadows on the cold, deadly wall of the inevitable. It is conceivable, therefore, that the pragmatic philosophy of Mohamedan Law thought it wise to put under eclipse the acts and dispositions done under the promptings of a phychosis indicating apprehension or clear fear of death."

11–23 The court recognised at page 170 that, depending on the facts of a case, "an old man meeting a natural death may be well disposed to see that the matters are settled in his lifetime and such dispositions would be perfectly valid and would not answer marz-ul-maut". However, in the present case, the old man, apprehending his end, showed a sense of helplessness rather than purposive action. Thus, as stated at page 170:

> "All this raises a clear possibility that while he was making the gift which is about 24 hours before death, he was seized or gripped by the subjective and imminent apprehension of his death. In fact, the signs of such psychosis had already set in."

In the judge's own romantic language, at page 170, "the bed on which he rested proved to be the death-bed and at the mellowed age of eighty this leaf fell from the tree of life". There was, thus, no doubt that his gift could not be sanctioned.

Testate succession

The traditional rules

11–24 In pre-Islamic times, individuals could will or give away their property as they pleased. The Qur'anic system introduced more protection for close relatives and thus restricted the power of individuals to make wills or gifts of various kinds. Bharatiya ((1996), p. 270) emphasises this balancing of competing expectations from a different perspective:

> "A will offers to the testator the means of correcting to a certain extent the law of succession, and enabling some of those relatives who are excluded from inheritance to obtain a share in his property, and of recognizing the services rendered to him by a stranger. At the same time, the Prophet has declared that the power should not be exercised to the injury of the lawful heirs, and restricted the testator from bequeathing more than one-third of his estate."

Nasir (1990a, p. 264) writes that the most common definition of a will is that it is "a transfer of ownership for no consideration to take effect after death".[17] The general rule is that every adult Muslim with reasoning ability has capacity to make a will. A Hanafi, Hanbali or Shafi'i Muslim is adult for this purpose as soon as he has

---

[17] Nasir (1990a), pp. 264–273 treats this subject in a separate chapter with many references to modern Muslim jurisdictions.

attained puberty; the presumption in Sunni law is 15 years old at a maximum. The Shi'i law and the Maliki doctrine place the emphasis on the age of discernment, namely 10 years old. A will may be made either verbally or in writing. While the latter is preferred, there was traditionally much recognition of oral arrangements between people.[18]

11-25 There are two restrictions on the power to make bequests. The two rules dealing with *ultra vires* bequests in Sunni law are that no bequests can be made which involve disposition beyond one third of the net estate (unless the heirs agree) and that no bequest can be made in favour of an heir. The limitation for testamentary disposition to one third of the estate is seen, in the classical doctrine, as a fundamental rule deriving from the *hadith* of the Prophet.[19] Schacht (1979, p. 201) suggested that this restriction originates from the Umayyad period, connected as it is to a fiscal interest, so important at that time. The rule, nonetheless, is of prime significance, and no Muslim country has restricted its scope.

11-26 If the bequest, or the addition of various bequests, should exceed one third of the net estate, the rights of the compulsory heirs in the estate would be directly interfered with. Thus the distribution of the estate to legatees beyond the one third available for distribution by testamentary succession lies in the hands of the compulsory heirs. In Hanafi law, the consent of the heirs to such a distribution has to be obtained, if it can be, after the death of the *propositus*. In the Shi'i doctrine, however, where the legatee acquires a 'contingent interest' as soon as the bequest is made, consent of the heirs can be obtained before the *propositus* dies. When some of the heirs grant their consent to such a distribution, but others do not, the bequests are payable beyond the one third out of the shares of the consenting heirs alone.

11-27 In cases where the legacies amount to more than one third of the net estate, and when none of the surviving heirs consent, these legacies must be reduced. A testator can validly specify the order in which several bequests he has made are to be administered, and thus the bequests take effect in the order specified until the bequeathable one third is exhausted. If no specification has been given by the testator, the abatement in Sunni law is proportionate; for as the will speaks from death, the rights of the legatees all mature at the same point in time.[20] The only exception to this rule relates to an instance where two or more bequests have been made for a pious purpose. The abatement with respect to the pious purposes themselves is not proportionate. So-called 'voluntary charities' abate before 'recommended charities', which themselves take second place to 'obligatory charities'. In the Shi'i tradition, because of the emphasis given to the contingent rights of the legatees, the simple rule is 'the first in time prevails'. As between pious and secular bequests, normal rules of proportional abatement apply.

11-28 The second limiting factor for wills, that there can be no bequest in favour of an heir, has been subject to important reforms. Nasir (1990a, p. 269) refers to this rule as giving rise to "a great controversy" and writes (*id.*):

> "At one extreme, the Zahiris and some Malikis, Shafiis and Hanbalis rule that a will to an heir is utterly void, on the authority of a Tradition of the Prophet to that effect. They deem it as an act of injustice against the other heirs who may allow it, in which case it shall not be a bequest but a gift . . . On the other

---

[18] See Coulson (1971), pp. 215–216; briefly Nasir (1990a), p. 265.

[19] Obviously, all writers on the subject make reference to this rule. For some useful details see Nasir (1990a), pp. 170–171, Bharatiya (1996), p. 275 and esp. Fyzee (1974), pp. 360–363.

[20] The rules in this respect relate to debts to be paid out of the estate. For details see Coulson (1971), pp. 250–251.

extreme, the Shia Ithna-Asharis and Zaidis accept as valid a will to an heir within one-third of the net estate without requiring the consent of the other heirs. A middle course is steered by the Hanafis, the Hanbalis, the Shafiis and the majority Malikis, who hold that a will to an heir is valid subject to the consent of the other heirs."

This divergence of opinion arises because the interpretation of Sura II verse 180 in the Qur'an appears to permit a testator, within the one third limit, to bequeath to whomsoever he desires. Sura II, verse 180, provides:

"It is prescribed, when death approaches any of you, if he leave any goods, that he make a bequest to parents and next of kin, according to reasonable usage this is due from the God-fearing."

Most of the Sunnis believe that this verse has been abrogated by the verse which details the specific fractions of the estate to particular relatives of the deceased (see pages 453–454 below). In much of Sunni law, a bequest to an heir is therefore treated as *ultra vires*, and its efficacy depends, as in the first limiting factor, on the agreement to the distribution by the heirs. The more generous Shi'i law has been adopted in various jurisdictions, including Egypt, Iraq and Sudan.

11–29 If a will is procured by fraud or duress, it will be void. Bequests which are opposed to Islam, such as a bequest to a gambling house or to a bar, are void. Bequests which are outwardly unquestionable, but which have been made for an immoral purpose are not void in Hanafi law, where the emphasis is on the form, but are void in Hanbali law where, because of the strong moralism of that school, a bequest inspired by an improper motive is ineffective. An example of the Hanbali rule, which was adopted in Egypt in 1946, is a bequest by the testator to Mr X which, although not stated, is in gratitude for having kept him supplied with liquor, or a bequest to Miss Y, which is impliedly granted in recognition of her services as his mistress (see also Nasir (1990a), p. 265).

11–30 The legatee must be in existence at the time the bequest is made. This raises the particular problem of the child *en ventre sa mere*. Such a child has a legal existence and is entitled to take a bequest if born within the maximum period of gestation from the date of the bequest.[21]

11–31 In Sunni law, the will must be accepted by the legatee after the legator's death; thus it is necessary for the legatee to survive the deceased. Acceptance may be either express or implied. If the legatee dies after the legator but before he has had the opportunity of accepting the will, the view of the Hanafi law is that the property devolves on the heirs of the legatee. Presumably, this situation is acceptable because the will is deemed to be completed on the death of the legator, and there can be no opportunity to repudiate the will. The other Sunni schools adopt a slightly different approach. They say that an option (*khiyar*) arises in this situation and the option to accept or repudiate devolves on the heirs of the legatee. Thus if these heirs of the deceased legatee accept the legacy, it is valid, otherwise it is void (*batil*).

11–32 It may be convenient at this stage to summarise the major differences between Sunni and Shi'i law (of the Ithna 'Ashari school) on testamentary succession.[22]

---

[21] For details see Nasir (1990a), pp. 267–268.
[22] Several of these issues are discussed in more detail in paras 11–37—11–134, below with particular reference to intestate succession. For the views of the other Sunni schools and modern legislation, readers are referred to Coulson (1971), pp. 229–231.

(1) Capacity to make a will:
    Hanafi law – puberty and sane
    Shi'i law – 10 (age of discernment)

(2) Consent of heirs to distribution of an otherwise *ultra vires* will:
    Hanafi law – consent after the death of the testator
    Shi'i law – consent can be given either after the testator's death or during his lifetime

(3) Abatement:
    Hanafi law – proportionate reduction
    Shi'i law – first in time prevails

(4) Bequests to an heir:
    Hanafi law – bequests to an heir are *ultra vires*
    Shi'i law – a bequest can be made in favour of an heir within one third of the distribution

(5) Legatee predeceases testator:
    Hanafi law – legacy lapses
    Shi'i law – the heirs of the legatee have the option of accepting or rejecting the legacy

(6) Homicide:
    Hanafi law – if the legatee caused the death of the legator in a direct manner, whether intentional or otherwise, the bequest is *ultra vires*
    Shi'i law – only intentional homicide will deprive the legatee of the bequest, although in this case the bequest is *batil*, and the legatee is absolutely barred.

Muslim bequests in South Asian law

11–33 With regard to wills, the minimum age of capacity on the Indian subcontinent is established by section 3 of the Indian Majority Act 1875 as eighteen years.[23] Cases of procurement, such as undue influence, or even coercion, often occur in cases where heirs allege that the deceased was a woman who observed strict seclusion (*purdah*). In the Anglo-Mohammedan system, the rule in this situation is that the burden lies on the beneficiary of the estate to prove that the secluded woman (*pardanashin*) knew what she was doing. The burden is discharged if the beneficiary proves that the *propositus* acted after receiving independent advice. Wills may therefore be challenged on the grounds of undue influence (see Mannan (1990), p. 174).

11–34 Wills may be made verbally or in writing.[24] More important in practice has been the one third rule. Bharatiya (1996, p. 270) refers briefly to the fact that the one third rule regarding wills was recognised by the British Indian courts in a number of cases as early as 1806. Mannan (1990, p. 182–185) discusses this rule in some detail with reference to its origins and decided cases. Whereas many other writers trace this rule back to Roman law, Mannan (1990, p. 182) refers to *sunna* as a source in this respect. South Asian law, being Hanafi-dominated, accepts the one third rule and makes any excess bequest (as indeed any bequest to an heir, too) subject to consent by the heirs.

---

[23] In certain situations, the age of majority is actually 21 years. For details see Mannan (1990), pp. 173–174.
[24] For details on this aspect see especially Mannan (1990), pp. 174–176 with reference to some decided cases.

11–35   The second important legal subject in this context has been the question of bequest to an heir. The general rule in South Asian Muslim law is that "a bequest to an heir is not valid unless the other heirs consent to the bequest after the death of the testator" (Mannan (1990), p. 176). The leading case in South Asian law regarding this matter is the Privy Council decision in *Ghulam Mohammad v. Ghulam Husain*, A.I.R. 1932 P.C. 81. Here, a Hanafi Muslim made a will which included the following terms:

> "I, Shaikh Khadim Husain, son of Munshi Aman Ullah, deceased . . . I have two sons . . . three daughters . . . and one wife. My elder son shall remain in proprietary possession [of certain property] acquired by my deceased father given to me under the will dated 1866."

Sir George Lowndes, in the Privy Council, said that it was not in dispute that under Hanafi law a will conferring beneficial interests to heirs is invalid unless consented to by other heirs after the testator's death. In a dispute between the two sons, the Privy Council formed the view that the younger son should be entitled to share equally with the elder son in the property mentioned.

11–36   This case was more recently referred to as an authority in a case coming before the Kerala High Court, which also made reference to other cases on the subject.[25] Here, a Muslim father had partitioned the family's property during his lifetime in a kind of family arrangement. This was challenged after the father's death. The court commented on the relationship between family arrangement and wills and it was stated, at page 204:

> "It is notorious that a testament is invariably designed to avoid a scramble among the heirs; but nobody ever said that all testaments are family arrangements. The test of a family arrangement is the give and take involved in the transaction."

In this case, it was held that in the absence of agreement by the other heirs, the purported bequest to one of the heirs could not be upheld as valid. In both Indian and Pakistani law today, therefore, it appears that the traditional rules of Muslim law are operated by the courts. The fact that most such disputes never reach the courts points to the continued importance of local and customary traditions.

Compulsory succession

The traditional concepts and their operation in practice

11–37   This section covers the basic principles of intestate succession law among Muslims and illustrates them with numerous examples. While emphasis is again placed on the Hanafi law, Shi'i principles are referred to, as well as some modern reforms.

11–38   In pre-Islamic Arabia, the rules of succession were connected directly with the system of tribal warfare, that is, the participation in combat of the man, and the non-participation in combat of the woman.[26] Doi (1984, p. 272) discussed the basic features of the system:

> "The rules regarding inheritance . . . are based on the principle that property which belonged to the deceased should devolve on those who by reason of

---

[25] See also *Valanhiyil Kunhi Avulla v. Eengayil Peetikayil Kunhi Avulla*, A.I.R. 1964 Ker. 200.
[26] For some indications see Nasir (1990a), pp. 218–219.

consanguinity or marital relations have the strongest claim to be benefited by it and in proportion to the strength of such claim."

Nasir (1990a, p. 219) emphasises the composite nature of the rules which evolved over time and sought to harmonise several conflicting principles:

"The Islamic law of inheritance has not entirely abolished the customary pre-Islamic law, but rather introduced radical changes to it. The doctrine of shares then becomes understandable once it is realized that the sharers consist of those who were not entitled to succeed under the customary law, in the circumstances in which they are granted the right to take their respective shares."

Those who normally inherited the estate in the pre-Islamic system were able to trace their relationship with a *propositus* exclusively by male links. These agnatic relatives, the *'asaba*, provided the cohesive unit of the Arabian tribe. In a competition between two male agnate relatives, the simple rule was that the one 'nearest' to the *propositus* inherited to the exclusion of those more remote.

Table 2

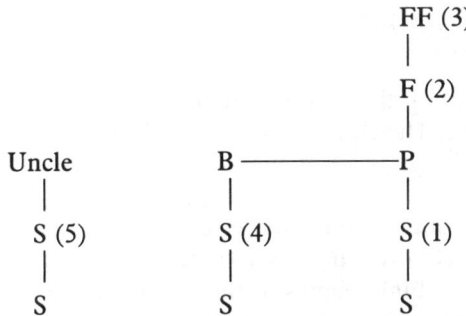

P = *Propositus*

11–39 One of the Prophet's major political objectives was to favour the nuclear family over the tribal unit. It is believed that the first Qur'anic provision in this area is Sura II, verse 180, which we cited at page 450 above. This verse introduced the moral obligation that Muslims must make satisfactory provision for parents and next of kin. This revelation, quite general in scope, was filled in by other verses in Sura IV, revealed during the time of the early desperate battles with the unbelievers.[27] These provisions allot specific fractions of the estate, for the first time, to the widows and orphans and other relatives who were not entitled to inherit through the agnatic tie. The old agnatic system is not totally excluded, however. Indeed Sura IV, verse 11, itself recognises that sons still inherit under the new system and provides:

"Allah thus directs you
as regards your children's
inheritance: to the male
a portion equal to that
of two females."

The Qur'anic system of inheritance, therefore, complements the old agnatic system. The synthesis of the two systems as worked out initially by the *sunna* of

---

[27] For details see Nasir (1990a), pp. 219–221.

Mohammed, represents the Sunni law of inheritance. First, the Qur'anic heirs are given their share, and then the residue is distributed to the nearest agnate.

The Qur'anic heirs

11–40 In our outline below, emphasis is given to the Hanafi law but the main provisions of Shi'i law are considered, too. The basic principle is that there are 12 so-called Qur'anic heirs in Sunni law.[28]

(1) Husband (H)
(2) Wife (W)
(3) Father (F)
(4) True grandfather (FF)[29]
(5) Mother (M)
(6) True grandmother (MM; FM)[30]
(7) Daughter (D)
(8) Son's daughter (howsoever low, *i.e.* SD, SSD, etc.)
(9) Full sister (sometimes referred to as the germane sister, Sis)
(10) Consanguine sister (children of the same father but different mothers) (Cons Sis)
(11) Uterine brother (Ut Br)
(12) Uterine sister (Ut Sis)[31]

We now proceed with a brief discussion of each of these relatives in turn, in order to build up a picture of the Hanafi succession rules. Readers are also referred to the simplified chart of Hanafi succession, found at the end of this section (below, page 466).

11–41 The husband's share is one quarter of the net estate. When there are no children or agnatic grandchildren, his share is increased to one half of the estate. It is immaterial whether the child belongs to the spouse relict (the surviving spouse) or is the issue of another marriage of the deceased spouse.

11–42 The share of the wife is one eighth of the net estate. If there are two wives, they share the one eighth between them. Where there are no children, or agnatic grandchildren, the wife or wives take one quarter.

Table 3

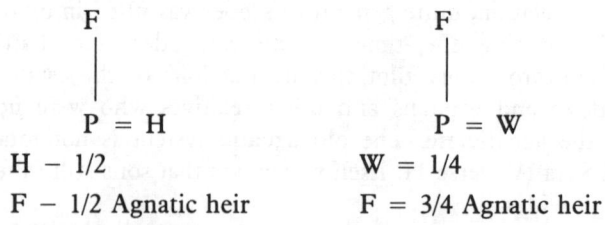

<hr />

[28] These are also sometimes referred to as class 1 heirs. The agnates comprise class 2, and more distant kinsmen constitute class 3. Distant kinsmen very rarely inherit, and the rules of distribution within this group are not discussed in this book. Readers may refer to Coulson (1971) for detailed provisions.

[29] A true grandfather is a male ancestor between whom and the *propositus* no female intervenes, that is, a paternal grandfather. A false grandfather would be a male ancestor between whom and the *propositus* a female intervenes, *e.g.* a maternal grandfather.

[30] A true grandmother is a female ancestor between whom and the *propositus* no false grandfather intervenes. Both the maternal and the paternal grandmother can inherit. A false grandmother is a mother's father's mother (MFM). She is excluded from any entitlement to inherit in this category in any circumstances.

[31] The latter two are children of the same mother, but of different fathers.

11–43   The father can inherit in three possible categories. If the son is alive, the father's share is limited to one sixth. If the daughter or son's daughter is alive, but not the son, he receives one sixth plus any residue as the nearest agnate. If there is no son or daughter or son's daughter, he simply inherits as the nearest agnate.

Table 4

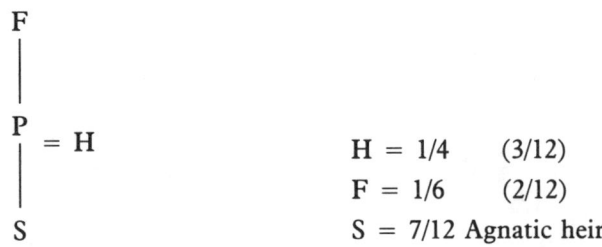

H = 1/4   (3/12)
F = 1/6   (2/12)
S = 7/12 Agnatic heir

Table 5

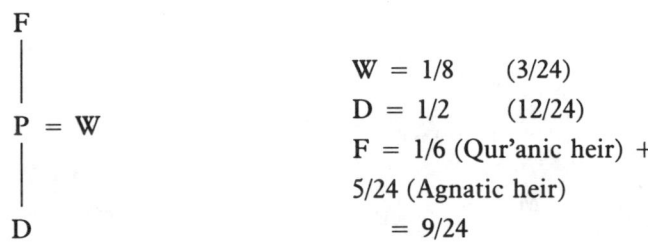

W = 1/8   (3/24)
F = 1/6   (4/24)
S = 17/24 Agnatic heir

Table 6

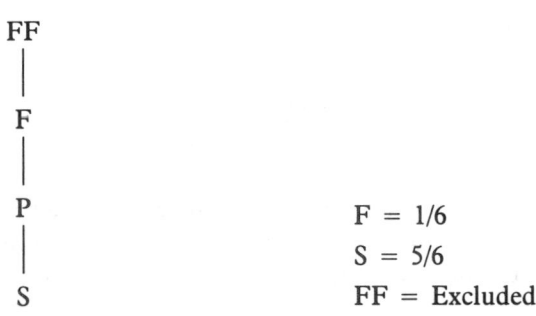

W = 1/8   (3/24)
D = 1/2   (12/24)
F = 1/6 (Qur'anic heir) +
5/24 (Agnatic heir)
      = 9/24

11–44   The true grandfather, as we have seen, is a slightly archaic term which refers to the single line of father's father, even though it is highly unlikely that an ancestor beyond the second generation from the propositus would ever inherit. The grandfather was added by *sunna* and was not expressly mentioned in the Qur'an. His share is one sixth. If, however, the father is alive, he is excluded. In the absence of the father, the son, daughter, or any child of the son, he will inherit as the nearest agnate. As in the case of the father, the presence of the daughter or son's daughter and the grandfather enables the grandfather to inherit in both capacities.

Table 7

FF
|
F
|
P
|
S

F = 1/6
S = 5/6
FF = Excluded

11–45 The mother is given a 'normal' share of one sixth which she inherits when her child dies leaving surviving his or her own child or agnatic grandchild. The mother's share is capable of increase. In the event of no child or agnatic grandchild of the *propositus* being alive at the moment of the death of the *propositus*, the share of the mother is increased to one third of the estate.

Table 8

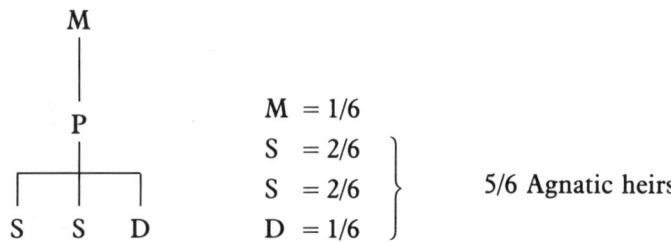

11–46 The daughter, incidentally, inherits in this situation as the agnatic heir rather than the Qur'anic heir, for the presence of the son pulls her over to agnatic inheritance. She inherits in the proportion one to two with the son in accordance with the Qur'anic provision in Sura IV, verse 11. This concept, known as *ta'sib*, is an extremely important provision, illustrating as it does the strength of the agnatic link.

Table 9

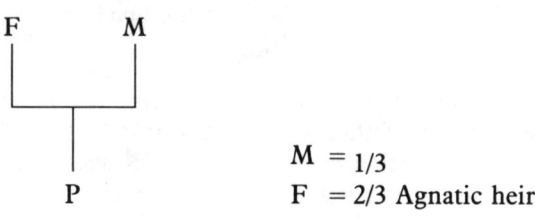

Table 10

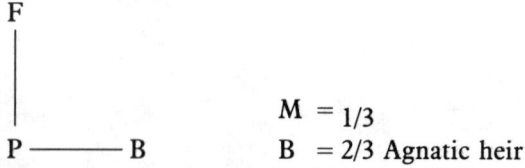

11–47 Where the *propositus* dies survived by his mother and one brother or one sister, then the mother's share is one third. If, however, there are two collaterals, be they brothers, sisters or a combination, the mother's share is reduced to the normal one sixth.

Table 11

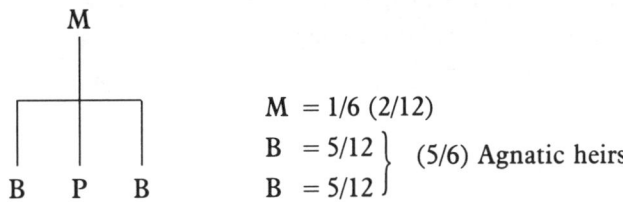

$$M = 1/6 \ (2/12)$$
$$B = 5/12 \ \bigg\} \ (5/6) \ \text{Agnatic heirs}$$
$$B = 5/12 \ \bigg/$$

11–48 A particular problem arises when the *propositus* is survived by the mother, the father, and the surviving spouse. If the normal rules are applied on the death of the wife, then the result of the distribution of the estate would be as shown in Table 12:

Table 12 (incorrect)

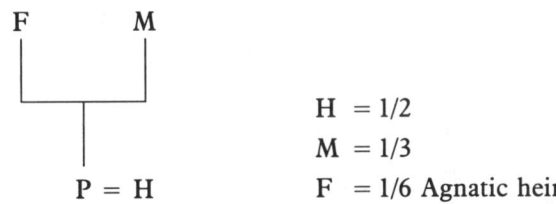

$$H = 1/2$$
$$M = 1/3$$
$$F = 1/6 \ \text{Agnatic heir}$$

11–49 This case was brought before Caliph 'Umar. Faced with the obvious illogicality in Islamic principle in this result, and bearing in mind the Qur'anic provision requiring distribution of twice the share to a male as compared to that of the female when they are of equal degree from the *propositus*, he solved the problem in the following manner. He first gave the surviving spouse his share of the estate, and distributed to the mother one third of the residue (*i.e.* one third of one half = one sixth). He then distributed the remainder of the estate (one third) to the father as the agnatic heir.

Table 12 (correct)

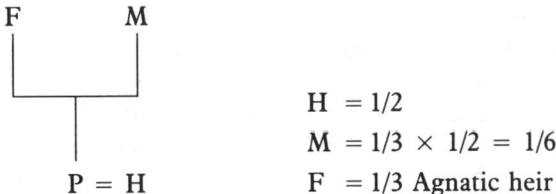

$$H = 1/2$$
$$M = 1/3 \times 1/2 = 1/6$$
$$F = 1/3 \ \text{Agnatic heir}$$

11–50 In this case, the Qur'anic provisions are subjected to a forced and restricted interpretation, primarily to preserve the customary pre-eminence of the father as the agnatic heir. The same approach is applied in the case of the death of the husband.

Table 13

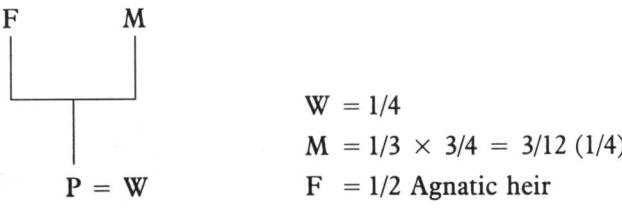

$$W = 1/4$$
$$M = 1/3 \times 3/4 = 3/12 \ (1/4)$$
$$F = 1/2 \ \text{Agnatic heir}$$

11–51 It should be noted also that the paternal grandfather does not have the same capacity or authority to reduce the mother's share.

Table 14

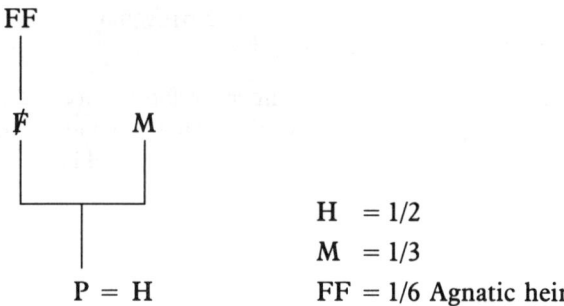

H = 1/2
M = 1/3
FF = 1/6 Agnatic heir

Table 15

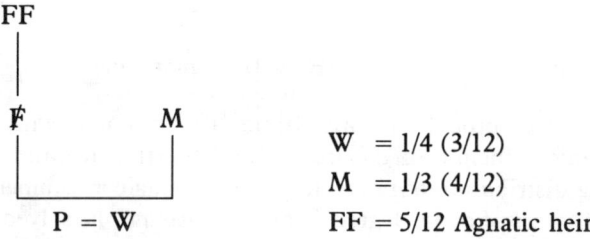

W = 1/4 (3/12)
M = 1/3 (4/12)
FF = 5/12 Agnatic heir

11–52 The true grandmother is treated very much as a secondary heir. When the mother is alive, then the true grandmother is excluded entirely. The Hanafi school treats all true grandmothers as a group; when two are equally entitled, they share the one sixth share, although the basic principle is that the nearer in degree will exclude the more remote. Thus, the maternal true grandmother is excluded by the nearer maternal or paternal true grandmother. Also, at least in India, the paternal true grandmother is excluded by the father or the near true grandfather as well as the above-mentioned relatives. The true grandmother does not appear in the Qur'anic revelation and, like the grandfather, this category is added by the *sunna*.

11–53 The Qur'anic share for the daughter is one half of the net estate. If two or more daughters survive the *propositus*, then that share is increased to a collective two-thirds. As we have seen already, however, the presence of the son agnatises the daughter, and she inherits with the son as an agnate, without regard to her Qur'anic status in the proportion of two shares to the son and one share to the daughter.

Table 16

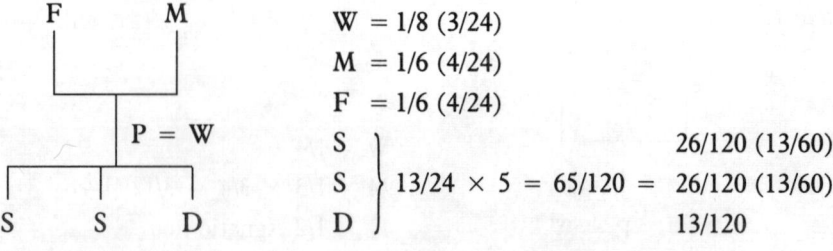

W = 1/8 (3/24)
M = 1/6 (4/24)
F = 1/6 (4/24)
S ⎫
S ⎬ 13/24 × 5 = 65/120 =
D ⎭

26/120 (13/60)
26/120 (13/60)
13/120

11-54 The daughter is described as the *'asaba bi ghayriha*; the son as the *'asaba bi nafsihi*. Two other examples will suffice to illustrate the principle in Tables 17 and 18.

Table 17

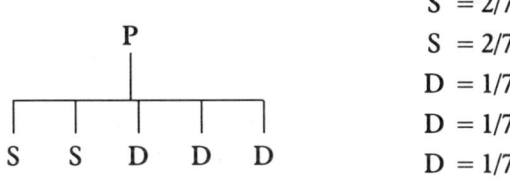

S = 2/7
S = 2/7
D = 1/7
D = 1/7
D = 1/7

Table 18

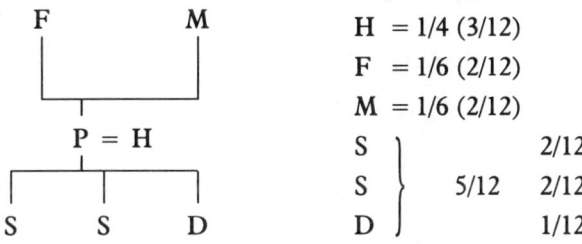

H = 1/4 (3/12)
F = 1/6 (2/12)
M = 1/6 (2/12)

S		2/12
S	5/12	2/12
D		1/12

11-55 The rules relating to the daughter are intertwined with those for the son's daughter (the son being deceased). The share of the son's daughter is one half, if there are two or more such daughters, it is two thirds. But if there is a daughter and a son's daughter, the daughter and the son's daughter receive a collective portion of two thirds in the proportion of one half to the daughter as opposed to one sixth to the son's daughter. If, however, there are more than two daughters, the collective portion of two thirds is exhausted by the presence of the daughters, and nothing will remain for the agnatic granddaughter.

Table 19

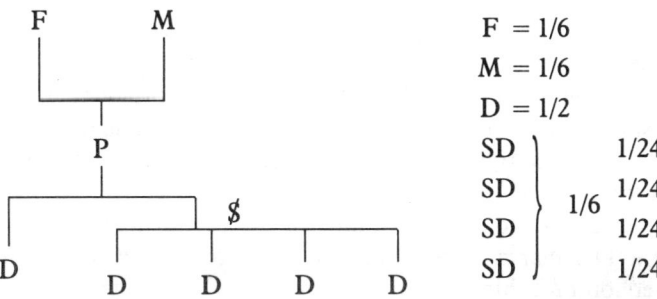

F = 1/6
M = 1/6
D = 1/2

SD		1/24
SD	1/6	1/24
SD		1/24
SD		1/24

Table 20

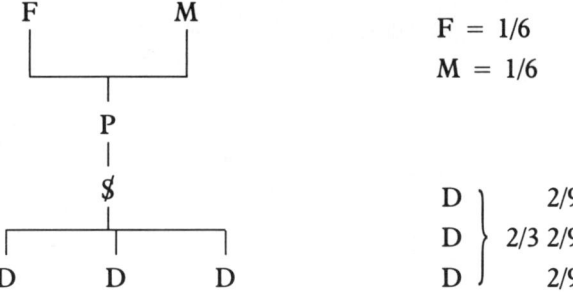

F = 1/6
M = 1/6

D ⎫   2/9
D ⎬ 2/3 2/9
D ⎭   2/9

Table 21

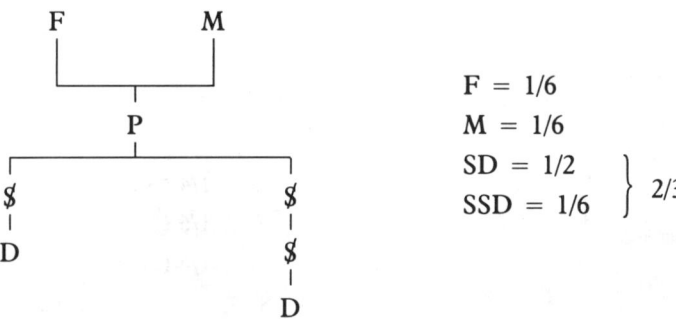

F = 1/6
M = 1/6
SD = 1/2 ⎫
SSD = 1/6 ⎬ 2/3

Table 22

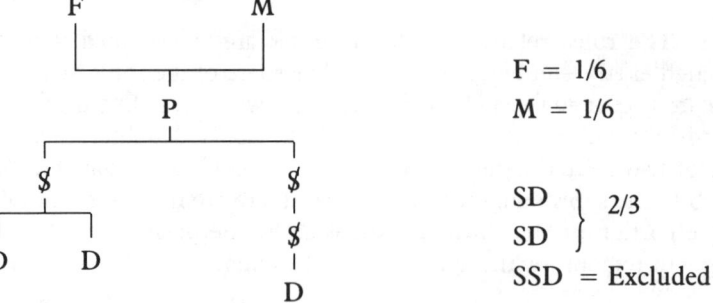

F = 1/6
M = 1/6

SD ⎫ 2/3
SD ⎭

SSD = Excluded

11–56 An important point to make at this stage is that a son's daughter is agnatised by an equidistant son's son in exactly the same way as a daughter is agnatised by a son. This principle, that of *ta'sib*, may be to the advantage of the son's daughter, but on the other hand may in some instances operate to her disadvantage.

11–57 It would operate to her advantage in the case where, under the Qur'anic principles, the existence of two daughters exhausts the share of the Qur'anic estate available for distribution to the son's daughter. However, the existence also of the son's son 'reactivates' the son's daughter as an heir and she can thus participate in the distribution of the agnatic residue in the proportion of one share to the son's daughter to two shares to the son's son. This point is made clear in the second and correct version of Table 23.

Table 23 (incorrect)

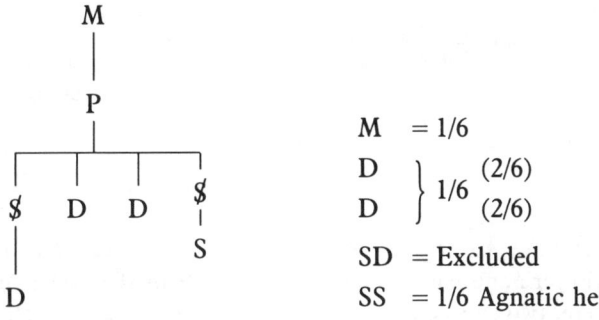

M   = 1/6

D   } 1/6   (2/6)
D   }   (2/6)

SD = Excluded

SS = 1/6 Agnatic heir

Table 23 (correct)

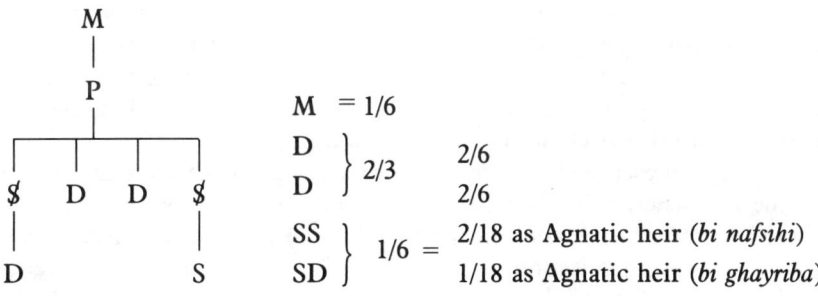

M = 1/6

D } 2/3   2/6
D }   2/6

SS } 1/6 = 2/18 as Agnatic heir (*bi nafsihi*)
SD }   1/18 as Agnatic heir (*bi ghayriba*)

11–58 If, in contrast, the son's daughter could inherit under the Qur'anic rules together with one daughter, the presence of the son's son nonetheless will pull her on to agnatic inheritance. In some instances, the residue may in fact be very small; in other even more unfortunate circumstances, the residue available for agnatic inheritance may indeed be non-existent. If this is the case she is indeed an unlucky kinswoman, as shown below:

Table 24 (correct)

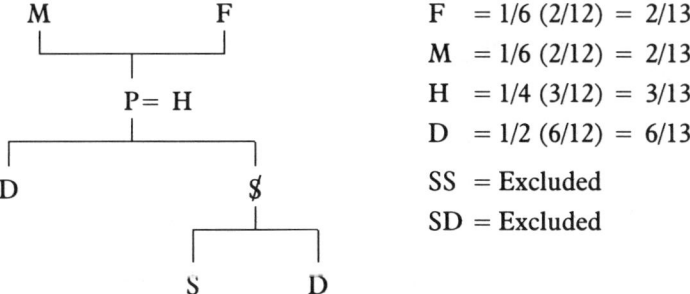

F = 1/6 (2/12) = 2/13
M = 1/6 (2/12) = 2/13
H = 1/4 (3/12) = 3/13
D = 1/2 (6/12) = 6/13

SS = Excluded
SD = Excluded

11–59 It will be noticed that in this case there has to be a proportionate reduction according to rules which we shall consider briefly later in this Chapter. It must be mentioned, of course, that the presence of a son or indeed a higher son's son excludes the son's daughter completely.

Table 25

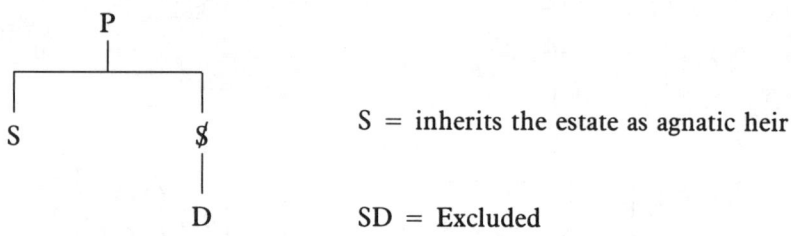

S = inherits the estate as agnatic heir

SD = Excluded

11–60 The germane sister and the consanguine sister can be considered together. The full (germane) sister's share is one half of the estate or, if there are two or more of them, two thirds. Similarly, the consanguine sister's share is one half (or if there are two or more of them, two thirds). Like the grandfather, the grandmother and the son's daughter, the full and consanguine sisters are, at times, excluded entirely. The full sister and the consanguine sister are excluded by the son, the son's son however low in degree, the father, and (notwithstanding minority opinions) by the true grandfather. The view of Abu Bakr that in a competition between the grandfather and the full sister the grandfather excludes the full sister, is accepted by way of consensus (*ijma*) in Hanafi law.[32] It needs to be emphasised that the full brother excludes the consanguine sister.

11–61 The presence of the brother, the daughter, or the son's daughter, together with the full sister, will affect the latter's share. It does not, however, necessarily exclude her from the rights of inheritance. In each of these circumstances, the sister will be subject to agnatisation, although in different ways and for different reasons.

Table 26

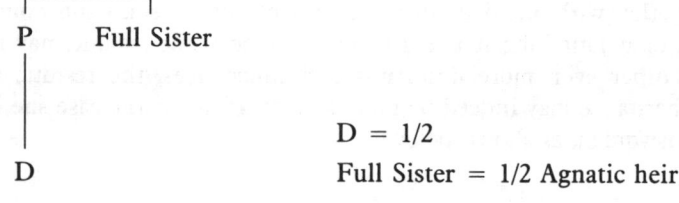

D = 1/2

Full Sister = 1/2 Agnatic heir

Table 27

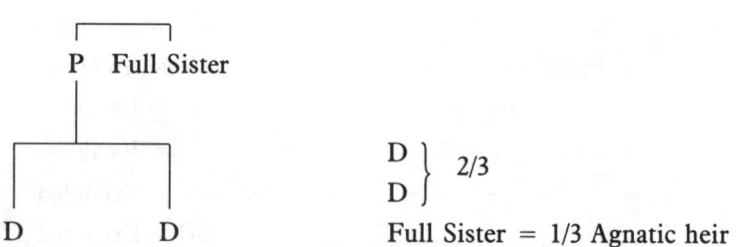

D } 2/3
D

Full Sister = 1/3 Agnatic heir

11–62 In these two illustrations, the daughter takes her primary share as a Qur'anic heir, forcing the sister on to agnatic inheritance. In the first illustration, the sister is in no way disadvantaged. In the second illustration, however, the presence of the two daughters will reduce the share of the sister to one third of the

---

[32] For a detailed discussion of the minority opinions and the juristic arguments which led the Hanafi jurists to accept Abu Bakr's solution to this problem, see Coulson (1971), pp. 68–78.

estate as agnatic heir. The son's daughter has the same capacity to 'push out' the collateral on to agnatic inheritance. The same rule applies also when the son's daughter or the daughter inherits with the consanguine sister.

11–63 When a full brother and a full sister co-exist, they take collectively as agnatic heirs, the brother taking a double share. Similarly, a consanguine sister co-existing with a consanguine brother takes agnatically, the brother receiving the double share of the sister. A full brother, as already stated, excludes the consanguine sister.

11–64 As in the case of the daughter and the son's daughter, the co-existence of the full sister and the consanguine sister enables the combined share of two thirds to be distributed to these collaterals in the proportion of one half to the full sister, to one sixth to the consanguine sister. Where there are two full sisters, however, the consanguine sister is excluded, for the two thirds of the estate available for distribution has been exhausted. The presence of a consanguine brother, however, affects the distribution for he has the capacity to agnatise the consanguine sister. There is, therefore, scope for distribution of the estate in such a way as would, in some cases, be to the advantage of the consanguine sister, and in other cases, to her disadvantage. There is a parallel here with the son's son who co-exists with the son's daughter. Thus we have the case of the lucky kinswoman in Table 28 below, while the case of the unlucky kinswoman is illustrated in Table 29.

Table 28

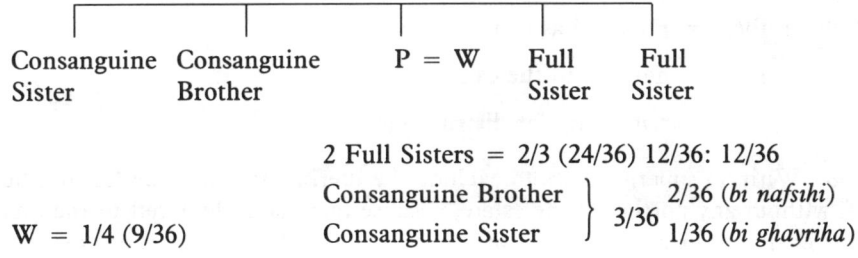

Table 29

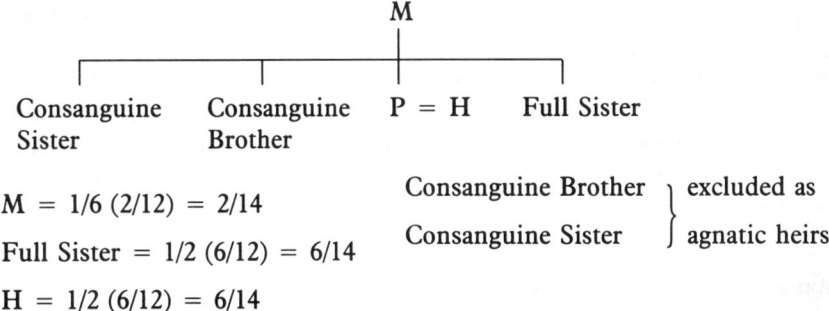

11–65 In this situation, the totality of the shares amounts to more than the whole, so there has to be reduction in the amounts received by the Qur'anic heirs, and the agnatic heirs, including the consanguine sister, are excluded from participating in the estate. A short description of how the reduction takes place is given further below (see page 468).

11–66 The list of Qur'anic heirs is concluded by the uterine collaterals, uterine brothers and uterine sisters. In a system of relatively easy divorce, uterine relationships are fairly common. As collaterals, the uterine collaterals are excluded by the superior heirs, namely son, daughter, son's daughter, father and true grandfather. If none of these people are present, the uterine collaterals will take one sixth; or if two or more survive, one third. All uterines take an equal share in the estate. Thus the general rule that a male heir takes twice the amount of the female heir of equal degree from the *propositus* does not apply to the uterine relationships.

11–67 A particularly interesting problem occurs when the full brother co-exists with the uterine brother; for instance, when the *propositus* dies leaving surviving her a husband, the mother, and uterine and full brothers. One way to distribute the estate is to apply the normal principle of distribution; thus the Qur'anic heirs receive their fractions, and any residue is distributed to the *'asaba*.

Table 30

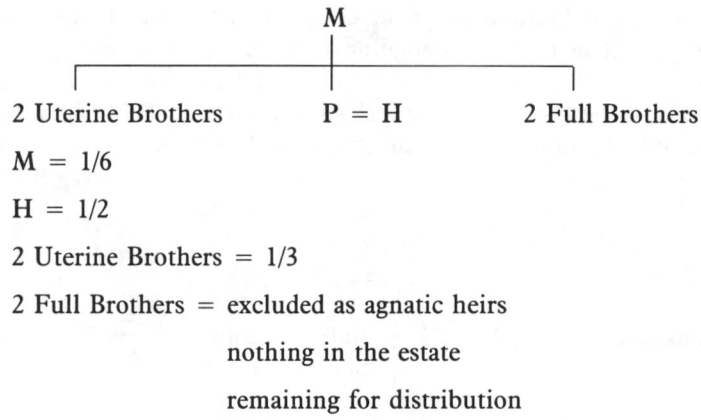

M

2 Uterine Brothers   P = H   2 Full Brothers

M = 1/6

H = 1/2

2 Uterine Brothers = 1/3

2 Full Brothers = excluded as agnatic heirs

nothing in the estate

remaining for distribution

11–68 With no superior heirs to exclude the uterine brothers, the full brothers are left without any portion of the estate, because there is nothing left in the estate for agnatic inheritance. The rights of the husband and of the mother are not in dispute, and thus the conflict is clearly between the uterine brothers and the full brothers. As Coulson ((1971, p. 73) observed, this conflict illustrates the head-on clash between pre-Islamic customary principles favouring the old tribal heirs (the full brothers) and the claims of the new heirs introduced by the Qur'anic revelations (the uterine brothers).

11–69 This led to the famous *Donkey* case.[33] The argument on behalf of the full brothers before Caliph 'Umar was to the effect that, as the uterine brothers and they themselves all had the same mother, they should be allowed to ignore their agnatic tie, and thus stand on a parity with the uterines. They put their argument in the following way:

> "O commander of the faithful!
> Suppose our father were a donkey (a *himar*);
> Do we not have the same mother as the deceased?"

We are told that 'Umar reversed his previous decision, and ordered that the one third be distributed to all the brothers, both full and uterine. This case, known as the *Himariyya* case, can be illustrated as follows:

---

[33] On this case see in detail Coulson (1971), pp. 73–78.

Table 31
The Himariyya Case

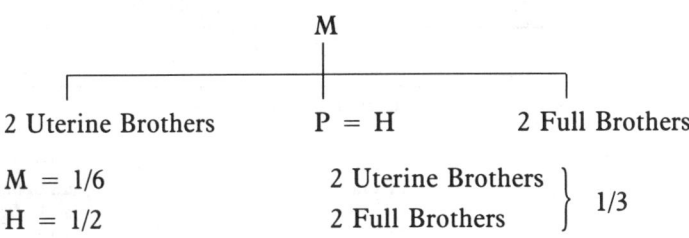

M = 1/6	2 Uterine Brothers ⎫
H = 1/2	2 Full Brothers ⎬ 1/3

11-70 A further complication arises in the situation where the grandfather is alive together with the uterine and full brothers. Some opinion allows the grandfather to inherit collectively with the full brothers in agnatic inheritance. The grandfather, however, excludes the uterine brothers from inheritance, and therefore the full brothers attempt to move back to the agnatic link. Given the exclusionary powers of the grandfather, the full brothers are in a stronger position if they can be treated as agnates rather than as Qur'anic heirs. The rule, which is known to us as Malik's rule, illustrated in Table 32 below, prevents such a development. A brother, it is held, cannot be uterine for one purpose and germane for another. Thus the grandfather takes the residue, and the full and the uterine brothers are excluded entirely.

Table 32
Malik's rule

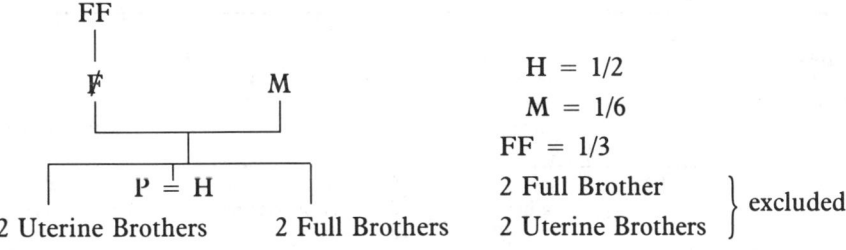

H = 1/2	
M = 1/6	
FF = 1/3	
2 Full Brother	⎫ excluded
2 Uterine Brothers	⎬

11-71 These two rules, the *Himariyya* and Malik's rule, are applied in Maliki law, but they are not followed in the Hanafi law. The Hanafi jurists uphold the consistent view that someone who is once an 'asaba, is always an 'asaba. Thus the full brother must remain as such, and in the situation illustrated by Table 30, the full brothers are excluded.

11-72 The Hanafis do not permit a full brother to inherit agnatically with the paternal grandfather. If the grandfather is alive at the opening of succession together with uterine brothers and full brothers, then, in the Hanafi law, uterine brothers are excluded by the superior heir, and the germane brothers are excluded because the Hanafi jurists acknowledge the pre-eminent agnatic claim of the paternal grandfather.

Table 33
Overview of the main rules in tabular form

Heir	Share	Excluded by	Affected by	In Which Case	Notes
Husband	1/4	—	no child or child of son	1/2	
Wife	1/8	—	no child or child of son	1/4	
Father	1/6	—	no child or child of son	agnatised	Father is both an agnatic and a Qur'anic heir
True grandfather	1/6	lower g/f or father	no child or child of son	agnatised	added by Sunna
Mother	1/6	—	1. no child or child of son	1/3	
			2. *one* brother or sister (and no child)	1/3	
			3. coexisting with father and spouse (and no child and not more than one collateral)	1/3 of residue	'Umariyyatam decision
True grandmother	1/6	*maternal true g/m:* mother, nearer maternal or paternal g/m *paternal true g/m:* these plus father, nearer true g/f.			added by Sunna (at least in India)
Daughter	1/2 (if 2 = 2/3)	—	son	agnatised	
Son's daughter however low i.e.: SSD, SSSD	1/2 (if 2 = 2/3)	son, more than one daughter, more than one higher son's daughter	1. one daughter 2. one higher SD 3. equal son's son	1. 1/6 2. 1/6 3. agnatised	Reactivisation can operate lucky or unlucky kinsmen
Full sister	1/2 (if 2 = 2/3)	son, son's son, father, true g/f	full brother, daughter or son's daughter	agnatised	in differing ways
Consanguine sister	1/2 (if 2 = 2/3)	son, son's son, father, true g/f, brother (full) more than one full sister	1. full sister 2. consanguine brother 3. daughter or son's daughter	1. 1/6 2. agnatised 3, agnatised	lucky and unlucky kinsmen cases
Uterine brother Uterine sister	1/6 (if 2 = 1/3)	child, child of son, father, true g/f	—	—	See Himariyya decision and Malik's rule

Rules of exclusion and agnatic linkage

11–73 The Muslim law of inheritance has developed a number of rules of exclusion, which need to be discussed briefly at this point. Although the surviving spouse is the primary Qur'anic heir in that s/he can never be excluded, the presence of the spouse relict does not affect the rights of inheritance of any other heir in the sense that it does not exclude other heirs. Some heirs, of course, do exclude others entirely, or at least have the capacity to push less fortunate relations to agnatic inheritance. Sometimes the presence of relations reduces the share of others even though it does not benefit themselves. The best example of this is the case of a mother, father and two sisters. The two sisters reduce the share of the mother to one sixth, even though they themselves do not benefit, for they are excluded by the father.

Table 34

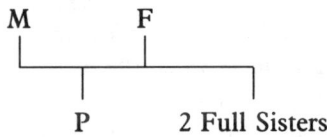

P   2 Full Sisters

M = 1/6

F = 5/6 Agnatic heir

2 Full Sisters = Excluded

11–74 The rules regulating agnatic inheritance, in summary form, are as follows:

(1) *Preference is given to the order:*
    descendants, ascendants, collaterals

(2) *Preference is then given to the degree:*
    the nearer in degree excludes the more remote

(3) *Preference is finally given to the blood tie:*
    the full blood excludes the consanguine blood.

This has a number of important implications in practice. The son of the deceased is a descendant, thus in a competition with the father, the son excludes the father. It is for this reason that the Qur'an lays down a specific fraction for the father when the *propositus* dies leaving both the son and the father. If the father co-exists with a collateral, the father excludes this collateral. In Hanafi law, notwithstanding variant opinions, the grandfather excludes the brother.

11–75 The nearer in degree always excludes the more remote. Thus a son's son is excluded by a son.

Table 35

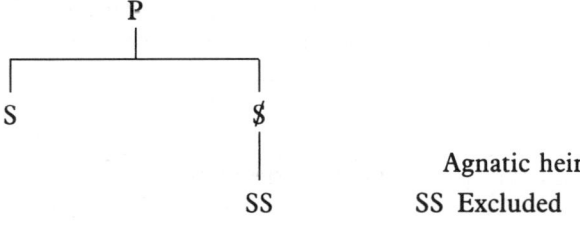

SS   SS Excluded

Agnatic heir

11-76 This problem has caused considerable difficulty, and indeed some hardship and suffering in the changed circumstances of today. The family is no longer the strongly cohesive unit that it was, and there is no guarantee that the nephews and nieces will be treated on a basis of equality with sons and daughters. This is an area of succession law which has been the subject of important reforms in Egypt, in Pakistan and elsewhere. These are discussed in some detail in paragraphs 11-122—11-129, below.

11-77 The position of distant kinsfolk may attract some attention in this context, too. When there is no Qur'anic heir other than possibly the spouse relict alive at the opening of the succession, and there are no agnates either, then the estate is distributed amongst any surviving distant kinsmen, that is, those blood relations who are neither Qur'anic nor agnatic heirs. The most important distant kinsmen, of course, are female agnates, and male and female cognates. In Maliki law, the distant kinsmen are never admitted. In Hanafi law, problems of inheritance within the distant kinsmen category may occur, but this will be rare.[34]

11-78 When there are no members of the *'asaba* or distant kinsmen alive at the moment of the death of the *propositus* in circumstances when the distribution to the Qur'anic heirs in their allotted fractions does not exhaust the estate, the problem arises as to what to do with the remainder. The simple answer, at least in Hanafi law, is that the residue 'returns' to the Qur'anic heirs in the proportion of their shares. This principle is known as *radd*. In the classical law, the husband or wife are not allowed to share in the return, unless there is no other heir alive at the opening of the succession, their share being expressly fixed in the Qur'anic revelations.[35]

11-79 In Maliki law, the doctrine of *radd* does not apply, not the least reason being that the *propositus* in Maliki law is never without an heir, since the Treasury is treated as an heir in its own right, and will therefore inherit any residue.

11-80 When the fractions amount to more than unity, the estate is distributed by a system of proportionate reduction of the shares by a principle known as *'awl*. So, for instance, in Table 24 (page 461, above) the shares of the heirs add up to 13 12ths. (2/12 = mother; 2/12 = father, 3/12 = husband; 6/12 = daughter). Under the principle of *'awl*, the denominator is adjusted to 13 and the mother's share is then 2/13, the father's share is 2/13, the husband receives 3/13, and the daughter takes 6/13. Similarly, in the situation given in Table 29 (see page 463, above), the mother ultimately receives 2/14, the husband 6/14, and the sisters 6/14 collectively.

Limitations on inheritance

11-81 We must now turn our attention to a number of problems relating to the competence of individual heirs to inherit the share allotted to them according to the rules of distribution which we have outlined. There will be circumstances where an heir, otherwise qualified to inherit a share, will find himself or herself excluded from succession because of a particular rule of Muslim law.

11-82 The first exclusion rule relates to religious differences.[36] When a Muslim dies, all non-Muslim heirs are excluded from any entitlement to participate in the

---

[34] Readers are referred to Chap. 7 in Coulson (1971, pp. 91–107) for relevant details.
[35] For the position when the only heir alive at the time of opening of the succession is the spouse relict, see the discussion by Tanzil-ur-Rehman J. at *In Re Zainab*, P.L.D. 1986 Kar. 269.
[36] See in detail Coulson (1971), pp. 185–193; Nasir (1990a), p. 232 also refers briefly to modern jurisdictions.

division of the estate. In contrast to this provision, a bequest from the estate can be made to a non-Muslim (Coulson (1971), p. 229).

11–83 The rules relating to exclusion on the basis of murder are discussed in detail by Coulson (1971, pp. 176–185). It is important to emphasise here the considerable differences of opinion among the Sunni schools.[37] The Hanafi and Shafi'i doctrine excludes from inheritance not only the person who has deliberately killed the *propositus*, but also excludes the person who has killed the *propositus* by accident; so long as there is a causal connection. Thus, the Hanafi law concentrates on excluding the direct killer, emphasing the act rather than the *animus*, so that an heir who has murderous intent and leaves poison around is not excluded from inheriting from his victim. However, if an heir shoots someone inadvertently, the killing is seen as direct, and the heir is not competent to inherit. In contrast, the Hanbali, Maliki and Shi'i schools apply the rule that only the deliberate killer is barred from rights of inheritance following the death of the *propositus*.

11–84 On illegitimacy, the short point to make here is that the illegitimate child in Sunni law has no right of inheritance from the father. However, such children can inherit from their mother.[38] As stated already, a child in the womb has a right of inheritance even though s/he is not alive at the moment of death. Again, for the detailed rules readers are referred to Coulson (1971, pp. 204–212).

11–85 We have already considered problems associated with the 'disease of death'. Of particular interest in this context is the case of the unfortunate wife who is repudiated by *talaq* by her husband at a time when he is aware that his death is imminent. The presumption adopted by Hanafi law is that a repudiation pronounced during death sickness involves an improper motive, namely to interfere with the laws of compulsory succession. Thus, the wife's right of inheritance will not be extinguished. This presumption, however, is not absolute. In Hanafi law, it lasts only for the period of the *'idda*. Thus a *talaq* in Hanafi law pronounced during 'death sickness' is treated as a revocable *ahsan talaq* regardless of the mode of pronouncement. The other schools enable the wife's right of inheritance under these circumstances to last for one year.

The Shi'i law of compulsory succession

11–86 Whereas the Sunni law of entitlement rests on the sophisticated interaction of the Qur'anic and agnatic heirs, the Shi'i jurists recognise just one basis of entitlement, namely the Qur'anic rules.[39] In Shi'i law, the spouse always takes the Qur'anic share, but otherwise, all relatives fall into one of three classes, with sub-sections in each class, as detailed below. The agnate, therefore, has no distinctive place in the scheme of Shi'i inheritance, and indeed it is often said that the Shi'i treat the *'asaba* with little sympathy, so much so that "dust into the jaws of the *'asaba*" has become a standard phrase.[40] The son will always have the same entitlement in Shi'i law as in Sunni law, but other agnatic heirs are much less favourably placed in the Shi'i system, which looks like this:

---

[37] See also *ibid.*, 231; Bharatiya (1996), p. 316.
[38] For details see Coulson (1971), pp. 172–176.
[39] For details of Shi'i law and Iranian law see also Nasir (1990a), pp. 245–263.
[40] For its origin see Coulson (1971), p. 108.

Class 1a   Parents
Class 1b   Lineal descendants
Class 2a   Grandparents
Class 2b   Brothers, sisters and their issue
Class 3a   Paternal uncles and aunts and those of parents and their descendants
Class 3b   Maternal uncles and aunts and those of parents and their descendants.

The general rules, subject to one politically motivated exception which we briefly discuss further below, are as follows: In each section of class 1 and class 2, the nearest to the *propositus* absolutely excludes the more remote, and the nearest members of the two subsections inherit together regardless of their comparative degree removed from the deceased. The existence of an heir in class 1 will exclude any heir from class 2. Likewise, the existence of an heir in class 2 will exclude any heir in class 3. In class 3, the nearest in degree in either section excludes all other claimants. Unlike the Sunnis, the Shi'is include females and their descendants in all classes. To illustrate the operation of the Shi'i law, and to contrast it with the Sunni law, we provide a number of examples.

Table 36

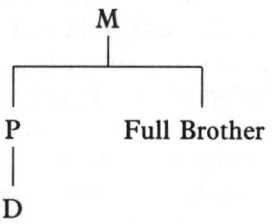

11–87 In Hanafi law, the mother will receive one sixth, the daughter will receive one half and the brother will receive one third in his capacity as the nearest agnatic relative. In Shi'i law, mother and daughter are heirs in classes 1a and 1b respectively. The brother (class 2b) is therefore excluded and the mother and daughter take their respective Qur'anic shares; one sixth and one half plus a return by *radd*. Thus the mother emerges with 2/12 + 1/12 and the daughter takes 6/12 + 3/12.

Table 37

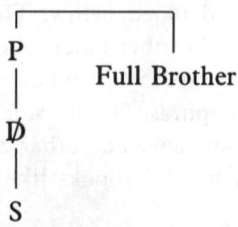

11–88 In Hanafi law, of course, the brother inherits the entire estate. The Shi'i, however, reach a result which is the exact opposite. The brother is a class 2 heir, whereas the daughter's son is a class 1 heir. The daughter's son therefore, succeeds to the estate, a result which is unthinkable in this context in Sunni jurisprudence.

Table 38

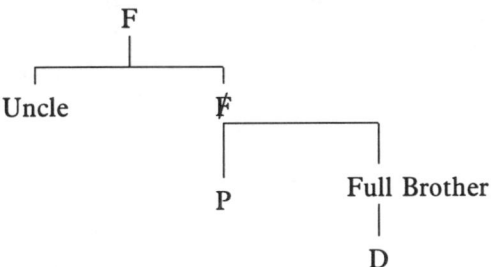

11–89 The brother's daughter has no rights in Hanafi law, and the uncle, the nearest agnate, inherits the estate. In Shi'i law, however, the brother's daughter, as a class 2 heir, excludes the uncle, who is a class 3 heir.

11–90 These three examples illustrate that there are fundamental differences between Sunni and Shi'i law. Indeed, it is hard not to agree with Coulson (1971, p. 125) who asserts that the major reason for the difference is the rejection by the Shi'i jurists of the notion of the continuing validity of pre-Islamic practice. There are, of course, political reasons for the differences, not the least being to give priority to a daughter's children. Perhaps the major reason for the disparity must be sought in the continuity of the tribal aristocracy of the Sunnis as compared with the limited family grouping of the Shi'i.[41] One important exception to the general Shi'i distribution, it must be conceded, is purely political. This occurs when a man is survived by his consanguine uncle and his paternal full uncle's son. In this case, the paternal full uncle's son alone will inherit, notwithstanding that the consanguine uncle is nearer in degree to the deceased. When the Prophet died, the question arose whether 'Ali, the son of Abu Talib, a full paternal uncle of the Prophet, had priority over 'Abbas, a consanguine paternal uncle. The Shi'i, of course, accept the religious headship of the Imams descending from 'Ali and thus they make this exception to the general rule.

11–91 Below we provide a number of other examples of the differences between the Sunni and Shi'i groups, adapted from Coulson (1971, pp. 124–125).

Table 39

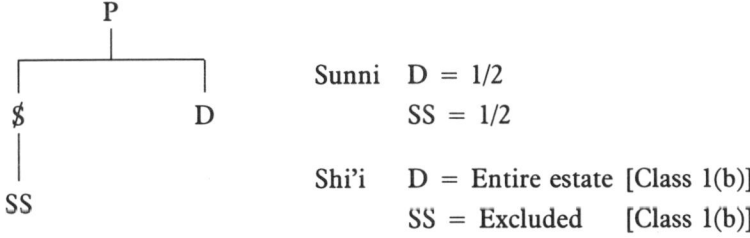

---

[41] Professor Schacht in his writings tended to emphasise the political nature of the difference of approach and minimised juristic divisions. See in detail Schacht, *The origins of Muhammadan jurisprudence* (1979), pp. 262–268.

Table 40

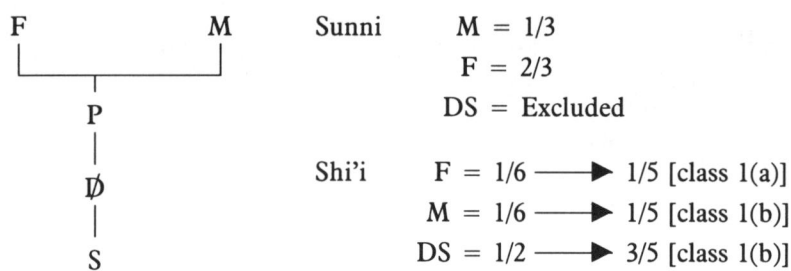

	Sunni	M = 1/3
		F = 2/3
		DS = Excluded
	Shi'i	F = 1/6 ⟶ 1/5 [class 1(a)]
		M = 1/6 ⟶ 1/5 [class 1(b)]
		DS = 1/2 ⟶ 3/5 [class 1(b)]

Table 41

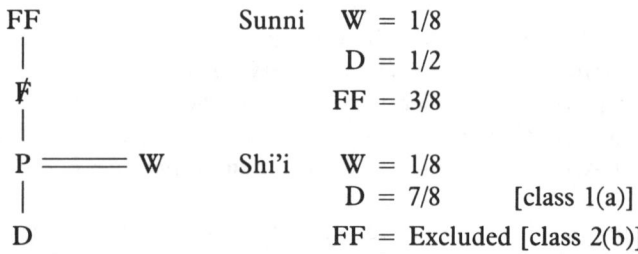

	Sunni	W = 1/8
		D = 1/2
		FF = 3/8
	Shi'i	W = 1/8
		D = 7/8 [class 1(a)]
		FF = Excluded [class 2(b)]

Table 42

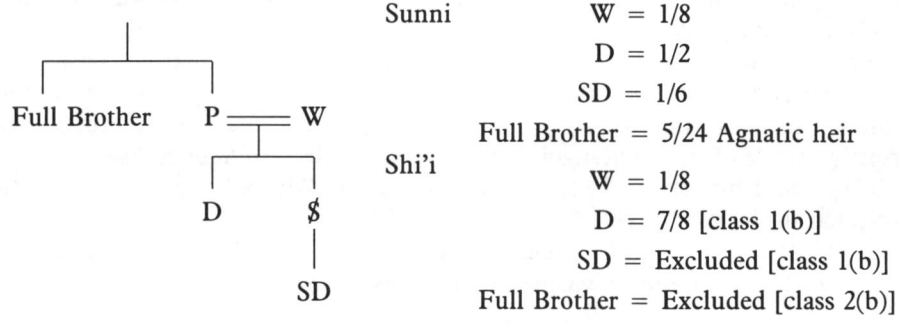

	Sunni	W = 1/8
		D = 1/2
		SD = 1/6
		Full Brother = 5/24 Agnatic heir
	Shi'i	W = 1/8
		D = 7/8 [class 1(b)]
		SD = Excluded [class 1(b)]
		Full Brother = Excluded [class 2(b)]

Table 43

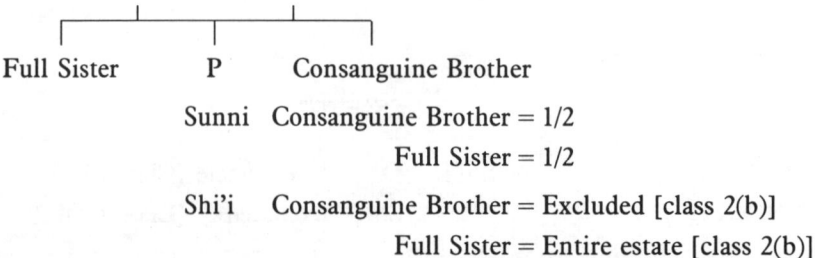

	Sunni	Consanguine Brother = 1/2
		Full Sister = 1/2
	Shi'i	Consanguine Brother = Excluded [class 2(b)]
		Full Sister = Entire estate [class 2(b)]

11–92 The Shi'i law permits a principle of representation, which is particularly relevant when the immediate children are dead, leaving orphaned grandchildren. The grandchildren step into the shoes of their parents and receive the share their parents would have received if alive. The son's daughter is, therefore, really an heir in her own right in Shi'i law, but will inherit the son's share if there is no surviving child of the *propositus*. In Sunni law, this issue has given rise to interesting reforms which we discuss in paragraphs 11–122—11–129, below.

Reforms in the Muslim law of inheritance

11–93 It is no accident that the major reforms in Muslim inheritance law have taken place in the Sunni countries, for it is here that the extended distributory system with its emphasis on agnatic inheritance still continues to play an important role. Professor Sir Norman Anderson, while emphasising the excellence of the system (Anderson (1965), p. 349), discussed what he saw as five major criticisms of Sunni inheritance law. These relate to rigidity, problems over the wife's share, the shares of daughters or the son's daughters, fragmentation of estates, and lastly lack of representation, leading to interesting debates about the position of the orphaned grandchild.

11–94 The argument that the system is far too rigid arises because it does not permit the prescribed shares to be augmented, even by will, however much the particular circumstances of the family may require such an augmentation. There have been changes, of course, notably in Sudan (1945), Egypt (1946) and Iraq (1959), permitting the testator complete freedom to make whatever legacies he likes within the bequeathable third.

11–95 Professor Anderson's second observation was that the Muslim wife has an inadequate share. An interesting attempt to improve this position occurred in Tunisia in 1959. The Tunisians, as Malikis, had no doctrine of return (*radd*). The Public Treasury in that system always inherits rather than acquires any residue by way of an administrative device (*escheat*). In 1959, the Tunisians abandoned this rule, and adopted the principle of *radd*, but went beyond the Hanafi law by allowing the wife the right to participate in the return regardless of whether other heirs were alive at the opening of the succession. This extension of the *radd* doctrine applies also now in Sudan, Egypt and Syria. A more radical reform was introduced in Somalia, where males and females, including husbands and wives, were placed on a completely equal footing (for details see Mahmood (1982b), pp. 263–266).

11–96 A third criticism is that the daughter or son's daughter receives only one half of the estate (or if there are two or more such heirs, two thirds), and the residue will often vest in a distant agnate. This was felt to be wrong and unjust in modern conditions. Thus, in Iraq legislation was passed in 1963 to enable female descendants of the deceased to exclude totally any collateral male agnate. This again is an adoption of Shi'i law and a rejection of Sunni doctrine, of course in a country where there is a fairly equal division between Sunni and Shi'i adherents. The 1959 Tunisian legislation is not as wide as that of Iraq, although, by Tunisian law, a daughter or son's daughter now excludes a collateral male agnate.

11–97 The fourth major criticism relates to fragmentation of the estate. One often hears criticism that the Muslim succession law permits fragmentation of holdings below a viable economic unit. Certain countries have sought to tackle this problem within the framework of general land reform by laying down a minimum limit of land-holding. Below that limit, heirs must take as co-owners. Some apologists, of course, believe that fragmentation is a powerful check on capitalism and that it provides a sensible alternative to socialism on the one hand as well as capitalism on the other. A discussion of this important issue is outside the scope of this book.

11–98 The fifth major criticism relates to the lack of representation in Sunni law, and the very serious problem of the orphaned grandchild. The Egyptian Will

Act, No. 71 of 1946 adopted a system generally referred to as 'obligatory bequests' or the 'mandatory will'.[42] The Egyptian law provides that the *propositus* is obliged to make a bequest in favour of a grandchild by any son or daughter who has predeceased him, if they would not be entitled to any share on intestacy, provided that this bequest does not exceed the limit of one third for legacies or the equivalent of the share of the predeceased son or daughter, whichever is less. The principle applies to all lineal descendants of the *propositus* in the male line, but in the case of predeceased daughters, only the immediate grandchildren can benefit. Should the grandfather fail to make a bequest, the court will act as if he had done so, and such an implied or obligatory bequest will have priority over any voluntary bequests which the *propositus* may have actually provided for in his will.[43]

11–99   The justification for the Egyptian law is based on Sura II, verses 176–180 which enjoin Muslims to make bequests in favour of parents and close relatives. The consensus is that these verses have been abrogated by the later provisions in Sura IV. The Egyptians, however, exercised *ijtihad* and reinterpreted the provisions in order to cope with the particular problem of the orphaned grandchild.

11–100   The 'obligatory legatees' in the Egyptian system are never legal heirs in their own right, so the system appears to harmonise well with the general scheme of Sunni inheritance. Certainly, when legacies to the extent of one third of the estate have been bequeathed, the obligatory bequests can be extracted from the estate at the expense of the voluntary bequests, and the rights of the compulsory heirs are in no way affected. However, if bequests have not been made, the amount received by the heirs will be reduced; and the extraction of the obligatory bequest will change the quantified amounts, although not the fractions, received by the heirs.

11–101   There are a number of different ways to implement the scheme. By the 'court method', so called because Egyptian courts initially adopted this method, the estate is distributed as if the deceased son or daughter were still alive, and that share, or one third, whichever is less, is then allocated to the grandchildren. Under this method, the distribution produces an unfortunate distortion. Thus, a method suggested initially by the Egyptian jurist, Abu Zahra, is now applied by the Egyptian courts. In the Abu Zahra method, the distribution is as follows: rather like the classical 'Umariyyatan decision (spouse relict, mother and father), one ascertains the exact amount which the predeceased son or daughter would have received if he or she had survived, and having subtracted this amount (or one third) from the estate and allocated it to the grandchildren, the balance is divided up without regard to the predeceased son or daughter on the basis that he or she is in fact dead. Two examples can be given, adapted from Coulson (1971, pp. 147, *et seq.*):

Table 44

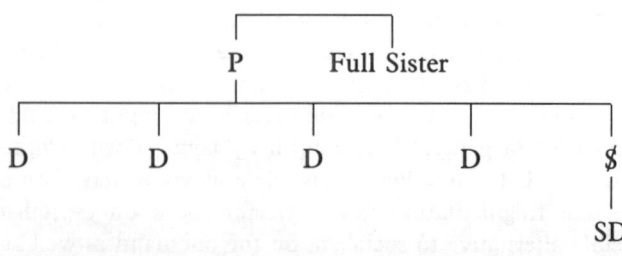

[42] For details see Nasir (1990a), pp. 271–273, also with examples from other jurisdictions.
[43] For details see also Faruki [1965] 4, No. 3 *Islamic Studies* 253–274; Chowdhury [1964] 3 *Islamic Studies* 375–391.

11–102 By the 'court method', the son is fictitiously reactivated in order to discover his interest. The son, if alive, would have excluded the sister and would have inherited agnatically with the daughters on a one to two basis, the son taking one third and the daughters one sixth each. The 'court method' simply adopts a system of substitution. Abu Zahra's method, in contrast, gives the son's daughter one third, and the residual two thirds are distributed as if the son were not alive. The daughters, therefore, receive four ninths between them (two thirds × two thirds) and the germane sister receives the residue of two-ninths (one third × two thirds).

Table 45

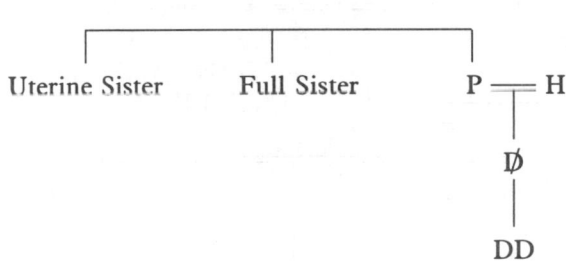

11–103 In this example, the 'court method' would produce the following fractions: H = one quarter; DD = one third (the share of D reduced down to one third); the uterine sister is excluded by the reactivated D; and the surplus of five twelfths is given to the germane sister as the residuary heir. The method proposed by Abu Zahra would provide a more equitable result, for there is no real justification for the uterine grandchild to exclude the uterine sister. Abu Zahra, therefore, would provide the one third to the DD; one half × two thirds = 2/18 to the H; one sixth × two thirds = 2/18 to the uterine sister, and one half × two thirds = 2/6 to the germane sister. The shares would then have to be reduced by the principles of 'awl, but all surviving relatives would be entitled to a part of the estate.

11–104 The system of obligatory bequests has been adopted in Syria, Morocco, Tunisia, and Kuwait, although in Syria and Morocco the reformers were a little more cautious for they confined the operation of the principle to children of the deceased's son, while children of the deceased's daughter do not benefit. As we shall see in paragraphs 11–122—11–129, below, Pakistani law has sought to tackle this problem as well.

South Asian Muslim laws of inheritance

11–05 Because of the strong Qur'anic base of the Muslim system of inheritance, and their balanced approach as to who should take a share, the basic rules have not really been put into question in South Asian laws. We have already referred to the important role of custom in this field generally. As far as statute law and the Anglo-Muslim case law is concerned, some changes have been made and require some comment here.

An illustrative case

11–106 Before we turn to some more specific issues in the South Asian Muslim law of succession, it may be useful to discuss one particular case which illustrates how the law works in practice, *Nur Ali v. Malka Sultana*, P.L.D. 1961 (W.P.) Lah. 431. This case is also typical in that it raises a number of interconnected issues, particularly because of the several local complications (such as religion and caste) which it introduces.

11–107 The case concerned the entitlement to property which was once owned by a Hindu, one Sahib Ditta Mal, who had died in 1933. The precise family relationship between the Sahib and the disputants in the case is rather complicated, and a family tree should be of assistance:

Table 46

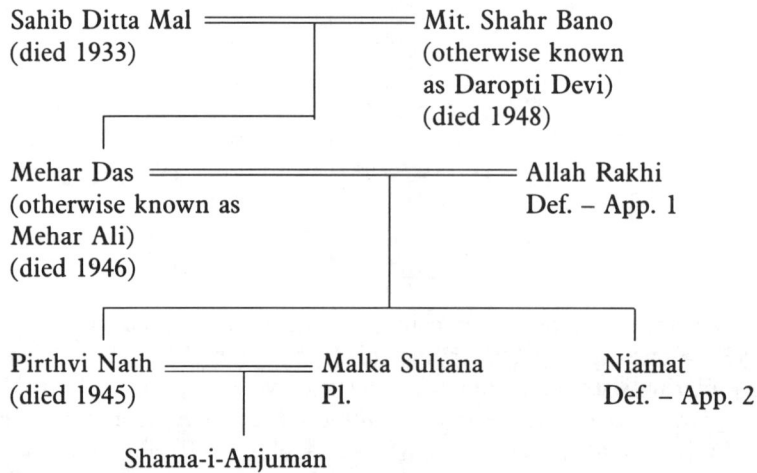

11–108 It was common ground that Sahib Ditta Mal had been born a Hindu and had not embraced Islam during his lifetime. However, his family members had later converted to Islam, which is why the suit now concerned Muslim law. The parties were in agreement that Sahib Ditta Mal's son, Mehar Das alias Mehar Ali, and his widow Shahr Bano had embraced Islam. It was also agreed that the parties were followers of the Aga Khan. Apparently, the Aga Khan allowed considerable liberty of religious profession to his followers throughout the subcontinent. Pirthi or Pirthvi Nath, the Sahib's grandson, had never embraced Islam but his death in 1945 during the lifetime of his father and his paternal grandmother enabled the court to overlook this particular complication. There was no doubt, therefore, that all the parties to the present suit were Muslim. But what kind of Muslim law should apply to the inheritance questions before the court?

11–109 The first issue, in point of time, arose out of a document executed by Sahib Ditta Mal in September 1933, some 10 weeks before his death, with which he purported to leave to his wife by will all the property which was now the subject of the dispute. The dispute revolved around whether this document conferred an absolute title or only a limited life interest on the wife. The trial judge had held that the document made the wife the full owner of the property. On appeal, the Lahore High Court came to the opposite conclusion after an examination of the terms of the document, holding that the Sahib intended no more than to make his wife the manager of his property after his death. Having decided on this point, the court distributed the property to the various contestants using as the starting point Hindu law, the personal law of Sahib Ditta Mal. The trial judge had distributed the estate using as his starting point the personal law of Shahr Bano, which at the time of her death was Muslim law.

11–110 The second issue involved the effect of the conversion to Islam by the widow and the son. Did their act of apostasy deprive them of their inheritance rights under Hindu law to the property of Sahib Ditta Mal? Any possible interpersonal conflict between substantive Hindu law and substantive Muslim law over this question was regulated by the Caste Disabilities Removal Act 1850. If in Hindu law Mehar Ali and Mst. Shahr Bano could have inherited any property from Sahib Ditta Mal, they would not be deprived of these rights by reason of their change of religion. The estate is distributed in accordance with the personal law of the *propositus*, but no account is taken of any rule of the personal law which attempts to exclude from the succession an apostate from the religion.

11–111 According to the interpretation of the court of the Hindu law in force at that time (1933) in the then province of the Panjab, neither Shahr Bano nor Malka Sultana, in any event, had any share in the property left by the Sahib. Mehar Das alias Mehar Ali was the only son and, therefore, according to Hindu law, he became the owner of the whole of Sahib Ditta Mal's estate. Mehar, of course, had converted to Islam and for this reason, on his own death in 1946, the property devolved according to the rules of his personal law, Muslim law, thus excluding any non-Muslims who happened to be alive at the time. This is how the existence of Pirthvi Nath at the time became irrelevant to this dispute.

11–112 The court had to take one more important decision. It was contended that Mehar Ali had been a Shi'i Muslim and that as a result Shi'i rules of inheritance should govern the distribution of the property on his death. The trial judge, who had come to a different conclusion with regard to the document executed by the Sahib, came also to a different conclusion with respect to the school of Muslim law to be applied. He held that the parties had converted to Shi'i Islam and therefore applied the Shi'i law. According to the Shi'i law, the entire estate devolved on the nearest class 1b heir, the son's daughter, Mst. Niamat, who would exclude all other competitors. It was basically this decision that the other ladies appealed against.

11–113 The Lahore High Court held, at page 438, that Mehar Ali should be presumed to have been a Sunni. This was so because of a well-known general presumption in favour of the application of Hanafi law and because of the fact that the Aga Khan had allowed his followers in the Panjab to remain Sunnis and to be governed by Sunni rules of Muslim law. The contesting heirs were as follows:

Table 47

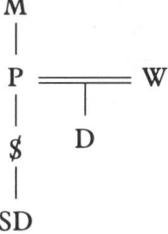

11–114 The result of the application of the Sunni law to this scenario was that Allah Rakhi (Mehar's widow) received one eighth of the property, while Mst. Niamat (Mehar's daughter) received one half, and Mst. Shama-i-Anjuman (Mehar's granddaughter) received one sixth. Strictly, the court should have considered the rights of the mother, Shahr Bano, who was still alive in 1946 – the year of Mehar's death. The mother should have been entitled to her Qur'anic share of one sixth which would have been distributed on her death in 1948 to the son's daughter (Niamat) and the son's son's daughter (Shama-i-Anjuman) in the proportion 1/2 : 1/6. In fact, the position of the mother was ignored. The shares of 1/8, 1/2 and 1/6 add up to 19/24. The residue, 5/24, is distributed in proportion to the shares of Shama-i-Anjuman and Niamat. Allah Rakhi, as the wife, was held to be entitled only to a fixed Qur'anic portion of 1/8 which cannot be increased by any 'return' of the residue. The final result was therefore that Mst. Niamat received 63/96 of the estate, Mst. Shama-i-Anjuman received 21/96, and Allah Rakhi took 12/96.

Specific issues relating to Muslim inheritance

11–115 One focal point, as the *Nur Ali* case above already illustrated, concerns change of religion. On the Indian subcontinent, the law on intestate succession was changed with respect to apostate heirs from Islam by the Caste Disabilities Removal Act 1850. An heir who leaves Islam will still be entitled to inherit on the death of a Muslim relation. The law, however, has not been altered with respect to a Muslim who subsequently dies. Thus if a person converts to Islam and then dies, his estate is distributed in accordance with Muslim law, and all the non-Muslim relations alive at the opening of succession are disbarred.[44]

11–116 In Pakistan, the effect of the Caste Disabilities Removal Act 1850 was taken away by a 1963 amendment,[45] to the effect that nothing contained in the 1850 Act shall apply to the rights of inheritance to the property of a Muslim, thus explicitly restoring the Muslim law which excludes all non-Muslim heirs, including those who were once Muslims and have apostacised, from any right to participate in the division of the estate. Finally, it should be mentioned that in India, if a Muslim marries under the provisions of the Special Marriage Act 1954, the Muslim law of succession is thereby abandoned, and that law no longer applies to the distribution of either spouse's estate on their death.

11–117 Concerning the exclusion of the murderer from inheritance, an interesting early case from Pakistan is *Beguman v. Saroo*, P.L.D. 1964 (W.P.) Lah. 451.[46] Applying the principles of justice, equity and good conscience, rather than analysing Muslim jurisprudence, it was held that a murderer or his progeny could not benefit by this crime of murder when it came to succession. This decision deviates from the traditional Muslim doctrine which, as applied by all schools and sects, appears to debar only the actual killer from inheriting from the victim. In this case, one Dara had been convicted and executed for the murder of his two nephews, the sons of his brother, some time in 1948. When Dara's brother died in 1951, he was survived by his widow and two daughters. The two sons of Dara claimed the residue of the estate as the nearest agnatic heirs. Their case was that their father had been innocent of the murders and, at any rate, the Muslim law of inheritance gave them entitlements to succession as collaterals.

11–118 The lower courts had decided that their claim should be disallowed only regarding the property of the two murdered sons, and not the share of their father. On appeal, the Lahore High Court held, at page 452:

---

[44] See *Mitar Sen Singh v. Maqbul Hasan Khan* [1930] 57 L.R. I.A. 313; *K. P. Chandrasekharappa v. Govt. of Mysore*, A.I.R. 1955 Mysore 26.

[45] This is the Caste Disabilities Removal (West Pakistan Amendment) Act 1963 (Act X of 1963).

[46] See earlier *Khan Gul Khan v. Karam Nishan*, A.I.R. 1940 Lah. 172, where it was held that the rule of exclusion of the murderer applies even where a life-estate intervenes and that the motive for the murder was immaterial.

"The rule of law is well-settled that under principles of justice, equity and good conscience a murderer or his progeny cannot be allowed to benefit by his crime of murder. The murderer may be the father alone but if the descendants claim through him even though not merely from him their title becomes tainted as the source or the channel through which the inheritance has to flow to them becomes blocked and extirpated by reason of the crime committed by that source."

It was therefore concluded, at page 453, that to uphold the claims of these two men "would certainly amount to giving them the benefit of the crime committed by their father . . . which is repugnant to all principles of natural justice and good conscience". The Lahore High Court, in this somewhat controversial decision, appeared to be superimposing the concept of a 'tainted' line upon the well-established principle in Muslim law that only the immediate killer is barred from succession.

11–119 It seemed doubtful if courts would follow the decision in *Beguman v. Saroo*, given that it was perceived as contrary to traditional doctrine. In *Maheea v. Shaiya*, P.L.D. 1991 S.C. 724, the Supreme Court of Pakistan had a further opportunity to decide the question whether the heirs of a murderer would also be excluded from inheriting a share of the victim's property. In this case a son had killed his father, and the son, as well as his descendants, were claiming inheritance to the property of the deceased. The case was subject to very long delays until it was finally heard in 1991. Nasim Hasan Shah J., speaking for the court, cited the judgment in *Beguman v. Saroo*, as quoted above, and indicated at page 726 that leave to appeal to the Supreme Court had been granted because it was contended that there was a difference of opinion among the Muslim jurists on the point at issue. However, the learned judge stated, at pages 726–727, that by 1991 the situation in Pakistani law was altogether different:

"Even if there was some difference of opinion amonst the Muslim Jurists on this question but now this question is only of academic interest in Pakistan. The reason being that Ordinance I of 1991 (commonly referred to as the Qisas and Diyat Ordinance), which is now in force in Pakistan, has settled this controversy, if there was any, by a specific provision."

The judgment is extremely brief but makes reference, at page 727, to the relevant provisions of the Ordinance, indicating that sections 299–338-H, constituting Chapter XVI (of offences relating to the human body) of the Pakistan Penal Code 1860 were substituted by new provisions based on Islamic injunctions by Ordinance I of 1991.[47] The relevant provision for the present case is found in section 317 of the Code:

"317. Persons committing Qatl debarred from succession.
Where a person committing Qatl-i-Amd or Qatl Shibh-i-Amd is an heir or a beneficiary under a will, he shall be debarred from succeeding to the estate of the victim as an heir or a beneficiary."[48]

Nasim Hasan Shah J. concluded at page 727 by saying that "in view of these statutory provisions, the question no longer remains res integra" and dismissed the

---

[47] Since then, the Criminal Law (Amendment) (Qisas & Diyat) Ordinance 1993 (XXXIX of 1993) has made further changes.
[48] ss.299, 300 and 315 of the Code provide details on these various forms of murder or manslaughter.

appeal of the murderous claimant and his offpsring. It could be suggested that this is a surprising judgment, particularly in view of Pakistan's declared objective to 'islamise' its legal system, since the statutory provision itself clearly refers only to the person committing the murder as excluded from inheritance. However, there are some other cases on the matter which fortify this public policy approach taken by Pakistan.[49] This appears to be the real reason why the Pakistani Supreme Court did not re-open this question. This view is also confirmed by Balchin (1994, p. 288), where the conscious departure from "certain principles of established Muslim jurisprudence" is also noted.

11–120   The problem of the repudiated wife in relation to 'death sickness' was discussed by the Pakistani Supreme Court in *Nazar Muhammad v. Shahzada Begum*, P.L.D. 1974 S.C. 22. The substantial property which was the subject of this litigation belonged originally to one Ch. Ghulam Haider of Chakwal, who died on November 10, 1959, survived by his two widows, Shahzada Begum and Musahiban. The latter had one son, Nazar Mohammad, of whom Ghulam Haider was the father. Shahzada Begum gave birth to a daughter, Khalida Begum, shortly after Ghulam's death. Musahiban died prior to the action in the courts. Shahzada Begum and her daughter Khalida Begum claimed to be heirs of Ghulam, while Nazar Mohammad denied their entitlement, relying upon a document of divorce dated November 6, 1959, in which it was stated that eight or nine months before this date, the deceased had pronounced a *talaq* purporting to divorce Shahzada Begum, by whom he had no child and who did not carry a child at that time. In other words, it was claimed that Shahzada was not the widow of Ghulam Haider, since the deceased had divorced her nine months prior to his death. The deed executed in November was claimed to be confirmation of the factum of divorce. Thus, as the daughter was born some two months after the man's death, she could not possibly be his daughter. In reply, Shahzada Begum submitted that she had not been divorced. She argued further, and in the alternative, that if indeed she had been divorced, then the relevant date was November 6, 1959, when her husband was in his death sickness. As her daughter was born within two months of the death of the husband, she was a legitimate child and therefore entitled to inherit.

11–121   On examination of the evidence, the Supreme Court came to the conclusion that Shahzada Begum had been divorced on November 6, 1959, but not earlier. It held also that the husband, suffering from severe paralysis, was in his death sickness when he divorced the wife. Shahzada Begum, therefore, was entitled to inherit, as was her daughter, the legitimate child of the deceased. The distribution of the estate was as follows:

Table 48

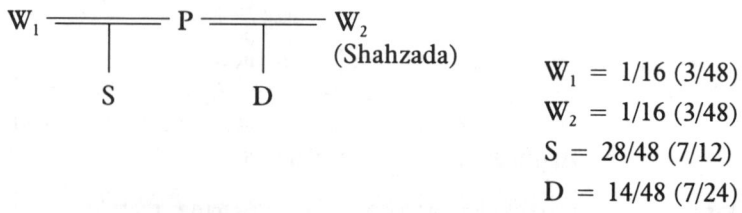

$$W_1 = 1/16\ (3/48)$$
$$W_2 = 1/16\ (3/48)$$
$$S = 28/48\ (7/12)$$
$$D = 14/48\ (7/24)$$

---

[49] It is surprising that the pre-Independence case of *Khan Gul Khan v. Karam Nishan* A.I.R. 1940 Lah. 172, was not cited. In that case, it was submitted that the exclusion applies only to a murderer and does not affect the rights of his children. However, it was held that considerations of public policy would exclude a murderer and his descendants from succession. See also *Muhammad Yusuf v. Muhammad Yusuf*, P.L.D. 1981 A.J.K. 49.

The orphaned grandchild in Pakistani law

11–122 Pakistan tackled the problem of lack of representation and of the orphaned grandchild by a radical departure from the classical Hanafi law of inheritance. Section 4 of the Muslim Family Laws Ordinance 1961 provides in this respect:

> "In the event of the death of any son or daughter of the *propositus* before the opening of succession, the children of such son or daughter, if any, living at the time the succession opens, shall *per stirpes* receive a share equivalent to the share which such son or daughter, as the case may be, would have received if alive."

This provision has come in for considerable criticism. In a specialist study, Anderson (1965, p. 357) raised the objection that the Pakistani reform "radically upsets the whole structure of the Islamic law of inheritance". Another study (Anderson (1968b), p. 233) referred to the Pakistani innovation as "a revolutionary provision" but argued that "this problem of the disinherited grandchild has been dealt with rather more intelligently, perhaps, though much less drastically, in several of the Arab countries". Anderson's considerable reservations about the Pakistani method are also reflected in secondary writing.[50] Anderson and Coulson (1967, p. 84) found that the new law involves and creates distinct anomalies in the distribution of an estate, concluding that "it is difficult therefore to avoid the conclusion that the effects of this reform go far beyond the original intention of its proponents". Coulson (1971, p. 150) also noted that this reform "effects a clean and total break with traditional Shari'a doctrine, orthodox or sectarian".[51] Further, Coulson (1971, pp. 150–151) criticised the reasoning of the 1955 Pakistani Commission as well as similar arguments by Faruki (1965) as unjustified attempts to discredit the traditional law which are in fact unnecessary and unconvincing (Coulson (1971), p. 152). He also found, however, that the Pakistani provisions worked well, to a certain extent, taking care of anomalies and thus making "more consistent and equitable provision for orphaned grandchildren" (Coulson (1971), p. 155).

11–123 South Asian reactions have been more favourable. Fyzee (1974, p. 393) welcomed the Pakistani reforms and even expressed hope that Indian legislation would follow suit. A simple scenario will illustrate the point of these controversies. In the table below, the *propositus* is survived by a germane brother and a son's daughter.

Table 49

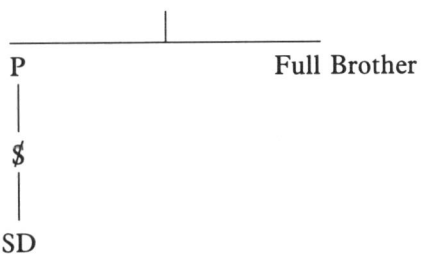

[50] For some interesting details see Bharatiya (1996), p. 313.
[51] For details see Coulson (1971), pp. 150–158; Balchin (1994), pp. 281–282.

11–124   In the classical Hanafi law, the son's daughter will receive one half of the estate and the brother receives the other half. The position, of course, is not altered in Egypt. In Pakistan, however, the son, if alive, would have excluded the brother; thus now the son's daughter takes the entire estate to the exclusion of the brother. The 1961 Ordinance introduces also children of daughters as primary heirs. This dramatic change has certainly upset the religious elements in Pakistani society.[52]

11–125   A succession problem of this kind arose in *Yusuf Abbas v. Ismat Mustafa*, P.L.D. 1968 Kar. 480, which involved a complex scenario with part of the properties left abroad and resulting conflicts of laws issues.[53] This case also reiterates, at pages 502 and 506, the basic principle that Muslim law makes no distinction between movable and immovable properties for the purpose of succession. A further issue was whether the 1961 Ordinance had any retrospective effect. At page 508, the judge firmly held that this was an improper view, highlighting the reformist intentions of section 4 of the MFLO:

> "The only condition is that the death should occur before the succession has opened, and if the succession opens after the promulgation of the Ordinance, section 4 would apply with full force . . . One consideration which has to be borne in mind in construing section 4 of the Ordinance is the purpose for which this law was passed. The Ordinance aims at alleviating the sufferings of the children whose unfortunate lot is to lose their father or mother during the lifetime of their grandfather, or grandmother as the case may be. The construction of such statutes should be just sensible and liberal, so as to give effect to the purpose for which they are passed."

Since the argument that the claimants, as foreign nationals, should be debarred from succession under this section also failed, it was held that the plaintiffs were entitled to a decree for the administration of the estate, a resounding victory for the application of the principle introduced through section 4 of the MFLO.

11–126   Later, attempts have been made in the Pakistani courts to attack the basis of section 4 of the Ordinance as being contrary to the principles of Islam as laid down in the Qur'an and Sunna.[54] However, all such attempts have ultimately failed. In *Farishta v. Federation of Pakistan*, reported at, P.L.D. 1980 Pesh. 47, the Shariat Bench of the High Court of Peshawar had accepted the argument that section 4 of the MFLO was against the injunctions of Islam and was therefore invalid.[55] However, this case went on appeal and in *Federation of Pakistan v. Farishta*, P.L.D. 1981 S.C. 120, the Shariat Bench of the Supreme Court of Pakistan made some very pertinent comments, at page 122, about the meaning of 'Muslim personal law' and discussed various concepts in detail. It was finally held, at page 127:

> ". . . section 4 of the Muslim Family Laws Ordinance VIII of 1961 is a special statutory provision which is intended to be applied only to Muslims of Pakistan as a class by itself, and from that point of view, constitutes a personal law for the Muslims . . . with the result, that its scrutiny was outside the jurisdiction of the High Court . . ."

An interesting and controversial case was *Kamal Khan v. Zainab*, P.L.D. 1983 Lah. 546, which involved the distribution of the estate of one Sufaid Khan who had died

---

[52] See in detail Chowdhury (1964), p. 375.
[53] We have already discussed this case in the context of conflicts of laws, see above paras 4–73—4–75.
[54] See paras 2–55—2–60, above for the Islamic nature of Pakistani law today. We saw earlier in paras 9–167—9–188, above that s.7 of the MFLO also faced similar attacks, which have remained unsuccessful.
[55] On this case, see the discussion by A. Ali (1986).

in 1972. In 1977, the entire estate was transferred to Zenib, the surviving granddaughter and the daughter of Rajoo, a predeceased son. An action was brought by the nephew, Kamal Khan, challenging the status of Zenib and this transfer. The scenario looks like this:

Table 50

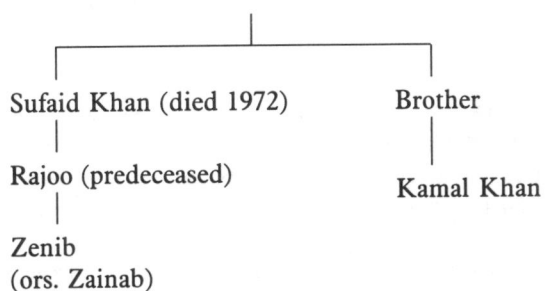

11-127 The Court found no reason to challenge the legitimacy of the granddaughter but stated, at page 547, that the interpretation of section 4 of the MFLO requires further consideration. Reliance was placed on an earlier case to support the granddaughter's claim to the entire estate.[56] The judge turned to the provisions of section 4 and stated, at page 548:

> "It can be safely assumed that this was meant to remedy the discrimination which was believed to exist against a grandchild whose parent had died before the succession opened. The law provides that the parent of such a grandchild will be deemed to be alive for the purpose of succession. It cannot, however, be assumed that the law ever intended to give a share to the grandchild more than what would have been his due if the parent was actually alive when the succession opened."

The judge rightly found that the calculation depended on the fiction that the predeceased son was deemed to be alive at the death of the propositus. However, if that was the case, then the daughter could not take the entire estate in accordance with Islamic law. Following this train of thought, the judge therefore found that he could not agree with the earlier Peshawar case and held, at page 548:

> "With utmost respect and in all humility, I am unable to share this view because the Legislature never intended to give greater benefit to the grandchild of a predeceased parent than would have been his due if the parent was alive. The starting point is, that notionally the off-spring of the propositus is deemed to be alive for the purpose of succession, at the time of the death of the propositus, and the succession of the grandchild is to be calculated again notionally as if the parent of the grandchild died after the death of the original propositus."

It was further held, at page 548, that "in the event of there being a single surviving grandchild the principle of *per stirpes* is pushed to the background but cannot be employed to support a principle which militates against the Islamic Law of Inheritance". Applying this double legal fiction, it was therefore decided that

---

[56] See *Zarina Jan v. Akbar Jan* P.L.D. 1975 Pesh. 252. See also *Sakhi Muhammad v. Ahmad Khan*, 1980 C.L.C. 1006.

Zenib, as a sole surviving grandchild, could not receive more than one half of the estate of her father, and the remaining half must revert to the collaterals, in this case the only nearest agnate, Kamal Khan.

11–128 In *Iqbal Mai v. Falak Sher*, P.L.D. 1986 S.C. 228, the Supreme Court of Pakistan refused to grant leave to appeal in a case which also concerned the rights of the children of a predeceased son. However, here the facts were quite different since the succession in this case had opened many years before the promulgation of the MFLO in 1961. However, with reference to *Kamal Khan*, Muhammad Afzal Zullah J. raised the question, at page 231,

> ". . . whether it was not the intention of the law-maker in section 4 of the Muslim Family Laws Ordinance to provide an opportunity, of obtaining only Islamic law shares, to the children of predeceased son or daughter of propositus and that the intention was not to increase their Islamic law shares."

Thus, the Supreme Court was waiting for a fit and proper case to give the matter a full hearing. Two such cases came up for hearing during 1990. In *Farid v. Manzooran*, P.L.D. 1990 S.C. 511, the conflict in the decisions of *Kamal Khan* and *Zarina Jan* was noted by Abdul Shakurul Salam J., who granted leave for a full hearing and authoritative decision before the Supreme Court on this matter. Here the facts were that a grandmother had died, the question being what the precise share of the sole daughter of her predeceased daughter would be in the inheritance, as opposed to the claims of the reversionaries, among whom was the petitioner in this case.

11–129 A unique chance to re-assess the whole subject presented itself when the *Kamal Khan* case went on appeal to the Supreme Court of Pakistan and was heard in July 1990. In *Zainab v. Kamal Khan*, P.L.D. 1990 S.C. 1051, the daughter of the predeceased son apparently tried to oust the rival claimant altogether, claiming that the interpretation of section 4 of the MFLO, as given in this case by the Lahore High Court, was incorrect.[57] The Supreme Court found itself in agreement with the interpretation of section 4 as given by the Lahore High Court. Abdul Qadeer Chaudhry J. said, at page 1055:

> "The law presupposes that legislature presumes that enactment will operate fairly, justly and equitably and not unreasonably, therefore, a construction has to be made which would be beneficial to the widest maximum extent."

The learned judges took care to distinguish the principle of *per stirpes*, as indicated in section 4 of the MFLO, from *per capita*, its antithesis. The consequence for succession under section 4 of the MFLO was then explained by the judge, at page 1057:

> "It means that the distribution has to be made to a group of shareholders taking the share of their ascendants. On the opening of succession, each group of children of the deceased sons/daughters would inherit the share of their father/mother and each individual would not get the share in his/her individual capacity. Section 4 has been added to cater to the needs of grand-children and to remove their sufferings but it cannot be interpreted so as to decrease the share of the other descendants. According to Section 4, share from the deceased grandfather's property has been bestowed upon the children of his

---

[57] Two further cases were cited in support of this contention, *Yussuf Abbas v. Ismat Mustafa*, P.L.D. 1968 Kar. 480 and *Ibrahim v. Nehmat Bi*, P.L.D. 1988 Lah. 186.

predeceased son but this does not mean that the other heirs of the deceased would be excluded from their share of inheritance. Under Section 2 of the Muslim Personal Laws (Shariat) Application Act 1962, the rule of decision shall be the Muslim Personal Law (Shariat) (in cases where parties are Muslim). In spite of the non-obstante clause section 4 is to be interpreted in the light of section 2 of the Act [of] 1962. Both thus can stand together."

The Supreme Court then considered the facts of the case again and decided that a sole surviving grandchild could not inherit the entire share of her father. It was held, at page 1057:

"Section 4 could not, therefore, be construed against the interest of the other heirs of the deceased who were entitled to share the inheritance in accordance with the principles of Muslim Law of Inheritance."

As a result, the granddaughter's appeal failed and the Supreme Court re-affirmed the position that a grandchild is not entitled to a higher share than could be inherited from the predeceased parent according to Muslim law. This constitutes a conscious compromise between reformist ambitions and a desire to keep to the principles of Muslim law. The result achieves also an equitable balance and it appears therefore, about 30 years after its promulgation, that the provisions contained in section 4 of the MFLO can no longer be seen as a limitless bonus for the orphaned grandchild in Pakistan.

Muslim law of succession in Britain

11-130 Migrant populations have traditionally tended to be young, so that the first issues coming up for legal adjudication among them related to marriage and divorce rather than matters of inheritance.[58] Today, as the original immigrants grow older inheritance questions are gaining in importance.

11-131 Ahsan (1995, p. 27) emphasises that "distribution of inheritance is another crucial issue on which Muslims cannot practise the Sharia in Britain or any part of Europe". However, for Muslims in Britain, it appears, also when it comes to matters of succession law, the preservation of *shariat* rules in England has been fairly easy. In this context, *angrezi shariat* in Britain is achieved by an intricate combination of selective use of English legal rules and Muslim legal principles. Again this confirms our observation that formal use is made of English law by British Muslims today to maintain the conceptual and actual superiority of *sharia* and to construct *angrezi shariat*.

11-132 It seems that many religious or community leader in Britain have been advising Muslim individuals to make wills.[59] This has been seen as desirable, as outlined by Ahsan (1995, p. 27), for a number of reasons:

"Since Western laws of inheritance are completely different and in many aspects contrary to the established principles of Islam, a member of the Muslim community has no other option other than to make a will to the effect that after his death his property and wealth should be distributed according to the Islamic law."

---

[58] See Nielsen (1993a), pp. 3–4.
[59] For details see *ibid.*, p. 3 and Badawi (1995), pp. 79–80. Haqq and Thomson, *The Islamic Will* (1995) show continued activity in popularising the making of wills.

These observations refer in an indirect manner to the freedom of the individual under English law to decide who should inherit property. In a sense, of course, this is similar to the pre-Islamic situation. Poulter (1990a, p. 72) writes:

> "English law (unlike Muslim law, for example) does not insist that any fixed part or portion must be allocated to specified relations of the deceased. A person who makes a will is basically entitled to choose freely to whom his property should pass by way of inheritance, subject only to claims for 'family provision'."

Close relatives of a deceased person are, therefore, not entirely unprotected by English law and the basic rule is that certain relatives and dependants of the deceased can be awarded 'reasonable provision' by the courts.[60] It would be wrong to suggest, therefore, that the two legal systems are totally different with regard to inheritance and the capacity to make wills.

11–133 Dr Ahsan's observations as cited above confirm the existence of what we have called *angrezi shariat*.[61] Muslims in Britain who want to ensure that Muslim law applies to an inheritance in England, rather than the English legal rules, have basically two options, either to make a will laying down that succession should take place in accordance with Muslim law, as Dr Ahsan suggests,[62] or to distribute their property *inter vivos*. The technique of making wills under English law is extremely simple. One writes such a will under the English Wills Act 1837 and stipulates in it how the property shall be distributed. Muslims can obviously use these same provisions to lay down that their property shall be distributed according to *shariat*. Poulter (1990a, p. 74) advises:

> "If such a will specifies which 'school' of Islamic law is to govern the distribution, so that the deceased's intentions are clear and unambiguous, then the will should basically be recognised as valid by English law."

11–134 Poulter (1990a, p. 74) also confirms that "approval has been given to such forms of wills by Muslim leaders in England and it appears that the directions given in these wills have been duly carried out by the executors". He envisages, however, some situations in which an English court might not uphold the details of certain testamentary provisions on public policy grounds, basically because they discriminate against women, giving them unequal shares, or non-Muslims, who are excluded from intestate succession, not however from taking property through a will, as we saw in paragraphs 11–24—11–32 above. Since Muslims themselves are not unaware of such reservations, it seems rather likely that disputes of such a nature would not reach English courts and will instead be dealt with by unofficial bodies like the Shariat Council.[63] Indeed, Badawi (1995, pp. 79–80) confirms this:

> "We have a great number of problems coming to us in the Sharia Council concerning inheritance and the distribution of wealth within the family, that is to say, preferring a particular child or heir over another. In 1979 we negotiated with the authorities over inheritance and were told that it was quite simple; all

---

[60] Details of this are found in all major family law books. With special reference to ethnic minorities, see Poulter (1986), pp. 54 and 88–89; Poulter, *Asian traditions and English law* (1990a), pp. 75–77; Pearl (1986a), p. 47.

[61] Ahsan (1995), p. 27 also indicates that the practice of appointing well-qualified persons as executors to ensure compliance with Muslim law is not yet widespread.

[62] The same suggestion is made by Poulter (1990a), pp. 74–75, with detailed advice on how to go about this.

[63] Poulter (1990a), p. 75 confirms that no such case has yet reached the English courts.

you need to do is to get a solicitor who would draft a will, which would be acceptable to us, and we would go ahead and implement Muslim law. At the time we negotiated with a lawyer who agreed to do this for the sum of £7 and we agreed that we would pay for the first 100 applicants to encourage Muslims to come forward. Only seventeen did so and at the time I received a delegation of Muslim women who said, 'We don't want it, because it militates against our interests. We are better off under English intestacy law'."

Research will need to be conducted to ascertain the substantive rules that are being developed in this field within the ambit of *angrezi shariat*. Given that most of the Muslims in Britain are of South Asian origin, it would not be surprising if a tendency to disinherit women by not actually giving them their due shares in accordance with traditional Muslim law was also found to be a feature of *angrezi shariat*.

Muslim law of gifts

The traditional law

11–135   We have seen in detail in earlier sections of this chapter that Muslim law seeks to protect the lawful rights of heirs who are close relatives of the deceased. As we saw already in relation to 'death sickness', attempts to dispose of property *inter vivos* have to some extent been treated as devices to evade the Muslim system of inheritance rules and have been accompanied by some strict legal requirements which must be satisfied in order to create an effective transfer of property. Not surprisingly, different schools of Muslim jurisprudence differ on details. However, whereas Muslim law allows testamentary disposition only within the limit of one third of one's property, it allows individuals to give away the whole of their property during their lifetime.[64]

11–136   Nasir (1990a, p. 281) defines a gift (*hiba*) generally as "a contract by which a person (the donor), disposes, without consideration, of property belonging to him during his lifetime to another person" and refers to a number of modern Muslim jurisdictions. Bharatiya (1996, pp. 216–217) lists a number of definitions given by earlier authors and considers the important topic of the essentials of a valid gift. Fyzee (1974, p. 218) defines *hiba* as "the immediate and unqualified transfer of the corpus of the property without any return". The basis of the doctrine of *hiba* is found in Sura II, verse 215.

11–137   There are three important incidents to the law of *hiba*. There has to be a declaration of offer (*ijab*), a declaration of acceptance (*qabul*) and actual delivery of possession (*qabda*). However, it appears that Muslim jurists and the provisions in modern jurisdictions differ considerably on these basics.[65] There is agreement, however, that offer and acceptance do not have to be in writing.[66]

11–138   Several other important conditions need to be stressed.[67] First, the donor must possess legal capacity and the donee must be actually alive at the time of the gift (Nasir (1990a), p. 284). Further, the property given must be in existence when the declaration of *hiba* is made. When a gift is of an undivided part (*musha'*),[68]

---

[64] For details see Bharatiya (1996), pp. 216–217. See also Hidayatullah and Hidayatullah (1990), p. 112, adding the comment that such gifts may be made even to an heir.
[65] For details see Nasir (1990a), pp. 282–283.
[66] *ibid.*, p. 282; Fyzee (1974), p. 219; Bharatiya (1996), p. 217.
[67] For details see Nasir (1990a), pp. 283–285.
[68] Every joint undivided property subject to the right of more than one individual is a *musha'*.

and the undivided part is in fact divisible, it is an irregular (*fasid*) gift, rendered valid by subsequent separation and delivery. If the undivided part is indivisible, the gift is valid (*sahih*). Nasir (1990a, p. 284) emphasises that in Hanafi law a gift of joint property is not valid.

11–139 As to the question whether possession of the gift is an essential condition for completion of the transaction, a minority of traditional jurists argued that possession is not a condition of validity.[69] However, Abu Hanifa and Shafi'i took the view that possession is a condition for the validity of a gift and modern Arab law, as well as South Asian Muslim law, have tended to follow this view. Accordingly, until possession is taken by the donee, the property remains entirely at the disposal of the donor. If a donor makes a declaration of *hiba* which is accepted by the donee, but without delivery of possession, then, on the death of the donor, the property will descend to the donor's heirs.

11–140 Revocation of gifts was frowned upon in Muslim law,[70] illustrated by the fact that there is a *hadith* saying that "if anyone seeks to take back a gift he is like a dog who returns to its vomit" (Doi (1984), p. 335). It is, however, possible to revoke a *hiba* in certain circumstances although it is not favoured and Fyzee (1974, p. 265) compares it in this respect to the *talaq* as a permitted action which is not ideal. The rules on this subject in the various school traditions are clearly not uniform and many allowances are made for specific situations.[71]

11–141 A full gift of the substance (*hiba*) is distinguished from a gift of the usufruct or profits only (*'ariyya*).[72] The latter may be accompanied by conditions limiting the period of enjoyment of the property in the sense of creating a limited interest. It follows that an *'ariyya* is revocable at any time by the donor.[73]

11–142 Our section on *hiba* is concluded by a brief discussion of two particular concepts — *hiba bi'l-iwad* and *hiba bi-sharti'l-iwad*. The former is a transaction consisting of (a) a *hiba* and (b) a return (*iwad*). As soon as the return gift is made, both gifts become irrevocable. *Hiba bi'sharti'l-iwad* is a gift made with a stipulation (*shart*) for a return (*iwad*). The basic difference between this institution and *hiba bi'l-iwad* is that in *hiba bi'l-iwad*, a voluntary gift is followed by a voluntary return, whereas in the *sharti'l-iwad*, the gift itself is made with a stipulation. The donee is free to accept or to reject the stipulation. If he accepts the stipulation, then he is under a legal duty to complete the gift in favour of the donor. If the donee rejects the stipulated condition, the original gift is effective as a simple gratuitous transfer, and the stipulation simply does not take effect.[74]

South Asian legal developments

11–143 While traditional Muslim jurists argued, to some extent, about whether acceptance is an essential element of a gift, all South Asian legal texts take offer and acceptance as essentials and emphasise in addition that "ordinarily, delivery of possession is an essential and substantive condition of a valid hiba" (Mahmood (1982a), p. 196). This principle has been highlighted in several early leading cases.[75]

---

[69] See Nasir (1990a), pp. 286–287.
[70] For details see Nasir (1990a), pp. 286–288.
[71] For details see Fyzee (1974), p. 265; Doi (1984), p. 336 *ibid.*; Mahmood (1982a), p. 203. For Pakistan see Mannan (1990), pp. 207–214.
[72] Nasir (1990a), p. 281 refers in this context to *aariya* as a "loan for use".
[73] On this concept see also Fyzee (1974), p. 267; Bharatiya (1996), p. 231.
[74] For further details see Mahmood (1982), pp. 208–209.
[75] For details see *ibid.*, pp. 196–197; Hidayatullah and Hidayatullah (1990a), pp. 118–121; Fyzee (1974), pp. 218 and 230–239.

11–144 A good example is *Mohammad Abdul Ghani v. Fakhr Jahan Begam* [1922] 49 L.R. I.A. 195. The donor had made a gift of the corpus of the property, but continued in physical possession enjoying the profits. The donee, however, paid all the government taxes in respect of the land after the date of the gift. It was held that this factor amounted to constructive possession of the property, and thus there was indeed a valid gift. One can compare this case with the earlier decision in *Ranee Khujooroonissa v. Mussamut Roushun Jehan* [1875–1876] 3 L.R. I.A. 291. A father had attempted to defeat the operation of the law of succession by divesting himself before his death of some of his property to his son. There was no question of the father being in death sickness at the time. It was held that the intention of this deed was that the transfer of the corpus was only to operate after the death of the donor and, therefore, there was no actual nor constructive possession.

11–145 An illustrative case from Pakistan on gifts and on the question of delivery of possession is *Zeenat Bi v. Zaman Mehdi*, P.L.D. 1956 (W.P.) Lah. 760.[76] In this case, two successive husbands and a lover had attempted, in turn, to persuade Mst. Zeenat to donate to them a gift of particularly valuable property. The judge in this case made reference to the fact that the principles of law in this respect were well-established and said therefore, at page 763:

> "It is unnecessary to point out that if the actual possession cannot be given by the donor to the donee, but the donor has done all that he could do to divest himself of the gifted property, the gift would be considered to be complete and effective according to law. This is a question of fact in each case and no judicial authority can bind the Court in coming to its own conclusions on the facts of the particular case under investigation."

The judge accepted evidence to the effect that the woman had intended to make a gift to her lover, Zaman Mehdi, who had taken constructive possession and had thus become the absolute owner of the property.

11–146 An interesting Supreme Court decision from India is *Maqbool Alam Khan v. Khodaija*, A.I.R. 1966 S.C. 1194. Shaik Ahmad Ali owned tenanted property in Dumraon. He died in 1910, leaving surviving him as his heirs his mother, his second wife, three sons and two daughters from this wife, and two sons and four daughters from his first wife. In tabular form this scenario looks as follows:

Table 51

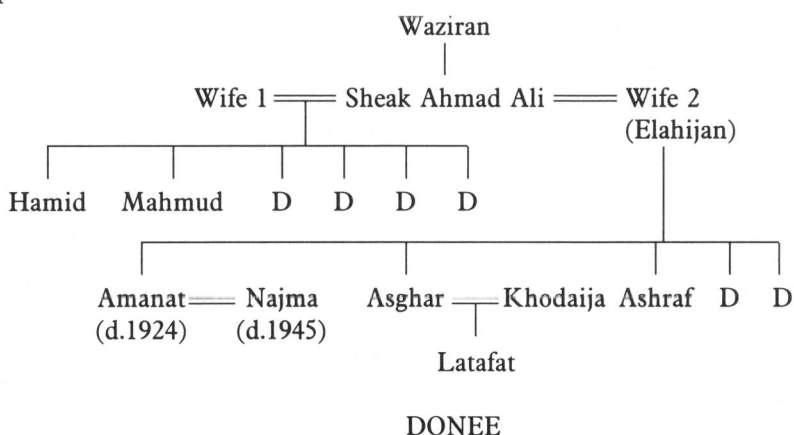

DONEE

---

[76] See also *Eidun Nisa Begum v. Member, Board of Revenue*, P.L.D. 1973 Pesh. 1.

11-147 All the heirs were co-sharers of this property, but only the names of Hamid and Mahmud were recorded as tenure-holders in the 'record of rights' published in 1911. In 1915, a decree for rent was obtained by the Maharaja of Dumraon against both Hamid and Mahmud. After considerable litigation connected with the rights and entitlements of the co-sharers in the tenure, Najma, the wife of Amanat, obtained by way of a compromise a share in the tenure.

11-148 Subsequently, the decree for rent was executed, and Latifat, the son of Asghar, purchased the tenure at the execution sale. Latafat, of course, was the Shaik's grandchild. The next stage of the litigation commenced in 1937, when Najma instituted proceedings against Latafat, seeking a declaration that her share in the tenure was not affected by the sale. Subsequently, the Maharaja returned to the scene by seeking an order for rent against Latafat. The Maharaja was successful in this endeavour and obtained a decree of execution from the court. There was a further execution sale in 1940, on which occasion Khodaija, the second wife of Asghar, successfully purchased the tenure.

11-149 In February 1943, Najma died. After her death, a certain Maqbool Alam, the appellant in the present proceedings, filed a petition praying for the substitution of his interest in the property in place of Najma, on the ground that before her death Najma had made an oral gift of her share to him. Maqbool Alam was successful and thus, in June 1943, he obtained possession of the land, dispossessing Khodaija in the process.

11-150 Further legal action continued during the 1940s, resulting finally in a reversal of the substitution decision. This stimulated the appellant to bring the present suit. The appellant based his claim to title upon the alleged oral gift to him by Najma. In response, Khodaija disputed both the factum and the validity of the gift. The appellant's evidence was that the gift was made on February 10, 1943, a fortnight before Najma's death, in the presence of witnesses. It was not shown, however, that he took possession of the properties; indeed this was not possible because at the time of the purported gift, Najma had already been dispossessed of the tenure. In the context of these facts, Bachawat J., giving judgment for the Supreme Court, said at page 1197:

> ". . . a gift of a property in the possession of a trespasser is not established by mere declaration of the donor and acceptance by the donee. To validate the gift, there must also be either delivery of possession or failing such delivery, some overt act by the donor to put it within the power of the donee to obtain possession. If, apart from making a declaration, the donor does nothing else, the gift is invalid."

It was found that Najma had done nothing at all after the alleged declaration. She did not even file a petition seeking substitution of the appellant in her place in the context of the proceedings which were then before the courts. In these circumstances, it was evident that the gift was invalid, and the appellant lost his case.

11-151 Recent reported decisions from India, a few almost every year, continue to rehearse the basic principles and apply them to the facts of the respective case. In *Hussenabi v. Husensab Hasan Sab*, A.I.R. 1989 Kant 218, property had been gifted by a grandfather to several minor grandchildren who were living with him. The court found that there was implied acceptance of the gift by the donor on behalf of his minor grandchildren and it was therefore accepted that these gifts were valid. However, a gift in favour of a fourth, major grandson without express or implied acceptance was liable to be set aside. This decision has been criticised as unfair on the fourth grandson, who was also living with the grandfather.[77]

11–152 *Maimuna Bibi v. Rasool Mian*, A.I.R. 1991 Pat. 203, is undoubtedly a most interesting case concerning the rights of the child of a pre-deceased son under Muslim law in India, where of course section 4 of the MFLO does not apply. Here, the purchasers of a property allegedly owned by three Muslim women appealed to the High Court after losing their claim in the lower court. The facts were that the father of the three women also had a son, who predeceased him, since he was presumed dead. The son's son, who had stayed with his grandfather all along and had cultivated the land together with him, claimed certain properties on the basis of a gift. Following lengthy examination of the evidence, the High Court came to the conclusion, at page 211, that the grandson's plea of an oral gift was based on an afterthought and that the three daughters had a claim to the properties in question. This case is discussed by Latifi (1991a, p. 553), who finds that on the facts, it is difficult to fault the reasoning and conclusions of the judge. However, to exclude the grandson from the inheritance altogether seemed hard. Latifi commented (*id.*):

> "The classical authorities of the Muslim law hold that there is an obligation on the grandfather, in such a case, to make a will (not exceeding his bequeathable third of his estate) in favour of the grandson. Egypt has enacted a law making such a compulsory bequest a statutory creature of law. This is held to be consistent with the *Shariat* principles. Pakistan has done something bolder and put the grandson in place of his predeceased father by importing the principle of succession *per stirpes* into the Hanafi law."

In Indian Muslim law today, as the above case illustrates, it is not sufficient for Muslim grandparents to make informal family arrangements to protect the interests of an orphaned grandchild in their care who is otherwise not entitled to succession. It would be advisable to either make a formal will, within the recognised one third limit and with the consent of all the heirs, or to make arrangements through gifts which are, preferably, properly executed and fulfil the well-recognised criteria of the law about acceptance of the gift and actual delivery of possession.

11–153 In *Y. S. Chen v. Batulbai*, A.I.R. 1991 M.P. 90, another point arose for consideration. Here, a tenant sought to oppose eviction proceedings by challenging the validity of the gift of the property in question by a mother to her daughter, on the ground that there had not been delivery of possession. The High Court found that the tenant had in fact paid rent to the new landlady and had recognised her as such. It was therefore not open to him to question the validity of the gift, which had been made in accordance with Muslim law. Other recent cases from India reiterate the basic principle that, in Muslim law, a gift need not be in writing. In *Mahboob Sahab v. Syed Ismail*, A.I.R. 1995 S.C. 1205, it was reiterated at pages 1207–1208 that the three essentials to the validity of a gift were the declaration by the donor, acceptance of the gift by or on behalf of the donee, and delivery of possession of the subject of the gift. It was held, at page 1208:

> "On proof of these essential conditions, the gift becomes complete and valid. In case of immovable property in the possession of the donor, he should completely divest himself physically of the subject of the gift."

This explains to some extent why the judge in *Maimuna Bibi v. Rasool Mian*, A.I.R. 1991 Pat. 203 (see above), did not accept the claim of the orphaned grandson,

---

[77] Mahmood (1989), p. 236, argues that this distinction was "rather unreasonable" and illogical.

because in that case both grandfather and grandson jointly managed the property and dealt with it in various ways which destroyed the claim of the grandson to a proper title.

11–154 Indian judges prior to 1948 ignored the distinction inherent in the traditional Muslim law between *hiba* (the gift of the substance) and *'ariyya* (the gift of the usufruct). When confronted with attempts by donors to make gifts for life, they declared such attempts void because they saw such devices as imposing a void condition on the enjoyment of the gift of the substance. The judges, therefore, struck out the limitation in the gift deeds, and allowed the donee to acquire an absolute interest. They were probably misled because of the English law concept of the 'life estate' which is a transfer of ownership of the property for a limited period, and which was introduced into Anglo-Hindu law. Influenced by such English concepts, the Indian judges could not conceive that Islamic law permitted the transfer of the *usus*, and interpreted all the gifts as transfers of the corpus subject to a condition which was void, for it was contrary to the Islamic law of *hiba*. The early cases are further complicated by the different views of the Shi'i as opposed to the Sunni law on the point. The whole episode was concluded by the Privy Council decision in *Nawazish Ali Khan v. Ali Raza Khan* [1948] 75 L.R. I.A. 62, when Sir John Beaumont stated the position as follows, at page 78:

> ". . . though the same terms may be used in English and Muslim law, to describe much the same things, the two systems of law are based on quite different conceptions of ownership. English law recognises ownership of land limited in duration; Muslim law admits only ownership unlimited in duration, but recognizes interests of limited duration in the use of property."

It is, therefore, a matter of construction whether the gift was intended as a transfer of the corpus or the *usus*. If it is the transfer of the *usus* only, any limitations imposed upon the duration of the donee's interest are valid and effective.[78]

11–155 There are three important exceptions to the classical rules about undivided parts (*musha'*), at least in India and Pakistan.[79] First, a gift made by one co-heir to another; secondly, a gift to two or more persons; and thirdly, a gift of freehold property in a town or shares in a land company. In all three cases, a gift of an undivided share capable of division is valid. In any event, the concept of *musha'* can be overcome by the use of a legal fiction (*hiyal*). An undivided share capable of division is sold by A to B and immediately thereafter A absolves B of his debt.

11–156 In India, various types of transaction involving in effect reciprocity of gifts have been recognised.[80] Mahmood (1989, p. 236), who discusses some recent cases, refers to such arrangements as "gifts for an exchange or with consideration" and confirms that *hiba bi'l-iwad* or *hiba bi'l-iwaz* is well-known in Indian law. An early example is found in *Muhammad Faiz Ahmad Khan v. Ghulam Ahmad Khan*, I.L.R. [1880/81] 3 Al. 490. In this case, a widow surrendered her claims over her husband's estate in favour of her brother-in-law, but only after a transfer of other property was made by the brother-in-law in her favour.[81]

11–157 The Indian case law on this subject has been criticised by Tahir Mahmood, who argues that where the transaction conforms to the Islamic form of

---

[78] Mahmood (1982a), pp. 206–207, suggests that these concepts are considered to be unislamic.

[79] See *Kasim Husain v. Sharif-un-Nissa*, I.L.R. [1883] 5 Al. 285. The gift in this case included the right to the use of a staircase used jointly by the donor and the owner of the adjoining house. As the *musha'* was not capable of division, the gift was valid.

[80] For details see Mahmood (1982a), pp. 208–211. Some of these transactions have evolved into a form of contract similar to sale and are therefore governed by general law rather than Muslim law.

[81] See also *Ashidbai v. Abdulla Haji Mahomed* I.L.R. [1906] 31 Bom. 271.

hiba bi'l-iwad, then the courts should apply the Muslim personal law because of the overriding provision of the Shariat Act. However, where the transaction amounts neither to *hiba* nor to the Islamic concept of *hiba bi'l-iwad*, then the court should simply apply the Indian general legislation, namely the Contract Act 1872 and the Transfer of Property Act 1882.

Waqf

The classical law

11-158 The Muslim religious endowment or *waqf*, a word which "literally means 'detention' and connotes tying up of property in perpetuity" (Bharatiya (1996), p. 185), is defined as follows by Islamic jurists[82]:

> ". . . the permanent dedication by a Muslim of any property, in such a way that the appropriator's right is extinguished, for charity or for religious objects or purposes, or for the founder of the waqf during his lifetime and after his death, for his descendants, and on their extinction to a purpose defined by the founder."

In effect, the settlor (*waqif*) withdraws from circulation the substance of the property (*'ayn*) and spends the proceeds (*manfa'a*) for a charitable purpose. Nasir (1990a, p. 274) draws a clear distinction between the two categories of *waqf*, a charity *waqf* and a family endowment. In either case, the property in question becomes the property of God Almighty.[83] If the income is devoted for charitable purposes from the beginning, it is called a *waqf khayri*. If it is designed primarily for the benefit of the settlor's descendants, with an ultimate benefit for a charitable purpose, it is a family *waqf* (a *waqf dhurri*). The emphasis in our discussion is placed on the second of these two institutions, often referred to as *waqf al-awlad*.

11-159 Although there are Qur'anic verses recommending gifts of property to charity, the institution of *waqf* is not expressly mentioned in the Qur'an, and its development appears to be a product of the jurists. The body of rules relating to *waqf* was built up around *hadith* during the first two centuries of Islam on the basis of *ijma*.[84]

11-160 It is a agreed that a *waqf* may be created orally or in writing. All that is necessary for the creation of a *waqf* is for the *waqif* to indicate the intention to make the property *waqf* property, and to specify the particular charitable purposes to which it is to be devoted. According to Abu Yusuf, the dedication of *waqf* is complete after this declaration.[85] In his view, no delivery of possession to the guardian (the *mutawali*) is necessary, which is the general view of the Hanafi school, although there is a minority opinion of Imam Muhammad Shaybani to the effect that delivery of possession is necessary prior to the creation of the *waqf*.[86] The Shi'i school demands delivery of the property.

11-161 Nasir (1990a, p. 275) provides a list of three essentials of a valid *waqf* according to Sunni law and of four essentials under the Shia law.[87] The Sunni

---

[82] Nasir (1990a), p. 274. See similarly Doi (1984), p. 339.

[83] There is a minority view that the *waqf* is a juristic person in its own right. Still others, as in the case of particular Shi'i jurists, vest ownership in the beneficiaries.

[84] For some details see Bharatiya (1996), pp. 183–184. It has been debated in some detail whether the institution has some roots in pre-Islamic concepts. For details see *ibid.*, p. 184; Fyzee (1974), p. 276.

[85] There is one apparent exception to this rule which relates to the *waqf* created by will. Such a *waqf* is subject to the law relating to testamentary succession, dedication beyond one third of the property being *ultra vires*. As the will speaks from death, the *waqf* only comes into operation on the death of the testator.

[86] On the various juristic opinions see in detail Fyzee (1974), pp. 278–280.

[87] Doi (1981), pp. 340–341, lists seven conditions but does not make specific reference to the Shia position. On the essentials of a *waqf* see in much detail Fyzee (1974), pp. 281–301.

criteria emphasise that the dedication of the property must be permanent (also a Shia essential), which includes irrevocability,[88] that the dedicator must be fully qualified in all respects to make the dedication, and that the *waqf* should be for a purpose recognised by Muslim law as religious, pious or charitable. The Shia criteria, apart from permanency, are that the dedication must be absolute and unconditional, that possession of the items dedicated must be given, and finally that the dedicator should not retain any interest. This means that the Shias insist on transfer of possession and/or control to an administrator (*mutawali*) in much stricter terms than the Sunnis.

11–162   The important point that the object of the *waqf* must be pleasing to Allah need only be achieved in a general sense. In the case of the *waqf khayri* the charitable object is the immediate beneficiary, but in the *waqf dhurri* the profits can be reserved for the benefit of the settlor's children or even for the benefit of strangers. In the case of the *waqf dhurri*, the perpetuity principle is achieved by allocating the proceeds of the *waqf* to the poor after the death of the individuals who are to benefit from the *waqf*. The examples of charitable purposes are very extensive, but will often include provisions to benefit a mosque, a school, a hospital, or the general welfare of the poor.

11–163   Linked to the perpetuity principle is the rule that the *waqf*, with a few exceptions, must be inalienable. The corpus of the property made the subject of the *waqf* cannot be sold, mortgaged, donated or alienated, even by inheritance, in any way. The only two exceptions are that it can be exchanged or sold on the authority of the *Qadi* in order to purchase new property and, secondly, it can be leased although usually for only a limited period of a year, or three years in the case of agricultural land.

11–164   One problem, which disturbed the jurists, and which is indeed of troublesome complexity, relates to the question of the vesting of ownership of the *waqf*. The disciples of Abu Hanifa (Shaybani and Abu Yusuf) as well as Shafi'i propounded the theory that the *waqif*'s right of ownership ceased on the dedication of the *waqf*. The Maliki school however, as well as Abu Hanifa himself, considered that the founder and his heirs retained rights of ownership. The *ijma* of the Hanafi school, as so often, has been to adopt the views of Abu Yusuf and Shaybani.

11–165   Regarding succession of beneficiaries, the founder has an unlimited power of laying down rules (Nasir (1990a), p. 278). The basic principles of succession in the absence of specific directions are interesting: both males and females have the same share, agnates and cognates share alike, and the children of deceased beneficiaries represent their parents (*id.*).

11–166   The powers and duties of the *mutawali*, the administrator of the *waqf* can be summed up in the statement that a *mutawali* is merely appointed to be a manager of the trust property. The *mutawali* may be a non-Muslim, blind, mute, male or female (Nasir (1990a), p. 279). No legal ownership vests in the *mutawali*, and it is this point which distinguishes the power of the *mutawali* from those of a trustee under an English trust. Essentially, the duty of the *mutawali* is to do everything necessary and proper for the protection of the *waqf* property and for the administration of the *waqf*. In particular, the *mutawali* is responsible for distributing the proceeds amongst the beneficiaries. Quite often, founders of a *waqf* will declare themselves as the first *mutawali*. If no *mutawali* is designated, the *waqif* becomes the *mutawali*.

11–167   With regard to succession to the position of *mutawali*, in the absence of any rules laid down in the *waqfnama* itself, the general rule is that during his own

---

[88] The view of Abu Hanifa, which represents a minority and divergent opinion within Hanafi law, is that a *waqf* can be revoked up until it is confirmed by a *Qadi*. The Maliki jurists also permit revocation.

lifetime, the *waqif* possesses the power to designate a successor to the *mutawali*. Otherwise, the *Qadi* has responsibility to designate the *mutawali*. Once a *mutawali* has been appointed, the settlor has no power of removal, although in a particular case of unfitness, the general supervisory role of the *Qadi* would allow for removal of the *mutawali*.

11–168 Regarding modern reforms, it is noteworthy that while Kenya was busy dismantling the restrictive interpretations of *waqf* by reverting to the classical Hanafi position,[89] several Muslim countries were indulging in attempts to bring *waqf* property back on to the commercial market and prevent further *waqfs* from being created.[90] Thus, in Egypt, an Act of 1946 provided that a *waqf khayri* may be either perpetual or temporary at the option of the *waqif*. More important, the perpetual *waqf dhurri* was abolished, although a *waqif* could still establish a *waqf dhurri* so long as it was restricted to two generations or to a period not exceeding 60 years from the date of the *waqif*'s death. In addition, the *waqif* was given the power to revoke the *waqf* either wholly or in part, in addition to the right to alter conditions of the *waqf*. In 1952 the next step was taken, in the context of more general land reform, to abolish *waqf dhurri* completely, so that in Egypt today only *waqf khayri* is permitted. In the Lebanon in 1947, the Egyptian law of 1946 was followed. After two generations, the *waqf dhurri* property reverts to the *waqif* or to his heirs. Moveable property and shares of stock were made the possible subject of *waqf*. In Syria in 1949, the creation of further *waqf dhurri* was prohibited, and existing *waqf dhurri* property was liquidated. All *waqf* ownership was expropriated in Tunisia in 1957. Major reforms in the administration of *waqf* property have been introduced in many Muslim countries, in particular Libya, Algeria and Kuwait (for some further details see Nasir (1990a), pp. 274–278).

Waqf in South Asian laws

11–169 Not surprisingly, several authors refer explicitly to the immense social and economic importance of the institution of *waqf* in South Asia.[91] Bharatiya (1996, p. 182) highlights its potential benefits for the educational and economic development of the Muslim community in India, given that there are well over 100,000 *waqfs*, worth more than a billion rupees (see also Doi (1984, p. 341).

11–170 Mahmood (1982), p. 263) emphasises that the subject is still to a large extent regulated by Muslim law, as an aspect of Muslim personal law. Bharatiya (1996, pp. 182–183) refers in some detail to the fact that, in India, *waqf* administration is protected under Article 26(d) of the Constitution as part of the right to freedom of religion.[92] However, *waqf* management must be in accordance with state law.

11–171 Mahmood (1982a, p. 263) says that there is no officially recognised, exhaustive, comprehensive or conclusive definition of *waqf* in India. Generally speaking, Indian courts have accepted the views of Abu Yusuf rather than Abu Hanifa (Bharatiya (1996), p. 185) and have taken the view that even in a family *waqf* the property vests in God (see Bharatiya (1996), p. 187). Various distinctions between public, quasi-public and private *waqfs* have been made.[93]

---

[89] See Pearl (1987a), pp. 204–205, and earlier Anderson (1955a), pp. 81–121.
[90] Note in contrast the view of Doi (1984), p. 341, that many successful public welfare activities have been carried out through *waqfs* and that the institution should be used more actively, especially in Africa.
[91] A very detailed study of *waqf* in India is Qureshi, *Waqfs in India. A study of administrative and legislative control* (1990).
[92] On this see in impressive detail *ibid.*, pp. 483–553.
[93] For details see Bharatiya (1996), pp. 188–189, and especially Qureshi (1990).

11–172 The starting point for a discussion of the law of *waqf* in South Asian laws must be the leading case of *Abul Fata Mahomed Ishak v. Russomoy Dhur Chowdhry* [1894–1895] 22 L.R. I.A. 76. The facts of this case are that a *waqfnama* was purportedly made in December 1868. The settlors were two brothers, Abdur Rahman and Abdool Kadir. The question before the court was simply whether this settlement was valid as a *waqfnama*. The settlement began as follows (page 83):

> "Committing ourselves to the mercy and kindness of the Great God, and relying upon the bounty of Providence for the perpetuation of the names of our forefathers and for the preservation of our properties, we . . . have made this permanent wakf according to our Mahomedan law . . . for the benefit of our children, the children of our children, and the members and relatives of our family and their descendants in male and female lines, and, in their absence, for the benefit of the poor and beggars and widows and orphans of *Sylhet* . . ."

Evidently, the two brothers had appointed themselves as *mutawali*, stating further in the document, as cited at page 83:

> "We, two brothers, have for our lifetime taken upon ourselves the management and supervision of the same in the capacity of matwalis, and taken out the wakf properties from our ownership and enjoyment in a private capacity, and we have put them in our possession and under our control in our capacity as matwalis."

Toward the end of the document, the general object of the *waqf* is stated, reproduced at page 84 of the case report:

> "The object of this wakf of properties is that the properties may be protected against all risks, the name and the prestige of the family maintained, and the profits of these properties appropriated towards the maintenance of the name and prestige of the family, the support of the persons for whose benefit the wakf is made, and religious purposes, & c."

At first instance, the judge had held the *waqf* valid, but on appeal the High Court had reversed the decision. The High Court's negative decision was upheld by the Privy Council. Lord Hobhouse, in the Privy Council, was apparently concerned by the illusory nature of the gift to the poor and saw this arrangement as an expedient device to benefit the family alone. Lord Hobhouse said, at pages 84–85:

> "Such is the instrument which is propounded as a wakfnama. The motives stated are, regard for the family name, and preservation of the property in the family. Every specific trust is for some member of the family. The family is to be aggrandized by accumulations of surpluses, and apparently by absorption into the settlement of after-acquired properties; and no person is to have any right of calling the managers to account. These possessions are to be secured for ever for the enjoyment of the family, so far as the settlors could accomplish such a result, by provisions that nobody's share shall be alienated, or be attached for his debts. There is no reference to religion unless it be the invocation of the Deity to perpetuate the family name and to preserve their property, and the casual mention of unspecified, religious purposes, & c., at the end of the sentence last quoted. There is a gift to the poor and to widows and orphans, but they are to take nothing, not even surplus income, until the total extinction of the blood of the settlors, whether lineal or collateral."

11–173 Their Lordships were certainly aware of the basic principles of the institution of *waqf*, since the history of the dispute over the acceptability of family *waqfs* was presented to them in detail, as reported at pages 80–81:

> "A wakf is simply a permanent benefaction for the good of God's creatures; so long as the dedication is permanent there is a free choice as to the beneficiaries; the descendants of the settlor being preferable objects of his bounty to the general body of the poor. That was the view of the old Mahomedan authorities, and it appears to have been acted on in early cases by the Indian Courts ... It was contended that not until the Mahomedan law officers ceased in 1864 to be consulted by the Law Courts was the doctrine laid down that a wakf on the members of one's family was invalid. After 1864 the cases were somewhat difficult to reconcile ... there is no trace of any distinction in Mahomedan law books between a wakf for one's family and a wakf for any other purpose. In this case the wakfnama is only in part for the wakif's family and descendants, and such an endowment cannot be held to be invalid without imposing disabilities upon Mahomedans which would conflict with their religious customs."

However, the suspicion that this particular family arrangement lacked religious integrity was evidently very strong. The other passage of Lord Hobhouse's speech deserving full quotation is found at page 86:

> "As regards precepts which are held up as the fundamental principles of Mahomedan law, their Lordships are not forgetting how far law and religion are mixed up together in the Mahomedan communities; but they asked during the argument how it comes about that by the general law of *Islam*, at least as known in *India*, simple gifts by a private person to remote unborn generations of descendants, successions that is of inalienable life interests, are forbidden; and whether it is to be taken that the very same dispositions, which are illegal when made by ordinary words of gift, become legal if only the settlor says that they are made as a wakf, in the name of God, or for the sake of the poor. To those questions, no answer was given or attempted, nor can their Lordships see any."

Turning to decided cases, it was stated, at page 87, that "clearly the Mahomedan law ought to govern a purely Mahomedan disposition of property". Their Lordships were obviously aware of an important *hadith* of the Prophet, to the effect that the most excellent of gifts (*sadaqa*) is that which a man bestows upon his family,[94] but placed their own interpretation on this. Lord Hobhouse said, at page 87:

> "Those precepts may be excellent in their proper application. They may, for aught their Lordships know, have had their effect in moulding the law and practice of wakf ... But it would be doing wrong to the great lawgiver to suppose that he is thereby commending gifts for which the donor exercises no self-denial; in which he takes back with one hand what he appears to put away with the other; which are to form the centre of attraction for accumulations of income and further accessions of family property; which carefully protect so-called managers from being called to account; which seek to give to the donors

---

[94] Fyzee (1974), p. 268, confirms that in traditional texts the term *sadaqa* refers both to *waqf* and to ordinary gifts.

and their family the enjoyment of property free from all liability to creditors; and which do not seek the benefit of others beyond the use of empty words."

The Privy Council therefore interpreted the purported ultimate gift to the poor as an illusory gesture, designed to benefit only the family itself. As we have seen, however, all schools of Muslim law are united in accepting that the settlor's own family may be validly designated as beneficiaries in a *waqf dhurri* and that such a *waqf* has to be both perpetual and inalienable. No distinction is drawn between the *waqf dhurri* and the *waqf khayri* in the above decision. Indeed, according to Abu Yusuf and accepted as Hanafi doctrine, the settlor can validly designate himself as the first beneficiary so that he can enjoy the income of the *waqf* property as a life tenant. The Privy Council, however, placed its own interpretation on the *sunna* of the Prophet, rather than following, by *taqlid*, the authoritative interpretations of the Hanafi school.

11–174 There was outrage in the Muslim community over this decision. Fyzee (1974, p. 302) reports that it created a storm in the country because "it was deemed to go against the fundamental notions of Islamic law". Apart from giving rise to a vigorous academic and religious debate, as Fyzee (*id.*) reports, one effect of this judgment was the promulgation of the Musalman Wakf Validating Act 1913 (bought into force on March 7, 1913), whose purpose was to restore the Hanafi law on the subject. However, as we shall see, not all of the Hanafi law was restored by the 1913 Act. Section 2(1) defines *waqf* as "the permanent dedication by a person professing the Mussalman faith of any property for any purpose recognized by the Mussalman law as religious, pious or charitable". This definition, of course, throws us back to the old texts for what is recognised as religious, pious or charitable. Examples would be money for pilgrimage (*haj*), for the relief of poverty, for a school, a mosque, or for public charitable purposes. Section 3 of the Act states:

> "It shall be lawful for any person professing the Mussalman faith to create a wakf which in all other respects is in accordance with the provisions of Mussalman law, for the following, among other, purposes: –
> (a) for the maintenance and support wholly or partially of his family, children or descendants, and
> (b) where the person creating a wakf is a Hanafi Mussalman, also for his own maintenance and support during his life-time or for the payment of his debts out of the rents and profits of the property dedicated:
> Provided that the ultimate benefit is in such cases expressly or impliedly reserved for the poor or for any other purpose recognized by the Mussalman law as a religious, pious or charitable purpose of a permanent character."

It appears from this section, since the ultimate benefit has to be reserved, either expressly or impliedly, for the poor or for any other purpose of a religious, pious or charitable nature, that the view of Abu Yusuf, to the effect that the benefit can be impliedly reserved, has been accepted.

11–175 Further, while the immediate purpose may be for 'maintenance and support', a reservation for members of the family absolutely is not valid as a *waqf*. In *Abdul Karim Adenwalla v. Rahimabai*, A.I.R. 1946 Bom. 342, the effect of the 1913 Act was discussed and it was held, at page 344:

"That Act makes it lawful for a Mussalman to create a wakf for the maintenance and support wholly or partially of his family, children or descendants, provided that the ultimate benefit is in such cases expressly or impliedly reserved for the poor or for any other purpose recognised by the Muhammadan law as a religious, pious or charitable purpose of a permanent character."

A slightly wider interpretation of section 3 has been given in *Mohammad Sabir Ali v. Tahir Ali*, A.I.R. 1957 Al. 94, where the ultimate bequest for charity was not in doubt, on the basis that the entire income of the *waqf* property may be reserved for maintenance and support of the beneficiaries. In this case, where part of the dispute concerned expenses for marriage, it was also held, at page 101, that "the words 'maintenance and support' are not to be limited to the necessities of life. The phrase includes maintenance of one's position in life". Under the Shi'i law, however, the *waqif* has no power to reserve the income for his own use. Section 3(b) of the 1913 Act only applies to Hanafis.[95]

11-176 Section 4 of the 1913 Act, in explaining section 3, expressly repeals the *Abul Fata* decision of 1894 when it states:

"No such wakf shall be deemed to be invalid merely because the benefit reserved therein for the poor or other religious, pious or charitable purpose of a permanent nature is postponed until after the extinction of the family, children or descendants of the person creating the wakf."

Section 5 of the Act provides that "nothing in this Act shall affect any custom or usage whether local or prevalent among Mussalmans of any particular class or sect". However, the application of section 5 is restricted by section 2 of the Shariat Act 1937 to cases of *waqfs* to charities, charitable institutions, and charitable and religious endowments. Family *waqfs* are governed by Hanafi law as contained in the 1913 Act.

11-177 Following the 1913 Act, there have been several further enactments in this field, found in the Mussalman Wakf Act 1923 (August 5, 1923),[96] the Mussalman Wakf Validating Act 1930 (July 25, 1930) and the Wakf Act 1954 in India. The 1930 Act had only one limited aim, namely to give retrospective effect to the 1913 Act, while the 1954 Act introduced a detailed regulatory scheme regarding the management of *waqf* property in India.[97] The Waqf Act 1954 was amended by the Waqf (Amendment) Act 1984. This central Act now applies throughout India except Jammu and Kashmir, where there is local legislation. Some consideration needs to be given, in brief, to the taxation and land legislation which reduces significantly the importance of the Musalman Wakf Validating Act 1913. For instance, in *Ahmed G. H. Ariff v. The Commissioner of Wealth Tax Calcutta*, A.I.R. 1971 S.C. 1691, it was held that where a Hanafi creates a family *waqf* of properties, the right to receive the income of these properties is an asset within the meaning of section 2(e) of the Wealth Tax Act 1957 and is therefore subject to tax legislation.

11-178 The case law on *waqf* in South Asia has been voluminous and continues to be fairly extensive and complex, especially as far as public *waqfs* are concerned.[98]

---

[95] *Shahban Mohib v. Hemraj Raghavyi* A.I.R. 1942 Sind. 14.
[96] This important Act, and the Mussalman Wakf Rules 1924 do not apply to family *waqfs*. They regulate the management of *waqf* properties and make provisions for proper accounts. For the full text see Haq, *The manual of Auqaf laws* (1992); for some comments Fyzee (1974), p. 318.
[97] For the full text of the 1930 and 1954 Acts see Mahmood (1982a), p. 300–324.
[98] The sections on Muslim law in the *Annual Surveys of Indian Law* are an excellent source of detailed information. Latifi, "Muslim Law", in *Annual Survey of Indian Law 1992* (1992), p. 179 emphasises the growing importance of this branch of the law.

We have already covered the negative approach of the Privy Council to family *waqfs*.[99] In general, in earlier cases the High Courts of Madras and Allahabad have tended to adopt a flexible approach,[1] whereas other courts have been more restrictive. For example, in *Abdul Fazal v. S. Sayeeda Khatun*, P.L.D. 1963 Dacca 343, the expression 'heir of the children' was used in a *waqfnama*. It was held that such an expression would include persons who are not members of the family, and thus the *waqf* was invalid.

11–179   An interesting line of cases considered the problem of the definition of 'family'. In *Ismail Haji Arat v. Umar Abdulla*, A.I.R. 1942 Bom. 155, it was held that a nephew who resided in the settlor's house could be considered to be within the term 'family', so long as that person was dependent on the settlor. A 'stranger', however, does not appear to be a member of the family within section 3(a) of the 1913 Act. This restriction seems contrary to the Hanafi law. In *Mohammad Afzal v. Din Mohammad*, I.L.R. [1946] 27 Lah. 300, it was held that 'kindred' also does not come within the definition of family.

11–180   Other recent cases concerned the rights of the *mutawali* to file a suit on behalf of the *waqf*.[2] A large number of reported cases provide evidence of power struggles between managers of *waqfs* and various State Wakf Boards, alleging mismanagement and seeking to exercise greater control, a topic to which we cannot devote space here.[3] The validity of a *waqf* made by a non-Muslim was at issue in *Tamilnadu Wakf Board v. S. Syed Inam Saheb*, A.I.R. 1983 Mad. 297. A detailed analysis of this case, focused on the fact that non-Muslims have always been able to create a *waqf* under Muslim law, is given by Latifi (1983, pp. 323–324). In one case, the rights of Muslim women as managers of shrines were solemnly confirmed by the Indian Supreme Court. This prompted Mahmood (1989, p. 237), who briefly discusses this case, to state:

> "The position and rights of women in Muslim law are, in fact, not all that bad as it is often believed. The culprits in this regard are those who have misunderstood and misconstrued the law, and not the noble makers of the law."

11–181   In India, despite a number of attempts to control it, the *waqf dhurri* is still a powerful force. It is often used as a legal device (*hiyal*) to overcome the particular rules of succession and it is probably mainly for this reason that attempts in India to reform the *waqf dhurri* have failed. At the same time, it is evident that the *waqf* legislation, together with the constant attempts by the courts to restrict the family *waqf* by making it subject to tax laws and other controls, has placed some restraints on the economic impact of *waqf* property.[4] In *Fazlul Rabbi Pradhan v. State of West Bengal*, A.I.R. 1965 S.C. 1722, it was stated, at pages 1727–1728:

---

[99] A good summary of the judicial reservations is found in Bharatiya (1996), pp. 213–215, with interesting reference to the views of Danial Latifi, who argued that a vigorous control of *waqf* would be preferable, since it would increase economic activity among Muslims. Hidayatullah and Hidayatullah (1990), pp. 148–151 provide a good summary; see also Qureshi (1990).

[1] See for instance *Muhammad Azam Khan v. Hamid Shah*, I.L.R. (1946) Al. 575, and *Asha Bibi v. Nabissa Sahib* A.I.R. (1957) Mad. 583.

[2] See *Maulvi Reza Ansari v. Shyamlal Shah*, A.I.R. (1983) Pat. 299, wrongly decided according to Latifi (1983), p. 322, who affirms that it has always been a principle of Muslim law that a *mutawali* has standing to protect the *waqf* property.

[3] For details see Qureshi (1990). A very positive example of judicial vigilance in this area is found in *Karnataka Board of Wakfs, Bangalore v. B. C. Nagaraja Rao*, A.I.R. 1991 Kant. 400, discussed in Latifi (1991a), pp. 554–555.

[4] For some examples of the hostile approach of the tax authorities see Latifi (1983), p. 329.

". . . the intention of the Validating Act was not to give a new meaning to the word "charity" which in common parlance is a word denoting a giving to someone in necessitous circumstances and in law a giving for public good. A private gift to one's own self or kith and kin may be meritorious and pious but is not a charity in the legal sense and the Courts in India have never regarded such gifts as for religious or charitable purposes even under the Mahomedan Law."[5]

In this case, it was found that the two deeds were not exclusively for charitable purposes. It was stated, in conclusion, at page 1728:

"They do provide in part for objects which are religious or charitable or both but mingled with those purposes are some which are secular and some which are family endowments very substantial in character. If the latter benefits had ceased or the families had become extinct, leaving only the charities or if the provisions were for poor and needy though belonging to the wakif's family, other considerations might conceivably have arisen . . . The deeds as they stand cannot, however, be said to come within the exemption claimed."

The High Court of Assam, in *Fazal Sheikh v. Abdur Rahman Mea*, A.I.R. 1991 Gau. 17, had to decide a case where the object of the *waqf* was only laid down in very general terms. The decision in this case confirms that, provided appropriate and genuine arrangements have been made, Indian Muslims can continue to create *waqfs* which will be recognised as valid and genuine. It was held, at page 21, that the explicit mention of the phrase 'permitted by the Shariat' made this a valid arrangement and Dr B. P. Saraf J. said:

"What is necessary for a valid Wakf is that the purpose of the Wakf must be one recognised by Mahomedan law as 'religious, pious and charitable'. A person who dedicates his property by way of Wakf may, instead of enumerating the objects for which the income of the Wakf may be used, provide that it may be used for any welfare works permitted by the Shariat, that is, the Mahomedan law. Such provision, in my opinion, is absolutely clear and there is no vagueness or uncertainty in it. The only difference is that instead of restricting the use of the income of the Wakf to some of the specified objects, the Wakf has allowed it to be used for any of the objects which are recognised by Shariat to be welfare works. No exception can be taken to such declaration."

For Pakistan, Mannan (1990, pp. 254–325) now provides the most authoritative summary of the relevant law.[6] The learned editor reiterates the basic principles and emphasises, at pages 256–257, that a valid *waqf* may be made "not only of immovable property, but also of movables, such as shares in joint stock companies, Government promissory notes, and even money". Regarding invalidity of a *waqf* for uncertainty, much material is provided on older cases. A close comparison of Mannan (1990, pp. 263–265) and Hidayatullah and Hidayatullah (1990, pp. 148–151) indicates that Pakistani law has not developed any significant differences from the Anglo-Indian law on this subject, although a number of decided cases create the impression that courts in Pakistan are less suspicious of the motives of *waqifs* than the Privy Council used to be.[7]

---

[5] It was also held in this case, at p. 1728, that English authorities on the subject should not be taken as a guide.

[6] A comprehensive, very useful collection of the relevant Pakistani law is found also in Haq (1992).

[7] For details on relevant cases see Mannan (1990), pp. 268–270.

11–182   The Pakistani Supreme Court decision of *Ghulam Shabbir v. Nur Begum*, P.L.D. 1977 S.C. 75, illustrates further how the 1913 Act works in practice. The dispute in this case related to a house and three shops in Multan. On May 10, 1939, Haji Faiz Bakhsh executed a deed transferring a one eighth share of the property in favour of Bakht Ilahi, wife of his son Hussain Bakhsh, in lieu of a dower. On November 30, 1948, he registered a *waqfnama* with respect to the residue of the property, appointing himself as the *mutawali* and his brother-in-law, Abdul Ghafar, as his successor. He died in April 1949, leaving surviving him a son, a widow (Hayat) and a daughter (Gulzar). After the death of Haji Faiz Bakhsh, his son started to interfere with the property and sold one third of the property to a third party. The dispute in this case was between this third party and the *mutawali* as to the ownership of the property. Thus the court had to determine whether there had been a valid *waqf*. It was held, first, that the *waqf* was not pronounced in death sickness. The Supreme Court then examined in detail the *waqfnama*. The *waqif* had declared that he had voluntarily decided to create the *waqf*. He had emphasised that henceforth he would have no right to sell the property and that he and his descendants would have only the right to enjoyment of the income of the property and to reside therein. He stated that he would be the first *mutawali* and that he would feed himself and his family from its income. He stated also that his son would have no right to any of the money from the property except for three rupees a day as his wages. The final paragraph of the *waqfnama* provided:

> "If, God forbid his family became extinct then half of [the] income of the factory will be given to the orphanage and the other half will be given to Madrisa Diniyat in Masjid Chattarhat."

It was obvious that the dominant, indeed the only, object with which the *waqif* executed the deed was to preserve and protect the property from the clutches of a son who, in his father's opinion, was reckless. The Supreme Court held that the *waqf* could not be struck down merely on the ground that it had as its object the exclusion of one who was profligate. There was one other difficulty preventing recognition for the *waqf*, however, namely that neither the orphanage nor the school attached to the mosque existed. The Supreme Court nevertheless held that such a problem can be overcome by applying the *cy pres* rule, to the effect that the charitable basis of the *waqf* can be satisfied by ensuring that the ultimate benefit would be for an object similar to the object which had failed. The *waqf*, therefore, was valid, and as the son had no title in the property, the third party took no interest and lost the case.

11–183   In Pakistan and also in Bangladesh, *waqf* has been made subject to restrictions on upper limits of land holdings. More important, in what was then West Pakistan, changes were made by the West Pakistan Land Reform Regulations 1959. These provided, in essence, that all agricultural land included in a *waqf dhurri* should forthwith, if the *waqif* were alive, be vested in him. If the *waqif* were dead, the *waqf* would be divided between the heirs, and others, nominated by the government. Since 1959, therefore, it has been impossible in Pakistan to make agricultural land the subject of a *waqf dhurri*. The *waqf khayri* is now controlled by a central administration of *waqf* under the West Pakistan Waqf Properties Ordinance 1959. In addition, a number of statutory controls of *waqfs* have been introduced in the various provinces of Pakistan.[8]

11–184   Finally, one other topic, pre-emption, could have been discussed here if it had not been for reasons of space. There continues to be much litigation in South

---

[8] For details see Mannan (1990), pp. 312–313.

Asian laws, particularly in Pakistan, on questions related to pre-emption, often related to succession. A number of useful collections of material exist and offer a reasonable overview.[9] Here is another fertile field for more detailed research, especially in view of the fact that there are so many recent judicial decisions on the subject.[10]

---

[9] For Indian law, see in particular Hidayatullah and Hidayatullah (1990), pp. 203–222; Fyzee (1974), pp. 333–354; Bharatiya (1996), pp. 248–268; Mahmood (1982a), pp. 211–218. On Pakistan, Mannan (1990), pp. 326–361, provides an excellent discussion, with ample evidence of recent case law, in particular the leading case of *Government of N.W.F.P. v. Said Kamal Shah*, P.L.D. 1986 S.C. 360.

[10] For important recent cases and further details see *e.g. Ghulam Nabi v. Member III, Board of Revenue*, P.L.D. 1990 S.C. 1043 and *Sikandar v. Muhammad Ayub*, P.L.D. 1991 S.C. 1041.

Bibliography

Abedin, Syed Z. and Ziauddin Sardar (eds), *Muslim minorities in the West* (1995, Grey Seal, London).

Abid, S. Ali, *Manual of family laws in Pakistan* [*as amended up-to-date with case laws*] (1993, Civil and Criminal Law Publication, Lahore).

Afshar, Haleh, "Fundamentalism and women in Iran", in *The rights of subordinated peoples* (1994, Mendelsohn, Oliver and Upendra Baxi (eds.), Delhi et al., Oxford University Press), pp. 276–294.

Afshar, Haleh, "Islam empowering or repressive to women?", in *God's law versus state law. The construction of an Islamic identity in Western Europe* (1995, King, Michael ed., Grey Seal, London), pp. 54–61.

Agarwala, B. R. (ed.), *Plight of a Muslim woman. The Shah Bano case* (1995, Arnold Heinemann, New Delhi).

Ahmad, Alia, *Women and fertility in Bangladesh* (1991, Sage, New York et al.).

Ahmad, Ejaz, *Cases and materials on law of maintenance* (1990, 3rd rev. & enl. ed., Ashoka Law House, Allahabad).

Ahmad, Furqan, *Triple talaq. An analytical study with emphasis on socio-legal aspects* (1994, Regency Publications, New Delhi).

Ahmad, Imtiaz (ed.), *Family, kinship and marriage among Muslims in India* (1976, South Asian Books, Columbia).

Ahmad, Muhammad Basheer, *The administration of justice in medieval India* (1951, A.M.U., Aligarh).

Ahmad, Masud, *Pakistan, a study of its constitutional history: 1857–1975* (1978, Research Society of Pakistan, Lahore).

Ahmad, Qazi Kholiquzzaman et al. (eds), *Situation of women in Bangladesh* (1985, Ministry of Social Welfare and Women's Affairs, Dacca).

Ahmad, Shaikh Mahmud, *Social justice in Islam* (1992, Adam Publishers, Delhi).

Ahmed, A. F. Salahuddin, *Bangladesh. Tradition and transformation* (1987, UPL, Dhaka).

Ahmed, Ishtiaq, *The concept of an Islamic state: An analysis of the ideological controversy in Pakistan* (1987, Frances Pinter, London).

Ahmed, Kazi Nasir-ud-din, *The Muslim law of divorce* (1972, Islamic Research Institute, Islamabad).

Ahmed, Kazi Nasir-ud-din, *The Muslim law of divorce* (1978, Kitab Bhavan, New Delhi).

Ahmed, Moudud, *Bangladesh: Constitutional quest for autonomy* (1992, UPL, Dhaka).

Ahsan, Manazir, "The Muslim family in Britain", in *God's law versus state law. The construction of an Islamic identity in Western Europe* (1995, King, Michael ed., Grey Seal, London), pp. 21–30.

Akhtar, Saleem, *Shah Bano judgement in Islamic perspective: A socio-legal study* (1994, Kitab Bhavan, New Delhi).

Al-Alwani, Taha J., "The rights of the accused in Islam" (1995) 10 *Arab Law Quarterly* 3–16.

Alam, Syed Iqbal, "Age at marriage in Pakistan" [1968] 8 *The Pakistan Development Review* 489–498.

Ali, Ahmad, "Case book: Mst. Farishta vs. The Federation of Pakistan" [1986] 5 No. 6 *Journal of Law and Society (Peshawar)* 73–85.

Ali, Ahmed, Shaheen Sardar Ali and Fayyaz-Ur-Rehman, "Sociological difficulties in the implementation of legislation pertaining to women in Pakistan" [1990] Vol. IX No. 14 [January] *Journal of Law & Society (Peshawar)* 9–31.

Ali, Firasat and Furquan Ahmad, *Divorce in Mohammedan law: The lar of "triple divorce"* (1983, Deep & Deep, New Delhi).

Ali, Shaheen Sardar, "Case book – Supreme Court on khula" [1985] 4 No. 4 *Journal of Law and Society (Peshawar)* 51–61.

Ali, Syed Ameer, *Mahommedan law* (1885, Thaker, Spink & Co., Calcutta; 1912–1917, 4th ed., Thaker, Spink & Co., Calcutta; 1976, 7th ed., P.L.D. Publishers, Raja Said Akbar Khan, Lahore).

Ali, Syed Mumtaz, "Establishing guardianship: The Islamic alternative to family adoption in the Canadian context" [1994] 14 Nos. 1–2 [Jan.–July 1994] *Journal of Muslim Minority Affairs* 202–218.

Ali, Syed Mumtaz and Enab Whitehouse, "The reconstruction of the Constitution and the case for Muslim personal law in Canada" [1992] 13 No. 1 [January 1992] *Journal of Muslim Minority Affairs* 156–172.

Al-Maqatei, Mohammed, "The philosophy of marriage in Islam" (1985) 7 *Warwick Law Wording Papers* No. 3 (University of Warwick, Coventry).

Allott, Anthony, *The limits of law* (1980, Butterworths, London).

Al-Zwaini, Laila and Rudolph Peters, *A bibliography of Islamic law, 1980–1993* (1994, Brill, Leiden).

Amin, Mohammad, *Islamization of laws in Pakistan* (1989, Sang-e-Meel, Lahore).

Amin, Sayed Hassan, *Middle East systems* (1985, Royston, Glasgow).

Ammah, Rabiatu, *Dhimmis in Islam. A review* (1996, Selly Oak Colleges, Birmingham, CSIS Papers No. 10).

Anderson, J. N. D., Invalid and void marriages in Hanafi law" [1950] Vol. XIII B.S.O.A.S. 357–366.

Anderson, J. N. D., *Islamic law in Africa* (1954a, HMSO, London; Reprint 1970, Frank Cass, London).

Anderson, J. N. D. "The shari'a and civil law" [1954b] 1 No. 1 *The Islamic Quarterly* 29–46.

Anderson, J. N. D., *Islamic law in Africa* (1955a, Frank Cass, London; New impression 1970 and 1978).

Anderson, J. N. D., "The Syrian law of personal status" [1955b] Vol. XVIII B.S.O.A.S. 34–49.

Anderson, J. N. D., "Law as a social force in Islamic culture and history" [1957] Vol. XX B.S.O.A.S. 15–40.

Anderson, J. N. D., "Reforms in family law in Morocco" [1958a] 2 *Journal of African Law* 146–159.

Anderson, J. N. D., "The Tunisian law of personal status" [1958b] 7 [April] I.C.L.Q., 262–279.

Anderson, J. N. D., *Islamic law in the modern world* (1959, Stevens and New York U.P., London and New York).

Anderson, J. N. D., "A law of personal status for Iraq" [1960a] 16 I.C.L.Q., 542–563.

Anderson, J. N. D., "The significance of Islamic law in the world today" [1960b] 9 No. 2 Spring *The American Journal of Comparative Law* 187–198.

Anderson, J. N. D., "Changes in the law of personal status in Iraq" [1963] 12 I.C.L.Q., 1026–1031.

Anderson, J. N. D., "Recent reforms in the Islamic law of inheritance" [1965] 14 I.C.L.Q., 349–365.

Anderson, J. N. D., "Codification in the Muslim world" [1966] 30 *Rabels Zeitschrift* 241–253.

Anderson, J. N. D., "Pakistan: An Islamic state?", in *Law, justice and equity* (1967, Holland, R. H. C. and G. Schwarzenberger (eds), Sir Isaac Pitman & Sons Ltd., London), pp. 127–136.

Anderson, J. N. D. (ed.) *Family law in Asia and Africa* (1968a, George Allen and Unwin, London).

Anderson, J. N. D., "The eclipse of the patriarchal family in contemporary Islamic law", in *Family law in Asia and Africa* (1968b, Anderson, J. N. D. (ed.), George Allen and Unwin, London), pp. 221–234.

Anderson, J. N. D., "Reforms in the law of divorce in the Muslim world" [1970] 31 *Studia Islamica* 41–52.

Anderson, J. N. D., "Modern trends in Islam: Legal reforms and modernisation in the Middle East" [1971] 20 [January] I.C.L.Q., 1–21.

Anderson, J. N. D., "Muslim personal law in India", in *Islamic law in modern India* (1972b, Mahmood, Tahir ed., pp. 34–49.

Anderson, Sir Norman, *Law reform in the Muslim world* (1976, Athlone Press, London).

Anderson, J. N. D. and Noel J. Coulson, "Islamic law in contemporary cultural change" [1967] 18 Nos. 1–2 *Saeculum* 13–92.

Anderson, Michael R., "Islamic law and the colonial encounter in British India", in *Islamic family law* (1990, Mallat, Chibli and Jane Connors eds.), pp. 205–223.

Anjum, Mohini (ed.), *Muslim women in India* (1992, Radiant, New Delhi).

An-Naim, Abdullahi A., "Religious minorities under Islamic law and the limits of cultural relativism" [1987] 9 *Human Rights Quarterly* 1–18.

Ansari, Iqbal A. (ed.), *The Muslim situation in India* (1989, Oriental University Press, London).

Ansay, Tugrul and Don Wallace Jr. (eds), *Introduction to Turkish law* (1996, Kluwer Law Publishers, Dordrecht).

Anwar, Muhammad, *Muslim burials – A policy paper* (1975, Community Relations Council, London).

Anwar, Muhammad, *The myth of return* (1979, Heinemann, London).

Anwar, M., *Young Muslims in Britain: Attitudes, educational needs & policy implications* (1994, The Islamic Foundation, Leicester).

Arora, K. K. , "Polygamy – A negation of Quran", in *Social policy, law and protection of weaker sections of society* (1986, Saraf, D. N. ed.), pp. 368–375.

Australian Law Reform Commission, *Multiculturalism: Family law* (1991, Discussion Paper 46, January 1991, Sydney).

Azami, M. M., *Studies in early Hadith literature with a critical edition of some early texts* (1992, 3rd ed., American Trust Publications, Indianapolis).

Aziz, Ahmad, *Studies in Islamic culture in the Indian environment* (1964, Clarendon Press, Oxford).

Badawi, Zaki, "Muslim justice in a secular state", in *God's law versus state law. The construction of an Islamic identity in Western Europe* (1995, King, Michael ed.), pp. 73–80.

Baillie, Neil B. E., *A digest of Moohummudan law* (1865, Vol. 1, 1st ed., Smith, Elder & Co, London).

Bakar, Khondaker Md. Abu, *A handbook on the Dowry Prohibition Act 1980 and the Cruelty to Women (Deterrent Punishment) Ordinance 1983* (1989, Rangpur: Author.

Balchin, Cassandra (ed.), *A handbook on family law in Pakistan* (1994, 2nd ed., Shirkat Gah, Lahore).

Ballard, Catherine, "Arranged marriages in the British context" [1978] 6 No. 3 [Spring] *New Community* 181–196.

Ballard, Roger (ed.), *Desh pardesh. The South Asian presence in Britain* (1994, Hurst, London).

Ballard, Roger, "Negotiating race and ethnicity: Exploring the implications of the 1991 Census" [1996] 30 No. 3 [July] *Patterns of Prejudice* 3–33.

Ballard, Roger, "The construction of a conceptual vision: 'Ethnic groups' and the 1991 U.K. Census" (Review article) [1997] 20 No. 1 [January] *Ethnic and Racial Studies* 182–194.

Ballard, Roger and Virinder Singh Kalra, *The ethnic dimensions of the 1991 Census. A preliminary report* (1994, Manchester University, Manchester).

Balogun, Ismail A. B., *Islam versus Ahmadiyyah in Nigeria* (1977, Sh. Muhammad Ashraf, Lahore).

Banatwalla, G. M., *Religion and politics in India* (1992, Banatwalla, Bombay).

Banerjee, Anil Chandra, *English law in India* (1984, Abhinav, New Delhi).

Barton, Rachel, *The scarlet thread. An Indian woman speaks* (1987, Virago, London).

Bassam, Tibi, *Islam and the cultural accommodation of social change* (1990, Westview Press, Boulder, Colorado).

Basu, K. K., "Hindu-Muslim marriages" [1948] 2 Nos. 3–4 *The Indian Law Review* 249–257.

Bauböck, Rainer (ed.), *From aliens to citizens. Redefining the status of immigrants in Europe* (1994, Aldershot et al., Avebury).

Beck, L. and N. Keddie (eds.), *Women in the Muslim world* (1978, Harvard University Press, London and Cambridge, Mass.).

Beevi, M. Fathima, "Muslim women. Problems and prospects", in *Muslim women. Problems and prospects* (1993, Siddiqi, Zakia A. and Anwar Jahan Zuberi eds, MD Publications, New Delhi), pp. 7–10.

Bellefonds, Y. Linant de, *Traite de droit musulman compare* (1965–1973, 3 Vols. Mouton, The Hague and Paris).

Berkovits, Bernard, "Transnational divorces: The Fatima decision" [1988] 104 [January] *The Law Quarterly Review* 60–93.

Berkovits, Bernard, "Get and talaq in English law: Reflections on law and policy", in *Islamic family law* (1990, Mallat, Chibli and Jane Connors eds), pp. 119–146.

Bharatiya, V. P., *Syed Khalid Rashid's Muslim law* (1996, 3rd rev. and enl. ed., Eastern Book Company, Lucknow).

Bhattacharjee, A. M., *Muslim law and the constitution* (1985, Eastern Law House, Calcutta).

Bhattacharjee, A. M., *Muslim law and the constitution* (1994, 2nd ed., Eastern Law House, Calcutta and New Delhi).

Bhattacharjee, A. M., *Matrimonial laws and the Constitution* (1996, Eastern Law House, Calcutta and New Delhi).

Bhuiyan, Rabia, "Legal status of women in Bangladesh", in *Situation of women in Bangladesh* (1985, Ahmad, Q. K. et al. eds), pp. 231–250.

Bistolfi, Robert and François Zabbal (eds.), *Islams d'Europe. Integration ou insertion communautaire?* (1995, Éditions de l'Aube, Paris).

Boland, Bernard J., *The struggle of Islam in modern Indonesia* (1982, Martinus Nijhoff, Den Haag).

Boumidienne, Halima, "African Muslim women in France: The emergence of a new identity", in *God's law versus state law. The construction of an Islamic identity in Western Europe* (1995, King, Michael ed.), pp. 49–53.

Bowen, David G. (ed.), *The Satanic Verses: Bradford responds* (1992, Bradford & Ilkley Community College, Ilkley).

Bradford, Keith, "Marriage by proxy" [1975] 4 No. 2 [Summer] *New Community* 254–255.

Bradley, David, "Duress and arranged marriages" [1983] 46 [July] *The Modern Law Review* 499–504.

Bradney, A., *Religions, rights and laws* (1993, Leicester et al., Leicester University Press).

Brah, Avtah, "Women of South Asian origin in Britain: Issues and concerns" [1987] 7 No. 1 [May] *South Asia Research* 39–54.

Brasted, Howard, "The politics of stereotyping. Western images of Islam" [1997] 98 [Jan.–Feb.] *Manushi* 6–16.

Bromley, P. M. and N. V. Lowe, *Family law* (1992, 8th ed., Butterworths, London et al.).

Burton, John, *The sources of Islamic law: Islamic theories of abrogation* (1990, Edinburgh University Press, Edinburgh).

Calder, Norman, *Studies in early Muslim jurisprudence* (1993, Oxford U.P., Oxford)

Canton, E. M. Clare, "Where is the lex loci divortii?" [1976] 25 [Oct.] I.C.L.Q. 909–912.

Canton, E. M. Clare, "Financial relief after talak divorce" [1983] *New Law Journal*, October 21, 1983, pp. 928–930.

Carroll, Lucy, "The Muslim Family Laws Ordinance, 1961: Provisions and procedures – A reference paper for current research" [1979] 13 No. 1 *Contributions to Indian Sociology (NS)* 117–143.

Carroll, Lucy, "Further notes on Pakistani and Indian *talaqs* in English law" [1981a] 23 No. 4 [Oct.–Dec.] J.I.L.I. 588–595.

Carroll, Lucy, "Muslim family law in South Asia: The right to avoid an arranged marriage contracted during minority" [1981b] 23 No. 2 [April–June] J.I.L.I. 149–180.

Carroll, Lucy, "Talaq-i-Tafwid and stipulations in a Muslim marriage contract: Important means of protecting the position of the South Asian Muslim wife" [1982a] 16 No. 2 *Modern Asian Studies* 277–309.

Carroll, Lucy, "Nizam-i-Islam: Process and conflict in Pakistan's programme of islamization, with special reference to the position of women" [1982b] 20 No. 1 *Journal of Commonwealth and Comparative Politics* 57–95.

Carroll, Lucy, "Pakistani talaqs: The requirement of notification" [1983] 99 [Oct.] *The Law Quarterly Review* 515–518.

Carroll, Lucy, "Mahr and Muslim divorcee's right to maintenance" [1985a] 27 No. 3 [July–Sept.] J.I.L.I. 487–495.

Carroll, Lucy, "Muslim women and judicial divorce: An apparently misunderstood aspect of Muslim law" [1985b] 5 Nos. 3–4 *Islamic and Comparative Law Quarterly* 226–245.

Carroll, Lucy, "Wife's right to notification of talaq under Muslim Law Ordinance, 1961" [1985c] P.L.D. 1985, Journal section, 272–276.

Carroll, Lucy, "Divorced Muslim women and maintenance" [1986a] P.L.D. 1986, Journal section, pp. 1–6.

Carroll, Lucy, "A note on the Muslim wife's right to divorce in Pakistan and Bangladesh" [1986b] Vol. XIII No. 1 [Spring/Summer] *New Community* 94–98.

Carroll, Lucy, "Consensual divorces and the Muslim Family Laws Ordinance, 1961" [1987a] P.L.D. 1987 Journal section, pp. 121–127.

Carroll, Lucy, "The Muslim woman's right to divorce" [1987b] 38 *Manushi* 37–38.

Carroll, Lucy, "Muslim women and 'Islamic divorce' in England" [1997a] 17 No. 1 *Journal of Muslim Minority Affairs* 97–115.

Carroll, Lucy, "Section 127(3)(b), Cr.P.C., 1973; The Muslim Women (Protection of Rights on Divorce) Act, 1986; and the Muslim woman's right to mataa" 1997b (1) K.L.T., Journal section, pp. 5–10.

Castles, Stephen, "Democracy and multicultural citizenship. Australian debates and their relevance for Western Europe", in *From aliens to citizens. Redefining the status of immigrants in Europe* (1994, Bauböck, Rainer ed.), pp. 3–27.

Chaudhry, Muhammad Sharif, *Women's rights in Islam* (1991, Muhammad Ashraf, Lahore).

Chaudhury, Rafiqul Huda and Nilufer Raihan Ahmed, *Female status in Bangladesh* (1981, Bangladesh Institute of Development Studies, Dacca).

Chehata, Chafik, *Droit musulman* (1970, Dalloz, Paris).

Chiba, Masaji, *Asian indigenous law in interaction with received law* (1986, Kegan Paul International, London and New York).

Chirane, Abdelhamid, "Conflict and division within Muslim families in France", in *God's law versus state law. The construction of an Islamic identity in Western Europe* (1995, King, Michael ed.), pp. 16–20.

Choudhury, Dilara, *Constitutional development in Bangladesh: Stresses and strains* (1995, UPL, Dhaka).

Choudhury, G. W., *Constitutional development in Pakistan* (1969, 2nd ed., Longman, Lahore).

Chowdhury, A. B. M. Sultanul Alam, "Problems of representation in the Muslim law of inheritance" [1964] 3 *Islamic Studies* 375–391.

Choudry, Salma, "Pakistani women's experience of domestic violence in Great Britain", in *Home Office Research Findings, No. 43* (1996, HMSO, London).

Christie, Clive John, "The rope of god: Muslim minorities in the West and Britain" [1991] 17 No. 3 [April] *New Community* 457–466.

Churches' Committee for Migrants in Europe (CCME), "Islamic law and its significance for the situation of Muslim minorities in Europe", in *Research Papers: Muslims in Europe* (September 1987, No. 35, Selly Oak Colleges, Birmingham).

Commission for Racial Equality, *Law, blasphemy and the multi-faith society. Report of a seminar* (1989, CRE, London).

Conway, Helen, "Divorce and religion" [1995] *New Law Journal*, November 3, 1995, pp. 1618–1619.

Cotterell, Roger, *The politics of jurisprudence* (1992, 2nd ed., Butterworths, London).

Coulson, Noel J., "Reform of family law in Pakistan" [1957] Vol. VII *Studia Islamica* 135–155.

Coulson, Noel J., *A history of Islamic law* (1964, Edinburgh U.P., Edinburgh; Repr. 1978).

Coulson, Noel J., "Islamic law", in *An introduction to legal systems* (1968, Derrett, J. D. M. ed. (1968a)), pp. 54–79.

Coulson, Noel J., *Conflicts and tensions in Islamic jurisprudence* (1969, University of Chicago, Center for Middle Eastern Studies, Chicago).

Coulson, Noel J., *Succession in the Muslim family* (1971, Cambridge U.P., Cambridge).

Coulson, Noel J., *Commercial law in the Gulf States* (1984, Graham & Trotman, London).

Coulson, Noel J. and Doreen Hinchcliffe, "Women and law reform in contemporary Islam", in *Women in the Muslim world* (1978, Beck, L. and N. Keddie eds), pp. 37–51.

Cretney, S. M. and J. M. Masson, *Principles of family law* (1997, 6th ed., Sweet & Maxwell, London).

Dallal, Ahmad, "Yemeni debates on the status of non-Muslims in Islamic law" [1996] 7 No. 2 [June] *Islam and Christian-Muslim Relations* 181–192.

Das, Man Singh (ed.), *The family in the Muslim world* (1991, M. D. Publications, New Delhi).

Datta, Jatindra Mohan, "How far is it lawful to chastise a wife under the Mahomedan law" [1940] A.I.R., Journal section, pp. 25–27.

Daura, Bello, "The limit of polygamy in Islam" [1969] 3 *Journal of Islamic and Comparative Law* 21–26.

Derrett, J. D. M., "Justice, equity and good conscience in India" [1962] 64 Bom.L.R., Journal section, pp. 129–138 and 145–152.

Derrett, J. D. M., "Justice, equity and good conscience", in *Changing law in developing countries* (1963, Anderson, J. N. D. ed., Allen & Unwin, London), pp. 114–153.

Derrett, J. D. M. (ed.), *An introduction to legal systems* (1968a, Sweet & Maxwell, London).

Derrett, J. D. M., *Religion, law and the state in India* (1968b, Faber and Faber, London).

Derrett, J. D. M., "A Hindu judge's animadversions on Muslim polygamy" [1970] 72 Bom.L.R. 61–63.

Derrett, J. D. M., "Some current problems in maintenance" [1977] 79 Bom.L.R., Journal section, pp. 4–5 and 1977 K.L.T., Journal section, pp. 11–12.

Desai, Kumud, *Indian law of marriage and divorce* (1993, 5th ed., N. M. Tripathi, Bombay).

Dhagamwar, Vasudha, *Towards the uniform civil code* (1989, N. M. Tripathi, Bombay).

Dhagamwar, Vasudha, *Law, power and justice. The protection of personal rights in the Indian Penal Code* (1992, 2nd ed., Sage, New Delhi et al.).

Diwan, Paras, *Muslim law in modern India* (1977, Allahabad Law Agency, Allahabad).

Diwan, Paras, "Who is a Muslim" [1978] 4 No. 1 *Indian Socio-Legal Journal* 75–85.

Diwan, Paras and Peeyushi Diwan, *Muslim law in modern India* (1991, 5th ed., Allahabad Law Agency, Allahabad).

Diwan, Paras and Peeyushi Diwan, *Private international law. Indian and English* (1993, 3rd rev. and enl. ed., Deep & Deep, New Delhi).

Diwan, Paras and Peeyushi Diwan, *Children and legal protection* (1994, Deep & Deep, New Delhi).

Doi, Abdur Rahman I., *Introduction to the Qur'an* (1981, Arewa, Sevenoaks.

Doi, Abdur Rahman I., *Shariah: The Islamic law* (1984, Ta Ha Publishers, London).

Douglas, Gillian and L. Seddon (eds.), *Children's rights and traditional values* (1998, Ashgate, Aldershot).

Eberhard, Wolfram, "Modern tendencies in Islam in Pakistan" [1959–1960] 9/10 *Sociologus* 139–152.

Edge, Ian, "A comparative approach to the treatment of non-Muslim minorities in the Middle East, with special reference to Egypt", in *Islamic family law* (1990, Mallat, Chibli and Jane Connors eds), pp. 31–53.

Edge, Ian (ed.), *Coulson's succession in the Muslim family* (1999, forthcoming, 2nd ed., Edinburgh University Press, Edinburgh).

Edwards, Lilian, "The Family Law Act 1986: A lost opportunity?" [1988] *Family Law* 419–426.

Edwards, Susan, "Vindication v. compensation" [1990] 140 *New Law Journal*, May 25, 1990, p. 747.

El Alami, Dawoud S., *The marriage contract in Islamic law in the shari'ah and personal status laws of Egypt and Morocco* (1992, Graham & Trotman, London).

El Alami, Dawoud and Doreen Hinchcliffe, *Islamic marriage and divorce laws of the Arab world* (1996, Kluwer Law, London et al.).

Ellis, Jean, "Local government and community needs: A case study of Muslims in Coventry" [1991] 17 No. 3 [April] *New Community* 359–376.

Endress, Gerhard, *An introduction to Islam* (1988, Edinburgh University Press, Edinburgh).

Engineer, Asghar Ali, *The rights of women in Islam* (1992, Sterling, New Delhi).

Engineer, Asgar Ali, "Muslim family law", in *Women and law. Contemporary problems* (1994, Sarkar, Lotika and B. Sivaramayya eds, Vikas, New Delhi), pp. 50–62.

Esposito, John L., "Muslim family law reform: Towards an Islamic methodology" [1976] 15 No. 1 *Islamic Studies* 19–51.

Esposito, John L., "Muslim family law reform in Pakistan" [1977] 4 Pt 2 [Dec.] *Journal of Malaysian and Comparative Law [Jernal Undang-Undang]* 293–310.

Esposito, John L., "Pakistan: Quest for Islamic identity", in *Islam and development* (1980a, Esposito, John L. ed., Syracuse U.P., Syracuse), pp. 139–162.

Esposito, John L., "Perspectives on Islamic law reform: The case of Pakistan" [1980b] 13 No. 2 *New York University Journal of International Law and Politics* 217–245.

Esposito, John L., "Islamization: Religion and politics in Pakistan" [1982a] 72 [July–Oct.] *The Muslim World* 197–223.

Esposito, John L., *Women in Muslim family law* (1982b, Syracuse University Press, Syracuse).

Esposito, John L. (ed.), *Islam in Asia. Religion, politics, and society* (1987, Oxford U.P., New York et al.)

Esposito, John L., *Islam. The straight path* (1988, Oxford U.P., New York et al.)

Esposito, John L. (ed.), *The Oxford encyclopedia of the modern Islamic world* (1995, 4 Volumes, Oxford U.P. New York et. al.).

Esposito, John L. (ed.), *Voices of resurgent Islam* (1983, Oxford U.P., New York et al.)

Esposito, John L. and John O. Voll, *Islam and democracy* (1996, Oxford U.P., New York et al.).

Evans, Della, *International families and the law* (1988, Jordan & Sons, Bristol).

Fadl, K. A. E., "Islamic law and Muslim minorities: The juristic discourse on Muslim minorities from the 2nd/8th to the 11th/17th centuries" [1994] 1 No. 2 *Islamic Law and Society* 141–187.

Farani, M., *Manual of family laws in Pakistan* (1992, Law Times Publications, Lahore).

Faruki, Kemal, *Islamic jurisprudence* (1962, Pakistan Publishing House, Karachi; Reprint 1975, Karachi).

Faruki, Kemal, "Orphaned grandchildren in Islamic succession law. A comparison of modern Muslim solutions" [1965] 4 No. 3 *Islamic Studies* 253–274.

Faruki, Kemal, "The Islamic resurgence: Prospects and implications", in *Voices of resurgent Islam* (1983, Esposito, John L. ed.), pp. 277–291.

Faruki, Kemal A., "Pakistan: Islamic government and society", in *Islam in Asia. Religion, politics, and society* (1987, Esposito, John L. ed.), pp. 53–78.

Fawcett, Charles, *The first century of British justice in India* (1934, Clarendon, Oxford).

Feldman, Herbert, *Revolution in Pakistan: A study of the martial law administration* (1967, Oxford U.P., London).

Feroze, Muhammad Rashid, "The reform in family laws in the Muslim world" [1962] 1 No. 1 *Islamic Studies* 107–130.

Fisch, Jörg, *Cheap lives and dear limbs* (1983, Franz Steiner Verlag, Wiesbaden).

Foblets, Marie–Claire, "Community justice amongst immigrant family members in France and Belgium", in *Law and anthropology* (1994a, Kuppe, René and Richard Rotz eds, Martinus Nijhoff, Dordrecht), pp. 371–385.

Foblets, Marie–Claire, *Les familles maghrébines et la justice en Belgique. Anthropologie juridique et immigration* (1994b, Éditions Karthala, Paris).

Foblets, Marie–Claire, *Familles – Islam – Europe. Le droit confronte au changement* (1996, Éditions L'Harmattan, Paris).

Forsyth, Christopher F., "Recognition of extra-judicial divorces: The transnational divorce" [1985] 34 [April] I.C.L.Q. 398–402.

Fyzee, Asaf A. A., "The Muslim wife's right of dissolving her marriage" [1936] 38 Bom.L.R. 113–123.

Fyzee, A. A. A., *A modern approach to Islam* (1963, Asia Publishing House, Bombay).

Fyzee, A. A. A., *Cases in the Muhammadan law of India and Pakistan* (1965, Oxford U.P., Oxford; Reprint Oxford 1981).

Fyzee, Asaf A. A., *Outlines of Muhammadan law* (1974, 4th ed., Oxford U.P., Oxford et al.)

Gadre, G. D. , *The role of Islam in South Asia* (1990, Al Fatiha, Pune).

Galanter, Marc, *Law and society in modern India* (1989, Oxford U.P., Delhi et al.)

Ganai, Nisar Ahmad, "Privileged position of dukhtar khana nashin among Muslim female heirs in Kashmir: An empirical study" [1985] 27 No. 3 [July–Sept.] J.I.L.I. 387–422.

Gandhi, B. M. (ed.), *V. D. Kulshreshtha's Landmarks in Indian legal and constitutional history* (1995, 7th ed., Eastern Book Co., Lucknow).

Gani, H. A., *Reform of Muslim personal law. The Shah Bano controversy and the Muslim Women (Protection of Rights on Divorce) Act 1986* (1988, Deep & Deep, New Delhi).

Gardezi, Hassan N., "Resurgence of Islam, Islamic ideology and encounters with imperialism" [1982] 12 No. 4 *Journal of Contemporary Asia* 451–463.

Gardner, Katy and Abdus Shukur, "I'm Bengali, I'm Asian, and I'm living here. The changing identity of British Bengalis", in *Desh pardesh. The South Asian presence in Britain* (1994, Ballard, Roger ed.), pp. 142–164.

Geertz, Clifford, *The religion of Java* (1960, Free Press, Glencoe, Illinois).

Gibb, H. A. R., *Mohammedanism: An historical survey* (1949, Oxford U.P., London; 1969, 2nd ed., Oxford U.P., London).

Goldziher, Ignaz, *Muslim studies* (1910, S. M. Stern, ed.; translated from German by C. R. Barber and S. M. Stern, Allen & Unwin, London).

Goldziher, I., *Muslim studies* (1967–1971, S. M. Stern, ed., translated from German by C. R. Barber and S. M. Stern, 2 Vols, George Allen & Unwin, Albany, NJ and London).

Goldziher, I., *Introduction to Islamic theology and law* (1981, Princeton U.P., Princeton).

Gordon, David, "Extra-judicial divorces revisited – a radical approach" [1986a] 37 No. 2 [Summer] *Northern Ireland Legal Quarterly* 151–169.

Gordon, David, "Ghulam Fatima: Extra-judicial divorces and the House of Lords" [1986b] 16 [July] *Family Law* 169–172.

Gordon, David, *Foreign divorces: English law and practice* (1988, Avebury, Aldershot et al.).

Gravells, Nigel P., "Recognition of extra-judicial divorces: Theoretical problems realised" [1976] 92 [July] *The Law Quarterly Review* 347–353.

Graveson, R. H., *Conflict of laws. Private international law* (1974, 7th ed., Sweet & Maxwell, London).

Griffiths, John, "What is legal pluralism?" [1986] 24 *Journal of Legal Pluralism and Unofficial Law* 1–55.

Haddad, Yvonne and A. T. Lummis, *Islamic values in the United States* (1987, Oxford U.P., New York and Oxford).

Haeri, Shahla, "The institution of mut'a marriage in Iran: A formal and historical perspective", in *Women and revolution in Iran* (1983, Nashat, G. ed., Westview Press, Boulder, Colorado), pp. 231–251.

Haeri, Shahla, "Power of ambiguity: Cultural improvisation on the theme of temporary marriage" [1986] 19 No. 2 *Iranian Studies* 123–154.

Hallaq, Wael B., "Was the gate of ijtihad closed?" [1984] 16 No. 1 [March] *International Journal of Middle East Studies* 3–41.

Hallaq, Wael B., "The development of logical structure in Sunni legal theory" [1987] 64 *Der Islam* 42–67.

Hallaq, Wael B., *A history of Islamic legal theories* (1997, Cambridge University Press, Cambridge).

Halliday, Fred, *Arabs in exile* (1992, I. B. Tauris & Co., London and New York).

Hamilton, Carolyn, *Family, law and religion* (1995, Sweet & Maxwell, London).

Hamilton, Charles, *The Hedaya, or guide: A commentary on the Mussulman laws* (1891, Vol. I–IV, T. Bensley, London).

Haq, M. Fazlul, "Polygamy in Islam: Misrepresented and ill-judged" 1990(2) K.L.T., Journal section, pp. 14–18.

Haq, Muhammad Waqar-ul, *The manual of auqaf laws* (1992, Nadeem Law Book House, Lahore).

Haqq, A., B. Aisha and Ahmad Thomson, *The Islamic will: A practical guide to being prepared for your death and writing your will according to the Shari'a of Islam and English law* (1995, Dar al-Taqwa Ltd, London).

Hasan, Ahmad, *The doctrine of ijm' in Islam. A study of the juridical principle of consensus* (1984, Reprint, Islamic Research Institute, Islamabad).

Hasan, Ayesha, "Islamic family law in the English courts" [1998] February *Family Law* 100–103.

Hastings, Donnan, *Marriage among Muslims: Preference and choice in Northern Pakistan* (1988, Brill, Leiden).

Hayes, Mary and Catherine Williams, *Family law. Principles, policy and practice* (1995, Butterworths, London, Dublin and Edinburgh).

Heer, Nicholas (ed.), *Islamic law and jurisprudence* (1990, University of Washington Press, Seattle and London).

Helie-Lucas, Marie-Aimee, "Strategies of women and women's movements in the Muslim world vis-à-vis fundamentalisms", in *The rights of subordinated peoples* (1994, Mendelsohn, Oliver and Upendra Baxi eds, Oxford U.P., Delhi et al.), pp. 251–275.

Hidayatullah, M. and A. Hidayatullah (ed.), *Mulla's Principles of Mahomedan law* (1990, 19th ed., N. M. Tripathi, Bombay).

Hill, Jonathan, "Recognition of the 'bare' talaq: The last word?" [1985] *Family Law* 290–291.

Hinchcliffe, D., "Divorce in Pakistan: Judicial reform" [1968a] 2 *Journal of Islamic and Comparative Law* 13–25.

Hinchcliffe, D., "The Iranian Family Protection Act" [1968a] 17 [April] I.C.L.Q., 516–521.

Hinchcliffe, Doreen, "Polygamy in traditional and contemporary Islamic law" [1970] 1 No. 3 [November] *Islam and the Modern Age* 13–38.

Hinchcliffe, Doreen, "The widow's dower debt in India" [1973] 4 No. 3 [August] *Islam and the Modern Age* 5–22.

Hodkinson, Keith, "Islamisation of law in Pakistan: Ways, means, and the Constitution" [1981] 40 [April] *Cambridge Law Journal* 248–251.

Hodkinson, Keith, *Muslim family law: A sourcebook* (1984, Croom Helm, London and Canberra).

Hoggett, B., D. Pearl, E. Cooke and P. Bates, *The family, law and society. Cases and materials* (1996, 4th ed., Butterworths, London et al.).

Hooker, M. B., *Legal pluralism* (1975, Clarendon Press, Oxford).

Hoque, Azizul, *The legal system of Bangladesh* (1980, BILIA, Dhaka).

Hossain, Sara, Shahdeen Malik and Bushra Musa (eds), *Public interest litigation in South Asia. Rights in search of remedies* (1997, UPL, Dhaka).

Husain, Sheikh Abrar, *Marriage customs among Muslims in India. A sociological study of Shia marriage customs* (1976, Sterling, New Delhi).

Husain, S. M., "Grandchildren whose father is dead – share in grandfather's estate" [1962] P.L.D. Journal section, pp. 1–8.

Hussain, Freda (ed.), *Muslim women* (1984, Croom Helm, London and Sydney).

Hussain, Faqir, "Public interest litigation in Pakistan" [1993] P.L.D., Journal section, pp. 72–83.

Hussain, Mohd. Ahsanuddin, "Marriage and khula in Islam" [1978] 9 No. 2 *Islam and the Modern Age* 86–88.

Hussain, Syed Jaffer, "Legal modernism in Islam: Polygamy and repudiation" [1965] 7 *Journal of the Indian Law Institute* 384–398.

Hussain, Syed Jaffer, *Marriage breakdown and divorce law reform in contemporary society* (1983, Concept, New Delhi).

Ibrahim, Ahmad, "Provision for divorced women under Islamic law" [1986] P.L.D., Journal section, pp. 234–239.

Ibrahim, Ahmad and Abdullah Abu Bakar, "Recent amendments to the Egyptian family law" [1980] 7 *Journal of Malaysian and Comparative Law [Jernal Undang-Undang]* 65–98.

Iqbal, Afzal, *Islamisation of Pakistan* (1986, Vanguard, Lahore).

Iqbal, Allama Muhammad, *The reconstruction of religious thought in Islam* (1989, 2nd ed., Iqbal Academy Pakistan and Institute of Islamic Culture, Lahore).

Iqbal, Javid, "Crimes against women in Pakistan" [1988] P.L.D., Journal section, pp. 195–203.

Iqbal, Safia, *Women and Islamic law* (1997, Adam, Delhi).

Islamic Shari'a Council, *The Islamic Shari'a Council: An introduction* (1995, ISC, London).

Iyer, V. R. Krishna, *The Muslim Women (Protection of Rights on Divorce) Act, 1986* (1987, Eastern Book Company, Lucknow).

Jacobson, Jessica, "Religion and ethnicity: Dual and alternative sources of identity among young British Pakistanis" [1997] 20 No. 2 [April] *Ethnic and Racial Studies* 238–256.

Jahangir, Asma and Hina Jalani, *The Hudood Ordinances. A divine sanction?* (1990, Rhotas Books, Lahore).

Jain, Kiran B., "Writs against, rulings under and suggested amendments to the Muslim Women (Protection of Rights on Divorce) Act 1986: An overview" [1988] 8 No. 4 *Islamic and Comparative Law Quarterly* 289–313.

Jain, M. P., *Outlines of Indian legal history* (1990, 5th ed., N. M. Tripathi, Bombay).

Jain, S. N. and Usha Loghani, *Child and the law* (1979, N. M. Tripathi for Indian Law Institute, New Delhi, Bombay).

Juynboll, Th. W., *Handbuch des islamischen Gesetzes* (1910, Brill and Harrassowitz, Leiden and Leipzig).

Kabbani, Rana, "Family matters", in *God's law versus state law. The construction of an Islamic identity in Western Europe* (1995, King, Michael ed.), pp. 44–48.

Kamali, M. Hashim, "Divorce and women's rights: Some Muslim interpretations of S. 2: 228" [1984] 74 *The Muslim World* 85–99.

Kamali, M. H., *Principles of Islamic jurisprudence* (1989, Penlanduk, Petaling Jaya; 2nd rev. ed., Islamic Text Society, Cambridge).

Kamali, M. Hashim, *Freedom of expression in Islam* (1997, Rev. ed., Islamic Texts Society, Cambridge).

Kandiyoti, Deniz (ed.), *Women, Islam and the state* (1991, Macmillan, Basingstoke).

Kannan, C. T., *Cultural adaptation of Asian immigrants: First and second generation* (1978, Author, London).

Karsten, I. G. F., "Child marriages" [1969] 32 [March] *The Modern Law Review* 212–217.

Kassen, Yousuf and M. Elshahhat Algindi, "Egyptian family law reform and the improvement of the status of women", in *The International Survey of Family Law* (1996, Martinus Nijhoff, The Hague et.al), pp. 1947–1956.

Katz, J. S. and R. S. Katz, "The new Indonesian marriage law: A mirror of Indonesia's political, cultural and legal systems" [1975] 23 *The American Journal of Comparative Law* 653–681.

Kaushik, Surendra Nath, *Politics of islamization in Pakistan: A study of Zia regime* (1993, South Asian Publishers, New Delhi).

Kelly, J. M., *A short history of Western legal theory* (1992, Clarendon Press, Oxford).

Kelly, Patricia, "Muslim Canadians: Immigration policy and community development in the 1991 census" [1998] 9 No. 1 *Islam and Christian Muslim Relations* 83–102.

Kennedy, Charles H., "Islamisation in Pakistan: Implementation of the Hudood Ordinances" [1988] 28 No. 3 [March] *Asian Survey* 307–316.

Kennedy, Charles H., "Islamization and legal reform in Pakistan 1979–1989" [1990] 63 No. 1 *Pacific Affairs* 62–77.

Kennedy, Charles H., "Islamic legal reform and the status of women in Pakistan" [1991] 2 No. 1 *Journal of Islamic Studies* 45–55.

Kennedy, Charles H., *Islamization of laws and economy. Case studies on Pakistan* (1996, IPS, Islamabad).

Kettani, M. Ali, *Muslim minorities in the world today* (1986, Mansell, London).

Kettani, M. Ali, "Muslims in non-Muslim societies: Challenges and opportunities" [1990] 11 No. 2 [July] *Journal of Muslim Minority Affairs* 226–233.

Khadduri, Majeed, *The Islamic conception of justice* (1984, John Hopkins University Press, Baltimore).

Khadduri, Majid K. and Herbert J. Liebesny (eds), *Law in the Middle East. Vol. 1. Original development of Islamic law* (1955, Middle East Institute, Washington D.C.).

Khambata, K. J., "Dissolution of a Mahomedan marriage at the instance of the wife" [1934] 11 *Bombay Law Journal* 290–291.

Khan, Bodiuzzaman, *Muslim Family Laws Ordinance* (1992, Kazi Anwara Khatoon, Jessore).

Khan, Hamid, *Islamic law of inheritance: A comparative study with emphasis on contemporary problems* (1980, Lahore Law Times Publications, Lahore).

Khan, M. Mustafa Ali, "Islamic polygamy – A blessing in disguise" 1989(1) K.L.T., Journal section, pp. 47–58.

Khan, Mansoor Hassan, "The concept of public interest litigation and its meaning in Pakistan" [1992] P.L.D., Journal section, pp. 84–95.

Khan, Mansoor Hassan, *Public interest litigation: Growth of the concept and its meaning in Pakistan* (1993, Pakistan Law House, Karachi).

Khan, Maulana Wahiduddin, *Woman between Islam and Western society* (1995, Al-Risala, New Delhi).

Khan, Raja Said Akbar, "Polygamy in Islam: A humane institution" [1972] P.L.D., Journal section, pp. 1–16.

Khanam, Firdous, *Attitudes of men and women towards polygyny* (n.y.c. [1960], Author, Lahore).

Khel, Muhammad Nazeer Kaka, "Status of non-Muslim minorities in Pakistan" [1984] 23 No. 1 *Islamic Studies* 45–54.

Khosa, Asif Saeed Khan, "Islamic provisions in the constitution of Pakistan" [1995] P.L.D., Journal section, pp. 17–22.

King, Michael (ed.), *God's law versus state law. The construction of an Islamic identity in Western Europe* (1995, Grey Seal, London).

Knott, Kim and Sajda Khokher, "Religious and ethnic identity among young Muslim women in Bradford" [1993] 19 No. 4 [July] *New Community* 593–610.

Korson, Henry J., "Age and social status at marriage: Karachi, 1961–64" [1965] 5 *The Pakistan Development Review* 586–600.

Korson, J. Henry and Michelle Maskiell, "Islamization and social policy in Pakistan. The constitutional crisis and the status of women" [1985] 25 No. 6 *Asian Survey* 589–612.

Kusum, "Maintenance of a divorced Muslim wife: A critique of the proposed law" [1980] 22 No. 3 [July–Sept.] J.I.L.I. 408–413.

Kusum, *Harassed husbands* (1993, Regency, New Delhi).

Lateef, Shahida, *Muslim women in India. Political and private realities* (1990, Kali for Women/Zed Books, New Delhi).

Latifi, Danial, "Muslim law", in *Annual Survey of Indian Law 1983* (1983, Indian Law Institute, New Delhi), pp. 318–336.

Latifi, Danial, "Muslim law", in *Annual Survey of Indian Law 1985* (1985, Indian Law Institute, New Delhi), pp. 385–404.

Latifi, Danial, "Muslim law", in *Annual Survey of Indian Law 1986* (1986, Indian Law Institute, New Delhi), pp. 615–636.

Latifi, Danial, "Muslim law", in *Annual Survey of Indian Law 1987* (1987, Indian Law Institute, New Delhi), pp. 312–318.

Latifi, Danial, "Muslim law", in *Annual Survey of Indian Law 1990* (1990, Indian Law Institute, New Delhi), pp. 153–162.

Latifi, Danial, "Muslim law", in *Annual Survey of Indian Law 1991* (1991a, Indian Law Institute, New Delhi), pp. 551–556.

Latifi, Danial, "Women, family law and social changes" [1991b] [January] *The Lawyers* 26–29.

Latifi, Danial, "Muslim law", in *Annual Survey of Indian Law 1992* (1992, Indian Law Institute, New Delhi), pp. 177–179.

Latifi, Danial, "Muslim law", in *Annual Survey of Indian Law 1993* (1993, Indian Law Institute, New Delhi), pp. 169–180.

Lau, Martin, "Introduction to the Pakistani legal system, with special reference to the law of contract", in *Yearbook of Islamic and Middle Eastern Law* (1995a, Vol 1. Kluwer Law International, The Hague), pp. 3–28.

Lau, Martin, "Pakistan – Zaheer-ud-din v. The State", in *Yearbook of Islamic and Middle Eastern Law* (1995b, Vol. 1, Kluwer Law International, London et al.), pp. 565–573.

Lau, Martin, "Islam and judicial activism: Public interest litigation and environmental protection in the Islamic Republic of Pakistan", in *Human rights approaches to environmental protection* (1996, Boyle, Alan E. and Michael R. Anderson eds, Clarendon Press, Oxford), pp. 285–302.

Lau, Martin, "Pakistan — Abdul Waheed v. Alma Jehargit (the Saima Waheed case)" [1997] 3 *Yearbook of Islamic and Middle Eastern Law* 518–531.

Layish, Aharon, "Qadis and Shari'a in Israel" [1971] 7 *Asian and African Studies* 237–272.

Layish, Aharon, "Ulama and politics in Saudi Arabia", in *Islam and politics in the modern Middle East* (1984, Heper, Metin and Raphael Israeli eds, Croom Helm, London), pp. 29–63.

Lester, Anthony and Geoffrey Bindman, *Race and law* (1972, Penguin Books Ltd, Harmondsworth).

Levy, R., *The social structure of Islam* (1957, Cambridge University Press, Cambridge).

Lewis, B., *The Arabs in history* (1950, Hutchinson, London; 1993, new ed., Oxford U.P., Oxford).

Lewis, Bernard, *The Jews of Islam* (1984, Routledge & Kegan Paul, London).

Lewis, Bernard, "Legal and historical reflections on the position of Muslim populations under non-Muslim rule" [1992] 13 No. 1 [January] *Journal of Muslim Minority Affairs* 1–16.

Lewis, Bernard, "Legal and historical reflections on the position of Muslim populations under non-Muslim rule", in *Muslims in Europe* (1994, Lewis, Bernard and D. Schnapper eds), pp. 1–18.

Lewis, Bernard and Dominique Schnapper (eds), *Muslims in Europe* (1994, Pinter, London and New York).

Libson, Gideon, "On the development of custom as a source of law in Islamic law" [1997] 4 No. 2 *Islamic Law and Society* 131–155.

Liebesny, Herbert J., "Religious law and westernisation in the Moslem Near East" [1953] 2 *The American Journal of Comparative Law* 492–504.

Liebesny, Herbert J., *The law of the Near and Middle East: Readings, cases & materials* (1975, State University of New York Press, Albany, New York).

Liebesny, Herbert J., "English common law and Islamic law and Islamic law in the Middle East and South Asia: Religious influences and secularization" [1985/86] 34 *Cleveland State Law Review* 19–33.

Liebesny, Herbert J., "Stability and change in Islamic law" [1967] 21 No. 1 *The Middle East Journal* 16–34.

Lohlker, Rudiger, *Schari'a und Moderne. Diskussionen über Schwangerschaftsabbruch, Versicherung und Zinsen* (1996, DMG and Franz Steiner, Stuttgart).

Lutz, Helma, "Cultural/ethnic identity in the safety net of cultural hegemony" [1990] 1 No. 2 *The European Journal of Intercultural Studies* 5–13.

Mahieddin, M. N., "Marriage: Its formation and effects in Algerian substantive law", in *The International Survey of Family Law* (1994, Martinus Nijhoff, The Hague, et. al), pp. 1–28.

Mahmood, Ch. M., *The Manual of family laws* (1991, Pakistan Law Times Publications, Lahore).

Mahmood, Shaukat, *Principles and digest of Muslim law* (1967, Legal Research Centre, Lahore; 4th ed., 1993, Nadeem Shaukat Mahmood).

Mahmood, S. and S. Nadeem Shaukat, *Constitution of the Islamic Republic of Pakistan, 1973* (1992, Legal Research Centre, Lahore).

Mahmood, Tahir, "Custom as a source of law in Islam" [1965] 7 J.I.L.I. 102–106.

Mahmood, Tahir, *Family law reform in the Muslim world* (1972a, N.M. Tripathi and Indian Law Institute, New Delhi and Bombay).

Mahmood, Tahir (ed.), *Islamic law in modern India* (1972b, N. M. Tripathi, Bombay).

Mahmood, Tahir, *An Indian civil code and Islamic law* (1976, N. M. Tripathi, Bombay).

Mahmood, Tahir, *Muslim personal law. Role of the state in the subcontinent* (1977, Vikas, New Delhi et al.).

Mahmood, Tahir, "Family law and succession" in *Annual Survey of Indian Law 1980* (1980, Vol. XVI, Indian Law Institute, New Delhi), pp. 70–80.

Mahmood, Tahir, *The Muslim law of India* (1982a, 2nd ed., Allahabad Law Book Co., Allahabad).

Mahmood, Tahir, "The Somali experiment with family law reform" [1982b] 2 *Islamic and Comparative Law Quarterly* 251–266.

Mahmood, Tahir, *Personal laws in crisis* (1986, Metropolitan, New Delhi).

Mahmood, Tahir, "Law in the Qur'an – A draft code" [1987] 7 No. 1 *Islamic and Comparative Law Quarterly* 1–32.

Mahmood, Tahir, "Muslim law", in *Annual Survey of Indian Law 1989* (1989, Indian Law Institute, New Delhi), pp. 227–239.

Mahmood, Tahir, "Islamic family law. Latest developments in India", in *Islamic family law* (1990, Mallat and Connors eds), pp. 295–320.

Mahmood, Tahir, *Uniform Civil Code. Fictions and facts* (1995, India and Islam Research Council, New Delhi).

Mahmudunnasir, S., "Polygamy in Islam" [1968] P.L.D., Journal section, pp. 60–66.

Maidment, Susan, "The legal effect of religious divorces" [1974] 37 [November] *The Modern Law Review* 611–626.

Makdisi, G., *The rise of colleges: Institutions of learning in Islam and the West* (1981, Edinburgh University Press, Edinburgh).

Makdisi, John, "Legal logic and equity in Islamic law" [1985] 33 *The American Journal of Comparative Law* 63–92.

Malik, A. R., "Problems of women and young people", in *Pakistanis in Europe* (1982, New Century Publishers, London), pp. 79–81.

Malik, Shahdeen, "Saga of divorced women: Once again Shah Bano. Maintenance, and the scope for marriage contracts" [1990] 42 D.L.R., Journal section, pp. 34–40.

Malik, Shahdeen, *The transformation of colonial perceptions into legal norms: Legislating for crime and punishment in Bengal, 1790s to 1820s* (1994, S.O.A.S., London). [Unpublished PhD thesis].

Malik, Vijay, *Muslim law of marriage, divorce and maintenance* (1988, 2nd ed., Eastern Book Company, Lucknow).

Mallat, Chibli, *Islam and public law* (1993a, Graham & Trotham, London).

Mallat, Chibli , *The renewal of Islamic law* (1993b, Cambridge U.P., Cambridge).

Mallat, Chibli and Jane Connors (eds), *Islamic family law* (1990, Graham & Trotman, London).

Mandelbaum, David Goodman, *Women's seclusion and men's honour: Sex roles in North India, Bangladesh and Pakistan* (1998, University of Arizona Press, Tucson).

Mannan, M. A., *D. F. Mulla's Principles of Mahomedan law* (1990, Pakistan ed., P.L.D. Publishers, Lahore).

Marlow, Louise, *Hierarchy and egalitarianism in Islamic thought* (1997, Cambridge U.P., Cambridge)

Matin, Abdul, *The children's law of Bangladesh* (1993a, Rose, Dhaka).

Matin, Abdul, *The women's law* (1993b, Rose, Dhaka).

Maududi, Abu'l A'la, "Islamic and Western laws on divorce – A comparative historical perspective" [1981] 1 *Islamic and Comparative Law Quarterly* 17–23.

Mayer, A., "Libyan legislation in defense of Arabo-Islamic sexual mores" [1980] 28 *The American Journal of Comparative Law* 287–313.

Mayer, Ann Elizabeth, "Islamic law", in *Islam – the religious and political life of a world community* (1984, Marjorie Kelly ed., Praeger, New York), pp. 226–242.

Mayer, Ann Elizabeth, "The Shari'ah: A methodology or a body of substantive rules?", in *Islamic law and jurisprudence* (1990, Nicholas Heer ed.), pp. 177–198.

Mayer, Ann Elizabeth, *Islam and human rights: Traditions and politics* (1991, Westview Press, Boulder, Colorado and San Francisco).

Mayer, Ann Elizabeth, "Universal versus Islamic human rights: A clash of cultures or a clash with a construct?" [1994] 15 *Michigan Journal of International Law* 307–404.

Mazari, Shireen, " 'Islamisation' and the status of women in Pakistan: A note" [1983] 3 No. 1 Spring *South Asia Bulletin* (University of California) 79–82.

McClean, J. David, *Morris: The conflict of laws* (1993, 4th ed., Sweet & Maxwell, London).

Mehdi, Rubya, "The offence of rape in the Islamic law of Pakistan" [1990] 18 *International Journal of the Sociology of Law* 19–29.

Mehdi, Rubya, *The islamization of the law in Pakistan* (1994, Curzon Press, Richmond).

Menski, Werner F., "Legal pluralism in the Hindu marriage", in *Hinduism in Great Britain* (1987, Burghart, Richard ed., Tavistock, London), pp. 180–200.

Menski, Werner F., "English family law and ethnic laws in Britain" 1988a (1) K.L.T., Journal section, pp. 56–66.

Menski, Werner F., "Uniformity of laws in India and England" [1988b] Vol. VII No. 11 July *Journal of Law and Society* (Peshawar) 11–26.

Menski, Werner F., "Comparative legal training in action: A reluctant defence of polygamy" 1990a (1) K.L.T., Journal section, pp. 50–69.

Menski, Werner F., "The reform of Islamic family law and a uniform civil code for India", in *Islamic family law* (1990b, Mallat, Chibli and Jane Connors eds), pp. 253–293.

Menski, Werner F., "Uniform civil code in India: A false model for development?" 1990c (2) K.L.T., Journal section, pp. 3–10.

Menski, Werner F., "Crocodile tears and Muslim polygamy in India" 1991(2) K.L.T., Journal section, pp. 20–24.

Menski, Werner F., "Asians in Britain and the question of adaptation to a new legal order: Asian laws in Britain?", in *Ethnicity, identity, migration: The South Asian context* (1993a, Israel, Milton and Narendra Wagle eds, University of Toronto, Toronto), pp. 238–268.

Menski, Werner F., "Much water has flowed down the Ganges: Muslim polygamy, the Special Marriage Act and judicial collusion" 1993b (2) K.L.T., Journal section, pp. 19–22.

Menski, Werner F., "Maintenance for divorced Muslim wives" 1994(1) K.L.T., Journal section, pp. 45–52.

Menski, Werner F., "Introduction: The democratisation of justice in India", in *Law of consumer protection in India. Justice within reach* (1996, Singh, Gurjeet, Deep & Deep, New Delhi), pp. xxv–liv.

Menski, Werner, "South Asian Muslim law today: An overview" [1997] 9 No. 1 July *Sharqiyyat* 16–36.

Menski, Werner F. and Tahmina Rahman, "Hindus and the law in Bangladesh" [1988] 8 No. 2 [Nov.] *South Asia Research* 111–131.

Mernissi, Fatima, *Women and Islam. An historical and theological enquiry* (1993, Indian reprint, Kali for Women, New Delhi).

Meron, Ya'akov, *L'obligation alimentaire entre épaux* (1971, CNRS, Paris).

Meron, Ya'akov, "L'accommodation de la repudiation musulmane" [1995] 4 *Revue Internationale de Droit Comparé* 921–939.

Miftahi, Mufti Zafeeruddin, *Modesty and chastity in Islam* (1993, Qazi, New Delhi).

Miller, Roland E., *Mappila Muslims of Kerala. A study in Islamic trends* (1992, Reprint of 1976 ed., Orient Longman, Madras).

Mir-Hosseini, Ziba, *Marriage on trial. A study of Islamic family law: Iran and Morocco compared* (1993, Tauris, London).

Mirza, Kauser, *The silent cry. Second generation Bradford Muslim women speak* (1989, No. 43, Muslims in Europe; C.S.I.C., Birmingham)

Modood, Tariq, *Not easy being British. Colour, culture and citizenship* (1992, Runnymede Trust and Trentham Books, Stoke-on-Trent).

Modood, Tariq, "Muslim views on religious identity and racial equality" [1993] 19 No. 3 [April] *New Community* 513–519.

Mohammadi, A., "The custom and its significance in Islamic law" [1977] 8 No. 2 [May] *Islam and the Modern Age* 32–38.

Mole, Nuala, *Immigration: Family entry and settlement* (1987, Jordan & Sons, Bristol).

Momen, Md. Abdul, *The Muslim Family Laws Ordinance 1961 (with commentaries)* (1993, New Didar Publishing House, Dhaka).

Monsoor, Taslima, *From patriarchy to gender equity: Family law and its impact on women in Bangladesh* (1994, S.O.A.S., London; Unpublished PhD thesis).

Monsoor, Taslima, *From patriarchy to gender equity: Family law and its impact on women in Bangladesh* (1998, UPL, Dhaka).

Moore, Kathleen M., *Al-Mughtaribūn. American law and the transformation of Muslim life in the United States* (1995, State University of New York Press, Albany).

Moors, Annelies, *Women and property in Islam. Palestinian experiences 1920–1990* (1996, Cambridge University Press, Cambridge).

Mortimore, Claudia, *Immigration and adoption* (1994, Trentham Books, Stoke-on-Trent), pp. 48–51.

Muhith, A. M. A., *Bangladesh: Emergence of a nation* (1992, U.P.L., Dhaka).

Mujeeb, M., *The Indian Muslims* (1st ed. 1967, George Allen and Unwin, London; 1985, Reprint Munshiram Manoharlal, New Delhi).

Mumtaz, Khawar and Farida Shaheed, *Women of Pakistan. Two steps forward, one step back?* (1987, Zed Books, London and New Jersey).

Mundy, Marsha, "The family, inheritance, and Islam: A re-examination of the sociology of fara'id law", in *Islamic law: Social and historical contexts* (1988, Al-Azmeh, Aziz ed., Routledge, London and New York), pp. 1–123.

Naseem, Farogh, *The Shah Bano case x-rayed* (1988, Karachi Legal Research Centre, Karachi).

Nasir, Jamal J., *The Islamic law of personal status* (1990a, 2nd ed., Graham & Trotman, London).

Nasir, Jamal, *The status of women under Islamic law and under modern Islamic legislation* (1990b, Graham & Trotman, London).

Nasr, Seyyed Vali Reza, *Mawdudi and the making of Islamic revivalism* (1996, Oxford U.P., New York et al.).

Newberg, Paula, *Judging the state: Courts and constitutional politics in Pakistan* (1995, Cambridge University Press, Cambridge).

Nielsen, Jørgen S. (ed.), *Islam in English law and administration. A symposium* (1981, Selly Oak Colleges, Birmingham). [4 Muslims in Europe, No. 9].

Nielsen, Jørgen S., "Family law and multi-cultural Britain" [1985] 14 [Nov.] *Newsletter of the Centre for the Study of Islam and Christian-Muslim Relations* (Selly Oak Colleges, Birmingham), pp. 15–18.

Nielsen Jørgen S., "Islamic communities in Britain", in *Religion, state, and society in modern Britain* (1989, Badham, Paul ed., Edwin Mellen Press, Lewiston et al.), pp. 225–241.

Nielsen, Jørgen S., "A Muslim agenda for Britain: Some reflections" [1991a] 17 No. 3 [April] *New Community* 467–475.

Nielsen Jørgen S., "Muslim organizations in Europe: Integration or isolation?", in *The integration of Islam and Hinduism in Western Europe* (1991b, Shadid, W. A. and P. S. van Koningsveld eds, Kok Pharos, Kampen), pp. 43–59.

Nielsen, Jørgen S., "Islam and Islamic law in the United Kingdom" [1992a] 10 *Recht Van de Islam* 92–99.

Nielsen, Jørgen S., *Islam, Muslims and British local and central government* (1992b, CSIC-MR, Birmingham; C.S.I.C. Papers No. 6).

Nielsen, Jørgen S., *Muslims in Western Europe* (1992c, Edinburgh University Press, Edinburgh).

Nielsen, Jørgen S., *Emerging claims of Muslim populations in matters of family law in Europe* (1993a, CSIC-MR, Birmingham; C.S.I.C. Paper No. 10, Nov. 1993).

Nielsen, Jørgen S., "State, religion and laicite: The Western European experience", in *Muslims and Christians in Europe: Breaking new ground* (1993b, Speelman, Gé et al. eds, Kok Pharos, Kampen), pp. 90–99.

Nielsen, Jørgen S., *Muslims in Western Europe* (1995a, 2nd ed., Edinburgh University Press, Edinburgh).

Nielsen, Jørgen S., "*Shari'ah*, change and plural societies", in *Religion, law and society: A Christian-Muslim discussion* (1995b, Mitri, Tarek ed., WCC and Kok Pharos, Geneva and Kampen), pp. 27–32.

Nielsen, Jørgen S., "State, religion and laicite: The Western European experience", in *Religion, law and society: A Christian-Muslim discussion* (1995c, Mitri, Tarek ed., WCC and Kok Pharos, Geneva and Kampen), pp. 100–110.

Nielsen, Jørgen S., "Muslim in Europe: History revisited or a way forward?" [1997] 8 No. 2 [July] *Islam and Christian-Muslim Relations* 135–143.

Nonneman, Gerd et al. (eds) *Muslim communities in Europe* (1996, Ithaca Press, Reading).

North, P. M., "Recognition of extra-judicial divorces" [1975] 91 [January] *The Law Quarterly Review* 36–67.

North, P. M. and J. J. Fawcett, *Cheshire and North's Private international law* (1992, 12th ed., Butterworths, London, Dublin, Edinburgh).

Ostrorog, L., *The Angora reform* (1927, London University Press, London).

Pakistanis in Europe (1982, London Centre for Pakistan Studies, London).

Parashar, Archana, *Women and family law reform in India* (1992, Sage, New Delhi et al.).

Parihar, Lalita, "Right to maintenance of Muslim divorcees", in *Women and law. Contemporary problems* (1994, Sarkar, Lotika and B. Sivaramayya eds), pp. 219–236.

Patel, Rashida, *Women and law in Pakistan* (1979, Faiza Publishers, Karachi).

Patel, Rashida, *Islamization of laws in Pakistan* (1986, Faiza Publishers, Karachi).

Patel, Rashida, *Socio-economic political status and women and law in Pakistan* (1991, Faiza Publishers, Karachi).

Patwari, A. B. M. Mafizul Islam, *Legal system of Bangladesh* (1991, Humanist and Ethical Association of Bangladesh, Dhaka).

Peach, Ceri, *Ethnicity in the 1991 Census. Vol. 2: The ethnic minority populations of Great Britain* (1996, HMSO, London).

Peach, Ceri and Günther Glebe, "Muslim minorities in western Europe" [1995] 18 No. 1 *Ethnic and Racial Studies* 26–45.

Pearl, David, "Family law in Pakistan" [1969a] 9 *Journal of Family Law* 165–189.

Pearl, David, "Internal conflict of laws in Pakistan (A comment on *Marina Jatoi v. Nuruddin Jatoi*)" [1969b] 11 No 3 [July–September] *Journal of the Indian Law Institute* 362–370.

Pearl, David, "Arranged marriages" [1971a] *Cambridge Law Journal* 206–207.

Pearl, David, "The impact of the Muslim Family Laws Ordinance (1961) in Quetta (Baluchistan) Pakistan" [1971b] 13 J.I.L.I. 561–569.

Pearl, David, "Modernising the personal laws in India" [1972a] 5 No. 2 [January] *South Asian Review* 147–153.

Pearl, David, "Muslim marriages in English law" [1972b] 30 Part 1 [April] *Cambridge Law Journal* 120–143.

Pearl, David, "Immigrant marriages: Some legal problems" [1972–1973] 2 No. 1 [Winter] *New Community* 67–73.

Pearl, David, "Bangladesh: Islamic laws in a secular state" [1974] 8 No. 1 [October] *South Asian Review* 33–41.

Pearl, David, "Foreign marriages and divorces: Recent English legislation" [1974–1975] 4 No. 1 [Winter/Spring] *New Community* 119–121.

Pearl, David, "The legal rights of Muslim women in India, Pakistan and Bangladesh" [1976] 5 Nos. 1–2 [Summer] *New Community* 68–74.

Pearl, David, "Interpersonal conflict of laws between two classes" [1978a] 4 No. 1 *Indian Socio-Legal Journal* 52–74.

Pearl, David, "Social security and the ethnic minorities" [1978b] *Journal of Social Welfare Law* 24–35.

Pearl, David, "Codification in Islamic law" [1979a] 2 *The Jewish Law Annual* 162–167.

Pearl, David, "Legal decisions affecting ethnic minorities and discrimination – No. 11" [1979b] 7 No. 3 [Winter] *New Community* 463–468.

Pearl, David, *A textbook on Muslim law* (1979c, Croom Helm, London).

Pearl, David, "Legal problems of immigrants: A case study in Peterborough (U.K.)" [1980] 22 No.1 *Journal of the Indian Law Institute* 81–107.

Pearl, David, "Legal decisions affecting ethnic minorities and discrimination – No. 12" [1980] 8 Nos. 1&2 [Spring/Summer] *New Community* 146–153.

Pearl, David, *Interpersonal conflict of laws in India, Pakistan and Bangladesh* (1981a, Stevens & Sons and N. M. Tripathi, London and Bombay).

Pearl, David, "Islam in English family law", in *Islam in English law and administration. A symposium* (1981b, Nielsen, Jørgen S. ed.), pp. 6–10.

Pearl, David, "The wife's right to divorce in Muslim law" [1981c] 4 *The Jewish Law Annual* 226–231.

Pearl, David, "Islamic family law and Anglo-American public policy" [1985/1986] 34 *Cleveland State Law Review* 113–127.

Pearl, David, *Family law and the immigrant communities* (1986a, Jordan & Sons, Bristol).

Pearl, David, "Immigration and unilateral divorces" [1986b] 1 No. 3 [October] *Immigration and Nationality Law and Practice* 81–84.

Pearl, David, *A textbook on Muslim personal law* (1987a, 2nd ed., Croom Helm, London et al.).

Pearl, David, "South Asian immigrant communities and English family law: 1971–1987" [1987b] 14, Nos. 1/2 [Autumn] *New Community* 161–169.

Pearl, David, "Family Law Act 1986, Part II" [1987c] *Cambridge Law Journal* 35–38.

Pearl, David, "Executive and legislative amendments to Islamic family law in India and Pakistan", in *Islamic law and jurisprudence* (1990a, Heer, Nicholas ed.), pp. 199–220.

Pearl, David, "Three decades of executive, legislative and judicial amendments to Islamic family law in Pakistan", in *Islamic family law* (1990b, Mallat, Chibli and Jane Connors eds), pp. 321–337.

Pearl, David, "The application of Islamic law in the English courts" [1995] II *Yearbook of Islamic and Middle Eastern law* (1996, Kluwer International, London et al.), pp. 3–11.

Pearl, David, "A note on Islamic law and the child", in *Children's rights and traditional values* (1998, Douglas, Gillian and L. Seddon eds, Ashgate, Aldershot), pp. 86–92.

Perry, Thomas Erskine, *Cases illustrative of Oriental life and the application of English law to India* (1853, S. Sweet, London).

Pilkington, M. P., "Transnational divorces under the Family Law Act 1986" [1988] 37 [January] I.C.L.Q. 131–143.

Pirzada, Shams, *Triple talaq in the light of Quran and Sunnah* (1996, Idara Dawat Ul Quran, Mumbai).

Piscatori, J., *Islam in a world of nation-states* (1986, Cambridge U.P., Cambridge)

Poulter, Sebastian, "Talaq divorces" [1977] *New Law Journal*, January 6, 1977, pp. 7–10.

Poulter, Sebastian M., "The definition of marriage in English law" [1979] 42 *Modern Law Review* 409–429.

Poulter, Sebastian M., *English law and ethnic minority customs* (1986, Butterworths, London).

Poulter, Sebastian M., "Ethnic minority customs, English law and human rights" [1987] 36 I.C.L.Q. 589–615.

Poulter, Sebastian M., "The significance of ethnic minority customs and traditions in English criminal law" [1989] 16 No. 1 [October] *New Community* 121–128.

Poulter, Sebastian M., *Asian traditions and English law* (1990a, Runnymede Trust and Trentham Books, Stoke-on-Trent).

Poulter, Sebastian M., "The claim to a separate Islamic system of personal law for British Muslims", in *Islamic family law* (1990b, Mallat, C. and Jane Connors eds), pp. 147–166.

Poulter, Sebastian M., "The limits of legal, cultural and religious pluralism", in *Discrimination: The limits of law* (1992a, Hepple, Bob and Erika M. Szyszczak eds, Mansell, London), pp. 172–192.

Poulter, Sebastian M., "The Muslim community and English law" [1992b] 3 No. 2 [December] *Islam and Christian-Muslim Relations* 259–273.

Poulter, Sebastian M., "Minority rights", in *Individual rights and the law in Britain* (1994, McCrudden, Christopher and Gerald Chambers eds, Oxford U.P., Oxford et. al.), pp. 457–489.

Poulter, Sebastian M., "Multiculturalism and human rights for Muslim families in English law", in *God's law versus state law. The construction of an Islamic identity in Western Europe* (1995, King, Michael ed.), pp. 81–87.

Poulter, Sebastian, "Muslim headscarves in school: Contrasting legal approaches in England and France" [1997] 17 [Spring] *Oxford Journal of Legal Studies* 43–74.

Poulter, Sebastian M., *Ethnicity, law and human rights* (1998, Clarendon Press, Oxford).

Powers, David S., *Studies in Qur'an and hadith. The formation of the Islamic law of inheritance* (1986, University of California Press, Berkeley et al.).

Powers, David, "The Islamic inheritance system: A socio-historical approach", in *Islamic family law* (1990, Mallat, Chibli and Jane Connors eds), pp. 11–29.

Prince of Wales, H. R. H., "Islam and the West" [1994] 9 *Arab Law Quarterly* 135–143.

Quadianis are not Muslims (1987, Darul Ilm, Islamabad).

Qureshi, M. A., *Waqfs in India. A study of administrative and legislative control* (1990, Gian Publishing House, New Delhi).

Rahim, Abdur, *Principles of Muhammadan jurisprudence* (1984, reprint Mansoor, Lahore; 1st ed. Madras 1911).

Rahim, Abdur, *Principles of Muhammadan jurisprudence* (1994, reprint Kitab Bhavan, New Delhi).

Rahman, A. F. M. A., *Bangladesh laws on Muslim marriage and divorce* (1989, Legal Aid Forum, Dhaka).

Rahman, Fazlur, "The controversy over the Muslim family laws", in *South Asian politics and religion* (1966, Smith, Donald Eugene ed., Princeton U.P., Princeton), pp. 414–427.

Rahman, S. A., *Punishment of apostacy in Islam* (1996, Kitab Bhavan, New Delhi).

Rahman, Sheikh Shamsur, "Family Court and Muslim Family Law Ordinance" [1988] 40 D.L.R., Journal section, pp. 24–26.

Rahman, Tanzilur, "Polygamy in Pakistan and other Muslim countries" [1967] P.L.D., Journal section, pp. 38–40.

Rahman, Tanzil-ur, *Islamization of Pakistan law* (1978, Hamdard Academy, Karachi).

Rahman, Tanzil-ur, *A code of Muslim personal law* (1978–1980, Vols I and II. Hamdard Academy and Islamic Publishers, Karachi).

Rahman, Tanzil-ur, "Succession under Muslim Family Laws Ordinance, 1961" [1982] P.L.D., Journal section, pp. 99–113.

Rankin, C., "Custom and the Muslim personal law in British India" [1939] 25 *Transactions of the Grotius Society* 89–118.

Rao, P. Koteswar, "Shah Bano's case and uniform civil code – A survey of public opinion among Muslim community at Tirupati" [1985] 27 No. 4 [Oct.–Dec.] J.I.L.I. 572–577.

Rehman, Tanzil-ur, "Constitution and the freedom of religion" [1989a] P.L.D., Journal section, pp. 17–20.

Rehman, Tanzil-ur, "Family Laws Ordinance and the Constitution" [1989b] P.L.D., Journal section, pp. 20–28.

Renteln, Alison Dundes, *International human rights. Universalism versus relativism* (1990, Sage, Newbury Park, London and New Delhi).

Rosen, Lawrence, "I divorce thee" [1970] 7 No. 8 *Transaction* 34–37.

Rosen, Lawrence, *The anthropology of justice. Law as culture in Islamic society* (1989, Cambridge University Press, Cambridge et al.).

Rutten, Susan, *Moslims in de Nederlandse rechtspraak* (1988, Uitgeversmaatschappij J. H. Kok, Kampen).

Sagade, Jaya, "Law and social reforms in rural India with special reference to child marriages" [1981] 1 S.C.J., Journal section, pp. 27–35.

Sahgal, G. and Nira Yuval-Davis, *Refusing holy orders. Women and fundamentalism in Britain* (1992, Virago, London).

Saleh, Nabil A., *Unlawful gain and legitimate profit in Islamic law* (1986, Cambridge U.P., Cambridge)

Saleh, Nabil A., *Unlawful gain and legitimate profit in Islamic law* (1992, 2nd ed., Graham & Trotman, London).

Saraf, D. N. (ed.), *Social policy, law and protection of weaker sections of society* (1986, Eastern Book Company, Lucknow).

Sarkar, Lotika and B. Sivaramayya (eds), *Women and law. Contemporary problems* (1994, Vikas, New Delhi).

Schacht, Joseph, *The origins of Muhammadan jurisprudence* (1950, Clarendon Press, Oxford; reprint 1979).

Schacht, J., "Islamic law in contemporary states" [1959] 8 *The American Journal of Comparative Law* 133–147.

Schacht, Joseph, *An introduction to Islamic law* (1964, Clarendon Press, Oxford; reprint 1984).

Schacht, Joseph, "Modernism and traditionalism in a history of Islamic law" [1965] 1 No. 4 [July] *Middle Eastern Studies* 388–400.

Schleifer, Aliah, *Motherhood in Islam* (1986, The Islamic Academy, Cambridge).

Schnapper, Dominique, "Muslim communities, ethnic minorities and citizens", in *Muslims in Europe* (1994, Lewis, Bernard and Dominique Schnapper eds), pp. 148–160.

Schuz, Rhona, "Divorce and ethnic minorities", in *Divorce: Where next?* (1996, Freeman, Michael ed., Dartmouth, Aldershot et al.), pp. 131–157.

Sehgal, Neeru, "Civil vs. religious marriages: Reflections on a recent Bombay ruling" [1982] 2 No. 4, *Islamic and Comparative Law Quarterly* 306–309.

Setalvad, M. C., *The common law in India* (1960, Stevens, London; Hamlyn Lectures No. 12).

Setalvad, M. C., *The role of English law in India* (1966, Magnes Press, Jerusalem).

Shabbir, Mohammad, *Muslim personal law and judiciary* (1988, Law Book Company, Allahabad).

Shadid, W. A. R. and P. S. van Koningsveld (eds), *The integration of Islam and Hinduism in Western Europe* (1991, Kok Pharos, Kampen).

Shadid, W. A. R. and P. S. van Koningsveld (eds), *Religious freedom and the position of Islam in Western Europe* (1995, Kok Pharos, Kampen).

Shah, Nasim Hasan, *Constitution, law and Pakistan affairs* (1986, Wajidalis, Lahore).

Shah, Nasim Hasan, *Law justice & Islam* (1989, Wajidalis, Lahore).

Shah, Nasim Hasan, "Islamisation of law in Pakistan" [1995] P.L.D., Journal section, pp. 37–53.

Shah, Prakash, "Legal pluralism – British law and possibilities with Muslim ethnic minorities" [1994] Nos. 66/67 *Retfaerd* 18–33.

Shaham, Ron, "Judicial divorce at the wife's initiative: The Shari'a Courts of Egypt, 1920–1955" [1994] 1 No. 2 [August] *Islamic Law and Society* 217–257.

Shaham, Ron, "Custom, Islamic law and statutory legislation: Marriage registration and minimum age at marriage in the Egyptian Shari'a Courts" [1995] 2 No. 3 [Oct.] *Islamic Law and Society* 258–281.

Shaikh, Sitara and Alison Kelly, "To mix or not to mix: Pakistani girls in British schools" [1989] 31 No. 1 [February] *Educational Research* 10–19.

Shams, Shamsuddin (ed.), *Women, law and social change* (1991, Ashish, New Delhi).

Shaw, Alison, "The Pakistani community in Oxford", in *Desh pardesh. The South Asian presence in Britain* (1994, Ballard, Roger ed.), pp. 35–57.

Shourie, Arun, *The world of fatwas or the shariah in action* (1995, ASA, Delhi).

Siddiqi, M. Mazheruddin, *Women in Islam* (1980, Adam, New Delhi).

Siddiqi, M. M., *A preliminary report of incidence of divorce among Indian Muslims* (1996, Institute of Objective Studies, New Delhi).

Siddiqui, N. U. A., *Studies in Muslim law. Vol. I. Batil and fasid marriages* (1955, Iqbal Uddin Ahmad, Dacca).

Singh, Alka, *Women in Muslim personal law* (1992, Rawat, Jaipur and New Delhi).

Smart, P. St. J., "Recognition of extra-judicial divorces" [1985] 34 [April] I.C.L.Q. 392–397.

Smith, Donald Eugene (ed.), *South Asian politics and religion* (1969, Princeton University Press, Princeton).

Smith, W. Robertson, *Kinship and marriage in early Arabia* (1907, 3rd ed., Beacon Press, Boston; 1885, 1st ed., Cambridge University Press, Cambridge; 1903, 2nd ed., A. & C. Black, London).

Sobhan, Salma, *Legal status of women in Bangladesh* (1978, BILIA, Dacca).

Spencer, Sarah, *Strangers and citizens. A positive approach to migrants and refugees* (1994, IPPR and Rivers Oram Press, London).

Spencer, Sarah, *Migrants, refugees and the boundaries of citizenship* (1995, IPPR, London).

Stowasser, Barbara Freyer, *Women and the Qur'an, traditions and interpretation* (1996, OUP USA, New York et al.).

Surty, Muhammad Ibrahim H. I., "The Shari'ah family law courts in Britain and the protection of women's rights in Muslim family law with special reference to the dissolution of marriage at the instance of the wife" [1991] 9 No. 1 *Muslim Educational Quarterly* 59–68.

Sylvester, M. P., "The Islamic talaq: Problems and perspectives for the future" [1980] *Journal of Social Welfare Law* 282–292.

Taylor, Charles (ed.), *Multiculturalism: Examining the politics of recognition* (1994, Princeton University Press, New Jersey).

Taylor, J. H., *The half-way generation. A study of Asian youths in Newcastle upon Tyne* (1976, NEFR, London).

Tayyibji, Muhsin (ed.), *Muslim law. The personal law of Muslims in India and Pakistan* (1968, by Faiz Badruddin Tyabji, 4th ed., N. M. Tripathi, Bombay).

Udovitch, A., *Partnership and profit in medieval Islam* (1970, Princeton U.P., Princeton)

Ullah, Al-Haj Mahomed, *The administration of justice in Islam. An introduction to the Muslim conception of the state* (1986, Kitab Bhavan, New Delhi).

Verma, B. R., *Muslim marriage, dissolution and maintenance* (1988, 2nd ed., Law Book Company, Allahabad).

Verma, Ved Prakash, "Conflict of personal law in divorce cases in India" [1969] *The Law Review* 78–93.

Vertovec, Steven, "Muslims, the state, and the public sphere in Britain", in *Muslim communities in Europe* (1996, Nonneman, Gerd et al. eds, Ithaca Press, Reading), pp. 169–186.

Visram, Rozina, *Ayahs, lascars and princes. The story of Indians in Britain 1700–1947* (1986, Pluto, London et al.).

Wahab, I., *Muslims in Britain: Profile of a community* (1989, Runnymede Trust, London).

Wakin, Jeanette A., *The function of documents in Islamic law* (1972, NY:SUNY, Albany).

Walter, H. A., *The Ahmadiya movement* (1991, Manohar, New Delhi).

Watson, James L. (ed.), *Between two cultures. Migrants and minorities in Britain* (1977, Blackwell, Oxford).

Weiss, Anita M., "Women's position in Pakistan" [1985] 25 No. 8 *Asian Survey* 863–880.

Weiss, Anita M. (ed.), *Islamic reassertion in Pakistan* (1986, Syracuse U.P., Syracuse)

Weiss, Anita M., "Benazir Bhutto and the future of women in Pakistan" [1990] 30 No. 5 [May] *Asian Survey* 433–445.

Welch, Alford T., "Islam", in *A handbook of living religions* (1984, Hinnells, John R. ed., Penguin, London et al.), pp. 123–170.

Welchman, Lynn, "The development of Islamic family law in the legal system of Jordan" [1988] 37 I.C.L.Q. 868–886.

Welchman, Lynn, *The Islamic law of marriage and divorce in the occupied West Bank* (1992, S.O.A.S., London; Unpublished PhD thesis).

Welchman, Lynn, "Special stipulations in the contract of marriage: Law and practice in the occupied West Bank" [1994] 11 *Recht van de Islam* 55–77.

Werbner, Pnina, "Avoiding the ghetto: Pakistani migrants and settlement shifts in Manchester" [1979] 7 No. 3 [Winter] *New Community* 376–389.

Werbner, Pnina and Tariq Modood (eds), *Debating cultural hybridity. Multicultural identities and the politics of anti-racism* (1997, Zed Books, London and New Jersey).

Wink, André, *Al Hind – The making of the Indo-Islamic world* (Vol. 1: Early medieval India and the expansion of Islam, 7th–11th centuries; 1990, Brill, Leiden et al.).

Wink, André, *Al Hind – The making of the Indo-Islamic world* (Vol. 2: The slave kings and the Islamic conquest, 11th–13th centuries; 1997, Brill, Leiden et al.).

Wolffe, John, "Fragmented universality: Islam and Muslims", in *The growth of religious diversity: Britain from 1945* (1994, Vol. II., Parsons, Gerald ed., Routledge and Open University Press, London), pp. 133–172.

Zafar, Fareeha (ed.), *Finding our way. Readings on women in Pakistan* (1991, A.S.R., Lahore)

Zaheer, Hasan, *The separation of East Pakistan: The rise and realisation of Bengali Muslim nationalism* (1994, U.P.L., Dhaka).

Zaid, Abdulaziz Mohammed, *The Islamic law of bequest* (1986, Scorpion, London).

Zingel, Wolfgang Peter and Stephanie Zingel-Ave Lallemant (eds), *Pakistan in the 80s. Ideology, regionalism, economy, foreign policy* (1985, Vanguard Books, Lahore).

Ziring, Lawrence, *Bangladesh: From Mujib to Ershad: An interpretive study* (1994, U.P.L., Dhaka).

Index